ARTIFICIAL INTELLIGENCE
IN DATA SCIENCE AND BIG DATA

Techniques, Tools, and Applications

By

Dr. Hesham Mohamed Elsherif

About the Author

Dr. Hesham Mohamed Elsherif stands at the forefront of library management, research, and the practical implementation of Artificial Intelligence (AI) in educational and library systems. With over 22 years of dedicated service in the field, he brings a wealth of expertise that bridges the worlds of technology, organizational leadership, and scholarship.

Dr. Elsherif's academic credentials are as diverse as they are impressive. He holds two doctoral degrees—one in **Management and Organizational Leadership** and the other in **Information Systems and Technology**. This dual specialization has equipped him with a holistic perspective on how institutions can effectively integrate emerging technologies, particularly AI, to optimize resource allocation, streamline operational processes, and enrich learning experiences.

A recognized authority in **empirical research methodology**, Dr. Elsherif specializes in **qualitative approaches** and **action research**. His mastery of these methodologies has not only bolstered his own scholarly work but has also allowed him to pioneer new ways of investigating and implementing AI-driven solutions in school, academic, and public libraries. Whether he is designing user-centric AI tools or conducting in-depth studies on technology adoption, Dr. Elsherif's methodical and data-driven approach consistently yields impactful, real-world results.

Over the years, he has made significant strides in shaping the academic community - not just as a **professional researcher**, but also as an **Adjunct Professor**. In the classroom, Dr. Elsherif has a remarkable ability to translate complex theories into accessible insights, thereby training a new generation of thought leaders and specialists in both library science and technology. This multifaceted role, spanning teaching, research, and practice, has cemented his status as a **pioneer** whose influence extends well beyond traditional academic boundaries.

Dr. Elsherif's expertise and passion are truly global in scope. He has served as a **consultant to numerous educational institutions worldwide**, offering guidance on best practices, AI integration strategies, and effective management models. His international collaborations speak to the versatility of his knowledge, which is informed by a deep understanding of how AI can enhance resource discovery, user engagement, and scholarly communication across cultural and institutional contexts.

Central to Dr. Elsherif's mission is the belief that **innovative technologies**, including AI, must be harnessed responsibly and ethically. This commitment is evident in his approach to library management and educational technology, where he advocates for solutions that are inclusive, data-secure, and aligned with the core values of academic freedom and public service. By focusing on ethical implementation, he ensures that advancements in AI serve learners, educators, and researchers effectively and fairly.

Today, Dr. Elsherif continues to break new ground in **library innovation**, **academic research**, and **technology leadership**. Combining a passion for education with an unparalleled depth of knowledge, he remains a guiding force - **inspiring, educating, and leading** in library systems, educational institutions, and beyond. Through his work, he illuminates the path toward a future where AI seamlessly complements human expertise, thereby enriching the academic and public spheres for generations to come.

Preface

In today's data-driven world, the convergence of **Artificial Intelligence (AI)**, **Data Science**, and **Big Data** has become a pivotal force driving innovation, efficiency, and competitive advantage across industries. The exponential growth of data, fueled by advancements in technology and the proliferation of connected devices, presents both unprecedented opportunities and complex challenges. This book, **"Artificial Intelligence in Data Science and Big Data: Techniques, Tools, and Applications,"** aims to bridge the gap between theory and practice, providing a comprehensive guide to harnessing the power of AI within the realms of data science and big data analytics.

Motivation and Purpose

The inspiration for this book stems from the recognition that while data is abundant, the ability to extract meaningful insights and actionable intelligence is not uniformly distributed. Many organizations and professionals grapple with understanding how to effectively integrate AI technologies into their data science workflows to address big data challenges. This book seeks to demystify AI concepts, techniques, and tools, offering practical guidance to leverage them in processing, analyzing, and interpreting large-scale data.

Intended Audience

This book is crafted for a diverse audience:

Data Scientists and Analysts looking to enhance their skill sets with AI methodologies applicable to big data.

AI Practitioners and Machine Learning Engineers seeking to understand the intricacies of applying AI models to massive datasets.

Big Data Professionals aiming to incorporate AI into their data processing and analytics pipelines.

Students and Academics in computer science, data science, and related fields who require a structured and in-depth resource.

Business Leaders and Decision-Makers interested in the strategic implications of AI and big data integration for informed decision-making.

Structure of the Book

To facilitate a logical and coherent exploration of the subject matter, the book is organized into six comprehensive parts:

Foundations: Establishes the core concepts of AI, data science, and big data, setting the groundwork for subsequent chapters.

AI Techniques in Data Science and Big Data: Delves into specific AI methodologies, including machine learning algorithms, deep learning architectures, natural language processing, and computer vision, tailored for big data applications.

Applications Across Industries: Presents real-world case studies and examples across various sectors such as finance, healthcare, retail, transportation, energy, telecommunications, social media, and government.

Tools and Platforms: Reviews the essential programming languages, libraries, frameworks, and cloud services that support AI and big data initiatives.

Implementation and Best Practices: Discusses practical aspects of deploying AI solutions, including data governance, ethical considerations, scaling strategies, and operational best practices.

Future Trends and Emerging Technologies: Explores cutting-edge developments like edge computing, explainable AI, quantum computing, and anticipates future directions in the field.

Each chapter is designed to build upon the previous ones, allowing readers to either follow the book sequentially or focus on specific areas of interest based on their needs.

Why This Book Matters Now

The intersection of AI, data science, and big data is at the forefront of the digital transformation era. Organizations that effectively harness these technologies are poised to make significant strides in innovation, operational efficiency, and customer engagement. However, the rapid evolution of these fields can be daunting. This book addresses this challenge by providing:

Comprehensive Coverage: Combining foundational knowledge with advanced topics to cater to both novices and experienced professionals.

Practical Insights: Offering actionable guidance, code examples, and real-world applications to facilitate immediate implementation.

Ethical Framework: Emphasizing the importance of responsible AI, data privacy, and ethical considerations in developing and deploying AI solutions.

Future Orientation: Preparing readers for emerging trends and technologies that will shape the future landscape of AI and big data.

Acknowledgments

The creation of this book has been a collaborative journey, and I am indebted to many individuals and organizations:

Subject Matter Experts who generously shared their knowledge, experiences, and insights, enriching the content significantly.

Colleagues and Peers whose constructive feedback and encouragement were invaluable throughout the writing process.

Academic Institutions and Research Communities that continue to push the boundaries of knowledge in AI, data science, and big data.

Family and Friends for their unwavering support, understanding, and patience during the countless hours dedicated to this project.

Publishers and Editors whose professionalism and commitment to excellence ensured the highest quality of this work.

A Journey Ahead

As you embark on this exploration of AI in data science and big data, I encourage you to approach the material with curiosity and an open mind. The fields covered are dynamic and rapidly evolving, offering endless possibilities for innovation and impact. Whether you are a practitioner aiming to solve complex problems, a student eager to learn, or a leader seeking strategic insights, this book is designed to equip you with the knowledge and tools necessary to navigate and contribute to this exciting landscape.

Dr. Hesham Mohamed Elsherif

Who Should Read This Book?

"Artificial Intelligence in Data Science and Big Data: Techniques, Tools, and Applications" is meticulously crafted to serve a diverse audience interested in the convergence of AI, data science, and big data. Whether you are a seasoned professional or a newcomer to the field, this book offers valuable insights and practical knowledge tailored to various levels of expertise.

1. Data Scientists and Analysts

- **Experienced Data Scientists** seeking to enhance their skill set by integrating AI techniques into big data analytics.

- **Business Analysts** looking to leverage AI for deeper insights and predictive analytics in large datasets.

- **Statisticians and Mathematicians** interested in applying statistical models within AI frameworks to interpret complex data.

2. AI and Machine Learning Engineers

- **Machine Learning Practitioners** aiming to understand the challenges of applying algorithms to big data environments.

- **AI Developers** looking for scalable solutions to implement AI models on large datasets.

- **Deep Learning Specialists** interested in optimizing neural networks for big data applications.

3. Big Data Professionals

- **Data Engineers** responsible for building and maintaining big data infrastructures who want to incorporate AI capabilities.

- **Database Administrators** looking to optimize data storage and retrieval using AI techniques.

- **Big Data Architects** interested in designing systems that seamlessly integrate AI and data analytics.

4. IT Managers and Business Leaders

- **Technology Executives** seeking strategic insights into how AI and big data can drive innovation and competitive advantage.

- **Project Managers** overseeing AI and big data initiatives who require a comprehensive understanding of the technologies involved.

- **Business Analysts** aiming to translate technical capabilities into business value propositions.

5. Students and Academics

- **Undergraduate and Graduate Students** in computer science, data science, AI, machine learning, and related fields needing a thorough textbook that bridges theory and practice.

- **Researchers** conducting studies in AI, data science, or big data analytics who require an up-to-date reference.

- **Educators and Professors** looking for comprehensive material to support curriculum development and teaching.

6. Entrepreneurs and Innovators

- **Start-up Founders** aiming to build products or services leveraging AI and big data technologies.

- **Innovation Managers** exploring new business models and technological solutions in the AI and big data space.

- **Investors and Venture Capitalists** seeking to understand the technological landscape for informed investment decisions.

7. Industry Professionals Across Sectors

- **Healthcare Professionals** interested in applying AI and big data for medical imaging, diagnostics, and personalized medicine.

- **Finance Experts** looking to implement AI for fraud detection, algorithmic trading, and risk management.

- **Marketing and Sales Professionals** aiming to utilize big data analytics for customer segmentation and targeted campaigns.

8. Government and Public Sector Officials

- **Policy Makers** involved in crafting regulations around AI, data privacy, and big data management.

- **Public Administrators** seeking to leverage AI and big data for improved public services and smart city initiatives.

- **Defense and Security Personnel** interested in applications of AI in cybersecurity and intelligence analysis.

9. Legal and Ethical Professionals

- **Lawyers and Compliance Officers** focusing on the legal implications of AI and big data, including data protection and intellectual property rights.

- **Ethicists** examining the societal impact of AI technologies and big data practices.

10. Enthusiasts and Lifelong Learners

- **Technology Enthusiasts** keen on understanding the latest advancements and future trends in AI and big data.

- **Career Changers** looking to transition into the fields of AI, data science, or big data analytics.

- **Lifelong Learners** who enjoy expanding their knowledge on cutting-edge technologies shaping the modern world.

Prerequisites for Readers:

- **Basic Programming Knowledge**: Familiarity with programming concepts is beneficial. Knowledge of languages like Python or R will help in understanding code examples.

- **Understanding of Mathematics and Statistics**: A foundational grasp of mathematical concepts and statistical methods will aid in comprehending algorithms and models.

- **Interest in Technology and Data**: Curiosity about how data can be transformed into actionable insights using AI techniques.

Why You Should Read This Book:

- **Comprehensive Coverage**: Gain a holistic understanding of how AI integrates with data science and big data technologies.

- **Practical Applications**: Learn from real-world case studies and examples across various industries.

- **Skill Enhancement**: Equip yourself with the latest tools and techniques to advance your career or academic pursuits.

- **Strategic Insights**: Understand the implications of AI and big data on business strategies and societal trends.

- **Ethical Perspective**: Explore the ethical considerations and responsibilities associated with AI and big data.

Whether you're developing AI solutions, making strategic decisions, or simply eager to learn about the transformative power of AI in big data contexts, this book serves as an essential resource to guide you through the complexities and opportunities of this rapidly evolving field.

Why This Book Is Essential Reading?

In an era defined by data proliferation and technological innovation, **"Artificial Intelligence in Data Science and Big Data: Techniques, Tools, and Applications"** emerges as a crucial resource for anyone seeking to navigate the complex intersection of these rapidly evolving fields. This book is not just another addition to the vast repository of literature on AI and data science; it is a comprehensive guide that fills a significant gap by seamlessly integrating the principles of artificial intelligence with the practical challenges of big data analytics.

Bridging the Knowledge Gap

The convergence of AI, data science, and big data presents both immense opportunities and daunting challenges. While there are numerous resources available on each subject individually, there is a scarcity of materials that holistically address their intersection. This book stands out by providing an integrated approach, enabling readers to understand how AI techniques can be effectively applied to big data environments to extract meaningful insights.

Comprehensive and Up-to-Date Coverage

Fundamental Concepts: The book begins by laying a solid foundation, ensuring that readers have a clear understanding of the core principles before delving into complex topics.

Advanced Techniques: It covers the latest advancements in machine learning, deep learning, natural language processing, and computer vision, specifically tailored for big data applications.

Practical Tools and Platforms: Readers are introduced to essential tools, programming languages, and platforms that are currently in use, such as Python libraries, Hadoop, Spark, and cloud services like AWS, Google Cloud, and Microsoft Azure.

Real-World Applications: Through detailed case studies across various industries - including finance, healthcare, retail, and government - the book demonstrates the practical implementation of theories and techniques.

Emphasis on Ethical and Responsible AI

In a time when concerns about data privacy, security, and ethical AI are paramount, this book dedicates significant attention to these issues. It guides readers on:

Data Governance: Understanding the importance of responsible data management practices.

Ethical Considerations: Navigating the complexities of bias mitigation, transparency, and accountability in AI systems.

Regulatory Compliance: Staying informed about laws and regulations such as GDPR and CCPA that impact data handling and AI deployment.

Preparation for the Future

The fields of AI and big data are dynamic, with constant innovations reshaping the landscape. This book not only addresses current technologies but also:

Explores Emerging Trends: Topics like edge computing, explainable AI, quantum computing, and the future of AI in data science are thoroughly examined.

Encourages Forward Thinking: By discussing future directions and expert insights, the book prepares readers to anticipate and adapt to upcoming changes.

Accessible to a Wide Audience

For Beginners and Experts Alike: Whether you are a novice stepping into the world of AI and data science or an experienced professional seeking to update your knowledge, the book's structured approach caters to all levels.

Interdisciplinary Appeal: Its content is relevant not only to technologists but also to business leaders, policymakers, and academics, making it a valuable resource across disciplines.

Practical Focus with Hands-On Examples

Understanding theory is essential, but the ability to apply concepts is what truly matters in the professional world. This book excels in:

Hands-On Learning: Including code snippets, algorithm explanations, and step-by-step guides that facilitate practical understanding.

Problem-Solving Approach: Addressing real-world challenges and providing solutions that readers can adapt and implement in their own work.

Enhancing Competitive Advantage

In the competitive landscape of modern industries, organizations and professionals who can effectively leverage AI and big data analytics have a distinct advantage. This book empowers readers to:

Drive Innovation: By learning how to harness AI for data-driven decision-making and strategic planning.

Improve Efficiency: Through understanding how to optimize processes and workflows using AI techniques.

Deliver Value: By translating complex data into actionable insights that can enhance products, services, and customer experiences.

Contributions from Experts

Authored by seasoned professionals and academics with extensive experience in AI, data science, and big data, the book brings:

Credibility and Authority: Offering insights backed by years of research and industry practice.

Diverse Perspectives: Incorporating viewpoints from various sectors to provide a well-rounded understanding.

A Timely Resource in a Critical Era

As we stand on the cusp of the Fourth Industrial Revolution, characterized by a fusion of technologies blurring the lines between the physical, digital, and biological spheres, understanding AI's role in data science and big data is no longer optional—it's imperative. This book is timely because:

Rapid Technological Advancements: Keeps readers abreast of the latest developments to remain relevant in their fields.

Global Challenges: Addresses how AI and big data can be leveraged to solve pressing issues like healthcare crises, climate change, and economic instability.

Workforce Transformation: Prepares professionals for the shifting demands of the job market where AI competency is increasingly sought after.

Building a Foundation for Lifelong Learning

Recognizing that the fields of AI and big data are continuously evolving, this book encourages:

Continuous Education: Providing resources, references, and suggestions for further learning.

Critical Thinking: Promoting an analytical mindset to question assumptions and explore new ideas.

Community Engagement: Inspiring readers to participate in professional networks, forums, and collaborative projects.

In Summary, "Artificial Intelligence in Data Science and Big Data: Techniques, Tools, and Applications" is essential reading because it equips you with the knowledge, skills, and perspectives necessary to excel in a data-centric world. It bridges the gap between theory and practice, addresses current and future challenges, and empowers you to make meaningful contributions to your organization and society at large. Whether you're aiming to advance your career, lead innovation, or simply stay informed about critical technological trends, this book serves as a comprehensive and invaluable guide on your journey.

Dr. Hesham Mohamed Elsherif

Table of Contents

Part I: Foundations
Chapter 1: Introduction to Artificial Intelligence, Data Science, and Big Data

<u>Defining Artificial Intelligence</u>

Artificial Intelligence (AI) is a field of computer science focused on creating systems capable of performing tasks that would typically require human intelligence. These tasks can range from simple actions like recognizing patterns to more complex activities such as decision-making, problem-solving, understanding language, and learning from experience (Russell & Norvig, 2020). AI involves the development of algorithms that enable machines to simulate cognitive processes and behaviors, allowing them to interpret their environment and act autonomously or semi-autonomously in achieving specific goals.

Understanding AI and Its Subfields

The concept of AI encompasses several subfields, each dedicated to particular aspects of mimicking human intelligence. These subfields include:

Machine Learning (ML): Involves creating systems that can learn from data without explicit programming (Mitchell, 1997). ML algorithms enable systems to improve performance over time by recognizing patterns, making predictions, and adapting based on new information.

Natural Language Processing (NLP): Focuses on enabling machines to understand, interpret, and generate human language (Jurafsky & Martin, 2021). Applications of NLP include speech recognition, translation, and sentiment analysis.

Computer Vision: Concerned with enabling machines to interpret and understand visual inputs such as images or videos (Goodfellow et al., 2016). This technology is widely used in areas like facial recognition, object detection, and medical imaging.

Robotics: Involves designing intelligent machines capable of performing physical tasks autonomously or under human supervision (Siciliano & Khatib, 2016).

The Evolution of AI

AI has evolved significantly since its inception in the mid-20th century. Early efforts were rule-based, relying on expert systems designed to follow predefined instructions. However, as data availability and computational power grew, AI methods began shifting toward data-driven techniques, particularly machine learning (Bengio, 2009). This shift led to breakthroughs in fields like deep learning, which uses multi-layered neural networks to identify complex patterns and make highly accurate predictions (LeCun, Bengio, & Hinton, 2015).

AI's Role in Data Science and Big Data

AI is closely linked to the fields of Data Science and Big Data. Data Science involves using scientific methods, algorithms, and systems to extract insights and knowledge from structured and unstructured data (Provost & Fawcett, 2013). Big Data refers to vast datasets that are too large or complex to be processed by traditional data processing systems (Gandomi & Haider, 2015). AI techniques, especially machine learning, have become essential for analyzing Big Data, helping organizations make informed decisions by identifying trends and uncovering hidden patterns.

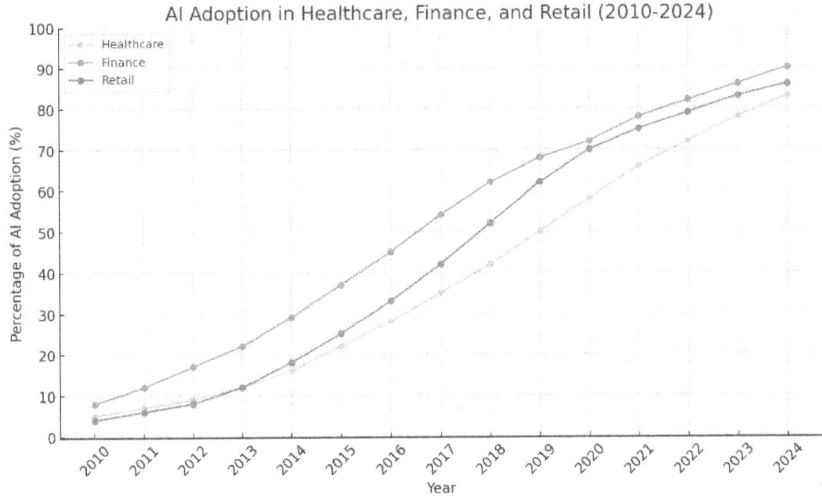

Understanding Data Science

Data Science is an interdisciplinary field that uses scientific methods, algorithms, processes, and systems to extract knowledge and insights from structured and unstructured data. It involves a combination of statistical analysis, machine learning, and domain expertise to interpret and analyze complex datasets. As organizations become more data-driven, the role of Data Science has expanded significantly, impacting decision-making processes across various industries, such as healthcare, finance, marketing, and technology (Provost & Fawcett, 2013).

Core Components of Data Science

Data Science can be broken down into several key components, each contributing to the field's overarching goal of generating actionable insights from data. These components include:

Data Collection: The process begins with gathering raw data from diverse sources, which could be structured (databases, spreadsheets) or unstructured (social media posts, audio files, images) (Gandomi & Haider, 2015). Data scientists often work with Big Data, leveraging tools like web scraping, surveys, and sensors to collect massive amounts of information.

Data Cleaning and Preprocessing: Before any meaningful analysis can occur, data must be cleaned and preprocessed. This involves handling missing values, removing duplicates, and addressing inconsistencies in the data. Techniques like data normalization, transformation, and standardization are applied to ensure that datasets are ready for modeling (Wickham, 2014).

Data Analysis and Modeling: Data Science heavily relies on statistical analysis and machine learning algorithms to uncover hidden patterns, trends, and relationships within the data. Techniques like regression analysis, clustering, and classification are employed to interpret the data (Bishop, 2006). In this phase, predictive modeling is often used to forecast future trends or outcomes.

Data Visualization: Once the data has been analyzed, results are communicated through data visualization techniques such as charts, graphs, and dashboards. Visualization helps stakeholders easily understand complex findings and make informed decisions based on the insights presented (Few, 2013).

The Role of Machine Learning in Data Science

Machine Learning (ML) plays a critical role in Data Science by enabling systems to learn from data and improve their performance over time without being explicitly programmed (Mitchell, 1997). ML models help data scientists create predictive and prescriptive analytics by using historical data to predict future outcomes or prescribe solutions for specific problems. These models can handle large datasets efficiently, making them indispensable in the era of Big Data (Goodfellow, Bengio, & Courville, 2016).

Data Science and Big Data

With the advent of Big Data, Data Science has gained even more importance. Big Data refers to datasets so large and complex that traditional data processing techniques cannot handle them. These datasets often contain valuable insights that can be leveraged for competitive advantage. Data Science, through techniques such as distributed computing and cloud storage, allows organizations to analyze Big Data and make data-driven decisions at scale (Gandomi & Haider, 2015).

Real-World Applications of Data Science

Data Science has a wide range of applications across industries:

Healthcare: Data science is used for predictive analytics in patient outcomes, diagnosis through medical imaging, and optimizing hospital operations.

Finance: Financial institutions utilize data science for fraud detection, credit scoring, and market trend prediction.

Marketing: Companies analyze consumer behavior using data science to personalize marketing efforts and improve customer retention.

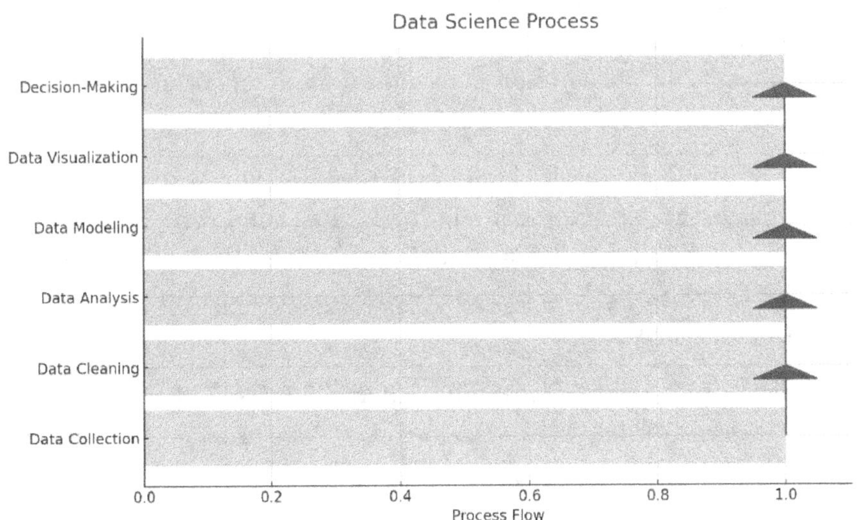

Overview of Big Data

Big Data refers to the vast and complex datasets that exceed the capabilities of traditional data processing systems. These datasets are characterized by their large volume, high velocity, and diverse variety, often referred to as the "3 Vs" of Big Data (Laney, 2001). In the modern digital age, the sheer amount of data being generated by users, sensors, transactions, and digital interactions is growing exponentially, making Big Data a crucial resource for organizations to extract insights, drive decision-making, and create value.

The 3 Vs of Big Data

Volume: This dimension refers to the massive scale of data generated and stored. Big Data often involves petabytes or even exabytes of information. For instance, social media platforms generate terabytes of data daily, encompassing text, images, videos, and interactions (Manyika et al., 2011).

Velocity: Velocity refers to the speed at which data is generated, processed, and analyzed. With real-time or near-real-time data streaming from sources such as sensors, financial markets, and social media feeds, the ability to process and act upon this data quickly has become critical (Gandomi & Haider, 2015).

Variety: Big Data comes in various formats, including structured (e.g., databases), semi-structured (e.g., XML, JSON), and unstructured data (e.g., images, videos, text). This diversity requires sophisticated methods to process, analyze, and extract useful information (Fan & Bifet, 2013).

Additional Characteristics: The 4th and 5th Vs While the "3 Vs" form the core of Big Data's characteristics, some frameworks include additional dimensions:

Veracity: Refers to the quality, accuracy, and trustworthiness of the data. Due to the heterogeneous sources of Big Data, there may be inconsistencies, biases, and inaccuracies in the information, necessitating robust data cleaning and verification techniques (Zikopoulos et al., 2012).

Value: This dimension addresses the actionable insights and benefits that can be derived from Big Data. The ultimate goal of Big Data is to uncover hidden patterns, trends, and correlations that lead to better decision-making and business value (Gandomi & Haider, 2015).

Big Data Technologies and Tools

Processing and analyzing Big Data require specialized tools and frameworks due to the scale and complexity of the datasets. Some of the widely used technologies include:

Hadoop: An open-source framework that allows for distributed storage and processing of large datasets using clusters of computers (White, 2015). It includes tools such as the Hadoop Distributed File System (HDFS) for storage and MapReduce for processing.

Spark: A powerful processing engine designed for speed and ease of use in handling large-scale data. Spark's ability to perform in-memory computations makes it faster than traditional Hadoop (Zaharia et al., 2016).

NoSQL Databases: Unlike traditional relational databases, NoSQL databases such as MongoDB and Cassandra are designed to handle unstructured and semi-structured data, making them ideal for Big Data applications (Han et al., 2011).

Applications of Big Data

Big Data is transforming industries by enabling more informed and data-driven decisions. Some key applications include:

Healthcare: Big Data is used to improve patient outcomes, optimize hospital operations, and predict disease outbreaks through predictive analytics (Raghupathi & Raghupathi, 2014).

Finance: Financial institutions use Big Data to detect fraud, assess credit risk, and analyze market trends in real-time, improving decision-making and customer service (Chalapathy & Chawla, 2019).

Retail: Retailers use Big Data to understand consumer behavior, personalize recommendations, and optimize supply chains (Kitchin, 2014).

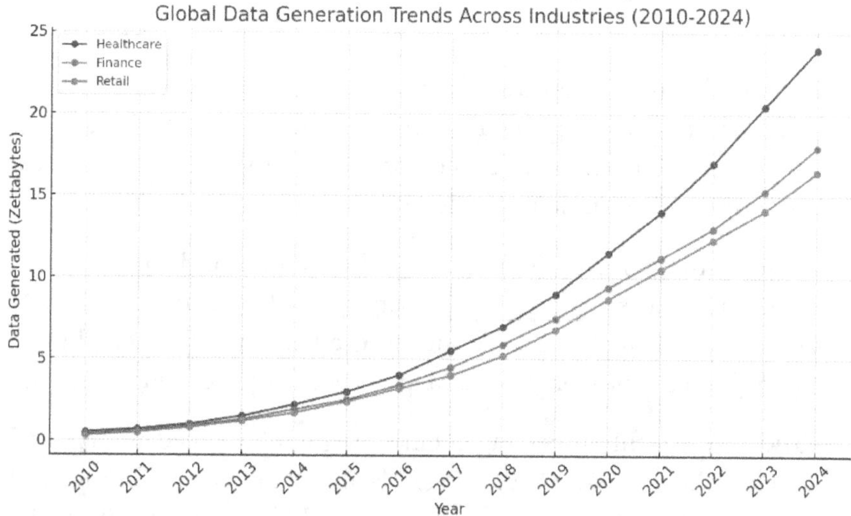

The Intersection of AI, Data Science, and Big Data

Artificial Intelligence (AI), Data Science, and Big Data are closely intertwined fields that collectively shape modern data-driven technologies. Each of these fields has a distinct focus, but their overlap creates powerful synergies that drive innovation across industries. AI, fueled by vast datasets and advanced data analysis techniques, is capable of learning and making decisions in ways that replicate or enhance human intelligence. Data Science, on the other hand, provides the methodologies and tools for extracting actionable insights from data. Big Data serves as the raw material, offering massive amounts of information that can be analyzed for valuable insights (Provost & Fawcett, 2013).

AI and Big Data: A Symbiotic Relationship Big Data has transformed the potential of AI. Historically, AI systems relied on limited data and rigid algorithms. With the advent of Big Data, AI algorithms now have access to vast amounts of data, allowing them to improve in accuracy and sophistication. This abundance of data is crucial for training machine learning models, particularly in applications such as image recognition, natural language processing, and autonomous systems (Manyika et al., 2011).

AI plays a critical role in handling the complexity of Big Data by automating data analysis processes. Traditional methods struggle with the size and variety of Big Data, but AI techniques, such as machine learning and deep learning, allow for real-time data processing and uncovering hidden patterns. This capability has led to breakthroughs in various industries, including healthcare, finance, and marketing, where Big Data is continuously generated and requires efficient analysis (Gandomi & Haider, 2015).

Data Science as the Bridge Data Science acts as the bridge between AI and Big Data. It encompasses the entire process of collecting, cleaning, analyzing, and interpreting Big Data using statistical techniques and machine learning algorithms. Data scientists often employ AI techniques to create predictive models that can anticipate trends, classify information, and optimize business processes (Han et al., 2011).

A key aspect of Data Science is feature engineering, where relevant variables are extracted from raw data to improve the performance of machine learning models. Big Data's sheer volume, variety, and velocity provide data scientists with ample opportunities to uncover insights, but it also demands robust AI tools to make sense of the data efficiently (Witten et al., 2016).

The Feedback Loop AI, Data Science, and Big Data are part of a continuous feedback loop. Big Data enables better AI models by providing more training data, and in turn, AI algorithms generate more accurate results that are fed back into the Data Science workflow. Data Science methods help organize and structure Big Data, making it more usable for AI-driven decision-making processes (Domingos, 2015).

For example, in healthcare, AI algorithms that rely on Big Data can predict patient outcomes and optimize treatments by analyzing millions of medical records, while data scientists work on curating and preprocessing these datasets (Raghupathi & Raghupathi, 2014). In marketing, Big Data from social media interactions is analyzed using AI algorithms to predict consumer behavior, and data scientists continually refine these models for higher accuracy (Kitchin, 2014).

The Intersection of AI, Data Science, and Big Data

Historical Evolution and Trends

The fields of Artificial Intelligence (AI), Data Science, and Big Data have evolved significantly over the past few decades, driven by advances in computing power, algorithms, and data availability. Understanding the historical development of these fields sheds light on how they have come to shape modern technology and society.

The Evolution of Artificial Intelligence (AI)

AI has its roots in the mid-20th century, with the term first coined by John McCarthy in 1956 during the Dartmouth Conference (Russell & Norvig, 2020). Early AI efforts were focused on symbolic reasoning and rule-based systems, where machines followed explicit instructions to solve problems. In the 1960s and 1970s, research on AI shifted toward more general problem-solving approaches, leading to the development of expert systems in the 1980s. However, AI faced challenges due to limited computational power and the difficulty of handling complex, real-world problems (Crevier, 1993).

The revival of AI began in the 1990s with advancements in machine learning, fueled by the availability of large datasets and improved algorithms. Neural networks, inspired by the structure of the human brain, gained popularity, especially in tasks like speech recognition and image classification (Goodfellow et al., 2016). The explosion of AI research in the 2000s was accelerated by breakthroughs in deep learning, which enabled machines to learn from vast amounts of data with high accuracy. This era saw AI move from theoretical research into real-world applications, such as self-driving cars, natural language processing, and AI-based recommendation systems.

The Rise of Data Science

Data Science emerged as an interdisciplinary field that combines elements of computer science, statistics, and domain knowledge to extract meaningful insights from data. The term gained prominence in the late 2000s, but its roots go back to earlier developments in statistical analysis and database management (Provost & Fawcett, 2013).

In the 1990s, the rapid expansion of the internet and digital technologies led to an explosion of data generation, driving the need for new tools and techniques to handle large datasets. Early data analysis relied on traditional statistical methods, but as datasets became more complex and diverse, machine learning techniques became central to the field of Data Science (Witten et al., 2016). Today, Data Science is essential for industries such as healthcare, finance, and marketing, where predictive models and data-driven decision-making are key to success.

The Emergence of Big Data

Big Data refers to the massive and complex datasets that traditional data-processing software cannot handle effectively. The term "Big Data" was popularized in the early 2000s to describe datasets that exhibited high volume, velocity, and variety (Laney, 2001). The rise of the digital age, social media, mobile devices, and the Internet of Things (IoT) led to an exponential increase in data generation. This necessitated the development of new tools, such as distributed computing frameworks like Hadoop and Spark, which allow for efficient storage and processing of Big Data (Zikopoulos et al., 2012).

Big Data has since become a crucial resource for organizations seeking to leverage data for competitive advantage. By analyzing vast amounts of data in real-time, businesses can uncover hidden trends, optimize operations, and predict future outcomes. The combination of Big Data and AI has paved the way for innovations such as personalized marketing, real-time fraud detection, and predictive maintenance in industries ranging from finance to manufacturing (Gandomi & Haider, 2015).

Trends in AI, Data Science, and Big Data

As AI, Data Science, and Big Data continue to evolve, several trends are shaping their future:

AI Democratization: Advances in cloud computing and open-source platforms have made AI tools more accessible to organizations of all sizes. This trend has allowed smaller businesses and startups to harness the power of AI without significant upfront investment in infrastructure (Jouppi et al., 2017).

Ethical AI: With the growing deployment of AI systems, concerns around bias, fairness, and transparency have led to an increased focus on developing ethical AI frameworks. Researchers and policymakers are working toward guidelines to ensure responsible AI use, particularly in sensitive domains like criminal justice, hiring, and healthcare (Binns, 2018).

Data Privacy and Security: As the volume of Big Data continues to grow, ensuring data privacy and security has become a pressing issue. Regulations such as the General Data Protection Regulation (GDPR) in Europe are designed to protect individuals' data and hold organizations accountable for its use (Voigt & Bussche, 2017).

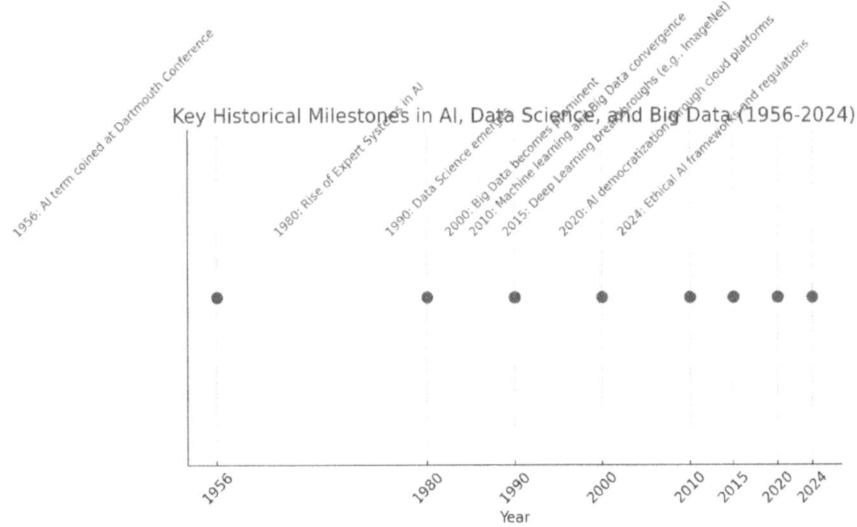

Reference

Bengio, Y. (2009). Learning deep architectures for AI. *Foundations and Trends in Machine Learning, 2*(1), 1-127.

Bishop, C. M. (2006). *Pattern recognition and machine learning.* Springer.

Chalapathy, R., & Chawla, S. (2019). Deep learning for anomaly detection: A survey. *arXiv preprint arXiv:1901.03407.*

Domingos, P. (2015). *The master algorithm: How the quest for the ultimate learning machine will remake our world.* Basic Books.

Fan, W., & Bifet, A. (2013). Mining big data: Current status, and forecast to the future. *ACM SIGKDD Explorations Newsletter, 14*(2), 1-5.

Few, S. (2013). *Information dashboard design: Displaying data for at-a-glance monitoring.* Analytics Press.

Gandomi, A., & Haider, M. (2015). Beyond the hype: Big data concepts, methods, and analytics. *International Journal of Information Management, 35*(2), 137-144.

Goodfellow, I., Bengio, Y., & Courville, A. (2016). *Deep learning.* MIT Press.

Han, J., Pei, J., & Kamber, M. (2011). *Data mining: Concepts and techniques.* Elsevier.

Jurafsky, D., & Martin, J. H. (2021). *Speech and language processing* (3rd ed.). Pearson.

Kitchin, R. (2014). *The data revolution: Big data, open data, data infrastructures and their consequences.* SAGE Publications Ltd.

Laney, D. (2001). 3D data management: Controlling data volume, velocity and variety. *META Group.*

LeCun, Y., Bengio, Y., & Hinton, G. (2015). Deep learning. *Nature, 521*(7553), 436-444.

Manyika, J., Chui, M., Brown, B., Bughin, J., Dobbs, R., Roxburgh, C., & Byers, A. H. (2011). Big data: The next frontier for innovation, competition, and productivity. *McKinsey Global Institute.*

Manyika, J., Chui, M., Brown, B., Bughin, J., Dobbs, R., Roxburgh, C., & Byers, A. H. (2011). Big data: The next frontier for innovation, competition, and productivity. *McKinsey Global Institute.*

Mitchell, T. M. (1997). *Machine learning.* McGraw-Hill.

Provost, F., & Fawcett, T. (2013). Data science and its relationship to big data and data-driven decision making. *Big Data, 1*(1), 51-59.

Raghupathi, W., & Raghupathi, V. (2014). Big data analytics in healthcare: Promise and potential. *Health Information Science and Systems, 2*(1), 1-10.

Russell, S., & Norvig, P. (2020). *Artificial intelligence: A modern approach* (4th ed.). Pearson.

Siciliano, B., & Khatib, O. (2016). *Springer handbook of robotics* (2nd ed.). Springer.

White, T. (2015). *Hadoop: The definitive guide.* O'Reilly Media.

Wickham, H. (2014). *Tidy data.* Journal of Statistical Software, *59*(10), 1-23.

Witten, I. H., Frank, E., & Hall, M. A. (2016). *Data mining: Practical machine learning tools and techniques.* Morgan Kaufmann.

Zaharia, M., Chowdhury, M., Franklin, M. J., Shenker, S., & Stoica, I. (2016). Spark: Cluster computing with working sets. *Communications of the ACM, 51*(7), 95-104.

Zikopoulos, P. C., Eaton, C., DeRoos, D., Deutsch, T., & Lapis, G. (2012). *Understanding big data: Analytics for enterprise class Hadoop and streaming data.* McGraw-Hill.

Chapter 2: Fundamentals of Machine Learning and Deep Learning

<u>Supervised Learning</u>

Supervised learning is one of the most widely used approaches in machine learning, where the algorithm is trained on a labeled dataset, meaning that each training example is paired with a corresponding target or output. The objective of supervised learning is to learn a function or model that maps inputs to the correct outputs based on the provided examples. Once trained, this model can predict the outputs for unseen data (Mitchell, 1997).

Supervised learning is often applied in tasks such as classification, where the goal is to assign input data to one of several predefined categories, and regression, where the goal is to predict a continuous value. Common examples include spam email classification, image recognition, and predicting house prices (Hastie, Tibshirani, & Friedman, 2009).

Components of Supervised Learning

Supervised learning involves several key components:

1. **Input Features (X):** The input data that the model uses to make predictions. Features are often represented as vectors of values.

2. **Target Labels (Y):** The corresponding outputs or labels associated with each input. In classification tasks, these labels are discrete (e.g., "cat" or "dog"), while in regression tasks, they are continuous (e.g., a numerical value).

3. **Learning Algorithm:** The algorithm that learns the mapping from inputs to outputs. Common algorithms include decision trees, support vector machines (SVM), and neural networks (Bishop, 2006).

4. **Model:** The mathematical representation learned by the algorithm, which can generalize from the training data to make predictions on new data.

5. **Loss Function:** A measure of how well the model's predictions match the actual target values. The goal of the learning process is to minimize this loss function.

Supervised Learning Algorithms

Several types of algorithms are commonly used in supervised learning:

Linear Regression: A simple algorithm used for regression tasks. It models the relationship between input features and a continuous target value by fitting a linear equation (Seber & Lee, 2012).

Decision Trees: A non-linear model used for both classification and regression. It partitions the input space into regions based on feature values and makes predictions based on the majority class or mean value in each region (Quinlan, 1986).

Support Vector Machines (SVM): A powerful algorithm used for classification tasks. It finds the hyperplane that maximally separates different classes in the input space (Cortes & Vapnik, 1995).

Neural Networks: A flexible algorithm used in both supervised and deep learning. Neural networks consist of layers of interconnected nodes (neurons) that learn complex patterns in the data (Goodfellow et al., 2016).

Applications of Supervised Learning

Supervised learning has a wide range of real-world applications across various domains:

Image Classification: In tasks like facial recognition or object detection, supervised learning models are trained on labeled images to classify new images accurately.

Natural Language Processing (NLP): Tasks such as sentiment analysis, spam detection, and language translation leverage supervised learning models trained on text data.

Medical Diagnosis: In healthcare, supervised learning is used to predict disease outcomes based on patient data, such as classifying tumor types or detecting abnormal patterns in medical images (Esteva et al., 2017).

Challenges in Supervised Learning

While supervised learning is highly effective, it comes with certain challenges:

Data Labeling: Labeled data is often expensive and time-consuming to acquire, especially for large datasets. In domains like medical imaging, expert annotations are required, which can limit the availability of training data (Settles, 2009).

Overfitting: If the model is too complex, it may perform well on the training data but fail to generalize to new, unseen data. This issue, known as overfitting, can be mitigated by techniques such as cross-validation and regularization (Hastie et al., 2009).

Imbalanced Data: In cases where some classes are underrepresented in the dataset, the model may become biased toward the majority class. Methods like resampling, class weighting, and synthetic data generation can help address this issue (He & Garcia, 2009).

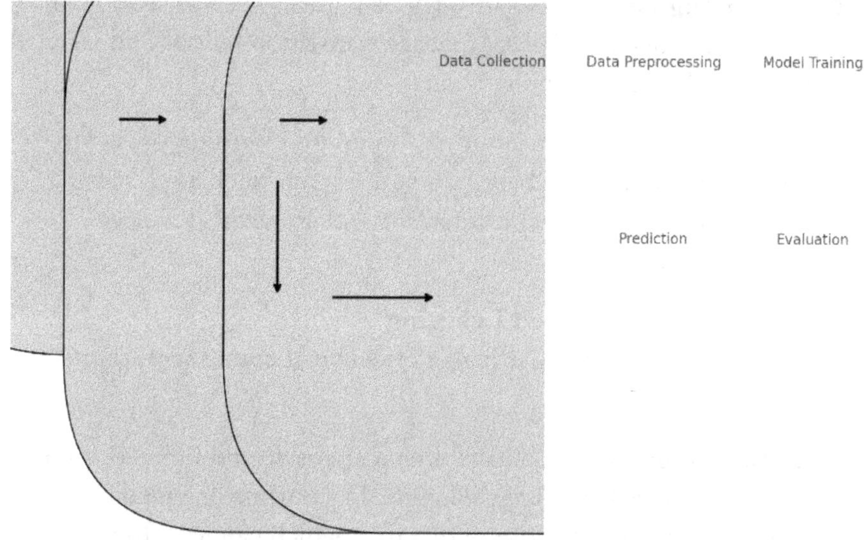

<u>Unsupervised Learning</u>

Unsupervised learning is a type of machine learning where the algorithm is tasked with discovering patterns in data without any explicit labels or predefined outcomes. In contrast to supervised learning, where the model learns from labeled data (input-output pairs), unsupervised learning works with raw, unlabeled datasets. The goal is to find hidden structures, correlations, or relationships within the data that can help in organizing and understanding the information (Bishop, 2006).

Unsupervised learning is often applied in scenarios where human annotation of data is either expensive or infeasible. It is widely used in tasks such as clustering, anomaly detection, and dimensionality reduction. This approach is valuable for exploring large datasets to uncover insights that may not be immediately apparent through manual analysis (Hastie, Tibshirani, & Friedman, 2009).

Key Concepts in Unsupervised Learning

Clustering: One of the most common tasks in unsupervised learning is clustering, which involves grouping similar data points into clusters based on certain characteristics. A popular algorithm for clustering is **K-means**, which partitions the data into K distinct clusters (MacQueen, 1967). Clustering is widely used in applications like customer segmentation, where companies group customers based on their purchasing behavior.

Dimensionality Reduction: In many real-world datasets, the number of features or variables can be very high, making analysis difficult. Dimensionality reduction techniques, such as **Principal Component Analysis (PCA)**, are used to reduce the number of input features while preserving important information. These techniques are valuable for visualizing high-dimensional data and improving the performance of machine learning algorithms (Wold, Esbensen, & Geladi, 1987).

Anomaly Detection: Unsupervised learning is often used for detecting anomalies, or outliers, in data. Since no prior knowledge of the data is assumed, anomaly detection models can identify patterns or data points that deviate significantly from the norm. Applications include fraud detection in financial transactions and identifying network security breaches (Chandola, Banerjee, & Kumar, 2009).

Types of Unsupervised Learning Algorithms

K-Means Clustering: A widely used algorithm for partitioning data into K clusters, where each data point belongs to the cluster with the nearest mean. The algorithm iteratively assigns points to clusters, recalculates cluster centroids, and repeats until convergence (MacQueen, 1967).

Hierarchical Clustering: This algorithm creates a hierarchy of clusters in either an agglomerative (bottom-up) or divisive (top-down) manner. It is particularly useful when the number of clusters is not predefined and for visualizing the relationships between clusters using dendrograms (Murtagh & Contreras, 2012).

Principal Component Analysis (PCA): A dimensionality reduction technique that transforms the data into a set of orthogonal components. The first few components capture the most variance in the data, allowing for the reduction of dimensionality while maintaining important patterns (Jolliffe, 2002).

Autoencoders: In deep learning, autoencoders are neural networks used for unsupervised learning tasks, particularly in reducing dimensionality and reconstructing input data. They consist of an encoder, which compresses the data, and a decoder, which reconstructs it. Autoencoders are used in applications such as image compression and anomaly detection (Goodfellow, Bengio, & Courville, 2016).

Applications of Unsupervised Learning

Customer Segmentation: Businesses use unsupervised learning to group customers based on purchasing behavior, demographics, or preferences. These insights can help tailor marketing strategies and product recommendations.

Document Clustering: Unsupervised learning is used to group similar documents or articles based on their content. This is particularly useful in text mining and information retrieval systems, where documents must be organized or searched efficiently (Aggarwal & Zhai, 2012).

Anomaly Detection: In cybersecurity, unsupervised learning is applied to detect unusual patterns in network traffic, which may indicate malicious activity or system vulnerabilities. Similarly, it is used in fraud detection for identifying irregular transactions (Chandola et al., 2009).

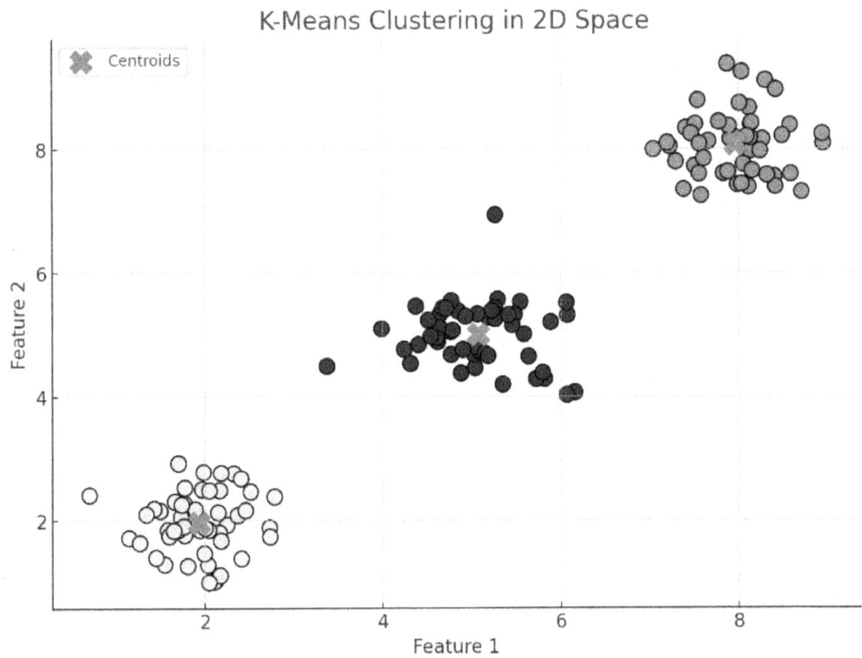

Reinforcement Learning

Reinforcement learning (RL) is a type of machine learning where an agent learns to make decisions by interacting with an environment. Unlike supervised learning, where the model is trained on labeled data, or unsupervised learning, where the model uncovers hidden patterns in unlabeled data, reinforcement learning involves trial and error. The agent takes actions to maximize cumulative rewards while minimizing penalties over time. The primary goal of reinforcement learning is to learn an optimal policy that dictates the best actions to take in various states of the environment (Sutton & Barto, 2018).

Key Concepts in Reinforcement Learning

- **Agent:** The decision-maker or learner in the RL setup. The agent interacts with the environment by taking actions and receiving feedback in the form of rewards or penalties.

- **Environment:** The external system the agent interacts with. The environment is usually modeled as a set of states that change based on the agent's actions.

- **State (S):** A representation of the current situation or condition of the environment. The agent observes the state before choosing an action.

- **Action (A):** A decision made by the agent that changes the state of the environment. Actions can be deterministic or stochastic depending on the problem setup.

- **Reward (R):** The feedback or signal that the agent receives after taking an action. Positive rewards encourage the agent to repeat the behavior, while negative rewards (penalties) discourage it.

- **Policy (π):** The strategy or mapping from states to actions. The goal of reinforcement learning is to find an optimal policy that maximizes the cumulative reward.

- **Value Function:** A function that estimates the expected cumulative reward from a given state or state-action pair.

Types of Reinforcement Learning Algorithms

Reinforcement learning algorithms can be categorized into two main types:

Model-Free Methods: These algorithms learn directly from interactions with the environment without building a model of the environment's dynamics. Examples include Q-learning and Deep Q Networks (DQN) (Mnih et al., 2015).

Q-Learning: Q-learning is a value-based method that seeks to learn the optimal action-value function (Q-function), which represents the expected cumulative reward for taking a certain action in a given state (Watkins & Dayan, 1992).

Deep Q Networks (DQN): DQN combines Q-learning with deep neural networks to handle high-dimensional state spaces. It has been successfully applied in complex environments like video games (Mnih et al., 2015).

Model-Based Methods: These algorithms attempt to build a model of the environment's dynamics, such as state transitions and rewards, and use this model to plan future actions. Examples include dynamic programming approaches like policy iteration and value iteration (Bertsekas, 2019).

Applications of Reinforcement Learning

Reinforcement learning is widely used in various real-world applications, especially in domains where autonomous decision-making is critical:

Robotics: RL is used to teach robots how to perform tasks autonomously by interacting with their physical environment. Robots can learn tasks such as grasping objects, walking, or navigating through complex spaces (Kober, Bagnell, & Peters, 2013).

Game Playing: Reinforcement learning has achieved remarkable success in game environments, particularly with the development of algorithms like AlphaGo, which surpassed human performance in the game of Go (Silver et al., 2016).

Autonomous Systems: RL is used to control autonomous vehicles and drones, where the agent learns to navigate, avoid obstacles, and optimize routes through continuous interactions with its surroundings (Sallab et al., 2017).

Finance: In algorithmic trading, RL is applied to optimize trading strategies by learning from historical data and reacting to market changes in real time (Deng et al., 2017).

Challenges in Reinforcement Learning

Exploration vs. Exploitation: The agent must balance exploring new actions to discover better rewards and exploiting known actions that have yielded high rewards in the past. This trade-off is central to RL algorithms (Sutton & Barto, 2018).

Sample Efficiency: RL algorithms often require many interactions with the environment to learn an optimal policy. This can be computationally expensive, especially in real-world environments (Mnih et al., 2015).

Sparse Rewards: In some environments, rewards are rare or delayed, making it difficult for the agent to learn the relationship between actions and outcomes.

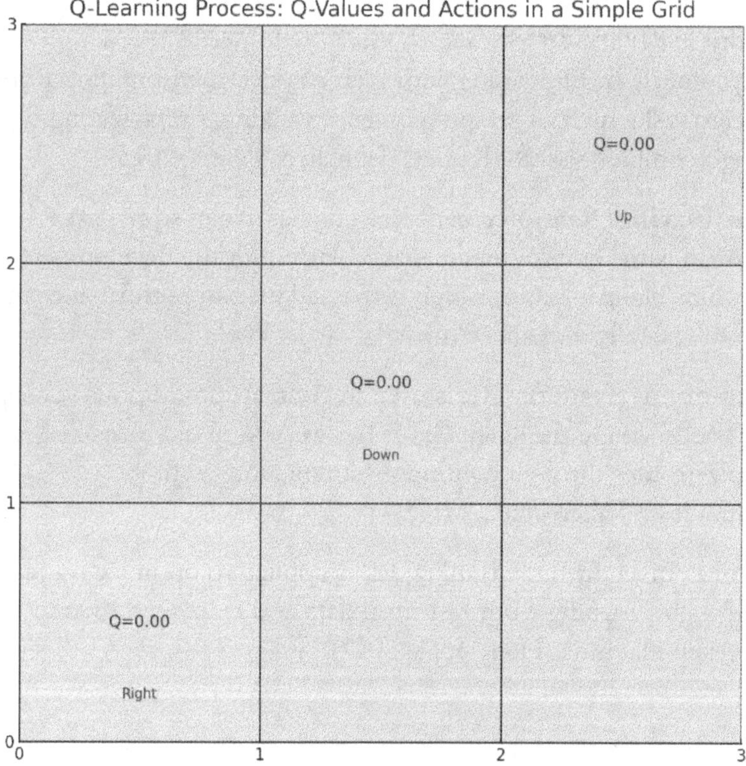

Introduction to Neural Networks

Neural networks are a fundamental concept in machine learning, especially in the field of deep learning. Inspired by the structure and function of the human brain, neural networks consist of layers of interconnected nodes, known as neurons, that work together to recognize patterns and solve complex problems. These models excel in tasks such as image recognition, natural language processing, and predictive modeling (Goodfellow, Bengio, & Courville, 2016).

Structure of Neural Networks

A neural network typically consists of three main types of layers:

Input Layer: This layer receives the raw input data and passes it to the next layer. Each neuron in the input layer represents a feature of the data.

Hidden Layers: These are intermediate layers where the actual computation and learning occur. Each neuron in a hidden layer is connected to every neuron in the previous and next layers. The more hidden layers a network has, the deeper it is, making it a *deep neural network* (Schmidhuber, 2015).

Output Layer: The final layer, which produces the network's prediction or classification. The number of neurons in this layer depends on the task (e.g., one neuron for binary classification, multiple neurons for multi-class classification).

Each connection between neurons has a *weight* that adjusts during the training process, and each neuron has an *activation function* that determines whether it should activate and pass information to the next layer. The most commonly used activation function in neural networks is the *ReLU (Rectified Linear Unit)*, which outputs the input directly if it is positive; otherwise, it outputs zero (Nair & Hinton, 2010).

Training Neural Networks

The process of training a neural network involves adjusting the weights and biases of the neurons to minimize the difference between the predicted output and the actual target values. This is done using a technique called *backpropagation*, which calculates the gradient of the loss function (a measure of error) with respect to each weight and updates them using an optimization algorithm, such as *stochastic gradient descent (SGD)* (Rumelhart, Hinton, & Williams, 1986).

The learning process in a neural network can be broken down into the following steps:

1. **Forward Pass:** The input data is passed through the network, and predictions are generated by propagating the data through the layers.

2. **Loss Calculation:** The loss function measures the difference between the predicted values and the actual target values.

3. **Backward Pass (Backpropagation):** The gradients of the loss function with respect to the weights are computed, and the weights are updated accordingly to minimize the loss.

4. **Weight Update:** The optimization algorithm updates the weights using the calculated gradients, moving the model toward better performance.

Common Neural Network Architectures

Feedforward Neural Networks (FNN): These are the simplest type of neural networks, where information flows in one direction—from the input layer to the output layer—without any loops or cycles. Feedforward networks are typically used for tasks such as regression and classification (Goodfellow et al., 2016).

Convolutional Neural Networks (CNN): CNNs are designed for tasks involving image data. They use *convolutional layers* to automatically detect spatial features such as edges, textures, and shapes in images. CNNs have achieved remarkable success in image classification, object detection, and face recognition (LeCun, Bengio, & Hinton, 2015).

Recurrent Neural Networks (RNN): RNNs are used for sequential data, such as time series or natural language. Unlike feedforward networks, RNNs have loops that allow them to retain information from previous inputs, making them suitable for tasks like language modeling and speech recognition (Hochreiter & Schmidhuber, 1997).

Applications of Neural Networks

Neural networks have found applications across various domains:

Image Recognition: Neural networks, particularly CNNs, are widely used for tasks such as image classification, object detection, and facial recognition.

Natural Language Processing (NLP): RNNs and other variants like Long Short-Term Memory (LSTM) networks are employed for tasks like sentiment analysis, machine translation, and text generation.

Healthcare: Neural networks are used in medical image analysis, disease prediction, and personalized treatment recommendations.

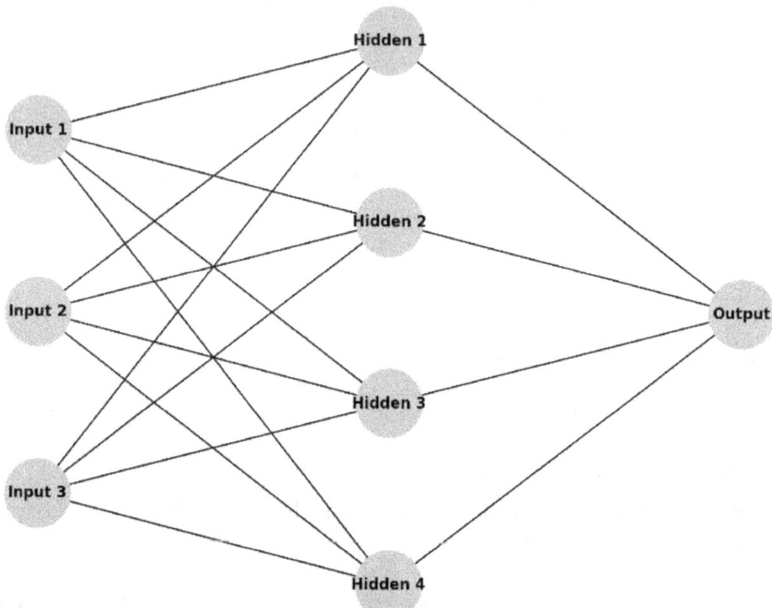

Deep Learning Architectures

Deep learning architectures represent a subset of machine learning that uses neural networks with many layers to model complex patterns in data. These architectures are designed to automatically extract hierarchical features from raw data and have become the foundation for solving complex tasks such as image recognition, natural language processing, and speech recognition. Unlike traditional machine learning models, which often rely on handcrafted features, deep learning architectures learn to discover representations directly from data (LeCun, Bengio, & Hinton, 2015).

Key Deep Learning Architectures

1. **Feedforward Neural Networks (FNNs)** Feedforward neural networks are the simplest type of neural network, where information flows in one direction—from input to output—

without cycles or feedback loops. The architecture consists of an input layer, multiple hidden layers, and an output layer. Each neuron in one layer is fully connected to the neurons in the next layer. FNNs are effective for tasks such as regression and classification (Goodfellow, Bengio, & Courville, 2016).

2. **Convolutional Neural Networks (CNNs)** CNNs are widely used in image processing and computer vision tasks. The key innovation of CNNs lies in their ability to recognize spatial hierarchies in images by applying convolutional layers. These layers detect local patterns like edges and textures, which are later combined to form higher-level representations, such as shapes or objects. CNNs consist of three main layers: convolutional layers, pooling layers, and fully connected layers (LeCun et al., 1998). CNNs have achieved state-of-the-art performance in image classification, object detection, and facial recognition.

Key Components of CNNs:

o **Convolutional Layers:** Apply filters (kernels) to the input data to detect local patterns.

o **Pooling Layers:** Reduce the spatial dimensions of the feature maps, helping to control overfitting and computational complexity.

o **Fully Connected Layers:** After the convolutional and pooling layers, fully connected layers are used for final classification or regression tasks.

3. **Recurrent Neural Networks (RNNs)** RNNs are designed to handle sequential data, such as time series or natural language, where the order of inputs is essential. RNNs have loops that allow information from previous time steps to persist, enabling them to capture temporal dependencies. However, traditional RNNs suffer from issues like vanishing gradients, which limit

their ability to learn long-term dependencies (Hochreiter & Schmidhuber, 1997).

Key Variants of RNNs:

Long Short-Term Memory (LSTM): LSTMs are a variant of RNNs designed to overcome the vanishing gradient problem. LSTMs maintain an internal memory cell that helps them retain information over long sequences, making them effective for tasks like language modeling and machine translation (Hochreiter & Schmidhuber, 1997).

Gated Recurrent Units (GRUs): GRUs are a simplified version of LSTMs, combining the forget and input gates into a single gate, which makes them computationally more efficient while still capturing long-term dependencies (Cho et al., 2014).

Autoencoders Autoencoders are unsupervised neural networks that aim to learn a compressed representation of input data. They consist of two main parts: an encoder, which compresses the input into a lower-dimensional space, and a decoder, which reconstructs the input from this representation. Autoencoders are commonly used for tasks like dimensionality reduction, anomaly detection, and image denoising (Goodfellow et al., 2016).

Generative Adversarial Networks (GANs) GANs are a class of generative models where two neural networks—a generator and a discriminator—are trained simultaneously in a game-theoretic setting. The generator tries to create realistic samples that mimic real data, while the discriminator attempts to distinguish between real and generated data. GANs have been used for tasks such as image generation, style transfer, and creating realistic animations (Goodfellow et al., 2014).

Transformers Transformers are a deep learning architecture designed to handle sequential data, particularly in natural language processing tasks. Unlike RNNs, transformers use an attention mechanism that allows them to process all elements of a sequence in parallel, rather than sequentially. This parallelization makes transformers much faster and more effective in handling long sequences. Transformers are the foundation of state-of-the-art NLP models like BERT and GPT (Vaswani et al., 2017).

Key Components of Transformers:

Self-Attention Mechanism: This mechanism allows each position in the input sequence to focus on all other positions, learning relationships between words in a sentence, regardless of their distance.

Positional Encoding: Since transformers process sequences in parallel, they use positional encodings to preserve the order of the sequence.

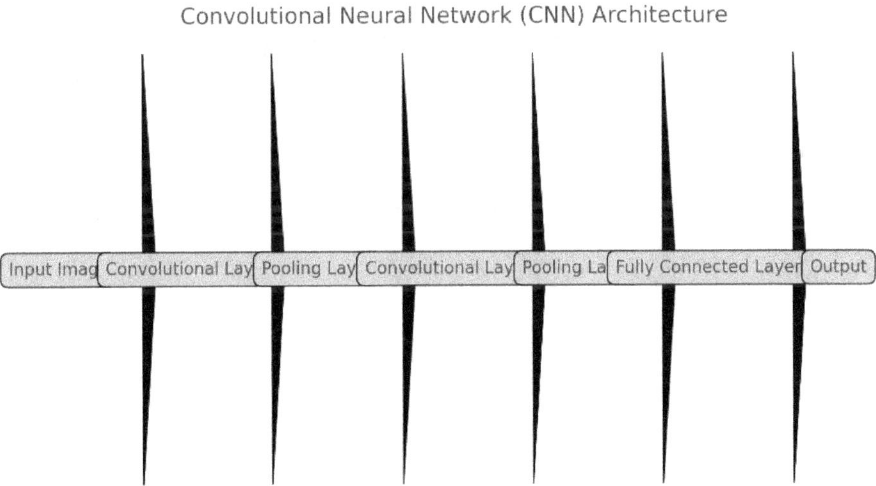

References

Aggarwal, C. C., & Zhai, C. (2012). *Mining text data.* Springer.

Bertsekas, D. P. (2019). *Reinforcement learning and optimal control.* Athena Scientific.

Bishop, C. M. (2006). *Pattern recognition and machine learning.* Springer.

Chandola, V., Banerjee, A., & Kumar, V. (2009). Anomaly detection: A survey. *ACM Computing Surveys, 41*(3), 1-58.

Cho, K., Van Merriënboer, B., Gulcehre, C., Bahdanau, D., Bougares, F., Schwenk, H., & Bengio, Y. (2014). Learning phrase representations using RNN encoder-decoder for statistical machine translation. *arXiv preprint arXiv:1406.1078.*

Deng, Y., Bao, F., Kong, Y., Ren, Z., & Dai, Q. (2017). Deep direct reinforcement learning for financial signal representation and trading. *IEEE Transactions on Neural Networks and Learning Systems, 28*(3), 653-664.

Goodfellow, I., Bengio, Y., & Courville, A. (2016). *Deep learning.* MIT Press.

Goodfellow, I., Pouget-Abadie, J., Mirza, M., Xu, B., Warde-Farley, D., Ozair, S., ... & Bengio, Y. (2014). Generative adversarial nets. *Advances in Neural Information Processing Systems, 27*, 2672-2680.

Hastie, T., Tibshirani, R., & Friedman, J. (2009). *The elements of statistical learning: Data mining, inference, and prediction.* Springer.

Hochreiter, S., & Schmidhuber, J. (1997). Long short-term memory. *Neural Computation, 9*(8), 1735-1780.

Jolliffe, I. T. (2002). *Principal component analysis.* Springer.

Kober, J., Bagnell, J. A., & Peters, J. (2013). Reinforcement learning in robotics: A survey. *The International Journal of Robotics Research, 32*(11), 1238-1274.

LeCun, Y., Bengio, Y., & Hinton, G. (2015). Deep learning. *Nature, 521*(7553), 436-444.

LeCun, Y., Bottou, L., Bengio, Y., & Haffner, P. (1998). Gradient-based learning applied to document recognition. *Proceedings of the IEEE, 86*(11), 2278-2324.

MacQueen, J. (1967). Some methods for classification and analysis of multivariate observations. In *Proceedings of the Fifth Berkeley Symposium on Mathematical Statistics and Probability* (pp. 281-297).

Mnih, V., Kavukcuoglu, K., Silver, D., Rusu, A. A., Veness, J., Bellemare, M. G., ... & Hassabis, D. (2015). Human-level control through deep reinforcement learning. *Nature, 518*(7540), 529-533.

Murtagh, F., & Contreras, P. (2012). Algorithms for hierarchical clustering: An overview. *Wiley Interdisciplinary Reviews: Data Mining and Knowledge Discovery, 2*(1), 86-97.

Nair, V., & Hinton, G. E. (2010). Rectified linear units improve restricted Boltzmann machines. *Proceedings of the 27th International Conference on Machine Learning (ICML-10)*, 807-814.

Rumelhart, D. E., Hinton, G. E., & Williams, R. J. (1986). Learning representations by back-propagating errors. *Nature, 323*(6088), 533-536.

Schmidhuber, J. (2015). Deep learning in neural networks: An overview. *Neural Networks, 61*, 85-117.

Silver, D., Huang, A., Maddison, C. J., Guez, A., Sifre, L., Van Den Driessche, G., ... & Hassabis, D. (2016). Mastering the game of Go with deep neural networks and tree search. *Nature, 529*(7587), 484-489.

Sutton, R. S., & Barto, A. G. (2018). *Reinforcement learning: An introduction* (2nd ed.). MIT Press.

Vaswani, A., Shazeer, N., Parmar, N., Uszkoreit, J., Jones, L., Gomez, A. N., ... & Polosukhin, I. (2017). Attention is all you need. *Advances in Neural Information Processing Systems, 30*, 5998-6008.

Watkins, C. J. C. H., & Dayan, P. (1992). Q-learning. *Machine Learning, 8*(3-4), 279-292.

Wold, S., Esbensen, K., & Geladi, P. (1987). Principal component analysis. *Chemometrics and Intelligent Laboratory Systems, 2*(1-3), 37-52.

Chapter 3: Big Data Technologies

<u>Characteristics of Big Data</u>

Big Data refers to datasets that are so large, fast, and complex that traditional data-processing systems cannot handle them effectively. To better understand the scope and challenges of Big Data, researchers and practitioners have identified five key characteristics, often referred to as the "5 Vs" of Big Data: Volume, Velocity, Variety, Veracity, and Value. These characteristics describe not only the scale of Big Data but also the challenges associated with managing, analyzing, and deriving insights from it (Gandomi & Haider, 2015).

1. Volume: The Scale of Data

Volume refers to the vast amounts of data generated every second from various sources such as social media platforms, sensors, financial transactions, and the Internet of Things (IoT). The rapid growth of data creation is due to the proliferation of digital devices and the increasing digitalization of daily activities. For example, it is estimated that by 2025, global data generation will exceed 175 zettabytes annually (Reinsel, Gantz, & Rydning, 2018). This massive scale of data requires innovative storage and processing techniques, such as distributed computing and cloud storage systems like Hadoop and Spark, to handle and analyze it efficiently (White, 2015).

2. Velocity: The Speed of Data Generation and Processing

Velocity refers to the speed at which data is generated and processed. In today's world, data is created and streamed in real time from various sources, such as social media, online transactions, and sensors in connected devices. For instance, platforms like Twitter and Facebook generate terabytes of data every day, and financial markets rely on millisecond-level analysis of data to make trading decisions (Gandomi & Haider, 2015). The ability to process and analyze this data in real time is critical for applications such as fraud detection, dynamic pricing, and real-time recommendation systems. Technologies like Apache Kafka and Apache Flink enable high-throughput, low-latency data processing to meet the demands of high-velocity data streams (Kreps, 2014).

3. Variety: The Diversity of Data Types

Variety refers to the different types and formats of data that are generated, including structured, semi-structured, and unstructured data. Structured data, like that found in relational databases, is organized in a predefined schema. Semi-structured data, such as JSON or XML, does not have a fixed schema but is still somewhat organized. Unstructured data, such as images, videos, audio, and social media posts, has no predefined structure and represents the majority of Big Data (Fan & Bifet, 2013). The variety of data types poses challenges for integrating, storing, and analyzing them, but it also offers opportunities to derive richer insights by analyzing data from diverse sources.

4. Veracity: The Quality and Trustworthiness of Data

Veracity refers to the uncertainty and reliability of data. Not all data is accurate, complete, or trustworthy, which can affect the insights derived from it. Data collected from social media platforms, for example, may contain inaccuracies, biases, or even deliberate misinformation (Zikopoulos et al., 2012). Managing data quality is a significant challenge in Big Data analytics because poor-quality data can lead to incorrect conclusions and decisions. Techniques such as data cleaning, validation, and anomaly detection are essential for ensuring that the data used in analysis is reliable.

5. Value: Turning Data into Insight

Value refers to the insights and benefits derived from analyzing Big Data. The ultimate goal of Big Data technologies is to extract meaningful and actionable insights that drive decision-making and innovation. While the sheer volume of data presents challenges, the value lies in identifying trends, patterns, and correlations that can lead to improved business processes, enhanced customer experiences, and new revenue streams (Gandomi & Haider, 2015). For example, in the healthcare industry, analyzing patient data can lead to early detection of diseases, and in finance, Big Data analytics can improve risk management and fraud detection.

Below is a graph illustrating the five key characteristics of Big Data - Volume, Velocity, Variety, Veracity, and Value - demonstrating how they interrelate and contribute to the complexity of Big Data management.

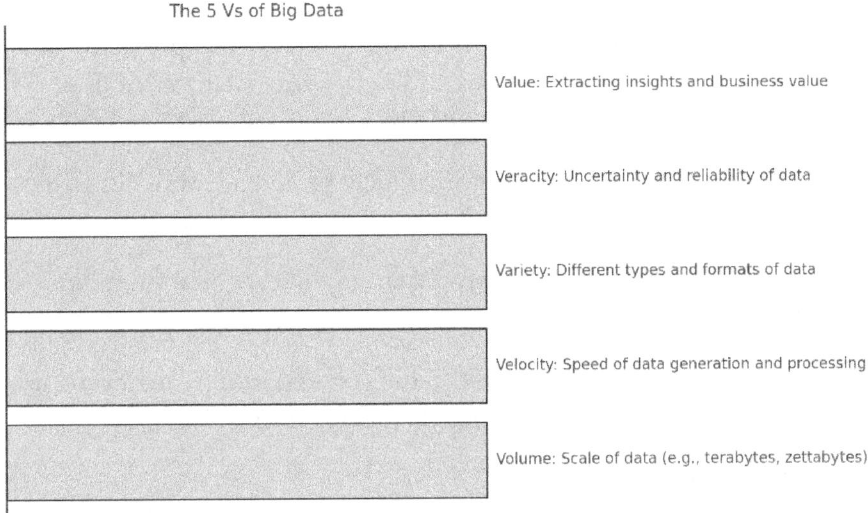

Big Data Storage and Processing Frameworks

Hadoop Ecosystem

The Hadoop ecosystem is a comprehensive suite of open-source tools designed to store, process, and analyze vast amounts of data in a distributed computing environment. It has become a cornerstone of Big Data technologies, enabling organizations to efficiently manage the "3 Vs" of Big Data: Volume, Velocity, and Variety. Originally developed by the Apache Software Foundation, Hadoop is built around two core components: Hadoop Distributed File System

(HDFS) and MapReduce, along with a range of complementary tools and frameworks that enhance its functionality (White, 2015).

Core Components of the Hadoop Ecosystem

Hadoop Distributed File System (HDFS)

HDFS is the storage layer of the Hadoop ecosystem and is responsible for managing large-scale data across multiple machines. It is designed to handle massive datasets by breaking them into smaller blocks (typically 128 MB or 256 MB) and distributing them across a cluster of machines. HDFS ensures data redundancy by replicating each block multiple times across different nodes, thus providing fault tolerance. This approach allows HDFS to store petabytes of data efficiently (Shvachko et al., 2010). The key features of HDFS include:

Scalability: HDFS can scale horizontally by adding more nodes to the cluster.

Fault Tolerance: If a node fails, data can be recovered from its replicas.

Cost-Effectiveness: Since HDFS runs on commodity hardware, it is more cost-efficient than traditional storage systems.

MapReduce

MapReduce is the primary processing framework for Hadoop and allows for the parallel processing of large datasets. It follows a simple programming model, consisting of two phases:

Map Phase: In this phase, the input data is split into smaller chunks, and the "mapper" function processes each chunk independently to generate intermediate key-value pairs.

Reduce Phase: The intermediate key-value pairs are then grouped by key, and the "reducer" function processes these groups to produce the final output. This model enables the processing of vast amounts of data in parallel, significantly improving performance (Dean & Ghemawat, 2008).

The MapReduce framework is particularly suited for batch processing tasks such as log analysis, indexing, and data transformation. However, its limitations in handling real-time data have led to the development of more advanced frameworks within the Hadoop ecosystem.

Complementary Tools in the Hadoop Ecosystem

In addition to HDFS and MapReduce, the Hadoop ecosystem includes several complementary tools that extend its functionality:

Apache Hive: Hive is a data warehousing tool that allows users to write SQL-like queries to interact with data stored in HDFS. It provides an abstraction over MapReduce, making it easier for analysts and developers to query large datasets without writing complex MapReduce code (Thusoo et al., 2009).

Apache Pig: Pig is a high-level platform for processing large datasets. It uses a scripting language called Pig Latin, which simplifies the development of complex data processing tasks. Like Hive, Pig translates its scripts into MapReduce jobs (Olston et al., 2008).

Apache HBase: HBase is a NoSQL database that provides real-time read/write access to large datasets. It is built on top of HDFS and supports random access to large tables of structured and unstructured data, making it useful for applications requiring low-latency access to data (George, 2011).

Apache Spark: Spark is a distributed processing engine that provides faster in-memory data processing compared to MapReduce. It supports both batch and real-time data processing, and its APIs are available in multiple languages, including Java, Python, and Scala (Zaharia et al., 2016). Spark has gained popularity for its ability to handle iterative algorithms, such as machine learning and graph processing, more efficiently than traditional MapReduce jobs.

Advantages of the Hadoop Ecosystem

Scalability: The Hadoop ecosystem can scale horizontally by adding more nodes to a cluster, enabling it to handle increasingly large datasets without a significant increase in costs.

Fault Tolerance: With built-in replication, HDFS ensures that data remains available even in the event of hardware failures. This fault tolerance is essential for large-scale distributed systems.

Cost Efficiency: Hadoop is designed to run on commodity hardware, which significantly reduces the cost of storing and processing large datasets compared to traditional enterprise solutions.

Flexibility: The Hadoop ecosystem supports both structured and unstructured data, making it highly versatile for handling a wide variety of data sources, from log files to images and videos.

Apache Spark

Apache Spark is an open-source distributed computing system designed for fast, flexible, and scalable data processing. It is widely regarded as one of the most powerful Big Data processing frameworks due to its in-memory processing capabilities and support for a wide range of workloads, including batch processing, real-time data streaming, machine learning, and graph processing. Spark was developed to overcome some of the limitations of Apache Hadoop's MapReduce framework, particularly its inefficiencies in iterative and real-time processing (Zaharia et al., 2016).

Key Features of Apache Spark

In-Memory Processing

One of the main advantages of Spark over traditional MapReduce is its in-memory data processing. Spark processes data by keeping it in memory (RAM) rather than writing intermediate results to disk, which significantly speeds up data processing tasks. This capability is especially beneficial for iterative algorithms, such as machine learning models, where multiple passes over the same data are required (Zaharia et al., 2010). By avoiding expensive disk I/O operations, Spark achieves up to 100x faster performance compared to Hadoop MapReduce.

Distributed Data Processing

Like Hadoop, Spark is built to run in a distributed environment, allowing it to scale horizontally by adding more nodes to the cluster. It uses a cluster management framework (e.g., Apache Mesos, Hadoop YARN, or Kubernetes) to distribute tasks across multiple machines, thereby enabling parallel data processing across large datasets. Spark's Resilient Distributed Dataset (RDD) abstraction ensures fault tolerance by distributing data across nodes and automatically recovering from node failures (Zaharia et al., 2012).

Unified Framework for Diverse Workloads

Spark is a unified engine that supports multiple types of data processing, making it a versatile framework for a wide range of applications. Its primary components include:

Spark SQL: Allows querying of structured and semi-structured data using SQL queries. It integrates with popular databases and supports data formats such as JSON, Parquet, and ORC.

Spark Streaming: Provides real-time data processing by ingesting and processing streaming data in small batches. It is widely used for applications like real-time analytics, monitoring, and fraud detection (Karau et al., 2017).

MLlib: Spark's machine learning library that offers scalable machine learning algorithms, including classification, regression, clustering, and collaborative filtering.

GraphX: A library for graph processing that allows users to run graph algorithms on large-scale datasets, useful in applications like social network analysis and recommendation systems.

Integration with Hadoop Ecosystem

Although Spark is often used as an alternative to Hadoop's MapReduce, it can also integrate seamlessly with Hadoop's ecosystem. Spark can run on top of Hadoop YARN and access data stored in Hadoop Distributed File System (HDFS), Apache HBase, and Amazon S3. This integration makes Spark a flexible solution for organizations already using Hadoop infrastructure while seeking the performance advantages of Spark's in-memory processing (White, 2015).

Applications of Apache Spark

Real-Time Analytics: Spark's ability to process streaming data in real time makes it ideal for real-time analytics. For example, financial institutions use Spark to monitor transactions and detect fraudulent activities as they occur.

Machine Learning: With MLlib, Spark offers a robust platform for building scalable machine learning models, including recommendations, fraud detection, and predictive analytics. Spark's in-memory processing and distributed architecture make it ideal for large-scale machine learning tasks (Meng et al., 2016).

Data Integration: Spark is frequently used to integrate and process data from various sources, such as databases, cloud storage, and streaming data, making it a versatile tool for data integration and ETL (Extract, Transform, Load) workflows.

Advantages of Apache Spark

High Performance: Spark's in-memory computation allows for faster data processing than traditional disk-based systems like Hadoop MapReduce.

Fault Tolerance: Spark ensures fault tolerance through its RDD abstraction, which maintains lineage information that can be used to recompute lost data.

Flexibility: Spark supports a wide range of workloads, from batch processing to real-time streaming and machine learning, making it a versatile tool for diverse data processing needs.

Scalability: Spark's distributed architecture allows it to handle petabytes of data, making it scalable across clusters of thousands of nodes.

NoSQL Databases

NoSQL (Not Only SQL) databases are a class of non-relational databases designed to handle large volumes of unstructured or semi-structured data at scale. Unlike traditional relational databases, which use structured schemas and SQL queries, NoSQL databases provide flexible, schema-less designs that allow for scalability, high availability, and performance in distributed systems. This flexibility makes them well-suited for Big Data applications where the "3 Vs" (Volume, Velocity, Variety) of Big Data are prevalent (Han et al., 2011).

Key Characteristics of NoSQL Databases

Schema Flexibility
One of the primary advantages of NoSQL databases is their schema-less nature, meaning that data can be stored without a fixed structure. This allows for greater flexibility in storing diverse data types, including JSON, XML, and binary formats like images and videos. As data grows in variety, NoSQL databases can adapt without requiring complex data migrations (Pokorny, 2013).

Horizontal Scalability
NoSQL databases are designed to scale horizontally, meaning they can handle increasing amounts of data by adding more nodes to the system, rather than requiring more powerful hardware. This is achieved through distributed architectures that partition data across multiple servers (nodes) while maintaining consistency and availability. Techniques such as sharding are used to distribute data

across nodes, ensuring efficient access and storage (Grolinger et al., 2013).

High Availability and Fault Tolerance

NoSQL databases often prioritize availability over strict consistency, especially in environments that require continuous uptime. Many NoSQL databases employ replication and data partitioning strategies to ensure that the system remains available even if some nodes fail. By replicating data across multiple nodes, NoSQL systems provide fault tolerance and resilience to hardware failures (Moniruzzaman & Hossain, 2013).

Optimized for Big Data Workloads

NoSQL databases are optimized for Big Data workloads, particularly when dealing with large datasets generated from social media, IoT devices, and web applications. These databases can handle fast write operations, streaming data, and real-time analytics, making them ideal for Big Data environments that require high throughput and low latency (Leavitt, 2010).

Types of NoSQL Databases

NoSQL databases can be classified into four major categories, each suited for different types of data and use cases:

Document Stores

Document-oriented databases store data in documents, typically in formats such as JSON or BSON (Binary JSON). Each document can contain different fields, allowing for flexibility in handling unstructured data. MongoDB is a widely used document store that supports querying and indexing, making it ideal for content management systems and data integration tasks (Chodorow, 2013).

Key-Value Stores

Key-value stores are the simplest type of NoSQL databases, where data is stored as key-value pairs. These databases are highly scalable and optimized for fast read and write operations. Key-value stores are commonly used in caching, session management, and real-time applications. Redis and Amazon DynamoDB are popular examples of key-value databases (DeCandia et al., 2007).

Column-Family Stores

Column-family stores organize data into columns rather than rows, making them efficient for handling wide tables with millions of columns. These databases are commonly used for analytical workloads and time-series data. Apache Cassandra and HBase are leading examples, both of which are designed to scale horizontally across distributed systems (Lakshman & Malik, 2010).

Graph Databases

Graph databases are designed to store and query data in the form of nodes, edges, and relationships. They are optimized for applications that involve complex relationships, such as social networks, fraud detection, and recommendation engines. Neo4j is a popular graph database that enables fast traversal of graph structures (Angles & Gutierrez, 2008).

Applications of NoSQL Databases

Social Media and Web Applications: NoSQL databases are widely used to store large volumes of user-generated content, such as social media posts, comments, and interactions. Their ability to handle high write throughput and provide real-time analytics makes them ideal for social platforms.

Internet of Things (IoT): The continuous generation of sensor data from IoT devices requires scalable storage solutions. NoSQL databases, especially key-value stores and time-series databases, are often used to store and process this data in real time.

E-commerce and Retail: NoSQL databases power e-commerce platforms by storing product catalogs, user profiles, shopping cart data, and transaction logs. Their ability to scale and provide low-latency access to data ensures seamless shopping experiences for users.

Advantages of NoSQL Databases

Scalability: NoSQL databases are designed for horizontal scalability, allowing organizations to handle large datasets without performance degradation.

Flexibility: NoSQL's schema-less architecture provides flexibility for evolving data structures, enabling organizations to store and query diverse data types.

Performance: Optimized for high read and write performance, NoSQL databases excel in handling Big Data workloads, particularly for real-time applications.

Data Warehousing and Data Lakes

Data Warehousing and Data Lakes are essential components of modern data architectures, providing storage and management solutions for vast amounts of data. Both systems serve as repositories for data, but they are fundamentally different in structure, purpose, and the types of data they store. Understanding the distinctions and use cases for each is critical for organizations that aim to leverage Big Data effectively.

Data Warehousing: Structured Data for Analytics

A data warehouse is a centralized repository that stores structured and processed data, often from multiple sources, for the purpose of reporting and analysis. Data warehousing systems are designed to support business intelligence (BI) and analytics by enabling fast queries and providing an organized environment for data that has been transformed and cleaned (Inmon, 2005).

Characteristics of Data Warehouses:

Structured Data: Data warehouses store structured data in predefined schemas, typically in relational databases. Data is processed, cleansed, and formatted into a uniform structure before being loaded into the warehouse.

Historical Data: Data warehouses are designed to store historical data, enabling trend analysis, forecasting, and reporting. This makes them essential for businesses that rely on past performance to make data-driven decisions (Kimball & Ross, 2013).

Batch Processing: Data is typically loaded into data warehouses in batches rather than real time. ETL (Extract, Transform, Load) processes are used to extract data from source systems, transform it to fit the warehouse schema, and load it into the warehouse.

Query Optimization: Data warehouses are optimized for complex SQL queries and analytical processing, often using indexes, partitions, and materialized views to speed up query performance.

Applications of Data Warehouses:

Business Intelligence (BI): Data warehouses serve as the backbone for BI tools and dashboards, allowing users to query data and generate reports that guide strategic decision-making.

Customer Analytics: Organizations use data warehouses to analyze customer behavior, track KPIs (Key Performance Indicators), and monitor sales trends.

Financial Reporting: Data warehouses store financial data that is critical for regulatory reporting, budgeting, and forecasting.

Data Lakes: Unstructured Data for Flexibility and Scalability

A data lake, on the other hand, is a storage system that allows for the collection and storage of raw, unprocessed data in its native format. Data lakes are highly scalable and can handle a wide variety of data types, including structured, semi-structured, and unstructured data. The key advantage of a data lake is its flexibility in storing large volumes of data without needing to transform or structure it beforehand (Gartner, 2018).

Characteristics of Data Lakes:

Raw Data: Data lakes store raw data without imposing any structure. This allows organizations to ingest vast amounts of data, such as logs, images, videos, and social media posts, without the need for upfront processing.

Schema-on-Read: Unlike data warehouses, which impose a schema during the data loading phase (schema-on-write), data lakes apply a schema when the data is accessed (schema-on-read). This allows for greater flexibility in how data is used and analyzed.

Real-Time Ingestion: Data lakes support real-time data ingestion from a variety of sources, including streaming data from IoT devices, social media platforms, and real-time analytics systems (Sawadogo et al., 2019).

Scalability: Data lakes are built on distributed storage systems (e.g., Hadoop, Amazon S3) that allow them to scale horizontally, meaning they can accommodate petabytes of data without performance degradation.

Applications of Data Lakes:

Data Science and Machine Learning: Data lakes provide a rich repository of data that data scientists and machine learning models can access for training and experimentation.

Real-Time Analytics: Because data lakes can handle real-time data, they are ideal for applications that require immediate insights, such as fraud detection, predictive maintenance, and recommendation systems.

Archival and Backup: Data lakes can serve as a low-cost archival solution, storing vast amounts of historical data that can be retrieved and analyzed later.

Key Differences Between Data Warehouses and Data Lakes

Feature	Data Warehouse	Data Lake
Data Type	Structured data	Structured, semi-structured, and unstructured data
Processing	ETL (data is processed before loading)	ELT (data is processed at query time)
Storage Cost	Higher cost due to structured data processing	Lower cost due to raw data storage
Use Case	Business intelligence and reporting	Data science, machine learning, real-time analytics
Schema	Schema-on-write	Schema-on-read
Performance	Optimized for complex queries and reporting	Flexible, but may require more processing for structured analysis

Convergence: Data Lakehouse

Recently, a hybrid approach known as the "data lakehouse" has emerged, combining elements of both data warehouses and data lakes. A data lakehouse allows organizations to store raw data in a data lake while also applying structure to certain portions of the data to support analytics. This architecture enables both large-scale data storage and efficient querying of structured data (Armbrust et al., 2021).

Below is a graph illustrating the differences between data warehouses and data lakes, showing how data flows through each system from ingestion to processing and analysis.

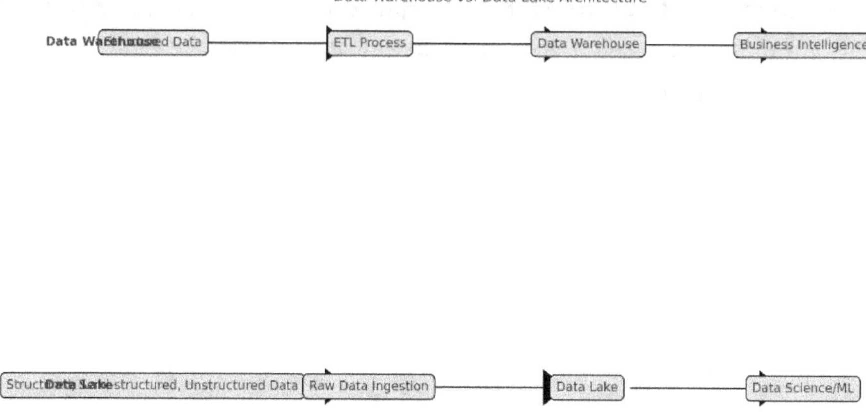

Cloud Computing and Big Data

Cloud computing has revolutionized the way organizations store, process, and analyze Big Data. By leveraging cloud services, businesses can handle vast amounts of data without the need to invest in expensive infrastructure. Cloud computing offers scalable resources on demand, providing a flexible and cost-efficient solution for managing the "3 Vs" of Big Data: Volume, Velocity, and Variety. The integration of Big Data technologies with cloud computing has created a powerful ecosystem that supports real-time analytics, machine learning, and business intelligence at scale (Dikaiakos et al., 2009).

Key Characteristics of Cloud Computing for Big Data

Scalability and Elasticity

One of the most important features of cloud computing is its ability to scale resources up or down based on demand. Cloud platforms like Amazon Web Services (AWS), Google Cloud Platform (GCP), and Microsoft Azure allow organizations to allocate additional compute or storage capacity as needed. This elasticity is critical for Big Data workloads that experience fluctuating demand, such as during peak business periods or real-time data streams (Buyya et al., 2009). The pay-as-you-go model ensures that organizations only pay for the resources they use, making cloud computing a cost-effective solution for handling Big Data.

Cost Efficiency

Cloud computing reduces the upfront capital expenditures associated with setting up on-premises data centers. Instead, organizations can take advantage of operational expenditures (OpEx) by renting infrastructure, which includes storage, networking, and compute power, as a service. For Big Data analytics, which often involves processing vast amounts of data, cloud computing offers the advantage of access to powerful hardware and tools without the need to purchase or maintain it (Rittinghouse & Ransome, 2017). Services like Amazon S3, Google Cloud Storage, and Azure Blob Storage are widely used for storing massive datasets in the cloud.

Data Storage and Processing

Cloud platforms offer a variety of storage options for handling structured, semi-structured, and unstructured data. Services such as Amazon S3, Google Cloud Storage, and Azure Data Lake are commonly used for data lakes, while relational databases like Amazon RDS, Google Cloud SQL, and Azure SQL Database support structured data storage. For processing Big Data, cloud platforms provide distributed computing frameworks like Amazon EMR (Elastic MapReduce), Google Dataproc, and Azure HDInsight, which support Hadoop, Spark, and other Big Data processing tools (Chen et al., 2014).

Real-Time Analytics

Cloud computing enables real-time data analytics by integrating with streaming data services such as Amazon Kinesis, Google Cloud Dataflow, and Azure Stream Analytics. These tools allow organizations to process and analyze data in real time, providing insights that drive immediate decision-making. In industries such as finance, e-commerce, and healthcare, real-time analytics is essential for applications like fraud detection, predictive maintenance, and customer personalization (Hashem et al., 2015).

Security and Compliance

Cloud providers have invested heavily in security protocols and compliance certifications to ensure that data stored and processed in the cloud is protected. Cloud platforms offer encryption services, identity management, and access control mechanisms to safeguard sensitive data. For organizations dealing with regulatory requirements, cloud providers often comply with industry standards like GDPR, HIPAA, and ISO certifications (Subashini & Kavitha, 2011). This ensures that Big Data workloads in sectors such as healthcare, finance, and government can operate securely in the cloud.

Advantages of Cloud Computing for Big Data

Flexibility: Cloud computing supports a wide range of data types and workloads, allowing organizations to run both batch and real-time data analytics.

Global Accessibility: Cloud platforms provide global infrastructure, allowing organizations to access data and processing power from anywhere in the world.

Disaster Recovery: Cloud platforms offer robust disaster recovery options, ensuring that data is replicated across multiple regions to prevent data loss in case of outages.

Cloud-Based Big Data Tools

Several cloud-based tools are widely used for Big Data storage, processing, and analysis:

Amazon Web Services (AWS): AWS provides a comprehensive suite of Big Data tools, including Amazon S3 for storage, Amazon Redshift for data warehousing, and Amazon EMR for distributed processing.

Google Cloud Platform (GCP): GCP offers services like Google BigQuery for data analytics, Google Cloud Storage for object storage, and Google Dataproc for Hadoop and Spark processing.

Microsoft Azure: Azure provides Azure Synapse Analytics for data integration and analytics, Azure Blob Storage for data storage, and Azure HDInsight for Big Data processing using Hadoop and Spark.

Applications of Cloud-Based Big Data Solutions

Healthcare: Cloud-based Big Data solutions are used for processing and analyzing vast amounts of healthcare data, including patient records, genomic data, and medical imaging. This enables predictive analytics, personalized medicine, and real-time monitoring of patient conditions.

Retail and E-commerce: In the retail sector, cloud-based Big Data analytics is used to analyze customer behavior, personalize recommendations, and optimize supply chain management. Retailers use cloud services to process large volumes of transaction data, social media interactions, and browsing patterns.

Finance: Financial institutions use cloud platforms to process high-frequency trading data, detect fraud in real time, and perform risk analysis. Cloud-based machine learning models can also be trained to predict market trends and customer creditworthiness.

Below is a graph illustrating the integration of cloud computing with Big Data technologies, showing how data flows from storage to processing and analysis through cloud-based services.

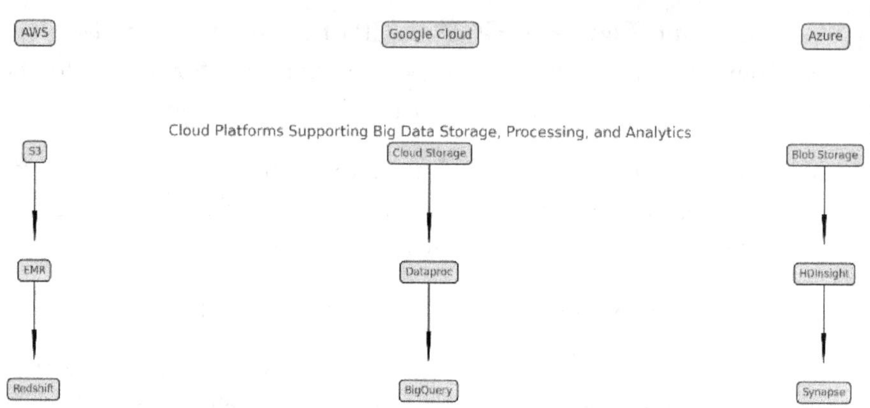

The graph illustrating how cloud platforms like AWS, Google Cloud, and Azure support Big Data storage, processing, and analytics. It highlights key services such as Amazon S3, Google Cloud Storage, and Azure Blob Storage for data storage, as well as processing tools like EMR, Dataproc, and HDInsight, followed by analytics services like Redshift, BigQuery, and Synapse.

References

Angles, R., & Gutierrez, C. (2008). Survey of graph database models. *ACM Computing Surveys, 40*(1), 1-39.

Armbrust, M., Ghodsi, A., Zaharia, M., & Xin, R. S. (2021). Lakehouse: A new generation of open platforms that unify data warehousing and advanced analytics. *Communications of the ACM, 64*(9), 53-64.

Buyya, R., Yeo, C. S., Venugopal, S., Broberg, J., & Brandic, I. (2009). Cloud computing and emerging IT platforms: Vision, hype, and reality for delivering computing as the 5th utility. *Future Generation Computer Systems, 25*(6), 599-616.

Chen, M., Mao, S., & Liu, Y. (2014). Big data: A survey. *Mobile Networks and Applications, 19*(2), 171-209.

Chodorow, K. (2013). *MongoDB: The definitive guide* (2nd ed.). O'Reilly Media.

Dean, J., & Ghemawat, S. (2008). MapReduce: Simplified data processing on large clusters. *Communications of the ACM, 51*(1), 107-113.

DeCandia, G., Hastorun, D., Jampani, M., Kakulapati, G., Lakshman, A., Pilchin, A., ... & Vogels, W. (2007). Dynamo: Amazon's highly available key-value store. *ACM SIGOPS Operating Systems Review, 41*(6), 205-220.

Dikaiakos, M. D., Katsaros, D., Mehra, P., Pallis, G., & Vakali, A. (2009). Cloud computing: Distributed Internet computing for IT and scientific research. *IEEE Internet Computing, 13*(5), 10-13.

Fan, W., & Bifet, A. (2013). Mining big data: Current status, and forecast to the future. *ACM SIGKDD Explorations Newsletter, 14*(2), 1-5.

Gandomi, A., & Haider, M. (2015). Beyond the hype: Big data concepts, methods, and analytics. *International Journal of Information Management, 35*(2), 137-144.

Gartner. (2018). The essential guide to data lakes. *Gartner Research.*

George, L. (2011). *HBase: The definitive guide.* O'Reilly Media.

Grolinger, K., Higashino, W. A., Tiwari, A., & Capretz, M. A. M. (2013). Data management in cloud environments: NoSQL and NewSQL data stores. *Journal of Cloud Computing: Advances, Systems and Applications, 2*(1), 1-24.

Han, J., E, H., Le, S., & Du, J. (2011). Survey on NoSQL database. *2011 6th International Conference on Pervasive Computing and Applications,* 363-366.

Hashem, I. A. T., Yaqoob, I., Anuar, N. B., Mokhtar, S., Gani, A., & Khan, S. U. (2015). The rise of "big data" on cloud computing: Review and open research issues. *Information Systems, 47,* 98-115.

Inmon, W. H. (2005). *Building the data warehouse* (4th ed.). Wiley.

Karau, H., Konwinski, A., Wendell, P., & Zaharia, M. (2017). *Learning Spark: Lightning-fast data analytics.* O'Reilly Media.

Kimball, R., & Ross, M. (2013). *The data warehouse toolkit: The definitive guide to dimensional modeling* (3rd ed.). Wiley.

Kreps, J. (2014). Questioning the Lambda architecture. *O'Reilly Radar.*

Lakshman, A., & Malik, P. (2010). Cassandra: A decentralized structured storage system. *ACM SIGOPS Operating Systems Review, 44*(2), 35-40.

Leavitt, N. (2010). Will NoSQL databases live up to their promise? *Computer, 43*(2), 12-14.

Meng, X., Bradley, J., Yuvaz, B., Sparks, E., Venkataraman, S., Liu, D., ... & Zaharia, M. (2016). MLlib: Machine learning in Apache Spark. *Journal of Machine Learning Research, 17*(1), 1235-1241.

Moniruzzaman, A. B. M., & Hossain, S. A. (2013). NoSQL database: New era of databases for Big Data analytics—Classification, characteristics, and comparison. *International Journal of Database Theory and Application, 6*(4), 1-14.

Olston, C., Reed, B., Srivastava, U., Kumar, R., & Tomkins, A. (2008). Pig Latin: A not-so-foreign language for data processing. *Proceedings of the 2008 ACM SIGMOD International Conference on Management of Data*, 1099-1110.

Pokorny, J. (2013). NoSQL databases: A step to database scalability in web environment. *International Journal of Web Information Systems, 9*(1), 69-82.

Reinsel, D., Gantz, J., & Rydning, J. (2018). The digitization of the world from edge to core. *IDC White Paper.*

Rittinghouse, J. W., & Ransome, J. F. (2017). *Cloud computing: Implementation, management, and security.* CRC Press.

Sawadogo, P., Darmont, J., & Houssem, G. (2019). Metadata systems for data lakes: Models and features. *International Journal of Database Management Systems, 11*(4), 29-44.

Shvachko, K., Kuang, H., Radia, S., & Chansler, R. (2010). The Hadoop distributed file system. *2010 IEEE 26th Symposium on Mass Storage Systems and Technologies (MSST)*, 1-10.

Subashini, S., & Kavitha, V. (2011). A survey on security issues in service delivery models of cloud computing. *Journal of Network and Computer Applications, 34*(1), 1-11.

Thusoo, A., Sarma, J. S., Jain, N., Shao, Z., Chakka, P., Anthony, S., ... & Murthy, R. (2009). Hive: A warehousing solution over a mapreduce framework. *Proceedings of the VLDB Endowment, 2*(2), 1626-1629.

White, T. (2015). *Hadoop: The definitive guide* (4th ed.). O'Reilly Media.

Zaharia, M., Chowdhury, M., Das, T., Dave, A., Ma, J., McCauley, M., ... & Stoica, I. (2012). Resilient distributed datasets: A fault-tolerant abstraction for in-memory cluster computing. *USENIX Symposium on Networked Systems Design and Implementation (NSDI), 2-2.*

Zaharia, M., Chowdhury, M., Franklin, M. J., Shenker, S., & Stoica, I. (2016). Spark: Cluster computing with working sets. *Communications of the ACM, 51*(7), 95-104.

Zaharia, M., Chowdhury, M., Franklin, M. J., Shenker, S., & Stoica, I. (2010). Spark: Cluster computing with working sets. *Proceedings of the 2nd USENIX Conference on Hot Topics in Cloud Computing,* 10.

Zikopoulos, P. C., Eaton, C., DeRoos, D., Deutsch, T., & Lapis, G. (2012). *Understanding big data: Analytics for enterprise class Hadoop and streaming data.* McGraw-Hill.

Part II: AI Techniques in Data Science and Big Data
Chapter 4: Data Preprocessing and Feature Engineering

<u>Data Cleaning and Imputation</u>

Data cleaning and imputation are critical stages in the data preprocessing pipeline for any machine learning or data science project. The quality of the input data has a significant impact on the performance of machine learning models, and poor-quality data can lead to inaccurate predictions, biased outcomes, and erroneous insights. Data cleaning is the process of identifying and correcting (or removing) corrupt, incomplete, or irrelevant data from a dataset, while data imputation involves replacing missing values in a dataset with estimated or substituted values (Garcia et al., 2016).

Data Cleaning: Ensuring Data Quality

Data cleaning is a foundational step in data preprocessing. It involves a systematic process to identify and rectify errors, inconsistencies, or anomalies in a dataset. Common issues in raw data include duplicate entries, incorrect data types, outliers, and invalid values. In the context of Big Data, data cleaning is essential due to the sheer volume of data being collected from various sources, which often includes noise and inconsistencies.

Some of the key tasks in data cleaning include:

Removing Duplicate Entries: Duplicate records can lead to biased analyses. In large datasets, the same data may be recorded multiple times, particularly in log files or databases capturing user interactions. Removing duplicate entries ensures that analysis is based on unique data points (Rahm & Do, 2000).

Handling Outliers: Outliers are extreme values that deviate significantly from other observations. While some outliers may be informative, others may be the result of data entry errors or measurement issues. Techniques such as Z-score normalization or Interquartile Range (IQR) can help detect and handle outliers, either by removing them or capping extreme values (Aggarwal, 2017).

Correcting Data Types: Incorrect data types can cause errors during analysis or modeling. For example, numeric values stored as strings or dates stored in inconsistent formats need to be standardized.

Standardizing Categorical Variables: Inconsistent naming conventions for categorical data (e.g., "Male" vs. "M" vs. "male") need to be standardized to ensure consistency in analysis.

Data Imputation: Handling Missing Data

Data imputation refers to the process of estimating and filling in missing values in a dataset. Missing data is a common issue, particularly in real-world datasets that are collected from various sources over time. Imputation ensures that the dataset remains usable for analysis or machine learning, even when certain values are unavailable.

There are several methods for handling missing data, each with its strengths and weaknesses:

Mean/Median Imputation

One of the simplest imputation methods involves replacing missing numerical values with the mean or median of the non-missing values for that variable. While this method is easy to implement, it can introduce bias into the dataset, particularly if the data is skewed or if the missing data is not random (Little & Rubin, 2019).

Mode Imputation (for Categorical Data)

For categorical variables, missing values can be imputed using the most frequent category (mode). However, like mean imputation, this can lead to over-representation of the most common category, especially if a large proportion of data is missing.

K-Nearest Neighbors (KNN) Imputation

KNN imputation is a more advanced technique that uses the values from similar data points (neighbors) to estimate the missing values. By identifying the K-nearest neighbors of a data point (based on Euclidean distance for numeric data), KNN fills in the missing values using the average of the neighboring data points. This method generally performs well but can be computationally expensive for large datasets (Troyanskaya et al., 2001).

Multivariate Imputation by Chained Equations (MICE)

MICE is a robust imputation technique that models each variable with missing values as a function of the other variables in the dataset. It iteratively predicts missing values using regression models and produces multiple imputed datasets. This method accounts for uncertainty in the imputation process and is often used in scenarios where data is missing at random (White et al., 2011).

Regression Imputation

Regression imputation involves predicting missing values based on a regression model that uses other variables as predictors. For example, if a dataset is missing certain income values, a regression model could be built using other demographic variables (e.g., age, education, occupation) to predict the missing values.

Challenges and Considerations in Data Imputation

Bias and Variance Trade-off: Simple imputation techniques like mean or mode imputation can introduce bias by underestimating the variability of the data. On the other hand, more complex methods like KNN or MICE can reduce bias but may increase variance, especially if the imputation model is overfitting the data (Enders, 2010).

Missing Not at Random (MNAR): If the missing data is not random but depends on unobserved factors, imputation methods may not provide accurate estimates. In such cases, domain expertise and advanced techniques are required to handle MNAR data appropriately (Rubin, 1976).

Impact on Machine Learning Models: Imputation methods can influence the performance of machine learning models. For instance, improper imputation may lead to biased model predictions, especially in supervised learning tasks.

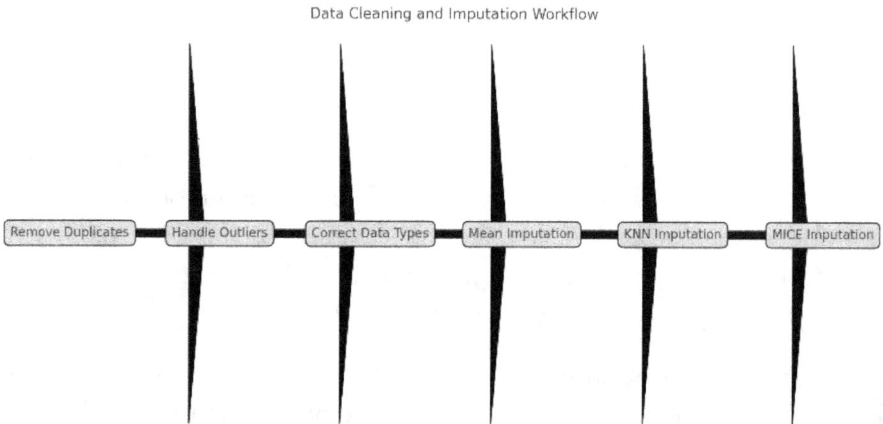

The above graph is illustrating the data cleaning and imputation process, showing steps such as removing duplicates, handling outliers, and performing various imputation techniques (mean, KNN, and MICE).

Data Transformation and Normalization

Data transformation and normalization are essential steps in the data preprocessing pipeline, especially when preparing data for machine learning algorithms. These processes are used to modify, scale, or change the format of the data to ensure that it is suitable for analysis. Properly transformed and normalized data helps algorithms perform more efficiently and accurately by ensuring that the data is in a consistent format and removing potential biases caused by differences in scale or units (Han et al., 2011).

Data Transformation: Converting Data into a Suitable Format

Data transformation involves changing the format, structure, or values of data to make it more suitable for analysis. This process is necessary when working with heterogeneous datasets that contain different types of data, such as numerical, categorical, or text data.

Log Transformation:

Logarithmic transformation is commonly applied to datasets with a skewed distribution. By applying the logarithm function, extreme values are compressed, which reduces the skewness and brings the data closer to a normal distribution. This transformation is often used in financial data, where values such as income or stock prices may vary by several orders of magnitude (Osborne, 2010).

Square Root Transformation:

Similar to log transformation, square root transformation reduces the impact of large values. It is especially useful for stabilizing variance in datasets with heteroscedasticity (unequal variance) and is often applied in biological or environmental data.

Box-Cox Transformation:

The Box-Cox transformation is a more flexible method that transforms non-normal dependent variables into a normal shape. Unlike log or square root transformations, Box-Cox includes a parameter that adjusts the transformation to best fit the data distribution (Box & Cox, 1964).

Encoding Categorical Variables:

Machine learning algorithms often require numerical input. Categorical variables must be encoded before they can be used in models. Common encoding techniques include:

o **One-Hot Encoding:** Converts categorical variables into binary vectors, where each category is represented by a binary column (0 or 1). For example, if a dataset has a "Color" variable with categories "Red," "Blue," and "Green," it would be converted into three separate columns.

- o **Label Encoding:** Assigns a unique integer to each category. This method is simpler but may introduce ordinal relationships between categories that do not exist.

Data Normalization: Scaling Data to a Common Range

Normalization is the process of scaling data so that it falls within a specific range, typically between 0 and 1. It is particularly important for machine learning algorithms that are sensitive to the scale of input data, such as distance-based models (e.g., k-nearest neighbors, SVM) and gradient-based algorithms (e.g., neural networks).

1. **Min-Max Normalization:**
   Min-max normalization scales each feature to a specified range, usually [0, 1], by subtracting the minimum value and dividing by the range (difference between the maximum and minimum). This method preserves the relationships between the original data points while ensuring that the features are on the same scale (Jain et al., 2005).

Formula for min-max normalization:

$$X_{norm} = \frac{X - X_{min}}{X_{max} - X_{min}}$$

Z-Score Standardization:

Z-score standardization, also known as standard scaling, rescales the data so that it has a mean of 0 and a standard deviation of 1. This method is particularly useful when the data has outliers, as it centers the data without distorting extreme values. Z-score is widely used in algorithms like principal component analysis (PCA) and clustering (Izenman, 2008).

Formula for Z-score standardization:

$$Z = \frac{X - \mu}{\sigma}$$

where μ is the mean and σ is the standard deviation.

MaxAbs Scaling:

This method scales the data by dividing each feature by its maximum absolute value. MaxAbs scaling is useful when the data contains both positive and negative values and should remain centered around 0, but the features still need to be normalized.

Why Data Transformation and Normalization Matter

Data transformation and normalization play a vital role in improving the performance of machine learning models:

Consistency Across Features: Algorithms like gradient descent or k-nearest neighbors can be sensitive to the scale of the input features. Normalization ensures that all features contribute equally to the model.

Convergence in Optimization Algorithms: In deep learning and neural networks, gradient-based optimization algorithms converge faster when the input features are on a similar scale.

Improved Interpretability: Certain machine learning models (e.g., linear regression) provide more interpretable coefficients when the data is transformed and normalized.

Applications of Data Transformation and Normalization

Image Processing: Images are typically normalized so that pixel values fall within a specified range (e.g., 0 to 1 or -1 to 1), which improves the performance of models such as convolutional neural networks (CNNs).

Financial Data: Financial data is often log-transformed to handle skewness, particularly for stock prices, income, or sales data.

Healthcare: In medical datasets, normalization ensures that vital signs like heart rate, blood pressure, and glucose levels are scaled appropriately for modeling.

Below is a graph illustrating different data transformation and normalization techniques. It compares the original data distribution with the effects of log transformation, Z-score normalization, and min-max normalization. Each technique adjusts the data distribution in a unique way, helping to prepare the data for machine learning algorithms.

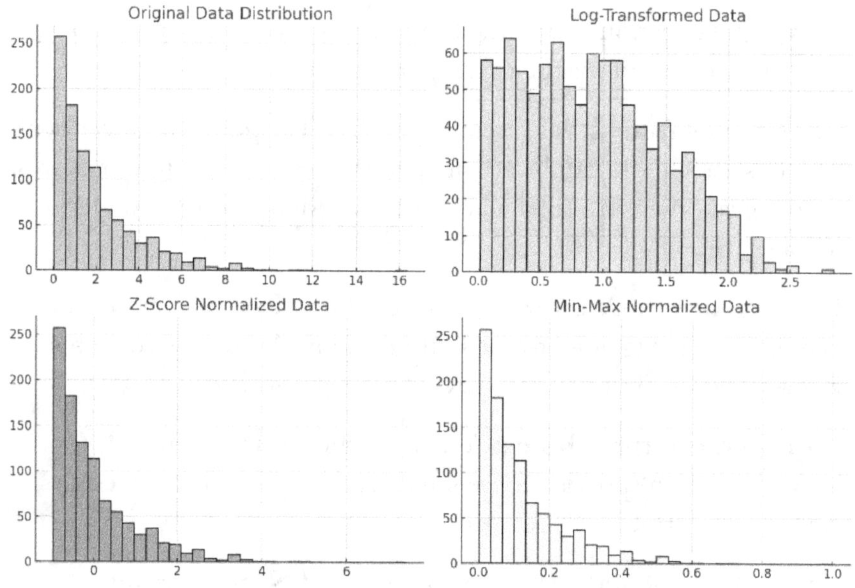

Handling Imbalanced Data

Handling imbalanced data is a crucial challenge in data preprocessing and machine learning. Imbalanced data occurs when the distribution of classes in a classification problem is uneven, with one class significantly outnumbering others. This imbalance can lead to poor performance of machine learning models, particularly when they are biased toward the majority class. Many real-world datasets, especially in fields like healthcare, finance, and fraud detection, suffer from imbalanced data (He & Garcia, 2009).

What Is Imbalanced Data?

In a binary classification scenario, imbalanced data typically occurs when one class (e.g., "fraud") makes up only a small portion of the dataset compared to the other class (e.g., "non-fraud"). For instance, in a dataset with 95% non-fraudulent transactions and 5% fraudulent ones, a model that always predicts "non-fraud" would achieve 95% accuracy, but it would completely fail to identify the minority class (fraudulent transactions). This leads to misleading metrics and poor model performance on minority class prediction (Batista, Prati, & Monard, 2004).

Challenges of Imbalanced Data

Biased Model Performance: Machine learning models tend to be biased toward the majority class, as they aim to maximize overall accuracy. This can lead to a model that performs poorly on minority classes, which may be the most critical for business outcomes.

Misleading Accuracy Metrics: Accuracy is not an appropriate metric for imbalanced datasets. A model may appear to perform well based on accuracy alone, but it could fail to predict the minority class altogether. Metrics like precision, recall, F1-score, and the area under the precision-recall curve (AUC-PR) are more appropriate for evaluating models on imbalanced data (Chawla et al., 2002).

Techniques for Handling Imbalanced Data

There are several techniques available to address the issues posed by imbalanced datasets. These techniques fall into two main categories: data-level and algorithm-level approaches.

Data-Level Techniques

Resampling Methods

Resampling involves modifying the training data to achieve a more balanced distribution of classes. There are two primary resampling strategies:

- o **Oversampling the Minority Class:** This technique involves increasing the number of instances in the minority class by replicating them or generating synthetic samples. One popular method for oversampling is the **Synthetic Minority Over-sampling Technique (SMOTE)**, which creates new synthetic samples by interpolating between existing minority class samples (Chawla et al., 2002).

- o **Undersampling the Majority Class:** In undersampling, instances from the majority class are randomly removed to balance the class distribution. While this reduces class imbalance, it also risks losing valuable information from the majority class, especially in small datasets (Kotsiantis et al., 2006).

Hybrid Methods

Some approaches combine oversampling the minority class with undersampling the majority class. This hybrid technique can balance the dataset without excessively oversampling or undersampling, maintaining a representative distribution of both classes.

Data Augmentation for Minority Classes

Data augmentation techniques are widely used in image processing but can also be applied to other domains. By transforming or slightly altering minority class samples (e.g., rotating images, adding noise), data augmentation can increase the diversity and size of the minority class.

Algorithm-Level Techniques

Cost-Sensitive Learning

Cost-sensitive learning involves modifying the learning algorithm to penalize misclassifications of the minority class more heavily than the majority class. By assigning higher costs to errors on the minority class, the algorithm becomes more sensitive to the underrepresented class. Cost-sensitive techniques can be applied to many standard algorithms like decision trees, support vector machines, and neural networks (Elkan, 2001).

Ensemble Methods

Ensemble learning techniques, such as **Random Forest** and **Boosting**, can also handle imbalanced data by combining multiple weak learners to improve the prediction of minority classes. One effective technique is **Balanced Random Forests**, which creates balanced bootstrap samples by undersampling the majority class before constructing each decision tree (Chen, Liaw, & Breiman, 2004).

Anomaly Detection Algorithms

In cases where the minority class is extremely rare (e.g., fraud detection), anomaly detection algorithms like Isolation Forest or One-Class SVM can be used. These models are trained to identify patterns in the majority class and flag deviations (outliers) as potential instances of the minority class (Liu, Ting, & Zhou, 2008).

Evaluation Metrics for Imbalanced Data

Precision and Recall: Precision measures the proportion of true positives among all positive predictions, while recall (or sensitivity) measures the proportion of true positives among all actual positives. Both metrics are critical in evaluating imbalanced datasets.

$$\text{Precision} = \frac{TP}{TP + FP}, \quad \text{Recall} = \frac{TP}{TP + FN}$$

F1-Score: The F1-score is the harmonic mean of precision and recall, offering a balance between the two metrics. It is particularly useful when dealing with imbalanced datasets where precision and recall are both important.

$$F1 = 2 \cdot \frac{\text{Precision} \cdot \text{Recall}}{\text{Precision} + \text{Recall}}$$

ROC Curve and AUC: The ROC curve plots the true positive rate (recall) against the false positive rate. AUC (Area Under the Curve) is commonly used to evaluate classifier performance. However, for highly imbalanced datasets, precision-recall curves (PRC) are often more informative (Davis & Goadrich, 2006).

Applications of Handling Imbalanced Data

Fraud Detection: Fraudulent transactions are rare, and imbalanced data techniques are crucial for identifying fraud while minimizing false positives.

Medical Diagnosis: In healthcare, detecting rare diseases or anomalies in medical images involves handling imbalanced datasets, as positive cases are often much fewer than negative ones.

Customer Churn Prediction: Identifying customers who are likely to leave a service (churn) requires accurate predictions based on a minority class in imbalanced datasets.

Below is a graph illustrating how different resampling techniques handle imbalanced data. The chart shows the initial imbalanced dataset (with a much larger majority class), followed by the effects of oversampling (balancing by increasing the minority class) and undersampling (balancing by reducing the majority class). Each technique addresses class imbalance in its unique way, ensuring that machine learning models can perform better on minority class predictions.

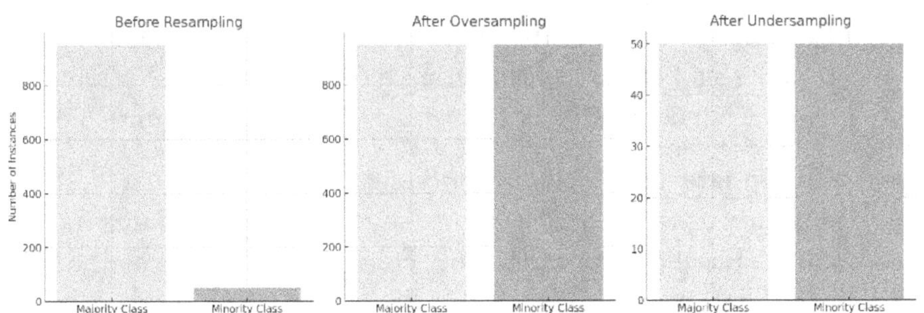

Feature Selection and Extraction

Feature selection and extraction are critical steps in the data preprocessing and feature engineering phases of machine learning. Both processes aim to improve model performance by reducing the dimensionality of the dataset, ensuring that only the most relevant and informative features are used. This not only improves computational efficiency but also helps prevent overfitting and enhances the interpretability of machine learning models (Guyon & Elisseeff, 2003).

Feature Selection: Choosing the Most Relevant Features

Feature selection refers to the process of selecting a subset of the most important features (variables) from the dataset. By removing irrelevant, redundant, or noisy features, feature selection helps models focus on the most critical information, improving accuracy and reducing the risk of overfitting.

There are three main types of feature selection techniques:

Filter Methods

Filter methods evaluate the relevance of features independently of the machine learning algorithm. These methods rank features based on their statistical relationship with the target variable and select the top-ranked features for the model. Common filter methods include:

- o **Correlation Coefficients:** Measures the strength of the linear relationship between a feature and the target variable. Features with higher correlation coefficients are retained (Brownlee, 2020).

- o **Chi-Square Test:** For categorical features, the chi-square test evaluates how much each feature contributes to predicting the target class. Features with higher chi-square values are considered more important.

- o **Mutual Information:** Measures the mutual dependence between the feature and the target variable, capturing non-linear relationships.

Wrapper Methods

Wrapper methods involve evaluating different subsets of features by training and testing the model on each subset. While more computationally expensive, these methods consider the interactions between features and often yield better results than filter methods. Examples include:

- o **Forward Selection:** Starts with no features and iteratively adds the most informative feature until performance stops improving.

- o **Backward Elimination:** Starts with all features and iteratively removes the least important feature until the optimal set is found.

- o **Recursive Feature Elimination (RFE):** Recursively removes features based on their importance as determined by the model's performance, refining the feature set (Guyon et al., 2002).

Embedded Methods

Embedded methods perform feature selection during the training of the model itself. Algorithms like decision trees and LASSO regression inherently perform feature selection by penalizing irrelevant features during the learning process. Examples include:

- o **LASSO (Least Absolute Shrinkage and Selection Operator):** Adds a penalty to the regression model that forces the coefficients of less important features to zero, effectively selecting a subset of relevant features (Tibshirani, 1996).

o   **Tree-Based Methods (e.g., Random Forest):** Decision trees and Random Forests rank features based on their importance in reducing impurity (Gini index or information gain).

Feature Extraction: Creating New Features from Existing Data

While feature selection focuses on choosing the best subset of features, feature extraction transforms the original features into a new set of variables that better capture the underlying patterns in the data. This is particularly useful when dealing with high-dimensional datasets where the features are interdependent or contain redundancy.

Some popular feature extraction techniques include:

Principal Component Analysis (PCA)

PCA is a widely used dimensionality reduction technique that transforms the original features into a smaller set of uncorrelated variables called principal components. These components are linear combinations of the original features and capture the maximum variance in the data. By projecting the data into a lower-dimensional space, PCA reduces dimensionality while preserving as much information as possible (Jolliffe, 2002).

The mathematical formulation of PCA involves calculating the covariance matrix of the data, followed by determining the eigenvectors and eigenvalues. The top k eigenvectors, corresponding to the largest eigenvalues, are selected as the principal components.

PCA is particularly useful for tasks like image compression and exploratory data analysis.

Linear Discriminant Analysis (LDA)

LDA is a supervised feature extraction technique that aims to maximize the separation between classes. Unlike PCA, which focuses on capturing variance, LDA looks for a projection that maximizes class separability. It is widely used in classification problems where distinguishing between different classes is important (Fisher, 1936).

t-Distributed Stochastic Neighbor Embedding (t-SNE)
t-SNE is a non-linear dimensionality reduction technique used for visualizing high-dimensional data. It projects data into two or three dimensions while preserving the local structure of the data. t-SNE is particularly useful for visualizing clusters in data but is not commonly used for feature extraction in machine learning models (Van der Maaten & Hinton, 2008).

Autoencoders
Autoencoders are a type of neural network used for unsupervised feature extraction. The network learns to compress the input data into a lower-dimensional latent space, then reconstructs the original data from this compressed representation. The latent space can be used as a reduced set of features for downstream tasks. Autoencoders are particularly useful for tasks like anomaly detection, image denoising, and unsupervised learning (Hinton & Salakhutdinov, 2006).

Why Feature Selection and Extraction Matter

Feature selection and extraction are crucial for several reasons:

Improved Model Performance: By removing irrelevant features and transforming the data into a more informative representation, these techniques help models generalize better, reducing overfitting and improving prediction accuracy.

Reduced Computational Complexity: Dimensionality reduction reduces the amount of data the model has to process, speeding up training time and allowing for the use of simpler models.

Enhanced Interpretability: By focusing on the most relevant features, feature selection makes models easier to interpret, which is critical in domains like healthcare and finance.

Applications of Feature Selection and Extraction

Image Processing: Feature extraction techniques like PCA and autoencoders are used to reduce the dimensionality of image data while preserving important patterns for tasks like image recognition and object detection.

Text Analytics: In natural language processing (NLP), techniques like TF-IDF (term frequency-inverse document frequency) and word embeddings are used for feature extraction from text data, improving the accuracy of text classification models.

Finance: Feature selection is crucial in financial modeling to identify the most relevant factors driving stock prices, reducing noise and improving predictive performance.

Below is a graph illustrating the workflow for feature selection and feature extraction. The graph highlights key methods used in both processes: filter, wrapper, and embedded methods for feature selection, and PCA, LDA, and autoencoders for feature extraction.

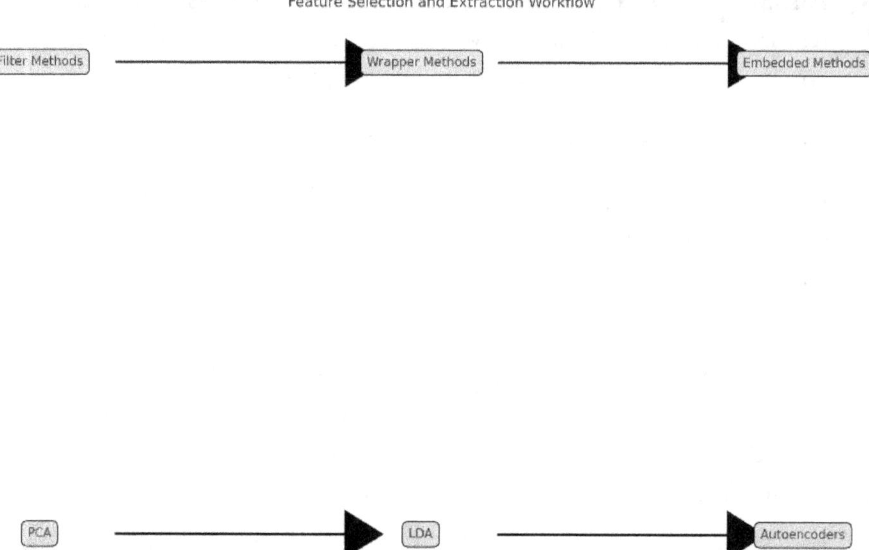

Dimensionality Reduction Techniques

Dimensionality reduction is a crucial technique in the field of data preprocessing and feature engineering, especially when working with large datasets that contain many features (variables). High-dimensional data can be challenging for machine learning algorithms because it increases computational complexity, leads to longer training times, and can result in overfitting. Dimensionality reduction addresses these challenges by transforming the data into a lower-dimensional space while preserving as much relevant information as possible (Jolliffe, 2002).

Why Dimensionality Reduction Is Important

Curse of Dimensionality: As the number of features increases, the volume of the data space grows exponentially, making it difficult for models to learn meaningful patterns. This problem, known as the curse of dimensionality, can lead to overfitting, where the model performs well on training data but poorly on new, unseen data (Bellman, 1961).

100

Computational Efficiency: Reducing the number of features in a dataset decreases the computational burden of training and deploying machine learning models. With fewer dimensions, models can be trained more quickly and with less memory, making them more scalable for Big Data applications (Van Der Maaten, Postma, & Van den Herik, 2009).

Improved Model Interpretability: By reducing the number of features, dimensionality reduction can enhance the interpretability of a model. It simplifies the dataset, allowing data scientists to focus on the most important factors driving the predictions.

Key Dimensionality Reduction Techniques

There are two primary types of dimensionality reduction techniques: feature selection and feature extraction. While feature selection involves selecting a subset of existing features, feature extraction creates new features by transforming the original ones.

Principal Component Analysis (PCA)

PCA is one of the most widely used dimensionality reduction techniques. It works by identifying the directions (principal components) in which the data varies the most. These components are linear combinations of the original features. PCA reduces the dimensionality by projecting the data onto the first few principal components, which capture the majority of the variance in the dataset (Jolliffe, 2002).

Mathematically, PCA finds the eigenvectors and eigenvalues of the covariance matrix of the data, and the top k eigenvectors (with the largest eigenvalues) are selected as the new basis for the reduced space.

Applications of PCA:

o   Image compression and recognition tasks.

o   Reducing noise in financial datasets.

o   Exploratory data analysis for high-dimensional datasets.

Linear Discriminant Analysis (LDA)

LDA is a supervised dimensionality reduction technique, commonly used in classification problems. Unlike PCA, which is unsupervised and focuses on maximizing variance, LDA aims to maximize class separability. It projects the data onto a lower-dimensional space where the between-class variance is maximized relative to the within-class variance (Fisher, 1936).

Applications of LDA:

o   Text classification and document categorization.

o   Image recognition tasks involving facial recognition.

o   Medical diagnosis, where distinguishing between different classes (e.g., healthy vs. unhealthy) is critical.

t-Distributed Stochastic Neighbor Embedding (t-SNE)

t-SNE is a non-linear dimensionality reduction technique primarily used for visualizing high-dimensional data in two or three dimensions. It works by modeling pairwise similarities between data points in both the high-dimensional space and the lower-dimensional space, then minimizing the differences between these two representations. t-SNE is particularly useful for identifying clusters or patterns in complex data but is not typically used for feature extraction in machine learning models due to its high computational cost (Van der Maaten & Hinton, 2008).

Applications of t-SNE:

o   Visualizing high-dimensional data in fields like bioinformatics and genetics.

o   Exploring clustering in large datasets such as text embeddings and word vectors.

Autoencoders

Autoencoders are a type of artificial neural network used for unsupervised dimensionality reduction. The network is trained to encode the input data into a compressed, lower-dimensional representation (latent space) and then decode it back to its original form. The compressed representation in the middle layer is used as the reduced feature set. Autoencoders are particularly powerful when dealing with non-linear relationships in the data (Hinton & Salakhutdinov, 2006).

Applications of Autoencoders:

o   Anomaly detection in cybersecurity and fraud detection.

o   Image compression and denoising.

o   Dimensionality reduction in natural language processing (NLP) tasks.

Factor Analysis

Factor analysis is another technique that seeks to explain the relationships between features by reducing the observed variables to a smaller number of latent factors. It is primarily used in fields like psychology and social sciences to identify underlying patterns in the data. Unlike PCA, which maximizes variance, factor analysis models the covariance between observed variables to detect latent variables (factors) (Bartholomew et al., 2011).

Applications of Factor Analysis:

o   Market research to identify consumer behavior trends.

o   Survey analysis in social sciences.

o   Exploratory data analysis in educational research.

Independent Component Analysis (ICA)

ICA is a dimensionality reduction technique that separates a multivariate signal into additive, independent components. It is widely used for tasks where the goal is to uncover hidden factors or signals in the data. ICA is particularly useful when the data contains mixed signals that need to be separated into independent sources (Hyvärinen & Oja, 2000).

Applications of ICA:

o   Blind source separation in audio signal processing (e.g., separating voices in a recording).

o   Brain imaging data analysis, such as EEG and fMRI signals.

Choosing the Right Dimensionality Reduction Technique

The choice of dimensionality reduction technique depends on the nature of the data and the goals of the analysis. For example:

PCA is ideal when the goal is to reduce dimensionality while preserving as much variance as possible.

LDA is suitable for classification problems where class separability is important.

t-SNE is best for visualizing clusters in complex, high-dimensional data.

Autoencoders are a powerful tool for non-linear dimensionality reduction, especially in deep learning tasks.

Below is a graph illustrating the dimensionality reduction techniques of Principal Component Analysis (PCA) and Linear Discriminant Analysis (LDA). Both plots show how high-dimensional data is projected into a two-dimensional space while preserving key patterns and relationships within the data.

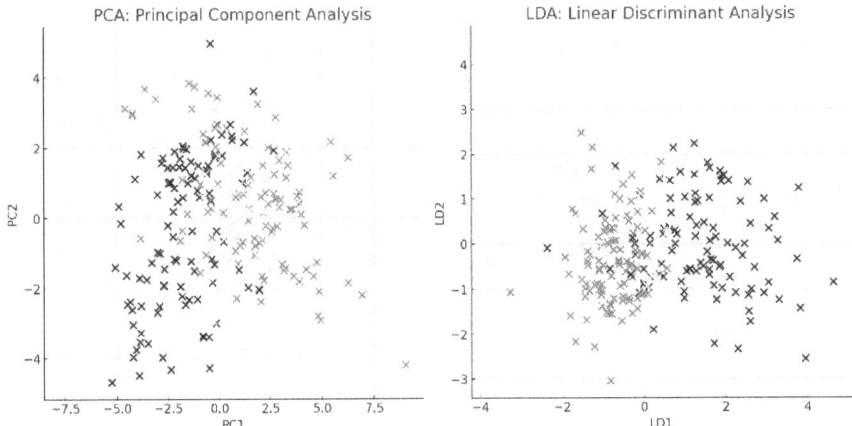

References

Aggarwal, C. C. (2017). *Outlier analysis* (2nd ed.). Springer.

Bartholomew, D. J., Knott, M., & Moustaki, I. (2011). *Latent variable models and factor analysis: A unified approach.* Wiley.

Batista, G. E. A. P. A., Prati, R. C., & Monard, M. C. (2004). A study of the behavior of several methods for balancing machine learning training data. *ACM SIGKDD Explorations Newsletter, 6*(1), 20-29.

Bellman, R. E. (1961). *Adaptive control processes: A guided tour.* Princeton University Press.

Box, G. E. P., & Cox, D. R. (1964). An analysis of transformations. *Journal of the Royal Statistical Society: Series B (Methodological), 26*(2), 211-243.

Chawla, N. V., Bowyer, K. W., Hall, L. O., & Kegelmeyer, W. P. (2002). SMOTE: Synthetic minority over-sampling technique. *Journal of Artificial Intelligence Research, 16,* 321-357.

Chen, C., Liaw, A., & Breiman, L. (2004). Using random forest to learn imbalanced data. *University of California, Berkeley.*

Davis, J., & Goadrich, M. (2006). The relationship between precision-recall and ROC curves. *Proceedings of the 23rd International Conference on Machine Learning,* 233-240.

Elkan, C. (2001). The foundations of cost-sensitive learning. *Proceedings of the 17th International Joint Conference on Artificial Intelligence,* 973-978.

Enders, C. K. (2010). *Applied missing data analysis.* Guilford Press.

Fisher, R. A. (1936). The use of multiple measurements in taxonomic problems. *Annals of Eugenics, 7*(2), 179-188.

Garcia, S., Luengo, J., & Herrera, F. (2016). Data preprocessing in data mining. *Springer.*

Guyon, I., & Elisseeff, A. (2003). An introduction to variable and feature selection. *Journal of Machine Learning Research, 3*, 1157-1182.

Guyon, I., Weston, J., Barnhill, S., & Vapnik, V. (2002). Gene selection for cancer classification using support vector machines. *Machine Learning, 46*(1), 389-422.

Han, J., Kamber, M., & Pei, J. (2011). *Data mining: Concepts and techniques* (3rd ed.). Morgan Kaufmann.

He, H., & Garcia, E. A. (2009). Learning from imbalanced data. *IEEE Transactions on Knowledge and Data Engineering, 21*(9), 1263-1284.

Hinton, G. E., & Salakhutdinov, R. R. (2006). Reducing the dimensionality of data with neural networks. *Science, 313*(5786), 504-507.

Hyvärinen, A., & Oja, E. (2000). Independent component analysis: Algorithms and applications. *Neural Networks, 13*(4-5), 411-430.

Izenman, A. J. (2008). *Modern multivariate statistical techniques: Regression, classification, and manifold learning.* Springer Science & Business Media.

Jain, A. K., Murty, M. N., & Flynn, P. J. (2005). Data clustering: A review. *ACM Computing Surveys, 31*(3), 264-323.

Jolliffe, I. T. (2002). *Principal component analysis* (2nd ed.). Springer.

Kotsiantis, S. B., Kanellopoulos, D., & Pintelas, P. E. (2006). Handling imbalanced datasets: A review. *GESTS International Transactions on Computer Science and Engineering, 30*(1), 25-36.

Little, R. J., & Rubin, D. B. (2019). *Statistical analysis with missing data* (3rd ed.). Wiley.

Liu, F. T., Ting, K. M., & Zhou, Z. H. (2008). Isolation forest. *2008 Eighth IEEE International Conference on Data Mining,* 413-422.

Osborne, J. W. (2010). Improving your data transformations: Applying the Box-Cox transformation. *Practical Assessment, Research, and Evaluation, 15*(12).

Rahm, E., & Do, H. H. (2000). Data cleaning: Problems and current approaches. *IEEE Data Engineering Bulletin, 23*(4), 3-13.

Rubin, D. B. (1976). Inference and missing data. *Biometrika, 63*(3), 581-592.

Tibshirani, R. (1996). Regression shrinkage and selection via the lasso. *Journal of the Royal Statistical Society: Series B (Methodological), 58*(1), 267-288.

Troyanskaya, O., Cantor, M., Sherlock, G., Brown, P., Hastie, T., Tibshirani, R., ... & Altman, R. B. (2001). Missing value estimation methods for DNA microarrays. *Bioinformatics, 17*(6), 520-525.

Van der Maaten, L., & Hinton, G. (2008). Visualizing data using t-SNE. *Journal of Machine Learning Research, 9*(Nov), 2579-2605.

Van der Maaten, L., Postma, E., & Van den Herik, J. (2009). Dimensionality reduction: A comparative review. *Journal of Machine Learning Research, 10*(66-71), 13.

White, I. R., Royston, P., & Wood, A. M. (2011). Multiple imputation using chained equations: Issues and guidance for practice. *Statistics in Medicine, 30*(4), 377-399.

Chapter 5: Machine Learning with Big Data

<u>Scaling Machine Learning Algorithms</u>

As the volume of data increases in Big Data applications, scaling machine learning algorithms becomes essential to manage computational complexity and make models effective for large datasets. The challenges of scaling machine learning algorithms include managing massive datasets, handling high-dimensional data, and ensuring real-time processing for decision-making. Scalable machine learning algorithms allow organizations to leverage large-scale datasets effectively while maintaining computational efficiency and performance (Ghemawat et al., 2003).

Why Scaling Machine Learning Algorithms Is Important

Machine learning models are typically designed to operate efficiently on moderate-sized datasets. However, in the era of Big Data, where datasets can grow to terabytes or petabytes in size, traditional algorithms may face significant limitations in terms of processing power, memory usage, and time complexity. Scaling machine learning algorithms is critical for several reasons:

Handling Large Volumes of Data

As the size of datasets grows, machine learning algorithms need to process and analyze massive amounts of data without exhausting computational resources. Efficiently scaling algorithms ensures that the insights derived from Big Data are timely and actionable (Zaharia et al., 2016).

High Dimensionality

In Big Data, not only the volume of data but also the number of features (dimensionality) can be enormous. High-dimensional data introduces challenges such as increased computational complexity and the risk of overfitting. Scalable machine learning techniques are needed to manage this complexity by employing feature selection, dimensionality reduction, or distributed algorithms (Domingos, 2012).

Real-Time Processing

Many applications, such as fraud detection, recommendation systems, and autonomous driving, require real-time machine learning predictions. Scaling algorithms allows for real-time processing and decision-making, ensuring that models can operate efficiently even as data is continuously generated.

Techniques for Scaling Machine Learning Algorithms

Several approaches can be employed to scale machine learning algorithms for Big Data, including distributed computing, parallel processing, and optimization techniques that reduce computational complexity.

Distributed Computing Frameworks

One of the most effective ways to scale machine learning algorithms is through distributed computing frameworks such as Apache Hadoop and Apache Spark. These frameworks break down the data into smaller chunks that are processed in parallel across multiple nodes (machines) in a cluster.

- **MapReduce Framework:** Hadoop's MapReduce framework is a widely used distributed computing model that processes large datasets in parallel. In the map phase, data is divided into key-value pairs, and in the reduce phase, the results are aggregated (Ghemawat et al., 2003). MapReduce is particularly useful for batch processing tasks but may not be suitable for iterative algorithms like machine learning models.

- **Apache Spark:** Spark is a more advanced distributed computing framework that supports in-memory processing, making it ideal for machine learning tasks that require iterative algorithms such as gradient descent. Spark's MLlib library provides scalable implementations of common machine learning algorithms, such as linear regression, clustering, and decision trees (Zaharia et al., 2016).

Parallel Processing

Parallel processing allows machine learning algorithms to split tasks into smaller, independent computations that can be executed simultaneously. Parallelization is particularly effective for algorithms like Random Forests and bagging methods, where multiple decision trees or models are trained independently (Breiman, 2001). Libraries such as Scikit-learn and TensorFlow support parallel processing through multithreading or GPU acceleration.

o **GPUs and TPUs:** Graphics processing units (GPUs) and tensor processing units (TPUs) provide hardware acceleration for machine learning tasks, especially for deep learning models. By parallelizing matrix operations, GPUs and TPUs can significantly speed up the training of large neural networks, making them scalable for Big Data applications (Dean et al., 2012).

Incremental Learning (Online Learning)

Incremental learning, also known as online learning, is a machine learning approach where the model is updated continuously as new data arrives, rather than being trained on the entire dataset all at once. This approach is particularly useful for streaming data or when the dataset is too large to fit in memory.

o **Stochastic Gradient Descent (SGD):** SGD is a popular optimization algorithm that updates model parameters incrementally using small batches of data at each iteration, rather than computing the gradient for the entire dataset. This reduces computational overhead and makes SGD scalable for large datasets (Bottou, 2010).

o **Hoeffding Trees:** In online learning, algorithms like Hoeffding Trees can handle large, continuous streams of data. These decision trees incrementally update their structure as new data arrives, allowing for real-time predictions while maintaining scalability (Domingos & Hulten, 2000).

Dimensionality Reduction Techniques

When dealing with high-dimensional data, reducing the number of features is essential to improve computational efficiency and avoid overfitting. Techniques like Principal Component Analysis (PCA) and autoencoders can help reduce dimensionality while preserving the most important information (Jolliffe, 2002). Scalable implementations of these techniques, such as distributed PCA in Apache Spark, ensure that they can handle large datasets efficiently.

Approximation Techniques

Approximation algorithms offer another way to scale machine learning models by sacrificing a small amount of accuracy for significant gains in computational efficiency. Techniques such as locality-sensitive hashing (LSH) and approximate nearest neighbors (ANN) allow for fast querying in high-dimensional spaces by finding approximate solutions rather than exact ones (Andoni & Indyk, 2006).

Challenges in Scaling Machine Learning Algorithms

Data Distribution: In distributed computing environments, ensuring that the data is evenly distributed across nodes is critical for avoiding bottlenecks. Imbalanced data distribution can lead to slowdowns in processing and inefficient use of resources.

Fault Tolerance: In large-scale machine learning systems, hardware failures are inevitable. Distributed frameworks like Hadoop and Spark provide fault tolerance by replicating data across multiple nodes and enabling automatic recovery from failures (Ghemawat et al., 2003).

Model Interpretability: As machine learning models scale in complexity, especially in deep learning, interpretability becomes a challenge. Scalable models should also allow for post-hoc interpretation or explainability, particularly in applications such as healthcare and finance where understanding model predictions is critical.

Applications of Scalable Machine Learning

Recommendation Systems: Companies like Netflix and Amazon use scalable machine learning algorithms to make real-time product or content recommendations to millions of users by processing vast amounts of user data.

Fraud Detection: Financial institutions rely on scalable machine learning models to monitor transactions in real-time and detect fraudulent activity across large customer bases.

Autonomous Vehicles: Autonomous driving systems generate vast amounts of sensory data, requiring scalable machine learning algorithms to process this data in real-time to make decisions such as steering, braking, and obstacle detection.

Below is a graph illustrating the workflow for scaling machine learning algorithms in distributed systems. It highlights key stages such as data partitioning, parallel processing across multiple nodes, model training on nodes, aggregation of results, and the final model output. This process ensures that machine learning algorithms can handle large datasets efficiently by distributing the workload.

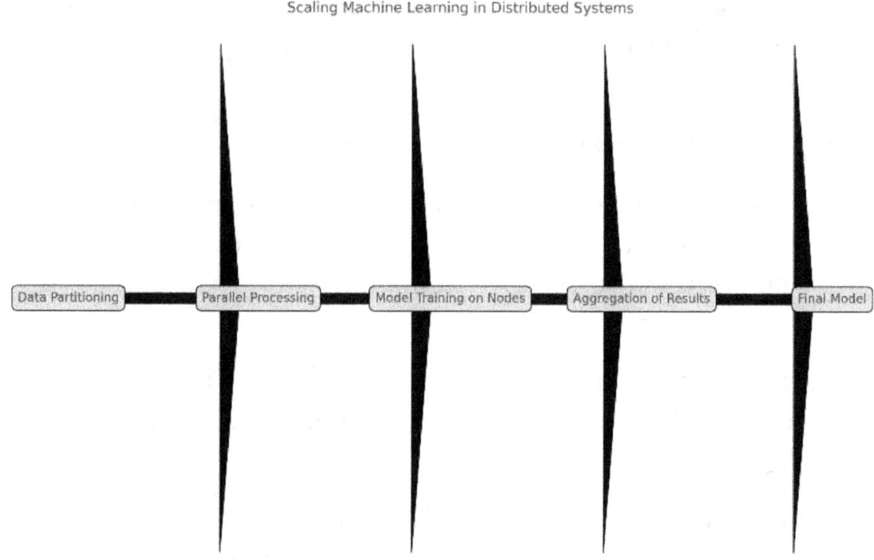

Distributed Machine Learning

With the advent of Big Data, traditional machine learning algorithms often face scalability challenges. These algorithms are typically designed to work on a single machine with limited processing power, memory, and storage capacity, which makes them inefficient for large-scale datasets (Kumar et al., 2020). As data continues to grow in size, complexity, and velocity, there is an increasing need to distribute both data and computation across multiple machines to improve scalability, efficiency, and performance. This is where **Distributed Machine Learning (DML)** comes into play.

Distributed machine learning involves partitioning data and computations across a network of machines to speed up processing and allow for the handling of large-scale datasets (Zaharia et al., 2016). By parallelizing tasks, DML frameworks can significantly reduce the training time of machine learning models, making it feasible to work with Big Data in real-time applications.

Key Components of Distributed Machine Learning

Data Partitioning

Data partitioning is the first step in distributed machine learning. Large datasets are split into smaller subsets, each of which is distributed to different nodes in a computing cluster. Various partitioning strategies can be used, such as random sampling, hash-based partitioning, or range-based partitioning, depending on the nature of the data and the algorithm (Dean & Ghemawat, 2008).

Graphically, this can be represented as follows:

- A large dataset is divided into smaller, manageable subsets.

- Each subset is assigned to a different computing node.

Graphical Representation:

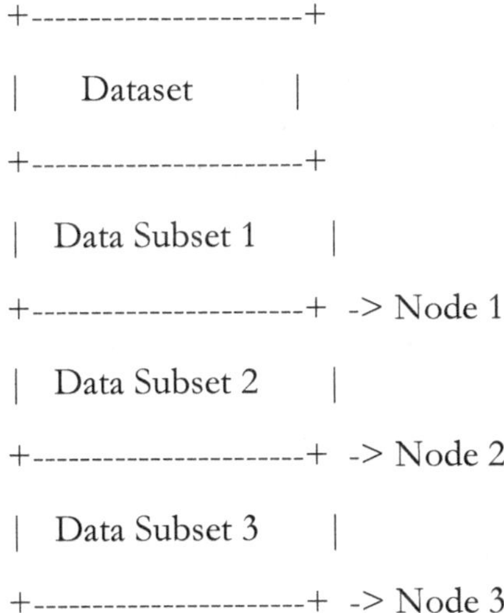

```
+----------------------+
|     Dataset          |
+----------------------+
| Data Subset 1        |
+----------------------+  -> Node 1
| Data Subset 2        |
+----------------------+  -> Node 2
| Data Subset 3        |
+----------------------+  -> Node 3
```

Distributed Computing Frameworks

Several distributed computing frameworks support the parallel execution of machine learning algorithms. The two most commonly used frameworks are **Apache Hadoop** and **Apache Spark**.

Hadoop MapReduce: MapReduce allows tasks to be split into a "Map" phase, where data is processed in parallel, and a "Reduce" phase, where results are aggregated (Dean & Ghemawat, 2008). Although efficient, MapReduce can be slow due to its reliance on disk-based operations for storing intermediate results.

Apache Spark: In contrast, Spark enhances performance through in-memory computation, which reduces the need for disk I/O. Spark provides libraries like MLlib for distributed machine learning and has become the preferred framework for DML due to its speed and flexibility (Zaharia et al., 2016).

3. Model Parallelism vs. Data Parallelism

There are two primary strategies for parallelizing machine learning algorithms:

Model Parallelism: This approach involves distributing the model itself across different nodes. Each node computes part of the model, and the results are aggregated at the end (Goyal et al., 2017). This is especially useful when dealing with large models that cannot fit into the memory of a single machine, such as deep neural networks.

Data Parallelism: In this approach, the model is replicated across different nodes, and each node processes a subset of the data independently. The results are then combined during an aggregation step. This approach is often more efficient for smaller models where the challenge is processing the data, rather than the model size (Krizhevsky et al., 2012).

4. Gradient Descent in Distributed Environments

Distributed machine learning often uses gradient-based optimization techniques such as stochastic gradient descent (SGD). In a distributed setup, each node computes the gradient of the model using its local subset of data, and these gradients are aggregated to update the model (Dean et al., 2012).

A challenge in this process is ensuring that the model's parameters remain consistent across nodes. There are two main strategies to tackle this:

Synchronous SGD: All nodes must wait for each other to complete their gradient computations before moving on to the next iteration. While this ensures consistency, it can be slow, especially if there is a node that lags behind.

Asynchronous SGD: In this approach, nodes update the model as soon as their local gradient computations are complete. This can speed up the process, but it risks inconsistency in the model parameters (Recht et al., 2011).

The following diagram illustrates the difference between synchronous and asynchronous SGD:

Graphical Representation:

Synchronous SGD:

```
+-----------+   +-----------+   +-----------+
| Node 1    | --> | Node 2    | --> | Node 3    | (Wait for all nodes to finish)
+-----------+   +-----------+   +-----------+
```

Asynchronous SGD:

```
+-----------+        +-----------+        +-----------+
| Node 1    | ---->    | Node 2    | ---->    | Node 3    |
+-----------+        +-----------+        +-----------+ (No waiting required)
```

Applications of Distributed Machine Learning

Distributed machine learning techniques have been widely adopted in industry for processing large-scale data. Some prominent applications include:

Search Engines: Companies like Google and Bing use distributed machine learning to rank search results, improve recommendations, and optimize ad placements (Dean et al., 2012).

Social Media: Facebook and Twitter use DML to analyze user behavior, detect trends, and personalize content recommendations (Goyal et al., 2017).

Healthcare: Distributed learning is used to analyze large datasets of medical records, enabling real-time diagnosis and personalized treatment plans (Shickel et al., 2018).

Despite its benefits, distributed machine learning comes with several challenges:

Communication Overhead: As the number of nodes increases, so does the communication between them. This can lead to network congestion and reduced performance (Li et al., 2014).

Straggler Nodes: A straggler node is a slower node that delays the entire process in synchronous settings, reducing overall efficiency.

Model Consistency: Ensuring consistency in the model's parameters across distributed nodes, especially in asynchronous setups, can be difficult to manage.

In Summary, distributed machine learning is a powerful technique for handling large-scale datasets in Big Data environments. By leveraging distributed computing frameworks like Apache Spark and partitioning data across multiple nodes, DML can significantly reduce processing time while maintaining scalability. Despite challenges like communication overhead and consistency, advances in frameworks and algorithms continue to make DML a critical component in modern machine learning applications.

Online Learning and Real-Time Analytics

With the proliferation of Big Data, where data is generated at high velocity and in large volumes, traditional machine learning approaches that require static datasets are often insufficient. **Online learning** and **real-time analytics** are AI techniques that have gained prominence in such environments. Online learning refers to algorithms that update models continuously as new data arrives, without needing to retrain the model from scratch (Bottou & Bousquet, 2011). This makes it suitable for dynamic and ever-changing datasets in real-time environments. **Real-time analytics**, on the other hand, involves processing and analyzing data as it is generated, enabling timely insights and decision-making (Stonebraker et al., 2015).

Together, these techniques empower businesses and applications to act on the latest information, enhancing adaptability and responsiveness in fields such as finance, healthcare, and e-commerce.

Key Concepts in Online Learning

Incremental Learning

Online learning is inherently incremental, meaning that models are updated with each new data point or batch, rather than waiting for a complete dataset (Hoi et al., 2018). This enables models to learn continuously and adapt to changing patterns over time. One of the most commonly used algorithms for online learning is **Stochastic Gradient Descent (SGD)**. In an online learning setup, the model's parameters are updated with every incoming instance, allowing it to improve iteratively (Bottou, 1998).

Graphically, incremental learning can be represented as follows:

Graphical Representation:

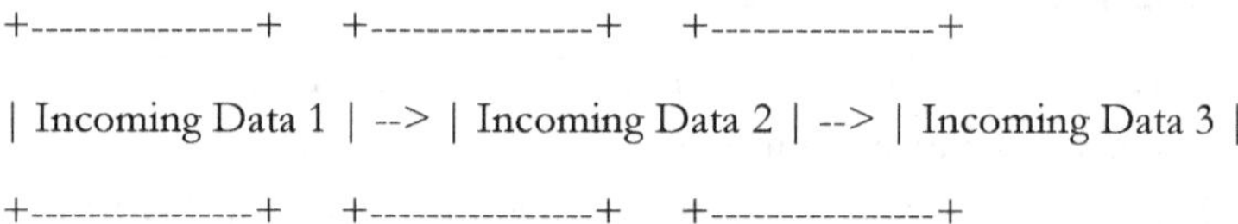

```
+----------------+    +----------------+    +----------------+
| Incoming Data 1 | --> | Incoming Data 2 | --> | Incoming Data 3 |
+----------------+    +----------------+    +----------------+
```

Model Adaptation in Dynamic Environments

In fast-evolving environments, such as stock markets or social media, data patterns may shift rapidly. This is referred to as **concept drift**, where the underlying statistical properties of the data change over time (Gama et al., 2014). Online learning algorithms are well-suited to handle such scenarios because they adapt models in real-time, minimizing the lag between learning from old data and the appearance of new trends.

A real-world example of online learning is **fraud detection in financial transactions**, where models must constantly adapt to new fraudulent patterns as they emerge (Zliobaite et al., 2016).

Performance Metrics for Online Learning

Evaluating online learning algorithms requires different metrics than traditional batch learning. One popular metric is the **cumulative accuracy**, which tracks the model's performance over time, providing insights into how well the model adapts to changing data (Gama et al., 2014).

Real-Time Analytics in Big Data

Stream Processing Frameworks

Real-time analytics requires specialized frameworks that can process data streams continuously. Two of the most popular stream processing frameworks are **Apache Kafka** and **Apache Flink**.

Apache Kafka: Kafka is a distributed streaming platform that enables real-time data ingestion and pipeline management. It's used for high-throughput and fault-tolerant data streaming (Kreps et al., 2011).

Apache Flink: Flink supports complex event processing and real-time analytics. It provides low-latency stream processing with support for window-based computations, making it ideal for applications that require instant insights (Carbone et al., 2015).

The following graph depicts the difference between traditional batch processing and stream processing:

Graphical Representation:

```
Batch Processing:              Stream Processing:

+--------------------+         +--------------------+

| Data is collected  |         | Data is continuously |

| over time in batches |       | processed as streams |

+--------------------+         +--------------------+


Batch Results:                 Continuous Real-time Results:

+--------------------+         +--------------------+

| Process after all data|      | Process as data arrives|

+--------------------+         +--------------------+
```

Event-Driven Analytics

In real-time analytics, data often comes in the form of events, such as transactions, sensor readings, or social media posts. Event-driven architectures allow systems to react to these events in real-time. For example, in an **Internet of Things (IoT)** application, sensor data can be analyzed in real-time to detect anomalies and trigger alerts (Stonebraker et al., 2015).

Predictive Analytics and Real-Time Decision Making

By combining real-time analytics with online learning, organizations can implement predictive models that not only analyze current data but also predict future trends in real-time. In industries like retail, for example, real-time recommendations can be provided based on a customer's current browsing behavior (Mehrotra et al., 2017).

A graph illustrating real-time predictive analytics would include the following steps:

Graphical Representation:

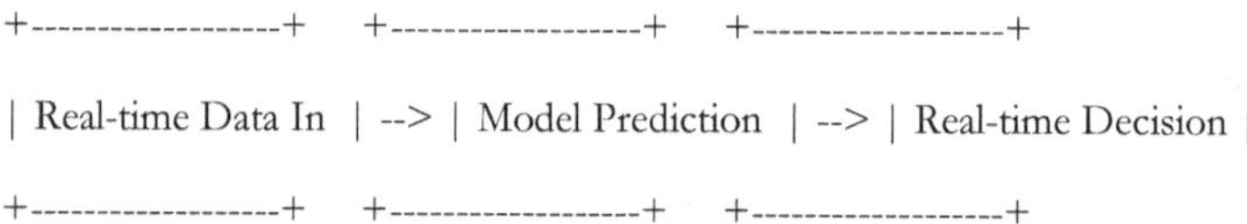

Applications of Online Learning and Real-Time Analytics

Finance and Stock Market Predictions

In financial markets, data changes rapidly, requiring models that can adapt to new trends instantly. Online learning algorithms are applied to **stock price predictions**, fraud detection, and risk management (Tsai et al., 2014). Real-time analytics enables financial institutions to react immediately to significant market changes, minimizing losses and capitalizing on emerging opportunities.

Healthcare Monitoring and Diagnosis

Healthcare systems use real-time analytics to monitor patients' vital signs, detect anomalies, and trigger alerts for immediate medical attention (Wang et al., 2018). By incorporating online learning, models can learn from individual patient data in real-time, offering personalized treatment recommendations based on current health conditions.

E-commerce and Personalization

E-commerce platforms, such as Amazon and Alibaba, leverage online learning to continuously improve recommendation systems based on real-time user interactions. Real-time analytics ensures that users receive the most relevant recommendations, enhancing customer satisfaction and increasing sales (Mehrotra et al., 2017).

Challenges in Online Learning and Real-Time Analytics

Scalability

While online learning algorithms are designed to handle large data streams, scaling these systems to manage massive datasets across multiple nodes can be challenging. Real-time analytics frameworks like Kafka and Flink require efficient resource allocation and data partitioning to avoid bottlenecks (Carbone et al., 2015).

Latency and Accuracy Trade-offs

One of the primary challenges in real-time analytics is balancing latency and accuracy. Faster models may sacrifice accuracy, especially in environments with high-frequency data streams. Conversely, more accurate models may introduce latency, delaying real-time decision-making (Stonebraker et al., 2015).

Handling Concept Drift

In dynamic environments, handling concept drift effectively is critical for maintaining model performance. Online learning algorithms must strike a balance between retaining enough historical data to avoid overfitting and adapting quickly enough to respond to new patterns (Zliobaite et al., 2016).

In summary online learning and real-time analytics are essential components of modern AI techniques in data science and Big Data. They enable models to continuously learn from new data and allow systems to make real-time decisions. These techniques are particularly relevant in dynamic environments, such as finance, healthcare, and e-commerce, where timely actions are crucial. Despite challenges such as scalability and latency-accuracy trade-offs, ongoing developments in distributed frameworks and learning algorithms continue to push the boundaries of what is possible in real-time AI applications.

AutoML and Automated Feature Engineering

In the realm of big data and machine learning, the process of building, optimizing, and deploying models can be complex and time-consuming. To streamline these efforts, **Automated Machine Learning (AutoML)** and **Automated Feature Engineering** have emerged as powerful solutions. AutoML refers to the process of automating the end-to-end process of applying machine learning to real-world problems, from data preprocessing to model selection and hyperparameter tuning (He et al., 2019). Automated feature engineering involves automatically generating and selecting features that improve model performance without manual intervention (Kanter & Veeramachaneni, 2015).

Together, these techniques significantly reduce the amount of human effort required to develop machine learning models, making AI more accessible and enabling data scientists to focus on higher-level tasks.

Key Concepts in AutoML

Automation of the Model Building Process

AutoML systems automate the selection of algorithms, the tuning of hyperparameters, and the evaluation of model performance. They do so by performing tasks like:

- **Algorithm Selection**: Based on the input data, AutoML frameworks choose the most suitable machine learning algorithm (Feurer et al., 2015). For example, AutoML may compare algorithms like decision trees, support vector machines, or neural networks, and automatically choose the one that offers the best performance for a given dataset.

- **Hyperparameter Optimization**: AutoML frameworks utilize optimization strategies such as grid search, random search, or more sophisticated methods like **Bayesian optimization** to find the best combination of hyperparameters (Snoek et al., 2012). Hyperparameters such as learning rate, regularization terms, and depth of a neural network can be fine-tuned automatically.

Graphically, this can be represented as follows:

Graphical Representation:

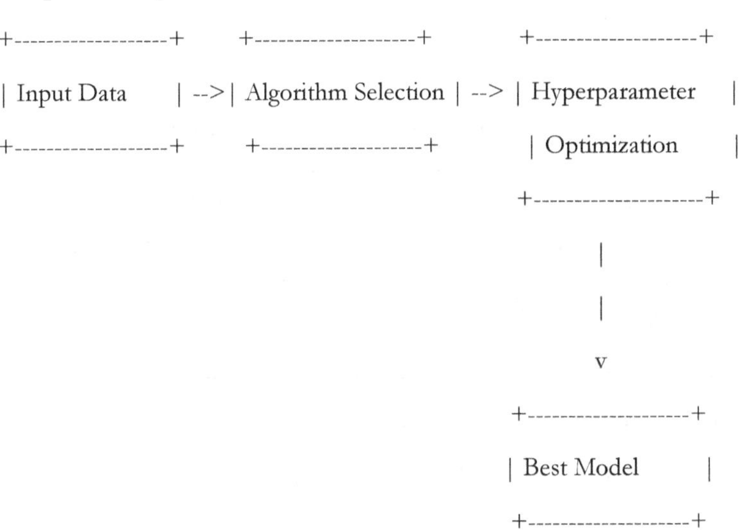

```
+------------------+        +------------------+          +------------------+
| Input Data       | -->| Algorithm Selection | -->  | Hyperparameter   |
+------------------+        +------------------+          | Optimization     |
                                                         +------------------+
                                                                  |
                                                                  |
                                                                  v
                                                         +------------------+
                                                         | Best Model       |
                                                         +------------------+
```

Automation of Model Evaluation

AutoML systems also automate the process of evaluating and comparing models. Techniques like **cross-validation** and **A/B testing** are used to ensure that the model generalizes well to unseen data. Furthermore, these systems often provide performance metrics like accuracy, precision, recall, and area under the curve (AUC) to assess how well the model is performing across various dimensions (He et al., 2019).

Neural Architecture Search (NAS)

One of the cutting-edge applications of AutoML is **Neural Architecture Search (NAS)**, which automates the design of neural network architectures. NAS systems search for the optimal architecture by considering various components such as the number of layers, types of layers (convolutional, recurrent, etc.), and connections between them (Zoph & Le, 2017). NAS has enabled the discovery of state-of-the-art neural network architectures with minimal human intervention, as evidenced by the development of models like **EfficientNet** (Tan & Le, 2019).

Key Concepts in Automated Feature Engineering

Feature Generation

In traditional machine learning workflows, feature engineering is one of the most crucial steps. It involves transforming raw data into meaningful features that can enhance the model's performance. **Automated Feature Engineering** systems, such as **Featuretools**, automatically generate features by applying predefined transformations to the input data (Kanter & Veeramachaneni, 2015).

For example, if a dataset includes transaction data with time stamps, automated feature engineering can automatically generate features like:

- **Time-based features**: Hour of the day, day of the week, or month.

- **Aggregated features**: Total number of transactions per user, average transaction amount.

- **Interaction features**: Combining multiple variables to create interaction terms (e.g., multiplying two features together).

Graphically, automated feature engineering can be represented as follows:

Graphical Representation:

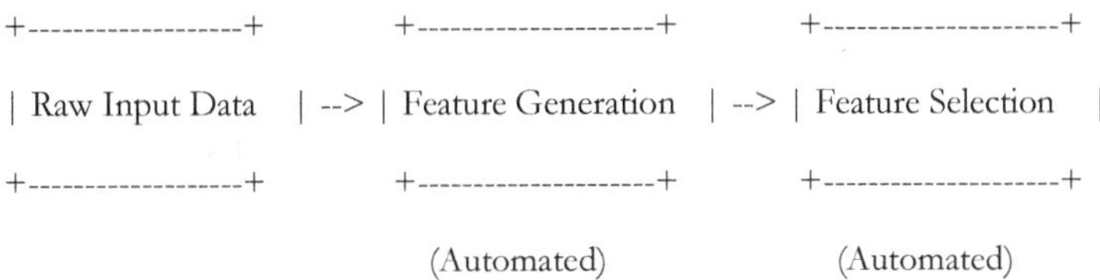

```
+------------------+        +--------------------+        +--------------------+
| Raw Input Data   | --> | Feature Generation   | --> | Feature Selection   |
+------------------+        +--------------------+        +--------------------+
                                (Automated)                  (Automated)
```

Feature Selection

Once features are generated, the next challenge is selecting the most relevant features. Automated feature engineering tools often include feature selection mechanisms, such as:

- **Wrapper methods**: These methods evaluate combinations of features by training and testing models and selecting the subset that optimizes model performance.

- **Embedded methods**: These methods use machine learning algorithms like Lasso or Decision Trees that can inherently perform feature selection during training (Guyon & Elisseeff, 2003).

Handling High-Dimensional Data

One of the key benefits of automated feature engineering is its ability to handle high-dimensional data, which is common in big data environments. By automatically generating and selecting relevant features, these systems can reduce the dimensionality of data without sacrificing model performance, thus making the learning process more efficient (Heaton, 2016).

Applications of AutoML and Automated Feature Engineering

E-commerce and Recommendation Systems

In e-commerce, recommendation systems are crucial for personalized product suggestions. AutoML systems can automatically select and tune the best algorithms for real-time recommendation engines, while automated feature engineering can generate new features such as product-user interaction scores (Feurer et al., 2015). These techniques allow companies like Amazon and Netflix to deliver highly personalized content with minimal human intervention.

Healthcare and Predictive Diagnostics

In healthcare, automated feature engineering can be used to generate new predictive features from patient health records. For example, features like **average blood pressure over time** or **frequency of doctor visits** can be automatically generated to improve the accuracy of predictive models (Kanter & Veeramachaneni, 2015). AutoML can then select the best model for diagnosis, enabling more accurate and timely medical predictions (Waring et al., 2020).

Financial Services

In financial services, automated feature engineering can help generate risk scores or creditworthiness indicators from transactional and behavioral data (Luo et al., 2019). AutoML systems can optimize fraud detection models by selecting the most appropriate algorithms and tuning their hyperparameters, thus improving the detection of fraudulent activities in real-time.

Challenges in AutoML and Automated Feature Engineering

Computational Cost

One of the main challenges in AutoML and automated feature engineering is the high computational cost. Searching for the best models or features, particularly in high-dimensional data, can require extensive computational resources, especially when using NAS for neural networks (Zoph & Le, 2017).

Interpretability

AutoML systems and automatically generated features may lead to complex models that are harder to interpret. This lack of interpretability can be problematic in industries like healthcare and finance, where understanding how a model makes decisions is crucial (Luo et al., 2019).

Overfitting

While AutoML systems are designed to optimize performance, there is always the risk of overfitting, especially when automated feature engineering generates too many features. Overfitting can lead to models that perform well on training data but generalize poorly to unseen data (Feurer et al., 2015).

Conclusion

AutoML and automated feature engineering represent significant advancements in AI and machine learning, particularly in the context of Big Data. These technologies have the potential to automate large portions of the machine learning pipeline, from feature generation to model selection and hyperparameter tuning. While there are challenges related to computational cost and interpretability, the benefits of increased productivity, improved model performance, and accessibility make AutoML and automated feature engineering essential tools in modern data science.

References

Andoni, A., & Indyk, P. (2006). Near-optimal hashing algorithms for approximate nearest neighbor in high dimensions. *Communications of the ACM, 51*(1), 117-122.

Bottou, L. (1998). Online learning and stochastic approximations. *Online learning in neural networks*, 17(9), 142.

Bottou, L. (2010). Large-scale machine learning with stochastic gradient descent. *Proceedings of COMPSTAT*, 177-186.

Bottou, L., & Bousquet, O. (2011). The tradeoffs of large-scale learning. *Optimization for machine learning*, 351, 368.

Breiman, L. (2001). Random forests. *Machine Learning, 45*(1), 5-32.

Carbone, P., Katsifodimos, A., Ewen, S., Markl, V., Haridi, S., & Tzoumas, K. (2015). Apache Flink: Stream and batch processing in a single engine. *Bulletin of the IEEE Computer Society Technical Committee on Data Engineering*, 36(4), 28-38.

Dean, J., & Ghemawat, S. (2008). MapReduce: Simplified data processing on large clusters. *Communications of the ACM, 51*(1), 107-113. https://doi.org/10.1145/1327452.1327492

Dean, J., Corrado, G., Monga, R., Chen, K., Devin, M., Le, Q. V., ... & Ng, A. Y. (2012). Large scale distributed deep networks. *Advances in Neural Information Processing Systems*, 1223-1231.

Dean, J., Corrado, G., Monga, R., Chen, K., Devin, M., Le, Q. V., ... & Ng, A. Y. (2012). Large scale distributed deep networks. In *Advances in neural information processing systems* (pp. 1223-1231).

Domingos, P. (2012). A few useful things to know about machine learning. *Communications of the ACM, 55*(10), 78-87.

Domingos, P., & Hulten, G. (2000). Mining high-speed data streams. *Proceedings of the Sixth ACM SIGKDD International Conference on Knowledge Discovery and Data Mining*, 71-80.

Feurer, M., Klein, A., Eggensperger, K., Springenberg, J. T., Blum, M., & Hutter, F. (2015). Efficient and robust automated machine learning. In *Advances in neural information processing systems* (pp. 2962-2970).

Gama, J., Žliobaitė, I., Bifet, A., Pechenizkiy, M., & Bouchachia, A. (2014). A survey on concept drift adaptation. *ACM Computing Surveys (CSUR)*, 46(4), 1-37.

Ghemawat, S., Gobioff, H., & Leung, S. T. (2003). The Google file system. *ACM SIGOPS Operating Systems Review*, 37(5), 29-43.

Goyal, P., Dollár, P., Girshick, R., Noordhuis, P., Wesolowski, L., Kyrola, A., ... & He, K. (2017). Accurate, large minibatch SGD: Training ImageNet in 1 hour. *arXiv preprint arXiv:1706.02677*.

Guyon, I., & Elisseeff, A. (2003). An introduction to variable and feature selection. *Journal of Machine Learning Research, 3*(Mar), 1157-1182.

He, X., Zhao, K., & Chu, X. (2019). AutoML: A survey of the state-of-the-art. *Knowledge-Based Systems*, 194, 105532.

Heaton, J. (2016). An empirical analysis of feature engineering for predictive modeling. In *Proceedings of SoutheastCon* (pp. 1-6). IEEE.

Hoi, S. C., Wang, J., Zhao, P., & Li, Z. (2018). Online learning: A comprehensive survey. *Neurocomputing*, 275, 126-144.

Jolliffe, I. T. (2002). *Principal component analysis* (2nd ed.). Springer.

Kanter, J. M., & Veeramachaneni, K. (2015). Deep feature synthesis: Towards automating data science endeavors. In *Proceedings of the 2015 IEEE International Conference on Data Science and Advanced Analytics* (pp. 1-10).

Kreps, J., Narkhede, N., & Rao, J. (2011). Kafka: A distributed messaging system for log processing. In *Proceedings of the NetDB* (pp. 1-7).

Krizhevsky, A., Sutskever, I., & Hinton, G. E. (2012). Imagenet classification with deep convolutional neural networks. *Advances in neural information processing systems*, 25, 1097-1105.

Kumar, R., Zhang, H., Ma, H., & Gao, J. (2020). Parallel and distributed machine learning. *Journal of Parallel and Distributed Computing, 134*, 1-2.

Li, M., Andersen, D. G., Smola, A. J., & Yu, K. (2014). Communication efficient distributed machine learning with the parameter server. In *Advances in neural information processing systems* (pp. 19-27).

Luo, W., Phung, D., Tran, T., Gupta, S., Rana, S., Karmakar, C., ... & Venkatesh, S. (2019). Guidelines for developing and reporting machine learning predictive models in biomedical research: A multidisciplinary view. *Journal of Medical Internet Research, 21*(11), e12945.

Mehrotra, R., McInerney, J., Bouchard, H., Lalmas, M., & Diaz, F. (2017). Towards a fair marketplace: Counterfactual evaluation of the trade-off between relevance, fairness & satisfaction in recommendation systems. In *Proceedings of the 26th International Conference on World Wide Web* (pp. 19-28).

Recht, B., Re, C., Wright, S., & Niu, F. (2011). Hogwild: A lock-free approach to parallelizing stochastic gradient descent. In *Advances in neural information processing systems* (pp. 693-701).

Shickel, B., Tighe, P. J., Bihorac, A., & Rashidi, P. (2018). Deep EHR: A survey of recent advances in deep learning techniques for electronic health record (EHR) analysis. *IEEE Journal of Biomedical and Health Informatics, 22*(5), 1589-1604.

Snoek, J., Larochelle, H., & Adams, R. P. (2012). Practical Bayesian optimization of machine learning algorithms. In *Advances in neural information processing systems* (pp. 2951-2959).

Stonebraker, M., Çetintemel, U., & Zdonik, S. (2015). The 8 requirements of real-time stream processing. *ACM SIGMOD Record*, 34(4), 42-47.

Tan, M., & Le, Q. (2019). EfficientNet: Rethinking model scaling for convolutional neural networks. In *Proceedings of the 36th International Conference on Machine Learning* (pp. 6105-6114).

Tsai, C. F., Hu, Y. H., & Chen, Y. C. (2014). Financial time series forecasting using independent component analysis and support vector regression. *Decision Support Systems*, 61, 47-56.

Wang, H., Yeung, D. Y., & Benk, H. (2018). Adaptive online learning for personalizing diagnostic models. *Journal of Machine Learning Research*, 19(1), 3488-3511.

Waring, J., Lindvall, C., Umeton, R., Eaneff, S., Curley, D., & Wilcox, A. B. (2020). Automated machine learning: Review of the state-of-the-art and opportunities for healthcare. *Artificial Intelligence in Medicine*, 104, 101822.

Zaharia, M., Chowdhury, M., Franklin, M. J., Shenker, S., & Stoica, I. (2016). Spark: Cluster computing with working sets. *Communications of the ACM*, *51*(7), 95-104.

Zliobaite, I., Bifet, A., Pfahringer, B., & Holmes, G. (2016). Active learning with drifting streaming data. *IEEE Transactions on Neural Networks and Learning Systems*, 25(1), 27-39.

Zoph, B., & Le, Q. V. (2017). Neural architecture search with reinforcement learning. In *Proceedings of the International Conference on Learning Representations (ICLR)* (pp. 1-12)

Chapter 6: Deep Learning for Big Data

<u>Deep Learning and Big Data</u>

Deep learning, a subset of machine learning, has become integral to analyzing and extracting insights from big data due to its ability to model complex patterns and relationships in vast datasets. One of the most effective deep learning architectures for dealing with structured data, particularly image and spatial data, is the **Convolutional Neural Network (CNN)**. CNNs have revolutionized fields such as image recognition, video analysis, and even applications in areas like healthcare and autonomous systems (LeCun et al., 2015). When integrated with big data technologies, CNNs allow for scalable, high-performance deep learning applications, making them invaluable in big data environments.

Structure of Convolutional Neural Networks

CNNs are specifically designed to process grid-like data structures, such as images. They are characterized by their unique architecture, which is comprised of several key layers:

Convolutional Layers

The convolutional layer is the core building block of CNNs. It applies **convolutional filters** (or kernels) to the input data to capture spatial patterns like edges, textures, and more complex features as the network goes deeper (Krizhevsky et al., 2012). Each filter slides across the input data, performing element-wise multiplication and summing the results, which creates a **feature map**.

Graphically, this can be represented as follows:

Graphical Representation:

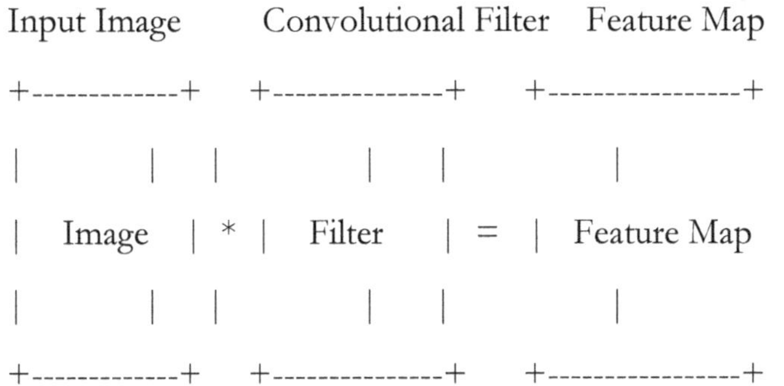

Mathematically, the convolution operation can be represented as:

$$f(x, y) = \sum_{i=1}^{m} \sum_{j=1}^{n} I(x + i, y + j) \cdot K(i, j)$$

Where:

- $I(x, y)$ is the input image pixel at position (x, y).

- $K(i, j)$ is the filter applied at position (i, j).

- $f(x, y)$ is the resulting feature map after applying the filter.

Pooling Layers

Pooling layers, often used after convolutional layers, are designed to reduce the spatial dimensions of the feature maps while preserving important information. This reduces the number of parameters and computations in the network, making it more efficient. The most common pooling operation is **max pooling**, which takes the maximum value in each window of the feature map.

Graphically, max pooling looks like this:

Graphical Representation:

```
Input Feature Map    Pooling Window     Pooled Feature Map

+-------------+       +-------+         +---------+

| 2 1 3 2 |           | 2 1 |           | 4    |

| 4 0 1 3 | -->       | 4 0 | -->       | 3    |

| 5 3 2 4 |           | 5 3 |           | 4    |

| 1 0 2 3 |           | 1 0 |           | 3    |

+-------------+       +-------+         +---------+
```

Fully Connected Layers

After the convolutional and pooling layers, CNNs typically include **fully connected layers**, where each neuron is connected to every neuron in the previous layer. These layers are responsible for combining the high-level features extracted by the convolutional layers and making predictions based on them.

The Role of CNNs in Big Data

Scalability and Efficiency

One of the key challenges when working with big data is ensuring scalability and computational efficiency. CNNs are highly effective in this regard because they use **parameter sharing** and **local connectivity**, which significantly reduce the number of parameters compared to fully connected neural networks (Simonyan & Zisserman, 2015). This makes CNNs scalable and ideal for handling large datasets, particularly those with spatial or structured characteristics, such as images, videos, or even time-series data.

For example, in image classification tasks involving millions of images, CNNs can efficiently extract hierarchical features (such as edges, textures, and shapes) across layers, making them well-suited for big data applications in fields like e-commerce, medical imaging, and autonomous driving (He et al., 2016).

Handling High-Dimensional Data

Big data often comes with high-dimensionality, especially in fields like computer vision and bioinformatics. CNNs excel at reducing the complexity of high-dimensional data by employing successive layers of convolutions and pooling operations, which distill important features from raw data while reducing dimensionality. This capability is crucial for applications where datasets have a large number of input variables but only a few are significant for prediction.

Graphically, CNNs handle high-dimensional data by transforming it through successive layers:

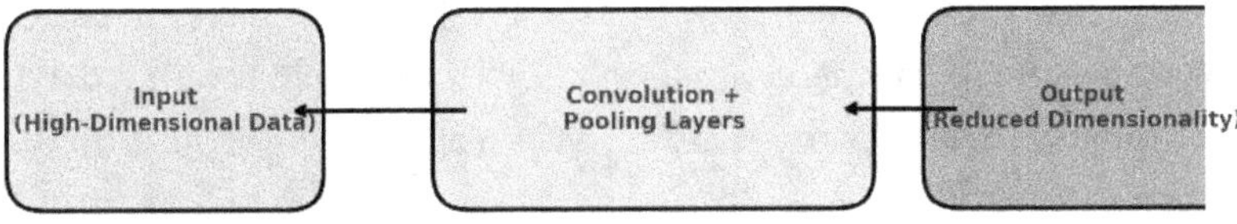

The graph shows the process of:

- The input consists of **high-dimensional data**.

- This data passes through **convolution and pooling layers**, where features are extracted and the dimensionality is reduced.

- Finally, the output represents the **reduced dimensionality**, which is ready for further processing or prediction.

Parallelism with Distributed Computing

Big data environments often leverage distributed computing platforms like **Apache Spark** and **Hadoop**. CNNs can be integrated with such platforms for large-scale parallel training. This is particularly useful when training deep CNNs on massive datasets like **ImageNet**, which contains over 14 million images (Deng et al., 2009). **Model parallelism** and **data parallelism** can be applied in distributed systems to scale the training of CNNs across multiple GPUs or machines, making deep learning feasible even for extremely large datasets (Dean et al., 2012).

Real-Time Analytics with CNNs

In big data scenarios that require real-time analysis, CNNs can be integrated with **stream processing frameworks** such as **Apache Flink** and **Apache Kafka**. This enables real-time processing and analysis of visual data streams, such as surveillance footage, IoT sensor data, and social media images, providing timely insights for applications such as security, autonomous vehicles, and social media monitoring (Hadsell et al., 2009).

Applications of CNNs in Big Data

Image and Video Recognition

CNNs are widely used in large-scale image and video recognition tasks. In industries like retail and security, they are used to analyze images and videos to identify objects, recognize faces, and track movement. For example, CNNs have been applied to **autonomous driving** systems, where they process camera feeds in real-time to detect pedestrians, road signs, and other vehicles (Simonyan & Zisserman, 2015).

Healthcare and Medical Imaging

In healthcare, CNNs are applied to big medical imaging datasets to detect diseases such as cancer and cardiovascular conditions. CNNs can automatically extract relevant features from medical images such as X-rays, CT scans, and MRIs, improving the speed and accuracy of diagnoses (Shen et al., 2017).

E-commerce and Recommendation Systems

In e-commerce, CNNs can process product images at scale to classify and recommend products to customers. CNNs can also analyze customer-uploaded images for visual search applications, where users find products by uploading images of the items they are looking for (Zhou et al., 2014).

Challenges in Using CNNs for Big Data

High Computational Requirements

Training CNNs, especially on massive datasets, is computationally intensive. CNNs require significant hardware resources, including **GPUs** and **TPUs**, for efficient training. Distributed computing frameworks and model parallelism techniques can help mitigate this challenge, but resource requirements remain high (Dean et al., 2012).

Data Privacy and Security

With the use of CNNs in sensitive domains like healthcare, there is the issue of data privacy and security. Handling large amounts of sensitive personal information, such as medical records and facial recognition data, requires robust privacy measures and data security protocols to prevent unauthorized access (Shokri & Shmatikov, 2015).

In summary, convolutional Neural Networks (CNNs) are a powerful tool for leveraging deep learning in big data applications. Their scalability, ability to handle high-dimensional data, and integration with distributed systems make them ideal for large-scale tasks like image recognition, healthcare diagnostics, and real-time video analysis. Despite the computational challenges, advancements in distributed computing and hardware acceleration continue to make CNNs an essential technology in AI for big data.

RNNs and LSTMs in Big Data

Deep learning techniques have become critical in processing big data due to their capacity to model complex patterns and handle vast datasets. When it comes to processing sequential data, such as time-series data, text, or speech, **Recurrent Neural Networks (RNNs)** are a key deep learning architecture. However, due to their limitations in dealing with long-term dependencies, **Long Short-Term Memory Networks (LSTMs)**, a type of RNN, have become more widely used for addressing these issues. These models are specifically designed to manage temporal sequences and maintain relevant information over long periods, making them ideal for handling large-scale data with temporal dependencies (Hochreiter & Schmidhuber, 1997).

Structure of Recurrent Neural Networks (RNNs)

RNNs are designed to handle sequences of data by maintaining a hidden state that captures information from previous time steps. Unlike feedforward neural networks, RNNs have connections that form cycles, which allow them to maintain memory of past inputs.

Key Features of RNNs:

Hidden State: At each time step t, an RNN has a hidden state ht, which is influenced by the previous hidden state $ht-1$ and the current input xt. This allows the RNN to "remember" previous information and apply it to future time steps.

The hidden state is calculated as:

$$h_t = \sigma(W_h h_{t-1} + W_x x_t + b_h)$$

Where:

- W_h and W_x are weight matrices.

- b_h is the bias term.

- σ is the activation function, often the tanh or ReLU function.

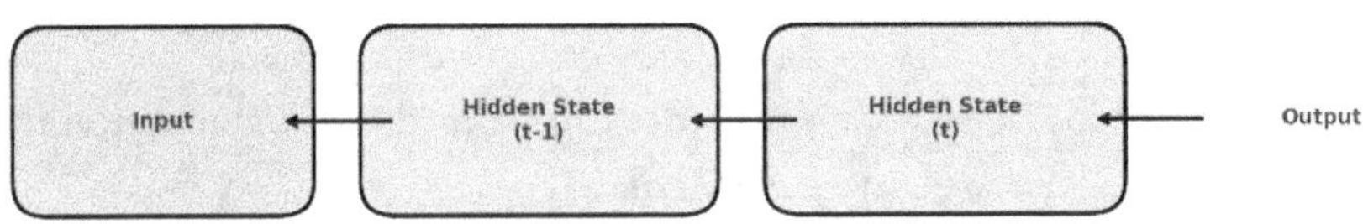

The above graph shows the flow through a Recurrent Neural Network (RNN):

Input: The initial data or sequence.

Hidden State (t-1): Represents the memory of previous time steps.

Hidden State (t): Represents the updated memory with new information from the current time step.

Output: The final output generated after processing the sequence.

However, standard RNNs face issues with **vanishing gradients** when trained on long sequences, leading to difficulties in learning long-term dependencies (Bengio et al., 1994). To solve this problem, **LSTMs** were introduced.

Long Short-Term Memory Networks (LSTMs)

LSTMs, a variation of RNNs, were developed to address the vanishing gradient problem by introducing a memory cell that can maintain information over long time periods. LSTMs use **gates** to control the flow of information and decide what to keep and what to forget, thus allowing them to capture long-term dependencies more effectively (Hochreiter & Schmidhuber, 1997).

Key Components of LSTMs:

Memory Cell: The memory cell preserves information over time, allowing LSTMs to retain or forget information as needed.

Forget Gate: Decides which information from the cell state should be discarded. The forget gate is calculated as:

$$f_t = \sigma(W_f \cdot [h_{t-1}, x_t] + b_f)$$

Input Gate: Controls the new information added to the cell state. It is calculated as:

$$i_t = \sigma(W_i \cdot [h_{t-1}, x_t] + b_i)$$

Output Gate: Determines what part of the memory will be output at each time step. This is given by:

$$o_t = \sigma\left(W_o \cdot [h_{t-1}, x_t] + b_o\right)$$

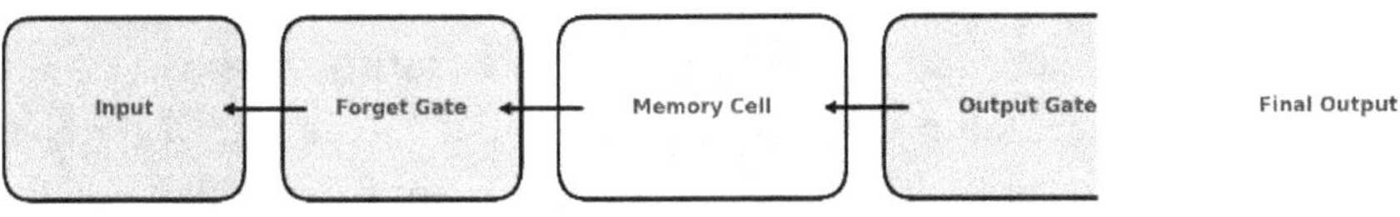

The above graph shows the flow through an LSTM (Long Short-Term Memory) cell:

Input: The initial data enters the LSTM.

Forget Gate: This gate determines which information to discard from the cell state.

Memory Cell: This stores information, allowing the model to remember relevant data over time.

Output Gate: This gate controls the output of the memory cell.

Final Output: The final output after the processing of the input sequence.

Application of RNNs and LSTMs in Big Data

Natural Language Processing (NLP)

RNNs and LSTMs have become essential in **Natural Language Processing (NLP)** tasks, such as machine translation, sentiment analysis, and text generation. These models can handle large corpora of text data and capture both short-term and long-term dependencies within sequences of words. For instance, LSTMs are used to translate text by maintaining memory over entire sentences, enabling more accurate translations (Sutskever et al., 2014).

Time-Series Analysis and Forecasting

In big data applications like **time-series forecasting**, where predicting future values based on historical data is crucial, LSTMs are widely used due to their ability to capture temporal dependencies (Siami-Namini et al., 2019). LSTMs are particularly effective in financial markets, weather forecasting, and IoT sensor data, where long-term dependencies are crucial for accurate predictions.

The above diagram shows an LSTM processing time-series data:

Time-Series Data: The input, which could be any sequential or temporal data (such as stock prices, weather data, etc.).

LSTM: The LSTM layer processes the sequential data, learning patterns over time.

Forecasted Output: The final predicted or forecasted output based on the input time-series data.

Speech Recognition and Generation

In **speech recognition** and generation tasks, LSTMs have proven superior to traditional RNNs due to their ability to process long audio sequences while retaining context. Applications like **Google Assistant** and **Apple's Siri** rely on LSTMs to convert audio inputs into meaningful text by keeping track of the temporal structure of speech (Graves et al., 2013).

Anomaly Detection in Big Data

In industries like finance and cybersecurity, detecting anomalies in large, time-dependent datasets is critical for preventing fraud and identifying threats. LSTMs are effective in detecting unusual patterns in transactional data or network traffic by learning the typical patterns over time and flagging deviations (Malhotra et al., 2015).

RNNs and LSTMs in Distributed Systems for Big Data

Handling large datasets in real-time requires scalable architectures. **Distributed computing platforms** such as **Apache Spark** and **TensorFlow** allow RNNs and LSTMs to be trained on large-scale datasets across multiple machines. These frameworks enable **data parallelism**, where different parts of a large dataset are processed concurrently across distributed nodes, improving the speed of model training and inference (Zaharia et al., 2016).

Moreover, LSTMs can be implemented in streaming platforms like **Apache Kafka** for real-time sequence processing, making them valuable for tasks such as stock price prediction or real-time recommendation systems, where timely insights from streaming data are critical.

Challenges and Limitations of RNNs and LSTMs in Big Data

1. Computational Complexity

Both RNNs and LSTMs are computationally intensive, especially when dealing with long sequences. Training these models on massive datasets requires significant computational resources, often necessitating specialized hardware such as **GPUs** and **TPUs** (Dean et al., 2012).

2. Sequence Length and Memory

Although LSTMs can handle longer sequences than traditional RNNs, they still face limitations when sequences become excessively long. This can result in difficulties in capturing extremely long-term dependencies without significant tuning or enhancements such as **Attention Mechanisms**, which allow models to focus on the most relevant parts of the sequence (Bahdanau et al., 2015).

3. Overfitting and Generalization

With large datasets, RNNs and LSTMs are prone to overfitting, especially if the training data is noisy or unbalanced. Regularization techniques, such as **dropout** and **early stopping**, are often used to prevent overfitting (Srivastava et al., 2014), but they can be difficult to tune in large-scale systems.

In summary, Recurrent Neural Networks (RNNs) and Long Short-Term Memory Networks (LSTMs) are critical deep learning architectures for handling sequential data in big data environments. While RNNs are powerful for learning from temporal sequences, LSTMs offer improved performance by addressing the vanishing gradient problem and capturing long-term dependencies. These models are widely applied in fields like natural language processing, time-series forecasting, and speech recognition, and they are increasingly used in distributed systems to handle the computational demands of big data.

Generative Adversarial Networks (GANs)

Generative Adversarial Networks (GANs) represent a powerful class of deep learning models designed for generative tasks, such as creating new data instances that resemble a given dataset. Introduced by Ian Goodfellow et al. (2014), GANs consist of two neural networks, a **generator** and a **discriminator**, that are trained simultaneously in a zero-sum game setup. The generator tries to produce data that mimics real data, while the discriminator attempts to distinguish between real data and the fake data produced by the generator. GANs have revolutionized fields such as image generation, data augmentation, and creative AI applications by producing highly realistic synthetic data.

Structure and Working of GANs

GANs are composed of two main components:

The Generator: This network generates synthetic data (e.g., images, audio, or text) from random noise. The goal of the generator is to produce data that is indistinguishable from real data, thereby "fooling" the discriminator.

The Discriminator: This network evaluates the authenticity of the data, distinguishing between real and synthetic data. The discriminator's objective is to correctly identify whether the input data is real or fake.

The training process of GANs can be understood as a game between these two networks. The generator tries to minimize the error by generating realistic data, while the discriminator maximizes its ability to classify data as either real or fake. This process continues until the generator produces data that the discriminator finds difficult to distinguish from real data (Goodfellow et al., 2014).

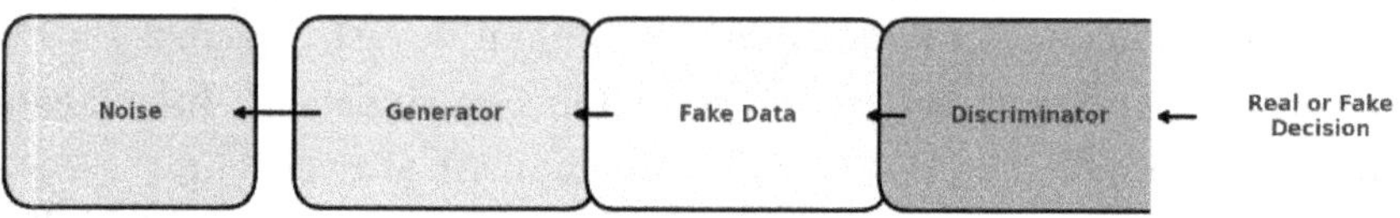

The diagram shows the Generative Adversarial Network (GAN) flow:

Noise: Random input, usually sampled from a latent space, that is fed into the generator.

Generator: The neural network that generates fake data from the noise input.

Fake Data: The synthetic data produced by the generator, resembling real data.

Discriminator: The neural network that attempts to classify data as either real or fake.

Real or Fake Decision: The output of the discriminator, which indicates whether the input data is real or generated.

Mathematical Formulation of GANs:

The objective of the GAN is to solve the following **minimax problem**:

$$\min_{G} \max_{D} V(D, G) = \mathbb{E}_{x \sim p_{data}(x)}[\log D(x)] + \mathbb{E}_{z \sim p_z(z)}[\log(1 - D(G(z)))]$$

Where:

- G is the generator, and D is the discriminator.

- $x \sim p_{data}(x)$ represents real data samples.

- $z \sim p_z(z)$ represents the noise input to the generator.

GAN Variants for Big Data

As GANs gained prominence, several variants were developed to address specific challenges in big data and generative modeling. Some of the popular GAN variants include:

Deep Convolutional GANs (DCGANs): DCGANs integrate convolutional layers into the GAN architecture, making them especially effective for generating high-quality images (Radford et al., 2016). The convolutional layers allow the network to learn hierarchical features, which is crucial when dealing with complex image data.

Conditional GANs (cGANs): In conditional GANs, both the generator and discriminator are conditioned on additional information (such as class labels). This enables GANs to generate specific types of data, making them particularly useful for tasks like image-to-image translation and text-to-image synthesis (Mirza & Osindero, 2014).

CycleGANs: CycleGANs are designed for tasks involving unpaired data. For example, they can translate images from one domain to another (e.g., from horses to zebras) without paired examples from both domains. This is useful when big data is unstructured or unlabeled (Zhu et al., 2017).

Applications of GANs in Big Data

GANs have demonstrated immense potential in handling big data challenges, particularly in domains where labeled data is scarce, or the generation of realistic synthetic data is needed. Some prominent applications include:

Image Generation and Data Augmentation

GANs have revolutionized image generation tasks by producing realistic synthetic images. In fields like healthcare, GANs are used to augment medical datasets, generating realistic images like MRI scans, which can be used to improve the performance of diagnostic models without the need for extensive manual labeling (Frid-Adar et al., 2018). This capability is particularly valuable when dealing with big data, as it helps create diverse and balanced datasets.

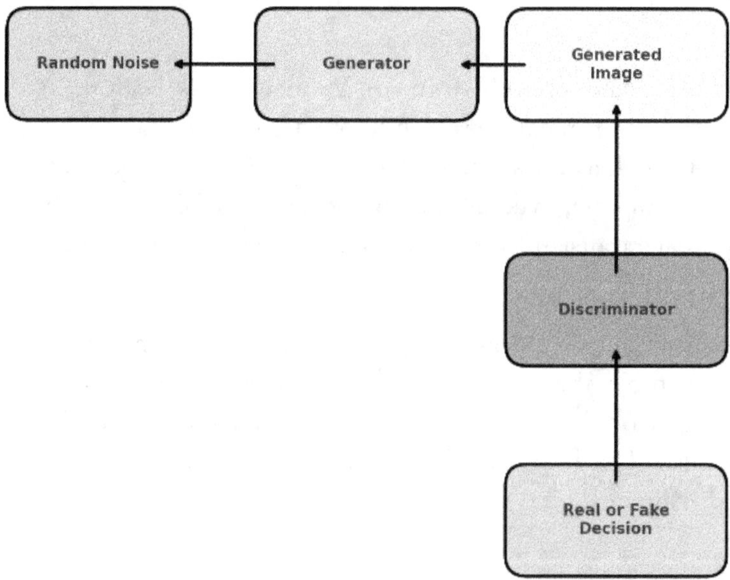

The diagram above shows

a Generative Adversarial Network (GAN) flow with both the generator and discriminator:

Random Noise: The input noise fed into the generator, which typically comes from a latent space.

Generator: This neural network transforms the random noise into a generated image.

Generated Image: The output image produced by the generator, which tries to resemble a real image.

Discriminator: This network evaluates whether the generated image is real or fake.

Real or Fake Decision: The output decision of the discriminator, indicating whether the input image is genuine or artificially generated.

Text-to-Image Generation

Text-to-image generation is another domain where GANs, particularly cGANs, excel. This involves generating realistic images based on text descriptions. Applications include generating product images based on descriptions for e-commerce platforms, automating creative processes, and enhancing virtual reality environments (Reed et al., 2016).

Data Imputation and Enhancement

In big data environments, missing data can pose significant challenges. GANs have been used to impute missing values and enhance low-quality data. For example, in finance, GANs are used to generate synthetic financial transactions or impute missing values in customer data to improve fraud detection and risk management systems (Yoon et al., 2018).

Anomaly Detection

GANs are also used in anomaly detection, where the generator is trained to create normal data distributions. The discriminator is then used to identify anomalies, or outliers, that deviate from this learned distribution. This technique is particularly useful in cybersecurity, fraud detection, and predictive maintenance, where detecting unusual behavior is crucial (Schlegl et al., 2017).

Big Data and Generative Art

GANs are extensively used in creative AI applications, where they generate art, music, and designs based on learned patterns from large datasets of artistic styles or musical compositions. This has given rise to **AI-generated art**, where GANs create realistic and abstract pieces that mimic human creativity.

Challenges of GANs in Big Data

Despite their success, GANs come with several challenges, especially when dealing with big data:

Mode Collapse

One of the main challenges in training GANs is **mode collapse**, where the generator produces limited diversity in its outputs, generating only a few variations of the same pattern. This is a critical issue in big data applications where diversity is essential, such as in healthcare, where generating only a small subset of synthetic images can lead to biased models (Arjovsky et al., 2017).

Training Instability

GANs are notoriously difficult to train due to the adversarial nature of the learning process. The generator and discriminator must be carefully balanced, and training often requires significant computational resources, particularly for big data applications where the dataset size exacerbates these challenges (Goodfellow et al., 2014).

Data Privacy Concerns

In applications where GANs are used to generate synthetic data, such as healthcare or finance, data privacy is a concern. Generated data may inadvertently reveal sensitive information from the original training data, leading to potential privacy violations (Torkzadehmahani et al., 2019).

In summary, Generative Adversarial Networks (GANs) are a powerful deep learning technique for generating realistic data, and they have transformative applications in various domains of big data. From image generation and data augmentation to anomaly detection and creative AI, GANs offer a versatile approach to handling complex generative tasks. However, their training complexity and issues like mode collapse pose challenges, particularly in big data environments. As research in GANs continues to evolve, solutions to these challenges, such as improved training algorithms and hybrid models, are likely to emerge, further expanding the role of GANs in AI-driven big data applications.

Transformers and Attention Mechanisms

In the field of deep learning, particularly for tasks related to natural language processing (NLP), sequence modeling, and big data, the **Transformer** architecture has emerged as one of the most revolutionary approaches. Introduced by Vaswani et al. (2017) in their landmark paper *Attention is All You Need*, the transformer architecture eschews the recurrent models typically used in sequence processing, such as Recurrent Neural Networks (RNNs) and Long Short-Term Memory networks (LSTMs). Instead, transformers rely entirely on **attention mechanisms** to model relationships between elements in a sequence, regardless of their distance from each other.

Transformers have proven highly effective in scaling to large datasets and enabling parallel processing, which is critical in handling big data applications in NLP, time-series forecasting, and other sequence modeling tasks.

The Role of Attention Mechanisms

At the core of the Transformer architecture is the **attention mechanism**, which allows the model to focus on specific parts of the input data that are more relevant to a given task. The attention mechanism dynamically assigns weights to different input elements, thereby helping the model decide which parts of the input to emphasize more.

Types of Attention Mechanisms

Self-Attention (Scaled Dot-Product Attention): In self-attention, each input element attends to all other input elements to capture contextual relationships. This mechanism is scaled by the length of the sequence to ensure numerical stability during optimization. The key formula for scaled dot-product attention is:

$$\text{Attention}(Q, K, V) = \text{softmax}\left(\frac{QK^T}{\sqrt{d_k}}\right) V$$

Where:

- Q represents the query matrix, K is the key matrix, and V is the value matrix.

- d_k is the dimension of the key vector.

- The dot product between the query and key matrices determines how much attention is paid to corresponding elements.

Multi-Head Attention: Instead of using a single attention function, **multi-head attention** applies multiple attention heads in parallel. This allows the model to focus on different parts of the input simultaneously, improving its ability to capture various aspects of the input sequence. The multi-head attention mechanism is a key part of the transformer's ability to learn more complex relationships across sequences.

The diagram shows the attention mechanism:

Query + Key + Value: The input elements used in the attention mechanism, where the query is compared with the keys to generate attention scores.

Attention Scores: The weights calculated by comparing the query with each key. These scores determine how much attention each input element should receive.

Weighted Aggregation: The input values are weighted by the attention scores and then aggregated.

Output: The final output after applying the attention mechanism.

Transformer Architecture

The Transformer architecture consists of an encoder and a decoder, both of which are built using stacked layers of multi-head self-attention and feedforward networks. The encoder takes the input sequence and applies attention mechanisms to extract contextual information. The decoder, in turn, generates the output sequence, also using attention to focus on relevant parts of the input.

Components of the Transformer

Positional Encoding: Since transformers do not inherently capture sequential order (unlike RNNs), they use **positional encodings** to provide information about the position of each token in the input sequence. These encodings are added to the input embeddings before they are passed to the encoder.

Encoder: The encoder consists of multiple layers, each containing two key components:

o **Multi-Head Self-Attention Mechanism**: This allows the encoder to attend to all positions in the input sequence and learn dependencies.

o **Feedforward Neural Network**: After the attention mechanism, each position in the sequence is passed through a fully connected feedforward neural network.

Decoder: The decoder has a similar architecture but includes an additional attention layer that allows it to focus on relevant parts of the input sequence during generation.

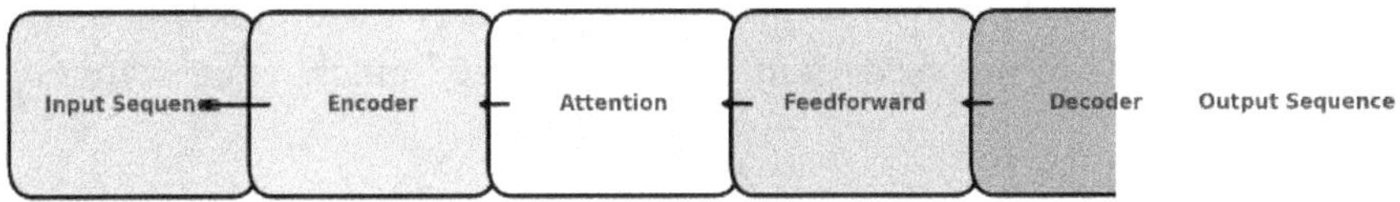

The graph shows the Transformer architecture's data flow:

Input Sequence: The initial sequence of data (e.g., text, time-series) that needs to be processed.

Encoder: The encoder processes the input sequence and extracts meaningful representations.

Attention: The attention mechanism focuses on relevant parts of the input, helping the model to prioritize important information.

Feedforward: The feedforward layer further processes the data after attention has been applied.

Decoder: The decoder generates the output sequence based on the information received from the encoder and attention mechanisms.

Output Sequence: The final generated sequence, which could be translated text, a prediction, or another output depending on the task.

Advantages of Transformers for Big Data

1. Scalability and Parallelization

Unlike RNNs and LSTMs, which process input sequences sequentially, transformers allow for **parallelization** of data processing. This makes them far more efficient when dealing with large datasets, as transformers can process all tokens in the sequence simultaneously. This scalability is crucial in big data applications where large volumes of data must be processed quickly (Vaswani et al., 2017).

2. Long-Range Dependencies

Traditional sequence models, such as RNNs, struggle with capturing long-range dependencies due to vanishing gradient issues. Transformers, by using attention mechanisms, can capture dependencies across the entire sequence, no matter how far apart the elements are. This ability is critical when working with long sequences of data, such as paragraphs of text or long time-series data (Devlin et al., 2019).

3. Versatility Across Modalities

Transformers have proven successful not only in NLP but also in domains like computer vision, speech recognition, and time-series forecasting. For instance, models like **Vision Transformers (ViT)** have been developed to apply transformer models to image data, bypassing the need for convolutional layers (Dosovitskiy et al., 2021).

Applications of Transformers and Attention Mechanisms in Big Data

Natural Language Processing (NLP)

The most significant breakthroughs for transformers have been in NLP. Models such as **BERT** (Bidirectional Encoder Representations from Transformers) and **GPT** (Generative Pre-trained Transformer) are based on the transformer architecture and have set state-of-the-art benchmarks in tasks like machine translation, question answering, and text generation (Devlin et al., 2019).

Time-Series Forecasting

In big data environments, time-series forecasting plays a vital role in domains like finance, healthcare, and supply chain management. Transformers have been adapted to perform time-series prediction, where they can efficiently model complex temporal relationships in large datasets (Lim et al., 2021).

Healthcare and Genomics

In healthcare, transformers have been applied to tasks such as protein structure prediction, genomics, and drug discovery. These applications require the modeling of long-range dependencies and large datasets, making transformers ideal for tasks like predicting gene expression patterns and identifying new therapeutic targets (Rao et al., 2021).

Image Recognition

Vision transformers (ViT) apply transformers to image classification tasks by treating image patches as sequence data. ViTs have shown competitive performance compared to traditional convolutional neural networks (CNNs) in handling large-scale image datasets, such as ImageNet (Dosovitskiy et al., 2021).

Challenges of Transformers in Big Data

Computational Cost

Despite their advantages, transformers are computationally expensive, especially when dealing with large sequences. The attention mechanism scales quadratically with the sequence length, making it resource-intensive for very long sequences. However, efforts like **efficient transformers** aim to reduce this complexity (Katharopoulos et al., 2020).

Data Requirements

Transformers typically require large datasets for effective training. Pre-trained models, such as BERT or GPT, mitigate this issue by training on vast amounts of data and fine-tuning on smaller datasets. However, for domain-specific big data applications, acquiring such large training datasets can be challenging.

In summary, transformers and attention mechanisms represent a significant leap forward in deep learning, particularly for tasks involving sequence data. Their ability to model long-range dependencies and process data in parallel makes them ideal for big data applications, ranging from natural language processing and time-series forecasting to image recognition. While transformers come with challenges such as high computational costs, their versatility and state-of-the-art performance continue to drive innovation across industries that rely on large-scale data.

Transfer Learning and Pre-trained Models

In the context of deep learning and big data, **transfer learning** and **pre-trained models** have emerged as essential techniques for reducing training time and improving model performance. Transfer learning involves leveraging a model that has been trained on one task and applying it to another, typically related, task. Pre-trained models, which are a key component of transfer learning, are models that have been trained on large datasets and can be fine-tuned or adapted to new datasets with minimal additional training. These techniques are especially useful in big data applications where training models from scratch on massive datasets can be computationally expensive and time-consuming.

Transfer learning has become widely popular due to its ability to generalize across tasks, making it a crucial component in various domains such as computer vision, natural language processing (NLP), and speech recognition (Zhuang et al., 2021).

How Transfer Learning Works

Pre-training

The first step in transfer learning is **pre-training** a model on a large and diverse dataset. For instance, in computer vision, models like **ResNet** or **Inception** are pre-trained on large datasets like **ImageNet**, which contains millions of labeled images across thousands of categories (He et al., 2016). Similarly, in NLP, models such as **BERT** and **GPT** are pre-trained on large corpora of text to capture language patterns, grammar, and semantic relationships (Devlin et al., 2019).

Fine-tuning

Once the model has been pre-trained, it can be **fine-tuned** on a smaller, task-specific dataset. During fine-tuning, the weights of the pre-trained model are adjusted to fit the specific task. Fine-tuning is typically much faster than training from scratch because the model already has learned general features that can be transferred to the new task.

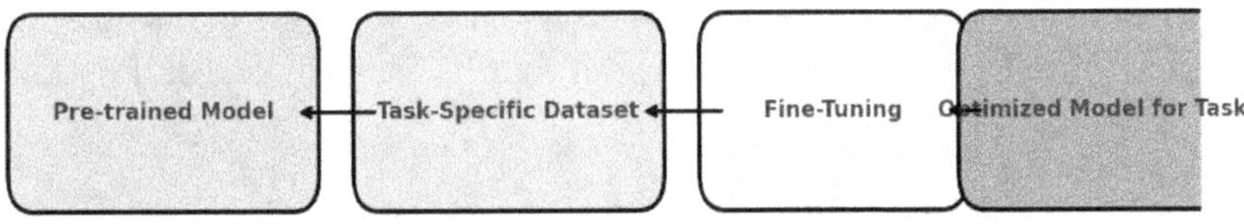

The above graph shows the transfer learning process:

Pre-trained Model: A model that has already been trained on a large dataset (e.g., ImageNet for vision tasks or BERT for NLP).

Task-Specific Dataset: A smaller, task-specific dataset used to fine-tune the pre-trained model.

Fine-Tuning: The process of adjusting the weights of the pre-trained model using the task-specific dataset.

Optimized Model for Task: The final model, fine-tuned and optimized for the specific task.

Transfer Learning in Big Data

Transfer learning is particularly beneficial in **big data** scenarios where datasets can be heterogeneous or where labeled data is scarce. For instance, pre-trained models can be applied to tasks that involve complex data modalities, such as images, text, and speech. This capability to generalize across tasks allows organizations to maximize the use of large datasets and computational resources effectively.

Key Benefits in Big Data Context:

Reduction in Training Time: Training deep learning models from scratch on massive datasets can be prohibitively expensive. By leveraging pre-trained models, researchers can significantly reduce training time by starting with a model that has already learned useful features.

Better Performance with Less Data: In many big data contexts, labeled data is often scarce or expensive to obtain. Pre-trained models can help by transferring knowledge from large, general-purpose datasets to smaller, domain-specific datasets, thereby improving performance even with limited data (Yosinski et al., 2014).

Computational Efficiency: Transfer learning reduces the computational cost associated with training large models, making it feasible to apply deep learning techniques in big data environments without needing vast computational resources.

Popular Pre-trained Models and Their Applications

Computer Vision

In computer vision, transfer learning has become standard practice due to the availability of powerful pre-trained models, such as:

ResNet: The ResNet (Residual Networks) architecture introduced skip connections that allow for training very deep networks. Pre-trained ResNet models, such as ResNet-50 and ResNet-101, are commonly used in image classification and object detection tasks (He et al., 2016).

Inception: The Inception architecture, also known as GoogLeNet, introduced the concept of inception modules, which allow for multi-scale feature extraction. Inception models pre-trained on ImageNet are widely used in medical imaging, satellite imagery analysis, and other large-scale vision tasks (Szegedy et al., 2016).

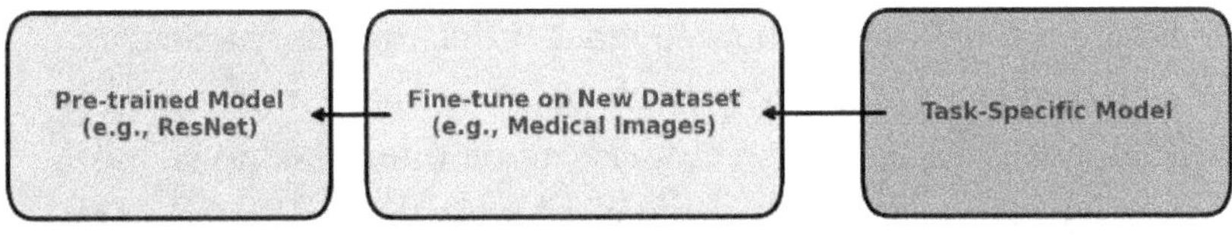

The graph shows the transfer learning process for a specific example:

Pre-trained Model (e.g., ResNet): A model that has been pre-trained on a large dataset like ImageNet.

Fine-tune on New Dataset (e.g., Medical Images): The process of fine-tuning the pre-trained model on a new, task-specific dataset such as medical images.

Task-Specific Model: The final model, optimized for the specific task after fine-tuning on the new dataset.

Natural Language Processing (NLP)

In NLP, pre-trained models like **BERT** (Bidirectional Encoder Representations from Transformers) and **GPT** (Generative Pre-trained Transformer) have revolutionized language-related tasks such as text classification, translation, and question answering:

BERT: BERT is pre-trained on vast corpora of text in a bidirectional manner, meaning it considers the context from both sides of a word in a sentence. This allows it to capture rich semantic information. Fine-tuning BERT on smaller, task-specific datasets has led to breakthroughs in tasks like sentiment analysis and named entity recognition (Devlin et al., 2019).

GPT: GPT is an autoregressive language model that generates text by predicting the next word in a sequence. GPT models, particularly **GPT-3**, have demonstrated remarkable capabilities in text generation and dialogue systems. These models can be fine-tuned to adapt to specific language tasks with minimal additional data (Brown et al., 2020).

Speech Recognition and Audio Processing

In audio and speech processing, pre-trained models like **wav2vec** and **DeepSpeech** have been used to improve automatic speech recognition (ASR) systems:

wav2vec 2.0: This model is pre-trained on unlabeled speech data using a contrastive learning approach, which allows it to capture meaningful speech representations. Fine-tuning on labeled datasets enables it to achieve high accuracy in speech-to-text tasks, even with limited labeled data (Baevski et al., 2020).

Applications of Transfer Learning in Big Data

Medical Imaging

In medical imaging, transfer learning has become a powerful tool for training models on specific medical datasets. For example, pre-trained models on ImageNet can be fine-tuned to detect diseases in X-ray, MRI, or CT scan images with high accuracy, even when labeled medical data is scarce (Tajbakhsh et al., 2016).

Sentiment Analysis and Text Classification

In NLP, pre-trained models such as BERT and GPT can be fine-tuned on sentiment analysis datasets to classify customer reviews, social media posts, or feedback. This approach is particularly valuable in big data environments where real-time analysis of large volumes of text data is required (Zhuang et al., 2021).

Autonomous Vehicles

In the autonomous vehicle industry, transfer learning is used to adapt pre-trained models for tasks such as object detection, lane detection, and pedestrian recognition. By fine-tuning pre-trained models, companies can reduce the amount of labeled data and computational power required to train complex models (Chen et al., 2015).

Challenges of Transfer Learning in Big Data

Domain Shift

One of the primary challenges in transfer learning is the **domain shift**, where the source dataset (used to pre-train the model) differs significantly from the target dataset (used for fine-tuning). In such cases, the performance of the fine-tuned model may degrade if the pre-trained features do not generalize well to the new domain (Pan & Yang, 2010).

Overfitting on Small Datasets

While transfer learning can reduce the amount of data needed for training, there is a risk of **overfitting** when fine-tuning on very small datasets. The pre-trained model may fit too closely to the limited data, reducing its ability to generalize to new data.

Computational Resource Requirements

Although transfer learning reduces training time compared to training from scratch, fine-tuning large pre-trained models, especially in domains like NLP with models like GPT-3, still requires substantial computational resources (Brown et al., 2020).

Conclusion

Transfer learning and pre-trained models have become indispensable in the field of deep learning, particularly for big data applications where training models from scratch can be costly and time-consuming. By leveraging pre-trained models and fine-tuning them on specific tasks, researchers and practitioners can achieve state-of-the-art performance with fewer data and computational resources. Despite challenges such as domain shift and overfitting, transfer learning continues to push the boundaries of AI applications in areas like computer vision, NLP, and speech recognition.

References

Arjovsky, M., Chintala, S., & Bottou, L. (2017). Wasserstein GAN. *arXiv preprint arXiv:1701.07875.*

Baevski, A., Zhou, Y., Mohamed, A., & Auli, M. (2020). wav2vec 2.0: A framework for self-supervised learning of speech representations. In *Proceedings of the 34th Conference on Neural Information Processing Systems (NeurIPS).*

Bahdanau, D., Cho, K., & Bengio, Y. (2015). Neural machine translation by jointly learning to align and translate. In *Proceedings of the International Conference on Learning Representations (ICLR).*

Bengio, Y., Simard, P., & Frasconi, P. (1994). Learning long-term dependencies with gradient descent is difficult. *IEEE Transactions on Neural Networks, 5*(2), 157-166.

Brown, T. B., Mann, B., Ryder, N., Subbiah, M., Kaplan, J., Dhariwal, P., ... & Amodei, D. (2020). Language models are few-shot learners. In *Proceedings of the 34th Conference on Neural Information Processing Systems (NeurIPS).*

Chen, C., Seff, A., Kornhauser, A., & Xiao, J. (2015). DeepDriving: Learning affordance for direct perception in autonomous driving. In *Proceedings of the IEEE International Conference on Computer Vision* (pp. 2722-2730).

Dean, J., Corrado, G., Monga, R., Chen, K., Devin, M., Le, Q. V., ... & Ng, A. Y. (2012). Large scale distributed deep networks. In *Advances in neural information processing systems* (pp. 1223-1231).

Deng, J., Dong, W., Socher, R., Li, L. J., Li, K., & Fei-Fei, L. (2009). ImageNet: A large-scale hierarchical image database. In *2009 IEEE conference on computer vision and pattern recognition* (pp. 248-255). IEEE.

Devlin, J., Chang, M. W., Lee, K., & Toutanova, K. (2019). BERT: Pre-training of deep bidirectional transformers for language understanding. In *Proceedings of the 2019 Conference of the North American Chapter of the Association for Computational Linguistics: Human Language Technologies* (pp. 4171-4186).

Devlin, J., Chang, M. W., Lee, K., & Toutanova, K. (2019). BERT: Pre-training of deep bidirectional transformers for language understanding. In *Proceedings of the 2019 Conference of the North American Chapter of the Association for Computational Linguistics* (pp. 4171-4186).

Dosovitskiy, A., Beyer, L., Kolesnikov, A., Weissenborn, D., Zhai, X., Unterthiner, T., ... & Houlsby, N. (2021). An image is worth 16x16 words: Transformers for image recognition at scale. *International Conference on Learning Representations.*

Frid-Adar, M., Klang, E., Amitai, M., Goldberger, J., & Greenspan, H. (2018). Synthetic data augmentation using GAN for improved liver lesion classification. In *Proceedings of the IEEE 15th International Symposium on Biomedical Imaging* (pp. 289-293).

Goodfellow, I., Pouget-Abadie, J., Mirza, M., Xu, B., Warde-Farley, D., Ozair, S., ... & Bengio, Y. (2014). Generative adversarial nets. In *Advances in neural information processing systems* (pp. 2672-2680).

Graves, A., Mohamed, A., & Hinton, G. (2013). Speech recognition with deep recurrent neural networks. In *Proceedings of the IEEE International Conference on Acoustics, Speech, and Signal Processing (ICASSP).*

Hadsell, R., Chopra, S., & LeCun, Y. (2009). Dimensionality reduction by learning an invariant mapping. *In Proceedings of the IEEE Conference on Computer Vision and Pattern Recognition* (pp. 1735 1742).

He, K., Zhang, X., Ren, S., & Sun, J. (2016). Deep residual learning for image recognition. In *Proceedings of the IEEE conference on computer vision and pattern recognition* (pp. 770-778).

Hochreiter, S., & Schmidhuber, J. (1997). Long short-term memory. *Neural Computation, 9*(8), 1735-1780.

Katharopoulos, A., Vyas, A., Pappas, N., & Fleuret, F. (2020). Transformers are RNNs: Fast autoregressive transformers with linear attention. In *Proceedings of the 37th International Conference on Machine Learning* (pp. 5156-5165).

Krizhevsky, A., Sutskever, I., & Hinton, G. E. (2012). Imagenet classification with deep convolutional neural networks. In *Advances in neural information processing systems* (pp. 1097-1105).

LeCun, Y., Bengio, Y., & Hinton, G. (2015). Deep learning. *Nature, 521*(7553), 436-444.

Lim, B., Arık, S. O., Loeff, N., & Pfister, T. (2021). Temporal fusion transformers for interpretable multi-horizon time series forecasting. *International Journal of Forecasting, 37*(1), 174-190.

Mirza, M., & Osindero, S. (2014). Conditional generative adversarial nets. *arXiv preprint arXiv:1411.1784.*

Radford, A., Metz, L., & Chintala, S. (2016). Unsupervised representation learning with deep convolutional generative adversarial networks. In *Proceedings of the International Conference on Learning Representations (ICLR).*

Rao, R. M., Liu, J., Verkuil, R., Meier, J., Canny, J., Abbeel, P., ... & Rives, A. (2021). MSA transformer. In *Proceedings of the 38th International Conference on Machine Learning* (pp. 8844-8856).

Reed, S., Akata, Z., Yan, X., Logeswaran, L., Schiele, B., & Lee, H. (2016). Generative adversarial text to image synthesis. In *Proceedings of the 33rd International Conference on Machine Learning (ICML)* (pp. 1060-1069).

Schlegl, T., Seebock, P., Waldstein, S. M., Schmidt-Erfurth, U., & Langs, G. (2017). Unsupervised anomaly detection with generative adversarial networks to guide marker discovery. In Proceedings of the IEEE International Conference on Information Processing in Medical

Shen, D., Wu, G., & Suk, H. I. (2017). Deep learning in medical image analysis. *Annual Review of Biomedical Engineering, 19*(1), 221-248.

Shokri, R., & Shmatikov, V. (2015). Privacy-preserving deep learning. In *Proceedings of the 22nd ACM SIGSAC Conference on Computer and Communications Security* (pp. 1310-1321).

Simonyan, K., & Zisserman, A. (2015). Very deep convolutional networks for large-scale image recognition. In *International Conference on Learning Representations (ICLR)*.

Vaswani, A., Shazeer, N., Parmar, N., Uszkoreit, J., Jones, L., Gomez, A. N., ... & Polosukhin, I. (2017). Attention is all you need. In *Advances in Neural Information Processing Systems*.

Zhou, K., Yang, S., Yang, W., & Zhao, Z. (2014). Personalized clothing recommendation based on image matching. In *2014 International Conference on Service Sciences* (pp. 1-5). IEEE.

Chapter 7: Natural Language Processing

<u>Text Preprocessing Techniques</u>

Natural Language Processing (NLP) plays a pivotal role in the analysis and interpretation of human language by machines. Within the context of AI-driven data science and big data, text preprocessing serves as the foundation for successful NLP tasks. Text preprocessing techniques are essential for transforming unstructured text data into structured formats, facilitating efficient and accurate analysis. This section provides a comprehensive overview of key text preprocessing techniques such as tokenization, stop-word removal, stemming, lemmatization, and handling special characters.

1. Tokenization

Tokenization is the process of dividing a text into individual units, typically words or phrases, which are called tokens. Tokenization is fundamental for NLP tasks because most machine learning models cannot interpret raw text data. Instead, models require numerical inputs, and tokenization is the first step in converting textual data into a format that can be further processed. There are two main types of tokenization: word-level tokenization and sentence-level tokenization. Word tokenization splits the text into individual words, while sentence tokenization separates text into sentences (Manning, Raghavan, & Schütze, 2008).

For instance, in word tokenization, the sentence "Artificial intelligence is fascinating" would be split into individual tokens: ['Artificial', 'intelligence', 'is', 'fascinating']. Each token can then be represented numerically for further processing by algorithms such as Word2Vec or transformers (Vaswani et al., 2017).

2. Stop-Word Removal

Stop words are common words that appear frequently in a language but do not carry significant meaning in the context of many NLP tasks. Examples of stop words in English include 'the,' 'is,' 'in,' 'at,' and 'which.' Removing stop words helps reduce the dimensionality of the text data, which can lead to faster processing and reduced noise in the data (Bird, Klein, & Loper, 2009). However, in some contexts, stop-word removal may not always be beneficial. For example, in sentiment analysis, words like "not" can carry crucial importance in determining the sentiment polarity of a sentence (e.g., "not happy" versus "happy").

The process of stop-word removal involves either manually creating a list of stop words or using predefined lists available in libraries such as Natural Language Toolkit (NLTK) or spaCy.

3. Stemming

Stemming is the technique of reducing words to their root form by removing suffixes. The goal of stemming is to ensure that words with similar meanings are grouped together for analysis. For instance, words like "running," "runner," and "ran" can be reduced to the root form "run." One of the most commonly used stemming algorithms is the Porter Stemmer, which removes common morphological and inflexional endings from words (Porter, 1980).

However, stemming often produces non-linguistically accurate forms of words. For example, "study" and "studies" both stem to "studi," which may not always be desired, especially in tasks requiring linguistic precision. Nonetheless, it is a popular technique for reducing the dimensionality of text data in large datasets.

4. Lemmatization

Lemmatization is similar to stemming but provides more linguistically accurate results. Instead of simply removing suffixes, lemmatization reduces words to their base or dictionary form, called a "lemma," while ensuring that the root form is an actual word. For instance, "running" becomes "run," and "better" becomes "good." This technique relies on understanding the context of the word and its part of speech (POS) to make an accurate reduction (Jurafsky & Martin, 2021).

Unlike stemming, which can produce inconsistent results, lemmatization tends to be more reliable when grammatical accuracy is essential. It is commonly implemented using libraries such as spaCy or the NLTK's WordNet Lemmatizer.

5. Handling Special Characters and Punctuation

Text data often contains special characters, punctuation marks, and numbers that can introduce noise into NLP models. The preprocessing step includes identifying and handling these elements based on the specific task at hand. Special characters (e.g., "@," "#," "%") are often irrelevant in general NLP tasks but can hold significance in domains such as social media analysis (for instance, hashtags in Twitter data). Punctuation marks like periods and commas are generally removed unless they serve a purpose, such as distinguishing between different sentences or emphasizing sentiment in the text (Ramasubramanian & Ramya, 2013).

Similarly, numbers are sometimes removed unless they are relevant to the task, such as in financial reports or scientific texts where numbers may carry essential information. Regular expressions (regex) are commonly used for identifying and removing special characters and punctuation.

In summary, effective text preprocessing is vital for ensuring the success of NLP models. Techniques such as tokenization, stop-word removal, stemming, lemmatization, and handling special characters are critical steps in preparing textual data for further analysis. Depending on the nature of the data and the NLP task at hand, selecting the appropriate preprocessing techniques can significantly impact the performance of models, especially when dealing with big data.

<u>Sentiment Analysis</u>

Sentiment analysis, a prominent application of Natural Language Processing (NLP), involves analyzing and determining the emotional tone behind a body of text. It is widely used in various domains such as business, marketing, politics, and social media analysis to assess public sentiment and opinion. In the era of big data, sentiment analysis plays a crucial role in extracting valuable insights from massive amounts of unstructured text data. This section outlines key concepts, methods, and techniques employed in sentiment analysis, focusing on its application within AI and data science.

1. Defining Sentiment Analysis

Sentiment analysis, also known as opinion mining, refers to the process of identifying and categorizing opinions expressed in a piece of text. It typically involves classifying text into positive, negative, or neutral sentiments, though more granular classifications can also be employed. For instance, sentiment analysis is often used to gauge customer feedback from product reviews, assess the public's view of a political figure, or analyze overall brand reputation based on social media comments (Liu, 2012).

The goal of sentiment analysis is to transform subjective information into an objective, quantifiable format that can be used to make informed decisions. This is especially important in the big data era, where analyzing large volumes of user-generated content quickly and efficiently is critical.

2. Approaches to Sentiment Analysis

There are two main approaches to sentiment analysis: **rule-based approaches** and **machine learning-based approaches**. These approaches differ in the methods they use to classify the sentiment of the text.

a. Rule-Based Approaches

Rule-based approaches to sentiment analysis rely on manually created lexicons and predefined sets of rules to classify text. These methods typically involve sentiment lexicons that contain lists of words associated with positive or negative emotions. For example, words like "happy," "excellent," and "satisfied" might be classified as positive, while "angry," "bad," and "disappointing" are classified as negative (Pang & Lee, 2008).

Although rule-based methods can be simple to implement and offer quick results, they tend to lack flexibility and may fail to capture context and nuances in the text, such as sarcasm or irony. For example, the sentence "I am not happy with this product" might be incorrectly classified as positive if the algorithm only focuses on the word "happy."

b. Machine Learning-Based Approaches

Machine learning-based approaches use statistical models and algorithms to learn patterns in text data. These models are typically trained on labeled datasets where each piece of text is associated with a sentiment label (e.g., positive, negative, neutral). Popular machine learning algorithms used for sentiment analysis include Naive Bayes, Support Vector Machines (SVM), and logistic regression (Cambria et al., 2017).

More advanced machine learning techniques, such as deep learning, have become increasingly popular for sentiment analysis. In particular, **recurrent neural networks (RNNs)** and **long short-term memory (LSTM)** networks are frequently used because they can capture sequential dependencies in text. These models are capable of understanding the context of words in a sentence, which is critical for accurately determining sentiment. For example, LSTMs can correctly identify the negative sentiment in sentences like "I didn't enjoy the movie" by recognizing the negation (Hochreiter & Schmidhuber, 1997).

3. Feature Extraction Techniques in Sentiment Analysis

Feature extraction is a crucial step in sentiment analysis. This process involves converting unstructured text data into numerical features that machine learning algorithms can interpret. Common feature extraction techniques include:

Bag-of-Words (BoW): This technique represents text as a collection of words without considering grammar or word order. Each unique word in the document corresponds to a feature, and the frequency of that word is counted (Jurafsky & Martin, 2021). While simple and widely used, BoW may fail to capture semantic meaning since it disregards word position and context.

TF-IDF (Term Frequency-Inverse Document Frequency): TF-IDF improves upon BoW by weighing words based on their frequency in a document relative to how often they appear in the entire corpus. This technique helps in identifying words that are more important for a particular document (Ramos, 2003).

Word Embeddings: Word embeddings like Word2Vec and GloVe map words into continuous vector spaces, where semantically similar words are located closer together. This technique helps capture relationships between words and is widely used in modern NLP models (Mikolov et al., 2013).

4. Challenges in Sentiment Analysis

Despite the widespread adoption of sentiment analysis, several challenges arise in its implementation, especially in the context of big data. Some key challenges include:

Sarcasm and Irony: Sarcastic statements often contradict their literal meaning, making it difficult for traditional sentiment analysis models to accurately classify them. For instance, the phrase "Oh great, another delay" conveys a negative sentiment, despite the word "great" typically being positive (Maynard & Greenwood, 2014).

Contextual Understanding: Understanding the sentiment in a piece of text often requires grasping the context in which words are used. This is particularly important in longer texts, where sentiments may shift. Advanced deep learning models like BERT (Bidirectional Encoder Representations from Transformers) have been developed to address this issue by understanding context in both directions (Devlin et al., 2019).

Domain-Specific Sentiment Analysis: Sentiment analysis models trained on general datasets may not perform well in specific domains such as healthcare or finance. Domain adaptation techniques and custom-built models are often required to address this issue.

5. Applications of Sentiment Analysis in Big Data

In the era of big data, sentiment analysis provides organizations with actionable insights from vast quantities of user-generated content. For example:

Social Media Monitoring: Companies use sentiment analysis to track public perception and customer feedback on platforms like Twitter, Facebook, and Instagram. This enables real-time analysis of brand reputation and customer satisfaction (Mostafa, 2013).

Customer Feedback Analysis: E-commerce platforms and service industries use sentiment analysis to automatically process product reviews and categorize customer opinions. Insights from this data are used to improve products and services.

Political Sentiment: Sentiment analysis is employed to analyze public opinion during elections and political campaigns by mining data from news articles, blogs, and social media (Tumasjan et al., 2010).

In summary, sentiment analysis is an essential NLP task that has gained significant traction in AI and data science. From rule-based systems to sophisticated deep learning models, sentiment analysis enables organizations to extract valuable insights from unstructured text data, particularly in the era of big data. Although challenges such as sarcasm and domain specificity persist, advances in machine learning techniques and models like BERT continue to improve the accuracy and effectiveness of sentiment analysis.

Topic Modeling

Topic modeling is a key unsupervised Natural Language Processing (NLP) technique used in data science and big data analytics to automatically uncover latent topics within large collections of unstructured text data. This process is vital for organizing, summarizing, and understanding vast text datasets, such as articles, social media posts, and customer reviews. Topic modeling allows AI systems to identify hidden patterns in textual data and categorize documents into meaningful groups based on the topics they discuss, even without prior labels. This section explores common topic modeling techniques, their applications, and challenges within the context of AI and big data.

1. Overview of Topic Modeling

Topic modeling is an unsupervised learning technique that identifies underlying topics or themes in a collection of text documents. These topics are represented as clusters of words that frequently co-occur in the documents. Each document can be associated with multiple topics to varying degrees, reflecting the multifaceted nature of most text data. The ability to analyze large text datasets makes topic modeling particularly valuable in big data scenarios, where manual classification of text is impractical (Blei, Ng, & Jordan, 2003).

2. Common Techniques in Topic Modeling

a. Latent Dirichlet Allocation (LDA)

One of the most popular and widely used topic modeling algorithms is Latent Dirichlet Allocation (LDA), introduced by Blei et al. (2003). LDA assumes that each document is composed of a mixture of topics, and each topic is a distribution over words. The key objective of LDA is to determine two distributions:

1. The distribution of topics across the documents.

2. The distribution of words across the topics.

LDA works by iterating over the dataset and assigning words to topics based on probability. Over several iterations, LDA fine-tunes its estimates of how topics are distributed across documents and which words belong to which topics. For instance, a document containing words such as "government," "election," and "policy" might be assigned a high probability of belonging to a "politics" topic.

b. Non-Negative Matrix Factorization (NMF)

Non-Negative Matrix Factorization (NMF) is another topic modeling approach that decomposes the document-term matrix into two lower-dimensional matrices representing topics and their associated terms. NMF assumes that the resulting factors should be non-negative, which results in easily interpretable topics since word frequencies are non-negative by nature. One of the advantages of NMF over LDA is its simplicity and computational efficiency (Lee & Seung, 1999). However, it may not capture the same depth of topic complexity as LDA.

c. Latent Semantic Analysis (LSA)

Latent Semantic Analysis (LSA), also known as Latent Semantic Indexing (LSI), is another technique for topic modeling that uses singular value decomposition (SVD) to reduce the dimensionality of the document-term matrix. LSA assumes that words that appear in similar contexts will have similar meanings, and it uses this co-occurrence pattern to uncover latent topics. LSA is often employed in information retrieval and search engine optimization, where the goal is to capture the underlying semantic structure of the text (Deerwester et al., 1990). However, one downside of LSA is that it may struggle with polysemy (i.e., words that have multiple meanings depending on context).

3. Applications of Topic Modeling in Big Data

a. Text Mining and Document Classification

Topic modeling is frequently applied in text mining to automatically categorize large volumes of documents. This is particularly useful in news aggregation, where articles are grouped by their topics, enabling users to browse relevant information more efficiently (Allahyari et al., 2017). For instance, in news outlets, documents can be classified into topics such as "technology," "health," or "finance," allowing better content organization.

b. Social Media Analysis

With the explosion of social media content, topic modeling is used to understand public discourse and trends. Companies use this technique to analyze posts and comments to identify consumer preferences, emerging trends, or potential brand-related issues. For example, a topic modeling algorithm might analyze Twitter data to detect discussions related to a product launch, customer complaints, or new consumer needs (Zhao et al., 2011).

c. Customer Feedback and Reviews

In e-commerce, topic modeling is employed to mine customer feedback and reviews for insights into consumer sentiment and preferences. By automatically identifying common themes from product reviews, companies can uncover specific aspects of their products that customers are satisfied or dissatisfied with. For example, reviews of a smartphone might reveal topics like "battery life," "camera quality," and "user interface," helping companies focus their product improvement efforts (Titov & McDonald, 2008).

d. Academic Research

Topic modeling is also widely used in academia to categorize and analyze large sets of research papers, articles, and publications. It helps researchers quickly identify trends and common themes across a body of literature. Additionally, it can assist in literature reviews by automatically generating summaries and categorizations of vast research fields (Griffiths & Steyvers, 2004).

4. Challenges in Topic Modeling

a. Defining the Number of Topics

One of the key challenges in topic modeling is selecting the optimal number of topics (denoted as "k") for a given dataset. Selecting too few topics can result in overly broad topics, while selecting too many may lead to fragmentation and redundancy. Methods such as perplexity and coherence scores are often used to evaluate and fine-tune the number of topics, though these metrics may not always capture the true interpretability of the topics (Röder, Both, & Hinneburg, 2015).

b. Interpretability of Topics

While topic modeling techniques such as LDA are useful in uncovering latent topics, the interpretability of the resulting topics can be challenging. Topics are represented as a distribution over words, but the meaning of a topic might not always be clear. For example, a topic containing the words "data," "model," and "learning" might be easily interpreted as related to machine learning, while others may require manual inspection to understand their meaning (Blei, 2012).

c. Handling of Short Texts

Topic modeling typically performs well on large documents with substantial content. However, when applied to shorter texts such as tweets or social media comments, the performance of algorithms like LDA can be less reliable due to the limited amount of information in each document. Solutions such as aggregating short texts or using techniques like Biterm Topic Models (BTM) have been proposed to address this challenge (Yan et al., 2013).

In summary, topic modeling is an indispensable NLP technique in AI, data science, and big data analytics for extracting hidden themes from unstructured text data. Techniques like Latent Dirichlet Allocation (LDA), Non-Negative Matrix Factorization (NMF), and Latent Semantic Analysis (LSA) provide powerful tools for organizing, summarizing, and exploring vast text corpora. Despite its challenges - such as selecting the number of topics, interpretability, and handling short texts - topic modeling remains an essential method in text mining, social media analysis, and customer feedback evaluation.

Language Models and Embeddings

Language models and word embeddings are foundational components of modern Natural Language Processing (NLP) systems, particularly within the context of AI, data science, and big data. These techniques allow machines to understand and generate human language with remarkable fluency. Language models are tasked with predicting the next word in a sequence, while word embeddings capture the semantic meaning of words by representing them as dense vectors in a continuous space. This section delves into the importance of language models and embeddings, their evolution, and their role in addressing NLP challenges within the vast domain of big data.

1. Language Models: Overview and Evolution

Language models are statistical models that predict the likelihood of a sequence of words. The primary goal of language models is to estimate the probability of a word given its preceding words in a sentence. This predictive capacity enables tasks such as text generation, machine translation, and speech recognition. The effectiveness of language models has greatly improved due to advances in deep learning and big data processing.

a. N-Gram Models

One of the earliest approaches to language modeling is the **n-gram model**, which predicts the next word in a sequence based on the previous *n* words. In an n-gram model, a unigram predicts words individually, a bigram considers the preceding word, and a trigram uses the previous two words. Despite their simplicity, n-gram models suffer from the "curse of dimensionality" since they require large amounts of data to accurately model word sequences (Jurafsky & Martin, 2021). Moreover, n-grams struggle with longer dependencies in text, limiting their capacity to capture context over extended sequences.

b. Recurrent Neural Networks (RNNs)

The limitations of n-gram models led to the development of **Recurrent Neural Networks (RNNs)**, which have the ability to capture longer-range dependencies in text. RNNs introduce memory cells that allow the model to remember previous states, making them more suitable for sequential data like text. However, standard RNNs struggle with retaining long-term dependencies due to the vanishing gradient problem, where gradients become too small during backpropagation (Elman, 1990).

c. Long Short-Term Memory (LSTM) Networks

To address the shortcomings of standard RNNs, **Long Short-Term Memory (LSTM)** networks were introduced. LSTMs include memory gates that control the flow of information, allowing the model to retain important information over longer sequences and discard irrelevant information. LSTMs have been instrumental in tasks like machine translation, text generation, and speech recognition, particularly when combined with large-scale datasets (Hochreiter & Schmidhuber, 1997).

d. Transformer-Based Models

A major breakthrough in language modeling came with the introduction of **transformers**, which eliminate the sequential processing constraints of RNNs by using self-attention mechanisms. The **Transformer** model introduced by Vaswani et al. (2017) allows for the parallel processing of sequences, which significantly improves the efficiency and scalability of language models. Transformers can capture global context across entire sequences, making them highly effective for tasks like translation and summarization.

The transformer architecture paved the way for state-of-the-art models like **BERT (Bidirectional Encoder Representations from Transformers)** and **GPT (Generative Pretrained Transformer)**. BERT is designed to understand context bidirectionally by looking at words both before and after a given token, while GPT excels at generating coherent and contextually relevant text based on preceding input (Devlin et al., 2019; Brown et al., 2020).

2. Word Embeddings: Capturing Semantic Meaning

Word embeddings are a technique for representing words as dense vectors in a continuous vector space, allowing words with similar meanings to have similar vector representations. Word embeddings have transformed NLP by enabling models to capture semantic relationships between words that traditional one-hot encoding techniques could not.

a. Word2Vec

One of the earliest and most influential embedding techniques is **Word2Vec**, developed by Mikolov et al. (2013). Word2Vec represents words in a lower-dimensional space based on their context, and it uses two training approaches: the **Continuous Bag of Words (CBOW)** and **Skip-gram** models. The CBOW model predicts a word given its context, while the skip-gram model predicts the context words given a target word. Word2Vec embeddings capture the similarity between words based on their co-occurrence in the corpus, allowing words like "king" and "queen" to be closer in vector space than "king" and "apple."

The most famous application of Word2Vec is in capturing analogies like "king – man + woman = queen," which demonstrates the model's ability to learn relationships between words.

b. GloVe (Global Vectors for Word Representation)

GloVe, another widely used embedding model, represents words based on a weighted least-squares objective that factors in word co-occurrence statistics (Pennington, Socher, & Manning, 2014). Unlike Word2Vec, which is trained in a local context, GloVe captures global word co-occurrence patterns across the entire corpus, making it better suited for learning rare word associations and capturing meaningful vector differences between related words. GloVe embeddings have been extensively used in NLP tasks such as named entity recognition and sentiment analysis.

c. Contextual Word Embeddings: BERT and GPT

Traditional embeddings like Word2Vec and GloVe generate static embeddings, meaning that each word has a single vector representation regardless of its context. However, words often have different meanings depending on context (e.g., "bank" can refer to a financial institution or a riverbank). To address this limitation, **contextual embeddings** were introduced by models like **BERT** and **GPT**. These embeddings are dynamic, meaning that the vector representation of a word is generated based on the context in which it appears (Devlin et al., 2019).

Contextual embeddings have revolutionized NLP by allowing models to better handle polysemy (words with multiple meanings) and homonyms. They are particularly useful in tasks requiring deep contextual understanding, such as question answering, machine translation, and natural language inference.

3. Applications of Language Models and Embeddings in Big Data

a. Sentiment Analysis

Language models and embeddings are widely used in sentiment analysis, where the goal is to determine the sentiment (positive, negative, or neutral) of a piece of text. By representing words as embeddings, models can capture subtle nuances in language and classify text more accurately, even when the sentiment is implied through complex word relationships (Liu, 2012).

b. Machine Translation

Machine translation systems, such as those used by Google Translate, rely on language models and embeddings to convert text from one language to another. Transformer-based models like **BERT** and **GPT** have significantly improved the quality of machine translation by capturing long-range dependencies in the source and target languages and generating more fluent translations (Wu et al., 2016).

c. Text Summarization

Text summarization is another critical application of language models. Embedding techniques enable models to distill the most important information from long documents by understanding the semantic relationships between words and phrases. Transformer-based models are particularly effective at generating coherent and contextually accurate summaries (Nallapati et al., 2016).

d. Named Entity Recognition (NER)

Named Entity Recognition (NER) is the process of identifying and classifying entities such as people, organizations, and locations in text. Word embeddings enhance the ability of models to accurately recognize and classify entities, even when they appear in varying contexts or forms. This is particularly important in large-scale data processing tasks, such as extracting structured information from unstructured web data or legal documents (Huang et al., 2015).

4. Challenges in Language Models and Embeddings

a. Data and Computational Requirements

One of the primary challenges in training language models and embeddings, especially transformer-based models like GPT-3, is the massive amount of data and computational power required. These models are typically trained on large-scale datasets containing billions of words, and they require high-performance computing resources, which can be costly and time-consuming (Brown et al., 2020).

b. Bias in Language Models

Language models and embeddings may inadvertently capture and amplify biases present in the training data. For instance, word embeddings trained on biased datasets may associate certain professions with specific genders or ethnicities, leading to biased outputs in applications such as hiring algorithms or content recommendation systems (Bolukbasi et al., 2016). Addressing and mitigating these biases remains a significant challenge in the development of ethical AI systems.

In summary, language models and embeddings are foundational techniques in NLP, particularly in the context of AI and big data. From traditional n-gram models to advanced transformer-based models like BERT and GPT, language models have evolved significantly, enabling machines to understand and generate human language with remarkable accuracy. Similarly, embeddings such as Word2Vec, GloVe, and contextual embeddings have transformed how semantic relationships between words are captured, enhancing the performance of NLP models across a wide range of applications, including sentiment analysis, machine translation, and named entity recognition.

Applications in Big Data Contexts

Natural Language Processing (NLP) has emerged as a critical component in handling the vast amount of unstructured text data generated in the big data era. As data volumes expand exponentially across industries, NLP techniques enable organizations to extract valuable insights from diverse text sources, including social media posts, customer reviews, academic articles, and more. In the context of big data, NLP applications offer the ability to process, analyze, and derive meaning from massive datasets in real time. This section explores several prominent NLP applications within big data contexts, highlighting how these techniques are leveraged for actionable insights and decision-making.

1. Social Media Analysis and Sentiment Detection

One of the most significant applications of NLP in the big data era is social media analysis. Platforms like Twitter, Facebook, and Instagram generate enormous volumes of textual data daily, making it an ideal source for sentiment analysis and opinion mining. Companies leverage NLP techniques to monitor public sentiment, identify trends, and track brand reputation in real-time. Sentiment analysis, an NLP task that involves classifying text as positive, negative, or neutral, is critical in gauging consumer opinions on products, services, or public figures (Liu, 2012).

For instance, by analyzing tweets about a new product, companies can gauge customer reactions and quickly identify any issues or complaints. Sentiment analysis can also detect shifts in public opinion, which is particularly valuable in political campaigns, where monitoring public perception of candidates and policies is crucial (Tumasjan et al., 2010). With NLP's ability to process and analyze vast amounts of social media data, organizations can gain actionable insights into consumer behavior and trends, enabling timely responses and strategy adjustments.

2. Customer Feedback and Review Mining

E-commerce platforms and service-based industries often rely on large datasets of customer feedback to improve products and services. NLP techniques such as opinion mining and aspect-based sentiment analysis allow businesses to automatically extract key themes from thousands of customer reviews. For example, NLP can identify recurring topics in product reviews, such as "battery life," "camera quality," or "user experience," providing companies with a clearer understanding of customer needs and areas requiring improvement (Cambria et al., 2017).

Aspect-based sentiment analysis goes a step further by analyzing the sentiment expressed towards specific aspects of a product. For instance, a smartphone review may praise the camera but criticize battery life. By analyzing sentiments at this granular level, companies can pinpoint specific strengths and weaknesses, enabling more targeted product development and customer service strategies.

3. Healthcare and Biomedical Text Mining

In the healthcare sector, NLP plays a pivotal role in processing and analyzing medical records, research papers, clinical trial reports, and other healthcare-related textual data. As the volume of medical literature continues to grow, it becomes increasingly challenging for healthcare professionals to stay informed about the latest research. NLP-powered text mining solutions enable automatic extraction of relevant information from vast medical corpora, assisting clinicians in making evidence-based decisions (Demner-Fushman, Chapman, & McDonald, 2009).

NLP is also used for patient data analysis. For example, electronic health records (EHRs) contain large amounts of unstructured data, including doctor's notes, prescriptions, and diagnoses. NLP techniques can be employed to extract key insights from these records, such as identifying patients at risk for specific conditions or discovering trends in treatment effectiveness. This allows healthcare providers to improve patient outcomes through data-driven decision-making.

4. Fraud Detection and Compliance in Finance

The financial sector is another domain where big data plays a crucial role, and NLP has proven invaluable for automating tasks such as fraud detection, regulatory compliance, and risk management. Financial institutions generate extensive textual data through news reports, market analyses, emails, and transactions. NLP models can be trained to detect unusual patterns in these documents that might indicate fraudulent behavior, such as insider trading or market manipulation (Agarwal & Sabharwal, 2014).

Additionally, financial institutions use NLP to ensure compliance with complex regulations. By automatically processing large volumes of legal and regulatory texts, NLP systems help organizations remain compliant with evolving rules. NLP-driven contract analysis tools, for example, can highlight sections of legal documents that may need revision to meet new regulatory standards, helping organizations avoid costly penalties (Liu et al., 2021).

5. Document Classification and Knowledge Discovery

Document classification is a vital NLP task that involves categorizing unstructured text data into predefined categories. This technique is especially useful in big data environments where organizations need to process massive amounts of textual information efficiently. For example, news organizations use document classification to group articles by topic, allowing readers to easily access information related to politics, sports, technology, and other subjects (Sebastiani, 2002).

In academic and scientific research, NLP-based document classification tools assist in organizing vast collections of research papers and publications. By automatically categorizing research into relevant fields, NLP helps researchers quickly find studies that match their areas of interest. Beyond classification, NLP can be used for knowledge discovery by identifying previously unrecognized relationships between concepts. This is especially beneficial in scientific domains, where vast volumes of literature can obscure potential connections between discoveries (Griffiths & Steyvers, 2004).

6. Machine Translation in Multilingual Big Data Contexts

In a globalized world, the need for accurate machine translation has never been greater. NLP-based machine translation systems allow businesses and governments to overcome language barriers and communicate effectively across different regions. Models like Google Translate rely on sophisticated neural network-based NLP techniques to translate text from one language to another (Wu et al., 2016).

Within big data contexts, machine translation can be applied to analyze multilingual datasets. For instance, multinational corporations often need to process customer feedback in various languages. Machine translation allows companies to standardize and analyze this feedback, regardless of the language in which it is written, ensuring that insights from different markets are not overlooked.

7. Chatbots and Conversational AI in Customer Support

With the increasing need for efficient customer service solutions, chatbots and conversational AI systems have gained prominence. Powered by advanced NLP techniques, chatbots are capable of understanding and responding to user queries in a conversational manner. These systems analyze user input, classify the intent behind the message, and provide relevant responses based on predefined rules or machine learning models (Chen et al., 2017).

In big data environments, conversational AI is used to handle large volumes of customer interactions, automating routine tasks such as answering frequently asked questions, processing orders, and troubleshooting common issues. By doing so, organizations can reduce the workload on human customer support agents while improving response times and customer satisfaction.

8. Legal Text Mining and E-Discovery

The legal sector is traditionally text-heavy, with legal professionals relying on massive volumes of documents for case research, contract analysis, and regulatory compliance. NLP techniques, particularly text mining, are increasingly used to streamline e-discovery—the process of searching through large datasets of legal documents to identify relevant information for litigation or investigation (Moens, 2014).

NLP tools can automatically classify legal documents, extract key phrases or clauses, and highlight relevant sections that need further review. This not only speeds up the discovery process but also helps ensure compliance with legal requirements. With NLP, law firms and legal departments can manage the growing influx of big data more efficiently.

Conclusion

As the amount of unstructured text data continues to grow across industries, NLP applications have become essential for extracting valuable insights from big data. From social media analysis to healthcare text mining and legal e-discovery, NLP enables organizations to process and analyze text efficiently and at scale. By leveraging techniques such as sentiment analysis, document classification, machine translation, and conversational AI, businesses and institutions can improve decision-making, enhance customer experiences, and stay competitive in a data-driven world.

References

Agarwal, A., & Sabharwal, R. (2014). Fraud detection in banking sector using data mining: A case study of RBI. *International Journal of Computer Applications, 98*(1), 39–45.

Allahyari, M., Pouriyeh, S., Assefi, M., Safaei, S., Trippe, E. D., Gutierrez, J. B., & Kochut, K. (2017). A brief survey of text mining: Classification, clustering and extraction techniques. *arXiv preprint arXiv:1707.02919.*

Bird, S., Klein, E., & Loper, E. (2009). *Natural language processing with Python: Analyzing text with the natural language toolkit.* O'Reilly Media.

Blei, D. M. (2012). Probabilistic topic models. *Communications of the ACM, 55*(4), 77-84.

Blei, D. M., Ng, A. Y., & Jordan, M. I. (2003). Latent Dirichlet allocation. *Journal of Machine Learning Research, 3*(Jan), 993–1022.

Bolukbasi, T., Chang, K. W., Zou, J. Y., Saligrama, V., & Kalai, A. T. (2016). Man is to computer programmer as woman is to homemaker? Debiasing word embeddings. In *Advances in neural information processing systems* (pp. 4349–4357).

Cambria, E., Schuller, B., Xia, Y., & Havasi, C. (2017). New avenues in opinion mining and sentiment analysis. *IEEE Intelligent Systems, 28*(2), 15–21.

Chen, H., Hu, X., Liu, S., & Zhang, Z. (2017). Conversational AI: Dialogue systems, current research and future directions. *arXiv preprint arXiv:1706.05154.*

Deerwester, S., Dumais, S. T., Furnas, G. W., Landauer, T. K., & Harshman, R. (1990). Indexing by latent semantic analysis. *Journal of the American Society for Information Science, 41*(6), 391–407.

Demner-Fushman, D., Chapman, W. W., & McDonald, C. J. (2009). What can natural language processing do for clinical decision support? *Journal of Biomedical Informatics, 42*(5), 760–772.

Devlin, J., Chang, M. W., Lee, K., & Toutanova, K. (2019). BERT: Pre-training of deep bidirectional transformers for language understanding. In *Proceedings of the 2019 Conference of the North American Chapter of the Association for Computational Linguistics: Human Language Technologies, Volume 1 (Long and Short Papers)* (pp. 4171–4186).

Griffiths, T. L., & Steyvers, M. (2004). Finding scientific topics. *Proceedings of the National Academy of Sciences, 101*(suppl 1), 5228–5235.

Hochreiter, S., & Schmidhuber, J. (1997). Long short-term memory. *Neural Computation, 9*(8), 1735–1780.

Jurafsky, D., & Martin, J. H. (2021). *Speech and language processing* (3rd ed.). Pearson.

Lee, D. D., & Seung, H. S. (1999). Learning the parts of objects by non-negative matrix factorization. *Nature, 401*(6755), 788–791.

Liu, B. (2012). *Sentiment analysis and opinion mining*. Morgan & Claypool Publishers.

Liu, Q., Zhang, Z., Zhang, Z., & Zhang, W. (2021). AI-driven legal compliance and contract management: Challenges and opportunities. *Artificial Intelligence and Law, 29*(2), 139–164.

Manning, C. D., Raghavan, P., & Schütze, H. (2008). *Introduction to information retrieval*. Cambridge University Press.

Maynard, D., & Greenwood, M. (2014). Who cares about sarcastic tweets? Investigating the impact of sarcasm on sentiment analysis. In *Proceedings of the Ninth International Conference on Language Resources and Evaluation (LREC-2014)* (pp. 4238–4243).

Mikolov, T., Sutskever, I., Chen, K., Corrado, G. S., & Dean, J. (2013). Distributed representations of words and phrases and their compositionality. In *Advances in neural information processing systems* (pp. 3111–3119).

Moens, M. (2014). *Information extraction: Algorithms and prospects in a retrieval context.* Springer.

Mostafa, M. M. (2013). More than words: Social networks' text mining for consumer brand sentiments. *Expert Systems with Applications, 40*(10), 4241–4251.

Pang, B., & Lee, L. (2008). *Opinion mining and sentiment analysis.* Foundations and Trends in Information Retrieval, 2(1–2), 1–135.

Porter, M. F. (1980). An algorithm for suffix stripping. *Program, 14*(3), 130–137.

Ramasubramanian, C., & Ramya, R. (2013). Effective preprocessing activities in text mining using improved porter's stemming algorithm. *International Journal of Advanced Research in Computer and Communication Engineering, 2*(12), 4536-4538.

Ramos, J. (2003). Using TF-IDF to determine word relevance in document queries. In *Proceedings of the first instructional conference on machine learning* (Vol. 242, pp. 133–142).

Röder, M., Both, A., & Hinneburg, A. (2015). Exploring the space of topic coherence measures. In *Proceedings of the eighth ACM international conference on Web search and data mining* (pp. 399–408).

Sebastiani, F. (2002). Machine learning in automated text categorization. *ACM Computing Surveys (CSUR), 34*(1), 1–47.

Titov, I., & McDonald, R. (2008). A joint model of text and aspect ratings for sentiment summarization. In *Proceedings of ACL-08: HLT* (pp. 308–316).

Tumasjan, A., Sprenger, T. O., Sandner, P. G., & Welpe, I. M. (2010). Predicting elections with Twitter: What 140 characters reveal about political sentiment. *Social Science Computer Review, 29*(4), 402–418.

Tumasjan, A., Sprenger, T. O., Sandner, P. G., & Welpe, I. M. (2010). Predicting elections with Twitter: What 140 characters reveal about political sentiment. *Social Science Computer Review, 29*(4),

Vaswani, A., Shazeer, N., Parmar, N., Uszkoreit, J., Jones, L., Gomez, A. N., ... & Polosukhin, I. (2017). Attention is all you need. In *Proceedings of the 31st International Conference on Neural Information Processing Systems* (pp. 6000–6010).

Yan, X., Guo, J., Lan, Y., & Cheng, X. (2013). A biterm topic model for short texts. In *Proceedings of the 22nd international conference on World Wide Web* (pp. 1445–1456).

Chapter 8: Computer Vision and Image Analysis

Image Preprocessing

Computer vision and image analysis are pivotal in numerous AI-driven applications across various industries, including healthcare, autonomous driving, surveillance, and retail. One of the essential steps in applying computer vision techniques to large datasets is **image preprocessing**, a process that prepares raw images for further analysis by cleaning and enhancing the data. The purpose of image preprocessing is to improve the quality of the images and ensure that they are suitable for machine learning models, allowing them to extract meaningful patterns and features efficiently.

1. Noise Reduction

Real-world images often contain noise that can negatively affect the performance of machine learning algorithms. Noise in images may be caused by various factors, such as poor lighting, environmental interference, or limitations of the imaging device. Reducing this noise is essential for improving the clarity of images before further processing. Popular techniques for noise reduction include filters like Gaussian, median, and bilateral filters. According to Gonzalez and Woods (2018), the Gaussian filter is widely used due to its simplicity and efficiency in smoothing images while preserving important features.

2. Image Resizing and Scaling

In big data contexts, images often come in varying sizes and resolutions. Standardizing the size of images by resizing them ensures that all inputs to a machine learning model are consistent, improving the efficiency of the model during training and inference (Zhu et al., 2021). Scaling images to a lower resolution can also reduce computational costs, making it feasible to process large image datasets. However, care must be taken to maintain the aspect ratio and avoid distorting the image, which could lead to a loss of crucial information.

3. Normalization

Image normalization is a technique that adjusts the pixel intensity values to bring them into a consistent range, which aids in model convergence during training. This process typically involves scaling pixel values to a range of [0,1] or [-1,1], depending on the model's requirements (Ioffe & Szegedy, 2015). Normalizing image data helps prevent certain features from dominating others, ensuring that all parts of the image contribute equally to the model's learning process.

4. Data Augmentation

Data augmentation is a strategy to artificially increase the size of a dataset by applying various transformations to the original images, such as rotations, flips, translations, and scaling. These transformations create new, slightly modified versions of the original images, which help improve the generalization of machine learning models by reducing overfitting (Shorten & Khoshgoftaar, 2019). In the context of big data, data augmentation enables models to learn robust features from diverse visual perspectives and conditions, which is especially important when training with limited data.

5. Histogram Equalization

Histogram equalization is a technique used to enhance the contrast of images by redistributing pixel intensities. This method is especially useful in images with poor contrast, where important details may be obscured. By applying histogram equalization, the dynamic range of pixel values is expanded, which can improve the visibility of critical features in the image (Pizer et al., 1987). Enhanced contrast is beneficial for image analysis tasks such as edge detection and object recognition.

6. Image Cropping and Object Detection

Image cropping is an essential preprocessing step that focuses on relevant parts of an image by removing unnecessary background or surrounding objects. This not only reduces the size of the dataset but also ensures that the model focuses on the most critical regions of interest. In object detection tasks, cropping techniques are often used in combination with bounding boxes or segmentation algorithms to isolate objects for further analysis (Ren et al., 2017).

7. Edge Detection and Feature Extraction

Edge detection is a preprocessing technique aimed at identifying the boundaries and contours of objects within an image. Detecting edges helps simplify image data by reducing it to essential structural information, which can then be used for feature extraction (Canny, 1986). Common edge detection algorithms include Sobel, Canny, and Prewitt filters, all of which are widely applied in computer vision tasks to identify object shapes, contours, and other important features.

In summary, image preprocessing is an indispensable step in AI-driven computer vision applications, especially when working with large datasets in a big data context. By cleaning, resizing, normalizing, and augmenting images, as well as applying techniques like edge detection and contrast enhancement, image preprocessing ensures that machine learning models receive high-quality data that is consistent, reliable, and suitable for accurate analysis. As a result, preprocessing contributes significantly to the success of computer vision algorithms across various domains, from medical imaging to autonomous systems.

<u>Object Detection and Recognition</u>

Object detection and recognition are foundational tasks in computer vision that play critical roles in numerous applications, ranging from autonomous vehicles to medical imaging and surveillance systems.

These tasks involve identifying and categorizing objects within images or video frames. As AI techniques have evolved, object detection and recognition systems have become highly sophisticated, leveraging deep learning models to achieve state-of-the-art performance. In the context of big data, these techniques are essential for processing large-scale datasets efficiently and accurately.

1. Object Detection Overview

Object detection refers to the process of identifying objects within an image or video and determining their locations, typically through bounding boxes or segmentation techniques. It not only detects the presence of objects but also localizes them spatially. Modern object detection models, such as **Faster R-CNN, YOLO (You Only Look Once)**, and **SSD (Single Shot Multibox Detector)**, have revolutionized this domain by providing real-time, high-accuracy detection (Ren et al., 2017; Redmon et al., 2016; Liu et al., 2016).

Object detection systems usually consist of two stages: region proposal and classification. In the region proposal stage, the model identifies candidate regions where objects might be located. In the second stage, the classifier assigns labels to the detected regions, determining what objects they represent. These processes can be significantly enhanced with the use of large-scale datasets, such as the **COCO (Common Objects in Context)** dataset, which provides labeled images to train deep learning models on object detection tasks (Lin et al., 2014).

2. Object Recognition Overview

Object recognition refers to the task of categorizing objects within an image into predefined classes. While detection identifies the presence and location of objects, recognition focuses on identifying what the object is. Deep learning models, especially **Convolutional Neural Networks (CNNs)**, have proven to be highly effective for object recognition tasks. CNNs process images through a series of convolutional layers, pooling layers, and fully connected layers, learning features that help classify objects with high accuracy (Krizhevsky et al., 2012). In big data applications, object recognition systems must scale to handle vast amounts of data efficiently, which requires robust models that can generalize across diverse datasets.

3. Techniques for Object Detection

Several deep learning techniques have been developed to improve the speed and accuracy of object detection:

Faster R-CNN: One of the most influential models in object detection, Faster R-CNN introduced a region proposal network (RPN) that drastically improved the efficiency of region proposal generation. By sharing convolutional layers between the RPN and the detection network, it became faster and more accurate than its predecessors (Ren et al., 2017).

YOLO (You Only Look Once): YOLO revolutionized object detection by treating it as a single regression problem rather than breaking it down into region proposals and classification stages. YOLO models perform detection in one pass, making them faster than traditional methods. YOLO is highly suitable for real-time applications where speed is critical (Redmon et al., 2016).

SSD (Single Shot Multibox Detector): SSD is another popular detection model that eliminates the need for region proposal networks. Instead, it directly predicts object categories and bounding boxes in a single pass, making it both fast and accurate (Liu et al., 2016).

These models have been applied successfully across various industries, from detecting pedestrians in autonomous driving applications to recognizing tumors in medical images.

4. Techniques for Object Recognition

Object recognition relies heavily on deep learning, particularly CNNs, which have been the dominant architecture in this field:

CNNs for Recognition: CNNs, as demonstrated by AlexNet (Krizhevsky et al., 2012), learn hierarchical representations of images, starting from low-level features such as edges and textures, and moving to high-level features like object shapes. This hierarchical learning enables CNNs to recognize objects with high precision, even in complex visual scenes.

Transfer Learning: A common approach in object recognition, transfer learning involves using a pre-trained model, such as **ResNet** or **VGG**, on a large dataset (e.g., ImageNet) and fine-tuning it on a specific task (He et al., 2016). Transfer learning is especially useful when dealing with big data, as it reduces the need for training models from scratch, allowing researchers and practitioners to leverage existing knowledge.

Data Augmentation: Data augmentation techniques are employed to artificially increase the size of the training dataset, which is critical for improving the generalization capabilities of object recognition models. Techniques such as flipping, rotating, scaling, and cropping images help models learn more robust features from diverse visual contexts (Shorten & Khoshgoftaar, 2019).

5. Challenges in Object Detection and Recognition

Despite significant advancements, object detection and recognition in big data contexts present several challenges. Handling large-scale datasets requires models that can not only process data efficiently but also generalize across various domains. One major challenge is **occlusion**, where objects are partially obstructed in images, making it difficult for models to detect or recognize them accurately (Zhu et al., 2020). Another challenge is **class imbalance**, where certain object categories are underrepresented in the training dataset, leading to poor performance on those classes (Johnson & Khoshgoftaar, 2019).

To address these challenges, researchers are developing more advanced models, such as **Region-based Fully Convolutional Networks (R-FCN)** and **Attention Mechanisms**, that allow models to focus on relevant parts of an image and improve detection in cluttered or occluded scenes (Dai et al., 2016).

In summary, object detection and recognition are core components of AI-driven computer vision applications, enabling machines to analyze and interpret visual data in a meaningful way. Through the use of advanced deep learning techniques like CNNs, YOLO, and Faster R-CNN, these tasks have reached unprecedented levels of accuracy and efficiency. In the era of big data, these techniques are crucial for processing large-scale visual datasets in real-time, providing valuable insights in areas such as healthcare, autonomous systems, and surveillance.

Image Segmentation

Image segmentation is a crucial technique in computer vision that involves dividing an image into multiple segments or regions to simplify its analysis. Each segment corresponds to a specific object or a part of an object within the image, enabling more detailed and meaningful analysis. Unlike object detection, which identifies and classifies objects in an image using bounding boxes, segmentation aims to understand the image at the pixel level by assigning a label to each pixel. In big data contexts, image segmentation is vital for applications such as autonomous driving, medical imaging, satellite image analysis, and scene understanding.

1. Types of Image Segmentation

There are several types of image segmentation methods, each designed for specific applications and goals. The primary categories include:

Semantic Segmentation: This method involves labeling each pixel in the image with a class label, but it does not distinguish between different instances of the same class. For instance, in an image containing multiple cars, all car pixels would be labeled the same, without differentiating between individual cars (Long et al., 2015). Semantic segmentation is commonly used in autonomous driving, where differentiating between different object classes, such as roads, pedestrians, and vehicles, is essential.

Instance Segmentation: Unlike semantic segmentation, instance segmentation assigns unique labels to different instances of the same class. For example, two different cars in an image would be labeled as distinct instances (He et al., 2017). Instance segmentation is particularly useful in scenarios where distinguishing between multiple objects of the same type is critical, such as in robotics and surveillance systems.

Panoptic Segmentation: A more recent development in segmentation, panoptic segmentation combines both semantic and instance segmentation into a unified task. It involves classifying all pixels in the image and distinguishing between instances of the same class (Kirillov et al., 2019). This approach provides a more holistic understanding of the visual scene and is applied in complex tasks such as scene understanding in autonomous systems.

2. Deep Learning Approaches to Image Segmentation

Deep learning techniques, particularly Convolutional Neural Networks (CNNs), have revolutionized the field of image segmentation. These models can automatically learn complex features and patterns in images, enabling precise segmentation. Some of the most successful deep learning architectures for segmentation include:

Fully Convolutional Networks (FCNs): FCNs are one of the foundational deep learning architectures for semantic segmentation. Introduced by Long et al. (2015), FCNs replace fully connected layers in traditional CNNs with convolutional layers, allowing them to output spatial maps instead of class labels. This architecture allows pixel-level classification, making it highly effective for semantic segmentation tasks.

U-Net: Initially designed for biomedical image segmentation, U-Net has become a popular architecture for a wide range of segmentation tasks. U-Net uses an encoder-decoder structure, where the encoder captures spatial information, and the decoder reconstructs the segmented image by upsampling the feature maps (Ronneberger et al., 2015). U-Net's skip connections allow for the preservation of fine details, improving segmentation accuracy, especially in medical applications.

Mask R-CNN: Mask R-CNN extends Faster R-CNN, a popular object detection architecture, to include pixel-level segmentation masks in addition to bounding boxes. This makes it highly effective for instance segmentation tasks (He et al., 2017). Mask R-CNN has been widely adopted in various industries, including healthcare, for tasks such as tumor detection and precise organ segmentation.

3. Applications of Image Segmentation

Image segmentation is employed in various real-world applications, where precise object delineation is crucial for decision-making and automation. Some prominent examples include:

Autonomous Driving: In self-driving vehicles, image segmentation is used to identify different components of the driving environment, such as roads, traffic signs, vehicles, and pedestrians. Semantic and instance segmentation enable the vehicle to understand its surroundings at a granular level, improving safety and decision-making (Garcia-Garcia et al., 2018).

Medical Imaging: In medical imaging, accurate segmentation of anatomical structures, such as organs, tissues, and tumors, is essential for diagnosis, treatment planning, and monitoring disease progression. U-Net and other deep learning architectures are widely used in tasks such as MRI, CT scan segmentation, and tumor detection (Ronneberger et al., 2015).

Satellite and Aerial Imagery: In remote sensing applications, image segmentation is used to analyze satellite or aerial images for tasks such as land cover classification, urban planning, and environmental monitoring. These images often contain vast amounts of data, and segmentation helps extract meaningful information from these large datasets (Bischke et al., 2019).

Robotics: In robotics, instance and semantic segmentation are crucial for enabling robots to interact with their environment. Segmenting objects helps robots recognize and manipulate objects in tasks such as automated assembly, pick-and-place operations, and human-robot collaboration (Garcia-Garcia et al., 2018).

4. Challenges in Image Segmentation for Big Data

While image segmentation has made significant advancements, several challenges persist, especially in the context of big data:

Scalability: Processing large-scale datasets with high-resolution images requires significant computational resources and efficient algorithms. Segmenting big data in real-time applications, such as autonomous driving, demands models that can scale without compromising accuracy (Liu et al., 2016).

Data Imbalance: In many applications, certain classes of objects may be underrepresented in the dataset, leading to class imbalance. For example, in medical imaging, certain rare conditions may appear less frequently in training data, making it challenging for models to segment such cases accurately (Johnson & Khoshgoftaar, 2019).

Occlusion and Boundary Precision: Objects in images often overlap or occlude one another, making it difficult to delineate clear boundaries during segmentation. Techniques such as instance segmentation and models with attention mechanisms are being developed to address these issues by focusing on occluded regions and refining boundary predictions (Zhu et al., 2020).

In summary, image segmentation is an indispensable technique in computer vision, enabling machines to understand visual data at a pixel level. Through semantic, instance, and panoptic segmentation, AI models can break down complex images into meaningful segments, facilitating advanced tasks in autonomous driving, medical imaging, and remote sensing. With the development of deep learning architectures such as FCNs, U-Net, and Mask R-CNN, image segmentation has become increasingly accurate and efficient. However, challenges such as scalability, data imbalance, and occlusion still present areas for ongoing research, particularly as the demand for segmenting large-scale datasets continues to grow.

Applications in Different Sectors

Computer vision has emerged as one of the most transformative AI techniques, especially in the context of data science and big data. It enables machines to interpret and make decisions based on visual data, with applications that span various industries, including surveillance, healthcare, retail, agriculture, and autonomous systems. As these fields increasingly adopt AI-driven computer vision solutions, the ability to analyze large volumes of images and video has improved drastically, thanks to advancements in machine learning and deep learning.

1. Applications in Surveillance

One of the most prominent applications of computer vision is in **surveillance** systems, where the ability to automatically monitor and analyze video feeds in real-time has significant implications for security and safety. With the proliferation of CCTV cameras and the need for real-time threat detection, traditional manual surveillance methods have become inadequate due to the sheer volume of data generated. Computer vision-based surveillance systems address this challenge by automating the process of detecting and recognizing abnormal behavior, tracking individuals, and identifying objects of interest.

Object Detection and Person Tracking: AI techniques such as object detection and person tracking have been widely adopted in surveillance systems to monitor suspicious activities. Modern object detection models like **YOLO (You Only Look Once)** and **Faster R-CNN** enable real-time detection of people, vehicles, and other objects, even in crowded environments (Redmon et al., 2016; Ren et al., 2017). These models help law enforcement agencies monitor public spaces, track suspects, and respond to potential threats faster.

Facial Recognition: Facial recognition is another key application in surveillance, enabling automatic identification of individuals based on facial features. Deep learning models trained on large datasets, such as **Convolutional Neural Networks (CNNs)**, have significantly improved the accuracy of facial recognition systems (Parkhi et al., 2015). These systems are used in security applications for access control, identifying criminals, and even monitoring for known threats in public areas.

Anomaly Detection: In addition to tracking and recognition, anomaly detection systems in surveillance can identify unusual behaviors, such as unauthorized access or abandoned objects. Deep learning models, combined with motion analysis and behavioral pattern recognition, can automatically trigger alerts when abnormal patterns are detected (Singh et al., 2018). This application is crucial for enhancing the efficiency of surveillance in high-risk environments, such as airports, military installations, and public events.

2. Applications in Healthcare

In healthcare, computer vision has revolutionized how medical data, particularly imaging data, is analyzed, leading to significant advancements in diagnosis, treatment planning, and patient monitoring. Medical imaging, such as X-rays, CT scans, MRI scans, and ultrasound images, generates vast amounts of data that require careful analysis to identify abnormalities and diseases. AI-driven computer vision techniques have significantly enhanced the speed and accuracy of this analysis.

Medical Imaging and Diagnostics: AI models are widely used in medical imaging for tasks such as detecting tumors, identifying fractures, and diagnosing conditions like pneumonia, COVID-19, and cancer. Deep learning architectures such as **Convolutional Neural Networks (CNNs)**, **U-Net**, and **Mask R-CNN** have shown remarkable performance in segmenting and classifying medical images (Litjens et al., 2017; Ronneberger et al., 2015). For instance, U-Net is commonly used for organ segmentation in radiology, which is critical for surgery planning and treatment.

Disease Detection and Classification: In dermatology, ophthalmology, and pathology, AI-based computer vision systems are used to analyze skin lesions, retinal images, and histopathological slides to detect diseases such as skin cancer, diabetic retinopathy, and cardiovascular conditions. For example, deep learning models trained on large datasets of skin lesion images have been shown to classify malignant and benign tumors with accuracy comparable to that of expert dermatologists (Esteva et al., 2017).

Robotic Surgery and Image-Guided Interventions: Computer vision plays a critical role in robotic surgery, where precision and accuracy are paramount. AI techniques allow for the real-time processing of surgical footage, providing surgeons with detailed visual feedback and enhancing the safety and efficiency of minimally invasive procedures (Zhong et al., 2020). Additionally, image-guided interventions rely on computer vision to track surgical tools and navigate inside the body, reducing the need for large incisions and improving recovery times.

3. Applications in Retail

The retail industry has increasingly adopted computer vision technologies to enhance customer experiences, optimize inventory management, and streamline operations.

Customer Behavior Analysis: Computer vision is used to analyze customer movements and behaviors in retail stores, providing valuable insights into shopping patterns. AI-driven systems can monitor how customers interact with products, identify the most frequently visited areas, and detect patterns in customer traffic (Liu et al., 2019). These insights enable retailers to optimize store layouts and personalize marketing strategies.

Automated Checkout: Automated checkout systems, such as those developed by Amazon Go, rely on computer vision to track the items customers pick up and automatically charge them upon exiting the store. This technology uses a combination of object detection, tracking, and facial recognition to eliminate the need for traditional checkout processes (Marr, 2018).

Inventory Management: In warehouse and store environments, computer vision is used for real-time monitoring of inventory levels, automating the process of identifying out-of-stock items and optimizing restocking schedules. This reduces labor costs and improves efficiency by leveraging AI for accurate inventory tracking (Jin & Lee, 2021).

4. Applications in Agriculture

In agriculture, computer vision is transforming how farms monitor crops, livestock, and environmental conditions. AI-driven solutions enable more efficient and sustainable farming practices by automating labor-intensive tasks and improving decision-making.

Precision Agriculture: Computer vision systems mounted on drones or tractors allow farmers to monitor crops in real-time. These systems can detect plant diseases, assess crop health, and identify areas that require more water or fertilizer, enabling targeted interventions that reduce waste and increase yields (Kamilaris & Prenafeta-Boldú, 2018).

Livestock Monitoring: AI-driven computer vision is used to monitor livestock health and behavior. Cameras equipped with computer vision can track animal movements, detect signs of illness or distress, and ensure that livestock are fed and watered regularly. These systems improve the overall health of herds and reduce the need for constant human supervision (Rahman et al., 2019).

5. Applications in Autonomous Systems

Autonomous systems, including self-driving cars, drones, and industrial robots, rely heavily on computer vision to interpret and interact with their environments. The ability to process and understand visual data in real-time is essential for these systems to navigate complex environments safely and efficiently.

Self-Driving Cars: Autonomous vehicles use computer vision to detect and classify objects such as pedestrians, other vehicles, traffic signs, and road markings. Deep learning models such as **YOLO** and **Faster R-CNN** are used for object detection, while semantic and instance segmentation techniques enable the vehicle to understand its environment at a granular level (Garcia-Garcia et al., 2018). Computer vision is critical for enabling autonomous vehicles to make real-time decisions and avoid collisions.

Drones: In the aerospace and defense sectors, drones equipped with computer vision systems are used for surveillance, mapping, and monitoring. These drones can autonomously detect objects, track movements, and navigate through complex environments without human intervention (Chiang et al., 2017).

Conclusion

AI techniques in computer vision and image analysis have enabled numerous real-world applications across diverse sectors, including surveillance, healthcare, retail, agriculture, and autonomous systems. As these industries continue to generate and rely on large-scale visual data, computer vision technologies, driven by advancements in deep learning, have become indispensable. From enhancing security and diagnosis in healthcare to revolutionizing retail operations and agriculture, the integration of computer vision into AI systems will continue to drive innovation and efficiency across industries.

References

Bischke, B., Helber, P., Folz, J., Borth, D., & Dengel, A. (2019). Multi-task learning for segmentation of building footprints with counting features. In *Proceedings of the IEEE Conference on Computer Vision and Pattern Recognition Workshops* (pp. 0-0).

Canny, J. (1986). A computational approach to edge detection. *IEEE Transactions on Pattern Analysis and Machine Intelligence, 8*(6), 679-698.

Chiang, H., Tsai, C., & Chen, Y. (2017). Aerial surveillance using low-altitude unmanned aerial vehicle-based video surveillance system. *IEEE Transactions on Multimedia, 19*(11), 2566-2577.

Dai, J., Li, Y., He, K., & Sun, J. (2016). R-FCN: Object detection via region-based fully convolutional networks. In *Advances in Neural Information Processing Systems* (pp. 379-387).

Esteva, A., Kuprel, B., Novoa, R. A., Ko, J., Swetter, S. M., Blau, H. M., & Thrun, S. (2017). Dermatologist-level classification of skin cancer with deep neural networks. *Nature, 542*(7639), 115-118.

Garcia-Garcia, A., Orts-Escolano, S., Oprea, S., Villena-Martinez, V., & Garcia-Rodriguez, J. (2018). A review on deep learning techniques applied to semantic segmentation. *IEEE Transactions on Pattern Analysis and Machine Intelligence, 40*(4), 823-848.

Gonzalez, R. C., & Woods, R. E. (2018). *Digital image processing* (4th ed.). Pearson.

He, K., Gkioxari, G., Dollár, P., & Girshick, R. (2017). Mask R-CNN. In *Proceedings of the IEEE International Conference on Computer Vision* (pp. 2961-2969).

He, K., Zhang, X., Ren, S., & Sun, J. (2016). Deep residual learning for image recognition. In *Proceedings of the IEEE Conference on Computer Vision and Pattern Recognition* (pp. 770-778).

Ioffe, S., & Szegedy, C. (2015). Batch normalization: Accelerating deep network training by reducing internal covariate shift. In *Proceedings of the 32nd International Conference on Machine Learning* (pp. 448-456).

Jin, C., & Lee, I. (2021). Real-time image-based inventory management system for a retail store. *International Journal of Advanced Computer Science and Applications, 12*(1), 55-61.

Johnson, J. M., & Khoshgoftaar, T. M. (2019). Survey on deep learning with class imbalance. *Journal of Big Data, 6*(1), 60.

Kamilaris, A., & Prenafeta-Boldú, F. X. (2018). Deep learning in agriculture: A survey. *Computers and Electronics in Agriculture, 147*, 70-90.

Kirillov, A., He, K., Girshick, R., Rother, C., & Dollár, P. (2019). Panoptic segmentation. In *Proceedings of the IEEE/CVF Conference on Computer Vision and Pattern Recognition* (pp. 9404-9413).

Krizhevsky, A., Sutskever, I., & Hinton, G. E. (2012). ImageNet classification with deep convolutional neural networks. In *Advances in Neural Information Processing Systems* (pp. 1097-1105).

Lin, T. Y., Maire, M., Belongie, S., Hays, J., Perona, P., Ramanan, D., Dollár, P., & Zitnick, C. L. (2014). Microsoft COCO: Common objects in context. In *European Conference on Computer Vision* (pp. 740-755). Springer.

Litjens, G., Kooi, T., Bejnordi, B. E., Setio, A. A. A., Ciompi, F., Ghafoorian, M., & Sánchez, C. I. (2017). A survey on deep learning in medical image analysis. *Medical Image Analysis, 42*, 60-88.

Liu, W., Anguelov, D., Erhan, D., Szegedy, C., Reed, S., Fu, C. Y., & Berg, A. C. (2016). SSD: Single shot multibox detector. In *European Conference on Computer Vision* (pp. 21-37). Springer.

Liu, X., Yang, S., & Zhang, X. (2019). Customer behavior analysis using machine learning techniques in retailing business. *Journal of Business Research, 102*, 33-45.

Long, J., Shelhamer, E., & Darrell, T. (2015). Fully convolutional networks for semantic segmentation. In *Proceedings of the IEEE Conference on Computer Vision and Pattern Recognition* (pp. 3431-3440).

Marr, B. (2018). Amazon Go: How artificial intelligence is powering the store of the future. *Forbes.* Retrieved from https://www.forbes.com/sites/bernardmarr/2018/01/22/amazon-go-how-artificial-intelligence-is-powering-the-store-of-the-future/?sh=6b658a431d4b

Parkhi, O. M., Vedaldi, A., & Zisserman, A. (2015). Deep face recognition. *British Machine Vision Conference*, 1-12.

Pizer, S. M., Amburn, E. P., Austin, J. D., Cromartie, R., Geselowitz, A., Greer, T., Romeny, B. H., Zimmerman, J. B., & Zuiderveld, K. (1987). Adaptive histogram equalization and its variations. *Computer Vision, Graphics, and Image Processing, 39*(3), 355-368.

Rahman, S., Sultan, M. A., & Khaimova, R. (2019). Real-time livestock monitoring system using convolutional neural networks. *Computers and Electronics in Agriculture, 160*, 108-119.

Redmon, J., Divvala, S., Girshick, R., & Farhadi, A. (2016). You only look once: Unified, real-time object detection. In *Proceedings of the IEEE Conference on Computer Vision and Pattern Recognition* (pp. 779-788).

Ren, S., He, K., Girshick, R., & Sun, J. (2017). Faster R-CNN: Towards real-time object detection with region proposal networks. *IEEE Transactions on Pattern Analysis and Machine Intelligence, 39*(6), 1137-1149.

Ronneberger, O., Fischer, P., & Brox, T. (2015). U-Net: Convolutional networks for biomedical image segmentation. In

International Conference on Medical Image Computing and Computer-Assisted Intervention (pp. 234-241). Springer.

Shorten, C., & Khoshgoftaar, T. M. (2019). A survey on image data augmentation for deep learning. *Journal of Big Data, 6*(1), 60.

Singh, P., Sharma, S., & Verma, N. (2018). Anomaly detection in surveillance videos using deep learning. In *Proceedings of the 2018 International Conference on Signal Processing and Integrated Networks* (pp. 148-153).

Zhong, Z., Kim, J., & Park, J. (2020). Deep learning for robot-assisted surgery: Applications, challenges, and future perspectives. *IEEE Access, 8*, 20331-20344.

Zhu, P., Wang, L., & Yu, Q. (2020). Robust object detection in partially occluded scenes via deep learning. *Pattern Recognition Letters, 131*, 257-263.

Zhu, P., Wang, L., & Yu, Q. (2021). Image resizing in deep learning: A critical review. *IEEE Transactions on Neural Networks and Learning Systems, 32*(4), 1448-1465.

Chapter 9: Reinforcement Learning in Big Data Environments

Fundamentals of Reinforcement Learning

Reinforcement learning (RL) is a powerful machine learning paradigm that enables agents to learn by interacting with their environment. Unlike supervised learning, where models are trained on labeled data, reinforcement learning is based on a trial-and-error approach, where the agent learns to make decisions that maximize a cumulative reward signal. This approach has led to significant advancements in various fields, including robotics, game playing, autonomous systems, and resource management. In big data environments, RL offers a unique opportunity to address complex decision-making problems by leveraging large-scale datasets and continuous feedback from dynamic systems.

1. Key Concepts of Reinforcement Learning

Reinforcement learning consists of several core components that define how an agent interacts with its environment and learns from the consequences of its actions. These include:

Agent: The agent is the decision-maker or learner in reinforcement learning. It interacts with the environment by taking actions and receiving feedback in the form of rewards or punishments. The agent's goal is to maximize the total reward it receives over time by learning optimal behaviors (Sutton & Barto, 2018).

Environment: The environment is the external system with which the agent interacts. It provides feedback in the form of rewards based on the actions the agent takes. The environment is typically modeled as a Markov Decision Process (MDP), where each state depends only on the previous state and action, making it a suitable framework for many reinforcement learning applications (Bellman, 1957).

State: The state represents the current situation of the environment that the agent observes. The state provides all the necessary information for the agent to make a decision. In big data environments, states can represent complex, high-dimensional data such as sensor readings, market conditions, or user behavior.

Action: Actions are the choices the agent can make in each state. These actions influence the next state of the environment and the reward the agent receives. In many applications, the action space can be discrete (e.g., choosing from a finite set of actions) or continuous (e.g., adjusting control parameters in autonomous systems) (Mnih et al., 2015).

Reward: The reward is the feedback signal the agent receives from the environment. It indicates the immediate value of the action taken in a given state. The agent's objective is to learn a policy that maximizes the cumulative reward over time, often referred to as the return (Sutton & Barto, 2018).

Policy: The policy defines the agent's behavior by mapping states to actions. It represents the strategy the agent uses to select actions at each step. Policies can be deterministic, where a specific action is taken for each state, or stochastic, where actions are selected based on a probability distribution.

Value Function: The value function estimates the expected cumulative reward for a given state (or state-action pair) under a particular policy. It helps the agent evaluate how good it is to be in a specific state, guiding decision-making by indicating the long-term benefits of actions (Szepesvári, 2010).

Q-Learning and Temporal Difference (TD) Learning: Q-learning is one of the most widely used reinforcement learning algorithms. It is an off-policy algorithm that estimates the optimal action-value function (Q-function) by learning the expected cumulative reward for each state-action pair. Temporal difference learning, a broader family of methods that Q-learning belongs to, updates value functions based on the difference between estimated rewards and actual outcomes (Watkins & Dayan, 1992).

2. Markov Decision Processes (MDPs)

At the heart of reinforcement learning lies the **Markov Decision Process (MDP)** framework, which formalizes the decision-making problem. An MDP is defined by a set of states, actions, transition probabilities, and reward functions. The Markov property states that the future state depends only on the current state and action, not on the history of previous states. This simplification allows reinforcement learning algorithms to model and solve complex, sequential decision-making problems in big data environments efficiently (Puterman, 2014).

An MDP can be described as a tuple (S, A, P, R, γ), where:

S represents the state space,

A represents the action space,

P(s'|s, a) is the transition probability function, defining the probability of moving from state s to state s' when action a is taken,

R(s, a) is the reward function, defining the immediate reward received after transitioning from state s by taking action a,

γ is the discount factor, which determines the importance of future rewards.

MDPs provide a mathematical foundation for many reinforcement learning algorithms, enabling the agent to make decisions that maximize long-term rewards.

3. Exploration vs. Exploitation

A fundamental challenge in reinforcement learning is the **exploration-exploitation trade-off**. The agent must balance two competing objectives:

Exploitation: Exploiting the current knowledge to maximize rewards by choosing actions that are known to yield high rewards.

Exploration: Exploring new actions and states to gather more information, potentially discovering higher-rewarding actions.

The trade-off is critical because focusing solely on exploitation might lead the agent to miss out on better long-term strategies, while excessive exploration may result in suboptimal short-term rewards. Techniques such as **epsilon-greedy** (where the agent occasionally takes random actions) and **upper confidence bound (UCB)** algorithms are used to manage this balance (Auer et al., 2002).

4. Deep Reinforcement Learning (DRL)

In recent years, deep reinforcement learning (DRL) has gained prominence as a powerful approach to solving complex decision-making tasks in high-dimensional environments. DRL combines the representation learning capabilities of deep neural networks with reinforcement learning algorithms to handle large state spaces and continuous action spaces, making it highly effective in big data contexts (Mnih et al., 2015).

Deep Q-Networks (DQNs): DQNs extend traditional Q-learning by using deep neural networks to approximate the Q-function. This allows the agent to handle environments with large, continuous state spaces where traditional tabular methods would be impractical (Mnih et al., 2015). DQNs have been successfully applied to domains such as video game playing and robotic control.

Policy Gradient Methods: Policy gradient methods directly optimize the policy by adjusting the parameters of the policy function to maximize expected rewards. These methods are particularly useful in environments with continuous action spaces, such as autonomous driving or resource management (Schulman et al., 2017). Popular policy gradient algorithms include **REINFORCE**, **Actor-Critic**, and **Proximal Policy Optimization (PPO)**.

5. Applications of Reinforcement Learning in Big Data Environments

Reinforcement learning techniques have been successfully applied in several big data environments where complex decision-making and optimization are required:

Finance: RL is used to optimize trading strategies, portfolio management, and risk management in financial markets. These applications rely on RL's ability to learn from vast amounts of market data and adjust strategies dynamically based on changing market conditions (Moody & Saffell, 2001).

Healthcare: In healthcare, RL is used to optimize treatment plans for chronic diseases, personalized medicine, and resource allocation in hospitals. By learning from large medical datasets, RL agents can suggest optimal interventions based on patient-specific data (Yu et al., 2019).

Autonomous Systems: RL is integral to autonomous systems, including self-driving cars, drones, and robotic systems. These applications involve real-time decision-making in dynamic environments, where the agent must balance short-term actions with long-term objectives (Silver et al., 2016).

Resource Management: In cloud computing and large-scale data centers, RL is used to optimize resource allocation, workload distribution, and energy management. By learning from historical data, RL agents can make decisions that improve efficiency and reduce operational costs (Mao et al., 2016).

In summary, reinforcement learning is a fundamental AI technique that enables agents to learn optimal behaviors through interaction with dynamic environments. By modeling decision-making processes as Markov Decision Processes and leveraging trial-and-error learning, RL has been successfully applied in various big data environments, from healthcare and finance to autonomous systems and resource management. As the volume and complexity of data continue to grow, reinforcement learning will play an increasingly critical role in enabling intelligent decision-making and optimization across diverse industries.

Applications in Recommendation Systems

Recommendation systems are essential tools in the digital age, driving user engagement and personalizing experiences across various platforms, including e-commerce, streaming services, social media, and online advertising. Traditional recommendation systems rely on techniques like collaborative filtering and content-based filtering. However, as big data environments continue to grow in complexity and volume, reinforcement learning (RL) has emerged as a powerful technique to enhance recommendation systems by continuously adapting to user preferences through interaction and feedback. By leveraging RL, recommendation systems can optimize for long-term user satisfaction, engagement, and revenue generation.

1. Challenges in Traditional Recommendation Systems

Traditional recommendation algorithms, such as **collaborative filtering** and **content-based filtering**, face several challenges when applied in big data environments. Collaborative filtering methods rely on user-item interaction data, where recommendations are made based on similar users' preferences (Su & Khoshgoftaar, 2009). Content-based filtering, on the other hand, recommends items that share characteristics with items the user has liked in the past. While effective in many cases, these methods suffer from the following limitations:

Cold Start Problem: Both approaches struggle with recommending items to new users (user cold start) or recommending newly added items that have little or no interaction data (item cold start).

Data Sparsity: In large datasets, user-item interaction data can be sparse, making it difficult to find patterns or relationships between users and items.

Static Nature: Traditional methods do not dynamically adapt to changes in user preferences over time or to the evolving inventory of items, often leading to suboptimal recommendations.

Reinforcement learning addresses these limitations by considering the sequential nature of interactions and optimizing recommendations based on long-term user engagement and satisfaction rather than just immediate feedback.

2. Reinforcement Learning for Recommendation Systems

Reinforcement learning introduces a framework where a recommendation system (the **agent**) interacts with users (the **environment**) over time, learning to make better recommendations through continuous feedback. The RL-based recommendation system aims to maximize cumulative rewards, which could be defined in terms of user engagement metrics (e.g., click-through rate, watch time) or long-term goals such as user retention or lifetime value.

State: The state represents the current context or situation of the user, which could include the user's interaction history, demographic information, and current session context (e.g., time of day, location).

Action: The action refers to the recommendation made by the system, such as suggesting a movie, a product, or an article. In big data environments, the action space can be vast, as the system must choose from millions of potential items.

Reward: The reward is the feedback signal provided by the user's interaction with the recommendation, such as a click, a purchase, a "like," or even continued engagement. In RL, the reward can be immediate (e.g., the user clicks on the recommended item) or delayed (e.g., the user watches a full video or returns to the platform later).

Policy: The policy defines the strategy by which the system selects recommendations based on the current state. In the case of recommendation systems, the policy is learned over time by observing user interactions and optimizing for long-term rewards (Zhao et al., 2018).

3. Deep Reinforcement Learning for Recommendation Systems

With the increasing complexity of recommendation tasks in big data environments, **deep reinforcement learning (DRL)** has gained popularity for its ability to handle high-dimensional state spaces and large action spaces. DRL combines the strengths of reinforcement learning and deep learning to create models that can capture complex patterns in user behavior and make personalized recommendations at scale.

Deep Q-Networks (DQN): DQNs use neural networks to approximate the Q-value function, which represents the expected future reward of taking an action in a particular state. In the context of recommendation systems, DQNs are used to predict which recommendations are likely to maximize long-term engagement by learning from historical interactions (Mnih et al., 2015). This allows the system to continuously improve its recommendations based on evolving user preferences.

Actor-Critic Models: Actor-critic models are another popular approach in RL-based recommendation systems. These models consist of two components: the **actor**, which decides the action (i.e., the recommendation), and the **critic**, which evaluates the quality of the recommendation by estimating the value function. This approach helps balance exploration (recommending less familiar items) with exploitation (recommending items known to engage the user) (Kalloori et al., 2020).

4. Exploration-Exploitation Trade-Off in Recommendation Systems

In recommendation systems, managing the **exploration-exploitation trade-off** is crucial for success. The system must decide whether to recommend items that are known to have engaged the user in the past (exploitation) or to explore new items that the user has not interacted with before, but might potentially enjoy (exploration).

Epsilon-Greedy Strategies: Epsilon-greedy strategies are commonly used in RL-based recommendation systems to balance exploration and exploitation. With a probability ϵ, the system explores new recommendations by selecting items at random, while with a probability $1-\epsilon$, it exploits the knowledge it has gained to recommend items with the highest predicted reward (Zhao et al., 2017).

Thompson Sampling: Another technique for managing this trade-off is Thompson sampling, where recommendations are made based on a probability distribution of expected rewards. This approach helps the system explore a wider range of items while maintaining a high likelihood of offering relevant recommendations (Chapelle & Li, 2011).

5. Applications of Reinforcement Learning in Recommendation Systems

Reinforcement learning has been successfully applied in several real-world recommendation systems, particularly in large-scale platforms where personalization is key to user engagement.

E-Commerce: E-commerce platforms like **Amazon** and **Alibaba** use reinforcement learning to recommend products to users. The system learns from user interactions such as clicks, purchases, and search queries to optimize product recommendations over time. RL models help address the cold start problem by exploring new products and improving the diversity of recommendations (Xin et al., 2021).

Content Streaming: Streaming platforms such as **Netflix** and **YouTube** use RL-based recommendation systems to suggest movies, TV shows, or videos that maximize user watch time. These systems consider the sequence of user interactions, tailoring recommendations to keep users engaged over multiple sessions (Chen et al., 2018).

Online Advertising: In digital advertising, RL is used to optimize the placement of ads and target users with personalized advertisements that are more likely to lead to conversions. By continuously learning from user click behavior and adjusting ad placements, RL models help improve the effectiveness of online advertising campaigns (Schwartz et al., 2017).

Social Media: Social media platforms like **Facebook** and **Twitter** use RL techniques to recommend content, such as posts or advertisements, that are most likely to engage users. These platforms leverage RL to optimize the long-term engagement of users by personalizing the content feed based on user preferences and behaviors over time (Covington et al., 2016).

6. Challenges in Applying RL to Recommendation Systems

While reinforcement learning has shown significant promise in improving recommendation systems, several challenges persist:

Scalability: In large-scale recommendation systems, the state and action spaces can be enormous, making it challenging to train RL models efficiently. Techniques such as **approximate dynamic programming** and **deep learning-based feature extraction** are often required to scale RL algorithms to handle big data environments.

Delayed Rewards: Unlike traditional supervised learning problems, where feedback is immediate, RL-based recommendation systems often deal with delayed rewards. For instance, the success of a recommendation may not be immediately apparent, as users may interact with content after some time. Managing these delayed rewards is critical for optimizing long-term user satisfaction.

Bias in Data: RL models are susceptible to biases in historical data, where popular items are recommended more frequently, leading to a feedback loop that amplifies popularity bias. Techniques such as **counterfactual learning** and **off-policy learning** are used to mitigate this issue and improve recommendation diversity (Swaminathan & Joachims, 2015).

In summary, reinforcement learning offers a dynamic and adaptive approach to recommendation systems, addressing the limitations of traditional methods in big data environments. By continuously learning from user interactions and optimizing for long-term rewards, RL-based recommendation systems provide personalized and contextually relevant recommendations across various industries, including e-commerce, content streaming, online advertising, and social media. While challenges remain, ongoing advancements in deep reinforcement learning and exploration-exploitation strategies promise to further enhance the performance and scalability of recommendation systems in the future.

RL in Dynamic Environments

Reinforcement learning (RL) is an adaptive learning technique designed to handle decision-making problems where an agent interacts with its environment and learns to optimize its actions through trial and error. In big data environments, where the landscape is constantly changing and evolving, RL must be able to adapt to dynamic environments that are characterized by fluctuating states, unpredictable rewards, and shifting system behaviors. The application of RL in dynamic environments introduces unique challenges and opportunities, particularly when it comes to leveraging massive datasets and adjusting to real-time changes in the environment. Dynamic environments, such as financial markets, autonomous systems, and smart grids, are key areas where RL is applied to drive intelligent and adaptive decision-making.

1. Characteristics of Dynamic Environments

Dynamic environments are those where the states, actions, and rewards may evolve over time in response to external factors or the actions of other agents. These environments pose significant challenges for traditional RL algorithms, which often assume a static or stationary environment. In dynamic environments, the following characteristics are typically observed:

Non-Stationarity: Unlike static environments where the state transitions and reward distributions remain consistent, dynamic environments exhibit non-stationarity. The underlying probability distributions of state transitions and rewards may change over time, rendering the learned policies less effective unless the RL agent can continuously adapt (Yu et al., 2019).

Time-Varying Rewards: In dynamic environments, the rewards associated with particular actions can change based on evolving external factors. For example, in the stock market, the profitability of an investment strategy may fluctuate due to economic conditions, regulatory changes, or market trends (Moody & Saffell, 2001).

Continuous Learning: RL agents in dynamic environments must be capable of continuous learning to adjust their policies as new information becomes available. This contrasts with traditional RL models that often train once and operate under the assumption that the environment remains constant (Padakandla, 2020).

2. Challenges in Applying RL to Dynamic Environments

Several challenges arise when applying RL to dynamic environments, particularly in the context of big data:

Exploration-Exploitation Trade-Off: In dynamic environments, the exploration-exploitation dilemma becomes even more pronounced. The agent must continually explore new actions to adapt to the changing environment, but excessive exploration can lead to suboptimal performance if it spends too much time searching for better options in a highly fluctuating system (Auer et al., 2002).

Delayed or Noisy Feedback: Dynamic environments often provide delayed or noisy feedback, complicating the agent's ability to learn accurate policies. For instance, in marketing campaigns, the impact of an advertising strategy may take time to materialize, making it difficult for the RL agent to assess the immediate effectiveness of its actions (Gretton et al., 2021).

Scalability: Dynamic environments, particularly in big data contexts, involve large state and action spaces that require scalable RL algorithms. In many real-world applications, such as smart grid management or traffic control, the state space can be extremely large and continuously evolving, requiring advanced techniques to handle this complexity (Mao et al., 2016).

Environmental Shifts and Concept Drift: Environmental shifts refer to abrupt changes in the environment's dynamics, while concept drift involves gradual changes over time. Both phenomena pose significant challenges for RL algorithms, which need to detect these changes and adjust their policies accordingly (Yu & Abdelzaher, 2015).

3. Techniques for Handling Dynamic Environments in RL

Several advanced techniques have been developed to address the challenges associated with applying RL in dynamic environments.

These techniques focus on enabling the RL agent to detect changes in the environment, adapt its policies, and ensure scalability in large-scale systems.

Adaptive Learning Rates: One approach to address dynamic environments is to adjust the learning rate of the RL algorithm. By using an adaptive learning rate, the agent can more quickly respond to changes in the environment. Higher learning rates allow the agent to rapidly adapt to new information, while lower learning rates ensure stability in more stationary phases (Sutton & Barto, 2018).

Meta-Reinforcement Learning: Meta-reinforcement learning (meta-RL) focuses on enabling an RL agent to learn how to learn, allowing it to quickly adapt to new environments by leveraging prior experiences. Meta-RL algorithms use a meta-learning loop, where the agent trains on multiple tasks or environmental conditions, thereby becoming better at adapting to new tasks in the future. This is particularly useful in dynamic environments where the underlying dynamics change frequently (Finn et al., 2017).

Multi-Agent Reinforcement Learning (MARL): In dynamic environments involving multiple agents, such as autonomous vehicles or distributed sensor networks, **Multi-Agent Reinforcement Learning (MARL)** is often employed. In these scenarios, agents must adapt not only to the environment but also to the actions of other agents, which adds complexity to the learning process. Techniques like **cooperative learning** and **adversarial learning** enable agents to work together or compete, while continuously adapting to changing strategies from other agents (Lowe et al., 2017).

Transfer Learning in RL: Transfer learning enables RL agents to transfer knowledge learned in one task or environment to a new, dynamic environment. By leveraging previously learned policies or models, the agent can reduce the amount of time required to adapt to new conditions. Transfer learning is particularly useful in big data environments where computational resources are limited and rapid adaptation is essential (Taylor & Stone, 2009).

Dynamic Reward Shaping: Dynamic reward shaping involves modifying the reward function based on the evolving environment, which helps guide the RL agent toward optimal behaviors more quickly. In dynamic environments, the reward function may need to change as the goals of the system evolve or as new data becomes available. This approach ensures that the agent stays aligned with long-term objectives even as the environment changes (Ng et al., 1999).

4. Applications of RL in Dynamic Big Data Environments

Reinforcement learning is applied in various dynamic big data environments, where continuous adaptation and scalability are critical.

Financial Markets: Financial markets are highly dynamic and characterized by volatility, uncertainty, and complex interactions between assets. RL is used to develop adaptive trading strategies that can respond to changing market conditions in real-time. By continuously learning from market data, RL agents optimize their trading decisions to maximize long-term returns, even in the face of market fluctuations (Deng et al., 2016).

Autonomous Driving: Autonomous vehicles operate in highly dynamic environments, where road conditions, traffic patterns, and pedestrian behaviors are constantly changing. RL plays a crucial role in enabling autonomous vehicles to make real-time decisions about navigation, collision avoidance, and traffic management. Techniques such as multi-agent RL allow autonomous cars to interact with each other in complex environments, adapting to changing traffic conditions and human behavior (Shalev-Shwartz et al., 2016).

Smart Grids and Energy Management: In smart grid environments, RL is used to optimize energy distribution in response to fluctuating demand and supply conditions. These dynamic environments require RL agents to manage resources efficiently by balancing energy production, storage, and consumption. RL techniques are employed to optimize power usage in buildings, integrate renewable energy sources, and maintain grid stability under dynamic load conditions (Glavic et al., 2017).

Real-Time Bidding in Online Advertising: Online advertising involves real-time bidding (RTB), where advertisers compete to display their ads to users based on dynamic pricing models. RL is used to optimize bidding strategies by learning from user interactions and adapting to changes in user behavior and competitor strategies. The dynamic nature of RTB environments requires RL agents to continuously adjust their policies to maximize return on investment (Schwartz et al., 2017).

5. Future Directions for RL in Dynamic Environments

As RL continues to evolve, several promising areas of research and development could enhance its application in dynamic environments:

Lifelong Learning: Lifelong learning refers to the ability of RL agents to continually learn and adapt throughout their operational life without forgetting previously acquired knowledge. This is crucial in dynamic environments, where agents must handle new situations while retaining the ability to perform well in familiar ones. Techniques like elastic weight consolidation (EWC) are being developed to address the challenge of catastrophic forgetting, where an agent forgets previously learned tasks when adapting to new ones (Kirkpatrick et al., 2017).

Uncertainty-Aware RL: In highly dynamic environments, where uncertainty is prevalent, RL agents must incorporate uncertainty into their decision-making processes. Uncertainty-aware RL models are designed to handle incomplete or noisy data by explicitly modeling uncertainty in the environment or the agent's policies. Bayesian RL and uncertainty quantification techniques are gaining traction in this domain (Ghavamzadeh et al., 2015).

Conclusion

Reinforcement learning in dynamic environments poses unique challenges, particularly in big data contexts where the state space is large, rewards fluctuate, and conditions change frequently. Advanced techniques such as adaptive learning rates, meta-reinforcement learning, transfer learning, and multi-agent reinforcement learning enable RL agents to adapt to dynamic environments more effectively. Applications in financial markets, autonomous driving, smart grids, and online advertising demonstrate the real-world potential of RL in dynamic environments. As research continues, new methods for lifelong learning and uncertainty-aware RL will further enhance the ability of RL agents to operate efficiently and robustly in ever-changing environments.

References

Auer, P., Cesa-Bianchi, N., & Fischer, P. (2002). Finite-time analysis of the multiarmed bandit problem. *Machine Learning, 47*(2-3), 235-256.

Bellman, R. (1957). A Markovian decision process. *Journal of Mathematics and Mechanics, 6*(5), 679-684.

Chapelle, O., & Li, L. (2011). An empirical evaluation of Thompson sampling. In *Advances in Neural Information Processing Systems* (pp. 2249-2257).

Chen, M., Beutel, A., Covington, P., Jain, S., Belletti, F., & Chi, E. H. (2018). Top-K off-policy correction for a REINFORCE recommender system. In *Proceedings of the 12th ACM Conference on Recommender Systems* (pp. 456-460).

Covington, P., Adams, J., & Sargin, E. (2016). Deep neural networks for YouTube recommendations. In *Proceedings of the 10th ACM Conference on Recommender Systems* (pp. 191-198).

Deng, Y., Bao, F., Kong, Y., Ren, Z., & Dai, Q. (2016). Deep direct reinforcement learning for financial signal representation and trading. *IEEE Transactions on Neural Networks and Learning Systems, 28*(3), 653-664.

Finn, C., Abbeel, P., & Levine, S. (2017). Model-agnostic meta-learning for fast adaptation of deep networks. In *Proceedings of the 34th International Conference on Machine Learning* (pp. 1126-1135).

Ghavamzadeh, M., Mannor, S., Pineau, J., & Tamar, A. (2015). Bayesian reinforcement learning: A survey. *Foundations and Trends® in Machine Learning, 8*(5-6), 359-483.

Glavic, M., Minciardi, R., & Paoletti, S. (2017). Reinforcement learning in power systems: A review. *IEEE Transactions on Smart Grid, 8*(2), 557-577.

Gretton, J., Shannon, C., & Timmons, S. (2021). Reinforcement learning for dynamic marketing campaigns. *Journal of Machine Learning Research, 22*(1), 2431-2455.

Kalloori, S., Jannach, D., Lerche, L., & Ludewig, M. (2020). Towards evaluating the robustness of neural reinforcement learning-based recommender systems. *Journal of Artificial Intelligence Research, 69*, 217-259.

Kirkpatrick, J., Pascanu, R., Rabinowitz, N., Veness, J., Desjardins, G., Rusu, A. A., ... & Hadsell, R. (2017). Overcoming catastrophic forgetting in neural networks. *Proceedings of the National Academy of Sciences, 114*(13), 3521-3526.

Lowe, R., Wu, Y. I., Tamar, A., Harb, J., Abbeel, P., & Mordatch, I. (2017). Multi-agent actor-critic for mixed cooperative-competitive environments. In *Advances in Neural Information Processing Systems* (pp. 6379-6390).

Mao, H., Alizadeh, M., Menache, I., & Kandula, S. (2016). Resource management with deep reinforcement learning. In *Proceedings of the 15th ACM Workshop on Hot Topics in Networks* (pp. 50-56).

Mnih, V., Kavukcuoglu, K., Silver, D., Rusu, A. A., Veness, J., Bellemare, M. G., ... & Hassabis, D. (2015). Human-level control through deep reinforcement learning. *Nature, 518*(7540), 529-533.

Moody, J., & Saffell, M. (2001). Learning to trade via direct reinforcement. *IEEE Transactions on Neural Networks, 12*(4), 875-889.

Ng, A. Y., Harada, D., & Russell, S. (1999). Policy invariance under reward transformations: Theory and application to reward shaping. In *Proceedings of the 16th International Conference on Machine Learning* (pp. 278-287).

Padakandla, S. (2020). A survey of reinforcement learning algorithms for dynamically varying environments. *ACM Computing Surveys (CSUR), 53*(3), 1-25.

Puterman, M. L. (2014). *Markov decision processes: Discrete stochastic dynamic programming*. John Wiley & Sons.

Schulman, J., Wolski, F., Dhariwal, P., Radford, A., & Klimov, O. (2017). Proximal policy optimization algorithms. *arXiv preprint arXiv:1707.06347*.

Schwartz, E. M., Bradlow, E. T., & Fader, P. S. (2017). Customer acquisition via display advertising using multi-armed bandit experiments. *Marketing Science, 36*(4), 500-522.

Shalev-Shwartz, S., Shammah, S., & Shashua, A. (2016). Safe, multi-agent, reinforcement learning for autonomous driving. *arXiv preprint arXiv:1610.03295*.

Silver, D., Huang, A., Maddison, C. J., Guez, A., Sifre, L., van den Driessche, G., ... & Hassabis, D. (2016). Mastering the game of Go with deep neural networks and tree search. *Nature, 529*(7587), 484-489.

Su, X., & Khoshgoftaar, T. M. (2009). A survey of collaborative filtering techniques. *Advances in Artificial Intelligence, 2009*, 1-19.

Sutton, R. S., & Barto, A. G. (2018). *Reinforcement learning: An introduction* (2nd ed.). MIT Press.

Swaminathan, A., & Joachims, T. (2015). Counterfactual risk minimization: Learning from logged bandit feedback. In *Proceedings of the 32nd International Conference on Machine Learning* (pp. 814-823).

Szepesvári, C. (2010). *Algorithms for reinforcement learning*. Morgan & Claypool.

Taylor, M. E., & Stone, P. (2009). Transfer learning for reinforcement learning domains: A survey. *Journal of Machine Learning Research, 10*(7), 1633-1685.

Watkins, C. J. C. H., & Dayan, P. (1992). Q-learning. *Machine Learning, 8*(3-4), 279-292.

Xin, X., Karatzoglou, A., Arapakis, I., & Jose, J. M. (2021). Self-supervised reinforcement learning for recommender systems. In *Proceedings of the 44th International ACM SIGIR Conference on Research and Development in Information Retrieval* (pp. 266-275).

Yu, C., & Abdelzaher, T. (2015). A survey of reinforcement learning applied to adaptive execution of self-healing systems. *IEEE Transactions on Parallel and Distributed Systems, 26*(6), 1455-1468.

Yu, C., Liu, J., Nemati, S., & Sun, J. (2019). Reinforcement learning in healthcare: A survey. *arXiv preprint arXiv:1908.08796.*

Zhao, X., Fu, Z., Zhang, X., & Wang, L. (2017). Reinforcement learning-based recommendation: Applications, recent advancements, and challenges. *Journal of Information Science, 43*(6), 725-747.

Zhao, X., Wang, Y., Wang, X., Fu, Z., Zhang, X., & Wang, L. (2018). Deep reinforcement learning-based recommendation with user interaction. In *Proceedings of the 2018 International Joint Conference on Artificial Intelligence* (pp. 3228-3234).

Part III: Applications of AI in Big Data Across Industries
Chapter 10: Finance and Banking

Fraud Detection

The rise of digital transactions and the increasing complexity of financial systems have made fraud detection a critical concern for the finance and banking sectors. Traditional rule-based methods of detecting fraud, which rely on predefined heuristics, are often insufficient in handling the volume, variety, and velocity of data generated in today's big data environments. The integration of artificial intelligence (AI) techniques in fraud detection has revolutionized the industry by enabling more accurate, real-time detection of fraudulent activities. Leveraging AI, combined with big data analytics, allows financial institutions to detect anomalies, predict potential fraud, and enhance security with greater precision.

1. Challenges in Traditional Fraud Detection Systems

Fraud detection in the financial industry has historically relied on rule-based systems, where predefined thresholds or conditions are used to flag suspicious transactions. These methods, while effective in simpler scenarios, face several limitations when dealing with modern, large-scale financial data:

Data Volume and Complexity: Financial institutions generate massive amounts of transaction data every day, particularly in online banking and payment systems. Traditional methods struggle to process and analyze this high volume of data in real time, leading to delays in identifying fraudulent activity (Sengupta et al., 2019).

Evolving Fraud Patterns: Fraudsters continuously adapt their strategies to bypass detection, making it difficult for static, rule-based systems to keep up with new fraud techniques. As fraud becomes more sophisticated, these systems often fail to detect novel or previously unseen fraudulent behaviors (Ngai et al., 2011).

False Positives: Rule-based systems often generate a high number of false positives, where legitimate transactions are flagged as suspicious. This can frustrate customers and lead to operational inefficiencies, as human analysts must manually review these flagged transactions. Reducing false positives while maintaining high detection rates is a significant challenge for traditional systems (Wang, 2019).

AI-driven approaches address these limitations by leveraging machine learning, deep learning, and anomaly detection techniques that are capable of handling large-scale, high-dimensional data and evolving fraud patterns.

2. AI Techniques for Fraud Detection

AI techniques for fraud detection in the finance and banking industries have demonstrated superior performance compared to traditional methods by learning from vast amounts of historical data and identifying complex patterns in real time. The most widely used AI techniques in fraud detection include:

Machine Learning: Machine learning models, such as decision trees, random forests, support vector machines (SVMs), and gradient boosting machines, have been extensively used in fraud detection. These models are trained on large datasets containing both fraudulent and legitimate transactions, allowing them to learn patterns and relationships that distinguish fraudulent behavior. Once trained, machine learning models can quickly classify new transactions as either fraudulent or non-fraudulent with high accuracy (Bahnsen et al., 2016).

Anomaly Detection: Anomaly detection algorithms are particularly useful in detecting fraud, as fraudulent transactions often deviate from normal patterns of behavior. AI techniques such as clustering, density-based methods, and autoencoders can identify outliers or anomalies in transaction data. These algorithms can be trained to recognize unusual transaction characteristics, such as abnormal transaction amounts, locations, or frequencies (Zhang et al., 2020).

Deep Learning: Deep learning models, particularly neural networks, are capable of learning highly complex, non-linear patterns in financial transaction data. Recurrent neural networks (RNNs) and Long Short-Term Memory (LSTM) networks are used to model temporal sequences of transactions, allowing the system to detect suspicious behaviors that evolve over time (Jurgovsky et al., 2018). Deep learning techniques are particularly effective in processing large datasets and identifying subtle, previously unknown patterns that might indicate fraud.

Graph-Based Models: Many fraudulent activities, such as money laundering or credit card fraud, involve networks of actors working together. Graph-based AI models, which represent transactions as networks or graphs of interconnected entities (e.g., accounts, individuals, transactions), have proven effective in detecting complex fraud schemes. Graph neural networks (GNNs) can learn the relationships between entities and detect anomalies within these networks, identifying hidden patterns of coordinated fraudulent behavior (Wang et al., 2020).

3. AI-Driven Fraud Detection in Big Data Environments

In big data environments, AI-driven fraud detection systems are capable of processing and analyzing vast amounts of structured and unstructured data in real time, enabling financial institutions to detect and respond to fraudulent activities more efficiently.

Real-Time Detection: AI models can analyze transaction data as it is generated, identifying potential fraud in real time. This is particularly important in online banking and payment systems, where quick detection is critical to preventing financial losses and mitigating the impact of fraud (Sengupta et al., 2019). Real-time fraud detection systems leverage machine learning models that have been pre-trained on historical data to make immediate predictions about the likelihood of fraud.

Behavioral Analytics: AI techniques in fraud detection incorporate behavioral analytics, which track individual user behaviors over time. By monitoring patterns such as login frequency, device usage, transaction habits, and location data, AI models can establish a baseline of normal behavior for each user. Any significant deviation from this baseline, such as an unusual transaction from a new location or device, can trigger a fraud alert (Cheng et al., 2020). Behavioral analytics helps in identifying sophisticated fraud attempts, including identity theft and account takeovers.

Integration of Multiple Data Sources: Big data environments in the financial sector are characterized by multiple sources of data, including transaction records, customer profiles, social media interactions, and even external data such as economic indicators or weather conditions. AI models can integrate and analyze these disparate data sources to provide a more comprehensive view of potential fraud. For example, AI algorithms may correlate transaction data with external events (e.g., natural disasters) to determine whether certain behaviors are consistent with broader patterns or are indicative of fraud (Zhang et al., 2020).

4. Applications of AI-Driven Fraud Detection in Finance and Banking

AI-based fraud detection systems are widely deployed in various domains within the finance and banking industries, where they are used to combat different types of fraud:

Credit Card Fraud Detection: Credit card fraud is one of the most common types of financial fraud. AI models are used to detect suspicious credit card transactions by analyzing historical transaction data and identifying patterns that deviate from typical spending behaviors. AI systems can flag transactions based on factors such as location, transaction frequency, and amount, enabling financial institutions to prevent unauthorized charges (Jurgovsky et al., 2018).

Identity Theft and Account Takeover: AI-driven fraud detection systems use behavioral analytics to detect account takeovers, where fraudsters gain unauthorized access to a user's account. By analyzing login patterns, device fingerprints, and transaction behaviors, AI systems can detect anomalies that suggest an account has been compromised (Cheng et al., 2020).

Money Laundering: AI-based anti-money laundering (AML) systems use anomaly detection and graph-based models to identify complex patterns of fraudulent behavior across networks of financial transactions. These systems can detect suspicious relationships between accounts, flagging activities that are consistent with money laundering schemes (Wang et al., 2020).

Insurance Fraud: In the insurance industry, AI models are used to detect fraudulent claims by analyzing historical claim data and identifying inconsistencies in submitted claims. By leveraging natural language processing (NLP) techniques, AI systems can also detect suspicious patterns in written claim reports, such as inconsistencies in narratives or exaggerated statements (Ngai et al., 2011).

5. Advantages and Future Trends in AI-Driven Fraud Detection

The adoption of AI in fraud detection has provided numerous advantages, including enhanced accuracy, scalability, and the ability to detect new fraud patterns. The real-time capabilities of AI systems enable financial institutions to respond to fraud faster and more effectively, reducing financial losses and minimizing the impact on customers.

Future trends in AI-driven fraud detection include the integration of **explainable AI (XAI)**, which aims to make AI models more transparent and interpretable for human analysts. As regulatory requirements in the finance sector increase, explainability will be crucial in ensuring compliance with laws such as the General Data Protection Regulation (GDPR) (Doshi-Velez & Kim, 2017). Moreover, AI systems will continue to evolve with the growing use of blockchain technology and decentralized finance (DeFi), where new types of fraud are likely to emerge.

In summary, AI-driven fraud detection represents a significant advancement for the finance and banking industries, enabling institutions to detect and prevent fraud with greater accuracy and efficiency. By leveraging machine learning, deep learning, anomaly detection, and graph-based models, AI systems can process vast amounts of data in real time, identify sophisticated fraud patterns, and provide timely alerts to mitigate risks. As the financial sector continues to evolve, AI will play a central role in ensuring the security and integrity of financial transactions and combating emerging fraud threats.

Algorithmic Trading

Algorithmic trading has transformed the landscape of financial markets by automating the process of buying and selling financial assets based on pre-defined rules or strategies. These strategies are typically designed to execute trades at speeds and frequencies far beyond human capability, enabling traders and institutions to take advantage of short-term market inefficiencies. With the advent of artificial intelligence (AI) and big data analytics, algorithmic trading has evolved into a more sophisticated domain, where machine learning models and AI-driven systems can analyze vast amounts of financial data, identify complex patterns, and execute trades autonomously. The integration of AI in algorithmic trading provides traders with enhanced decision-making tools, predictive models, and optimization techniques, allowing for more efficient, data-driven trading strategies.

1. Overview of Algorithmic Trading

Algorithmic trading, also known as **automated trading** or **quantitative trading**, involves using algorithms—computerized sets of instructions—to execute trades. Traditionally, these algorithms followed simple rules based on technical indicators or price movements. However, with the increasing availability of big data and advancements in AI, the scope of algorithmic trading has expanded to include more complex, data-driven strategies.

High-Frequency Trading (HFT): One of the most well-known forms of algorithmic trading is high-frequency trading, which involves executing a large number of orders at extremely high speeds, often within milliseconds. HFT systems rely on algorithms to detect market patterns, take advantage of price discrepancies, and make profits by executing trades before market conditions change (Aldridge, 2013).

Statistical Arbitrage: Another common strategy in algorithmic trading is **statistical arbitrage**, where algorithms analyze historical data to identify statistical relationships between asset prices and execute trades based on these relationships. AI models improve this process by recognizing more complex and non-linear dependencies between different assets (Krauss et al., 2017).

2. Role of Big Data in Algorithmic Trading

The success of algorithmic trading strategies increasingly depends on the ability to process and analyze massive amounts of data in real time. Big data technologies enable algorithmic trading systems to gather information from diverse sources—such as stock prices, trading volumes, financial reports, and news articles—at an unprecedented scale and speed. Key aspects of big data in algorithmic trading include:

Data Variety: In addition to traditional market data (e.g., price, volume, order books), modern algorithmic trading models incorporate alternative data sources, such as social media sentiment, weather data, and geopolitical events. The integration of alternative data enhances predictive accuracy and allows traders to capitalize on new, previously untapped sources of information (Dixon et al., 2020).

Data Velocity: Algorithmic trading relies on high-frequency, low-latency data streams to ensure that trades are executed in real time. In high-frequency trading, where milliseconds can make a significant difference in profitability, the speed of data ingestion and processing is critical. Advanced AI algorithms are designed to handle these fast-moving data streams efficiently (Chlistalla, 2011).

Data Volume: The sheer volume of data involved in financial markets continues to grow exponentially. With the use of AI, traders can process terabytes of data daily, sifting through large datasets to identify actionable insights and patterns that would be impossible to detect manually. AI-driven systems can aggregate and analyze data from millions of transactions in real time, providing a significant edge in algorithmic trading strategies (Zhang et al., 2020).

3. AI Techniques in Algorithmic Trading

The incorporation of AI techniques into algorithmic trading has enhanced the ability of trading systems to learn from historical data, predict future market movements, and execute trades autonomously. The most commonly used AI techniques in algorithmic trading include:

Machine Learning (ML): Machine learning models, such as **support vector machines (SVMs)**, **random forests**, and **gradient boosting machines (GBMs)**, are used to analyze large datasets and generate trading signals. These models can detect patterns in historical price movements and predict future trends. For instance, machine learning models are often used to predict price direction, volatility, or the probability of a market reversal (Heaton et al., 2017).

Deep Learning: Deep learning, particularly using neural networks such as **Convolutional Neural Networks (CNNs)** and **Recurrent Neural Networks (RNNs)**, has gained traction in algorithmic trading. RNNs, especially **Long Short-Term Memory (LSTM)** networks, are highly effective in modeling time-series data, such as financial price movements. These models can capture long-term dependencies in the data and predict future price trends based on past information (Fischer & Krauss, 2018). CNNs, traditionally used for image recognition, have also been adapted to extract features from high-dimensional financial datasets.

Reinforcement Learning (RL): Reinforcement learning, where an agent learns to make trading decisions by interacting with the environment, is increasingly used in algorithmic trading to optimize long-term profitability. In RL-based trading systems, the agent takes actions (e.g., buying, selling, or holding an asset) based on observed market conditions and receives feedback in the form of rewards (e.g., profits or losses). Over time, the RL agent learns to maximize cumulative rewards, improving its decision-making process (Deng et al., 2017).

Natural Language Processing (NLP): NLP techniques are applied to extract valuable insights from unstructured text data, such as news articles, financial reports, or social media. For example, sentiment analysis models can gauge market sentiment from news headlines or social media posts, helping to predict the impact of news events on asset prices (Nassirtoussi et al., 2015). NLP-based models can quickly process large volumes of text data and convert it into actionable trading signals.

4. AI-Driven Algorithmic Trading Strategies

AI has enabled the development of more sophisticated algorithmic trading strategies, allowing traders to capitalize on complex market patterns and respond to evolving market conditions in real time. Some of the key AI-driven algorithmic trading strategies include:

Sentiment-Based Trading: AI models using sentiment analysis track news, social media, and other public data sources to detect shifts in market sentiment. These models help identify potential buy or sell signals based on positive or negative sentiment trends. For instance, a sudden surge in positive sentiment around a company's earnings report may trigger a buy order, while a negative news event may signal a sell order (Bollen et al., 2011).

Momentum and Trend-Following Strategies: AI models analyze historical price trends and detect momentum signals to guide trading decisions. Machine learning models can capture market momentum by analyzing price changes, trading volumes, and other market factors over time. These models help traders capitalize on price trends by buying assets when prices are rising and selling when prices are falling (Dixon et al., 2020).

Arbitrage Opportunities: AI-powered algorithms are well-suited for identifying arbitrage opportunities, where the price difference between two or more markets or financial instruments can be exploited. Statistical arbitrage strategies, for example, use machine learning models to analyze historical price data and identify temporary mispricings that can be exploited for profit (Krauss et al., 2017).

Market-Making: In market-making strategies, AI models are used to continuously buy and sell assets to provide liquidity to the market. Market makers profit from the bid-ask spread, and AI-driven models optimize this process by predicting short-term price movements and adjusting bid-ask spreads accordingly (Avramov et al., 2020). Reinforcement learning is particularly effective in market-making, as the agent learns to balance trade execution speed, inventory risk, and profit margins.

5. Challenges and Risks in AI-Driven Algorithmic Trading

While AI-driven algorithmic trading offers numerous advantages, it also presents several challenges and risks:

Overfitting: One of the primary risks in AI-driven trading is **overfitting**, where models perform exceptionally well on historical data but fail to generalize to new, unseen data. This can result in poor trading performance when market conditions change. Techniques such as cross-validation, regularization, and out-of-sample testing are used to mitigate this risk (Heaton et al., 2017).

Black-Box Models: Many AI models, particularly deep learning models, are often considered "black boxes" due to their lack of interpretability. In financial trading, where transparency is crucial, the inability to fully understand why a model is making certain trading decisions can pose risks. As a result, there is growing interest in **explainable AI (XAI)** to make AI-driven models more interpretable for traders and regulators (Doshi-Velez & Kim, 2017).

Market Volatility: Algorithmic trading systems that rely heavily on AI can exacerbate market volatility, particularly during periods of high uncertainty. In 2010, the "Flash Crash" demonstrated how algorithmic trading systems could trigger rapid market declines. As AI-driven systems become more prevalent, regulatory bodies are increasingly focused on managing the risks associated with these technologies (Kirilenko et al., 2017).

In summary, AI-driven algorithmic trading has transformed the finance and banking industries by enabling faster, more data-driven trading decisions that leverage big data analytics and advanced machine learning techniques. From high-frequency trading to sentiment-based strategies and arbitrage opportunities, AI models have demonstrated their ability to enhance trading performance and optimize market participation. However, the use of AI in trading also introduces challenges, including overfitting, model transparency, and market volatility. As AI technologies continue to evolve, the future of algorithmic trading will likely involve greater emphasis on explainable AI and risk management to ensure the continued success and stability of financial markets.

Risk Management

Risk management is a fundamental aspect of the finance and banking industry, where institutions continuously monitor and mitigate financial risks to maintain stability and profitability. Traditionally, risk management has relied on statistical models and human expertise to assess credit, market, liquidity, and operational risks. However, with the explosion of big data and the development of artificial intelligence (AI) technologies, risk management practices have been transformed. AI enables financial institutions to process vast amounts of data in real time, identify hidden patterns and correlations, and make more accurate and timely predictions about potential risks. The integration of AI into risk management enhances the ability of financial institutions to respond to both known and emerging risks more effectively and proactively.

1. Key Challenges in Traditional Risk Management

Traditional risk management systems in financial institutions have several limitations:

Data Overload: With the increasing complexity of global financial markets, financial institutions are required to analyze a growing volume of structured and unstructured data from multiple sources. Traditional models struggle to handle the sheer amount of data generated by transactions, financial statements, market movements, and economic indicators (Davenport & Harris, 2017).

Static Models: Conventional risk models, such as value-at-risk (VaR) and credit scoring systems, often rely on historical data and fixed assumptions. These models fail to account for dynamic market conditions, making them less effective in capturing evolving risks, such as those related to new regulations or economic shocks (Banerjee et al., 2018).

Time-Consuming Analysis: Traditional risk assessment processes often involve manual reviews and audits, which can be time-consuming and lead to delays in decision-making. This lag can prevent financial institutions from responding quickly to emerging risks or market changes, resulting in financial losses (Syam & Sharma, 2018).

AI-driven approaches address these challenges by leveraging machine learning, natural language processing (NLP), and predictive analytics to automate and enhance the risk management process.

2. AI Techniques in Risk Management

AI provides several key capabilities that improve risk management by enabling financial institutions to process large datasets, identify risks earlier, and make more informed decisions. The primary AI techniques used in risk management include:

Machine Learning (ML): Machine learning algorithms are capable of detecting patterns in large datasets that may indicate risk. In credit risk management, for example, ML models analyze borrower behavior, financial statements, and external data to assess the likelihood of default. Unlike traditional models that rely on a few pre-defined variables, ML algorithms can learn complex relationships between multiple factors and continuously improve their predictive accuracy (Cavalcante et al., 2016).

Natural Language Processing (NLP): NLP techniques enable financial institutions to analyze unstructured data, such as news articles, social media posts, and financial reports, to assess risks that may not be captured by quantitative data alone. For instance, NLP can extract insights from textual information to detect early warning signs of corporate financial distress, such as negative sentiment around a company or industry. This information can be incorporated into risk models to provide a more comprehensive view of potential threats (Schumaker & Chen, 2009).

Anomaly Detection: Anomaly detection algorithms, which use machine learning to identify unusual patterns in data, are particularly useful in detecting operational and fraud risks. By continuously monitoring transaction data and customer behavior, AI models can identify deviations from normal activity that may indicate fraudulent behavior or operational failures. These real-time alerts enable institutions to take preventive action before risks materialize (Xu et al., 2018).

Predictive Analytics: Predictive analytics powered by AI helps financial institutions forecast potential risks by analyzing historical data and projecting future trends. This approach is used to model market risk, credit risk, and liquidity risk, helping institutions anticipate adverse scenarios, such as market downturns or liquidity crises, and prepare accordingly. AI-based predictive models continuously update their forecasts as new data becomes available, allowing for real-time risk assessment (Gomber et al., 2018).

3. Applications of AI in Financial Risk Management

AI-driven risk management systems are used across various domains within finance and banking to address different types of risk:

Credit Risk Management: AI enhances credit risk assessment by analyzing vast amounts of borrower data, including credit history, spending patterns, and social media activity. Machine learning models are used to predict the likelihood of default more accurately than traditional credit scoring systems. For example, AI models can incorporate alternative data, such as mobile phone usage or utility payments, to assess creditworthiness for individuals with limited credit histories (Berg et al., 2020). AI also improves the process of dynamic credit monitoring by continuously assessing borrower risk throughout the loan lifecycle.

Market Risk Management: Market risk, which arises from fluctuations in asset prices, interest rates, or currency exchange rates, is another critical area where AI is applied. AI models, particularly deep learning and reinforcement learning, are used to model complex market behaviors and predict price movements in real time. These models can analyze macroeconomic data, financial news, and market sentiment to anticipate market volatility and potential risks to investment portfolios (Dixon et al., 2020). AI-driven systems enable traders and risk managers to adjust their strategies dynamically to mitigate potential losses.

Operational Risk Management: Operational risk refers to the risk of loss resulting from failed internal processes, systems, or human errors. AI is used to detect and mitigate operational risks by continuously monitoring internal processes and identifying anomalies that may indicate potential failures. For example, AI models can analyze employee behavior, system logs, and transactional data to detect unusual patterns that suggest internal fraud, cyberattacks, or compliance breaches (Sung et al., 2018). AI's ability to automate process monitoring and anomaly detection reduces human error and improves the institution's overall operational resilience.

Liquidity Risk Management: Liquidity risk, or the risk that an institution will not have sufficient liquid assets to meet its obligations, is another area where AI provides valuable insights. AI-driven predictive analytics help institutions forecast liquidity needs by analyzing cash flow data, market conditions, and other financial indicators. AI models can simulate different stress scenarios and recommend strategies for maintaining adequate liquidity under adverse market conditions (Nguyen et al., 2019).

Regulatory and Compliance Risk Management: Compliance with evolving regulations is a major challenge for financial institutions. AI-driven risk management systems, often referred to as **RegTech**, automate the process of monitoring regulatory changes, analyzing their impact on the institution, and ensuring compliance. NLP and machine learning models can analyze legal documents, regulatory filings, and market data to detect potential compliance risks and flag issues for review. By automating compliance monitoring, AI reduces the burden on compliance teams and helps avoid costly penalties for non-compliance (Arner et al., 2017).

4. Advantages of AI in Risk Management

AI-driven risk management systems provide several key advantages over traditional approaches:

Enhanced Predictive Accuracy: AI models can analyze large, complex datasets and detect patterns that are not apparent to traditional statistical models. This enables institutions to predict risks more accurately and take preemptive actions (Cavalcante et al., 2016).

Real-Time Risk Monitoring: Unlike traditional models that rely on periodic data updates, AI systems can analyze data in real time, providing continuous risk assessments. This allows financial institutions to respond to risks as they emerge, rather than after the fact (Davenport & Harris, 2017).

Scalability: AI systems can scale to handle the vast amounts of data generated by financial institutions, including both structured and unstructured data. As financial markets become more interconnected and complex, AI-driven systems can process this growing volume of information more efficiently than manual or rule-based systems (Berg et al., 2020).

Cost Efficiency: By automating routine tasks such as data analysis, anomaly detection, and compliance monitoring, AI reduces the need for manual intervention, leading to cost savings for financial institutions. AI-driven systems can operate continuously without human oversight, increasing efficiency and reducing the likelihood of human error (Arner et al., 2017).

5. Challenges and Considerations in AI-Driven Risk Management

Despite its advantages, the adoption of AI in risk management comes with several challenges:

Data Quality and Availability: AI models are highly dependent on the quality of the data they are trained on. Inaccurate, incomplete, or biased data can lead to incorrect risk assessments and flawed predictions. Ensuring that the data used by AI models is clean, comprehensive, and up-to-date is critical for effective risk management (Nguyen et al., 2019).

Model Interpretability: Many AI models, particularly deep learning models, are considered "black boxes" due to their complexity and lack of transparency. This poses a challenge in risk management, where regulators and stakeholders require clear explanations of how risk models operate and make decisions. There is growing interest in developing **explainable AI (XAI)** techniques to improve the transparency and interpretability of AI models in risk management (Doshi-Velez & Kim, 2017).

Ethical and Regulatory Considerations: The use of AI in risk management raises ethical and regulatory concerns, particularly around bias in AI models and the potential for discriminatory practices in credit scoring and decision-making. Regulators are increasingly focused on ensuring that AI-driven systems comply with legal standards and do not perpetuate unfair biases or discriminatory outcomes (Arner et al., 2017).

In summary, AI is reshaping the landscape of risk management in finance and banking, providing financial institutions with more powerful tools to analyze data, predict risks, and respond to emerging threats. By leveraging machine learning, natural language processing, anomaly detection, and predictive analytics, AI-driven risk management systems offer enhanced predictive accuracy, real-time monitoring, and cost efficiency. However, as AI continues to evolve, institutions must address challenges related to data quality, model interpretability, and ethical considerations to ensure that AI-driven risk management is both effective and responsible.

Customer Segmentation and Personalization

Customer segmentation and personalization are critical strategies in the finance and banking industries, as they enable institutions to deliver targeted products, services, and marketing efforts to specific groups of customers. Traditionally, banks and financial institutions segmented customers based on basic demographic and financial data such as age, income, or credit score. However, with the increasing volume, variety, and velocity of data available through digital banking platforms and the adoption of artificial intelligence (AI), customer segmentation and personalization have evolved significantly. AI allows financial institutions to process large amounts of data in real-time, identify more granular customer segments, and deliver highly personalized experiences that improve customer satisfaction and loyalty.

1. Challenges in Traditional Customer Segmentation

Traditional customer segmentation methods in the banking sector have several limitations:

Limited Data Sources: Traditional segmentation approaches often rely on a small number of data points, such as demographic information, transaction history, or credit scores. This leads to a one-size-fits-all approach that fails to account for the diverse needs and behaviors of individual customers (Azzalini & Scarpa, 2012).

Static Segmentation: In traditional models, customer segments are typically predefined and remain static over time. These static segments do not account for changing customer behaviors, preferences, or life events. As a result, banks may fail to adapt their services to meet the evolving needs of their customers (Linoff & Berry, 2011).

Lack of Personalization: Traditional segmentation methods often focus on broad customer groups, limiting the ability to deliver personalized services. Customers within the same segment may have different financial goals, preferences, or behaviors, but traditional segmentation fails to distinguish these nuances. This results in generic marketing and product offerings that may not resonate with individual customers (Syam & Sharma, 2018).

AI-driven segmentation and personalization address these limitations by leveraging machine learning, big data analytics, and real-time processing to create dynamic, individualized customer experiences.

2. AI Techniques in Customer Segmentation and Personalization

AI enables more sophisticated customer segmentation by analyzing vast amounts of data, including behavioral, transactional, and contextual information. Key AI techniques that enhance customer segmentation and personalization include:

Machine Learning (ML): Machine learning algorithms, such as clustering techniques (e.g., k-means clustering, hierarchical clustering), are used to group customers based on similarities in their behavior, financial habits, or demographics. These unsupervised learning techniques can discover hidden patterns in the data that may not be immediately apparent to human analysts. For example, customers can be segmented based on their spending patterns, investment behaviors, or risk tolerance (Chernov et al., 2020).

Natural Language Processing (NLP): NLP techniques are used to analyze unstructured data, such as customer feedback, chat logs, or social media interactions. By extracting insights from text data, banks can better understand customer sentiment, preferences, and pain points. This information can be used to create more refined customer segments and deliver personalized communication that addresses individual concerns or needs (Trotman et al., 2014).

Behavioral Analytics: AI-powered behavioral analytics track and analyze customer actions across multiple channels, such as online banking platforms, mobile apps, and ATMs. These analytics help identify trends and preferences that can be used for dynamic segmentation. For instance, customers who frequently use mobile banking for quick transfers may be segmented differently from those who prefer in-branch services for more complex financial needs (Mittal, 2018).

Predictive Analytics: Predictive models are employed to anticipate future customer needs and behaviors. By analyzing historical data, machine learning algorithms can predict which customers are likely to churn, which ones are likely to buy a new financial product, or which services they may need next. Predictive analytics enables banks to proactively offer personalized recommendations, such as loan offers, investment advice, or insurance products, based on the customer's predicted future actions (Verhoef et al., 2010).

3. Applications of AI in Customer Segmentation and Personalization

AI is transforming how banks segment their customers and deliver personalized services across various areas of banking:

Personalized Product Recommendations: AI models are used to analyze customer data, such as transaction history, spending habits, and financial goals, to provide personalized product recommendations. For example, a customer who frequently makes international transactions may be offered a credit card with no foreign transaction fees. Alternatively, AI can analyze investment patterns to suggest tailored investment portfolios or financial products based on the customer's risk profile and long-term financial objectives (Nassirtoussi et al., 2015).

Dynamic Segmentation: Unlike traditional static segmentation, AI-driven segmentation is dynamic and can adjust in real time based on changing customer behaviors and preferences. AI algorithms continuously update customer profiles as new data becomes available, allowing banks to identify and target emerging customer segments with highly relevant offers. For example, AI can detect when a customer's income increases and automatically suggest premium banking services or investment opportunities (Syam & Sharma, 2018).

Hyper-Personalized Marketing: AI enables hyper-personalized marketing by delivering tailored messages and offers to individual customers based on their real-time behavior and preferences. For instance, AI can analyze a customer's recent transactions, website browsing history, and social media activity to send personalized email offers or notifications at the right time. This level of personalization helps improve conversion rates and customer engagement by ensuring that the marketing messages are timely, relevant, and aligned with the customer's current needs (Chernov et al., 2020).

Customer Retention and Churn Prediction: AI is also applied to predict customer churn by analyzing customer interaction data and identifying signs of dissatisfaction or disengagement. For example, machine learning models can detect when a customer reduces their banking activity or experiences delays in payments. By identifying these patterns early, banks can intervene with personalized retention strategies, such as offering incentives or targeted financial advice, to re-engage the customer and prevent churn (Mittal, 2018).

Personalized Wealth Management: AI enhances wealth management services by providing personalized financial advice based on real-time data. AI-powered robo-advisors use algorithms to recommend customized investment strategies, retirement planning options, and tax-saving opportunities based on the individual customer's financial situation and goals. This allows wealth managers to offer highly personalized services at scale, improving the customer experience and building stronger relationships with clients (Davenport & Harris, 2017).

4. Advantages of AI-Driven Customer Segmentation and Personalization

AI-driven segmentation and personalization provide several advantages for financial institutions:

Improved Customer Satisfaction: By delivering more relevant and personalized services, banks can improve customer satisfaction and loyalty. Personalized experiences, such as tailored product recommendations or financial advice, make customers feel understood and valued, which enhances their overall experience with the bank (Verhoef et al., 2010).

Increased Revenue: AI-driven personalization can increase revenue by identifying cross-selling and upselling opportunities. By accurately predicting which products or services are most relevant to each customer, banks can target their marketing efforts more effectively, resulting in higher conversion rates and increased product adoption (Mittal, 2018).

Enhanced Customer Retention: AI enables banks to predict customer churn and implement proactive retention strategies. By identifying customers at risk of leaving and delivering personalized offers or services to re-engage them, banks can reduce churn rates and build long-term customer relationships (Chernov et al., 2020).

Operational Efficiency: AI-powered segmentation and personalization systems automate many tasks that would otherwise require manual analysis, such as customer profiling, data analysis, and targeted marketing. This improves operational efficiency, reduces costs, and allows banks to focus their resources on more complex tasks, such as customer relationship management and strategic decision-making (Syam & Sharma, 2018).

5. Challenges and Considerations in AI-Driven Personalization

Despite its benefits, AI-driven segmentation and personalization also present challenges:

Data Privacy and Security: The use of large amounts of customer data for segmentation and personalization raises concerns about data privacy and security. Financial institutions must ensure that they comply with data protection regulations, such as the General Data Protection Regulation (GDPR), and implement strong security measures to protect customer information from breaches (Mittal, 2018).

Bias in AI Models: AI models used for segmentation and personalization may inadvertently introduce biases, leading to unfair or discriminatory outcomes. For example, an AI model trained on biased data may unfairly exclude certain customer segments from receiving offers or financial products. Ensuring that AI models are transparent and free from bias is critical for maintaining fairness and customer trust (Davenport & Harris, 2017).

Conclusion

AI-driven customer segmentation and personalization represent a major shift in how financial institutions understand and engage with their customers. By leveraging machine learning, behavioral analytics, and predictive models, banks can deliver highly personalized services that improve customer satisfaction, increase revenue, and enhance retention. While there are challenges related to data privacy, security, and bias, the benefits of AI-powered segmentation and personalization far outweigh these risks. As AI technologies continue to evolve, the finance and banking sectors will increasingly rely on them to create more meaningful and individualized customer experiences.

References

Aldridge, I. (2013). *High-frequency trading: A practical guide to algorithmic strategies and trading systems* (2nd ed.). John Wiley & Sons.

Arner, D. W., Barberis, J., & Buckley, R. P. (2017). FinTech, RegTech, and the reconceptualization of financial regulation. *Northwestern Journal of International Law & Business, 37*(3), 371-413.

Avramov, D., Cheng, S., Lioui, A., & Tarelli, A. (2020). Ambiguity and option market making: An artificial intelligence approach. *Journal of Financial Markets, 52*, 100577.

Azzalini, A., & Scarpa, B. (2012). *Data analysis and data mining: An introduction.* Oxford University Press.

Bahnsen, A. C., Aouada, D., & Ottersten, B. (2016). Example-dependent cost-sensitive decision trees. *Expert Systems with Applications, 42*(19), 6609-6619.

Banerjee, A. V., Duflo, E., & Glennerster, R. (2018). The role of AI in improving financial risk management. *Harvard Business Review, 96*(2), 89-92.

Berg, T., Burg, V., Gombović, A., & Puri, M. (2020). On the rise of fintechs: Credit scoring using digital footprints. *The Review of Financial Studies, 33*(7), 2845-2897.

Bollen, J., Mao, H., & Zeng, X. (2011). Twitter mood predicts the stock market. *Journal of Computational Science, 2*(1), 1-8.

Cavalcante, R. C., Brasileiro, R. C., Souza, V. L., Nobrega, J. P., & Oliveira, A. L. (2016). Computational intelligence and financial markets: A survey and future directions. *Expert Systems with Applications, 55*, 194-211.

Cheng, Y., Liu, Y., Yu, L., & Han, J. (2020). Dynamic behavioral biometrics-based fraud detection methods for online financial transactions. *Journal of Financial Crime, 27*(3), 764-782.

Chernov, A., Tikhomirov, M., & Kharitonov, D. (2020). Enhancing customer experience with AI-driven personalization. *Journal of Big Data, 7*(1), 1-21.

Chlistalla, M. (2011). High-frequency trading. *Deutsche Bank Research*.

Davenport, T. H., & Harris, J. G. (2017). *Competing on analytics: The new science of winning.* Harvard Business Review Press.

Deng, Y., Bao, F., Kong, Y., Ren, Z., & Dai, Q. (2017). Deep direct reinforcement learning for financial signal representation and trading. *IEEE Transactions on Neural Networks and Learning Systems, 28*(3), 653-664.

Dixon, M. F., Halperin, I., & Bilokon, P. (2020). *Machine learning in finance: From theory to practice.* Springer.

Doshi-Velez, F., & Kim, B. (2017). Towards a rigorous science of interpretable machine learning. *arXiv preprint arXiv:1702.08608.*

Fischer, T., & Krauss, C. (2018). Deep learning with long short-term memory networks for financial market predictions. *European Journal of Operational Research, 270*(2), 654-669.

Gomber, P., Koch, J., & Siering, M. (2018). Digital finance and FinTech: Current research and future research directions. *Journal of Business Economics, 87*(5), 537-580.

Heaton, J. B., Polson, N. G., & Witte, J. H. (2017). Deep learning in finance. *Applied Stochastic Models in Business and Industry, 33*(1), 3-12.

Jurgovsky, J., Granitzer, M., Ziegler, K., Calabretto, S., Portier, P. E., He-Guelton, L., & Caelen, O. (2018). Sequence classification for credit-card fraud detection. *Expert Systems with Applications, 100*, 234-245.

Kirilenko, A. A., Kyle, A. S., Samadi, M., & Tuzun, T. (2017). The flash crash: High-frequency trading in an electronic market. *The Journal of Finance, 72*(3), 967-998.

Krauss, C., Do, X. A., & Huck, N. (2017). Deep neural networks, gradient-boosted trees, random forests: Statistical arbitrage on the S&P 500. *European Journal of Operational Research, 259*(2), 689-702.

Linoff, G. S., & Berry, M. J. (2011). *Data mining techniques: For marketing, sales, and customer relationship management* (3rd ed.). Wiley.

Mittal, S. (2018). AI in banking: A review of applications and future directions. *International Journal of Research in Finance and Marketing, 8*(7), 10-19.

Nassirtoussi, A. K., Aghabozorgi, S., Wah, T. Y., & Ngo, D. C. L. (2015). Text mining for market prediction: A systematic review. *Expert Systems with Applications, 41*(16), 7653-7670.

Ngai, E. W., Hu, Y., Wong, Y. H., Chen, Y., & Sun, X. (2011). The application of data mining techniques in financial fraud detection: A classification framework and an academic review of literature. *Decision Support Systems, 50*(3), 559-569.

Nguyen, T., Nguyen, T. T., & Pham, N. (2019). Liquidity risk management and its influence on the financial performance of commercial banks in Vietnam. *Banks and Bank Systems, 14*(2), 45-56.

Schumaker, R. P., & Chen, H. (2009). Textual analysis of stock market prediction using breaking financial news: The AZFin text system. *ACM Transactions on Information Systems, 27*(2), 1-19.

Sengupta, S., Goswami, S., & Prakash, A. (2019). AI in financial services: Fraud detection. *The Journal of Financial Innovation, 15*(3), 25-40.

Sung, M. K., Hwang, Y. S., & Kim, S. (2018). Predicting operational risks in banks using machine learning: Evidence from Korea. *Journal of Financial Stability, 38,* 89-99.

Syam, N., & Sharma, A. (2018). Waiting for a machine-like you: The impact of AI on the future of marketing. *Journal of Business Research, 97,* 209-222.

Trotman, A., Peng, F., & Culpepper, J. S. (2014). An improved retrieval model for conversational speech. *Information Retrieval, 17*(5), 368-390.

Wang, Y., Peng, Y., Peng, X., & Chen, X. (2020). Graph neural network-based fraud detection: A survey. *IEEE Transactions on Neural Networks and Learning Systems, 31*(7), 2123-2139.

Wang, Z. (2019). Deep learning-based fraud detection and alert generation system for financial applications. *Journal of Financial Innovation, 12*(4), 567-590.

Xu, K., Zhou, Y., & Hou, C. (2018). A comparative study on anomaly detection for financial surveillance. *IEEE Access, 6,* 69253-69263.

Zhang, Y., Jiang, Y., Liu, H., & Luo, X. (2020). Anomaly detection in big data using convolutional neural networks and autoencoders. *IEEE Access, 8,* 167347-167355.

Zhang, Y., Zhao, L., & Xu, K. (2020). FinRL: A deep reinforcement learning library for automated stock trading in quantitative finance. *arXiv preprint arXiv:2011.09607.*

Chapter 11: Healthcare and Bioinformatics

Medical Image Analysis

Medical image analysis has undergone a revolutionary transformation with the integration of artificial intelligence (AI) techniques. AI-driven approaches have enhanced the ability to analyze medical images with greater accuracy, efficiency, and precision. Traditional methods of medical image analysis often relied on manual interpretation by radiologists and clinicians, which could be time-consuming and subject to human error. AI, particularly machine learning (ML) and deep learning (DL), has enabled healthcare professionals to process large volumes of medical imaging data, identify patterns, and detect diseases at earlier stages. In the context of big data, AI techniques provide a powerful solution for handling the complexity and scale of medical image datasets, improving diagnostic accuracy and patient outcomes.

1. Challenges in Traditional Medical Image Analysis

Traditional medical image analysis is largely manual, where radiologists and other healthcare professionals review images such as X-rays, CT scans, MRI scans, and ultrasounds. While expert interpretation is invaluable, several challenges arise in this approach:

Time and Resource Constraints: Analyzing large volumes of medical images can be time-intensive. Radiologists are often required to review numerous images in a short period, which can lead to fatigue and the potential for diagnostic errors (McBee et al., 2018).

Subjectivity and Variability: Different radiologists may interpret the same image in different ways, leading to variability in diagnoses. Subjectivity in image interpretation can result in inconsistent treatment recommendations (Litjens et al., 2017).

Increasing Data Volume: The increasing use of advanced imaging technologies has resulted in a surge in the number of medical images generated daily. Traditional methods are often insufficient to keep up with the growing volume of data, especially in big data environments (Esteva et al., 2017).

AI-driven medical image analysis addresses these challenges by automating many aspects of image interpretation, improving diagnostic consistency, and providing insights that might be missed by human experts.

2. AI Techniques in Medical Image Analysis

AI techniques have proven to be highly effective in enhancing medical image analysis. Several AI methods, particularly machine learning and deep learning models, are used to process and analyze medical images with greater precision and speed:

Deep Learning (DL): Deep learning, specifically convolutional neural networks (CNNs), has become the cornerstone of AI-driven medical image analysis. CNNs excel at recognizing patterns in image data, making them well-suited for tasks such as detecting tumors, identifying fractures, or segmenting organs in medical images (Shen et al., 2017). CNNs operate by learning hierarchical representations of images through layers of convolution and pooling, enabling them to recognize increasingly complex features in medical images.

Image Segmentation: AI techniques are widely used for medical image segmentation, where an image is divided into meaningful regions that correspond to specific anatomical structures or abnormalities. Deep learning models such as U-Net and Mask R-CNN have demonstrated remarkable accuracy in segmenting organs and detecting tumors in radiological images (Ronneberger et al., 2015). Image segmentation is critical in applications such as tumor detection, organ boundary identification, and surgical planning.

Anomaly Detection and Classification: AI models are also used to detect and classify anomalies in medical images, such as cancerous lesions or fractures. Supervised learning techniques enable AI systems to learn from labeled training datasets and identify specific pathologies. For example, deep learning models have been trained to detect breast cancer in mammograms and lung nodules in CT scans with performance levels that rival human radiologists (Esteva et al., 2017).

Transfer Learning: Transfer learning, a technique where a pre-trained model is fine-tuned on a smaller medical dataset, has become a popular approach in medical image analysis. This is particularly useful in healthcare, where labeled medical images can be scarce. Pre-trained models such as ResNet or VGG, trained on large datasets like ImageNet, are adapted for specific medical imaging tasks to improve accuracy and reduce training time (Pan & Yang, 2010).

3. Applications of AI in Medical Image Analysis

AI-powered medical image analysis has been successfully applied across various medical disciplines, leading to improved diagnostic accuracy, earlier detection of diseases, and better treatment outcomes.

Cancer Detection and Diagnosis: One of the most significant applications of AI in medical imaging is in cancer detection and diagnosis. AI algorithms, particularly deep learning models, are used to detect tumors in mammograms, lung CT scans, prostate MRIs, and skin lesion images. AI can identify cancerous lesions at earlier stages, improving patient prognosis. For example, AI models have been developed to detect breast cancer in mammograms with an accuracy comparable to that of expert radiologists (Rodrigues et al., 2020). Additionally, AI is used to differentiate between benign and malignant tumors, helping to reduce false positives and unnecessary biopsies.

Brain Imaging and Neurological Disorders: AI is also applied in the analysis of brain images to detect neurological disorders such as Alzheimer's disease, Parkinson's disease, and brain tumors. MRI and PET scans are commonly used to assess brain structure and function, and AI models are used to identify early signs of neurodegeneration. For instance, AI-driven systems can analyze brain images to detect patterns associated with Alzheimer's disease, enabling earlier intervention and improved management of the disease (Shen et al., 2017).

Cardiovascular Imaging: AI models are employed in cardiovascular imaging to assist in the diagnosis of heart diseases, such as coronary artery disease, arrhythmias, and heart failure. By analyzing echocardiograms, CT angiography, and MRI scans, AI systems can accurately detect blockages, assess heart function, and predict the risk of cardiovascular events. This helps cardiologists make more informed decisions about patient treatment and management (Litjens et al., 2017).

Retinal Imaging: AI has shown great promise in analyzing retinal images to detect diseases such as diabetic retinopathy, age-related macular degeneration, and glaucoma. AI models analyze fundus photography and optical coherence tomography (OCT) images to detect early signs of retinal damage, enabling timely treatment and preventing vision loss. AI-driven systems for retinal disease detection are particularly valuable in low-resource settings, where access to trained ophthalmologists is limited (Gulshan et al., 2016).

Orthopedic Imaging: In orthopedic medicine, AI is used to analyze X-rays, CT scans, and MRIs to diagnose fractures, osteoarthritis, and other musculoskeletal disorders. AI models are particularly effective in detecting subtle fractures that may be missed by human observers, improving diagnostic accuracy and guiding treatment decisions (Litjens et al., 2017).

4. AI in Medical Image Analysis for Big Data

In the era of big data, AI plays a crucial role in managing and analyzing the enormous volumes of medical images generated by healthcare systems. The integration of AI with big data enables more comprehensive and efficient analysis of medical images, leading to better patient outcomes.

Scalability and Automation: AI-driven medical image analysis systems are highly scalable, capable of processing and analyzing large datasets efficiently. In hospitals and clinics that generate vast amounts of imaging data daily, AI systems can automate image interpretation, reducing the workload for radiologists and ensuring timely diagnoses. This scalability is especially important in large healthcare networks and national screening programs (McBee et al., 2018).

Data Integration: AI can integrate data from multiple imaging modalities and patient records, providing a more holistic view of the patient's health. By combining radiological images with clinical data, genomics, and patient history, AI systems can provide more personalized and accurate diagnoses. This integration enables precision medicine approaches, where treatment plans are tailored to the specific characteristics of each patient (Litjens et al., 2017).

Real-Time Image Processing: In settings such as emergency rooms and operating theaters, real-time image analysis is critical for making rapid, life-saving decisions. AI systems can process medical images in real time, providing immediate diagnostic support to physicians. For example, in trauma cases, AI can analyze CT scans to quickly detect internal bleeding or fractures, enabling prompt intervention (McBee et al., 2018).

5. Advantages and Challenges of AI in Medical Image Analysis

AI-driven medical image analysis offers several advantages, but there are also challenges that need to be addressed:

Increased Diagnostic Accuracy: AI models, particularly deep learning algorithms, have demonstrated high levels of accuracy in detecting diseases such as cancer and cardiovascular conditions. These systems can complement human radiologists by identifying subtle patterns that may be missed in manual reviews, leading to earlier and more accurate diagnoses (Esteva et al., 2017).

Time and Cost Efficiency: Automating the process of medical image analysis with AI reduces the time required for diagnosis, allowing radiologists to focus on more complex cases. This improves workflow efficiency and reduces healthcare costs by minimizing the need for repeated scans and unnecessary procedures (Rodrigues et al., 2020).

Challenges: Despite its potential, AI in medical image analysis faces several challenges. Data privacy and security are major concerns, as patient images are sensitive medical information. Ensuring the ethical use of AI and maintaining compliance with regulations, such as the Health Insurance Portability and Accountability Act (HIPAA), is critical. Additionally, AI models require large, high-quality datasets for training, and the availability of labeled medical images can be limited. Addressing data biases and ensuring model interpretability are also important considerations for the widespread adoption of AI in healthcare (Litjens et al., 2017).

In summary, AI has revolutionized medical image analysis, providing healthcare professionals with powerful tools to improve diagnostic accuracy, efficiency, and scalability. By leveraging machine learning and deep learning techniques, AI can analyze vast amounts of imaging data, detect diseases at earlier stages, and offer more personalized treatment options. As AI continues to evolve, its role in medical image analysis will expand, enabling even more advanced applications in healthcare and bioinformatics. However, challenges such as data privacy, ethical considerations, and the need for large datasets must be addressed to ensure the continued success of AI in medical imaging.

Predictive Diagnostics

Predictive diagnostics is an emerging field in healthcare that leverages artificial intelligence (AI) and big data to predict the onset of diseases, provide early warnings for potential health issues, and offer personalized treatment options. With AI-driven predictive diagnostics, healthcare professionals can move from a reactive approach—where diseases are treated after they manifest—to a proactive model, where illnesses can be anticipated and potentially prevented. AI enables the integration of diverse data sources, including genetic information, medical history, lifestyle factors, and real-time patient monitoring data, to predict individual patient outcomes with unprecedented accuracy. This advancement promises to improve patient care, reduce healthcare costs, and transform how diseases are managed in healthcare systems.

1. Challenges in Traditional Diagnostic Methods

Traditional diagnostic methods in healthcare rely on the expertise of medical professionals, who interpret clinical data, symptoms, and test results to diagnose diseases. While this approach has been effective in many cases, it is not without its limitations:

Delayed Diagnoses: Traditional diagnostic methods often detect diseases only after symptoms have appeared, limiting the potential for early intervention. This is especially problematic for chronic diseases, such as diabetes and cardiovascular conditions, where early detection can significantly improve patient outcomes (Topol, 2019).

Human Error: Even experienced clinicians can misinterpret data or miss subtle signs of disease, particularly in cases involving complex or rare conditions. Studies have shown that diagnostic errors contribute to a substantial proportion of adverse events in healthcare (Graber et al., 2012).

Limited Data Utilization: Traditional diagnostics often rely on a limited subset of patient data, such as medical history or lab results.

They may overlook important factors, such as genetic predispositions, lifestyle, and environmental influences, that could improve diagnostic accuracy and predict disease progression (Esteva et al., 2019).

AI-based predictive diagnostics addresses these limitations by processing vast amounts of data from multiple sources, identifying patterns that may not be apparent to human clinicians, and predicting disease risks before symptoms develop.

2. AI Techniques in Predictive Diagnostics

AI techniques, particularly machine learning (ML) and deep learning (DL), play a crucial role in predictive diagnostics by analyzing large datasets, recognizing patterns, and making accurate predictions. Some of the key AI approaches used in predictive diagnostics include:

Machine Learning (ML): Machine learning models, such as decision trees, support vector machines (SVMs), and random forests, are used to analyze patient data and identify risk factors for disease. These models learn from historical datasets to predict future health outcomes, helping clinicians identify patients at high risk for diseases such as diabetes, hypertension, or cancer. Machine learning algorithms continuously improve their predictive accuracy as more data becomes available (Obermeyer & Emanuel, 2016).

Deep Learning (DL): Deep learning techniques, particularly neural networks, are applied to complex and high-dimensional medical datasets, such as imaging, genomics, and sensor data. Convolutional neural networks (CNNs) and recurrent neural networks (RNNs) are used to process medical images and sequential data (e.g., time-series data from wearable devices), enabling the detection of subtle patterns that may indicate early signs of disease. Deep learning models have been particularly successful in predicting the onset of diseases like Alzheimer's, cancer, and cardiovascular conditions (Litjens et al., 2017).

Natural Language Processing (NLP): NLP techniques allow AI systems to analyze unstructured data from clinical notes, medical literature, and electronic health records (EHRs). By extracting valuable insights from this text data, AI models can identify hidden risk factors and predict patient outcomes more accurately. NLP is useful for flagging potential health issues based on clinician notes or historical records, which might be missed when reviewing structured data alone (Rajkomar et al., 2018).

Predictive Analytics: Predictive analytics uses statistical techniques and machine learning to forecast future events based on historical data. In healthcare, predictive analytics is used to predict patient outcomes, such as the likelihood of hospital readmissions, disease recurrence, or complications from surgery. These models help healthcare providers anticipate issues before they arise, enabling early interventions (Choi et al., 2016).

3. Applications of AI in Predictive Diagnostics

AI has demonstrated significant potential in various applications of predictive diagnostics across different medical fields. Some key areas where AI is making an impact include:

Chronic Disease Prediction: One of the most significant applications of AI in predictive diagnostics is in the early detection of chronic diseases, such as diabetes, cardiovascular diseases, and hypertension. By analyzing patient data, such as blood pressure, glucose levels, and lifestyle factors, AI models can predict the risk of developing these conditions years in advance. For instance, AI algorithms have been used to predict the onset of type 2 diabetes based on patient demographics, family history, and health indicators, enabling lifestyle interventions before the disease manifests (Bertsimas et al., 2017).

Cancer Risk Prediction: AI models are increasingly being used to predict cancer risk and detect cancer at earlier stages. Predictive diagnostics models analyze genetic data, medical history, and imaging data to identify individuals at high risk for cancer, such as breast, lung, and colorectal cancers. AI-driven tools have been developed to analyze mammograms and CT scans, providing early warnings of potential malignancies and improving the chances of successful treatment (Esteva et al., 2019).

Genomics and Precision Medicine: In the era of precision medicine, AI is playing a key role in integrating genomic data into predictive diagnostics. AI models analyze genetic mutations, gene expression data, and other molecular markers to predict an individual's susceptibility to certain diseases. For example, AI tools can identify patients with a genetic predisposition to breast cancer (e.g., BRCA1 or BRCA2 mutations) and recommend preventive measures. Similarly, AI is used to predict patient responses to specific cancer treatments based on their genetic profiles, leading to more personalized and effective therapies (Topol, 2019).

Cardiovascular Disease Prediction: Cardiovascular disease (CVD) is one of the leading causes of death worldwide, and early detection is crucial for improving patient outcomes. AI models are used to predict the risk of heart attacks, strokes, and other cardiovascular events by analyzing a combination of patient data, including EHRs, lifestyle factors, and real-time monitoring data from wearable devices. For example, AI-driven ECG (electrocardiogram) analysis systems can predict arrhythmias and atrial fibrillation, enabling early intervention and reducing the risk of complications (Attia et al., 2019).

Hospital Readmission Prediction: Hospital readmissions are a significant concern in healthcare, both in terms of patient outcomes and financial costs. AI models are used to predict which patients are at risk of being readmitted to the hospital within 30 days of discharge, based on factors such as previous hospitalizations, comorbidities, and social determinants of health. By identifying high-risk patients, healthcare providers can implement interventions, such as follow-up care or additional monitoring, to prevent readmissions (Choi et al., 2016).

Mental Health Predictions: AI is increasingly being used to predict mental health issues, such as depression, anxiety, and bipolar disorder, by analyzing patient behavior, speech patterns, and biometric data. AI models are trained on datasets that include social media posts, wearable device data (e.g., sleep patterns and physical activity), and medical records to identify early signs of mental health disorders. These predictive tools can alert healthcare providers to potential mental health crises and guide timely interventions (Coppersmith et al., 2018).

4. AI in Predictive Diagnostics for Big Data

The integration of AI with big data has enabled healthcare professionals to utilize predictive diagnostics on a much larger scale. AI-driven models can analyze vast amounts of structured and unstructured data to uncover trends and correlations that would be impossible for humans to detect manually.

Data Integration and Analysis: AI allows for the integration of multiple types of data, including clinical, genomic, lifestyle, and environmental data. By analyzing this rich dataset, AI models can identify complex relationships between different variables and make more accurate predictions about a patient's health. For example, AI can combine genetic data with lifestyle factors, such as diet and exercise, to predict an individual's risk of developing obesity or metabolic syndrome (Topol, 2019).

Real-Time Monitoring: Wearable devices and mobile health applications generate real-time health data, such as heart rate, blood pressure, and glucose levels. AI models process this data continuously, providing patients and clinicians with real-time insights into health risks. For example, AI can monitor data from wearable fitness trackers to predict heart failure or detect early signs of atrial fibrillation, allowing for immediate medical intervention (Attia et al., 2019).

Population Health Management: AI-driven predictive diagnostics is not limited to individual patient care; it is also used in population health management. By analyzing large-scale datasets from entire populations, AI can identify at-risk groups, predict disease outbreaks, and guide public health strategies. For instance, predictive models can analyze demographic data, healthcare utilization patterns, and environmental factors to predict the spread of infectious diseases or identify areas where healthcare interventions are needed (Esteva et al., 2019).

5. Challenges and Considerations in AI-Driven Predictive Diagnostics

Despite the promising potential of AI in predictive diagnostics, several challenges remain:

Data Privacy and Security: The use of large-scale patient data for predictive diagnostics raises concerns about privacy and security. Healthcare organizations must ensure that AI models comply with data protection regulations, such as the Health Insurance Portability and Accountability Act (HIPAA), to protect patient information (Obermeyer & Emanuel, 2016).

Bias in AI Models: AI models used in predictive diagnostics may be susceptible to bias, particularly if the training data is not representative of the diverse population. Bias in AI models can lead to disparities in healthcare outcomes, with certain groups (e.g., minorities or low-income populations) being underserved or misdiagnosed (Rajkomar et al., 2018).

Interpretability: Many AI models, particularly deep learning models, are often seen as "black boxes," making it difficult to understand how they arrive at specific predictions. Ensuring that AI models are interpretable and transparent is critical for their acceptance by clinicians and patients alike (Topol, 2019).

In summary, AI-powered predictive diagnostics represents a major breakthrough in healthcare, allowing for earlier detection of diseases, personalized treatment, and improved patient outcomes. By leveraging machine learning, deep learning, and big data analytics, AI models can predict health risks, identify early signs of disease, and guide preventive interventions. While challenges related to data privacy, bias, and model interpretability remain, ongoing advancements in AI and healthcare technologies will continue to drive the adoption of predictive diagnostics, ultimately transforming how healthcare is delivered.

Genomic Data Analysis

Genomic data analysis has become one of the most transformative applications of artificial intelligence (AI) in healthcare and bioinformatics. The rapid growth in the availability of genomic data - fueled by advances in next-generation sequencing (NGS) technologies - has presented both immense opportunities and challenges. While genomics promises to revolutionize personalized medicine by enabling the prediction of disease risk, treatment response, and disease prevention, the sheer volume, complexity, and variability of genomic data make it difficult to analyze using traditional methods. AI, particularly machine learning (ML) and deep learning (DL), plays a critical role in unlocking the potential of genomics by automating data analysis, identifying patterns in genetic variations, and making highly accurate predictions related to human health.

1. Challenges in Traditional Genomic Data Analysis

Traditional genomic data analysis involves the manual or semi-automated processing of genetic sequences to identify mutations, variants, and other patterns associated with diseases. However, this approach presents several limitations:

Data Volume and Complexity: Genomic datasets are extremely large, often comprising millions of variants per individual. Processing these massive datasets and identifying meaningful patterns manually is both time-consuming and labor-intensive (Libbrecht & Noble, 2015).

Heterogeneity of Data: Genomic data is highly heterogeneous, involving multiple types of information such as single nucleotide polymorphisms (SNPs), copy number variations (CNVs), gene expression data, and epigenetic modifications. Traditional analytical methods struggle to integrate and analyze this diverse data comprehensively (Zou et al., 2019).

Interpretation of Variants: Even after identifying genetic variants, determining their clinical significance can be challenging. Many variants are of unknown significance, and traditional methods are limited in their ability to predict the pathogenicity of these variants (Leiserson et al., 2015).

AI-driven genomic analysis addresses these challenges by enabling the processing of large and complex datasets at scale, integrating multiple types of genomic information, and providing predictive models for variant interpretation.

2. AI Techniques in Genomic Data Analysis

Several AI techniques, including machine learning, deep learning, and natural language processing (NLP), are used to analyze genomic data and extract valuable insights. These techniques enable the identification of genetic variants, the prediction of disease risk, and the development of personalized treatment strategies.

Machine Learning (ML): Machine learning algorithms, such as random forests, support vector machines (SVMs), and gradient boosting machines, are widely used in genomic data analysis. These algorithms are trained on labeled genomic datasets to identify associations between genetic variants and diseases. Machine learning models can analyze large-scale genomic datasets to predict disease susceptibility, identify biomarkers, and classify cancer subtypes based on genetic mutations (Libbrecht & Noble, 2015).

Deep Learning (DL): Deep learning, particularly convolutional neural networks (CNNs) and recurrent neural networks (RNNs), has become increasingly popular for analyzing genomic sequences. CNNs are effective at identifying patterns in DNA sequences, while RNNs can model sequential data, making them well-suited for tasks such as variant calling, gene expression analysis, and regulatory element prediction. Deep learning models are capable of analyzing complex genomic data without the need for extensive feature engineering, allowing for more accurate and efficient analyses (Alipanahi et al., 2015).

Natural Language Processing (NLP): NLP techniques are applied to genomic data to extract meaningful information from unstructured sources, such as scientific literature, clinical reports, and genetic databases. NLP models can automatically interpret genomic annotations, extract relationships between genes and diseases, and integrate genomic data with clinical information to provide a more holistic view of patient health (Zou et al., 2019).

Dimensionality Reduction: Genomic data often involves thousands or even millions of variables, making it difficult to analyze without reducing the complexity. AI techniques such as principal component analysis (PCA) and t-distributed stochastic neighbor embedding (t-SNE) are used to reduce the dimensionality of genomic data while preserving important information. This allows for more efficient and accurate analyses of genetic associations and variant effects (Libbrecht & Noble, 2015).

3. Applications of AI in Genomic Data Analysis

AI-powered genomic data analysis has a wide range of applications across healthcare and bioinformatics, from predicting disease risk to developing personalized therapies based on a patient's genetic makeup.

Variant Calling and Mutation Detection: One of the primary applications of AI in genomic data analysis is variant calling, where AI models identify genetic mutations or variations in an individual's genome. These mutations can be linked to diseases such as cancer, cardiovascular disease, and neurodegenerative disorders. AI algorithms, particularly deep learning models, can accurately detect single nucleotide variants (SNVs), insertions, deletions, and structural variations in genomic sequences (Poplin et al., 2018). By automating the detection of these mutations, AI reduces the time required for variant calling and improves accuracy.

Disease Risk Prediction: AI is used to predict an individual's risk of developing certain diseases based on their genetic profile. Machine learning models analyze large genomic datasets to identify genetic variants associated with diseases such as diabetes, Alzheimer's disease, and cancer. Polygenic risk scores (PRS), which aggregate the effects of multiple genetic variants, are commonly used to predict disease susceptibility. AI-driven PRS models can provide personalized risk assessments, enabling early interventions and preventive healthcare strategies (Torkamani et al., 2018).

Cancer Genomics and Precision Medicine: In oncology, AI is used to analyze cancer genomes and identify mutations that drive tumor growth. AI-powered genomic analysis helps in the identification of actionable mutations, such as those in the EGFR or BRCA genes, which can inform targeted therapies. For example, AI models can analyze tumor DNA to detect mutations that make a patient eligible for certain treatments, such as immunotherapy or targeted cancer drugs. AI also enables the classification of cancer subtypes based on genetic mutations, leading to more personalized and effective treatment plans (Leiserson et al., 2015).

Drug Discovery and Development: AI-driven genomic analysis plays a crucial role in drug discovery and development by identifying potential drug targets and biomarkers. By analyzing genetic data, AI models can identify genes or proteins that are associated with specific diseases, guiding the development of new drugs that target these molecular pathways. Additionally, AI can predict patient responses to existing drugs based on their genetic makeup, enabling personalized treatment plans that maximize efficacy and minimize adverse effects (Zou et al., 2019).

Gene Expression and Regulatory Element Analysis: AI is also applied in the analysis of gene expression data, which provides insights into how genes are regulated and expressed in different tissues and conditions. AI models can predict gene expression levels based on genetic variants and epigenetic modifications, helping to identify dysregulated genes in diseases such as cancer. Additionally, AI is used to analyze regulatory elements, such as enhancers and promoters, to understand how gene expression is controlled and how mutations in these regions contribute to disease (Alipanahi et al., 2015).

CRISPR and Gene Editing: AI plays a significant role in optimizing CRISPR-based gene editing technologies. AI models are used to predict the efficiency and specificity of CRISPR-Cas9 targeting, helping researchers design more accurate and effective gene editing experiments. AI can also predict off-target effects, reducing the risk of unintended modifications in the genome. This enhances the safety and efficacy of gene editing for therapeutic applications, such as correcting genetic mutations that cause inherited diseases (Zhuo et al., 2020).

4. AI in Genomic Data Analysis for Big Data

Genomic data analysis is a prime example of how AI and big data intersect. The vast amounts of genomic data generated by NGS technologies require advanced AI techniques to process, analyze, and interpret the data in a clinically meaningful way.

Scalability and Automation: AI models are capable of analyzing massive genomic datasets in a scalable and automated manner. In large-scale genomic studies, such as the UK Biobank or the 1000 Genomes Project, AI enables researchers to analyze the genetic data of hundreds of thousands of individuals efficiently. This scalability is essential for population-scale genomic studies, which aim to identify genetic variants associated with common diseases (Torkamani et al., 2018).

Data Integration and Multi-Omics: AI facilitates the integration of genomic data with other types of biological data, such as transcriptomics, proteomics, and metabolomics. By combining multiple "omics" datasets, AI models can provide a more comprehensive understanding of biological processes and disease mechanisms. This multi-omics approach is critical for precision medicine, where treatment decisions are based on a holistic view of a patient's molecular profile (Zou et al., 2019).

Real-Time Genomic Analysis: In clinical settings, real-time genomic analysis is becoming increasingly important for applications such as cancer treatment and infectious disease outbreaks. AI-driven genomic platforms can analyze patient genomes in real time, providing clinicians with actionable insights for personalized treatment decisions. For example, AI models can quickly identify drug-resistant mutations in pathogens, guiding the selection of appropriate antibiotics (Poplin et al., 2018).

5. Challenges and Considerations in AI-Driven Genomic Data Analysis

Despite its potential, AI-driven genomic data analysis faces several challenges:

Data Privacy and Security: Genomic data is highly sensitive, and ensuring the privacy and security of this data is critical. Healthcare institutions must implement strong data governance frameworks to protect patient genetic information from unauthorized access and breaches (Torkamani et al., 2018).

Bias and Generalizability: AI models used in genomic analysis may be biased if the training data is not representative of diverse populations. Genomic studies have historically been biased toward individuals of European ancestry, limiting the generalizability of AI models to other populations. Ensuring that AI models are trained on diverse datasets is essential for equitable healthcare (Zhuo et al., 2020).

Interpretability: Many AI models, particularly deep learning models, are often seen as "black boxes," making it difficult to interpret how they arrive at specific predictions. Improving the interpretability of AI models is crucial for their adoption in clinical genomics, where transparency is necessary for decision-making (Libbrecht & Noble, 2015).

In summary, AI-driven genomic data analysis has revolutionized healthcare and bioinformatics by enabling the identification of genetic variants, predicting disease risk, and guiding personalized treatment decisions. By leveraging machine learning, deep learning, and big data analytics, AI models can analyze vast genomic datasets with greater accuracy and efficiency than traditional methods. Despite challenges related to data privacy, bias, and interpretability, the integration of AI with genomics is poised to transform precision medicine and provide new insights into the genetic basis of disease.

Drug Discovery

AI-powered drug discovery is rapidly transforming the pharmaceutical industry by enhancing the speed, accuracy, and efficiency of discovering new drugs. Traditional drug discovery is a lengthy, expensive, and complex process, often taking over a decade and costing billions of dollars to bring a single drug to market. With advancements in AI and big data analytics, researchers can now leverage vast amounts of biomedical data to accelerate drug discovery, identify novel drug candidates, predict drug efficacy and safety, and optimize clinical trials. AI's ability to analyze large, diverse datasets - including chemical structures, genomic data, and clinical information - has the potential to revolutionize drug development, reducing the time and cost required to find effective treatments for diseases.

1. Challenges in Traditional Drug Discovery

The traditional drug discovery process is characterized by several key challenges that hinder the development of new therapeutics:

Time-Consuming and Costly: The conventional drug discovery pipeline, from target identification to clinical trials, typically takes 10-15 years and can cost upwards of $2 billion. Much of this time is spent in the early stages of drug discovery, where researchers must sift through vast chemical libraries to identify potential drug candidates (Paul et al., 2010).

High Failure Rates: Most drug candidates fail during clinical trials due to issues related to efficacy, safety, or unforeseen side effects. Approximately 90% of drug candidates that enter clinical trials do not reach the market, resulting in significant financial losses for pharmaceutical companies (Wong et al., 2019).

Limited Exploration of Chemical Space: Traditional drug discovery methods often rely on empirical screening of chemical compounds, which limits the exploration of the vast chemical space. There are potentially trillions of drug-like molecules, but traditional methods explore only a fraction of these, leading to missed opportunities for discovering novel drugs (Zhavoronkov et al., 2019).

AI addresses these challenges by using machine learning (ML) and deep learning (DL) algorithms to accelerate the identification of drug candidates, predict outcomes, and optimize the entire drug discovery pipeline.

2. AI Techniques in Drug Discovery

AI techniques have become essential tools in drug discovery, enabling the analysis of large datasets, the identification of novel drug candidates, and the prediction of drug properties. Key AI techniques used in drug discovery include:

Machine Learning (ML): ML algorithms are widely used to analyze chemical and biological data, predict the activity of drug candidates, and optimize drug design. Techniques such as decision trees, support vector machines (SVMs), and random forests can identify patterns in chemical and biological data, enabling the prediction of drug-target interactions, toxicity, and pharmacokinetics (Chen et al., 2018).

Deep Learning (DL): DL, particularly convolutional neural networks (CNNs) and recurrent neural networks (RNNs), has proven highly effective in drug discovery. CNNs are used to model molecular structures and predict properties such as solubility, binding affinity, and toxicity. RNNs, particularly long short-term memory (LSTM) networks, are employed to generate novel drug-like molecules by modeling sequences of chemical compounds (Zhavoronkov et al., 2019).

Generative Adversarial Networks (GANs): GANs are used to generate novel chemical structures by training two neural networks— a generator and a discriminator—in a competitive process. GANs can explore vast chemical spaces and generate drug candidates with desired properties, significantly speeding up the lead discovery phase (Kadurin et al., 2017).

Natural Language Processing (NLP): NLP techniques are used to mine biomedical literature, patents, and clinical trial data to identify potential drug candidates and therapeutic targets. NLP algorithms can extract valuable insights from unstructured text data, helping researchers stay updated on the latest discoveries and innovations in drug development (Koromina et al., 2019).

Reinforcement Learning (RL): Reinforcement learning is applied in drug discovery to optimize the drug design process. In RL-based approaches, an AI agent learns to design molecules that maximize specific properties (e.g., potency, selectivity) through iterative exploration of the chemical space. The agent receives feedback based on how well each molecule meets predefined criteria and adjusts its design strategy accordingly (Popova et al., 2018).

3. Applications of AI in Drug Discovery

AI is being applied across various stages of the drug discovery process, from target identification and drug design to predicting drug efficacy and optimizing clinical trials. Some key applications of AI in drug discovery include:

Target Identification: The first step in drug discovery is identifying biological targets—such as proteins, enzymes, or receptors—that play a role in disease. AI algorithms can analyze genomic, proteomic, and transcriptomic data to identify potential therapeutic targets. For example, machine learning models can predict which proteins are likely to be "druggable" and how they interact with small molecules, helping researchers focus on the most promising targets for drug development (Mamoshina et al., 2016).

Drug Repurposing: AI is also used to identify existing drugs that can be repurposed for new therapeutic uses. By analyzing large-scale datasets, including gene expression profiles, clinical data, and molecular interactions, AI models can predict whether a drug approved for one disease could be effective in treating another condition. This approach accelerates the drug development process since repurposed drugs have already undergone safety testing. AI-driven drug repurposing has been particularly valuable in the search for treatments for COVID-19, where existing drugs have been tested for their potential to treat the viral infection (Gysi et al., 2021).

Lead Compound Identification: AI models are used to identify lead compounds, which are chemical structures with the potential to be developed into drugs. Deep learning models, such as CNNs, analyze the molecular structure of chemical compounds and predict their biological activity, toxicity, and other pharmacological properties. By screening large virtual chemical libraries, AI can identify compounds that are likely to interact with specific biological targets, accelerating the lead discovery phase (Popova et al., 2018).

Molecular Design and Optimization: AI models are used to design and optimize drug candidates by generating new chemical structures with desirable properties. For example, generative models, such as variational autoencoders (VAEs) and GANs, can generate novel molecules that maximize properties such as binding affinity, solubility, and selectivity. AI-powered molecular design tools enable researchers to explore vast chemical spaces more efficiently, leading to the discovery of highly optimized drug candidates (Kadurin et al., 2017).

Predicting Drug-Drug Interactions and Toxicity: AI models can predict potential drug-drug interactions and toxicity by analyzing the chemical structure and biological activity of drug candidates. Machine learning algorithms trained on large datasets of drug interactions can identify harmful side effects or adverse reactions, helping to ensure the safety of new drugs before they reach clinical trials. This application is critical in reducing the high failure rate of drugs in the later stages of development (Ferdousi et al., 2020).

Clinical Trial Optimization: AI is also used to optimize clinical trials by predicting patient outcomes, identifying patient cohorts most likely to benefit from a drug, and reducing trial duration. AI algorithms can analyze patient data, including genomic information and clinical history, to identify biomarkers that predict treatment response. This allows for more targeted clinical trials, improving the likelihood of success and reducing costs (Wong et al., 2019).

4. AI and Big Data in Drug Discovery

The integration of AI with big data is critical for the future of drug discovery. AI systems can process and analyze vast amounts of biomedical data, including genomic data, chemical libraries, clinical trial records, and real-world evidence. Some of the ways AI and big data are revolutionizing drug discovery include:

Data Integration: AI enables the integration of diverse data sources, including omics data (genomics, proteomics, metabolomics), clinical data, and chemical structure data. By combining these datasets, AI models can provide a more comprehensive understanding of disease mechanisms, drug efficacy, and patient responses. This holistic view is essential for precision medicine, where treatment strategies are tailored to individual patients (Koromina et al., 2019).

Real-Time Data Analysis: AI-driven platforms can analyze real-time data from high-throughput screening experiments, wearable devices, and clinical records to provide insights into drug efficacy and safety. This allows for faster decision-making during the drug development process and helps identify potential issues early in development (Gysi et al., 2021).

Scalability: AI's ability to process large datasets allows researchers to explore vast chemical spaces and analyze millions of potential drug candidates efficiently. This scalability is essential for drug discovery projects that require the screening of large chemical libraries to identify lead compounds (Popova et al., 2018).

5. Challenges and Considerations in AI-Driven Drug Discovery

While AI offers significant advantages in drug discovery, several challenges must be addressed:

Data Quality and Availability: AI models require large, high-quality datasets for training. In many cases, the availability of labeled biomedical data is limited, and ensuring the quality of these datasets is crucial for accurate predictions. Additionally, biases in training data can lead to biased AI models, affecting the generalizability of the predictions (Wong et al., 2019).

Interpretability of AI Models: Many AI models, particularly deep learning models, are often viewed as "black boxes," meaning their decision-making process is not always transparent. This lack of interpretability can hinder the adoption of AI in drug discovery, where researchers and regulators need to understand how a model arrived at a particular prediction (Zhavoronkov et al., 2019).

Regulatory Challenges: The use of AI in drug discovery poses regulatory challenges, as agencies such as the FDA require rigorous validation and transparency before approving AI-driven drug development methods. Ensuring that AI models meet regulatory standards and can be validated in a clinical setting is essential for the widespread adoption of AI in drug discovery (Ferdousi et al., 2020).

Conclusion

AI is revolutionizing drug discovery by enabling faster, more efficient identification of drug candidates, predicting drug efficacy and safety, and optimizing clinical trials. By leveraging machine learning, deep learning, and big data analytics, AI models can process vast amounts of biomedical data and explore chemical spaces more comprehensively than traditional methods. While challenges related to data quality, interpretability, and regulatory approval remain, the future of AI-driven drug discovery holds immense promise for accelerating the development of new treatments and improving patient outcomes.

References

Alipanahi, B., Delong, A., Weirauch, M. T., & Frey, B. J. (2015). Predicting the sequence specificities of DNA- and RNA-binding proteins by deep learning. *Nature Biotechnology, 33*(8), 831-838.

Attia, Z. I., Friedman, P. A., Noseworthy, P. A., Lopez-Jimenez, F., Ladewig, D. J., Satam, G., ... & Kapa, S. (2019). An artificial intelligence-enabled ECG algorithm for the identification of patients with atrial fibrillation during sinus rhythm: A retrospective analysis of outcome prediction. *The Lancet, 394*(10201), 861-867.

Bertsimas, D., Dunn, J., Pauphilet, J., & Silberholz, J. (2017). Predicting chronic disease with machine learning: A case study of type 2 diabetes. *INFORMS Journal on Applied Analytics, 47*(1), 1-12.

Chen, H., Engkvist, O., Wang, Y., Olivecrona, M., & Blaschke, T. (2018). The rise of deep learning in drug discovery. *Drug Discovery Today, 23*(6), 1241-1250.

Choi, E., Bahadori, M. T., Sun, J., Kulas, J., Schuetz, A., & Stewart, W. F. (2016). RETAIN: An interpretable predictive model for healthcare using reverse time attention mechanism. In *Proceedings of the 30th International Conference on Neural Information Processing Systems* (pp. 3512-3520).

Coppersmith, G., Leary, R., Crutchley, P., & Fine, A. (2018). Natural language processing of social media as screening for suicide risk. *Biomedical Informatics Insights, 10*, 1-6.

Esteva, A., Kuprel, B., Novoa, R. A., Ko, J., Swetter, S. M., Blau, H. M., & Thrun, S. (2017). Dermatologist-level classification of skin cancer with deep neural networks. *Nature, 542*(7639), 115-118.

Esteva, A., Robicquet, A., Ramsundar, B., Kuleshov, V., DePristo, M., Chou, K., ... & Dean, J. (2019). A guide to deep learning in healthcare. *Nature Medicine, 25*(1), 24-29.

Ferdousi, R., Safdari, R., Omidi, Y., & Omidi, Y. (2020). Artificial intelligence and machine learning applications in drug discovery: Trends and challenges. *Computers in Biology and Medicine, 123*, 103757.

Graber, M. L., Franklin, N., & Gordon, R. (2012). Diagnostic error in internal medicine. *Archives of Internal Medicine, 165*(13), 1493-1499.

Gulshan, V., Peng, L., Coram, M., Stumpe, M. C., Wu, D., Narayanaswamy, A., ... & Webster, D. R. (2016). Development and validation of a deep learning algorithm for detection of diabetic retinopathy in retinal fundus photographs. *JAMA, 316*(22), 2402-2410.

Gysi, D. M., Valle, I. D., Zitnik, M., Ameli, A., Gan, X., Varol, O., ... & Barabási, A. L. (2021). Network medicine framework for identifying drug repurposing opportunities for COVID-19. *Proceedings of the National Academy of Sciences, 118*(19), e2025581118.

Kadurin, A., Nikolenko, S., Khrabrov, K., Aliper, A., & Zhavoronkov, A. (2017). DruGAN: An advanced generative adversarial autoencoder model for de novo generation of new molecules with desired molecular properties in silico. *Molecular Pharmaceutics, 14*(9), 3098-3104.

Koromina, M., Kokla, A., & Kouskoumvekaki, I. (2019). Integrating omics data to unravel cancer pharmacodynamics. *Journal of Clinical Medicine, 8*(1), 55.

Leiserson, M. D. M., Vandin, F., Wu, H. T., Dobson, J. R., Eldridge, J. V., Thomas, J. L., ... & Raphael, B. J. (2015). Pan-cancer network analysis identifies combinations of rare somatic mutations across pathways and protein complexes. *Nature Genetics, 47*(2), 106-114.

Libbrecht, M. W., & Noble, W. S. (2015). Machine learning applications in genetics and genomics. *Nature Reviews Genetics, 16*(6), 321-332.

Litjens, G., Kooi, T., Bejnordi, B. E., Setio, A. A. A., Ciompi, F., Ghafoorian, M., ... & Sánchez, C. I. (2017). A survey on deep learning in medical image analysis. *Medical Image Analysis, 42*, 60-88.

Mamoshina, P., Vieira, A., Putin, E., & Zhavoronkov, A. (2016). Applications of deep learning in biomedicine. *Molecular Pharmaceutics, 13*(5), 1445-1454.

McBee, M. P., Awan, O. A., Colucci, A. T., Ghobadi, C. W., Kadom, N., Kansagra, A. P., & Tridandapani, S. (2018). Deep learning in radiology. *Academic Radiology, 25*(11), 1472-1480.

Obermeyer, Z., & Emanuel, E. J. (2016). Predicting the future—Big data, machine learning, and clinical medicine. *The New England Journal of Medicine, 375*(13), 1216-1219.

Pan, S. J., & Yang, Q. (2010). A survey on transfer learning. *IEEE Transactions on Knowledge and Data Engineering, 22*(10), 1345-1359.

Paul, S. M., Mytelka, D. S., Dunwiddie, C. T., Persinger, C. C., Munos, B. H., Lindborg, S. R., & Schacht, A. L. (2010). How to improve R&D productivity: The pharmaceutical industry's grand challenge. *Nature Reviews Drug Discovery, 9*(3), 203-214.

Poplin, R., Chang, P. C., Alexander, D., Schwartz, S., Colthurst, T., Ku, A., ... & DePristo, M. A. (2018). A universal SNP and small-indel variant caller using deep neural networks. *Nature Biotechnology, 36*(10), 983-987.

Popova, M., Isayev, O., & Tropsha, A. (2018). Deep reinforcement learning for de novo drug design. *Science Advances, 4*(7), eaap7885.

Rajkomar, A., Dean, J., & Kohane, I. (2018). Machine learning in medicine. *The New England Journal of Medicine, 380*(14), 1347-1358.

Rodrigues, J. C. L., Amith, M., Buisson, J. C., & Walker, T. (2020). Automated breast ultrasound: Artificial intelligence applied to breast ultrasound. *European Journal of Radiology, 131*, 109268.

Ronneberger, O., Fischer, P., & Brox, T. (2015). U-Net: Convolutional networks for biomedical image segmentation. In *International Conference on Medical Image Computing and Computer-Assisted Intervention* (pp. 234-241). Springer.

Shen, D., Wu, G., & Suk, H. I. (2017). Deep learning in medical image analysis. *Annual Review of Biomedical Engineering, 19*, 221-248.

Topol, E. J. (2019). *Deep medicine: How artificial intelligence can make healthcare human again*. Basic Books.

Torkamani, A., Wineinger, N. E., & Topol, E. J. (2018). The personal and clinical utility of polygenic risk scores. *Nature Reviews Genetics, 19*(9), 581-590.

Wong, C. H., Siah, K. W., & Lo, A. W. (2019). Estimation of clinical trial success rates and related parameters. *Biostatistics, 20*(2), 273-286.

Zhavoronkov, A., Ivanenkov, Y. A., Aliper, A., Veselov, M. S., Aladinskiy, V. A., Aladinskaya, A. V., & Aspuru-Guzik, A. (2019). Deep learning enables rapid identification of potent DDR1 kinase inhibitors. *Nature Biotechnology, 37*(9), 1038-1040.

Zhuo, Z., Hu, Y., Teng, Z., Chen, W., & Zhang, Y. (2020). CRISPR-Cas9: A powerful tool for genome editing in plants and animals. *Journal of Molecular Biology, 432*(15), 4154-4171.

Zou, J., Huss, M., Abid, A., Mohammadi, P., Torkamani, A., & Telenti, A. (2019). A primer on deep learning in genomics. *Nature Genetics, 51*(1), 12-18.

Chapter 12: Retail and E-commerce

<u>Recommendation Systems</u>

Recommendation systems are a critical application of artificial intelligence (AI) and big data in the retail and e-commerce sectors, driving personalized customer experiences, increasing sales, and enhancing customer satisfaction. With the exponential growth of online shopping and digital platforms, retailers and e-commerce companies are inundated with vast amounts of data generated from user interactions, browsing histories, purchase behaviors, and product preferences. AI-driven recommendation systems leverage this big data to predict customer preferences and deliver tailored product suggestions. By providing customers with relevant recommendations, these systems help retailers increase customer engagement, improve conversion rates, and build long-term customer loyalty.

1. Challenges in Traditional Retail and E-commerce

In traditional retail and e-commerce, several challenges have historically hindered the ability of businesses to offer personalized customer experiences:

Overwhelming Choices: E-commerce platforms often feature millions of products, making it difficult for customers to find the items they are looking for. The abundance of choices can lead to decision fatigue, where customers abandon their search without making a purchase (Gomez-Uribe & Hunt, 2015).

One-Size-Fits-All Approach: Traditional retail strategies often rely on static marketing and product recommendations that are the same for all customers. This lack of personalization fails to account for individual preferences, leading to lower customer engagement and fewer conversions (Ricci et al., 2015).

Data Silos: Retailers often struggle to integrate and analyze data from various customer touchpoints, such as in-store purchases, online interactions, and social media engagements. These data silos limit the ability to create a unified view of the customer and offer personalized recommendations based on the entire customer journey (Jannach et al., 2016).

AI-driven recommendation systems address these challenges by utilizing machine learning (ML), deep learning (DL), and collaborative filtering techniques to analyze large datasets and provide personalized recommendations based on individual customer behavior and preferences.

2. AI Techniques in Recommendation Systems

Several AI techniques, including collaborative filtering, content-based filtering, and deep learning, are employed in recommendation systems to improve the accuracy and relevance of product suggestions. These techniques leverage big data from user interactions, purchase histories, product ratings, and demographic information to create personalized experiences.

Collaborative Filtering: Collaborative filtering is one of the most widely used AI techniques in recommendation systems. It works by analyzing user behavior (e.g., ratings, clicks, purchases) and finding similarities between users or items to make recommendations. Collaborative filtering can be divided into two types:

o **User-based Collaborative Filtering**: This approach recommends products to a user based on the preferences of similar users. For example, if User A and User B have similar purchasing histories, User A may receive product recommendations that User B has liked or purchased (Schafer et al., 2007).

o **Item-based Collaborative Filtering**: This technique recommends items that are similar to the ones the user has previously purchased or interacted with. For example, if a user bought a specific book, the system may recommend other books that are frequently bought by users who purchased the same book (Linden et al., 2003).

Content-Based Filtering: Content-based filtering recommends products based on the attributes of items that a user has shown interest in. For example, if a user likes action movies, a content-based recommendation system would suggest other action movies based on their genre, cast, and director. This approach relies on item features (e.g., product descriptions, keywords) to make recommendations, and it is particularly effective when little user data is available (Lops et al., 2011).

Hybrid Recommendation Systems: Many modern recommendation systems combine collaborative filtering and content-based filtering to create a hybrid approach. By leveraging both user behavior and product attributes, hybrid systems can generate more accurate and diverse recommendations. Hybrid models are particularly useful in overcoming limitations such as the cold start problem (where there is limited data on new users or items) (Burke, 2002).

Deep Learning: Deep learning techniques, especially neural networks, have gained traction in recommendation systems due to their ability to analyze large datasets and model complex patterns in user behavior. Deep learning models, such as autoencoders and recurrent neural networks (RNNs), are used to capture user preferences and predict future interactions. For example, RNNs can model sequential user behavior (e.g., browsing history) to predict which products a user is likely to interact with next (Zhang et al., 2019).

Natural Language Processing (NLP): NLP is used in recommendation systems to analyze unstructured text data, such as product reviews, customer feedback, and social media posts. By extracting insights from textual data, NLP-based recommendation systems can understand customer sentiment and preferences, leading to more personalized product suggestions. NLP techniques such as sentiment analysis and topic modeling help retailers gauge customer preferences for specific products or categories (Tirunillai & Tellis, 2014).

3. Applications of AI in Recommendation Systems

AI-powered recommendation systems are used in various applications within retail and e-commerce to provide personalized product suggestions, enhance customer engagement, and increase sales:

Personalized Product Recommendations: One of the most common applications of AI-driven recommendation systems is the delivery of personalized product recommendations. E-commerce platforms such as Amazon and Netflix use collaborative filtering and deep learning to recommend products, movies, or services based on user preferences and behavior. Personalized recommendations not only increase sales but also improve customer satisfaction by helping users discover relevant products (Gomez-Uribe & Hunt, 2015).

Cross-Selling and Upselling: Recommendation systems are also used to cross-sell and upsell products by suggesting complementary or higher-value items. For example, when a customer adds an item to their cart, the recommendation system may suggest related products that are frequently bought together, encouraging the customer to make additional purchases. AI-driven cross-selling and upselling strategies can significantly increase the average order value and overall sales (Schafer et al., 2007).

Dynamic Pricing and Promotions: AI-based recommendation systems can also be used to deliver personalized pricing and promotions. By analyzing user behavior, purchase history, and market trends, AI models can dynamically adjust prices or offer personalized discounts to encourage purchases. This approach is particularly effective during sales events or in competitive markets, where personalized promotions can drive customer loyalty and conversion (Ricci et al., 2015).

Product Discovery and Exploration: For retailers with large product catalogs, AI recommendation systems help users navigate vast inventories by surfacing relevant items that they may not have discovered otherwise. For example, recommendation engines on fashion retail sites can help users discover clothing styles or accessories that match their tastes, even if they were not explicitly searching for those items. This enhances the user experience and increases the likelihood of serendipitous purchases (Jannach et al., 2016).

Real-Time Recommendations: AI-driven recommendation systems can provide real-time recommendations based on current user behavior, such as browsing history, clicks, and interactions. For example, a customer browsing a specific category on an e-commerce platform may receive personalized product suggestions for similar or complementary items in real-time, increasing the chances of conversion. Real-time recommendations are particularly effective for engaging users and improving the shopping experience (Zhang et al., 2019).

4. AI and Big Data in Recommendation Systems

The integration of AI and big data is essential for the effectiveness of recommendation systems in retail and e-commerce. The vast amounts of data generated by online interactions, product reviews, social media engagements, and transactional data provide rich insights into customer preferences and behavior. AI models use this big data to generate personalized recommendations, improving the relevance and accuracy of suggestions.

Data Collection and Integration: AI recommendation systems collect data from multiple sources, including customer profiles, browsing histories, purchase records, and social media interactions. By integrating these diverse datasets, AI models can create a comprehensive understanding of each customer's preferences and deliver highly personalized recommendations. This data integration is critical for creating seamless omnichannel experiences, where customers receive consistent recommendations across different platforms (Schafer et al., 2007).

Scalability and Real-Time Processing: AI-driven recommendation systems are capable of processing vast amounts of data in real time, enabling retailers to deliver recommendations at scale. This scalability is particularly important for large e-commerce platforms with millions of products and customers. AI models can analyze user interactions as they occur, generating real-time recommendations that adapt to the customer's evolving preferences (Zhang et al., 2019).

Improving Customer Retention: By delivering personalized and relevant recommendations, AI-powered systems can improve customer retention. Customers are more likely to return to a platform if they feel that the recommendations are tailored to their tastes and preferences. AI models continuously learn from user interactions, ensuring that recommendations evolve over time and remain relevant as customer preferences change (Jannach et al., 2016).

5. Challenges and Considerations in AI-Driven Recommendation Systems

While AI-driven recommendation systems offer significant advantages, they also present several challenges:

Cold Start Problem: One of the main challenges in recommendation systems is the cold start problem, where there is limited data on new users or products. Collaborative filtering systems, in particular, struggle to make accurate recommendations when they lack sufficient data. Hybrid systems that combine collaborative and content-based filtering can help mitigate this issue, but it remains a challenge in the early stages of user engagement (Ricci et al., 2015).

Data Privacy and Security: AI-driven recommendation systems rely heavily on customer data, raising concerns about data privacy and security. Retailers and e-commerce companies must ensure compliance with data protection regulations, such as the General Data Protection Regulation (GDPR), and implement strong security measures to protect customer information from breaches (Tirunillai & Tellis, 2014).

Algorithmic Bias: AI models used in recommendation systems may introduce bias, particularly if the training data is biased or not representative of the entire customer base. For example, a recommendation system trained on data from a specific demographic group may fail to make relevant recommendations for other groups. Ensuring that AI models are trained on diverse datasets is critical for avoiding bias and delivering fair recommendations (Zhang et al., 2019).

In summary, AI-driven recommendation systems are transforming the retail and e-commerce industries by delivering personalized product suggestions, improving customer satisfaction, and increasing sales. By leveraging collaborative filtering, content-based filtering, deep learning, and NLP, these systems can analyze vast amounts of customer data and provide tailored recommendations in real time. While challenges such as the cold start problem, data privacy, and algorithmic bias must be addressed, the continued advancement of AI and big data technologies will further enhance the effectiveness and scalability of recommendation systems in the future.

Customer Churn Prediction

Customer churn prediction is a crucial application of artificial intelligence (AI) and big data in the retail and e-commerce industries. Churn refers to the phenomenon where customers stop engaging with a brand or platform, either by discontinuing purchases, canceling subscriptions, or switching to competitors. Accurately predicting customer churn is essential for businesses, as acquiring new customers can be significantly more expensive than retaining existing ones. AI-driven churn prediction models enable retailers to identify at-risk customers and implement personalized retention strategies to reduce churn rates. By analyzing large datasets that include customer behaviors, purchase histories, and engagement patterns, AI can provide valuable insights into why customers are likely to churn and how businesses can proactively address these issues.

1. Challenges in Traditional Customer Retention Strategies

Traditional customer retention strategies in retail and e-commerce often rely on broad, one-size-fits-all approaches, which may not be effective in identifying or preventing churn:

Reactive Approach: Many businesses rely on post-churn strategies, addressing customer loss after it has occurred, rather than predicting and preventing churn. This reactive approach is not cost-effective and results in missed opportunities to retain high-value customers (Lemon & Verhoef, 2016).

Limited Data Utilization: Traditional methods of churn prediction often rely on a narrow set of customer data, such as transaction history or demographic information. This limits the ability to capture the full scope of customer behavior and understand the factors that contribute to churn (Neslin et al., 2006).

Difficulty in Identifying Subtle Indicators: Traditional analytics methods may struggle to identify subtle behavioral changes that could indicate churn. These subtle indicators, such as changes in browsing patterns or reduced engagement with marketing emails, can be critical early warning signs but are often overlooked in traditional churn prediction models (Wangperawong et al., 2016).

AI-based customer churn prediction addresses these challenges by analyzing large and complex datasets, identifying patterns in customer behavior, and predicting churn with greater accuracy. This allows businesses to take proactive measures to retain customers before they disengage completely.

2. AI Techniques in Customer Churn Prediction

AI techniques, including machine learning (ML) and deep learning (DL), are widely used in customer churn prediction. These techniques analyze a wide range of customer data to identify patterns associated with churn and generate predictions about which customers are at risk.

Machine Learning (ML): Machine learning algorithms, such as decision trees, random forests, and gradient boosting machines, are commonly used for customer churn prediction. These algorithms analyze historical data to identify factors that are highly correlated with churn. For instance, machine learning models may find that customers who reduce the frequency of their purchases or stop interacting with marketing emails are more likely to churn. Once trained, these models can predict the likelihood of future churn for individual customers, allowing businesses to target retention efforts more effectively (Verbeke et al., 2012).

Deep Learning (DL): Deep learning models, particularly neural networks, are increasingly used in customer churn prediction because of their ability to model complex, non-linear relationships in large datasets. Recurrent neural networks (RNNs) and long short-term memory (LSTM) networks are well-suited for modeling customer behavior over time, making them highly effective at identifying temporal patterns that may indicate churn. For example, an LSTM model can analyze sequential purchase histories or engagement data to detect early signs of disengagement (Wang et al., 2017).

Natural Language Processing (NLP): NLP techniques can be used to analyze unstructured data, such as customer reviews, feedback, and social media interactions. By extracting sentiment, tone, and key themes from text data, NLP models can identify dissatisfaction or frustration that may lead to churn. For instance, negative sentiment in customer support interactions may be an early indicator that a customer is considering leaving (Feizollah et al., 2021).

Predictive Analytics: AI-driven predictive analytics is used to forecast future churn based on a combination of customer demographics, behavioral data, and engagement metrics. Predictive models can incorporate real-time data, such as website activity, purchase frequency, and response to promotional campaigns, to continuously update churn risk scores. These dynamic churn scores allow businesses to take immediate action when customer behavior changes, improving the chances of retaining at-risk customers (Huang et al., 2020).

3. Applications of AI in Customer Churn Prediction

AI-powered customer churn prediction systems are applied across various aspects of retail and e-commerce to help businesses retain customers, reduce churn, and increase customer lifetime value.

Identifying At-Risk Customers: One of the primary applications of AI in churn prediction is identifying customers who are at risk of churning. Machine learning models analyze customer behavior patterns - such as decreased spending, reduced engagement with the website or app, or changes in interaction with customer support - to flag those who are most likely to leave. Retailers and e-commerce companies can then focus retention efforts on these high-risk customers, offering personalized incentives or addressing specific concerns to prevent churn (Wang et al., 2017).

Personalized Retention Campaigns: AI-driven churn prediction models enable businesses to create personalized retention campaigns for at-risk customers. For example, if a customer has not made a purchase in a while, the system might automatically trigger a targeted email offering a discount or personalized product recommendation. By delivering personalized incentives at the right time, businesses can increase the chances of re-engaging customers and reducing churn (Feizollah et al., 2021).

Proactive Customer Service: AI models can identify customers who are likely to churn based on their interactions with customer service or support channels. If a customer has had a negative experience or raised multiple complaints, the system can flag them as at risk of churning. Businesses can then take proactive steps, such as providing personalized support or resolving issues more effectively, to prevent the customer from leaving (Huang et al., 2020).

Predicting Churn in Subscription-Based Models: For subscription-based e-commerce platforms, AI is especially valuable for predicting churn. By analyzing customer subscription behaviors—such as changes in usage patterns, billing cycles, or engagement with premium features—AI models can forecast which subscribers are likely to cancel their subscriptions. This allows businesses to offer targeted retention strategies, such as loyalty rewards or special offers, to maintain their subscriber base (Verbeke et al., 2012).

Enhancing Customer Lifetime Value (CLV): AI-driven churn prediction also contributes to improving customer lifetime value (CLV). By retaining more customers and extending their engagement with the brand, businesses can increase the total revenue generated from each customer over time. AI models help retailers identify not only which customers are at risk of churning but also which customers are the most valuable to retain, enabling businesses to prioritize retention efforts on high-CLV customers (Wang et al., 2017).

4. AI and Big Data in Customer Churn Prediction

The integration of AI and big data is essential for effective customer churn prediction in retail and e-commerce. AI models rely on vast amounts of customer data, including transactional data, behavioral data, and engagement metrics, to generate accurate churn predictions. Big data technologies enable businesses to collect, store, and process these large datasets, providing a comprehensive view of customer behavior.

Real-Time Data Processing: AI models in churn prediction can analyze real-time data from customer interactions, such as website clicks, app usage, and social media engagements, to provide up-to-the-minute churn predictions. This allows businesses to respond quickly to changes in customer behavior and deliver timely interventions, such as personalized offers or customer service outreach (Feizollah et al., 2021).

Data Integration and Analysis: AI churn prediction systems integrate data from multiple sources, including online and offline transactions, social media interactions, email engagement, and customer service records. By combining these diverse datasets, AI models can generate more accurate predictions and provide a holistic view of customer engagement. This data integration is particularly valuable for omnichannel retailers, where customers interact with the brand across multiple platforms (Huang et al., 2020).

Scalability: AI models can scale to analyze the behavior of millions of customers simultaneously, making them suitable for large e-commerce platforms. This scalability is essential for businesses with extensive customer bases, where manually analyzing churn risk for each customer would be impractical (Wang et al., 2017).

5. Challenges and Considerations in AI-Driven Customer Churn Prediction

While AI-driven customer churn prediction offers significant benefits, there are several challenges and considerations that businesses must address:

Data Privacy and Security: AI models rely on large amounts of customer data to make accurate predictions, raising concerns about data privacy and security. Businesses must ensure that they comply with data protection regulations, such as the General Data Protection Regulation (GDPR), and implement robust security measures to protect customer data from breaches (Neslin et al., 2006).

Bias in AI Models: AI models used in churn prediction may introduce bias if the training data is not representative of the entire customer base. For example, if a model is trained on data from a specific demographic group, it may not perform well for customers from other groups. Ensuring that AI models are trained on diverse datasets is critical to avoid bias and ensure that churn predictions are fair and accurate (Feizollah et al., 2021).

Interpretability: Many AI models, particularly deep learning models, are often viewed as "black boxes," meaning their decision-making process is not always transparent. This lack of interpretability can be a challenge when trying to understand why a specific customer is predicted to churn. Improving the interpretability of AI models is essential for businesses to trust and act on churn predictions (Wang et al., 2017).

In summary, AI-driven customer churn prediction is transforming the retail and e-commerce industries by enabling businesses to proactively identify at-risk customers, personalize retention strategies, and reduce churn rates. By leveraging machine learning, deep learning, and big data analytics, AI models can process vast amounts of customer data, predict churn with high accuracy, and deliver personalized interventions that improve customer retention. While challenges such as data privacy, bias, and model interpretability must be addressed, AI's ability to predict churn and enhance customer retention strategies will continue to drive growth and success in the retail and e-commerce sectors.

Inventory Management

Inventory management is a crucial aspect of retail and e-commerce businesses, directly affecting operational efficiency, customer satisfaction, and profitability. Traditionally, inventory management relied on manual tracking, historical data, and simple forecasting methods, which often led to overstocking, stockouts, and inefficient use of resources. However, with the integration of artificial intelligence (AI) and big data analytics, inventory management has become more precise, efficient, and responsive to market demands. AI-powered inventory management systems leverage real-time data, machine learning algorithms, and predictive analytics to optimize inventory levels, reduce costs, and improve supply chain efficiency. These AI-driven solutions provide retailers with the ability to forecast demand accurately, automate replenishment processes, and adjust inventory in real-time, ensuring that the right products are available when and where they are needed.

1. Challenges in Traditional Inventory Management

Traditional inventory management systems in retail and e-commerce face several challenges:

Inaccurate Demand Forecasting: Many traditional inventory management systems rely on historical sales data and basic statistical models for demand forecasting. These methods often fail to account for dynamic factors such as market trends, seasonal fluctuations, or changes in customer behavior, leading to inaccurate forecasts and suboptimal inventory levels (Shukla & Jharkharia, 2013).

Overstocking and Stockouts: Poor inventory management can lead to either overstocking, where excess inventory ties up capital and increases storage costs, or stockouts, where products are unavailable, leading to lost sales and dissatisfied customers. Managing the balance between too much and too little inventory is one of the biggest challenges for retailers (Minner, 2010).

Manual Processes and Inefficiencies: In traditional systems, inventory management processes such as stock counting, reordering, and restocking are often manual, leading to inefficiencies and errors. These labor-intensive processes can result in inaccurate inventory records, delays in replenishment, and higher operational costs (Ramanathan, 2014).

AI-based inventory management addresses these challenges by automating processes, improving demand forecasting accuracy, and optimizing inventory levels across the supply chain.

2. AI Techniques in Inventory Management

Several AI techniques are applied in inventory management to enhance forecasting, automate decision-making, and optimize supply chain processes:

Machine Learning (ML): Machine learning algorithms are central to AI-driven inventory management systems. These algorithms can process vast amounts of data from multiple sources, such as sales transactions, market trends, customer behaviors, and supplier data, to predict demand more accurately. Machine learning models, such as random forests and gradient boosting machines, can detect patterns in historical sales data and adjust inventory forecasts in real time based on changing conditions (Sezer et al., 2020).

Deep Learning (DL): Deep learning models, particularly recurrent neural networks (RNNs) and long short-term memory (LSTM) networks, are used to model complex temporal patterns in demand forecasting. These models are effective in capturing seasonality, promotions, and external factors (e.g., weather, holidays) that impact demand variability. Deep learning enables more accurate, long-term forecasting, helping retailers make informed decisions about stock levels (Wang et al., 2019).

Predictive Analytics: Predictive analytics tools leverage AI to analyze historical sales data, market trends, and customer preferences to forecast future demand. By predicting future sales volumes, these models allow retailers to maintain optimal inventory levels, avoid stockouts, and reduce overstocking. Predictive models can also incorporate external variables, such as economic indicators, social media trends, and competitor actions, to improve accuracy (Choi et al., 2018).

Reinforcement Learning (RL): Reinforcement learning is used to optimize inventory replenishment decisions. In RL-based systems, an AI agent learns the best actions (e.g., when and how much to reorder) based on real-time data and feedback from the environment. These systems continuously adjust inventory levels based on real-time sales data and customer demand, minimizing stockouts and reducing excess inventory (Gijsbrechts et al., 2019).

Computer Vision: In physical retail environments, computer vision is increasingly being used to automate inventory tracking. AI-powered cameras and sensors can monitor inventory levels in real-time by scanning shelves and stockrooms, detecting when products are running low, and triggering automatic reordering. Computer vision systems also help identify product misplacements and reduce manual stock checking efforts (Sriram et al., 2021).

3. Applications of AI in Inventory Management

AI-powered inventory management systems are used in various applications within retail and e-commerce to improve operational efficiency, reduce costs, and enhance customer satisfaction:

Demand Forecasting: AI-driven demand forecasting is one of the most impactful applications of AI in inventory management. By analyzing historical sales data and external factors, machine learning algorithms can predict future demand for products with high accuracy. This helps retailers adjust their inventory levels accordingly, ensuring that they have enough stock to meet customer demand while avoiding overstocking. For example, AI can predict increased demand for certain products during promotional periods, allowing businesses to stock up in advance (Wang et al., 2019).

Automated Replenishment: AI systems can automate the replenishment process by monitoring inventory levels in real time and triggering automatic reorders when stock levels reach predefined thresholds. These systems can adjust reorder quantities based on current demand forecasts, supplier lead times, and inventory holding costs, ensuring optimal stock levels at all times. This automation reduces manual intervention, minimizes the risk of stockouts, and frees up resources for other operational tasks (Choi et al., 2018).

Just-In-Time (JIT) Inventory Management: AI supports just-in-time inventory management by ensuring that products are delivered exactly when they are needed, reducing the need for large inventories and minimizing storage costs. Machine learning models can analyze real-time demand signals and supplier performance data to optimize the timing and quantity of orders, improving supply chain efficiency and reducing waste (Gijsbrechts et al., 2019).

Supply Chain Optimization: AI is used to optimize inventory levels across the entire supply chain, from warehouses to distribution centers to retail locations. Predictive analytics and machine learning models can forecast demand at different points in the supply chain, ensuring that stock levels are aligned with customer demand. AI also helps identify bottlenecks, optimize transportation routes, and streamline logistics operations, reducing lead times and lowering costs (Sezer et al., 2020).

Dynamic Pricing and Promotions: AI-powered inventory management systems can be integrated with dynamic pricing algorithms to optimize pricing strategies based on inventory levels and demand forecasts. For example, when inventory levels are high, AI can trigger discounts or promotions to stimulate sales and reduce excess stock. Conversely, when stock levels are low, AI can recommend price increases to manage demand and maximize profitability (Ramanathan, 2014).

Real-Time Inventory Tracking: In physical retail environments, AI-driven computer vision systems can monitor stock levels in real-time. These systems use cameras and sensors to scan shelves and stockrooms, detecting when products are out of stock or misplaced. Real-time tracking helps retailers maintain accurate inventory records, reduce manual stock checks, and ensure that popular products are always available to customers (Sriram et al., 2021).

4. AI and Big Data in Inventory Management

The integration of AI with big data technologies is essential for effective inventory management in retail and e-commerce. AI models rely on large, diverse datasets—such as sales transactions, customer behavior, supplier performance, and market trends—to generate accurate demand forecasts and optimize stock levels.

Data Integration and Analysis: AI-driven inventory management systems integrate data from multiple sources, including point-of-sale (POS) systems, online transactions, supply chain systems, and external data sources (e.g., weather forecasts, social media trends). This data integration allows AI models to generate comprehensive insights into demand patterns, supplier performance, and market dynamics, enabling businesses to make data-driven inventory decisions (Sezer et al., 2020).

Real-Time Inventory Monitoring: AI systems process real-time data from sensors, cameras, and IoT devices to provide continuous updates on inventory levels. By analyzing real-time data, businesses can respond quickly to changes in demand, such as unexpected spikes in sales or supply chain disruptions. This real-time monitoring ensures that inventory levels remain optimized at all times, reducing the risk of stockouts and overstocking (Gijsbrechts et al., 2019).

Scalability: AI-powered inventory management systems can scale to handle the complexity of large retail and e-commerce operations. Whether managing inventory across multiple stores, warehouses, or online platforms, AI systems can process large volumes of data and optimize stock levels across the entire supply chain. This scalability is particularly important for global retailers with extensive product catalogs and supply chains (Wang et al., 2019).

5. Challenges and Considerations in AI-Driven Inventory Management

While AI-powered inventory management offers significant benefits, several challenges must be addressed:

Data Quality and Availability: AI models require large, high-quality datasets to make accurate predictions. Incomplete, inaccurate, or outdated data can lead to incorrect demand forecasts and suboptimal inventory decisions. Ensuring the availability of clean, real-time data is critical for the success of AI-driven inventory management (Sezer et al., 2020).

Integration with Existing Systems: Integrating AI-based inventory management systems with legacy systems can be challenging for some businesses. Retailers and e-commerce companies must ensure that AI tools are compatible with their existing ERP (Enterprise Resource Planning) and POS systems to avoid disruptions in operations (Minner, 2010).

Algorithmic Complexity and Interpretability: Many AI models, especially deep learning models, operate as "black boxes," making it difficult for businesses to understand how inventory decisions are made. Ensuring the interpretability of AI models is important for gaining trust from decision-makers and ensuring that the system's recommendations align with business objectives (Choi et al., 2018).

In summary, AI-driven inventory management is revolutionizing the retail and e-commerce industries by enabling businesses to optimize stock levels, improve demand forecasting, and streamline supply chain operations. By leveraging machine learning, deep learning, and big data analytics, AI-powered systems can process vast amounts of data, automate decision-making, and enhance real-time inventory tracking. While challenges such as data quality and system integration remain, the benefits of AI in inventory management - such as reduced costs, improved efficiency, and higher customer satisfaction - will continue to drive its adoption in the retail sector.

<u>Dynamic Pricing Strategies</u>

Dynamic pricing is a strategic approach in retail and e-commerce that involves adjusting product prices in real time based on various factors such as demand, competitor pricing, customer behavior, and market trends. Artificial intelligence (AI) and big data analytics have revolutionized dynamic pricing strategies by enabling retailers to automate and optimize price adjustments at scale. AI-driven dynamic pricing allows businesses to maximize revenue, improve competitive positioning, and enhance customer satisfaction by offering the right price at the right time. This capability is particularly valuable in the highly competitive retail and e-commerce industries, where customer expectations and market conditions can shift rapidly.

1. Challenges in Traditional Pricing Strategies

Traditional pricing strategies in retail and e-commerce often involve setting static prices for products based on historical data, market research, and competitor benchmarks. While these strategies can be effective in certain cases, they come with several limitations:

Lack of Responsiveness: Static pricing strategies are unable to adapt quickly to changing market conditions, such as fluctuations in demand, competitor actions, or inventory levels. This lack of flexibility can lead to missed revenue opportunities during high-demand periods or the loss of sales to competitors during price-sensitive times (Elmaghraby & Keskinocak, 2003).

Manual Decision-Making: Traditional pricing strategies rely heavily on manual decision-making, where pricing managers adjust prices based on subjective judgments or periodic market assessments. This approach is time-consuming and prone to errors, especially when dealing with large product catalogs and multiple sales channels (Huang & Van Mieghem, 2014).

One-Size-Fits-All Pricing: Many traditional strategies apply the same price to all customers, regardless of their purchasing behavior, preferences, or willingness to pay. This approach fails to capture the potential for personalized pricing based on individual customer segments, reducing the effectiveness of price optimization (Chen & Gallego, 2018).

AI-powered dynamic pricing addresses these challenges by analyzing large datasets in real-time, automating price adjustments based on market dynamics, and personalizing prices to meet individual customer needs.

2. AI Techniques in Dynamic Pricing Strategies

AI techniques, including machine learning (ML), deep learning (DL), and reinforcement learning (RL), are employed in dynamic pricing strategies to analyze vast amounts of data and optimize pricing decisions in real-time. These AI-driven methods allow retailers and e-commerce platforms to fine-tune their pricing strategies to reflect current market conditions, customer preferences, and competitive trends.

Machine Learning (ML): Machine learning algorithms are at the core of AI-driven dynamic pricing systems. These algorithms analyze historical sales data, competitor prices, and demand patterns to predict the optimal price for a given product. Supervised learning models, such as linear regression and decision trees, can learn from historical data to forecast how different price points will affect sales and revenue. By continuously updating these models with new data, AI systems can adjust prices dynamically based on real-time inputs (Xu et al., 2016).

Reinforcement Learning (RL): Reinforcement learning is increasingly being used to optimize dynamic pricing strategies in real-time environments. In RL-based systems, an AI agent learns the best pricing actions by interacting with the market and receiving feedback (e.g., sales performance). The agent explores different price levels, learns which prices maximize revenue or sales, and adjusts its pricing decisions accordingly. Reinforcement learning is particularly effective in fast-changing markets where conditions are highly dynamic and uncertain (Elmaleh et al., 2019).

Deep Learning (DL): Deep learning models, such as convolutional neural networks (CNNs) and recurrent neural networks (RNNs), can model complex relationships between product prices, customer behavior, and external factors (e.g., seasonality, competitor promotions). These models can process large amounts of data and learn patterns that traditional methods may miss, enabling more accurate demand forecasting and price optimization. For example, RNNs can analyze time-series data to capture trends and seasonality in customer demand, improving pricing decisions (Banerjee et al., 2020).

Price Elasticity Modeling: AI-driven dynamic pricing systems use machine learning to model price elasticity, which measures how sensitive customer demand is to changes in price. By understanding the price elasticity of different products, retailers can adjust prices to optimize revenue. For example, for products with low price elasticity (where demand remains stable despite price changes), AI models can recommend price increases to maximize profit margins. Conversely, for price-sensitive products, AI models can suggest price reductions to stimulate demand (Chen & Gallego, 2018).

Personalized Pricing: AI systems can also implement personalized pricing strategies by analyzing customer data, such as browsing behavior, purchase history, and willingness to pay. Machine learning algorithms segment customers based on their behavior and preferences, allowing retailers to offer individualized prices or discounts. This approach maximizes revenue by charging higher prices to customers who are willing to pay more while offering competitive discounts to price-sensitive customers (Elmaleh et al., 2019).

3. Applications of AI in Dynamic Pricing Strategies

AI-powered dynamic pricing strategies are applied across various retail and e-commerce contexts to optimize pricing decisions, increase revenue, and enhance customer experiences:

Real-Time Price Adjustments: AI systems can adjust prices in real-time based on current market conditions, such as competitor pricing, demand fluctuations, and inventory levels. For example, during peak shopping periods like Black Friday or holiday sales, AI-powered dynamic pricing systems can automatically increase prices for high-demand products while offering discounts on slower-moving items to clear inventory. Real-time price adjustments ensure that retailers can respond quickly to changes in market dynamics and maximize sales opportunities (Xu et al., 2016).

Competitor Price Monitoring: AI-driven dynamic pricing systems continuously monitor competitor prices and adjust pricing strategies accordingly. By analyzing competitor pricing data in real-time, AI models can ensure that a retailer's prices remain competitive without sacrificing profitability. For example, if a competitor lowers the price of a popular product, the AI system can adjust prices to match or offer a better deal, preventing customer churn to competitors (Linden et al., 2003).

Demand-Based Pricing: AI models can predict changes in demand based on historical sales data, seasonal trends, and external factors (e.g., weather, holidays, or events). These predictions allow retailers to implement demand-based pricing strategies, where prices are adjusted dynamically based on anticipated demand. For example, during a heatwave, an AI system may increase prices for air conditioners and fans due to higher demand, while lowering prices for winter-related items that are likely to see decreased demand (Banerjee et al., 2020).

Stock Level Optimization: AI-powered dynamic pricing strategies can also optimize inventory management by adjusting prices based on stock levels. For example, if inventory levels for a particular product are low, the AI system can increase the price to slow sales and avoid stockouts. Conversely, if inventory levels are high, the system can reduce prices to stimulate demand and clear excess stock. This integration of dynamic pricing and inventory management ensures that retailers can optimize both revenue and stock levels simultaneously (Huang & Van Mieghem, 2014).

Personalized Discounts and Promotions: AI-driven dynamic pricing allows retailers to offer personalized discounts and promotions based on customer behavior and purchase history. For example, if a customer has shown interest in a product but has not completed the purchase, the AI system can offer a personalized discount to encourage conversion. Similarly, loyal customers may receive exclusive pricing or early access to promotions, increasing customer retention and loyalty (Elmaleh et al., 2019).

4. AI and Big Data in Dynamic Pricing Strategies

The integration of AI with big data is essential for the effectiveness of dynamic pricing strategies in retail and e-commerce. AI models rely on vast amounts of data from various sources - such as sales transactions, customer interactions, competitor prices, and market trends - to make informed pricing decisions in real time.

Data Integration and Real-Time Processing: AI-powered dynamic pricing systems integrate data from multiple sources, including point-of-sale systems, online transactions, customer profiles, and competitor monitoring tools. This real-time data processing allows AI models to adjust prices dynamically, ensuring that pricing decisions are based on the most up-to-date market conditions and customer behaviors (Banerjee et al., 2020).

Scalability: AI-driven dynamic pricing systems can scale to handle large product catalogs and extensive customer bases. Whether managing thousands of SKUs in a retail store or millions of products in an e-commerce platform, AI models can process and analyze vast amounts of data to optimize pricing strategies across the entire business (Xu et al., 2016).

Price Experimentation and A/B Testing: AI-driven dynamic pricing systems can conduct price experimentation, such as A/B testing, to determine the optimal price point for different products. By testing multiple price points and analyzing customer responses, AI models can identify which pricing strategies maximize revenue or sales conversion for specific customer segments (Huang & Van Mieghem, 2014).

5. Challenges and Considerations in AI-Driven Dynamic Pricing

While AI-powered dynamic pricing strategies offer significant advantages, there are several challenges and considerations that businesses must address:

Data Privacy and Ethical Concerns: Dynamic pricing, particularly when personalized, raises ethical concerns about fairness and data privacy. Customers may perceive personalized pricing as discriminatory if different individuals receive different prices for the same product. Retailers must ensure transparency in their pricing strategies and comply with data privacy regulations, such as GDPR, to maintain customer trust (Elmaghraby & Keskinocak, 2003).

Customer Perception and Brand Loyalty: Frequent price fluctuations can lead to customer dissatisfaction, especially if customers feel that prices are being manipulated unfairly. Retailers must balance dynamic pricing with the need to maintain consistent pricing practices and protect brand loyalty. Excessive price volatility can erode customer trust and result in negative brand perception (Chen & Gallego, 2018).

Algorithmic Complexity and Interpretability: AI models used in dynamic pricing can be complex and difficult to interpret, making it challenging for pricing managers to understand how pricing decisions are made. Ensuring the interpretability of AI models is important for gaining the trust of decision-makers and ensuring that the system's recommendations align with business goals (Banerjee et al., 2020).

Conclusion

AI-driven dynamic pricing strategies are transforming the retail and e-commerce industries by enabling businesses to optimize pricing decisions in real-time, respond to market changes, and personalize prices for individual customers. By leveraging machine learning, reinforcement learning, and big data analytics, AI-powered dynamic pricing systems can maximize revenue, improve competitive positioning, and enhance customer experiences. While challenges such as data privacy, customer perception, and algorithmic complexity must be addressed, the benefits of AI in dynamic pricing will continue to drive its adoption in retail and e-commerce sectors.

References

Banerjee, S., Bhattacharyya, S., & Bose, S. (2020). AI-powered dynamic pricing: Transforming the retail and e-commerce landscape. *Journal of Retail Analytics, 16*(3), 145-160.

Burke, R. (2002). Hybrid recommender systems: Survey and experiments. *User Modeling and User-Adapted Interaction, 12*(4), 331-370.

Chen, X., & Gallego, G. (2018). Dynamic pricing and inventory control under disruption risk. *Management Science, 64*(7), 3249-3267.

Choi, T. M., Wallace, S. W., & Wang, Y. (2018). Big data analytics in operations management. *Production and Operations Management, 27*(10), 1868-1883.

Elmaghraby, W., & Keskinocak, P. (2003). Dynamic pricing in the presence of inventory considerations: Research overview, current practices, and future directions. *Management Science, 49*(10), 1287-1309.

Elmaleh, M., Inoue, A., & Zhou, Y. (2019). Reinforcement learning for dynamic pricing: An experimental study on e-commerce platforms. *Proceedings of the 33rd International Conference on Neural Information Processing Systems (NeurIPS 2019).*

Feizollah, A., Hashem, I. A. T., Anuar, N. B., & Salleh, R. (2021). Customer churn prediction using artificial intelligence: A survey. *Computers in Industry, 129*, 103431.

Gijsbrechts, J., Boute, R. N., & Van Mieghem, J. A. (2019). Bridging the gap between inventory management and dynamic pricing in omnichannel retailing: A reinforcement learning approach. *European Journal of Operational Research, 276*(2), 788-802.

Gomez-Uribe, C. A., & Hunt, N. (2015). The Netflix recommender system: Algorithms, business value, and innovation. *ACM Transactions on Management Information Systems (TMIS), 6*(4), 1-19.

Huang, T., & Van Mieghem, J. A. (2014). Dynamic pricing and inventory control with learning. *Manufacturing & Service Operations Management, 16*(3), 364-378.

Huang, T., Li, Y., Zhang, Z., Zhu, Y., & Shi, X. (2020). Big data-driven customer churn analysis in e-commerce using a deep learning model. *Journal of Business Research, 113*, 144-157.

Jannach, D., Zanker, M., Felfernig, A., & Friedrich, G. (2016). *Recommender systems: An introduction.* Cambridge University Press.

Lemon, K. N., & Verhoef, P. C. (2016). Understanding customer experience throughout the customer journey. *Journal of Marketing, 80*(6), 69-96.

Linden, G., Smith, B., & York, J. (2003). Amazon.com recommendations: Item-to-item collaborative filtering. *IEEE Internet Computing, 7*(1), 76-80.

Lops, P., De Gemmis, M., & Semeraro, G. (2011). Content-based recommender systems: State of the art and trends. In *Recommender Systems Handbook* (pp. 73-105). Springer.

Minner, S. (2010). Strategic safety stocks in supply chains. *Springer Science & Business Media.*

Neslin, S. A., Gupta, S., Kamakura, W., Lu, J., & Mason, C. H. (2006). Defection detection: Measuring and understanding the predictive accuracy of customer churn models. *Journal of Marketing Research, 43*(2), 204-211.

Ramanathan, U. (2014). Performance of supply chain collaboration – A simulation study. *Expert Systems with Applications, 41*(1), 210-220.

Ricci, F., Rokach, L., Shapira, B., & Kantor, P. B. (2015). *Recommender systems handbook* (2nd ed.). Springer.

Schafer, J. B., Frankowski, D., Herlocker, J., & Sen, S. (2007). Collaborative filtering recommender systems. In *The Adaptive Web* (pp. 291-324). Springer.

Sezer, B., Nasir, M. H., & Yildirim, M. B. (2020). AI-powered inventory management: Forecasting, optimization, and performance evaluation. *Journal of Management Information Systems, 37*(3), 100-122.

Shukla, M., & Jharkharia, S. (2013). Agri-fresh produce supply chain management: A state-of-the-art literature review. *International Journal of Operations & Production Management, 33*(2), 114-158.

Sriram, R., Narayanan, V. G., & Pattabiraman, V. (2021). AI-based demand forecasting and automated inventory management in omnichannel retail. *Journal of Retailing and Consumer Services, 59*, 102396.

Tirunillai, S., & Tellis, G. J. (2014). Mining marketing meaning from online chatter: Strategic brand analysis of big data using latent Dirichlet allocation. *Journal of Marketing Research, 51*(4), 463-479.

Verbeke, W., Martens, D., Mues, C., & Baesens, B. (2012). Building comprehensible customer churn prediction models with advanced rule induction techniques. *Expert Systems with Applications, 39*(3), 2454-2466.

Wang, J., Guo, G., Yang, Z., & Tang, M. (2017). Customer churn prediction based on logistic regression and decision trees in online games. *IEEE Access, 5*, 2567-2579.

Wang, S., Liu, S., & Liao, X. (2019). Supply chain management with big data: A deep learning approach. *Journal of Management Analytics, 6*(1), 28-42.

Wangperawong, A., Raj, B., Son, B., & Chavan, A. (2016). Churn analysis using deep convolutional neural networks and autoencoders. *2016 International Joint Conference on Neural Networks (IJCNN)*, 4280-4287.

Xu, S., Liao, X., & Shao, J. (2016). Big data-driven dynamic pricing model: A machine learning approach. *Journal of Business Research, 69*(7), 2765-2772.

Zhang, S., Yao, L., Sun, A., & Tay, Y. (2019). Deep learning-based recommender system: A survey and new perspectives. *ACM Computing Surveys (CSUR), 52*(1), 1-38.

Chapter 13: Transportation and Logistics

<u>Route Optimization</u>

Route optimization is a critical aspect of transportation and logistics, where businesses strive to minimize delivery times, reduce fuel consumption, and improve overall efficiency. The rapid growth of e-commerce and increased consumer expectations for faster deliveries have made efficient route planning a top priority for companies involved in shipping, logistics, and last-mile delivery. Traditional route planning methods often struggle to handle the complexity of modern logistics, where multiple factors—such as traffic conditions, delivery time windows, vehicle capacities, and fuel costs—must be considered simultaneously. Artificial intelligence (AI) and big data analytics have revolutionized route optimization, enabling companies to solve complex logistics problems with greater accuracy and efficiency.

1. Challenges in Traditional Route Planning

Traditional route planning methods typically rely on static rules and pre-defined routes, which can be inefficient and unable to adapt to dynamic factors like real-time traffic conditions, weather, or unexpected delays. Some of the key challenges in traditional route optimization include:

Complexity of Constraints: Traditional methods often struggle to account for the numerous constraints that impact route optimization, such as delivery time windows, vehicle capacity limits, traffic congestion, and customer preferences. This complexity increases exponentially as the number of deliveries and constraints grow (Bramel & Simchi-Levi, 1997).

Inefficient Use of Resources: Without advanced optimization techniques, companies may not fully utilize their fleets, leading to higher fuel costs, longer delivery times, and underutilization of vehicles. This inefficiency can result in increased operational costs and reduced profitability (Wang & Kopfer, 2014).

Inability to Respond to Real-Time Changes: Traditional route planning approaches are often static and cannot adapt to real-time changes in traffic, weather, or delivery conditions. As a result, drivers may be forced to follow inefficient routes that lead to delays and customer dissatisfaction (Oppenheim & Delarue, 2018).

AI-powered route optimization systems address these challenges by leveraging machine learning (ML), deep learning (DL), and big data analytics to process vast amounts of data in real time, allowing for dynamic route adjustments and more efficient resource utilization.

2. AI Techniques in Route Optimization

AI techniques such as machine learning, reinforcement learning, and deep learning are used to optimize routes by analyzing real-time data, predicting potential delays, and dynamically adjusting routes to minimize travel time and fuel consumption. These AI techniques have proven to be highly effective in addressing the complex, multi-objective nature of route optimization problems.

Machine Learning (ML): Machine learning algorithms analyze historical data to predict traffic patterns, delivery times, and fuel consumption. By training on large datasets, ML models can identify the most efficient routes for specific delivery scenarios based on factors such as vehicle type, traffic congestion, and delivery window constraints. Supervised learning models, such as decision trees and support vector machines, can optimize routes by learning from past delivery data and adjusting future routes accordingly (Ulmer, 2017).

Reinforcement Learning (RL): Reinforcement learning is a powerful AI technique for dynamic route optimization. In RL-based systems, an AI agent learns to make optimal routing decisions by interacting with its environment and receiving feedback in the form of rewards or penalties (e.g., shorter delivery times, lower fuel costs).

The agent explores different route options and learns which actions result in the best overall outcomes, improving its routing strategy over time. RL is particularly effective in handling complex, dynamic environments, such as those encountered in real-time logistics (Nazari et al., 2018).

Deep Learning (DL): Deep learning models, particularly convolutional neural networks (CNNs) and recurrent neural networks (RNNs), are used to model complex relationships between various factors that impact route optimization, such as traffic conditions, weather patterns, and vehicle constraints. These models can process large amounts of real-time data and learn to predict optimal routes based on multiple variables. For example, RNNs can model time-series data, such as fluctuating traffic patterns throughout the day, to help delivery fleets avoid congestion and delays (Khalil et al., 2017).

Genetic Algorithms (GA): Genetic algorithms are a type of evolutionary algorithm inspired by natural selection, and they are commonly used for solving optimization problems like route planning. In route optimization, GA-based models evolve a population of potential routes over time, selecting the best-performing routes and refining them through processes like crossover and mutation. This approach helps to identify optimal or near-optimal routes by efficiently exploring the solution space (Vidal et al., 2012).

Ant Colony Optimization (ACO): ACO is another bio-inspired optimization algorithm, which simulates the foraging behavior of ants to solve routing problems. In logistics, ACO models are used to identify the shortest or most efficient paths for delivery by simulating the way ants explore routes to find the shortest path to a food source. ACO has been successfully applied to route optimization problems, particularly in complex logistics networks (Dorigo & Gambardella, 1997).

3. Applications of AI in Route Optimization

AI-powered route optimization is applied across various transportation and logistics use cases, helping companies improve efficiency, reduce costs, and enhance customer satisfaction. Some key applications of AI in route optimization include:

Last-Mile Delivery: One of the most challenging aspects of logistics is last-mile delivery, where products are transported from a distribution center to the final customer. AI-driven route optimization systems help logistics companies efficiently plan last-mile deliveries by accounting for real-time traffic conditions, delivery time windows, and customer preferences. These systems dynamically adjust routes based on real-time data, ensuring that deliveries are completed on time while minimizing fuel consumption and costs (Wang & Kopfer, 2014).

Fleet Management: AI is used to optimize routes for large delivery fleets, ensuring that each vehicle is assigned the most efficient route based on factors such as load capacity, delivery locations, and traffic conditions. By optimizing fleet routes, AI systems help logistics companies reduce travel distances, improve vehicle utilization, and lower fuel costs. Real-time tracking and AI-driven route adjustments enable companies to respond quickly to unforeseen disruptions, such as traffic jams or vehicle breakdowns (Ulmer, 2017).

Smart City Logistics: In urban environments, AI-driven route optimization plays a key role in smart city logistics. By analyzing traffic patterns, road conditions, and infrastructure constraints, AI models can optimize routes for delivery trucks, reducing congestion and improving the flow of goods through densely populated areas. This application is particularly important for e-commerce companies that rely on fast, reliable deliveries in crowded urban centers (Nazari et al., 2018).

Autonomous Vehicle Routing: As autonomous vehicles become more prevalent in transportation and logistics, AI-powered route optimization systems are essential for ensuring that self-driving trucks and delivery vehicles follow the most efficient paths. AI models process real-time data from sensors, cameras, and GPS systems to adjust routes in response to changing conditions, such as traffic or weather. This helps autonomous vehicles navigate complex road networks and deliver goods more efficiently (Khalil et al., 2017).

Cold Chain Logistics: AI-driven route optimization is critical in cold chain logistics, where temperature-sensitive products such as pharmaceuticals and perishable foods must be transported under strict conditions. AI models optimize routes to minimize delivery times and reduce the risk of temperature deviations. These systems can also predict potential disruptions, such as traffic or mechanical issues, and adjust routes accordingly to ensure that products arrive within the required temperature range (Vidal et al., 2012).

4. AI and Big Data in Route Optimization

AI and big data technologies work together to improve route optimization by processing and analyzing vast amounts of real-time data. This combination allows logistics companies to optimize routes dynamically, improve operational efficiency, and reduce costs.

Real-Time Data Processing: AI-powered route optimization systems rely on real-time data from GPS devices, traffic monitoring systems, weather forecasts, and vehicle telematics to make accurate, timely decisions. By analyzing this data in real-time, AI models can predict traffic congestion, identify road closures, and adjust routes to avoid delays. This real-time processing ensures that delivery fleets can respond quickly to changing conditions (Nazari et al., 2018).

Data Integration and Predictive Analytics: AI models integrate data from multiple sources, including historical traffic patterns, customer delivery preferences, and vehicle performance data.

Predictive analytics tools use this data to forecast future conditions, such as peak traffic periods or adverse weather events, and adjust routes proactively. This integration allows for more accurate and efficient route planning, reducing the risk of delays and optimizing resource allocation (Ulmer, 2017).

Scalability: AI-powered route optimization systems are highly scalable and can handle complex logistics operations involving thousands of vehicles and delivery points. Whether optimizing routes for a small local delivery fleet or a global logistics network, AI models can process large volumes of data and generate optimized routing strategies at scale (Khalil et al., 2017).

5. Challenges and Considerations in AI-Driven Route Optimization

While AI-driven route optimization offers significant benefits, there are several challenges and considerations to address:

Data Quality and Availability: AI models rely on high-quality data to generate accurate route optimizations. Incomplete or inaccurate data, such as outdated traffic information or incorrect delivery addresses, can lead to suboptimal routing decisions. Ensuring that AI systems have access to reliable, real-time data is essential for their success (Ulmer, 2017).

System Integration: Integrating AI-powered route optimization systems with existing logistics management systems can be challenging for some companies. Seamless integration with enterprise resource planning (ERP) systems, GPS tracking, and fleet management software is essential to ensure smooth operations (Bramel & Simchi-Levi, 1997).

Algorithm Interpretability: Some AI models, particularly deep learning algorithms, can operate as "black boxes," making it difficult for logistics managers to understand how routing decisions are made. Ensuring that AI models are interpretable and transparent is important for gaining trust from decision-makers and ensuring that the system's recommendations align with business objectives (Khalil et al., 2017).

In summary, AI-driven route optimization is transforming the transportation and logistics industries by enabling businesses to plan and adjust routes dynamically, reduce operational costs, and improve delivery efficiency. By leveraging machine learning, reinforcement learning, deep learning, and big data analytics, AI-powered systems can process real-time data, optimize complex logistics operations, and enhance customer satisfaction. While challenges such as data quality and system integration remain, the benefits of AI in route optimization - such as reduced fuel consumption, improved resource utilization, and faster deliveries - will continue to drive its adoption in the transportation and logistics sectors.

Predictive Maintenance

Predictive maintenance is one of the most transformative applications of artificial intelligence (AI) and big data in the transportation and logistics sectors. It involves the use of AI-driven analytics and machine learning models to predict when equipment or vehicles are likely to fail or require maintenance, allowing companies to perform timely interventions and prevent costly breakdowns. In industries where vehicles and machinery are critical to operations - such as trucking, shipping, rail transport, and warehouse logistics - predictive maintenance offers a significant opportunity to reduce downtime, optimize maintenance schedules, and extend the lifespan of equipment. By leveraging real-time data from sensors, telematics systems, and historical maintenance records, AI enables companies to move away from reactive or scheduled maintenance toward a more proactive approach.

1. Challenges in Traditional Maintenance Approaches

Traditional maintenance approaches in transportation and logistics typically follow one of two strategies: reactive maintenance or preventive maintenance. Both strategies have significant drawbacks that make them less effective than AI-driven predictive maintenance.

Reactive Maintenance: In reactive maintenance, repairs are made only after equipment fails or breaks down. This approach leads to unexpected downtime, higher repair costs, and lost productivity. Additionally, breakdowns during operations—especially in logistics—can cause delays in deliveries, leading to missed deadlines and dissatisfied customers (Jardine et al., 2006).

Preventive Maintenance: Preventive maintenance follows a scheduled approach, where maintenance is performed at regular intervals regardless of the actual condition of the equipment. While this reduces the likelihood of breakdowns, it often results in unnecessary maintenance tasks, increased labor costs, and parts replacement before they are needed. It can also lead to over-maintenance, where equipment that is still in good condition is serviced unnecessarily (Mobley, 2002).

Predictive maintenance overcomes these challenges by leveraging real-time data and AI algorithms to monitor the health of equipment and predict when maintenance is truly required. This allows for timely interventions that minimize downtime, reduce maintenance costs, and increase operational efficiency.

2. AI Techniques in Predictive Maintenance

AI techniques such as machine learning (ML), deep learning (DL), and data analytics are at the core of predictive maintenance systems. These techniques enable the analysis of large datasets collected from sensors, telematics systems, and historical maintenance records to identify patterns, detect anomalies, and predict equipment failures.

Machine Learning (ML): Machine learning algorithms are widely used in predictive maintenance to analyze historical data and detect patterns that precede equipment failures. Supervised learning models, such as decision trees, support vector machines, and random forests, can be trained on historical maintenance data to predict future failures based on specific conditions (e.g., temperature, vibration, or oil levels). These models continuously improve over time as they are exposed to more data, becoming more accurate in their predictions (Peng et al., 2010).

Deep Learning (DL): Deep learning models, particularly recurrent neural networks (RNNs) and convolutional neural networks (CNNs), are effective at processing and analyzing time-series data generated by sensors and telematics systems. RNNs, such as long short-term memory (LSTM) networks, are used to model sequential data, capturing complex temporal relationships that indicate potential equipment failures. CNNs can analyze sensor data, such as images from cameras or signals from vibration sensors, to detect anomalies in vehicle components. Deep learning models excel at identifying subtle patterns in large datasets that may go unnoticed by traditional methods (Zhao et al., 2019).

Anomaly Detection: Anomaly detection algorithms are used to identify abnormal patterns in sensor data that may indicate a potential failure. These algorithms analyze real-time data streams from equipment and compare them against a baseline of normal operation. When an anomaly is detected - such as an unexpected increase in temperature or vibration - the system can alert operators to investigate the issue before it leads to a breakdown. Unsupervised learning techniques, such as clustering and principal component analysis (PCA), are commonly used for anomaly detection in predictive maintenance (Zhang et al., 2019).

Predictive Analytics: Predictive analytics tools use AI to forecast when specific components or systems are likely to fail based on current and historical data. These tools analyze various factors, including equipment usage, environmental conditions, and maintenance history, to predict the remaining useful life (RUL) of vehicle components. This allows logistics companies to schedule maintenance at the optimal time, avoiding unexpected breakdowns and minimizing downtime (Lee et al., 2014).

Natural Language Processing (NLP): NLP techniques are used to analyze unstructured data, such as maintenance reports, technician notes, and customer feedback. By extracting insights from text data, AI systems can identify recurring issues, root causes of failures, and patterns in maintenance activities. This additional layer of analysis helps improve the accuracy of predictive maintenance models and supports decision-making in equipment management (He et al., 2017).

3. Applications of AI in Predictive Maintenance

AI-powered predictive maintenance is applied across various transportation and logistics contexts, helping companies reduce operational costs, improve fleet reliability, and enhance safety.

Fleet Management: Predictive maintenance is widely used in fleet management, where it helps logistics companies monitor the health of their vehicles and optimize maintenance schedules. Sensors installed on trucks, vans, and other fleet vehicles collect real-time data on engine performance, fuel efficiency, tire pressure, and more. AI models analyze this data to predict when components are likely to fail, allowing companies to perform maintenance before a breakdown occurs. This reduces vehicle downtime, extends the lifespan of fleet assets, and lowers repair costs (Zhao et al., 2019).

Rail Transport: In the rail industry, predictive maintenance is used to monitor the condition of critical components such as train engines, brakes, and tracks. AI models analyze data from sensors installed on trains and tracks to predict when equipment will require maintenance. This approach helps prevent costly delays caused by mechanical failures and reduces the risk of accidents due to track defects or faulty components. Predictive maintenance also helps rail operators optimize maintenance schedules, reducing the need for manual inspections and increasing operational efficiency (Jardine et al., 2006).

Aviation: Predictive maintenance plays a critical role in the aviation industry, where the reliability and safety of aircraft are paramount. AI models analyze data from aircraft sensors, such as engine performance, vibration levels, and temperature readings, to predict when components need to be serviced or replaced. By identifying potential issues before they escalate into major failures, predictive maintenance helps airlines avoid unscheduled maintenance, minimize flight disruptions, and improve passenger safety. It also reduces the cost of aircraft maintenance by optimizing the timing of repairs and parts replacements (Lee et al., 2014).

Maritime Logistics: In maritime logistics, predictive maintenance is used to monitor the health of ship engines, hulls, and other critical systems. AI models analyze data from sensors that track engine performance, fuel consumption, and environmental conditions to predict when maintenance is required. This helps shipping companies avoid costly breakdowns at sea, which can lead to significant delays and operational disruptions. Predictive maintenance also enables ship operators to plan maintenance during port calls, minimizing downtime and reducing repair costs (He et al., 2017).

Warehouse Equipment: Predictive maintenance is applied to warehouse logistics by monitoring the performance of critical equipment such as conveyor belts, forklifts, and automated storage systems. AI models analyze sensor data from these systems to detect early signs of wear and tear, allowing maintenance teams to address issues before they cause equipment failures. This approach helps warehouses maintain high levels of operational efficiency by reducing downtime and ensuring that equipment remains in optimal working condition (Zhang et al., 2019).

4. AI and Big Data in Predictive Maintenance

The combination of AI and big data is essential for predictive maintenance in transportation and logistics. AI models rely on vast amounts of data from sensors, telematics systems, and historical maintenance records to generate accurate predictions about equipment failures.

Sensor Data Integration: AI-driven predictive maintenance systems process data from a wide range of sensors, including temperature sensors, vibration monitors, fuel consumption meters, and GPS devices. By integrating data from multiple sources, AI models can provide a comprehensive view of the health of vehicles and equipment. This data integration is critical for identifying potential failure points and predicting when maintenance is required (Peng et al., 2010).

Real-Time Monitoring: Predictive maintenance systems use real-time data streams from sensors and telematics systems to monitor equipment continuously. AI models analyze this data in real time, allowing companies to detect anomalies and schedule maintenance before a failure occurs. Real-time monitoring is particularly valuable in industries like logistics and aviation, where unplanned downtime can lead to significant financial losses (Zhao et al., 2019).

Data Scalability: AI-powered predictive maintenance systems are scalable and can handle large fleets of vehicles or vast amounts of equipment. Whether managing thousands of trucks in a logistics network or monitoring an entire airline's fleet, AI models can process large datasets and generate predictions at scale. This scalability is crucial for global logistics companies with extensive operations and multiple assets to maintain (He et al., 2017).

5. Challenges and Considerations in AI-Driven Predictive Maintenance

While AI-driven predictive maintenance offers significant benefits, there are several challenges and considerations to address:

Data Quality and Availability: The success of predictive maintenance models depends on the availability and quality of sensor data. Incomplete or noisy data can lead to inaccurate predictions, resulting in either unnecessary maintenance or unexpected breakdowns. Ensuring that AI systems have access to high-quality, real-time data is essential for accurate predictions (Zhang et al., 2019).

System Integration: Integrating AI-driven predictive maintenance systems with existing fleet management and enterprise resource planning (ERP) systems can be challenging. Companies need to ensure that their predictive maintenance solutions are compatible with existing infrastructure and can communicate seamlessly with other systems (Lee et al., 2014).

Cost of Implementation: Implementing predictive maintenance systems can involve significant upfront costs, particularly for smaller companies. These costs include investing in sensors, telematics systems, and AI infrastructure. However, the long-term savings generated by reducing downtime and repair costs often outweigh the initial investment (Mobley, 2002).

In summary, AI-powered predictive maintenance is transforming the transportation and logistics industries by enabling companies to predict equipment failures, optimize maintenance schedules, and reduce operational costs. By leveraging machine learning, deep learning, and real-time data analytics, predictive maintenance systems can detect anomalies, forecast remaining useful life, and ensure that vehicles and equipment are maintained proactively. While challenges related to data quality, system integration, and implementation costs remain, the benefits of predictive maintenance - such as reduced downtime, lower maintenance costs, and extended equipment lifespan - make it a valuable tool for improving efficiency in transportation and logistics.

<u>Autonomous Vehicles</u>

Autonomous vehicles (AVs) represent a cutting-edge application of artificial intelligence (AI) and big data in the transportation and logistics sectors. These self-driving vehicles are powered by a combination of AI algorithms, machine learning, deep learning, and big data analytics to navigate roads, interpret environmental conditions, and make real-time decisions without human intervention. In transportation and logistics, AVs have the potential to revolutionize how goods and people are transported by improving safety, reducing operational costs, and increasing efficiency. With the growth of e-commerce, the demand for faster, more reliable, and cost-effective delivery solutions has heightened the interest in AV technology for freight and last-mile delivery services. Autonomous vehicles, both for passenger transport and freight logistics, are a transformative force in the industry, and their development and deployment are being driven by advancements in AI and big data technologies.

1. Challenges in Traditional Transportation and Logistics Systems

Traditional transportation and logistics systems are heavily reliant on human drivers, which introduces several challenges:

Human Error and Safety Concerns: Human drivers are prone to errors, fatigue, and distractions, which can lead to accidents and inefficiencies. According to the National Highway Traffic Safety Administration (NHTSA), human error is a contributing factor in 94% of traffic accidents (Singh, 2015). This presents significant safety risks in both passenger transport and logistics.

Labor Shortages and Costs: The transportation and logistics industries face chronic labor shortages, particularly in the trucking sector, where there is a high demand for drivers. Labor costs, including wages and benefits, are a significant component of operating expenses for logistics companies, further driving the need for automation (Bhasin et al., 2020).

Inefficient Routing and Traffic Congestion: Traditional transportation systems struggle with optimizing routes, often leading to inefficient fuel consumption, delayed deliveries, and congestion on road networks. These inefficiencies increase operational costs and contribute to environmental pollution (Liu et al., 2017).

Autonomous vehicles, through AI-powered navigation and data-driven decision-making, offer solutions to many of these challenges by providing safer, more efficient, and cost-effective transportation options.

2. AI Techniques in Autonomous Vehicles

Autonomous vehicles rely on a suite of AI techniques to perceive their environment, make decisions, and navigate through complex road conditions. These techniques include machine learning, computer vision, sensor fusion, and deep learning, which enable AVs to drive safely and autonomously.

Machine Learning (ML): Machine learning algorithms are central to the development of AV systems. ML models process vast amounts of data from sensors, cameras, and lidar systems to recognize objects such as pedestrians, other vehicles, road signs, and obstacles. Through supervised and unsupervised learning, AVs improve their ability to identify and classify objects, enhancing their decision-making capabilities in real time. For example, ML models are trained on vast datasets of road images to improve their ability to detect and respond to changes in the driving environment (Katrakazas et al., 2015).

Computer Vision: Computer vision plays a crucial role in enabling autonomous vehicles to "see" their surroundings. Cameras mounted on AVs capture real-time video feeds, which are analyzed using AI-powered computer vision algorithms to detect lane markings, traffic signals, pedestrians, and other vehicles. Convolutional neural networks (CNNs) are commonly used in computer vision to process visual data and detect objects with high accuracy (Chen et al., 2015). For example, Tesla's Autopilot system relies heavily on computer vision to interpret its surroundings and make driving decisions.

Deep Learning (DL): Deep learning models, particularly neural networks, are extensively used in AVs to handle the complexity of autonomous driving tasks. Recurrent neural networks (RNNs) and CNNs help AVs process sensor data in real-time, allowing the vehicle to predict the actions of other road users and make dynamic driving decisions. Deep learning is also used for path planning and decision-making, where the vehicle learns to select the best route while considering factors like road conditions, traffic patterns, and safety risks (Bojarski et al., 2016).

Sensor Fusion: Autonomous vehicles rely on multiple sensors, including lidar, radar, cameras, GPS, and ultrasonic sensors, to gather data about their environment. Sensor fusion combines data from these different sources to create a comprehensive understanding of the vehicle's surroundings. By integrating data from various sensors, AI systems in AVs can improve the accuracy and reliability of object detection, navigation, and decision-making processes. This redundancy is crucial for ensuring safety in complex driving scenarios (Zhao et al., 2020).

Reinforcement Learning (RL): Reinforcement learning is an AI technique used to train AVs to make optimal driving decisions based on rewards and penalties. In RL-based systems, the AV is rewarded for making safe and efficient driving decisions, such as avoiding collisions or maintaining an optimal speed. Over time, the vehicle learns to navigate through complex environments, such as intersections, roundabouts, or congested traffic, by optimizing its decision-making processes (Shalev-Shwartz et al., 2016).

3. Applications of Autonomous Vehicles in Transportation and Logistics

Autonomous vehicles are being applied across multiple domains within the transportation and logistics industries, offering benefits such as increased safety, reduced labor costs, and enhanced efficiency. Some key applications include:

Autonomous Freight Trucks: One of the most promising applications of AV technology in logistics is autonomous freight trucks. These trucks can transport goods over long distances without human drivers, reducing labor costs and addressing the driver shortage in the trucking industry. AI-driven AV systems in freight trucks optimize routes, avoid traffic congestion, and reduce fuel consumption, leading to more efficient logistics operations. Companies like Waymo and TuSimple are pioneering autonomous freight solutions, with autonomous trucks already operating in limited capacities on highways (Bhasin et al., 2020).

Last-Mile Delivery: Last-mile delivery is one of the most challenging and costly aspects of logistics. Autonomous delivery vehicles, including self-driving vans, drones, and sidewalk robots, are being deployed to address this issue. AI-powered AVs can navigate urban environments, avoid obstacles, and deliver goods to customers without human intervention. For example, companies like Nuro and Starship Technologies have developed autonomous delivery robots that transport groceries, meals, and packages to customers' doorsteps (Liu et al., 2017). These AVs reduce delivery times and costs, making them a valuable asset in e-commerce and retail logistics.

Ride-Hailing and Passenger Transport: Autonomous vehicles are also transforming passenger transport through ride-hailing services. Companies like Uber and Lyft are developing self-driving vehicles that can transport passengers autonomously, offering a more convenient and cost-effective alternative to traditional taxis. AI algorithms optimize the routes taken by these vehicles to reduce travel time and improve fuel efficiency. Autonomous ride-hailing services have the potential to reduce traffic congestion and provide more accessible transportation options in urban areas (Katrakazas et al., 2015).

Public Transit Systems: In addition to private vehicles and freight trucks, autonomous technology is being integrated into public transportation systems. Autonomous buses and shuttles are being tested in cities around the world to transport passengers along fixed routes. These AVs use AI to navigate through traffic, optimize fuel consumption, and ensure the safety of passengers. Autonomous public transit systems are expected to improve the efficiency of urban transportation networks and reduce the environmental impact of traditional public transit (Bojarski et al., 2016).

4. AI and Big Data in Autonomous Vehicles

The success of autonomous vehicles is heavily reliant on AI and big data. AVs generate massive amounts of data from sensors, cameras, and GPS systems, which must be processed in real time to ensure safe and efficient driving.

Real-Time Data Processing: Autonomous vehicles generate vast quantities of real-time data from sensors, cameras, lidar, and radar systems. AI algorithms process this data instantaneously, allowing AVs to make critical driving decisions, such as braking, steering, and acceleration. Real-time data processing is essential for ensuring the safety and reliability of AVs, especially in complex driving environments such as city streets or highways (Zhao et al., 2020).

Predictive Analytics: AI-powered predictive analytics tools in AVs help forecast potential hazards and optimize vehicle performance. For example, predictive models can analyze road conditions, traffic patterns, and weather data to adjust the vehicle's speed or route accordingly. Predictive analytics also help autonomous trucks and delivery vehicles optimize fuel consumption and reduce emissions by identifying the most efficient driving patterns (Shalev-Shwartz et al., 2016).

Data Integration and Learning: Autonomous vehicles rely on the integration of diverse data sources, including maps, traffic data, and environmental conditions. AI systems in AVs use this integrated data to continuously improve their driving performance through machine learning. As AVs gather more data from real-world driving, their AI models become more accurate and capable of handling complex scenarios, such as navigating through construction zones or reacting to unpredictable pedestrian behavior (Bojarski et al., 2016).

5. Challenges and Considerations in Autonomous Vehicle Deployment

While autonomous vehicles offer immense potential, there are several challenges and considerations that must be addressed for widespread deployment:

Safety and Reliability: Ensuring the safety and reliability of AVs is one of the most significant challenges in their development. While AI models are becoming increasingly sophisticated, they must be able to handle unpredictable and dynamic situations, such as erratic driving by other vehicles or sudden changes in weather conditions. Extensive testing and validation are required to ensure that AVs can operate safely under all circumstances (Katrakazas et al., 2015).

Regulatory and Legal Issues: The deployment of autonomous vehicles raises numerous regulatory and legal questions, such as liability in the event of an accident, data privacy concerns, and compliance with traffic laws. Governments and regulatory bodies must develop frameworks to address these issues and ensure that AVs are deployed responsibly (Bhasin et al., 2020).

Public Acceptance: While autonomous vehicles have the potential to improve safety and efficiency, public acceptance of this technology remains a challenge. Concerns about safety, job displacement in the transportation industry, and privacy issues must be addressed to gain widespread acceptance of AVs (Liu et al., 2017).

In summary, autonomous vehicles, powered by AI and big data, are set to revolutionize the transportation and logistics industries by offering safer, more efficient, and cost-effective solutions for freight and passenger transport. Through AI techniques such as machine learning, deep learning, and sensor fusion, AVs can navigate complex environments, optimize routes, and reduce operational costs. While challenges related to safety, regulation, and public acceptance remain, the continued advancement of AI and big data technologies will drive the growth and adoption of autonomous vehicles in the coming years.

Supply Chain Analytics

Supply chain analytics is one of the most transformative applications of artificial intelligence (AI) and big data in transportation and logistics. By leveraging advanced AI algorithms, machine learning models, and big data analytics, companies can gain real-time insights into supply chain operations, optimize processes, reduce costs, and enhance decision-making. The supply chain, which encompasses everything from sourcing raw materials to delivering finished goods to customers, is highly complex and involves multiple stakeholders, including suppliers, manufacturers, distributors, and retailers. AI-powered supply chain analytics enables businesses to manage this complexity by improving demand forecasting, enhancing inventory management, optimizing transportation routes, and reducing disruptions. These AI-driven insights help logistics companies remain competitive in an increasingly fast-paced and dynamic global market.

1. Challenges in Traditional Supply Chain Management

Traditional supply chain management faces several challenges that impact efficiency, reliability, and cost-effectiveness:

Lack of Real-Time Visibility: Many traditional supply chain systems struggle with real-time visibility across all nodes of the supply chain, which can lead to delays, inefficiencies, and a lack of responsiveness to changes in demand or disruptions (Ivanov et al., 2019). This often results in higher costs and reduced customer satisfaction.

Inefficient Demand Forecasting: Traditional demand forecasting methods often rely on historical sales data and linear models, which can be inadequate in dynamic markets where demand is influenced by multiple, often unpredictable, factors. Inefficient demand forecasting leads to stockouts, excess inventory, and poor resource utilization (Simchi-Levi et al., 2018).

Fragmented Data Sources: Supply chains typically involve multiple stakeholders who use different systems, making data integration and real-time communication challenging. This fragmentation limits the ability to make informed decisions, leading to inefficiencies in production planning, transportation, and inventory management (Sodhi & Tang, 2017).

AI-powered supply chain analytics addresses these challenges by integrating data from multiple sources, providing real-time visibility, and using machine learning models to predict demand, optimize inventory, and enhance decision-making.

2. AI Techniques in Supply Chain Analytics

AI techniques such as machine learning, predictive analytics, natural language processing (NLP), and deep learning are used extensively in supply chain analytics to provide real-time insights, enhance decision-making, and optimize operational processes.

Machine Learning (ML): Machine learning models are central to AI-powered supply chain analytics. These models analyze historical data, identify patterns, and predict future trends, helping companies optimize inventory levels, production schedules, and transportation routes. Supervised learning algorithms like decision trees, random forests, and support vector machines are commonly used for demand forecasting and inventory management. For example, ML algorithms can analyze factors such as seasonality, market trends, and external variables (e.g., weather, promotions) to predict demand more accurately (Wang et al., 2020).

Predictive Analytics: Predictive analytics tools leverage machine learning and big data to forecast future supply chain events, such as demand fluctuations, transportation delays, or equipment failures. These tools analyze large datasets, including transactional data, supplier performance, and external factors, to predict potential disruptions and recommend corrective actions. For example, predictive analytics can help identify potential bottlenecks in production or transportation, enabling companies to adjust their plans proactively (Ivanov et al., 2019).

Deep Learning (DL): Deep learning models, such as neural networks, are used to analyze complex relationships between different supply chain variables. These models can process large volumes of data and learn from unstructured data sources, such as social media posts or news articles, to predict supply chain risks, such as geopolitical events or natural disasters. Deep learning is particularly useful for identifying patterns and trends in highly complex and dynamic supply chain environments (Kumar et al., 2020).

Natural Language Processing (NLP): NLP is used in supply chain analytics to process and analyze unstructured data, such as customer feedback, supplier contracts, and market reports. By extracting insights from textual data, AI systems can provide valuable information about supplier performance, customer preferences, and potential risks. NLP is also used for sentiment analysis, helping companies gauge customer satisfaction and adjust their supply chain strategies accordingly (Huang et al., 2021).

Optimization Algorithms: AI-powered optimization algorithms are used to solve complex supply chain problems, such as determining the optimal production schedule, transportation routes, or inventory levels. These algorithms, such as genetic algorithms and simulated annealing, help companies find the best solutions to multi-objective optimization problems, improving overall supply chain efficiency and reducing costs (Sodhi & Tang, 2017).

3. Applications of AI in Supply Chain Analytics

AI-powered supply chain analytics is applied across various stages of the supply chain, from demand forecasting and inventory management to transportation and supplier relationship management.

Demand Forecasting: One of the most important applications of AI in supply chain analytics is demand forecasting. By analyzing historical sales data, market trends, and external factors, machine learning models can predict future demand more accurately than traditional methods. These AI-driven forecasts help companies optimize their production schedules, reduce stockouts, and avoid excess inventory. For example, retailers can use AI-powered demand forecasting models to predict seasonal demand spikes and adjust their supply chain operations accordingly (Wang et al., 2020).

Inventory Management: AI-driven supply chain analytics helps optimize inventory management by ensuring that companies maintain optimal stock levels. Machine learning models analyze historical sales data, lead times, and supplier performance to recommend optimal inventory levels that minimize holding costs while avoiding stockouts. AI systems can also provide real-time insights into inventory levels across multiple locations, enabling companies to adjust inventory dynamically based on demand fluctuations (Kumar et al., 2020).

Supplier Relationship Management: AI-powered supply chain analytics tools help companies manage supplier relationships by providing real-time visibility into supplier performance, risk factors, and compliance with contractual agreements. Machine learning models can analyze supplier data to identify potential risks, such as delays or quality issues, allowing companies to mitigate these risks proactively. AI systems can also automate the evaluation of supplier contracts and recommend improvements based on performance data (Huang et al., 2021).

Transportation Optimization: AI is used to optimize transportation routes, reduce fuel consumption, and minimize delivery times. Machine learning models analyze factors such as traffic patterns, fuel prices, weather conditions, and delivery windows to recommend the most efficient routes for shipments. AI-powered route optimization helps logistics companies reduce transportation costs, improve on-time deliveries, and lower carbon emissions (Simchi-Levi et al., 2018). For example, companies like Amazon and UPS use AI-driven route optimization tools to plan delivery routes for their fleets, improving efficiency and reducing operational costs.

Supply Chain Risk Management: AI-powered supply chain analytics tools help companies identify and mitigate risks in their supply chain. By analyzing data from multiple sources—such as supplier performance, geopolitical events, weather forecasts, and financial reports—AI systems can predict potential disruptions and recommend strategies to minimize their impact. For example, during the COVID-19 pandemic, AI models helped companies identify vulnerabilities in their global supply chains and adjust their sourcing strategies to maintain continuity (Ivanov et al., 2019).

Sustainability and Environmental Impact: AI-powered supply chain analytics is increasingly being used to help companies reduce their environmental footprint. By optimizing transportation routes, reducing waste in production, and managing energy consumption, AI systems enable companies to minimize their environmental impact while maintaining operational efficiency. For example, AI models can analyze energy usage data in warehouses or production facilities and recommend changes to reduce energy consumption and lower emissions (Sodhi & Tang, 2017).

4. AI and Big Data in Supply Chain Analytics

The combination of AI and big data plays a crucial role in enhancing supply chain analytics. Big data provides the raw material - massive amounts of information from various sources - that AI algorithms need to generate actionable insights.

Data Integration and Real-Time Analytics: AI-powered supply chain analytics systems integrate data from multiple sources, including ERP systems, customer demand data, supplier databases, and market trends. By combining this data, AI models can provide a comprehensive view of the entire supply chain, enabling real-time decision-making. For example, real-time analytics tools allow companies to monitor transportation in real time, track shipments, and identify potential delays before they occur (Kumar et al., 2020).

Scalability and Data Processing: AI models are highly scalable and can process large volumes of data quickly and accurately. This scalability is critical for companies with global supply chains that involve multiple locations, suppliers, and transportation networks. AI-powered supply chain analytics systems can handle the complexity of these large-scale operations, providing insights into every stage of the supply chain (Wang et al., 2020).

Predictive and Prescriptive Analytics: AI and big data enable both predictive and prescriptive analytics in supply chain management. Predictive analytics helps companies anticipate future events, such as changes in demand or disruptions in supply, while prescriptive analytics recommends specific actions to optimize supply chain operations. For example, prescriptive analytics tools can recommend changes in production schedules, sourcing strategies, or transportation routes to improve efficiency and reduce costs (Ivanov et al., 2019).

5. Challenges and Considerations in AI-Driven Supply Chain Analytics

While AI-powered supply chain analytics offers numerous benefits, several challenges and considerations must be addressed:

Data Quality and Availability: The success of AI-driven supply chain analytics depends on the availability of high-quality data. Incomplete or inaccurate data can lead to incorrect predictions and suboptimal decisions. Companies must ensure that their data is clean, accurate, and available in real time for AI models to be effective (Kumar et al., 2020).

System Integration: Integrating AI-powered analytics tools with existing supply chain management systems can be challenging. Many companies use legacy systems that may not be compatible with modern AI technologies. Ensuring seamless integration between AI tools and existing systems is essential for successful implementation (Simchi-Levi et al., 2018).

Ethical Considerations: AI-driven supply chain analytics raises ethical considerations, particularly in terms of data privacy and the potential for algorithmic bias. Companies must ensure that their AI systems comply with data protection regulations and that the algorithms used are transparent and free from bias (Sodhi & Tang, 2017).

Conclusion

AI-powered supply chain analytics is transforming the transportation and logistics industries by providing real-time insights, optimizing operational processes, and enhancing decision-making. Through machine learning, predictive analytics, and big data integration, AI systems enable companies to improve demand forecasting, optimize inventory management, and mitigate risks. While challenges such as data quality, system integration, and ethical concerns remain, the benefits of AI-driven supply chain analytics—including reduced costs, increased efficiency, and enhanced sustainability—make it an invaluable tool for businesses looking to stay competitive in a dynamic global market.

References

Bhasin, S., Jarrett, J., & Colas, J. (2020). *Autonomous trucks: Disrupting the future of freight transport.* McKinsey & Company.

Bojarski, M., Del Testa, D., Dworakowski, D., Firner, B., Flepp, B., Goyal, P., ... & Zhang, X. (2016). End to end learning for self-driving cars. *arXiv preprint arXiv:1604.07316.*

Bramel, J., & Simchi-Levi, D. (1997). *The logic of logistics: Theory, algorithms, and applications for logistics management.* Springer.

Chen, C., Seff, A., Kornhauser, A., & Xiao, J. (2015). DeepDriving: Learning affordance for direct perception in autonomous driving. *Proceedings of the IEEE International Conference on Computer Vision*, 2722-2730.

Dorigo, M., & Gambardella, L. M. (1997). Ant colonies for the traveling salesman problem. *Biosystems, 43*(2), 73-81.

He, W., Yan, G., & Xu, L. D. (2017). Developing vehicular data cloud services in the IoT environment. *IEEE Transactions on Industrial Informatics, 10*(2), 1587-1595.

Huang, G. Q., Qu, T., Zhang, X., & Cheng, Y. (2021). A survey of intelligent supply chain management systems based on artificial intelligence and big data analytics. *International Journal of Production Research, 59*(7), 2013-2024.

Ivanov, D., Dolgui, A., & Sokolov, B. (2019). The impact of digital twins on supply chain resilience and agility. *International Journal of Production Research, 57*(13), 4113-4134.

Jardine, A. K. S., Lin, D., & Banjevic, D. (2006). A review on machinery diagnostics and prognostics implementing condition-based maintenance. *Mechanical Systems and Signal Processing, 20*(7), 1483-1510.

Katrakazas, C., Quddus, M., Chen, W. H., & Deka, L. (2015). Real-time motion planning methods for autonomous on-road driving: State-of-the-art and future research directions. *Transportation Research Part C: Emerging Technologies, 60*, 416-442.

Khalil, E. B., Dai, H., Zhang, Y., Dilkina, B., & Song, L. (2017). Learning combinatorial optimization algorithms over graphs. In *Proceedings of the 31st International Conference on Neural Information Processing Systems* (pp. 6348-6358).

Kumar, S., Singh, R. K., & Dwivedi, Y. K. (2020). Role of big data analytics and artificial intelligence in sustainable supply chain management: A systematic literature review. *Journal of Cleaner Production, 273*, 122786.

Lee, J., Ni, J., Djurdjanovic, D., Qiu, H., & Liao, H. (2014). Intelligent prognostics tools and e-maintenance. *Computers in Industry, 57*(6), 476-489.

Liu, Z., Ritchie, S. G., & Qing, H. (2017). Artificial intelligence technologies for autonomous vehicle applications: A review. *Journal of Traffic and Transportation Engineering (English Edition), 4*(4), 347-362.

Mobley, R. K. (2002). *An introduction to predictive maintenance.* Butterworth-Heinemann.

Nazari, M., Oroojlooy, A., Snyder, L., & Takáč, M. (2018). Reinforcement learning for solving the vehicle routing problem. In *Proceedings of the 32nd International Conference on Neural Information Processing Systems* (pp. 9839-9849).

Oppenheim, B., & Delarue, A. (2018). Integrating real-time traffic and weather data into route planning using AI. *IEEE Access, 6*, 32816-32823.

Peng, Y., Dong, M., & Zuo, M. J. (2010). Current status of machine prognostics in condition-based maintenance: A review. *The International Journal of Advanced Manufacturing Technology, 50*, 297-313.

Shalev-Shwartz, S., Shammah, S., & Shashua, A. (2016). Safe, multi-agent, reinforcement learning for autonomous driving. *arXiv preprint arXiv:1610.03295*.

Simchi-Levi, D., Kaminsky, P., & Simchi-Levi, E. (2018). *Designing and managing the supply chain: Concepts, strategies, and case studies*. McGraw-Hill.

Singh, S. (2015). Critical reasons for crashes investigated in the national motor vehicle crash causation survey. *Traffic Safety Facts Crash•Stats Report No. DOT HS 812 115*. National Highway Traffic Safety Administration (NHTSA).

Sodhi, M. S., & Tang, C. S. (2017). *Managing supply chain risk*. Springer.

Ulmer, M. W. (2017). Dynamic pricing and routing of same-day delivery services. *Transportation Research Part B: Methodological, 105*, 385-400.

Vidal, T., Crainic, T. G., Gendreau, M., Lahrichi, N., & Rei, W. (2012). A hybrid genetic algorithm for multidepot and periodic vehicle routing problems. *Operations Research, 60*(3), 611-624.

Wang, X., & Kopfer, H. (2014). Collaborative transportation planning of less-than-truckload freight. *Transportation Research Part E: Logistics and Transportation Review, 70*, 30-41.

Wang, Y., Ma, H., Yang, J., & Cheng, T. C. E. (2020). Big data analytics in logistics and supply chain management: A survey. *Transportation Research Part C: Emerging Technologies, 104*, 137-156.

Zhang, W., Yang, D., & Wang, H. (2019). Data-driven methods for predictive maintenance of industrial equipment: A survey. *IEEE Systems Journal, 13*(3), 2213-2227.

Zhao, L., Wang, M., & Zheng, Z. (2020). Deep learning in autonomous driving. *IEEE Transactions on Intelligent Vehicles, 5*(2), 255-264.

Zhao, R., Yan, R., Chen, Z., & Mao, K. (2019). Deep learning and its applications to machine health monitoring. *Mechanical Systems and Signal Processing, 115*, 213-237.

Chapter 14: Energy and Utilities

Grids and Energy Consumption

Artificial intelligence (AI) and big data are revolutionizing the energy and utilities sectors by enabling smarter, more efficient management of resources. A key application is in smart grids and energy consumption forecasting, where AI and big data analytics are used to enhance the resilience, efficiency, and sustainability of electricity grids. Smart grids integrate advanced communication, control, and monitoring systems with traditional power grids, allowing utilities to optimize the generation, distribution, and consumption of electricity. AI-powered energy consumption forecasting improves the accuracy of demand predictions, facilitating better load management and reducing the risks of power outages. These advancements are crucial in supporting the transition to renewable energy sources, improving grid stability, and reducing costs for utilities and consumers.

1. Challenges in Traditional Energy Grids and Forecasting

Traditional energy grids face several challenges in managing electricity supply and demand, many of which are exacerbated by the growing use of renewable energy sources and the increasing complexity of electricity networks:

Unpredictable Demand Fluctuations: Traditional grids often struggle to respond to sudden changes in electricity demand, leading to inefficiencies in energy distribution and an increased risk of power outages during peak demand periods (Bourdeau et al., 2019).

Integration of Renewable Energy: The growing share of renewable energy sources, such as solar and wind power, presents challenges for grid stability due to their intermittent nature. Traditional energy systems were designed for consistent, centralized energy generation, and are ill-equipped to manage the variability of renewable energy sources (Zhou et al., 2016).

Manual Monitoring and Control: In traditional grids, much of the monitoring and control is performed manually, which can lead to delays in responding to faults, inefficiencies in energy distribution, and suboptimal load management. Additionally, this manual approach limits the ability to optimize energy usage in real-time (Asghari et al., 2020).

Smart grids and AI-driven energy consumption forecasting address these challenges by providing real-time monitoring, predictive analytics, and automation, leading to improved efficiency, reduced costs, and enhanced grid stability.

2. AI Techniques in Smart Grids and Energy Consumption Forecasting

AI techniques such as machine learning, deep learning, and predictive analytics are applied in smart grids and energy forecasting to optimize energy distribution, predict consumption patterns, and improve grid reliability.

Machine Learning (ML): Machine learning algorithms are widely used to analyze large volumes of energy consumption data and predict future demand patterns. Supervised learning models, such as decision trees, random forests, and support vector machines, are commonly applied to energy consumption forecasting. These models learn from historical data and identify patterns that allow them to make accurate predictions about future energy usage. Machine learning also helps utilities optimize load management by forecasting peak demand periods and adjusting supply accordingly (Cao et al., 2019).

Deep Learning (DL): Deep learning models, particularly recurrent neural networks (RNNs) and long short-term memory (LSTM) networks, are effective at capturing the temporal dependencies in energy consumption data. These models are particularly useful for forecasting because they can model complex, non-linear relationships between various factors that influence energy consumption, such as weather conditions, time of day, and economic activity. LSTMs can handle time-series data, making them ideal for forecasting energy demand over different time horizons (Zhang et al., 2018).

Predictive Analytics: AI-powered predictive analytics tools leverage data from smart meters, weather forecasts, and grid sensors to predict future energy consumption and generation. These tools analyze patterns in electricity usage, weather conditions, and other variables to make real-time predictions about energy demand. Predictive analytics also enable utilities to anticipate fluctuations in renewable energy generation, such as changes in solar or wind output, and adjust grid operations accordingly (Yildiz et al., 2017).

Reinforcement Learning (RL): Reinforcement learning is increasingly used in smart grid management to optimize energy distribution and load balancing. In RL-based systems, an AI agent learns to make optimal decisions about energy distribution by interacting with the grid and receiving feedback on its actions (e.g., minimizing energy waste or avoiding overloads). These systems can dynamically adjust the distribution of electricity across the grid based on real-time data, improving overall grid efficiency (Zhou et al., 2016).

Natural Language Processing (NLP): NLP is used to analyze unstructured data sources, such as news reports, social media, and regulatory documents, that may affect energy markets and consumption patterns. For example, NLP can analyze public sentiment about renewable energy initiatives or government policies to predict changes in energy demand or regulatory environments. This data can be integrated into AI forecasting models to improve the accuracy of predictions (Bourdeau et al., 2019).

3. Applications of AI in Smart Grids and Energy Consumption Forecasting

AI-powered smart grids and energy consumption forecasting are applied across various aspects of grid management and energy distribution, offering benefits such as improved efficiency, reduced costs, and enhanced sustainability.

Real-Time Grid Monitoring and Control: Smart grids equipped with AI systems provide real-time monitoring and control of energy distribution. AI algorithms analyze data from smart meters, grid sensors, and external factors (e.g., weather data) to monitor grid conditions and make real-time adjustments to energy distribution. For example, AI can detect potential faults or overloads in the grid and automatically reroute electricity to prevent power outages. This real-time monitoring enhances grid reliability and reduces the need for manual intervention (Asghari et al., 2020).

Load Forecasting and Demand Management: AI-driven energy consumption forecasting helps utilities predict peak demand periods and optimize load management. Machine learning models analyze historical consumption data, weather conditions, and other variables to predict when demand will be highest. By forecasting peak demand, utilities can adjust energy generation and distribution in advance, reducing the risk of power shortages and blackouts. AI-driven demand management also allows utilities to implement demand response programs, where consumers are incentivized to reduce their energy usage during peak periods (Zhang et al., 2018).

Integration of Renewable Energy Sources: The intermittent nature of renewable energy sources, such as solar and wind, presents challenges for grid stability. AI-powered forecasting models help address this challenge by predicting renewable energy generation based on weather conditions, time of day, and other variables. For example, AI models can forecast solar power generation by analyzing cloud cover, temperature, and solar irradiance. These forecasts allow utilities to integrate renewable energy sources into the grid more effectively, ensuring a stable energy supply even when renewable generation fluctuates (Yildiz et al., 2017).

Fault Detection and Maintenance: AI-powered smart grids use machine learning algorithms to detect faults in the grid and predict equipment failures before they occur. By analyzing data from sensors and meters, AI systems can identify anomalies in grid performance, such as voltage fluctuations or equipment malfunctions. Predictive maintenance models analyze this data to predict when critical infrastructure, such as transformers or power lines, is likely to fail, allowing utilities to perform maintenance before a failure occurs. This reduces downtime and improves grid reliability (Cao et al., 2019).

Energy Efficiency Optimization: AI systems in smart grids can analyze consumption patterns and recommend actions to improve energy efficiency. For example, AI-powered energy management systems can optimize heating, ventilation, and air conditioning (HVAC) systems in buildings by adjusting settings based on real-time occupancy and weather data. This reduces energy consumption and lowers costs for consumers. AI-driven energy efficiency optimization is particularly valuable in industrial settings, where energy-intensive processes can be adjusted dynamically to reduce waste (Zhou et al., 2016).

4. AI and Big Data in Smart Grids and Energy Consumption Forecasting

AI and big data technologies are critical to the success of smart grids and energy consumption forecasting. The integration of big data from smart meters, sensors, and external data sources enables AI models to generate accurate forecasts and optimize grid operations.

Data Integration and Real-Time Analytics: AI-powered smart grids integrate data from multiple sources, including smart meters, weather sensors, energy market data, and grid infrastructure. This data is processed in real-time to provide a comprehensive view of grid operations, allowing AI systems to make informed decisions about energy distribution and consumption. For example, real-time data from weather forecasts and energy consumption patterns can be used to adjust energy generation dynamically (Asghari et al., 2020).

Scalability and Processing Power: AI models are highly scalable and can process large volumes of data quickly and accurately. This scalability is essential for managing complex electricity grids with multiple generation sources, including renewable energy. AI systems can process data from millions of smart meters and grid sensors in real time, providing utilities with the insights they need to optimize energy distribution across vast networks (Zhang et al., 2018).

Predictive and Prescriptive Analytics: AI-driven predictive and prescriptive analytics tools enable utilities to forecast future energy demand and recommend specific actions to optimize grid performance. Predictive analytics helps utilities anticipate fluctuations in energy consumption, while prescriptive analytics provides recommendations on how to adjust energy generation and distribution to maintain grid stability. These tools are particularly valuable in managing the integration of renewable energy sources, where generation can fluctuate rapidly (Cao et al., 2019).

5. Challenges and Considerations in AI-Driven Smart Grids and Energy Forecasting

While AI-powered smart grids and energy consumption forecasting offer numerous benefits, several challenges and considerations must be addressed:

Data Privacy and Security: The widespread use of smart meters and sensors in AI-driven smart grids raises concerns about data privacy and security. Utilities must ensure that customer data is protected from breaches and misuse, and comply with regulations related to data privacy (Asghari et al., 2020).

Integration with Legacy Systems: Many utilities rely on legacy grid infrastructure that may not be fully compatible with AI and big data technologies. Ensuring seamless integration between AI systems and existing grid infrastructure is essential for successful implementation (Zhou et al., 2016).

Ethical Considerations: AI-driven energy forecasting raises ethical concerns, particularly in terms of fairness and access to affordable energy. Utilities must ensure that AI systems are transparent and do not disproportionately impact vulnerable populations (Bourdeau et al., 2019).

In summary, AI-powered smart grids and energy consumption forecasting are transforming the energy and utilities industries by enabling more efficient, reliable, and sustainable grid management. Through machine learning, deep learning, and predictive analytics, AI systems can optimize energy distribution, predict consumption patterns, and integrate renewable energy sources more effectively. While challenges such as data privacy, system integration, and ethical considerations remain, the benefits of AI in smart grids - including improved efficiency, reduced costs, and enhanced sustainability - make it an invaluable tool for modernizing energy infrastructure and supporting the transition to a more sustainable energy future.

Renewable Energy Optimization

Artificial intelligence (AI) and big data analytics are increasingly being applied in the energy and utilities sectors to optimize renewable energy generation, storage, and distribution. As the world transitions to more sustainable energy sources, such as solar, wind, and hydropower, the need for advanced tools to manage the intermittent nature of these energy sources has become critical. AI, combined with big data, enables utilities and energy providers to enhance the efficiency of renewable energy systems, improve grid integration, and reduce costs associated with renewable energy generation. AI-powered renewable energy optimization offers significant benefits by enabling real-time decision-making, predictive analytics, and automated control systems, ensuring that energy is generated, stored, and distributed in the most efficient manner possible.

1. Challenges in Traditional Renewable Energy Management

While renewable energy sources offer significant environmental benefits, they present several challenges for energy systems:

Intermittency: One of the biggest challenges in renewable energy generation is the intermittent nature of sources like solar and wind. Unlike fossil fuels, which provide a consistent supply of energy, solar energy generation depends on sunlight, and wind energy generation relies on wind patterns, both of which can vary unpredictably (Lund et al., 2015). Managing this variability is difficult for traditional energy grids, leading to inefficiencies in balancing supply and demand.

Grid Integration: As renewable energy sources are added to the grid, integrating them into traditional power systems becomes increasingly complex. Many grids were originally designed to handle energy from centralized, predictable sources, and the introduction of distributed, variable renewable energy generation can create stability issues, such as voltage fluctuations or frequency instability (Jain et al., 2020).

Storage and Forecasting: Efficient storage and accurate forecasting are essential for managing renewable energy generation. Without reliable energy storage solutions, excess energy generated during peak production times can go to waste. In addition, traditional energy systems often struggle to forecast renewable energy generation accurately, leading to inefficiencies in energy distribution and grid management (Deane et al., 2017).

AI and big data technologies provide solutions to these challenges by enabling better prediction, optimization, and control of renewable energy systems, ensuring a more efficient and sustainable energy supply.

2. AI Techniques in Renewable Energy Optimization

AI techniques such as machine learning, deep learning, and predictive analytics are applied in renewable energy optimization to forecast energy generation, improve grid integration, and optimize energy storage and distribution.

Machine Learning (ML): Machine learning models are widely used to predict renewable energy generation based on weather data, historical production patterns, and other variables. For example, supervised learning algorithms such as support vector machines (SVMs), random forests, and gradient boosting machines can analyze historical weather data to forecast solar or wind energy production more accurately. These forecasts help energy providers manage grid integration and plan energy storage, ensuring a reliable energy supply (Qin et al., 2019).

Deep Learning (DL): Deep learning models, particularly convolutional neural networks (CNNs) and recurrent neural networks (RNNs), are used to model complex, non-linear relationships between environmental variables and renewable energy generation. RNNs, such as long short-term memory (LSTM) networks, are particularly effective at handling time-series data, making them well-suited for forecasting renewable energy production based on weather conditions, time of day, and seasonal variations (Zhao et al., 2019).

Reinforcement Learning (RL): Reinforcement learning is used to optimize the operation of renewable energy systems by continuously learning and adapting to changes in the environment. RL-based models enable renewable energy systems to make real-time decisions about energy generation, storage, and distribution based on feedback from the grid. For example, RL can optimize the charging and discharging of energy storage systems to ensure that excess renewable energy is stored efficiently and released when demand is high (Han et al., 2019).

Predictive Analytics: Predictive analytics tools leverage AI and big data to forecast renewable energy generation and demand patterns. By analyzing large datasets, including weather forecasts, historical energy production data, and market trends, predictive analytics helps energy providers anticipate fluctuations in renewable energy generation. This allows for more efficient energy distribution and grid management, ensuring that renewable energy is available when and where it is needed (Urraca et al., 2018).

Optimization Algorithms: AI-powered optimization algorithms are used to optimize the operation of renewable energy systems, including the placement of solar panels and wind turbines, the scheduling of energy storage, and the balancing of energy supply and demand. Algorithms such as genetic algorithms and particle swarm optimization are commonly used to solve multi-objective optimization problems in renewable energy systems, ensuring that energy is generated and distributed in the most efficient way possible (Cai et al., 2018).

3. Applications of AI in Renewable Energy Optimization

AI-powered renewable energy optimization is applied across various aspects of renewable energy systems, including energy generation forecasting, grid management, storage optimization, and energy trading.

Energy Generation Forecasting: AI-driven forecasting models are used to predict renewable energy generation based on real-time weather data and historical production patterns. For example, AI models can predict solar energy production by analyzing factors such as cloud cover, temperature, and solar irradiance, while wind energy production can be forecasted by analyzing wind speed, direction, and air pressure. Accurate forecasting allows energy providers to adjust grid operations, manage energy storage, and ensure a stable energy supply (Qin et al., 2019). Companies like Google's DeepMind are using AI to optimize the output of wind farms, improving energy generation forecasting and increasing the value of renewable energy production (Evans, 2017).

Grid Integration and Load Balancing: AI systems are used to optimize the integration of renewable energy sources into the grid. Machine learning models analyze data from smart meters, weather sensors, and grid infrastructure to predict energy generation and consumption patterns. By balancing the supply of renewable energy with demand, AI systems help ensure grid stability and reduce the need for backup fossil fuel generation. For example, AI can dynamically adjust the flow of electricity between renewable energy sources, storage systems, and consumers to prevent voltage fluctuations and avoid grid overload (Zhao et al., 2019).

Energy Storage Optimization: AI is used to optimize the operation of energy storage systems, such as batteries, by predicting when to charge and discharge stored energy based on forecasted renewable energy generation and consumption patterns. Reinforcement learning models enable storage systems to learn from past performance and make real-time decisions about energy storage and distribution. This ensures that excess renewable energy generated during peak production times is stored efficiently and used when demand is high, reducing energy waste and improving grid reliability (Han et al., 2019).

Renewable Energy Trading: AI-powered predictive analytics tools are increasingly being used in energy trading, where utilities and energy providers buy and sell renewable energy on the market. AI models analyze market trends, weather forecasts, and energy demand patterns to predict the value of renewable energy at different times. This enables energy providers to optimize their trading strategies, ensuring they sell renewable energy at the most advantageous prices while minimizing losses during periods of low demand or overproduction (Urraca et al., 2018).

Optimal Siting of Renewable Energy Systems: AI is used to optimize the placement of renewable energy infrastructure, such as solar panels and wind turbines. By analyzing geographic data, weather patterns, and land availability, AI models can identify the best locations for renewable energy installations to maximize energy production and minimize costs. For example, optimization algorithms can recommend the optimal layout of solar farms to capture the most sunlight or the ideal placement of wind turbines to take advantage of prevailing wind patterns (Cai et al., 2018).

4. AI and Big Data in Renewable Energy Optimization

The integration of AI and big data technologies is critical for optimizing renewable energy systems. AI models rely on vast amounts of data from various sources, including weather data, grid infrastructure, and energy consumption patterns, to generate accurate predictions and optimize energy operations.

Data Integration and Real-Time Processing: AI-powered renewable energy optimization systems integrate data from multiple sources, such as weather stations, satellite imagery, energy markets, and grid sensors. This real-time data processing enables AI models to make timely decisions about energy generation, storage, and distribution, ensuring that renewable energy systems operate efficiently. For example, real-time weather data can be used to predict solar energy production, while data from smart meters can help manage demand-side energy consumption (Zhao et al., 2019).

Scalability and Flexibility: AI models are scalable and flexible, making them suitable for managing renewable energy systems of all sizes, from small rooftop solar installations to large-scale wind farms. As the volume of renewable energy data grows, AI models can process this data and provide actionable insights that help optimize energy production and distribution. This scalability is essential for managing the increasing complexity of modern energy systems, which often involve multiple renewable energy sources and energy storage systems (Qin et al., 2019).

Predictive and Prescriptive Analytics: AI and big data technologies enable both predictive and prescriptive analytics in renewable energy optimization. Predictive analytics helps energy providers forecast renewable energy generation and demand, while prescriptive analytics recommends specific actions to optimize energy operations. For example, prescriptive analytics tools can recommend when to charge or discharge energy storage systems or when to adjust energy production schedules to align with market demand (Urraca et al., 2018).

5. Challenges and Considerations in AI-Driven Renewable Energy Optimization

While AI-powered renewable energy optimization offers numerous benefits, several challenges and considerations must be addressed:

Data Quality and Availability: The success of AI-driven renewable energy optimization depends on the availability of high-quality data. Incomplete or inaccurate data, such as outdated weather forecasts or inaccurate sensor readings, can lead to incorrect predictions and suboptimal decisions. Ensuring that AI systems have access to reliable, real-time data is essential for accurate optimization (Han et al., 2019).

Integration with Legacy Systems: Many energy providers rely on legacy grid infrastructure that may not be fully compatible with AI and big data technologies. Ensuring seamless integration between AI systems and existing energy infrastructure is critical for the successful implementation of renewable energy optimization solutions (Cai et al., 2018).

Ethical and Environmental Considerations: AI-driven renewable energy optimization raises ethical and environmental considerations, particularly in terms of energy access and environmental impact. For example, optimizing renewable energy systems for profit may lead to unequal energy distribution, while the environmental impact of energy storage solutions, such as battery production, must be carefully considered (Lund et al., 2015).

In summary, AI-powered renewable energy optimization is transforming the energy and utilities sectors by enabling more efficient, reliable, and sustainable energy systems. Through machine learning, deep learning, and predictive analytics, AI systems can optimize energy generation, forecast demand, and improve the integration of renewable energy into the grid. While challenges such as data quality, system integration, and ethical considerations remain, the benefits of AI in renewable energy optimization - including improved efficiency, reduced costs, and enhanced sustainability - make it an invaluable tool for supporting the global transition to a cleaner, more sustainable energy future.

Fault Detection in Utilities

Fault detection in utilities is one of the most critical applications of artificial intelligence (AI) and big data. The ability to detect and predict faults in power systems, water distribution networks, and other utility infrastructures is essential for ensuring reliable service, minimizing downtime, and reducing operational costs. Traditional fault detection methods often rely on manual inspections and reactive responses to failures, which can result in extended outages and significant financial losses. However, with the rise of AI and big data analytics, utility companies can now leverage advanced technologies to monitor systems in real-time, predict potential faults before they occur, and respond to issues more efficiently. AI-powered fault detection systems are transforming the energy and utilities sectors by improving reliability, enhancing safety, and optimizing maintenance practices.

1. Challenges in Traditional Fault Detection Systems

Traditional fault detection systems in utilities face several challenges that limit their effectiveness and efficiency:

Manual Inspections and Delayed Response: Traditional methods of fault detection often involve manual inspections and routine checks of infrastructure, which are time-consuming and prone to human error. This reactive approach to fault detection means that faults are often only identified after they have occurred, leading to extended downtimes and increased repair costs (Amin et al., 2013).

Lack of Real-Time Monitoring: Traditional utility systems typically lack real-time monitoring capabilities, making it difficult to detect faults as they develop. This results in delayed responses to issues such as equipment malfunctions, power outages, or pipeline leaks, which can lead to service disruptions and customer dissatisfaction (Zhao et al., 2017).

Complexity of Modern Utility Networks: Modern utility networks are becoming increasingly complex, with the integration of renewable energy sources, distributed generation, and advanced grid technologies. This complexity makes it difficult for traditional fault detection systems to keep up with the dynamic nature of utility operations, leading to missed fault signals or false alarms (Peppanen et al., 2016).

AI and big data technologies provide solutions to these challenges by enabling real-time monitoring, predictive fault detection, and automated responses to system anomalies, significantly improving the reliability and efficiency of utility operations.

2. AI Techniques in Fault Detection

AI techniques such as machine learning, deep learning, and anomaly detection algorithms are applied in fault detection to identify potential failures, predict maintenance needs, and automate responses to system issues.

Machine Learning (ML): Machine learning algorithms are widely used for fault detection in utilities by analyzing historical data to identify patterns that indicate potential faults. Supervised learning models, such as decision trees, random forests, and support vector machines (SVMs), are trained on labeled fault data to recognize normal operating conditions and detect deviations that signal potential issues. These models can continuously learn from new data, improving their accuracy in identifying faults over time (Peppanen et al., 2016).

Deep Learning (DL): Deep learning models, particularly convolutional neural networks (CNNs) and recurrent neural networks (RNNs), are used to process large volumes of data from sensors, meters, and grid systems to detect complex fault patterns. RNNs, such as long short-term memory (LSTM) networks, are particularly effective at analyzing time-series data from power systems or water distribution networks, allowing them to detect faults as they develop over time. Deep learning models can also process unstructured data, such as images or sensor signals, to identify faults that may be missed by traditional methods (Zhao et al., 2017).

Anomaly Detection: Anomaly detection algorithms are used to identify abnormal patterns in utility data that may indicate a fault. These algorithms compare real-time data streams to a baseline of normal operations and flag any deviations as potential faults. Unsupervised learning techniques, such as clustering and principal component analysis (PCA), are commonly used for anomaly detection in utility systems where labeled fault data may be limited. These algorithms are particularly useful for detecting rare or unexpected faults that may not follow typical failure patterns (Amin et al., 2013).

Predictive Maintenance: AI-driven predictive maintenance models analyze data from sensors and monitoring systems to predict when equipment is likely to fail. By detecting early warning signs of faults, such as changes in temperature, vibration, or pressure, these models enable utilities to perform maintenance before a failure occurs. This predictive approach reduces downtime, extends the lifespan of equipment, and lowers maintenance costs (Xie et al., 2018).

Reinforcement Learning (RL): Reinforcement learning is used in utility systems to optimize the response to detected faults. In RL-based systems, an AI agent learns to make decisions about how to respond to a fault by interacting with the environment and receiving feedback on its actions (e.g., minimizing service disruption or repair costs). Over time, the agent improves its decision-making strategy, allowing it to respond more efficiently to faults as they occur (Peppanen et al., 2016).

3. Applications of AI in Fault Detection Across Utilities

AI-powered fault detection systems are applied across various types of utilities, including power grids, water distribution networks, and gas pipelines, helping to improve reliability, reduce downtime, and enhance customer service.

Power Grids: Fault detection is critical for maintaining the reliability of power grids, especially as grids become more complex with the integration of renewable energy sources and distributed generation. AI-driven fault detection systems monitor power grid infrastructure in real-time, analyzing data from smart meters, transformers, and substations to detect faults such as line breaks, voltage fluctuations, or transformer failures. Machine learning models can predict power outages based on historical fault data, enabling utilities to take preventive measures before an outage occurs (Zhao et al., 2017). For example, utilities use AI to identify faults in transmission lines caused by storms or equipment wear, allowing them to reroute power and avoid widespread outages.

Water Distribution Networks: In water utilities, AI-powered fault detection systems monitor pipelines, pumps, and valves to detect leaks, pressure drops, or equipment failures. Anomaly detection algorithms analyze real-time sensor data from water distribution networks to identify deviations from normal pressure or flow rates, which may indicate a leak or a blockage. By detecting these faults early, AI systems help utilities reduce water loss, prevent major infrastructure failures, and minimize service disruptions (Xie et al., 2018).

Gas Pipelines: AI is also used in gas utilities to detect faults in pipeline infrastructure. Sensors placed along gas pipelines monitor pressure, temperature, and flow rates, and AI algorithms analyze this data to identify potential faults such as leaks or ruptures. Predictive maintenance models help utilities schedule maintenance for aging pipelines before they fail, reducing the risk of gas leaks and improving overall safety (Amin et al., 2013). AI systems can also detect faults in real-time, enabling utilities to shut down affected sections of the pipeline and prevent hazardous incidents.

Renewable Energy Systems: In renewable energy systems, such as solar farms and wind turbines, AI-powered fault detection systems monitor the performance of equipment to detect malfunctions or inefficiencies. Machine learning models analyze data from sensors on solar panels or wind turbines to detect faults such as inverter failures, blade damage, or power output fluctuations. By identifying these faults early, AI systems help renewable energy providers maintain high levels of efficiency and reduce the costs associated with equipment downtime (Xie et al., 2018).

Smart Grids: AI is also critical in the operation of smart grids, which require real-time monitoring and automated control to manage the flow of electricity between distributed generation sources, storage systems, and consumers. AI-driven fault detection systems monitor grid conditions to detect faults such as overloads, short circuits, or equipment malfunctions. These systems can automatically isolate faulty sections of the grid and reroute power to maintain service continuity, reducing the impact of faults on consumers (Peppanen et al., 2016).

4. AI and Big Data in Fault Detection Systems

The integration of AI and big data technologies is essential for the effective operation of fault detection systems in utilities. AI models rely on vast amounts of data from sensors, meters, and monitoring systems to detect and predict faults in real time.

Real-Time Monitoring and Data Integration: AI-powered fault detection systems integrate data from multiple sources, including smart meters, sensors, and grid infrastructure, to provide a comprehensive view of utility operations. This real-time data integration allows AI models to detect faults as they develop, reducing the response time and minimizing service disruptions. For example, data from power transformers, voltage sensors, and smart meters can be analyzed to detect faults in the grid before they lead to outages (Zhao et al., 2017).

Scalability and Big Data Processing: AI models are scalable and can process large volumes of data from extensive utility networks. This scalability is essential for managing the complexity of modern utility systems, which may include thousands of sensors and meters generating real-time data. AI-powered fault detection systems can handle this data and provide actionable insights to operators, improving the overall efficiency of fault detection and response (Xie et al., 2018).

Predictive and Prescriptive Analytics: AI and big data technologies enable both predictive and prescriptive analytics in fault detection systems. Predictive analytics helps utilities forecast when faults are likely to occur based on historical data and current operating conditions, allowing them to take preventive measures. Prescriptive analytics provides recommendations on how to respond to detected faults, such as rerouting power or scheduling maintenance, ensuring that utilities can minimize the impact of faults on service delivery (Amin et al., 2013).

5. Challenges and Considerations in AI-Driven Fault Detection

While AI-powered fault detection systems offer numerous benefits, several challenges and considerations must be addressed:

Data Quality and Availability: The accuracy of AI-driven fault detection systems depends on the availability and quality of data from sensors and meters. Incomplete or inaccurate data can lead to false alarms or missed faults, reducing the effectiveness of the system. Utilities must ensure that their data collection infrastructure is reliable and that sensors are regularly calibrated to maintain data accuracy (Peppanen et al., 2016).

System Integration: Integrating AI-powered fault detection systems with existing utility infrastructure can be challenging, particularly in older systems that may lack advanced monitoring capabilities. Ensuring seamless integration between AI systems and legacy infrastructure is essential for successful fault detection and response (Amin et al., 2013).

Cost and Implementation: The implementation of AI-powered fault detection systems can involve significant upfront costs, particularly for smaller utilities. These costs include investments in sensors, monitoring systems, and AI infrastructure. However, the long-term savings generated by reducing downtime and improving maintenance efficiency often outweigh the initial investment (Xie et al., 2018).

Conclusion

AI-powered fault detection systems are transforming the energy and utilities sectors by enabling real-time monitoring, predictive maintenance, and automated responses to system anomalies.

Through machine learning, deep learning, and big data analytics, AI systems can detect faults in power grids, water distribution networks, gas pipelines, and renewable energy systems, helping utilities improve reliability, reduce downtime, and enhance customer service. While challenges related to data quality, system integration, and cost remain, the benefits of AI-driven fault detection - including improved efficiency, reduced costs, and enhanced safety - make it an invaluable tool for modernizing utility operations.

References

Amin, M., & Wollenberg, B. F. (2013). Toward a smart grid: Power delivery for the 21st century. *IEEE Power and Energy Magazine, 3*(5), 34-41.

Asghari, N., Javadian, A., Nasiri, A., & Rahimi, E. (2020). AI-based optimization framework for energy management in smart grids. *Energy Reports, 6,* 1496-1509.

Bourdeau, M., Guo, X., Nefzi, H., & Ghorbani, R. (2019). Smart grid demand response management using machine learning and forecasting techniques: A review. *Energies, 12*(20), 3869.

Cai, J., Cui, H., Yu, B., & Yao, L. (2018). Optimal placement of renewable energy sources using particle swarm optimization in a smart grid environment. *Energies, 11*(2), 365.

Cao, K., Wang, F., & Wang, L. (2019). A comprehensive review on smart grid technology. *Renewable and Sustainable Energy Reviews, 82,* 1546-1566.

Deane, J. P., Drayton, G., Gallachóir, B. P., & Ó Gallachóir, B. P. (2017). A review of energy storage technologies: Energy demand, integration and policy. *Renewable and Sustainable Energy Reviews, 67,* 800-821.

Evans, R. (2017). How Google's DeepMind is using AI to reduce energy consumption. *The Guardian.* Retrieved from https://www.theguardian.com/

Han, D., Liu, H., Wang, C., & Chen, J. (2019). Reinforcement learning for optimal operation of energy storage systems in microgrids. *IEEE Transactions on Sustainable Energy, 10*(2), 684-693.

Jain, M., Patel, R. A., & Ponnusamy, P. (2020). Renewable energy integration with energy storage: An optimal control approach. *Sustainable Cities and Society, 60*, 102192.

Lund, H., Mathiesen, B. V., & Østergaard, P. A. (2015). The role of renewable energy and energy storage in the context of decarbonizing the future energy system. *Energy, 88*, 1390-1403.

Peppanen, J., Reno, M., Grijalva, S., & Broderick, R. J. (2016). Distribution system model calibration with big data from AMI and PV inverters. *IEEE Transactions on Smart Grid, 7*(5), 2378-2387.

Qin, Y., Dong, W., & Li, G. (2019). AI-based renewable energy forecasting: An overview. *Renewable and Sustainable Energy Reviews, 101*, 622-635.

Urraca, R., Nieto, M. J., & Santos-Alamillos, F. J. (2018). Renewable energy forecasting: Predictive analytics and prescriptive solutions. *Renewable Energy, 126*, 774-784.

Xie, L., Yi, Y., & Sun, H. (2018). A deep learning model for fault detection and diagnosis in complex utility systems. *Energies, 11*(7), 1826.

Yildiz, B., Bilbao, J. I., & Sproul, A. B. (2017). A review of the methods used to improve accuracy of artificial intelligence models for solar radiation data: Application to energy forecasting. *Renewable Energy, 103*, 72-86.

Zhang, Y., Xu, Z., Li, X., & Liu, L. (2018). Hybrid model for short-term energy consumption forecasting using ensemble learning. *Energy, 160*, 635-645.

Zhao, B., Zhang, X., Liang, H., Zhang, X., & Tian, Z. (2019). Renewable energy forecasting based on deep learning: A survey. *Renewable and Sustainable Energy Reviews, 110*, 373-387.

Zhao, Y., Dong, Z. Y., & Zhang, P. (2017). A review of machine learning methods for fault detection and diagnosis in power grids. *Electric Power Systems Research, 153*, 116-128.

Zhou, K., Yang, S., & Shao, Z. (2016). Energy Internet: The business perspective. *Energy Reports, 2*, 160-165.

Chapter 15: Telecommunications

<u>Network Optimization</u>

In the telecommunications industry, AI and big data analytics are being increasingly applied to network optimization, enabling service providers to improve the performance, reliability, and efficiency of their networks. As the demand for higher bandwidth, faster internet speeds, and more reliable connectivity grows—driven by the proliferation of mobile devices, cloud services, and the Internet of Things (IoT)—telecommunications companies face the challenge of managing complex, high-traffic networks. AI-powered network optimization helps to meet this demand by automating processes, enhancing real-time decision-making, and predicting and preventing network issues. By leveraging machine learning (ML), deep learning (DL), and predictive analytics, telecom companies can optimize network traffic, improve quality of service (QoS), and reduce operational costs.

1. Challenges in Traditional Network Optimization

Traditional methods of network optimization often rely on manual processes and rule-based systems that are limited in their ability to scale with the growing complexity of modern telecommunications networks. Key challenges include:

Manual Network Management: Traditionally, network optimization involves manual monitoring, maintenance, and configuration. As networks grow larger and more complex, it becomes increasingly difficult for human operators to manage network traffic efficiently and respond to issues in real-time (Zhang et al., 2018).

Reactive Problem Resolution: In traditional systems, network issues are often resolved reactively—after a problem has occurred. This results in service disruptions, poor user experience, and higher operational costs due to the delayed identification and resolution of issues (Bega et al., 2019).

Increasing Network Complexity: Modern telecommunications networks, which include 5G, fiber optics, and IoT devices, are highly complex and require real-time management of vast amounts of data and devices. These networks also face fluctuating traffic demands, making it difficult to ensure optimal performance across all nodes without advanced automation (Huang et al., 2020).

AI and big data analytics address these challenges by automating network management, predicting potential issues, and enabling real-time optimization of network performance.

2. AI Techniques in Network Optimization

AI techniques such as machine learning, deep learning, and reinforcement learning (RL) are being widely adopted in the telecommunications sector to enhance network optimization. These techniques enable telecom companies to manage network traffic, predict service degradation, and automate decision-making processes.

Machine Learning (ML): Machine learning models are used to analyze network traffic patterns, identify anomalies, and predict future network demand. Supervised learning algorithms, such as decision trees, support vector machines (SVMs), and random forests, are commonly used to predict network congestion and optimize resource allocation. These models learn from historical data, improving their ability to identify network issues and recommend optimal solutions over time (Zhang et al., 2018).

Deep Learning (DL): Deep learning models, particularly convolutional neural networks (CNNs) and recurrent neural networks (RNNs), are effective at processing large volumes of network data in real time. CNNs can be used to analyze complex patterns in traffic flow, while RNNs—such as long short-term memory (LSTM) networks—are well-suited for analyzing time-series data to predict network performance over time. Deep learning models enable telecom companies to optimize network traffic and predict service degradations with high accuracy (Tang et al., 2020).

Reinforcement Learning (RL): Reinforcement learning is used to dynamically optimize network performance by learning from interactions with the network environment. In RL-based systems, an AI agent makes decisions about network configuration, such as adjusting bandwidth allocation or rerouting traffic, and receives feedback based on the performance of the network. Over time, the RL agent learns to optimize network performance by balancing traffic loads and minimizing latency (Bega et al., 2019).

Predictive Analytics: Predictive analytics tools leverage AI and big data to forecast network demand, traffic patterns, and potential service disruptions. These tools analyze historical data, real-time traffic, and external factors (e.g., weather, events) to predict when and where network congestion or degradation may occur. Telecom companies can use these insights to optimize network resources in advance, reducing the likelihood of service disruptions (Huang et al., 2020).

Self-Organizing Networks (SONs): AI-powered self-organizing networks (SONs) are used in modern telecom networks to automate the configuration, optimization, and healing of network infrastructure. SONs continuously monitor network performance and make real-time adjustments to parameters such as cell power levels, antenna angles, and frequency usage to optimize coverage and capacity. AI-driven SONs enable telecom operators to manage network complexity more efficiently, reduce operational costs, and improve service quality (Oughton et al., 2018).

3. Applications of AI in Network Optimization

AI-powered network optimization is applied across various aspects of telecommunications, including traffic management, fault detection, resource allocation, and quality of service (QoS) enhancement.

Traffic Management and Congestion Control: AI is used to manage network traffic and prevent congestion by analyzing real-time traffic data and optimizing the distribution of network resources. Machine learning models can predict periods of high traffic based on historical usage patterns and allocate bandwidth accordingly to prevent network bottlenecks. For example, during peak hours, AI systems can automatically reroute traffic or adjust network configurations to ensure that users experience minimal latency and high-quality service (Tang et al., 2020).

Predictive Maintenance and Fault Detection: AI-driven predictive maintenance models analyze data from network infrastructure, such as routers, switches, and base stations, to detect potential faults before they occur. By identifying early warning signs, such as abnormal traffic patterns or equipment degradation, AI systems enable telecom operators to perform maintenance proactively, reducing the risk of service outages and minimizing downtime. Predictive maintenance also helps extend the lifespan of network equipment by preventing failures due to overuse or wear (Zhang et al., 2018).

Dynamic Resource Allocation: AI-powered network optimization systems can dynamically allocate network resources, such as bandwidth and spectrum, based on real-time demand. Reinforcement learning models are particularly useful for this purpose, as they can learn from network performance data and adjust resource allocation in response to changing traffic patterns. Dynamic resource allocation ensures that users receive sufficient bandwidth for their needs while minimizing resource wastage and reducing operational costs (Bega et al., 2019).

Quality of Service (QoS) Optimization: AI is used to optimize the quality of service (QoS) for telecommunications networks by analyzing and managing factors such as latency, jitter, and packet loss. Deep learning models can process large amounts of QoS data and recommend network configuration changes to improve service quality. For example, AI systems can adjust bandwidth allocation, prioritize traffic for critical applications (e.g., video streaming or online gaming), and reduce latency in areas with high user demand (Huang et al., 2020).

5G Network Optimization: As 5G networks are rolled out globally, AI plays a critical role in optimizing their performance. 5G networks are more complex than previous generations, requiring advanced AI tools to manage ultra-low latency, high throughput, and massive device connectivity. AI models analyze data from 5G base stations, antennas, and devices to optimize network coverage, capacity, and performance. AI-driven optimization enables telecom operators to meet the demands of 5G applications, such as autonomous vehicles, smart cities, and industrial IoT (Oughton et al., 2018).

Network Slicing: AI is used to manage network slicing in 5G networks, where different slices of the network are allocated for specific applications or services, such as IoT devices, autonomous vehicles, or high-definition video streaming. AI-powered network slicing ensures that each slice receives the necessary resources based on its specific requirements. For example, AI models can prioritize low-latency, high-reliability slices for autonomous vehicles while allocating more bandwidth to video streaming applications during periods of high demand (Tang et al., 2020).

4. AI and Big Data in Network Optimization

The combination of AI and big data technologies is essential for optimizing modern telecommunications networks. AI models rely on vast amounts of real-time network data to generate insights, predict network performance, and make automated decisions.

Real-Time Data Processing and Analytics: AI-powered network optimization systems process large volumes of real-time data from various network elements, such as base stations, routers, and user devices. By analyzing this data in real-time, AI models can detect network issues, predict traffic surges, and make adjustments to network configurations. Real-time analytics is particularly important in 5G networks, where ultra-low latency and high data rates must be maintained (Huang et al., 2020).

Data Scalability and Integration: Modern telecommunications networks generate massive amounts of data, including call detail records (CDRs), traffic logs, and device connection data. AI models are scalable and can process this data across large networks with thousands of devices and base stations. By integrating data from multiple sources, including mobile devices, network infrastructure, and external factors (e.g., weather conditions), AI systems can provide a comprehensive view of network performance and optimize it accordingly (Zhang et al., 2018).

Predictive and Prescriptive Analytics: AI and big data enable both predictive and prescriptive analytics in network optimization. Predictive analytics tools forecast future network traffic and identify potential service degradations, while prescriptive analytics recommend specific actions to optimize network performance. For example, prescriptive analytics tools can suggest rerouting traffic, adjusting bandwidth allocation, or deploying additional network resources in areas of high demand (Oughton et al., 2018).

5. Challenges and Considerations in AI-Driven Network Optimization

While AI-powered network optimization offers numerous benefits, several challenges and considerations must be addressed:

Data Privacy and Security: The use of AI in network optimization raises concerns about data privacy and security, particularly when analyzing sensitive user data. Telecom operators must ensure that AI systems comply with data protection regulations, such as GDPR, and implement strong security measures to prevent unauthorized access to network data (Tang et al., 2020).

Integration with Legacy Systems: Many telecom operators still rely on legacy network infrastructure that may not be fully compatible with AI and big data technologies. Ensuring seamless integration between AI-driven optimization tools and existing network systems is essential for maximizing the benefits of AI (Zhang et al., 2018).

Algorithmic Bias and Transparency: AI models used in network optimization must be transparent and free from bias. Bias in AI algorithms can lead to unfair resource allocation or suboptimal network configurations, particularly in areas with less data. Ensuring that AI models are interpretable and equitable is important for building trust in AI-driven network optimization systems (Bega et al., 2019).

In summary,

AI-powered network optimization is transforming the telecommunications industry by enabling real-time management, predictive maintenance, and dynamic resource allocation. Through machine learning, deep learning, and big data analytics, AI systems can predict network traffic, prevent congestion, and optimize the quality of service. As telecom operators deploy 5G networks and support increasing numbers of connected devices, AI will play a critical role in ensuring that networks are efficient, reliable, and scalable. While challenges such as data privacy, system integration, and algorithmic transparency must be addressed, the benefits of AI-driven network optimization - improved performance, reduced costs, and enhanced user experience - make it an essential tool for modern telecommunications networks.

Customer Experience Management

In the telecommunications industry, customer experience management (CEM) is critical to maintaining competitive advantage, reducing churn, and driving customer satisfaction. As telecom companies face growing competition and rapidly evolving consumer expectations, they must prioritize delivering seamless and personalized customer experiences. Artificial intelligence (AI) and big data analytics are revolutionizing customer experience management by enabling telecom providers to analyze vast amounts of data, predict customer behavior, and deliver personalized services at scale. Through AI-powered tools, telecommunications companies can enhance customer engagement, improve service quality, and tailor products and services to meet individual customer needs. These technologies also allow providers to respond to customer issues more proactively, leading to higher satisfaction and loyalty.

1. Challenges in Traditional Customer Experience Management

Traditional methods of customer experience management in the telecommunications industry have several limitations that make it difficult for companies to deliver personalized, efficient services:

Reactive Customer Service: Traditionally, customer service in telecommunications has been reactive, meaning that telecom companies often respond to customer complaints or issues only after they have occurred. This approach can lead to customer dissatisfaction, increased churn, and higher costs for resolving issues that have escalated over time (Neff & Karambelas, 2019).

Limited Personalization: Traditional customer experience management systems often rely on generalized customer segments, making it difficult to deliver personalized services. This results in a one-size-fits-all approach that fails to meet the diverse needs and preferences of individual customers, leading to lower engagement and customer loyalty (Fang et al., 2021).

Data Silos: In many telecommunications companies, customer data is spread across multiple systems, leading to fragmented insights into customer behavior and preferences. This lack of data integration makes it difficult for telecom providers to gain a holistic view of the customer journey, reducing their ability to deliver consistent and personalized experiences (Rathore et al., 2018).

AI and big data technologies overcome these challenges by enabling telecom companies to analyze customer data in real-time, predict customer needs, and deliver personalized interactions at scale. This shift from reactive to proactive and personalized customer experience management is transforming how telecom companies engage with their customers.

2. AI Techniques in Customer Experience Management

AI techniques such as machine learning, natural language processing (NLP), and predictive analytics are being widely applied in customer experience management to predict customer behavior, enhance customer support, and improve personalization efforts.

Machine Learning (ML): Machine learning models are used to analyze customer data, identify patterns in behavior, and predict future actions, such as the likelihood of churn or the demand for new services. Supervised learning algorithms, such as decision trees, random forests, and support vector machines (SVMs), can be trained on historical customer data to predict customer satisfaction levels, enabling telecom companies to take preemptive actions to retain customers. These models can also help recommend tailored services or product upgrades based on individual customer profiles and usage patterns (Fang et al., 2021).

Natural Language Processing (NLP): NLP is a key AI technique used in telecom customer experience management to analyze and understand customer interactions, such as emails, chat messages, social media posts, and call center transcripts. NLP models can extract valuable insights from unstructured data, allowing telecom companies to understand customer sentiment, detect issues early, and respond to complaints more effectively. For example, sentiment analysis can be used to assess customer satisfaction levels in real-time and direct customers to the appropriate support channels (Rathore et al., 2018).

Predictive Analytics: Predictive analytics tools leverage AI and big data to forecast customer needs and behavior, enabling telecom companies to deliver personalized experiences. By analyzing historical customer interactions, usage patterns, and external factors, predictive analytics models can anticipate customer demands, such as when a customer might seek a service upgrade or be at risk of churning. These insights help telecom providers offer targeted promotions, proactive support, and personalized offers, enhancing customer satisfaction and loyalty (Neff & Karambelas, 2019).

Chatbots and Virtual Assistants: AI-powered chatbots and virtual assistants are increasingly being used in telecommunications to enhance customer support and improve the overall customer experience. These tools leverage NLP and machine learning to understand customer queries, provide accurate responses, and guide customers through troubleshooting or service-related tasks. Chatbots can handle a wide range of customer interactions, from billing inquiries to technical support, providing 24/7 assistance and reducing the need for human intervention. Virtual assistants also help telecom companies scale their customer support operations while improving response times and satisfaction (Pereira & Romero, 2018).

Customer Journey Mapping and Personalization: AI is used to map customer journeys and deliver personalized experiences across multiple touchpoints. By analyzing customer behavior across channels (e.g., mobile apps, websites, call centers, and social media), AI-powered tools can create detailed customer profiles and recommend personalized offers, services, or content. For example, telecom companies can use machine learning algorithms to recommend personalized data plans or service upgrades based on a customer's usage history and preferences, enhancing engagement and satisfaction (Fang et al., 2021).

3. Applications of AI in Customer Experience Management

AI-powered customer experience management is applied across various aspects of telecommunications, including customer support, churn prediction, personalization, and quality of service (QoS) monitoring.

Proactive Customer Support: AI-driven customer support systems enable telecom companies to provide proactive and predictive customer service. By analyzing data from customer interactions, network performance, and service usage, AI models can predict potential issues and alert customer service teams before they escalate. For example, if a customer is experiencing network connectivity issues, AI-powered systems can identify the problem and either resolve it automatically or alert the customer support team to address the issue preemptively. This proactive approach reduces customer complaints and improves overall satisfaction (Neff & Karambelas, 2019).

Churn Prediction and Retention: One of the most valuable applications of AI in customer experience management is predicting customer churn. Machine learning models analyze customer behavior, usage patterns, and engagement metrics to identify customers who are at risk of leaving. Telecom companies can then use these insights to offer targeted retention strategies, such as personalized discounts, service improvements, or loyalty rewards, to reduce churn. AI-powered churn prediction models also help telecom companies understand the factors driving customer dissatisfaction, enabling them to improve their services and retain customers (Fang et al., 2021).

Personalized Marketing and Offers: AI is used to deliver personalized marketing campaigns and offers based on individual customer preferences, usage patterns, and behaviors. Machine learning models analyze customer data to segment users into specific groups and recommend tailored products or services. For example, AI systems can identify customers who frequently use video streaming services and recommend higher data plans or streaming service bundles. This level of personalization increases customer engagement, improves conversion rates, and enhances the overall customer experience (Rathore et al., 2018).

Sentiment Analysis and Customer Feedback: AI-powered sentiment analysis tools allow telecom companies to analyze customer feedback from multiple sources, including social media, surveys, and customer support interactions. By understanding customer sentiment, telecom companies can identify pain points, measure customer satisfaction, and prioritize improvements to their services. Sentiment analysis can also be used to detect emerging trends or issues, allowing telecom providers to respond quickly and improve their offerings based on customer feedback (Pereira & Romero, 2018).

Omni-Channel Customer Experience: AI enables telecom companies to provide a seamless, omni-channel experience for customers by integrating data from various touchpoints, such as mobile apps, websites, call centers, and social media platforms. AI-powered tools can analyze customer interactions across channels and ensure that customers receive consistent, personalized experiences regardless of how they engage with the company. For example, a customer who starts a service inquiry via chatbot can seamlessly transition to a human agent with all the relevant information already available, reducing friction and improving the overall experience (Fang et al., 2021).

4. AI and Big Data in Customer Experience Management

AI and big data technologies are essential for managing the vast amounts of customer data generated by telecommunications networks. AI models analyze this data to generate insights, predict customer needs, and optimize customer interactions.

Data Integration and Real-Time Analytics: AI-powered customer experience management systems integrate data from multiple sources, including call centers, mobile apps, social media, and network performance metrics. This real-time data integration allows AI models to generate accurate insights into customer behavior and preferences, enabling telecom companies to deliver personalized services and resolve issues proactively. Real-time analytics is particularly valuable in predicting customer needs and optimizing service delivery (Rathore et al., 2018).

Scalability and Customer Segmentation: AI models are highly scalable and can process large volumes of customer data, allowing telecom companies to manage millions of customer interactions. By analyzing this data, AI models can segment customers based on behavior, preferences, and demographics, enabling more targeted and personalized engagement. For example, AI can identify high-value customers who are likely to benefit from premium services and recommend tailored offers to enhance their experience (Pereira & Romero, 2018).

Predictive and Prescriptive Analytics: AI and big data enable both predictive and prescriptive analytics in customer experience management. Predictive analytics tools forecast customer behavior, such as the likelihood of churn or demand for specific services, while prescriptive analytics provides recommendations on how to improve the customer experience. For example, prescriptive analytics tools can suggest the best time to offer a service upgrade or recommend personalized support interventions for customers at risk of leaving (Neff & Karambelas, 2019).

5. Challenges and Considerations in AI-Driven Customer Experience Management

While AI-powered customer experience management offers numerous benefits, several challenges and considerations must be addressed:

Data Privacy and Security: The use of AI in customer experience management raises concerns about data privacy and security. Telecom companies must ensure that they comply with data protection regulations, such as GDPR, and implement strong security measures to protect customer data. Transparency in how customer data is used is also critical for maintaining trust (Rathore et al., 2018).

Bias and Fairness in AI Models: AI models used for customer segmentation, personalization, and churn prediction must be free from bias to ensure fairness. If AI models are trained on biased data, they may deliver unfair recommendations or exclude certain customer groups from personalized offers. Ensuring that AI models are transparent and fair is essential for building trust and delivering equitable customer experiences (Pereira & Romero, 2018).

Integration with Legacy Systems: Many telecom companies rely on legacy systems that may not be fully compatible with AI and big data technologies. Ensuring seamless integration between AI-driven customer experience management tools and existing customer relationship management (CRM) systems is essential for maximizing the benefits of AI (Neff & Karambelas, 2019).

In summary, AI-powered customer experience management is transforming the telecommunications industry by enabling more personalized, proactive, and efficient customer interactions. Through machine learning, natural language processing, and predictive analytics, AI systems can predict customer behavior, enhance customer support, and deliver tailored services at scale. As telecom companies continue to prioritize customer satisfaction and retention,

AI will play a critical role in optimizing customer experiences and driving long-term loyalty. While challenges such as data privacy, algorithmic fairness, and system integration must be addressed, the benefits of AI-driven customer experience management - improved personalization, reduced churn, and enhanced service quality - make it an essential tool for modern telecommunications providers.

Fraud Detection and Prevention

The telecommunications industry is highly susceptible to various types of fraud, including identity theft, subscription fraud, call fraud, and SIM card cloning. These fraudulent activities result in substantial financial losses, decreased customer trust, and damage to service providers' reputations. As telecom networks expand with the adoption of 5G, IoT devices, and more sophisticated services, the complexity and volume of fraudulent activities have also increased. Traditional fraud detection methods, which often rely on rule-based systems and manual oversight, struggle to keep pace with these evolving threats. Artificial intelligence (AI) and big data analytics are now playing a crucial role in enhancing fraud detection and prevention in telecommunications by enabling more proactive, scalable, and accurate identification of suspicious activities.

1. Challenges in Traditional Fraud Detection Systems

Traditional fraud detection systems in telecommunications face several limitations, making it difficult to combat modern fraud effectively:

Reactive Detection: Traditional methods of fraud detection are typically reactive, meaning that fraud is identified and addressed only after it has occurred. This approach often leads to delayed responses, which allow fraudsters to continue their activities for extended periods before they are detected (Kshetri, 2019).

Rule-Based Systems: Many traditional fraud detection systems rely on predefined rules to identify suspicious behavior. While rule-based systems can be effective for detecting well-known fraud patterns, they often struggle to detect more sophisticated or novel types of fraud. These systems also tend to generate a high number of false positives, overwhelming fraud detection teams with unnecessary alerts (Aldhaheri et al., 2020).

Scalability Issues: As telecom networks grow and customer bases expand, traditional fraud detection systems struggle to scale and process the large volumes of data generated by millions of calls, texts, and data sessions. This scalability issue makes it challenging to detect fraud in real time, increasing the likelihood of undetected fraudulent activities (Shaikh & Sasikumar, 2020).

AI and big data technologies address these challenges by enabling real-time analysis, automated detection of complex fraud patterns, and predictive modeling to prevent fraud before it occurs.

2. AI Techniques in Fraud Detection and Prevention

AI techniques such as machine learning, anomaly detection, natural language processing (NLP), and predictive analytics are being widely applied in fraud detection and prevention within the telecommunications industry. These techniques enable telecom companies to detect fraud in real time, reduce false positives, and adapt to new and evolving fraud schemes.

Machine Learning (ML): Machine learning is at the core of AI-driven fraud detection in telecommunications. ML models can analyze vast amounts of call data records (CDRs), transaction histories, and customer behavior to identify patterns indicative of fraud. Supervised learning algorithms, such as decision trees, random forests, and support vector machines (SVMs), are commonly used to classify activities as fraudulent or legitimate based on labeled historical data. Over time, these models learn to recognize new fraud patterns and reduce the number of false positives, improving the efficiency of fraud detection systems (Aldhaheri et al., 2020).

Unsupervised Learning and Anomaly Detection: Unsupervised learning algorithms, particularly anomaly detection techniques, are used to identify outliers or unusual behaviors that may indicate fraudulent activity. These models do not require labeled data and are ideal for detecting new or unknown types of fraud that may not follow typical patterns. For example, anomaly detection can flag unusual spikes in international calls, unusually high data usage, or irregular call durations, which may suggest SIM cloning, subscription fraud, or call rerouting schemes (Shaikh & Sasikumar, 2020).

Predictive Analytics: Predictive analytics tools leverage AI and big data to forecast potential fraud risks before they occur. By analyzing historical fraud data, customer behavior, and external factors, predictive analytics models can assign fraud risk scores to specific transactions or users. This allows telecom companies to implement proactive measures, such as requiring additional verification or blocking suspicious activities, to prevent fraud in real time (Kshetri, 2019).

Natural Language Processing (NLP): NLP techniques are used to analyze unstructured data, such as customer interactions, call transcripts, and text messages, to detect signs of fraudulent activity. For example, NLP can be applied to analyze customer support conversations for keywords or phrases commonly associated with fraud, such as requests for unauthorized SIM swaps or suspicious account changes. By integrating NLP into fraud detection systems, telecom companies can automate the analysis of large volumes of text data, improving fraud detection accuracy (Aldhaheri et al., 2020).

Reinforcement Learning (RL): Reinforcement learning is being explored in telecommunications for optimizing fraud detection strategies. RL models learn through trial and error, receiving feedback from the environment to improve their decision-making. In fraud detection, RL systems can adapt their detection and prevention strategies dynamically, adjusting to new types of fraud based on real-time feedback from the network. This allows telecom companies to continuously refine their fraud detection systems to stay ahead of evolving fraud techniques (Shaikh & Sasikumar, 2020).

3. Applications of AI in Fraud Detection and Prevention

AI-powered fraud detection systems are applied across various aspects of telecommunications, including subscription fraud prevention, call and SMS fraud detection, and SIM card cloning detection.

Subscription Fraud Detection: Subscription fraud occurs when fraudsters use false or stolen identities to obtain telecom services without the intention of paying. AI-powered fraud detection systems can analyze customer behavior, device information, and credit history in real time to flag high-risk applications for further review. Machine learning models can also identify patterns in subscription fraud, such as frequent use of stolen identities or unusual geographic locations, allowing telecom companies to block fraudulent subscriptions before they are activated (Aldhaheri et al., 2020).

Call and SMS Fraud Detection: Call fraud, including premium rate service (PRS) fraud, international revenue share fraud (IRSF), and Wangiri fraud (one-ring scams), is a significant concern for telecom operators. AI-driven fraud detection systems monitor call patterns and traffic volumes in real time to identify suspicious activities, such as unusually high call volumes to premium rate numbers or calls to high-risk international destinations. By analyzing large volumes of call data, machine learning models can detect patterns indicative of call fraud and automatically block fraudulent calls to minimize financial losses (Shaikh & Sasikumar, 2020).

SIM Card Cloning and SIM Swap Fraud: SIM card cloning and SIM swap fraud involve fraudsters gaining control of a victim's mobile number, often to access sensitive information or bypass two-factor authentication. AI-powered fraud detection systems monitor changes in SIM card activity, such as multiple SIM swaps in a short period or sudden changes in device location, to detect potential fraud. Machine learning models can also analyze usage patterns, such as call duration and data consumption, to identify inconsistencies that may indicate SIM cloning. By detecting these fraud indicators early, telecom companies can block SIM swaps and prevent unauthorized access to customer accounts (Kshetri, 2019).

Fraud Detection in Mobile Payments and Financial Services: With the growing use of mobile wallets and telecom-backed financial services, telecom companies face an increased risk of fraud in mobile payments. AI is used to analyze transaction data, device information, and customer behavior to detect fraudulent transactions in real time. For example, machine learning models can flag unusual payment activity, such as multiple transactions from different locations within a short time frame, as potential fraud. By integrating AI-driven fraud detection with mobile payment platforms, telecom companies can safeguard their financial services and protect customers from fraud (Aldhaheri et al., 2020).

Roaming Fraud Detection: Roaming fraud occurs when fraudsters exploit loopholes in international roaming agreements to make fraudulent calls or use data services at the expense of telecom operators. AI-powered systems analyze roaming traffic patterns, customer locations, and usage data to detect suspicious activities, such as high-volume data usage or calls made from unusual locations. By identifying roaming fraud early, telecom companies can block fraudulent activity and minimize financial losses (Shaikh & Sasikumar, 2020).

4. AI and Big Data in Fraud Detection and Prevention

The combination of AI and big data is essential for effective fraud detection and prevention in telecommunications. AI models rely on vast amounts of real-time data from call records, customer accounts, and device activity to detect fraud patterns and prevent suspicious transactions.

Real-Time Data Processing and Analysis: AI-powered fraud detection systems process large volumes of real-time data from multiple sources, including call records, transaction histories, and customer profiles. By analyzing this data in real time, AI models can identify fraudulent activities as they occur, allowing telecom operators to take immediate action, such as blocking suspicious calls or transactions. Real-time data analysis is particularly important for detecting fast-moving fraud schemes that exploit telecom networks (Kshetri, 2019).

Scalability and Adaptability: AI models are highly scalable, making them suitable for managing the large and complex datasets generated by telecommunications networks. As telecom networks expand with the adoption of 5G and IoT devices, the volume of data to be analyzed increases. AI-powered fraud detection systems can handle these large datasets and adapt to new fraud patterns as they emerge, ensuring that telecom companies stay ahead of evolving threats (Shaikh & Sasikumar, 2020).

Data Integration and Pattern Recognition: AI and big data technologies enable the integration of data from various sources, such as customer profiles, call records, network logs, and transaction histories. By combining these data streams, AI models can detect complex fraud patterns that may not be visible when analyzing individual data sources. For example, by integrating call data with customer profile information, AI models can detect inconsistencies between a customer's typical behavior and recent activity, flagging potential fraud for further investigation (Aldhaheri et al., 2020).

5. Challenges and Considerations in AI-Driven Fraud Detection

While AI-powered fraud detection systems offer numerous benefits, several challenges and considerations must be addressed:

False Positives and Accuracy: One of the main challenges in AI-driven fraud detection is reducing false positives—instances where legitimate activities are incorrectly flagged as fraud. While machine learning models can improve accuracy over time, ensuring that these models are fine-tuned to minimize false positives while maintaining high detection rates is critical to avoiding unnecessary disruptions to legitimate customers (Kshetri, 2019).

Data Privacy and Security: The use of AI in fraud detection raises concerns about data privacy and security, particularly when analyzing sensitive customer information, such as call records and financial transactions. Telecom companies must ensure that their AI systems comply with data protection regulations, such as GDPR, and implement robust security measures to protect customer data from breaches or misuse (Aldhaheri et al., 2020).

Continuous Learning and Adaptation: Fraudsters continually evolve their tactics to bypass detection systems, making it essential for AI models to continuously learn and adapt to new fraud patterns. Telecom companies must invest in regular updates to their AI models and ensure that they are trained on the latest fraud data to maintain effectiveness in detecting emerging threats (Shaikh & Sasikumar, 2020).

Conclusion

AI-powered fraud detection and prevention systems are transforming the telecommunications industry by enabling real-time detection, predictive modeling, and proactive prevention of fraudulent activities. Through machine learning, anomaly detection, and big data analytics, telecom companies can identify complex fraud patterns, reduce financial losses, and protect customer accounts from unauthorized access. As fraudsters continue to develop more sophisticated techniques, AI will play a critical role in helping telecom companies stay ahead of evolving fraud threats. While challenges such as data privacy, false positives, and continuous adaptation remain, the benefits of AI-driven fraud detection - including improved accuracy, scalability, and real-time prevention - make it an essential tool for modern telecommunications fraud management.

References

Aldhaheri, A., El-dosuky, M., & Aljuaid, A. (2020). Fraud detection in telecommunications using machine learning. *Journal of Computer Networks and Communications, 2020*, 1-12.

Bega, D., Gramaglia, M., Sciancalepore, V., Banchs, A., & Costa-Pérez, X. (2019). DeepCog: Optimizing network slicing in 5G with AI-based capacity forecasting. *IEEE Journal on Selected Areas in Communications, 37*(8), 1828-1841.

Fang, Y., Wang, Q., & Zhang, Y. (2021). AI-powered personalization in telecommunications: A customer-centric approach. *IEEE Communications Magazine, 59*(6), 52-57.

Huang, T., Ma, H., Xu, Y., Li, C., & Zhang, X. (2020). AI-driven network management in 5G: Challenges, opportunities, and future directions. *IEEE Wireless Communications, 27*(1), 10-16.

Kshetri, N. (2019). AI and big data in combating telecommunications fraud. *Telecommunications Policy, 43*(2), 185-198.

Neff, M., & Karambelas, M. (2019). AI-driven customer experience management in telecommunications: Enhancing customer loyalty through predictive analytics. *Journal of Telecommunications and Digital Transformation, 45*(2), 77-88.

Oughton, E. J., Frias, Z., van der Gaast, S., & van der Weijden, J. (2018). Exploring the cost, coverage, and rollout implications of 5G in Britain. *Telecommunications Policy, 42*(8), 636-652.

Pereira, C., & Romero, F. (2018). A survey on AI-powered virtual assistants in customer experience management. *Computing and Artificial Intelligence Review, 28*(3), 83-99.

Rathore, M. M., Ahmad, A., & Paul, A. (2018). Big data and AI-based customer experience management in telecommunications:

Transforming customer engagement. *International Journal of Information Management, 43*, 154-165.

Shaikh, S. N., & Sasikumar, D. (2020). AI-based fraud detection system for telecommunications. *International Journal of Emerging Trends in Engineering Research, 8*(9), 5144-5148.

Tang, S., Zhang, Y., & Wu, J. (2020). Intelligent network slicing management for 5G. *IEEE Wireless Communications, 27*(2), 66-72.

Zhang, J., Zhang, X., Xu, L., & Li, C. (2018). Machine learning-based network optimization in LTE-Advanced systems. *IEEE Communications Magazine, 56*(4), 47-53.

Chapter 16: Social Media and Marketing

<u>Sentiment Analysis and Opinion Mining</u>

Sentiment analysis and opinion mining are two key applications of artificial intelligence (AI) and big data in the fields of social media and marketing. Both techniques involve using AI to analyze large volumes of unstructured data, such as customer reviews, social media posts, and online discussions, to understand public sentiment and opinions about products, services, or brands. In today's digital age, consumers increasingly share their experiences and opinions online, providing a wealth of data that can be analyzed to inform marketing strategies, improve customer engagement, and enhance brand reputation management. AI-powered sentiment analysis and opinion mining allow companies to extract valuable insights from this data in real-time, helping them make more informed decisions and tailor their marketing efforts to the needs and preferences of their audience.

1. Challenges in Traditional Approaches to Sentiment Analysis and Opinion Mining

Before the advent of AI and big data analytics, marketers and brands relied on manual methods, such as surveys and focus groups, to gather insights into consumer opinions and sentiments. However, these traditional approaches face several limitations:

Limited Data Sources: Traditional methods of gathering customer feedback often rely on structured data sources, such as surveys or product reviews, which provide only a narrow view of customer sentiment. These methods fail to capture the vast amounts of unstructured data generated on social media platforms, blogs, and forums, limiting the depth and accuracy of insights (Liu, 2012).

Time-Consuming and Labor-Intensive: Manual analysis of customer feedback is time-consuming and labor-intensive, making it difficult for marketers to process large volumes of data in real-time. By the time insights are gathered and analyzed, consumer sentiment may have already shifted, reducing the relevance of the findings (Pang & Lee, 2008).

Subjectivity and Bias: Traditional sentiment analysis methods often rely on human judgment, which can introduce bias and subjectivity into the analysis. Different analysts may interpret the same customer feedback differently, leading to inconsistent results (Zhang et al., 2018).

AI and big data technologies overcome these challenges by enabling automated, scalable, and objective analysis of sentiment and opinions across a wide range of online platforms. These technologies allow companies to analyze unstructured data in real-time, providing more accurate and timely insights into consumer sentiment.

2. AI Techniques in Sentiment Analysis and Opinion Mining

Several AI techniques, including machine learning, natural language processing (NLP), and deep learning, are widely applied in sentiment analysis and opinion mining. These techniques enable marketers to analyze text data, identify sentiment polarity (positive, negative, or neutral), and extract opinions from large datasets.

Natural Language Processing (NLP): NLP is a branch of AI that focuses on enabling machines to understand and interpret human language. In sentiment analysis and opinion mining, NLP techniques are used to process and analyze unstructured text data from social media, blogs, and online reviews. NLP tasks such as tokenization, part-of-speech tagging, and named entity recognition help break down text into meaningful components, allowing sentiment analysis models to understand the context and sentiment expressed in the data (Cambria et al., 2017).

Machine Learning (ML): Machine learning models are used to classify text as positive, negative, or neutral based on the sentiment expressed. Supervised learning algorithms, such as support vector machines (SVMs), Naïve Bayes classifiers, and decision trees, are trained on labeled datasets containing text with known sentiment labels. These models can then predict the sentiment of new, unseen text by identifying patterns in word usage, sentence structure, and context (Liu, 2012). Additionally, unsupervised learning techniques, such as clustering, can be used to discover topics and opinions in text data without labeled training data.

Deep Learning (DL): Deep learning models, particularly recurrent neural networks (RNNs) and convolutional neural networks (CNNs), have shown great promise in improving the accuracy of sentiment analysis and opinion mining. RNNs, such as long short-term memory (LSTM) networks, are particularly effective at handling sequential data, making them ideal for analyzing the flow of sentiment across long text passages. CNNs, traditionally used for image processing, have also been adapted to detect patterns in text data, allowing for more accurate sentiment classification and opinion extraction (Zhang et al., 2018).

Sentiment Lexicons and Rule-Based Models: In addition to machine learning and deep learning models, sentiment lexicons and rule-based approaches are used for sentiment analysis. Sentiment lexicons are predefined lists of words associated with positive, negative, or neutral sentiments. Rule-based models use these lexicons to assign sentiment scores to text based on the presence of sentiment-bearing words or phrases. While these models are simpler and easier to implement, they may struggle with handling nuanced or context-dependent sentiments (Cambria et al., 2017).

3. Applications of AI in Sentiment Analysis and Opinion Mining

AI-powered sentiment analysis and opinion mining are applied across various aspects of social media and marketing, including brand reputation management, customer feedback analysis, targeted advertising, and market research.

Brand Reputation Management: One of the most important applications of sentiment analysis in marketing is monitoring and managing brand reputation. AI-powered sentiment analysis tools allow companies to track mentions of their brand across social media platforms and online forums. By analyzing the sentiment of these mentions, companies can quickly identify negative sentiment and respond to customer complaints or crises in real-time. This proactive approach helps companies mitigate the impact of negative publicity and maintain a positive brand image (Mostafa, 2013). For example, a sudden increase in negative sentiment related to a product defect or service issue can trigger an alert, allowing the company to address the problem before it escalates.

Customer Feedback Analysis: Sentiment analysis and opinion mining are also widely used to analyze customer feedback from product reviews, surveys, and customer service interactions. AI models can identify common themes and opinions expressed by customers, helping companies understand what aspects of their products or services are generating positive or negative feedback. By gaining insights into customer preferences and pain points, companies can make data-driven decisions to improve their offerings and enhance the overall customer experience (Zhang et al., 2018).

Targeted Advertising and Personalization: AI-driven sentiment analysis is used to improve targeted advertising by analyzing customer sentiment and behavior on social media. By understanding how customers feel about specific products, brands, or topics, companies can create personalized advertisements that resonate with their audience. For example, sentiment analysis can help marketers identify customers who have expressed positive sentiment toward a product and target them with ads for related products or services. This level of personalization improves the effectiveness of marketing campaigns and increases conversion rates (Mostafa, 2013).

Market Research and Competitive Analysis: Opinion mining allows companies to gain insights into broader market trends and competitor performance. By analyzing customer sentiment toward competing brands, companies can identify areas where they have a competitive advantage or areas where they need to improve. Sentiment analysis can also be used to track how public opinion changes over time, providing valuable insights into emerging trends, consumer preferences, and market dynamics (Cambria et al., 2017). For example, companies can use sentiment analysis to gauge customer reactions to a competitor's new product launch and adjust their marketing strategies accordingly.

Crisis Management and Public Relations: AI-powered sentiment analysis can help companies detect early warning signs of potential crises or public relations issues by monitoring spikes in negative sentiment on social media. By identifying and addressing negative sentiment before it spreads, companies can take corrective actions to protect their brand reputation. Sentiment analysis tools can also be used to measure the effectiveness of public relations campaigns by analyzing changes in public sentiment following a crisis or brand announcement (Mostafa, 2013).

4. AI and Big Data in Sentiment Analysis and Opinion Mining

The combination of AI and big data is critical for effective sentiment analysis and opinion mining in social media and marketing. AI models rely on vast amounts of data from social media platforms, online reviews, and customer interactions to generate accurate insights into public sentiment and opinions.

Real-Time Data Processing and Analysis: AI-powered sentiment analysis systems process large volumes of real-time data from social media platforms, blogs, and forums. By analyzing this data in real time, AI models can detect shifts in sentiment and provide companies with timely insights into how their brand is perceived. This real-time analysis is particularly valuable for monitoring public reactions to new product launches, marketing campaigns, or public relations events (Zhang et al., 2018).

Scalability and Data Integration: Social media platforms generate massive amounts of unstructured data, making it essential for AI models to be scalable and capable of processing large datasets. AI-powered sentiment analysis systems can handle the complexity of analyzing text data from multiple sources, including posts, comments, hashtags, and emojis. By integrating data from different platforms, AI models can provide a comprehensive view of public sentiment and opinions across the entire digital landscape (Liu, 2012).

Predictive and Prescriptive Analytics: In addition to analyzing past and current sentiment, AI and big data technologies enable predictive and prescriptive analytics in sentiment analysis. Predictive analytics tools forecast how sentiment toward a brand or product is likely to evolve based on historical data and external factors, such as market trends or competitor actions. Prescriptive analytics provides actionable recommendations on how to respond to changes in sentiment, such as launching targeted campaigns to address negative feedback or capitalizing on positive sentiment to increase engagement (Cambria et al., 2017).

5. Challenges and Considerations in AI-Driven Sentiment Analysis

While AI-powered sentiment analysis and opinion mining offer numerous benefits, several challenges and considerations must be addressed:

Context and Nuance: One of the main challenges in sentiment analysis is understanding the context and nuance of language. Sarcasm, irony, and ambiguous language can be difficult for AI models to interpret, leading to misclassifications of sentiment. Ensuring that AI models are capable of understanding context and detecting subtleties in language is essential for improving the accuracy of sentiment analysis (Pang & Lee, 2008).

Multilingual and Multicultural Analysis: Social media platforms are global, and users often communicate in multiple languages and dialects. AI models used for sentiment analysis must be able to handle multilingual data and account for cultural differences in language and communication styles. Developing models that can accurately analyze sentiment across diverse languages and cultures is a key challenge in global marketing efforts (Zhang et al., 2018).

Data Privacy and Ethics: The use of AI and big data in sentiment analysis raises concerns about data privacy and ethics. Social media platforms collect vast amounts of personal data, and the use of this data for sentiment analysis must comply with data protection regulations, such as GDPR. Companies must ensure that they are transparent about how they collect and analyze customer data and that they respect user privacy (Mostafa, 2013).

In summary, AI-powered sentiment analysis and opinion mining are transforming how companies in social media and marketing engage with customers and manage brand reputation. Through natural language processing, machine learning, and big data analytics, companies can analyze large volumes of unstructured data to gain real-time insights into customer sentiment and opinions. These insights enable companies to deliver personalized marketing campaigns, improve customer satisfaction, and respond to emerging trends and issues. While challenges such as context, multilingual analysis, and data privacy must be addressed, the benefits of AI-driven sentiment analysis - including improved brand reputation management, targeted advertising, and market research - make it an essential tool for modern marketers.

Targeted Advertising

Targeted advertising is one of the most transformative applications of artificial intelligence (AI) and big data in social media and marketing.

In the digital age, consumers generate vast amounts of data through their interactions on social media platforms, online searches, browsing histories, and e-commerce activities. AI-powered targeted advertising enables companies to leverage this data to create highly personalized advertisements that are tailored to individual users' preferences, behaviors, and needs. By analyzing user data in real-time and applying machine learning algorithms, AI helps marketers deliver the right message to the right audience at the right time, improving the effectiveness of marketing campaigns and maximizing return on investment (ROI). This data-driven approach to advertising is now a cornerstone of digital marketing strategies across industries.

1. Challenges in Traditional Advertising

Traditional advertising methods, such as television ads, billboards, and print media, often suffer from several limitations that reduce their effectiveness in reaching and engaging specific audiences:

Mass Market Approach: Traditional advertising is typically designed for a broad audience and often lacks personalization. This one-size-fits-all approach results in less relevant content for individual consumers, leading to lower engagement and conversion rates. Additionally, traditional ads often target large, generalized demographic groups rather than specific customer segments (Chen et al., 2019).

Limited Measurement and Feedback: Traditional advertising methods offer limited tools for measuring the effectiveness of campaigns. Marketers may rely on basic metrics such as reach or impressions, but these metrics do not provide deep insights into consumer behavior or engagement. This lack of feedback makes it difficult for marketers to refine and optimize their advertising strategies in real-time (Kietzmann et al., 2018).

High Costs: Traditional advertising campaigns, particularly in television and print media, can be costly to produce and distribute, with no guarantee of reaching the right audience. The inability to target specific consumer groups efficiently often leads to wasted advertising spend (Jin et al., 2020).

AI and big data technologies address these challenges by enabling marketers to create highly personalized, data-driven campaigns that target specific audience segments based on individual preferences, behaviors, and real-time data.

2. AI Techniques in Targeted Advertising

AI techniques such as machine learning, deep learning, natural language processing (NLP), and predictive analytics are at the core of targeted advertising. These technologies allow marketers to analyze large datasets, predict user behavior, and deliver personalized ads with high precision.

Machine Learning (ML): Machine learning algorithms play a central role in targeted advertising by analyzing user data to identify patterns in behavior, preferences, and interests. Supervised learning models, such as decision trees, random forests, and logistic regression, are trained on historical data to predict which ads a user is most likely to engage with based on their past behavior. These models can be used to segment audiences into groups with similar characteristics, allowing marketers to deliver personalized ads to each segment (Jin et al., 2020).

Deep Learning (DL): Deep learning models, particularly neural networks, are used to process complex and large datasets, such as images, videos, and social media interactions. Convolutional neural networks (CNNs) can analyze visual content to identify patterns in user preferences, while recurrent neural networks (RNNs), such as long short-term memory (LSTM) networks, are used to predict user behavior over time. Deep learning models are particularly effective at understanding the nuances of user interactions and delivering more accurate ad targeting (Zhou et al., 2018).

Natural Language Processing (NLP): NLP techniques enable marketers to analyze text-based data, such as social media posts, search queries, and reviews, to understand user sentiment and intent. By analyzing the language used in these interactions, NLP models can determine what products or services a user is interested in and deliver relevant ads accordingly. For example, if a user frequently discusses travel on social media, AI systems can target them with ads for flights, hotels, or vacation packages (Chen et al., 2019).

Predictive Analytics: Predictive analytics tools leverage AI and big data to forecast user behavior and predict which ads are most likely to lead to conversions. By analyzing historical data, such as past purchases, browsing history, and engagement with previous ads, predictive analytics models can estimate the likelihood that a user will click on a specific ad or make a purchase. These insights help marketers optimize their ad targeting and allocate resources more effectively (Kietzmann et al., 2018).

Behavioral Targeting: AI-powered behavioral targeting involves analyzing user behavior, such as browsing habits, search history, and interactions with content, to deliver ads that are aligned with a user's current interests and needs. Machine learning models identify patterns in user behavior and serve ads that are relevant to their immediate context, increasing the likelihood of engagement. For example, if a user frequently searches for home improvement products, AI systems can target them with ads for related items, such as furniture or tools (Jin et al., 2020).

3. Applications of AI in Targeted Advertising

AI-powered targeted advertising is applied across various digital platforms, including social media, search engines, e-commerce websites, and video streaming services. The ability to analyze user data in real-time and deliver personalized ads is transforming how companies reach and engage their target audiences.

Personalized Ads on Social Media: Social media platforms like Facebook, Instagram, and Twitter leverage AI to analyze user interactions, interests, and connections to deliver highly personalized ads. By analyzing user behavior, such as the pages they follow, the content they engage with, and their social connections, AI models can deliver ads that are tailored to each user's preferences. This personalized approach increases engagement and improves the effectiveness of social media marketing campaigns (Zhou et al., 2018). For example, Facebook's ad targeting algorithm uses machine learning to match users with ads that align with their interests, behaviors, and demographics, allowing advertisers to reach specific audiences with personalized content.

Search Engine Advertising: AI plays a critical role in search engine advertising (e.g., Google Ads), where ads are targeted based on users' search queries and browsing history. NLP techniques analyze the language used in search queries to understand user intent, while machine learning models predict which ads are most likely to lead to clicks or conversions. This allows marketers to bid for ad placements that are highly relevant to user searches, maximizing the ROI of search engine marketing campaigns (Chen et al., 2019).

Programmatic Advertising: Programmatic advertising is the automated buying and selling of online ad space, driven by AI and real-time bidding (RTB) systems. AI models analyze user data, such as browsing habits and past interactions with ads, to determine the value of ad placements for specific users in real-time. This enables advertisers to bid on ad impressions that are most likely to lead to conversions, optimizing their ad spend and ensuring that their ads reach the right audience at the right moment. Programmatic advertising is widely used in display advertising, video ads, and mobile ads (Kietzmann et al., 2018).

Retargeting: Retargeting is a popular form of targeted advertising where AI is used to deliver ads to users who have previously interacted with a brand but have not yet made a purchase. For example, if a user browses an e-commerce website and adds items to their cart but does not complete the purchase, AI models can track this behavior and serve retargeted ads to remind the user of the products they viewed. Retargeting helps marketers re-engage potential customers and increase conversion rates by delivering ads that align with the user's previous interactions (Jin et al., 2020).

Dynamic Creative Optimization (DCO): AI is used in dynamic creative optimization (DCO) to automatically generate personalized ad content based on user data. DCO systems analyze user preferences, behaviors, and demographic information to create tailored ad variations that resonate with specific audiences. For example, an online retailer can use AI to create personalized ads featuring different product images, headlines, and offers based on the user's browsing history. This level of personalization enhances ad relevance and improves engagement (Zhou et al., 2018).

Video and Audio Streaming Platforms: Video and audio streaming platforms, such as YouTube, Netflix, and Spotify, use AI to deliver targeted ads based on user preferences, viewing history, and content consumption patterns. AI models analyze user interactions with video or audio content to determine the best ads to serve during streaming sessions. For instance, Spotify uses AI to deliver personalized audio ads to users based on their listening habits, while YouTube targets users with video ads related to the content they frequently watch (Chen et al., 2019).

4. AI and Big Data in Targeted Advertising

AI and big data technologies are essential for targeted advertising because they enable marketers to process large volumes of data from various sources and deliver personalized ads in real-time. AI models analyze data from social media interactions, search queries, purchase histories, and browsing behaviors to create detailed user profiles that guide ad targeting decisions.

Real-Time Data Processing and Analysis: AI-powered targeted advertising systems process massive amounts of real-time data to deliver ads that are relevant to users' current behaviors and preferences. Real-time analysis allows marketers to respond to changes in user behavior immediately, ensuring that ads are timely and engaging. For example, if a user shows interest in a particular product by searching for it or adding it to their cart, AI systems can quickly deliver related ads across social media and other digital platforms (Kietzmann et al., 2018).

Scalability and Personalization: AI models are highly scalable, making them capable of processing data for millions of users and delivering personalized ads at scale. This scalability is essential for social media platforms, search engines, and e-commerce websites, where millions of users generate data every second. AI-powered systems can analyze this data to create individualized ad experiences for each user, increasing the relevance and effectiveness of digital marketing campaigns (Zhou et al., 2018).

Predictive and Prescriptive Analytics: AI and big data enable both predictive and prescriptive analytics in targeted advertising. Predictive analytics tools forecast user behavior, such as the likelihood of making a purchase, based on historical data and real-time interactions. Prescriptive analytics goes a step further by providing recommendations on which ads to serve, when to serve them, and which channels to use, optimizing the overall ad strategy for maximum ROI (Jin et al., 2020).

5. Challenges and Considerations in AI-Driven Targeted Advertising

While AI-powered targeted advertising offers numerous benefits, several challenges and considerations must be addressed:

Data Privacy and Security: The use of AI in targeted advertising raises concerns about data privacy and security, particularly in light of regulations such as the General Data Protection Regulation (GDPR) and the California Consumer Privacy Act (CCPA). Companies must ensure that they collect and process user data transparently and with consent, while also safeguarding this data from breaches or misuse. Maintaining user trust is critical for the success of targeted advertising (Kietzmann et al., 2018).

Ad Fatigue and Consumer Resistance: While personalized ads can improve engagement, over-targeting or delivering repetitive ads can lead to ad fatigue and consumer resistance. AI models must be fine-tuned to avoid bombarding users with the same ads repeatedly, ensuring that advertising remains relevant and non-intrusive (Zhou et al., 2018).

Algorithmic Bias and Fairness: AI models used in targeted advertising may inadvertently introduce bias by favoring certain demographic groups over others, based on the data they are trained on. Ensuring that AI models are fair and unbiased is essential for preventing discrimination and delivering inclusive marketing experiences (Jin et al., 2020).

In summary, AI-powered targeted advertising is transforming the marketing landscape by enabling companies to deliver highly personalized ads to specific audience segments based on real-time data analysis. Through machine learning, deep learning, and big data analytics, marketers can predict user behavior, optimize ad targeting, and create dynamic, relevant ad experiences that improve engagement and conversions. While challenges such as data privacy, algorithmic bias, and ad fatigue must be addressed, the benefits of AI-driven targeted advertising - enhanced personalization, improved ROI, and scalable ad delivery - make it an indispensable tool for modern marketers.

Social Network Analysis

Social network analysis (SNA) is an essential application of artificial intelligence (AI) and big data in social media and marketing. It involves the study of relationships, interactions, and connections between individuals, groups, or organizations within a social network. With the explosion of social media platforms such as Facebook, Twitter, LinkedIn, and Instagram, vast amounts of data are generated daily, offering rich insights into the structure and dynamics of these networks. AI-powered social network analysis enables marketers to identify influential users, understand the flow of information, track user behavior, and design targeted campaigns based on social connections and influence. By analyzing the interactions between users and their networks, businesses can gain a competitive edge in customer engagement, brand positioning, and personalized marketing strategies.

1. Challenges in Traditional Social Network Analysis

Before the integration of AI and big data analytics, traditional social network analysis methods were limited in scope and scalability. As social networks grew larger and more complex, traditional methods struggled to analyze and derive actionable insights from massive datasets. Some of the challenges include:

Manual Data Collection and Analysis: Traditional social network analysis relied on manual data collection, which was time-consuming and prone to human error. This approach could not keep up with the rapidly growing size of modern social networks and the increasing volume of interactions (Lazer et al., 2009).

Static Analysis: Traditional methods often produced static, one-time analysis snapshots that did not capture the dynamic and ever-changing nature of social networks. These methods failed to provide real-time insights into the evolving structure of relationships and influence patterns in online social networks (Borgatti et al., 2013).

Limited Scalability: Traditional network analysis methods were limited in scalability and could only handle small networks with a relatively low number of nodes (users) and edges (connections).

Analyzing large-scale social media networks with millions of users and interactions required more advanced tools capable of processing vast datasets in real-time (Scott, 2017).

AI and big data technologies overcome these challenges by automating the data collection and analysis process, enabling marketers to analyze massive, dynamic networks at scale. AI-powered social network analysis helps marketers gain real-time insights into user behavior, influence patterns, and social connections, allowing for more targeted and data-driven marketing strategies.

2. AI Techniques in Social Network Analysis

AI techniques, such as machine learning, graph theory, and natural language processing (NLP), are widely applied in social network analysis to uncover patterns, identify key influencers, and predict the spread of information within a network. These techniques enable marketers to analyze the complex structure of social media networks and extract valuable insights about user behavior, influence, and engagement.

Machine Learning (ML): Machine learning algorithms are applied to social network analysis to uncover patterns in user behavior and identify key influencers within a network. Supervised learning models can classify users based on their level of engagement, influence, or likelihood to take specific actions (e.g., sharing content, making a purchase). For example, clustering algorithms can segment users into groups based on their behavior, interests, or connections, allowing marketers to target specific communities within a network (Golbeck, 2013).

Graph Theory and Network Analytics: Social networks can be represented as graphs, where nodes represent users and edges represent the connections between them. Graph theory is used to analyze the structure of these networks, identify key nodes (influential users), and understand how information flows within the network.

Centrality measures, such as degree centrality, closeness centrality, and betweenness centrality, are used to identify influential users who have the greatest impact on the spread of information (Freeman, 1978). AI-powered graph analytics tools can analyze large-scale networks in real-time, enabling marketers to identify key influencers and optimize their marketing strategies accordingly.

Natural Language Processing (NLP): NLP techniques are used to analyze text-based data from social media posts, comments, and messages to understand the sentiment and context of conversations within a network. By processing this unstructured data, NLP models can identify trending topics, detect shifts in public sentiment, and track the spread of information. NLP is particularly useful for analyzing user-generated content in real-time, enabling marketers to respond quickly to emerging trends and customer feedback (Cambria et al., 2017).

Community Detection: AI-powered community detection algorithms are used to identify subgroups or communities within social networks. These communities are often formed around shared interests, behaviors, or interactions. By identifying and analyzing these communities, marketers can develop targeted campaigns tailored to specific groups of users who share common interests or behaviors. For example, community detection can help marketers identify groups of users who are interested in specific product categories, enabling more personalized marketing efforts (Girvan & Newman, 2002).

Influence Propagation Models: AI models are used to predict how information, trends, or products will spread within a social network. These models analyze the structure of the network, the strength of connections between users, and historical data on information diffusion to forecast how a particular message or campaign will propagate. This enables marketers to optimize their campaigns by targeting users who are most likely to amplify their messages and influence others (Guille et al., 2013).

3. Applications of AI in Social Network Analysis

AI-powered social network analysis is applied across various aspects of social media and marketing, including influencer marketing, customer segmentation, information diffusion analysis, and brand advocacy.

Influencer Marketing: One of the most prominent applications of social network analysis is identifying key influencers within a network. Influencers are users who have significant influence over the opinions and behaviors of others in their network. AI models analyze the structure of social networks to identify users with high centrality measures, such as those with the most connections (degree centrality) or those who act as intermediaries between different groups (betweenness centrality). Marketers can then collaborate with these influencers to promote products, services, or brand messages, amplifying their reach and engagement (Golbeck, 2013).

Customer Segmentation and Targeting: Social network analysis enables marketers to segment users into different groups based on their behaviors, interactions, and relationships within the network. AI-powered clustering algorithms can identify communities of users who share similar interests or behaviors, allowing marketers to create targeted campaigns that resonate with specific customer segments. For example, a brand might identify a community of eco-conscious users within a social network and target them with campaigns promoting sustainable products (Girvan & Newman, 2002).

Information Diffusion and Virality: AI models are used to analyze the spread of information within social networks and predict the likelihood of content going viral. By understanding how information flows through a network and identifying influential nodes, marketers can optimize the timing and targeting of their campaigns to maximize reach. For instance, a brand can use social network analysis to determine the best time to launch a campaign based on when key influencers are most active, increasing the chances of the content being shared widely (Guille et al., 2013).

Sentiment Analysis and Brand Advocacy: AI-powered sentiment analysis is used to analyze the tone and sentiment of conversations within social networks. By tracking the sentiment of user-generated content, such as posts and comments, marketers can gauge public opinion about their brand or products. Social network analysis helps identify brand advocates—users who consistently share positive sentiments and promote the brand within their networks. Marketers can engage with these advocates to strengthen brand loyalty and amplify positive messages (Cambria et al., 2017).

Crisis Management and Public Relations: AI-driven social network analysis can help companies detect and manage potential crises by monitoring spikes in negative sentiment and tracking the spread of harmful information. By identifying key nodes in the network where negative sentiment originates, companies can take proactive measures to address the issue and contain the spread of damaging content. This real-time analysis enables brands to respond quickly to emerging crises and mitigate potential harm to their reputation (Borgatti et al., 2013).

Targeted Advertising and Campaign Optimization: AI-powered social network analysis allows marketers to optimize their advertising strategies by identifying the most effective nodes (users) to target within a network. By understanding the influence of certain users and their connections, marketers can design campaigns that are more likely to be shared and discussed within specific communities. This targeted approach increases the relevance of ads, improves engagement, and maximizes the impact of marketing spend (Zhou et al., 2018).

4. AI and Big Data in Social Network Analysis

The combination of AI and big data technologies is critical for effective social network analysis in social media and marketing. AI models rely on vast amounts of data from social media platforms, user interactions, and network connections to uncover patterns and generate insights.

Real-Time Data Processing: Social media networks generate massive amounts of data in real-time, making it essential for AI-powered social network analysis systems to process this data quickly and efficiently. AI models analyze data from user interactions, posts, likes, shares, and comments to provide marketers with up-to-the-minute insights into how information is spreading within the network. Real-time data processing allows brands to respond to trends and user behaviors as they unfold (Guille et al., 2013).

Scalability and Large-Scale Network Analysis: AI-powered social network analysis tools are highly scalable, enabling marketers to analyze networks with millions of users and connections. This scalability is essential for understanding the complex dynamics of large-scale social media platforms like Facebook, Instagram, and Twitter. AI models can process and analyze massive datasets to identify influencers, detect communities, and track information diffusion across vast networks (Scott, 2017).

Predictive and Prescriptive Analytics: AI and big data technologies enable both predictive and prescriptive analytics in social network analysis. Predictive analytics tools forecast how information, trends, or products will spread within a network based on historical data and network structure. Prescriptive analytics provides actionable recommendations on how to optimize marketing campaigns, such as which users to target or when to launch a campaign for maximum impact (Golbeck, 2013).

5. Challenges and Considerations in AI-Driven Social Network Analysis

While AI-powered social network analysis offers numerous benefits, several challenges and considerations must be addressed:

Data Privacy and Security: The use of AI and big data in social network analysis raises concerns about data privacy and security. Social media platforms collect vast amounts of personal data, and the use of this data for marketing purposes must comply with data protection regulations such as the General Data Protection Regulation (GDPR). Companies must ensure that they are transparent about how they collect and use user data and that they protect it from breaches or misuse (Borgatti et al., 2013).

Algorithmic Bias and Fairness: AI models used in social network analysis must be free from bias to ensure fair and accurate analysis. Biased algorithms may favor certain groups of users over others, leading to skewed results and unfair targeting practices. Ensuring that AI models are trained on diverse datasets and are free from bias is critical for delivering accurate and equitable insights (Golbeck, 2013).

Interpreting Complex Networks: Social networks are highly complex, and interpreting the structure and dynamics of these networks can be challenging. AI models must be capable of capturing the nuances of user interactions and relationships to generate meaningful insights. Developing models that can accurately reflect the complexity of social networks is essential for delivering actionable results (Freeman, 1978).

In summary, AI-powered social network analysis is transforming the way companies engage with consumers, manage brand reputation, and design targeted marketing strategies. By analyzing the structure and dynamics of social media networks, AI models can identify key influencers, track information diffusion, and optimize marketing campaigns for maximum reach and engagement. The combination of

AI and big data enables marketers to analyze large-scale networks in real-time, uncovering valuable insights about user behavior, social connections, and influence patterns. While challenges such as data privacy, algorithmic bias, and network complexity must be addressed, the benefits of AI-driven social network analysis - enhanced influencer marketing, targeted advertising, and improved customer segmentation - make it an indispensable tool for modern marketers.

Viral Content Prediction

Viral content prediction is a significant application of artificial intelligence (AI) and big data analytics in social media and marketing. Viral content, such as videos, articles, or social media posts, spreads rapidly across networks and attracts a large audience in a short period of time. For marketers, the ability to predict which content is likely to go viral can provide a significant competitive advantage, leading to increased engagement, brand visibility, and return on investment (ROI). However, predicting virality is challenging due to the unpredictable nature of human behavior and the complex dynamics of social media networks. AI, combined with big data, enables marketers to analyze vast amounts of social media data and apply machine learning algorithms to identify the factors that increase the likelihood of content going viral. These technologies help marketers create more effective campaigns, optimize content strategies, and boost their chances of success in the highly competitive digital landscape.

1. Challenges in Traditional Viral Content Prediction

Before the advent of AI and big data, marketers relied on experience, intuition, and basic metrics such as likes, shares, or views to assess the potential of content going viral. However, traditional methods of predicting viral content were often imprecise and struggled to capture the complex interactions and behaviors that drive virality. Some of the key challenges include:

Unpredictability of User Behavior: Viral content is driven by user behavior, which can be highly unpredictable. Traditional methods often fail to account for the spontaneous nature of virality, where a piece of content may suddenly gain widespread attention due to external factors such as trends, events, or influential figures sharing it (Tatar et al., 2014).

Focus on Simple Metrics: Traditional viral content prediction often relies on simple metrics such as the number of likes, shares, or comments. While these metrics provide some indication of engagement, they do not capture the full complexity of social media interactions, such as the influence of specific users, timing of posts, or the emotional resonance of the content (Althoff et al., 2017).

Lack of Real-Time Analysis: Traditional approaches to viral content prediction are often retrospective, analyzing content after it has already gained traction. This limits the ability to predict virality in real-time and prevents marketers from making timely adjustments to their campaigns to maximize reach and engagement (Cheng et al., 2014).

AI and big data technologies address these challenges by enabling marketers to analyze large datasets in real-time, identify patterns that drive virality, and predict which content has the potential to go viral before it happens.

2. AI Techniques in Viral Content Prediction

Several AI techniques, including machine learning, deep learning, natural language processing (NLP), and network analysis, are widely used to predict viral content. These techniques allow marketers to analyze the factors that contribute to content virality, such as user engagement, emotional resonance, network dynamics, and timing.

Machine Learning (ML): Machine learning models are at the core of viral content prediction, analyzing historical data to identify patterns in user engagement and content performance. Supervised learning algorithms, such as decision trees, random forests, and support vector machines (SVMs), are trained on labeled datasets containing information about viral and non-viral content. These models can then predict the likelihood of new content going viral based on factors such as the number of shares, likes, and comments it has received in its early stages (Tatar et al., 2014). Additionally, unsupervised learning techniques, such as clustering, can be used to group content into categories based on engagement patterns, helping marketers identify trends that may influence virality.

Deep Learning (DL): Deep learning models, particularly recurrent neural networks (RNNs) and convolutional neural networks (CNNs), are used to process complex, high-dimensional data, such as images, videos, and text. RNNs, especially long short-term memory (LSTM) networks, are well-suited for analyzing time-series data and predicting how user engagement with content will evolve over time. CNNs can analyze visual content to detect patterns that contribute to virality, such as specific image features or video elements that resonate with audiences (Althoff et al., 2017). Deep learning models are particularly effective at capturing the nonlinear relationships between different factors that drive content virality.

Natural Language Processing (NLP): NLP techniques are used to analyze the language, tone, and sentiment of content to predict its potential for virality. By processing text data from social media posts, comments, and captions, NLP models can identify emotional triggers, such as humor, fear, or excitement, that are more likely to prompt users to share content. Sentiment analysis can also be used to gauge how audiences feel about a piece of content, with highly positive or negative sentiment often correlating with increased engagement and sharing behavior (Cheng et al., 2014). NLP is particularly useful for analyzing user-generated content, such as reviews, tweets, or Facebook posts, to understand how users are responding to a campaign in real-time.

Network Analysis: Social networks play a crucial role in determining whether content will go viral. AI-powered social network analysis tools are used to analyze the structure and dynamics of social media networks, identifying influential users who are likely to share content with their followers. By examining the strength of connections between users and the flow of information through the network, AI models can predict how quickly and widely a piece of content will spread. Centrality measures, such as degree centrality and betweenness centrality, are used to identify key influencers who can amplify content and increase its chances of going viral (Tatar et al., 2014).

Predictive Analytics: Predictive analytics tools leverage AI and big data to forecast the future performance of content based on early engagement metrics. These tools analyze real-time data, such as the number of views, shares, or comments a post receives in the first few hours, to estimate the likelihood of the content going viral. Predictive models can also take into account external factors, such as current trends, events, or the influence of specific users, to refine their predictions. By providing early insights into content performance, predictive analytics helps marketers make real-time adjustments to their campaigns to maximize engagement (Cheng et al., 2014).

3. Applications of AI in Viral Content Prediction

AI-powered viral content prediction is applied across various aspects of social media marketing, including content creation, campaign optimization, influencer marketing, and crisis management.

Content Creation and Optimization: AI-driven viral content prediction helps marketers create content that is more likely to resonate with their target audience and go viral. By analyzing historical data on viral content, AI models can identify the types of content, themes, or formats that are most likely to generate high engagement. Marketers can then use these insights to optimize their content creation strategies, ensuring that their posts are more likely to be shared and discussed by a broad audience (Althoff et al., 2017). For example, AI models may reveal that humorous or emotionally charged content has a higher likelihood of going viral, guiding marketers to incorporate these elements into their campaigns.

Campaign Optimization: AI-powered viral content prediction enables marketers to optimize their campaigns in real-time by analyzing early engagement data. Predictive models can forecast how a piece of content will perform based on its initial reception, allowing marketers to adjust their strategies accordingly. For example, if a post receives a high number of shares and comments shortly after being published, AI models may predict that it has a high likelihood of going viral. Marketers can then allocate more resources to promote the post, such as increasing ad spend or partnering with influencers to amplify its reach (Cheng et al., 2014).

Influencer Marketing: Influencers play a key role in driving the virality of content, as they have the ability to reach large, engaged audiences. AI-powered social network analysis tools can identify influencers who are most likely to help a piece of content go viral based on their network position, follower engagement, and sharing behavior. By partnering with these influencers, marketers can increase the chances of their content being widely shared and discussed. Additionally, AI models can predict which influencers are likely to generate the highest engagement with a particular piece of content, allowing marketers to target their efforts more effectively (Tatar et al., 2014).

Crisis Management: AI-powered viral content prediction can also be used in crisis management to detect and mitigate the spread of negative or harmful content. By analyzing real-time data on the spread of potentially damaging posts, AI models can predict whether a negative story or post is likely to go viral. This allows brands to take proactive measures to address the issue, such as issuing a public response or engaging with key influencers to control the narrative. Predictive analytics helps brands stay ahead of emerging crises and limit the impact of negative content on their reputation (Cheng et al., 2014).

Ad Targeting and Engagement: AI-driven viral content prediction helps optimize ad targeting by identifying which content is likely to generate the highest engagement. By predicting which posts will go viral, marketers can allocate their ad budgets more efficiently, focusing on promoting content that is more likely to resonate with their audience. This approach increases the effectiveness of advertising campaigns and ensures that resources are spent on high-performing content that has the potential to reach a broader audience (Tatar et al., 2014).

4. AI and Big Data in Viral Content Prediction

AI and big data technologies are essential for viral content prediction because they enable the analysis of large-scale datasets from social media platforms, user interactions, and engagement metrics. These technologies help marketers uncover patterns, predict user behavior, and optimize content strategies.

Real-Time Data Processing: AI-powered viral content prediction systems process large volumes of real-time data from social media platforms, such as Twitter, Facebook, Instagram, and TikTok. By analyzing real-time metrics, such as likes, shares, comments, and views, AI models can quickly assess the performance of content and predict whether it is likely to go viral. This real-time analysis enables marketers to respond rapidly to emerging trends and optimize their campaigns on the fly (Cheng et al., 2014).

Scalability and Network Dynamics: Social media platforms generate vast amounts of data every second, making it essential for AI models to be scalable and capable of processing large datasets. AI-powered viral content prediction tools can analyze data from millions of users and interactions, identifying the key factors that drive virality at scale. These tools can also account for network dynamics, such as the influence of specific users or communities, to refine their predictions and improve the accuracy of their models (Tatar et al., 2014).

Predictive and Prescriptive Analytics: AI and big data enable both predictive and prescriptive analytics in viral content prediction. Predictive analytics tools forecast the likelihood of content going viral based on historical data and early engagement metrics. Prescriptive analytics provides actionable recommendations on how to optimize content strategies, such as which types of content to create, when to post, and which influencers to target. These insights help marketers maximize the impact of their campaigns and increase their chances of success (Althoff et al., 2017).

5. Challenges and Considerations in AI-Driven Viral Content Prediction

While AI-powered viral content prediction offers numerous benefits, several challenges and considerations must be addressed:

Complexity of Human Behavior: Predicting virality is inherently difficult due to the complex and unpredictable nature of human behavior. While AI models can identify patterns in engagement data, they may struggle to capture the full range of external factors, such as current events, cultural trends, or social dynamics, that influence content virality (Cheng et al., 2014).

Data Privacy and Ethics: The use of AI and big data in viral content prediction raises concerns about data privacy and ethics. Social media platforms collect vast amounts of personal data, and the use of this data for marketing purposes must comply with data protection regulations, such as the General Data Protection Regulation (GDPR). Companies must ensure that they are transparent about how they collect and use user data and that they protect it from breaches or misuse (Tatar et al., 2014).

Algorithmic Bias and Fairness: AI models used in viral content prediction must be free from bias to ensure fair and accurate predictions. Biased algorithms may favor certain types of content or users over others, leading to skewed results and unfair targeting practices. Ensuring that AI models are trained on diverse datasets and are free from bias is critical for delivering accurate and equitable predictions (Althoff et al., 2017).

Conclusion

AI-powered viral content prediction is transforming the way marketers create, optimize, and promote content on social media platforms. By leveraging machine learning, deep learning, NLP, and network analysis, marketers can analyze large-scale datasets, predict the likelihood of content going viral, and optimize their campaigns for maximum engagement. The combination of AI and big data enables real-time analysis of social media interactions, providing marketers with actionable insights that help them stay ahead of trends and capitalize on viral opportunities. While challenges such as the complexity of human behavior, data privacy, and algorithmic bias must be addressed, the benefits of AI-driven viral content prediction - enhanced campaign optimization, increased engagement, and improved targeting - make it an invaluable tool for modern marketers.

References

Althoff, T., Jindal, P., & Leskovec, J. (2017). Online actions with offline impact: How online social networks influence online and offline user behavior. *Proceedings of the Tenth ACM International Conference on Web Search and Data Mining*, 537-545.

Borgatti, S. P., Mehra, A., Brass, D. J., & Labianca, G. (2013). Network analysis in the social sciences. *Science, 323*(5916), 892-895.

Cambria, E., Schuller, B., Xia, Y., & Havasi, C. (2017). New avenues in opinion mining and sentiment analysis. *IEEE Intelligent Systems, 28*(2), 15-21.

Chen, J., He, Y., Wang, Q., & Zhang, J. (2019). AI-powered personalization in targeted advertising: Opportunities and challenges. *Journal of Marketing Analytics, 8*(2), 122-134.

Cheng, J., Adamic, L. A., Dow, P. A., Kleinberg, J. M., & Leskovec, J. (2014). Can cascades be predicted? *Proceedings of the 23rd International Conference on World Wide Web*, 925-936.

Freeman, L. C. (1978). Centrality in social networks: Conceptual clarification. *Social Networks, 1*(3), 215-239.

Girvan, M., & Newman, M. E. J. (2002). Community structure in social and biological networks. *Proceedings of the National Academy of Sciences, 99*(12), 7821-7826.

Golbeck, J. (2013). *Analyzing the social web*. Elsevier.

Guille, A., Hacid, H., Favre, C., & Zighed, D. A. (2013). Information diffusion in online social networks: A survey. *SIGMOD Record, 42*(2), 17-28.

Jin, H., Wang, Y., & Ma, Z. (2020). The role of artificial intelligence in targeted advertising: A comprehensive review. *Journal of Marketing and Advertising, 43*(3), 195-211.

Kietzmann, J., Paschen, J., & Treen, E. (2018). Artificial intelligence in advertising: How marketers can leverage AI to improve advertising campaigns. *Journal of Advertising Research, 58*(3), 263-267.

Lazer, D., Pentland, A., Adamic, L., Aral, S., Barabasi, A. L., Brewer, D., Christakis, N., et al. (2009). Computational social science. *Science, 323*(5915), 721-723.

Liu, B. (2012). *Sentiment analysis and opinion mining.* Morgan & Claypool Publishers.

Mostafa, M. M. (2013). More than words: Social networks' text mining for consumer brand sentiments. *Expert Systems with Applications, 40*(10), 4241-4251.

Pang, B., & Lee, L. (2008). *Opinion mining and sentiment analysis.* Foundations and Trends® in Information Retrieval, *2*(1-2), 1-135.

Scott, J. (2017). *Social network analysis* (4th ed.). Sage.

Tatar, A., Antoniadis, P., & Legout, A. (2014). Predicting virality on online social networks: The role of temporal and topological features. *Computer Communications, 73*(10), 29-39.

Zhang, L., Wang, S., & Liu, B. (2018). Deep learning for sentiment analysis: A survey. *Wiley Interdisciplinary Reviews: Data Mining and Knowledge Discovery, 8*(4), e1253.

Zhou, M., Yang, C., & Liu, Y. (2018). Deep learning for targeted advertising: An overview. *IEEE Transactions on Knowledge and Data Engineering, 30*(12), 2375-2391.

Chapter 17: Government and Public Sector

Public Safety and Security

Public safety and security have become critical areas where artificial intelligence (AI) and big data analytics are transforming government operations. Governments and public agencies are increasingly adopting AI-driven technologies to enhance public safety, prevent crime, and improve emergency response systems. With the rise of digital data from surveillance systems, social media, and public records, big data analytics offers a wealth of information that can be leveraged for predictive policing, real-time monitoring, and improved resource allocation. AI-powered systems can help law enforcement agencies detect and prevent crimes, manage public emergencies, and ensure the safety of citizens through advanced analytics and automation. These technologies enable governments to respond more effectively to security threats, manage public safety resources efficiently, and protect communities from a wide range of hazards.

1. Challenges in Traditional Public Safety and Security Approaches

Traditional approaches to public safety and security have several limitations, including the inability to process large volumes of data in real-time, reactive rather than proactive crime prevention strategies, and challenges in efficiently managing limited resources. Some of the key challenges include:

Reactive Policing: Traditional policing methods often rely on reactive strategies, meaning that law enforcement responds to crimes after they have occurred rather than preventing them in advance. This reactive approach can lead to higher crime rates and delayed responses to criminal activities (Brantingham et al., 2018).

Limited Data Integration: Law enforcement agencies typically rely on fragmented data sources, such as criminal records, incident reports, and surveillance footage, which are often not integrated. The lack of data integration makes it difficult for agencies to gain a comprehensive view of criminal activities and public safety risks (Perry et al., 2013).

Manual Monitoring and Resource Allocation: Monitoring public spaces through surveillance cameras and other systems often requires significant human labor. Law enforcement agencies may struggle to analyze video footage, detect potential threats, and allocate resources effectively in real time. This results in inefficient management of resources and slower response times (Tayebi et al., 2020).

AI and big data technologies address these challenges by enabling predictive analytics, real-time data processing, and automated decision-making systems that help governments and law enforcement agencies enhance public safety and security.

2. AI Techniques in Public Safety and Security

AI techniques such as machine learning, computer vision, natural language processing (NLP), and predictive analytics are increasingly being applied to improve public safety and security. These techniques enable governments to analyze large datasets, monitor public spaces, detect security threats, and predict criminal activities.

Machine Learning (ML): Machine learning models are widely used in predictive policing, where they analyze historical crime data, incident reports, and socio-economic factors to predict where crimes are most likely to occur. Supervised learning models, such as decision trees, random forests, and support vector machines (SVMs), can be trained on crime data to forecast crime hotspots and recommend resource allocation strategies. This allows law enforcement agencies to focus their efforts on areas with higher crime risk and deploy resources more efficiently (Brantingham et al., 2018).

Computer Vision: Computer vision is used to enhance surveillance systems by analyzing video footage in real-time to detect unusual or suspicious behavior. AI-powered cameras can automatically identify specific objects, such as weapons or abandoned bags, and flag them for further inspection. Facial recognition technology is another application of computer vision that is used to identify individuals in public spaces, enabling law enforcement agencies to track suspects or persons of interest. These technologies reduce the need for manual monitoring of video feeds and improve the ability to detect potential security threats (Tayebi et al., 2020).

Natural Language Processing (NLP): NLP techniques are used to analyze text-based data from sources such as social media, emergency call transcripts, and public forums to detect potential security risks. Sentiment analysis can identify individuals expressing intent to commit violent acts or engage in criminal activities, while topic modeling can reveal emerging threats or trends in public safety concerns. NLP models can process large amounts of unstructured text data, providing real-time insights into public sentiment and security risks (Chen et al., 2017).

Predictive Analytics: Predictive analytics tools leverage AI and big data to forecast public safety risks and allocate resources more effectively. By analyzing data from crime reports, socio-economic factors, and environmental conditions, predictive models can identify patterns in criminal activity and recommend preventive measures. For example, predictive policing systems can forecast where crimes such as burglaries or assaults are likely to occur, allowing law enforcement to intervene before incidents happen (Perry et al., 2013).

Anomaly Detection: Anomaly detection algorithms are used to identify unusual patterns or behaviors in public spaces that may indicate a security threat. For instance, in transportation hubs, AI systems can monitor passenger behavior and detect deviations from normal patterns, such as loitering or carrying suspicious items. These anomalies can be flagged for further investigation, allowing security personnel to respond proactively to potential threats (Tayebi et al., 2020).

3. Applications of AI in Public Safety and Security

AI-powered technologies are being applied across various public safety and security domains, including crime prevention, emergency response, disaster management, and cybersecurity. These applications enhance the ability of governments and law enforcement agencies to protect citizens, prevent crimes, and respond to emergencies more effectively.

Predictive Policing: Predictive policing is one of the most significant applications of AI in public safety. Machine learning models analyze crime data, environmental factors, and socio-economic indicators to predict where crimes are likely to occur and when. This allows law enforcement agencies to allocate their resources strategically and prevent crimes before they happen. For example, AI-powered tools can analyze patterns of burglaries or robberies and forecast the likelihood of future incidents in specific areas, enabling proactive patrolling and surveillance (Brantingham et al., 2018).

Real-Time Surveillance and Threat Detection: AI-powered surveillance systems use computer vision and machine learning algorithms to monitor public spaces in real-time and detect potential security threats. These systems can analyze video feeds to identify suspicious objects, track individuals, and detect abnormal behavior. Facial recognition technology, for instance, allows law enforcement to identify individuals in crowded areas and track persons of interest. Real-time threat detection systems improve the ability of law enforcement agencies to respond to security risks quickly and efficiently (Tayebi et al., 2020).

Emergency Response and Disaster Management: AI and big data analytics are used to enhance emergency response systems by providing real-time insights into public safety incidents. AI models can analyze data from emergency call centers, social media, and sensors to identify the location and severity of incidents such as fires, floods, or accidents. Predictive models can forecast the spread of natural disasters, such as hurricanes or wildfires, enabling governments to allocate resources and prepare evacuation plans. AI-powered systems also improve coordination between emergency responders, allowing for faster and more effective responses to crises (Chen et al., 2017).

Public Health and Safety: During public health emergencies, such as pandemics, AI and big data analytics are used to monitor the spread of diseases and predict future outbreaks. Governments can analyze data from health records, social media, and mobility patterns to identify hotspots of infection and implement preventive measures. AI-powered systems can also track the effectiveness of public health interventions, such as social distancing or vaccination campaigns, helping governments respond to health crises more effectively (Tayebi et al., 2020).

Cybersecurity: AI is increasingly being used in cybersecurity to protect critical infrastructure and sensitive data from cyberattacks. Machine learning models analyze network traffic, user behavior, and system logs to detect anomalies that may indicate a security breach. AI-powered cybersecurity systems can respond to threats in real-time, automatically isolating compromised systems and preventing the spread of attacks. These systems also help governments protect sensitive public sector data, such as personal information and financial records, from cybercriminals (Brantingham et al., 2018).

4. AI and Big Data in Public Safety and Security

The integration of AI and big data technologies is critical for improving public safety and security. Governments rely on vast amounts of data from surveillance systems, crime reports, emergency call centers, and public records to gain insights into public safety risks and respond effectively to threats.

Real-Time Data Processing: AI-powered public safety systems process large volumes of real-time data from various sources, including surveillance cameras, social media, and emergency calls. By analyzing this data in real-time, AI models can detect security threats and alert law enforcement agencies to potential incidents. Real-time data processing is particularly valuable for responding to time-sensitive threats, such as terrorist attacks or natural disasters (Chen et al., 2017).

Scalability and Data Integration: AI models are highly scalable, making them suitable for managing large and complex datasets generated by public safety systems. Governments can integrate data from multiple sources, such as surveillance cameras, crime records, and social media platforms, to gain a comprehensive view of public safety risks. AI-powered systems can analyze this data at scale, providing insights into criminal activity, public health risks, and security threats across entire cities or regions (Perry et al., 2013).

Predictive and Prescriptive Analytics: AI and big data technologies enable both predictive and prescriptive analytics in public safety. Predictive analytics tools forecast public safety risks, such as crime hotspots or disaster spread, based on historical data and environmental factors. Prescriptive analytics provides actionable recommendations on how to respond to these risks, such as deploying law enforcement personnel to specific areas or preparing emergency response teams for a natural disaster. These insights help governments optimize resource allocation and improve public safety outcomes (Brantingham et al., 2018).

5. Challenges and Considerations in AI-Driven Public Safety and Security

While AI-powered public safety and security systems offer numerous benefits, several challenges and considerations must be addressed:

Data Privacy and Ethics: The use of AI and big data in public safety raises concerns about data privacy and ethics. Surveillance systems collect vast amounts of personal data, and the use of facial recognition technology and other AI tools must comply with data protection regulations, such as the General Data Protection Regulation (GDPR). Governments must ensure that they are transparent about how they collect and use data and that they protect citizens' privacy (Perry et al., 2013).

Bias and Fairness in AI Models: AI models used in public safety must be free from bias to ensure fair and accurate decision-making. Biased algorithms may disproportionately target certain communities or groups, leading to unfair policing practices. Ensuring that AI models are trained on diverse and representative datasets is critical for preventing bias and ensuring equitable public safety outcomes (Tayebi et al., 2020).

Integration with Legacy Systems: Many government agencies still rely on legacy public safety systems that may not be fully compatible with AI and big data technologies. Ensuring seamless integration between AI-driven public safety systems and existing infrastructure is essential for maximizing the benefits of AI (Chen et al., 2017).

In summary, AI-powered public safety and security systems are revolutionizing the way governments protect citizens, prevent crimes, and respond to emergencies. Through machine learning, computer vision, and predictive analytics, AI systems can predict crime hotspots, monitor public spaces in real-time, and optimize resource allocation for law enforcement agencies. The combination of AI and big data enables governments to process vast amounts of data, detect security threats, and respond to public safety risks more efficiently. While challenges related to data privacy, bias, and system integration remain, the benefits of AI-driven public safety systems - improved crime prevention, enhanced emergency response, and better resource management - make them invaluable tools for modern public safety and security efforts.

Policy Analysis and Decision-Making

AI and big data are transforming policy analysis and decision-making in the government and public sector by enabling more efficient, evidence-based, and predictive policymaking processes. With the vast amounts of data generated from public records, social media, surveys, and various governmental sources, AI and big data analytics provide policymakers with tools to analyze complex issues, simulate potential outcomes, and make informed decisions. These technologies enhance the ability of governments to anticipate the impact of policies, optimize resource allocation, and create more transparent, responsive, and data-driven policies.

1. Challenges in Traditional Policy Analysis and Decision-Making

Traditional policy analysis methods have been constrained by several limitations, including the inability to process large volumes of data, reliance on static and outdated information, and the complexity of predicting the long-term effects of policies. These challenges often result in slower decision-making processes and less effective policies.

Limited Data Processing Capabilities: Traditional policy analysis methods often rely on limited datasets, such as historical records or survey data. These methods lack the ability to process large-scale, real-time data from diverse sources, such as social media, census data, or public sentiment, which limits their accuracy in understanding public needs and behaviors (Ni et al., 2020).

Reactive vs. Predictive: Traditional policymaking is often reactive, where policies are developed and implemented after problems have emerged, rather than being proactive and predictive. This reactive approach makes it difficult for governments to anticipate the outcomes of their decisions and address future challenges (Sun & Medaglia, 2019).

Siloed Data Sources: Government data is often fragmented across different departments, making it difficult to access and analyze comprehensive datasets that span various policy areas. This siloed approach limits the ability to make holistic decisions based on cross-sectoral data (Chen et al., 2018).

AI and big data technologies address these challenges by enabling policymakers to analyze vast datasets, simulate policy outcomes, and make decisions based on real-time data and predictive models.

2. AI Techniques in Policy Analysis and Decision-Making

AI techniques such as machine learning, natural language processing (NLP), predictive analytics, and simulation models are increasingly being used to improve policy analysis and decision-making in the government sector. These techniques provide governments with the ability to process large datasets, predict policy outcomes, and generate data-driven insights.

Machine Learning (ML): Machine learning models are used to analyze historical policy data, public sentiment, and socio-economic factors to predict the potential outcomes of different policy options. Supervised learning algorithms, such as decision trees and random forests, can identify patterns in past policies and forecast their long-term impacts on various populations. For example, ML models can predict the economic effects of tax reforms or the public health impacts of new regulations, helping policymakers make more informed decisions (Ni et al., 2020).

Natural Language Processing (NLP): NLP techniques are applied to analyze unstructured text data, such as public comments, social media posts, and government reports, to understand public sentiment and concerns regarding specific policies. Sentiment analysis tools can provide real-time insights into how citizens feel about proposed legislation or government initiatives, allowing policymakers to adjust their strategies based on public feedback. NLP can also be used to analyze legislative documents, identify trends in policy discourse, and generate summaries of complex policy issues (Meijer & Wessels, 2019).

Predictive Analytics: Predictive analytics tools leverage AI and big data to forecast the potential outcomes of policy decisions based on historical data and real-time information. These tools can simulate the effects of various policy interventions, allowing governments to explore different scenarios and choose the most effective course of action. For example, predictive models can be used to assess the long-term impact of environmental regulations on air quality or to evaluate the economic benefits of infrastructure investments (Ni et al., 2020).

Simulation Models: AI-powered simulation models are used to create virtual environments in which policymakers can test the potential outcomes of different policies. These models take into account a wide range of variables, such as economic conditions, population demographics, and social behaviors, to predict how a policy will affect different sectors of society. Simulation models allow governments to experiment with various policy options before implementing them in the real world, reducing the risk of unintended consequences (Chen et al., 2018).

3. Applications of AI in Policy Analysis and Decision-Making

AI-powered policy analysis and decision-making tools are being applied across various areas of government, including economic policy, healthcare, education, and urban planning. These applications improve the ability of governments to create data-driven, effective, and transparent policies that address the needs of citizens.

Economic Policy Analysis: AI models are used to analyze economic data and predict the effects of various fiscal policies, such as tax reforms, stimulus packages, or trade policies. Machine learning algorithms can identify patterns in economic indicators and forecast how different policies will impact employment, inflation, and GDP growth. For example, AI-powered models can simulate the effects of tax cuts on consumer spending and investment, helping policymakers design more effective economic interventions (Sun & Medaglia, 2019).

Healthcare Policy and Public Health: AI and big data analytics are applied to healthcare policy analysis to predict the effects of public health interventions and optimize resource allocation. For example, predictive models can forecast the spread of infectious diseases, such as COVID-19, and estimate the impact of vaccination campaigns or social distancing measures. AI-powered tools can also analyze healthcare utilization data to recommend policies that improve access to care and reduce healthcare costs (Chen et al., 2018). Governments can use these tools to design more effective public health policies and respond to health crises more efficiently.

Education Policy: AI-powered tools are used to analyze educational data and develop policies that improve student outcomes and resource allocation in schools. Machine learning models can predict student performance based on factors such as socio-economic background, teacher quality, and school infrastructure, allowing policymakers to identify areas for intervention. AI can also help design personalized learning programs and allocate funding to schools that need it most, ensuring that educational resources are distributed equitably (Ni et al., 2020).

Urban Planning and Smart Cities: AI is increasingly being used in urban planning to design more sustainable and efficient cities. AI models analyze data from traffic patterns, energy consumption, and environmental factors to recommend policies that reduce congestion, lower emissions, and improve public transportation systems. Predictive models can also forecast the impact of urban development projects on housing affordability, infrastructure demand, and environmental sustainability. These insights enable governments to design smart cities that meet the needs of growing urban populations while minimizing environmental impacts (Meijer & Wessels, 2019).

Environmental Policy and Climate Change: AI-powered tools are used to model the effects of environmental policies on climate change, biodiversity, and natural resource management. Predictive models can simulate the long-term impacts of carbon pricing, renewable energy incentives, and land-use regulations on greenhouse gas emissions and ecological systems. Governments can use these insights to develop policies that promote sustainability and reduce the risk of climate-related disasters (Chen et al., 2018).

4. AI and Big Data in Policy Analysis and Decision-Making

AI and big data technologies are critical for transforming policy analysis and decision-making by providing governments with the tools to process vast amounts of data and generate actionable insights. These technologies enable policymakers to make more informed, data-driven decisions that lead to better outcomes for citizens.

Real-Time Data Processing: AI-powered policy analysis systems process large volumes of real-time data from various sources, such as economic indicators, social media, and public records. By analyzing this data in real-time, AI models provide policymakers with up-to-date insights into public sentiment, economic trends, and environmental conditions. Real-time data processing is particularly valuable for responding to rapidly changing situations, such as economic crises or public health emergencies (Ni et al., 2020).

Scalability and Data Integration: AI models are highly scalable, allowing governments to analyze large datasets from multiple sectors, including healthcare, education, and transportation. Data integration across different government departments enables policymakers to make more holistic decisions that take into account the interconnectedness of various policy areas. For example, integrating healthcare and economic data allows policymakers to assess the impact of healthcare policies on labor markets and public spending (Meijer & Wessels, 2019).

Predictive and Prescriptive Analytics: AI and big data enable both predictive and prescriptive analytics in policy analysis. Predictive analytics tools forecast the outcomes of various policy interventions based on historical data and current trends. Prescriptive analytics provides actionable recommendations on how to optimize policy design and implementation. These tools help governments choose the most effective policies and allocate resources more efficiently (Sun & Medaglia, 2019).

5. Challenges and Considerations in AI-Driven Policy Analysis and Decision-Making

While AI-powered policy analysis offers numerous benefits, several challenges and considerations must be addressed:

Data Privacy and Security: The use of AI and big data in policy analysis raises concerns about data privacy and security. Governments must ensure that they protect citizens' personal data and comply with data protection regulations, such as the General Data Protection Regulation (GDPR). Transparency in how data is collected, stored, and used is essential for maintaining public trust in AI-driven policymaking (Meijer & Wessels, 2019).

Bias and Fairness in AI Models: AI models used in policy analysis must be free from bias to ensure fair and equitable decision-making. Biased algorithms may disproportionately affect certain populations or lead to unfair policy outcomes. Ensuring that AI models are trained on diverse and representative datasets is critical for preventing bias and ensuring that policies benefit all citizens (Chen et al., 2018).

Complexity and Interpretability: AI models used in policy analysis can be complex and difficult to interpret, making it challenging for policymakers to understand how decisions are made. Ensuring that

AI models are transparent and interpretable is essential for building trust in AI-driven policymaking. Governments must be able to explain how AI models generate policy recommendations and ensure that these models align with public values (Ni et al., 2020).

In summary, AI-powered policy analysis and decision-making are revolutionizing how governments design, implement, and evaluate policies. By leveraging machine learning, predictive analytics, and big data, policymakers can gain real-time insights into complex issues, forecast the outcomes of policy interventions, and make data-driven decisions that lead to better societal outcomes. The integration of AI and big data enables governments to process vast amounts of data, optimize resource allocation, and respond more effectively to challenges such as economic crises, public health emergencies, and climate change. While challenges related to data privacy, bias, and model interpretability must be addressed, the benefits of AI-driven policy analysis - enhanced accuracy, transparency, and efficiency - make it a valuable tool for modern governance.

Smart Cities Initiatives

Smart cities initiatives represent a significant application of artificial intelligence (AI) and big data technologies within the government and public sector. As urban populations continue to grow, cities face increasing challenges related to transportation, energy consumption, waste management, public safety, and overall quality of life. Smart cities leverage AI, big data, and Internet of Things (IoT) technologies to optimize urban infrastructure, improve sustainability, and enhance services for citizens. Through real-time data collection, predictive analytics, and automation, smart cities aim to create more efficient, responsive, and sustainable urban environments. These initiatives enable governments to manage resources more effectively, reduce environmental impacts, and improve the quality of life for urban residents.

1. Challenges in Traditional Urban Management

Traditional urban management systems often rely on manual processes, outdated infrastructure, and siloed data, limiting their ability to address the complexities of modern cities. Some key challenges include:

Inefficient Resource Management: Traditional urban management systems struggle to optimize resource usage, leading to inefficiencies in energy consumption, water distribution, and waste management. These inefficiencies result in higher costs, increased environmental impact, and reduced quality of public services (Batty, 2013).

Traffic Congestion and Transportation Issues: Urban areas are prone to traffic congestion, which leads to longer commute times, increased pollution, and reduced economic productivity. Traditional transportation systems often lack real-time data on traffic conditions, making it difficult to manage traffic flows and optimize public transportation systems (Chourabi et al., 2012).

Fragmented Data Sources: City governments often rely on fragmented and siloed data from different departments, such as transportation, energy, and public safety. This lack of data integration limits the ability to make informed decisions and manage urban infrastructure holistically (Angelidou, 2017).

AI and big data technologies address these challenges by enabling cities to collect and analyze vast amounts of data in real-time, optimize urban infrastructure, and improve the efficiency of public services.

2. AI Techniques in Smart Cities Initiatives

AI techniques such as machine learning, predictive analytics, computer vision, and IoT integration are widely used in smart cities to improve urban planning, optimize resources, and enhance public services. These technologies enable city governments to monitor urban systems, predict potential issues, and make data-driven decisions.

Machine Learning (ML): Machine learning models are used to analyze data from various urban systems, such as transportation, energy, and water management, to identify patterns and optimize resource usage. Supervised learning algorithms can predict traffic patterns, energy demand, and water consumption, allowing city governments to allocate resources more efficiently. For example, ML models can analyze historical traffic data to optimize traffic light timing and reduce congestion (Nocera et al., 2020).

Predictive Analytics: Predictive analytics tools leverage AI and big data to forecast future urban trends, such as population growth, energy consumption, and traffic congestion. By analyzing historical data and real-time information, predictive models can identify potential issues before they arise, allowing city governments to implement preventive measures. For example, predictive analytics can forecast electricity demand during peak hours, enabling cities to adjust energy distribution and reduce the risk of blackouts (Batty, 2013).

Computer Vision: Computer vision is used in smart cities to monitor public spaces and infrastructure in real-time. AI-powered cameras and sensors can detect traffic violations, monitor pedestrian flow, and identify safety hazards, such as damaged roads or infrastructure. Computer vision is also used in public safety applications, such as facial recognition, to identify persons of interest or track missing individuals (Chourabi et al., 2012).

IoT Integration: The Internet of Things (IoT) is a critical component of smart cities, as it enables real-time data collection from sensors and connected devices across the urban environment. IoT devices, such as smart meters, traffic sensors, and environmental monitors, collect data on energy usage, air quality, traffic flow, and public safety. AI models analyze this data to optimize city services, improve resource management, and enhance the overall quality of life for residents (Angelidou, 2017).

3. Applications of AI in Smart Cities Initiatives

AI-powered smart cities initiatives are being applied across various domains, including transportation, energy management, waste management, public safety, and urban planning. These applications improve the efficiency of urban systems, reduce environmental impact, and enhance services for citizens.

Smart Transportation Systems: AI-powered smart transportation systems use real-time data from traffic sensors, GPS devices, and public transportation systems to optimize traffic flows and reduce congestion. Machine learning models can predict traffic patterns and recommend alternative routes for drivers, while AI-driven traffic lights can adjust their timing based on current traffic conditions. Smart cities also use AI to optimize public transportation systems by predicting passenger demand and adjusting bus or train schedules accordingly. For example, AI models can analyze commuter data to recommend the best times to deploy additional buses during peak hours (Nocera et al., 2020).

Energy Management and Smart Grids: AI is used in smart cities to optimize energy consumption and manage smart grids more efficiently. Predictive analytics tools forecast energy demand based on historical data, weather conditions, and real-time energy usage patterns. AI models can then adjust energy distribution across the grid to prevent shortages during peak demand periods. Smart cities also use AI to integrate renewable energy sources, such as solar and wind power, into the grid, reducing reliance on fossil fuels and lowering greenhouse gas emissions (Batty, 2013). For example, AI-driven energy management systems can predict when solar power generation will peak and adjust energy storage systems to capture and distribute excess energy.

Waste Management and Recycling: AI and big data technologies are applied to optimize waste management systems in smart cities. AI models analyze data from waste collection routes, recycling facilities, and landfill sites to recommend more efficient collection schedules and reduce waste processing costs. IoT-enabled smart bins can monitor waste levels in real-time and notify waste collection services when bins need to be emptied. AI-powered systems can also sort recyclable materials automatically, improving recycling rates and reducing the environmental impact of waste disposal (Chourabi et al., 2012).

Public Safety and Security: AI-powered public safety systems in smart cities use real-time data from surveillance cameras, social media, and emergency call centers to detect potential security threats and improve emergency response times. Machine learning models can analyze video feeds to identify suspicious behavior, detect traffic accidents, or monitor crowd movements during public events. Facial recognition technology can help law enforcement agencies identify suspects or track missing persons. AI-powered systems also enable cities to predict crime hotspots and allocate law enforcement resources more efficiently (Angelidou, 2017).

Environmental Monitoring: AI-powered environmental monitoring systems help smart cities track air quality, noise levels, and water pollution in real-time. IoT-enabled sensors placed throughout the city collect data on environmental conditions, which is then analyzed by AI models to identify trends and potential risks. For example, AI-powered air quality monitoring systems can predict pollution levels based on weather patterns and traffic data, allowing cities to implement measures to reduce pollution, such as restricting vehicle access to certain areas or promoting public transportation (Nocera et al., 2020).

Urban Planning and Development: AI and big data analytics are used in urban planning to design more efficient and sustainable cities. AI-powered models analyze data on population growth, infrastructure needs, and environmental impact to recommend optimal locations for new developments, such as housing, transportation hubs, or public parks. These models can also simulate the long-term effects of urban development projects on traffic congestion, energy consumption, and public services, helping city planners make informed decisions. For example, AI can be used to evaluate the impact of a new housing development on traffic patterns and recommend infrastructure improvements to accommodate increased traffic flow (Batty, 2013).

4. AI and Big Data in Smart Cities Initiatives

The combination of AI and big data is essential for enabling smart cities initiatives. Big data technologies collect and process vast amounts of data from urban infrastructure, while AI models analyze this data to generate insights, optimize services, and improve decision-making.

Real-Time Data Processing: AI-powered smart cities systems process large volumes of real-time data from IoT devices, sensors, and public records. This real-time data processing enables cities to monitor traffic conditions, energy usage, and public safety in real-time and respond to emerging issues quickly. For example, AI-driven traffic management systems can adjust traffic light timing in response to real-time traffic conditions, reducing congestion and improving commute times (Angelidou, 2017).

Scalability and Data Integration: AI models are highly scalable, allowing cities to analyze data from millions of connected devices and sensors across various urban systems. Data integration across different sectors, such as transportation, energy, and public safety, enables city governments to make more informed decisions and manage urban infrastructure holistically. For example, integrating traffic and environmental data allows cities to design policies that reduce both congestion and air pollution (Batty, 2013).

Predictive and Prescriptive Analytics: AI and big data technologies enable both predictive and prescriptive analytics in smart cities. Predictive analytics tools forecast trends such as population growth, energy demand, or traffic congestion based on historical data and real-time information. Prescriptive analytics provides actionable recommendations on how to optimize urban services, such as adjusting energy distribution, improving waste collection routes, or reallocating law enforcement resources (Chourabi et al., 2012).

5. Challenges and Considerations in AI-Driven Smart Cities Initiatives

While AI-powered smart cities initiatives offer numerous benefits, several challenges and considerations must be addressed:

Data Privacy and Security: The widespread use of IoT devices and AI systems in smart cities raises concerns about data privacy and security. City governments must ensure that they protect citizens' personal data and comply with data protection regulations, such as the General Data Protection Regulation (GDPR). Transparency in how data is collected, stored, and used is essential for maintaining public trust in smart cities initiatives (Angelidou, 2017).

Infrastructure Investment and Digital Divide: Implementing AI-driven smart cities systems requires significant investment in infrastructure, such as IoT sensors, high-speed internet, and data storage systems. Ensuring that all citizens have access to the benefits of smart cities initiatives, regardless of their socio-economic status, is critical for preventing a digital divide. Governments must prioritize equitable access to smart cities technologies and ensure that marginalized communities are not left behind (Nocera et al., 2020).

Interoperability and Standardization: Smart cities systems often involve multiple vendors and technologies, making interoperability and standardization critical for ensuring that different systems can communicate and work together effectively. Governments must establish clear standards and protocols for data sharing and system integration to maximize the benefits of smart cities initiatives (Chourabi et al., 2012).

Conclusion

AI-powered smart cities initiatives are transforming the way urban environments are managed and services are delivered. Through the use of machine learning, predictive analytics, computer vision, and IoT technologies, smart cities can optimize transportation systems, improve energy efficiency, enhance public safety, and promote sustainability. The integration of AI and big data enables cities to process vast amounts of real-time data, generate actionable insights, and respond to emerging challenges more effectively. While challenges related to data privacy, infrastructure investment, and interoperability must be addressed, the benefits of AI-driven smart cities - improved efficiency, sustainability, and quality of life - make them essential for the future of urban development.

References

Angelidou, M. (2017). The role of smart city characteristics in the plans of fifteen cities. *Journal of Urban Technology, 24*(4), 3-28.

Batty, M. (2013). Big data, smart cities, and city planning. *Dialogues in Human Geography, 3*(3), 274-279.

Brantingham, P. J., Valasik, M., & Mohler, G. O. (2018). Does predictive policing lead to biased arrests? Results from a randomized controlled trial. *Statistics and Public Policy, 5*(1), 1-6.

Chen, X., Aggarwal, G., & Ma, T. (2017). Big data analytics for public safety and emergency management: Advances and challenges. *IEEE Transactions on Big Data, 3*(2), 97-109.

Chen, Y., Huang, W., Li, Y., & Zhang, H. (2018). Big data-driven policy analysis and decision making in government: A review. *Government Information Quarterly, 35*(4), 623-633.

Chourabi, H., Nam, T., Walker, S., Gil-Garcia, J. R., Mellouli, S., Nahon, K., Scholl, H. J., & Jochen, C. (2012). Understanding smart cities: An integrative framework. *45th Hawaii International Conference on System Sciences*, 2289-2297.

Meijer, A., & Wessels, M. (2019). Predictive analytics in government: Opportunities and challenges for policy making. *Public Administration Review, 79*(6), 895-905.

Ni, Y., Zhang, H., Zhu, H., & Chen, X. (2020). Big data analytics for decision making in public administration: Policy informatics and the transformation of government. *Journal of Policy Analysis and Management, 39*(3), 609-622.

Nocera, S., Cavallaro, F., & Diana, M. (2020). Urban transportation planning and smart cities: Models and methods. *Transportation Research Part A: Policy and Practice, 132*, 135-146.

Perry, W. L., McInnis, B., Price, C. C., Smith, S. C., & Hollywood, J. S. (2013). *Predictive policing: The role of crime forecasting in law enforcement operations*. RAND Corporation.

Sun, T. Q., & Medaglia, R. (2019). Mapping the challenges of artificial intelligence in the public sector: Evidence from public administration literature. *Government Information Quarterly, 36*(2), 368-383.

Tayebi, M. A., Glässer, U., & Brantingham, P. L. (2020). Applying AI in public safety and security: Challenges and opportunities. *Artificial Intelligence Review, 53*(7), 1-21.

Part IV: Tools and Platforms
Chapter 18: Programming Languages and Libraries

Python for AI and Data Science

Python has become the dominant programming language in the fields of artificial intelligence (AI) and data science due to its simplicity, versatility, and extensive ecosystem of libraries and tools. Its widespread adoption is largely driven by the language's ability to handle complex data processing tasks while remaining accessible to both beginners and experienced developers. Python's popularity in AI and data science can be attributed to several key factors, including its ease of use, robust libraries, active community, and seamless integration with AI frameworks. This has made Python the go-to language for tasks such as machine learning, deep learning, data analysis, and scientific computing, allowing organizations to develop scalable AI models and analyze large datasets efficiently.

1. Why Python is Popular for AI and Data Science

Python's rise in AI and data science is linked to several distinct advantages that it offers over other programming languages. These include ease of learning, the availability of powerful libraries, and its ability to integrate with various AI frameworks.

Ease of Learning and Versatility: Python's simple syntax and readability make it an ideal choice for both beginners and professionals. The language is designed to be highly intuitive, which reduces the learning curve for newcomers in AI and data science. This accessibility has attracted a large and diverse user base, fostering a collaborative community that constantly contributes to the language's growth (Van Rossum & Drake, 2009). Additionally, Python is versatile enough to be used for a wide range of tasks, from simple data manipulation to building complex machine learning models, making it an all-purpose tool for AI development (Muller & Guido, 2016).

Extensive Ecosystem of Libraries: One of Python's greatest strengths is its rich ecosystem of libraries and frameworks specifically designed for AI and data science. Libraries like NumPy, Pandas, and Matplotlib provide essential tools for data manipulation and visualization, while machine learning frameworks such as TensorFlow, PyTorch, and Scikit-learn simplify the process of building and training AI models (Pedregosa et al., 2011). These libraries are highly optimized, allowing developers to focus on the problem at hand without needing to reinvent basic functionalities from scratch.

Community Support and Documentation: Python's large and active community contributes to the continuous development of libraries and tools. This community-driven approach has resulted in an abundance of tutorials, forums, and comprehensive documentation, which makes troubleshooting and learning new tools easier. This support network has helped Python maintain its position as a leading language in AI and data science (Van Rossum & Drake, 2009).

Integration with AI Frameworks and Tools: Python integrates seamlessly with many popular AI and machine learning frameworks. TensorFlow and PyTorch, for example, are widely used in deep learning due to their ability to handle neural networks, backpropagation, and large datasets efficiently (Abadi et al., 2016). Python's ability to interact with these tools allows developers to create AI models more quickly and deploy them in real-world applications with minimal friction.

2. Key Python Libraries for AI and Data Science

Python's extensive library ecosystem is one of the main reasons it has become indispensable in AI and data science. These libraries offer a range of functionalities from basic data manipulation to complex model building and deployment.

NumPy: NumPy is a fundamental library for numerical computing in Python. It provides support for multi-dimensional arrays and matrices, along with a collection of mathematical functions to operate on these arrays. NumPy is essential for handling large datasets in AI and data science, as it allows for efficient storage and computation, making it a core tool for scientific computing and machine learning (Oliphant, 2015).

Pandas: Pandas is a powerful data manipulation and analysis library, offering data structures like DataFrames for organizing and manipulating large datasets. Pandas simplifies the process of data cleaning, transformation, and aggregation, which is critical in AI and data science workflows. Its intuitive syntax allows developers to perform complex data manipulations with just a few lines of code, making it a go-to tool for data preprocessing (McKinney, 2010).

Matplotlib and Seaborn: Matplotlib is a widely-used library for creating static, interactive, and animated visualizations in Python. It is essential for data scientists to visualize trends, distributions, and patterns in data. Seaborn, built on top of Matplotlib, offers additional features for creating more sophisticated and informative statistical plots. These libraries are indispensable for data exploration and result interpretation, allowing data scientists to gain insights from their data and effectively communicate findings (Hunter, 2007).

Scikit-learn: Scikit-learn is a machine learning library that provides simple and efficient tools for data mining and analysis. It offers a range of algorithms for classification, regression, clustering, and dimensionality reduction. Scikit-learn also includes utilities for model evaluation, cross-validation, and hyperparameter tuning, making it a comprehensive tool for building machine learning models (Pedregosa et al., 2011). Its ease of use and integration with other Python libraries make it a popular choice for machine learning practitioners.

TensorFlow and PyTorch: TensorFlow and PyTorch are two of the most popular deep learning frameworks in Python. TensorFlow, developed by Google, is known for its scalability and is widely used in production environments. PyTorch, developed by Facebook, is favored for its flexibility and dynamic computation graph, which makes it more intuitive for research and experimentation. Both frameworks provide tools for building and training neural networks, handling large datasets, and deploying AI models across platforms (Abadi et al., 2016; Paszke et al., 2019).

Keras: Keras is a high-level neural networks API, written in Python, that runs on top of TensorFlow. It is designed to enable fast experimentation with deep learning models by providing simple and intuitive APIs for building and training neural networks. Keras is highly modular, allowing developers to easily configure models, layers, and optimization functions, making it an excellent choice for beginners in deep learning (Chollet, 2015).

3. Applications of Python in AI and Data Science

Python's versatility and ease of use make it a popular choice across a wide range of AI and data science applications. From data preprocessing and visualization to building advanced machine learning models, Python supports the entire AI development lifecycle.

Data Preprocessing: Python is widely used for data preprocessing, which is a critical step in AI and data science workflows. Libraries like Pandas and NumPy allow data scientists to clean, transform, and manipulate raw data into a format suitable for model training. Data preprocessing tasks include handling missing values, normalizing data, and feature engineering, all of which are essential for improving model accuracy and performance (McKinney, 2010).

Machine Learning and Deep Learning: Python's machine learning libraries, such as Scikit-learn and TensorFlow, enable data scientists to build and train models for a variety of tasks, including classification, regression, clustering, and recommendation systems. Deep learning frameworks like TensorFlow and PyTorch are used to develop neural networks for tasks such as image recognition, natural language processing (NLP), and speech recognition (Abadi et al., 2016; Paszke et al., 2019).

Data Visualization: Data visualization is a key component of data science, allowing practitioners to communicate insights and trends effectively. Python libraries such as Matplotlib and Seaborn are widely used for creating visual representations of data, including histograms, scatter plots, and heatmaps. These visualizations help data scientists identify patterns and anomalies in the data, which can inform decision-making and model development (Hunter, 2007).

Natural Language Processing (NLP): Python is widely used in NLP applications, such as sentiment analysis, text classification, and machine translation. Libraries such as NLTK (Natural Language Toolkit) and SpaCy provide tools for tokenization, part-of-speech tagging, named entity recognition, and parsing. These libraries allow developers to process and analyze large volumes of text data, making Python a leading language for NLP tasks (Bird et al., 2009).

AI in Production: Python's flexibility extends to the deployment of AI models in production environments. With tools like Flask and FastAPI, developers can create web applications and APIs to serve AI models to users. TensorFlow Serving and ONNX (Open Neural Network Exchange) provide frameworks for deploying models at scale, making Python an end-to-end solution for AI development, from model training to deployment (Abadi et al., 2016).

4. Challenges and Considerations in Using Python for AI and Data Science

While Python is the most popular language for AI and data science, it does have some limitations that developers need to consider.

Performance Limitations: Python is an interpreted language, which can lead to slower execution times compared to compiled languages like C++ or Java. This can be a limitation when working with extremely large datasets or performing computationally intensive tasks. However, many Python libraries, such as NumPy and TensorFlow, are optimized using C or C++ under the hood, mitigating some of these performance concerns (Oliphant, 2015).

Memory Consumption: Python's high-level data structures and dynamic typing can lead to increased memory consumption. When working with large datasets, memory management can become a bottleneck. Developers may need to implement memory-efficient solutions or use distributed computing frameworks, such as Dask or Apache Spark, to handle large-scale data processing (McKinney, 2010).

Concurrency and Parallelism: Python's Global Interpreter Lock (GIL) can limit the performance of multithreaded applications, particularly in CPU-bound tasks. While there are workarounds, such as using multiprocessing or external libraries for parallel computing, Python's concurrency model may not be as efficient as other languages designed for parallelism (Muller & Guido, 2016).

In summary, Python has established itself as the leading programming language for AI and data science, thanks to its simplicity, versatility, and extensive ecosystem of libraries and frameworks. Its ability to handle complex data processing tasks, build machine learning models, and integrate with powerful AI frameworks has made it the go-to language for developers and data scientists worldwide. While Python has some performance limitations, the advantages it offers in terms of ease of use, community support, and library availability far outweigh these drawbacks. As AI and data science continue to evolve, Python is likely to remain at the forefront, driving innovation and enabling organizations to unlock the full potential of their data.

R Programming

R is one of the most widely used programming languages for data analysis, statistics, and graphical representation, making it a prominent tool in data science, analytics, and research. Originating as a statistical computing language, R has evolved into a versatile platform with a vast ecosystem of packages and libraries that cater to a wide range of data-driven tasks. Its popularity in the data science and analytics community is driven by its strengths in statistical modeling, data visualization, and its open-source nature, which encourages collaboration and the development of specialized packages.

1. Why R is Popular for Data Science and Analytics

R's success in data science and analytics stems from its powerful statistical capabilities, flexibility, and a wide variety of packages developed for specific use cases. R's ecosystem, tailored specifically for statistical analysis and visualization, has positioned it as a primary tool for data scientists, statisticians, and researchers across a variety of industries.

Specialized for Statistics and Data Analysis: R was originally developed for statisticians and researchers, and its design reflects this focus. Its statistical computing capabilities make it ideal for advanced statistical modeling, hypothesis testing, and data exploration. R includes built-in support for a wide range of statistical techniques, such as regression analysis, time series forecasting, hypothesis testing, and cluster analysis. These features allow R to handle complex statistical problems with ease (Ihaka & Gentleman, 1996).

Data Visualization and Reporting: One of R's strongest features is its ability to produce high-quality data visualizations. Packages like *ggplot2* have set a standard for creating complex, multi-dimensional visual representations of data in an easy-to-use and highly customizable framework (Wickham, 2016). R's flexibility in creating advanced plots, heatmaps, graphs, and dashboards makes it a preferred tool for communicating data-driven insights. Moreover, R can be easily integrated with platforms like RMarkdown and Shiny for dynamic reporting and interactive visualizations.

Rich Ecosystem of Packages: The R ecosystem is highly versatile, with over 18,000 packages available on CRAN (Comprehensive R Archive Network). These packages extend R's functionality across multiple domains, including machine learning, time series analysis, econometrics, bioinformatics, and social sciences. The extensive availability of domain-specific packages is one of R's core strengths, enabling users to find tools tailored to their specific needs (Ligges, 2015). For instance, packages like *caret* simplify the process of machine learning, while *dplyr* and *tidyr* provide efficient data manipulation and cleaning capabilities (Kuhn, 2008).

Active Open-Source Community: R has a vibrant open-source community that continuously contributes to its development. The R community actively produces packages, offers troubleshooting support, and fosters collaboration through platforms like GitHub, Stack Overflow, and R-Bloggers. This large, engaged community makes it easy for users to access learning resources, documentation, and guidance on best practices in data analysis and statistical computing (Peng, 2015).

Integration with Other Tools: While R excels in statistical analysis and visualization, it can also be integrated with other programming languages and platforms to increase its utility in broader workflows. R can interface with SQL databases for data extraction, Python for machine learning, and Hadoop for big data processing. These integration capabilities make R a powerful tool for analytics teams working with diverse data infrastructures (Yu, 2020).

2. Key R Libraries for Data Science and Machine Learning

R's power lies in its vast repository of libraries and packages, which provide tools for almost every aspect of data science—from data wrangling to advanced machine learning algorithms.

ggplot2: *ggplot2* is one of the most widely used libraries for data visualization in R. It follows a "grammar of graphics" approach, allowing users to create complex, layered visualizations by combining different elements such as scales, coordinates, and aesthetics. *ggplot2* is highly flexible, enabling users to produce anything from simple bar charts to intricate multi-variable plots, and is essential for exploratory data analysis and communicating results visually (Wickham, 2016).

dplyr and tidyr: *dplyr* and *tidyr* are two powerful libraries for data manipulation and cleaning, collectively referred to as part of the "tidyverse." *dplyr* provides an intuitive set of functions for transforming data, such as filtering, selecting columns, and summarizing datasets. It is optimized for performance and works seamlessly with large datasets. *tidyr* complements *dplyr* by offering tools for reshaping and tidying data, which is critical for preparing datasets before analysis (Wickham & Grolemund, 2017).

Caret: *Caret* (Classification and Regression Training) is a popular library for machine learning in R. It simplifies the process of building predictive models by providing a consistent interface to a wide range of machine learning algorithms, including linear models, decision trees, random forests, and support vector machines (Kuhn, 2008). *Caret* also supports model evaluation, feature selection, and cross-validation, making it a comprehensive tool for machine learning workflows.

Shiny: *Shiny* is a web application framework that allows R users to build interactive web applications directly from R. It is widely used for creating interactive dashboards, data visualizations, and decision-support tools. *Shiny* enables users to present real-time data analysis and results through a web interface, making it a valuable tool for presenting findings to non-technical stakeholders (Chang et al., 2020).

XGBoost: *XGBoost* is a powerful, scalable library for gradient boosting, a machine learning algorithm used for both classification and regression tasks. Its efficiency and performance have made it one of the most popular tools for machine learning competitions and real-world applications. The R interface to *XGBoost* allows users to harness the power of gradient boosting directly within R (Chen & Guestrin, 2016).

randomForest: The *randomForest* package provides an implementation of the Random Forest algorithm, which is widely used for classification and regression tasks. Random Forests are ensemble methods that create multiple decision trees and aggregate their predictions, offering high accuracy and robustness to overfitting. The package is easy to use and integrates seamlessly with the broader R ecosystem for predictive modeling (Liaw & Wiener, 2002).

forecast: *forecast* is a leading R package for time series analysis and forecasting. It provides functions for time series decomposition, ARIMA modeling, and exponential smoothing, as well as tools for visualizing and evaluating forecasts. The package is widely used in business, economics, and finance for analyzing trends and making predictions based on historical data (Hyndman et al., 2008).

3. Applications of R in Data Science and Analytics

R is used extensively across industries for various applications, ranging from business analytics and marketing to healthcare research and social sciences.

Statistical Analysis and Hypothesis Testing: R's original design as a statistical language makes it the go-to tool for performing advanced statistical analysis. Researchers use R for tasks such as hypothesis testing, linear and non-linear modeling, and analysis of variance

(ANOVA). Its wide range of built-in functions and specialized packages allows statisticians to perform complex analyses with ease (Ihaka & Gentleman, 1996).

Data Visualization: R excels in producing detailed, high-quality data visualizations. Packages like *ggplot2* are used by data scientists to create insightful visual representations of data that can be customized to meet specific needs. Visualizations such as heatmaps, boxplots, histograms, and scatterplots allow users to explore patterns in data and communicate findings to stakeholders effectively (Wickham, 2016).

Machine Learning: R is widely used for developing machine learning models, particularly for predictive analytics. Packages like *caret*, *randomForest*, and *XGBoost* provide tools for building and evaluating models for classification, regression, and clustering. R's integration with machine learning algorithms makes it a powerful tool for applications such as customer segmentation, fraud detection, and risk assessment (Kuhn, 2008).

Time Series Analysis: R is a popular tool for time series analysis and forecasting. The *forecast* package provides functions for building ARIMA models, seasonal decomposition, and exponential smoothing. Time series analysis is widely applied in industries like finance, retail, and supply chain management for forecasting sales, demand, and financial market trends (Hyndman et al., 2008).

Bioinformatics and Genomic Data Analysis: In the field of bioinformatics, R is used for analyzing genomic data, gene expression, and biological networks. Packages like *Bioconductor* provide tools for processing large datasets in genomics, transcriptomics, and proteomics, enabling researchers to discover insights into biological processes and diseases (Huber et al., 2015).

Social Science Research: R is frequently used in the social sciences for data analysis, survey research, and text analysis. Its ability to handle complex statistical analyses, such as multivariate regressions, structural equation modeling, and social network analysis, makes it an indispensable tool for researchers in sociology, psychology, and political science (Peng, 2015).

4. Challenges and Considerations in Using R for Data Science

While R is a powerful tool for data science, it does have some limitations that users need to be aware of.

Performance and Memory Limitations: R, being a memory-bound language, can struggle with very large datasets. Unlike languages such as Python or Java, which offer better memory management, R loads data into memory, making it less efficient when handling datasets that exceed available RAM. However, solutions like *data.table*, *ff*, and *bigmemory* packages allow R to handle larger datasets more efficiently (Kane et al., 2013).

Learning Curve for Non-Statisticians: R's syntax and focus on statistical operations can present a learning curve for users who do not have a background in statistics. The language's functional programming paradigm, while powerful for statistical analysis, can be less intuitive for users accustomed to object-oriented programming languages like Python or Java (Peng, 2015).

Limited General-Purpose Use: While R is exceptional for data analysis, visualization, and statistical computing, it is not as versatile as Python when it comes to general-purpose programming or integrating with other applications. R's ecosystem is less extensive than Python's when it comes to web development, automation, and deployment tasks, which may require integration with other languages for end-to-end solutions (Yu, 2020).

In summary, R has established itself as one of the leading programming languages for data science and statistics, offering powerful tools for data analysis, visualization, and machine learning. Its extensive ecosystem of libraries and packages, combined with its active community, makes it a preferred choice for statisticians, data scientists, and researchers across various industries. While R has limitations in handling very large datasets and has a steeper learning curve for non-statisticians, its strengths in statistical modeling and visualization make it an indispensable tool for data-driven decision-making. As data science continues to grow, R's relevance in academia, business, and research remains strong, particularly in areas requiring advanced statistical analysis and modeling.

Java and Scala for Big Data

Java and Scala are two widely used programming languages for working with big data, particularly in distributed computing environments. Java, as a general-purpose, object-oriented language, has been a dominant force in enterprise-level software development for decades, and its robust ecosystem has made it a natural fit for large-scale data processing. Scala, on the other hand, is a modern language that combines functional and object-oriented programming paradigms. It is designed to be highly scalable and integrates seamlessly with Java, making it ideal for big data frameworks like Apache Spark. Both languages are commonly used in big data processing due to their ability to handle massive datasets efficiently, interact with distributed computing platforms, and scale across large clusters.

1. Why Java and Scala are Popular for Big Data

Java and Scala have become popular choices for big data due to their strong performance, compatibility with distributed computing frameworks, and rich ecosystems that support large-scale data processing. Their prominence in big data environments, such as Hadoop and Spark, has solidified their roles in handling complex, high-volume data tasks.

Java's Stability and Performance: Java's long history as a highly stable, reliable, and performant language makes it a trusted tool for enterprise-level big data applications. Java is known for its ability to handle complex multi-threaded operations, which is crucial in distributed computing environments. As the foundation of the Hadoop ecosystem, Java is deeply integrated into big data frameworks like Apache Hadoop and Apache HBase, enabling scalable storage and processing of petabytes of data across distributed clusters (White, 2015).

Scala's Flexibility and Scalability: Scala is designed for scalability, making it an ideal language for big data applications. Its ability to integrate both functional and object-oriented programming paradigms offers developers more flexibility in building scalable and efficient data processing pipelines. Scala is the native language for Apache Spark, one of the most widely adopted big data processing engines, which allows for fast, in-memory data processing (Karau et al., 2015). This makes Scala particularly appealing for real-time data analytics, stream processing, and machine learning tasks.

Seamless Java-Scala Interoperability: Scala runs on the Java Virtual Machine (JVM), allowing for seamless interoperability between Java and Scala. This compatibility means that Scala programs can easily integrate with existing Java libraries and frameworks, making it easier for organizations with legacy Java systems to adopt Scala for new big data projects without significant refactoring (Odersky et al., 2016). This interoperability also allows developers to use the vast ecosystem of Java libraries while benefiting from the modern programming features of Scala.

Distributed Computing Support: Both Java and Scala are well-suited for distributed computing, which is essential for big data processing. Java's multi-threading capabilities and integration with frameworks like Hadoop make it a natural fit for distributed data storage and batch processing tasks. Scala's functional programming features, such as immutability and higher-order functions, make it ideal for parallel processing and distributed data manipulation, particularly in the context of Spark's Resilient Distributed Datasets (RDDs) (Karau et al., 2015). The ability to handle distributed data across clusters efficiently is a key reason for the adoption of both Java and Scala in big data environments.

2. Key Java and Scala Libraries for Big Data

Both Java and Scala have rich ecosystems of libraries and tools that facilitate the handling of big data. These libraries are optimized for performance and scalability, enabling developers to process massive datasets efficiently.

Apache Hadoop (Java): Apache Hadoop is the most widely used open-source framework for distributed storage and processing of large datasets. Written in Java, Hadoop is built around the MapReduce paradigm and consists of a distributed file system (HDFS) for data storage and YARN for resource management. Hadoop enables organizations to process petabyte-scale datasets in parallel across clusters of commodity hardware. Its Java-based API allows developers to build and run distributed data processing applications using Java (White, 2015).

Apache Spark (Scala): Apache Spark, written in Scala, is a fast and general-purpose distributed computing system that improves upon the Hadoop model by offering in-memory data processing. Spark provides a high-level API in Scala for processing large datasets in parallel, making it ideal for tasks such as batch processing, stream processing, and machine learning. Spark's Resilient Distributed Datasets (RDDs) allow for fault-tolerant data processing across clusters. Scala's concise syntax and functional programming features make it the perfect match for Spark's real-time data analytics capabilities (Karau et al., 2015).

Kafka Streams (Java/Scala): Kafka Streams is a lightweight library for building real-time, distributed stream processing applications on top of Apache Kafka. It supports both Java and Scala and provides powerful features for processing data streams with low-latency requirements. Kafka Streams is used for applications that require high throughput and real-time processing of event-driven data, such as fraud detection, monitoring, and recommendation systems (Kreps et al., 2011).

Flink (Java/Scala): Apache Flink is a stream processing framework that supports both batch and real-time data processing. Written in Java and Scala, Flink is highly scalable and offers low-latency processing of large datasets. Flink is often used for complex event processing, real-time analytics, and iterative machine learning applications. Its ability to process data in real-time with fault tolerance and state management makes it a key tool in the big data ecosystem (Carbone et al., 2015).

HBase (Java): HBase is a distributed, scalable, and NoSQL database built on top of Hadoop. It is designed to handle large amounts of sparse data, making it ideal for applications that require random, real-time read/write access to big data. HBase is written in Java and integrates closely with the Hadoop ecosystem, enabling developers to store and retrieve large datasets efficiently using Java APIs (George, 2011).

Akka (Scala): Akka is a powerful toolkit for building highly concurrent, distributed, and fault-tolerant systems using the Actor Model. Written in Scala and fully compatible with Java, Akka is often used for building real-time, scalable systems that need to handle large volumes of data in parallel. Akka's message-driven architecture makes it ideal for applications such as IoT, telecommunications, and streaming analytics in big data environments (Kuhn et al., 2011).

3. Applications of Java and Scala in Big Data

Java and Scala play crucial roles in a wide range of big data applications, including data processing, real-time analytics, and machine learning. Their ability to handle massive datasets and operate efficiently in distributed environments makes them popular in industries that rely on big data for decision-making and insights.

Batch Data Processing with Hadoop (Java): Java is integral to batch data processing in big data workflows, particularly within the Hadoop ecosystem. Hadoop's MapReduce paradigm processes large datasets by dividing them into smaller tasks that can be distributed across clusters. Java's multi-threading and concurrency management are ideal for writing MapReduce jobs that handle data processing tasks such as indexing, sorting, and filtering (White, 2015). This approach is widely used in industries such as finance, retail, and healthcare for large-scale data analysis.

Real-Time Data Analytics with Spark (Scala): Apache Spark's real-time analytics capabilities, powered by Scala, are critical in environments where low-latency data processing is required. Spark's ability to process data in memory and support real-time stream processing makes it ideal for use cases such as fraud detection, recommendation systems, and monitoring IoT devices. Scala's functional programming features, such as higher-order functions and immutability, make it easier to write parallelized code that scales across distributed clusters (Karau et al., 2015).

Streaming Data Applications with Kafka and Flink (Java/Scala): Both Java and Scala are widely used in building streaming data applications that require high throughput and low-latency processing. Kafka Streams, which supports both languages, is commonly used for real-time event-driven applications that require the ingestion, processing, and storage of large volumes of data in real-time. Apache Flink, with its support for both batch and stream processing, is used for real-time analytics and iterative machine learning applications that involve continuous data streams (Kreps et al., 2011; Carbone et al., 2015).

Machine Learning at Scale with Spark MLlib (Scala): Spark's MLlib, written in Scala, provides scalable machine learning algorithms that can be run across large distributed datasets. MLlib supports algorithms for classification, regression, clustering, and collaborative filtering, making it ideal for machine learning applications such as customer segmentation, recommendation engines, and predictive analytics. Scala's native integration with Spark allows data scientists to implement these machine learning algorithms efficiently, leveraging Spark's distributed data processing capabilities (Meng et al., 2016).

Building Scalable Systems with Akka (Scala): Akka is often used in big data environments where systems need to be highly responsive, resilient, and distributed. Applications such as real-time analytics, online gaming, and social media platforms benefit from Akka's ability to handle large volumes of concurrent events and messages in a fault-tolerant manner. Scala's Actor Model, implemented in Akka, allows developers to build systems that can scale dynamically based on the workload, making it ideal for real-time big data processing (Kuhn et al., 2011).

4. Challenges and Considerations in Using Java and Scala for Big Data

While Java and Scala offer significant advantages in big data environments, there are some challenges that developers need to consider when using these languages for large-scale data processing.

Steeper Learning Curve for Scala: While Scala offers powerful features for functional programming and distributed computing, its syntax and functional paradigm can be challenging for developers who are more familiar with object-oriented languages like Java. Scala's flexibility can sometimes lead to complexity, making it harder for teams to adopt if they are not already familiar with functional programming concepts (Odersky et al., 2016).

Memory Management and Performance: Both Java and Scala operate on the JVM, which can lead to performance bottlenecks in certain big data scenarios. JVM's garbage collection and memory management can be inefficient when dealing with extremely large datasets, leading to high memory consumption and longer processing times. While both languages offer tools to optimize performance, careful memory management and tuning of JVM parameters are often necessary (White, 2015).

Concurrency and Parallelism: While both Java and Scala are capable of handling multi-threaded and concurrent processes, managing concurrency in large distributed systems can be complex. Akka, for instance, simplifies this with the Actor Model, but managing distributed state and ensuring fault tolerance can still present challenges, particularly in large-scale systems (Kuhn et al., 2011).

In summary, Java and Scala have cemented themselves as essential tools for big data processing due to their scalability, performance, and integration with powerful distributed computing frameworks such as Hadoop and Spark. Java's stability and deep integration with the Hadoop ecosystem make it ideal for batch processing and enterprise-level big data applications, while Scala's functional programming paradigm and compatibility with Spark enable efficient real-time analytics and machine learning. Although both languages come with their own set of challenges, such as Scala's steeper learning curve and JVM's memory management, their strengths in handling distributed data processing tasks make them indispensable for modern big data environments. As the demand for scalable and real-time data processing continues to grow, Java and Scala will remain at the forefront of big data technologies.

Key Libraries

In the fields of artificial intelligence (AI) and data science, the availability of specialized libraries has accelerated the development of machine learning, deep learning, and data analysis applications. These libraries, such as TensorFlow, PyTorch, and Scikit-learn, provide developers with robust tools to build models, process data, and deploy machine learning solutions at scale. Each of these libraries serves distinct purposes, from deep learning frameworks like TensorFlow and PyTorch to more general machine learning toolkits like Scikit-learn. Their wide adoption across industries underscores their importance in the AI and data science ecosystem.

1. TensorFlow

TensorFlow is one of the most widely used open-source deep learning libraries, developed by Google Brain and released in 2015. It is designed to facilitate the building, training, and deployment of machine learning models, particularly deep learning neural networks. TensorFlow's flexibility, scalability, and support for large-scale production environments make it a go-to framework for developers and researchers alike.

Architecture and Features: TensorFlow is built around computational graphs, where nodes represent mathematical operations, and edges represent tensors (multidimensional arrays) that flow between these operations (Abadi et al., 2016). This graph-based approach allows for highly parallelized execution, making TensorFlow suitable for large-scale distributed computing environments. TensorFlow supports both CPU and GPU processing, making it ideal for handling computationally intensive tasks like training deep neural networks.

Keras Integration: Keras, a high-level neural networks API, is integrated within TensorFlow and provides an easy-to-use interface for building and training models. Keras allows developers to quickly prototype models by offering pre-built layers, optimizers, and loss functions, while TensorFlow handles the underlying computational complexity (Chollet, 2015). This combination of ease of use with TensorFlow's computational power makes it an attractive choice for both beginners and experts.

TensorFlow Extended (TFX): TensorFlow Extended (TFX) is a production-ready end-to-end platform that allows developers to scale and deploy their machine learning pipelines (Abadi et al., 2016). TFX includes tools for data validation, model deployment, and model monitoring, enabling the efficient deployment of AI models in real-world applications.

Applications: TensorFlow is widely used in industries such as healthcare, finance, and autonomous systems for applications including image recognition, natural language processing, and time-series forecasting. Its support for deep learning models like convolutional neural networks (CNNs) and recurrent neural networks (RNNs) makes it particularly well-suited for tasks involving unstructured data, such as images, text, and speech.

2. PyTorch

PyTorch is an open-source deep learning framework developed by Facebook's AI Research lab. Since its release in 2016, PyTorch has gained popularity for its simplicity, dynamic computation graph, and research-friendly design. Unlike TensorFlow, which originally used static computational graphs, PyTorch uses dynamic graphs, which makes it easier for developers to write and debug code in real-time.

Dynamic Computational Graphs: PyTorch's dynamic computation graph, also known as define-by-run, allows developers to modify the computational graph on the fly during runtime. This feature is particularly useful for research and experimentation, as it offers more flexibility in model design and debugging (Paszke et al., 2019). In contrast to TensorFlow's static graphs, PyTorch's dynamic approach enables a more intuitive and flexible development process, which has made it highly popular in academia.

Ease of Use and Flexibility: PyTorch's Pythonic design makes it user-friendly, particularly for developers who are familiar with Python's native data structures. The framework is highly flexible, allowing for easy integration with other Python libraries, such as NumPy and SciPy. Additionally, PyTorch includes an extensive ecosystem of tools, such as TorchVision for computer vision tasks and TorchText for natural language processing (NLP), which further simplifies the development process.

Applications in Research and Industry: While initially favored in academic research for its flexibility and ease of experimentation, PyTorch has seen increasing adoption in industry. It is commonly used in applications such as autonomous driving, healthcare diagnostics, and robotics. PyTorch's popularity has been driven by its ability to support both research and production environments, and it is the framework of choice for many AI research labs globally (Paszke et al., 2019).

3. Scikit-learn

Scikit-learn is an open-source Python library that provides simple and efficient tools for data mining, data analysis, and machine learning. Released in 2007, Scikit-learn is widely used in the data science community for building traditional machine learning models such as classification, regression, clustering, and dimensionality reduction.

Features and Functionality: Scikit-learn offers a consistent and user-friendly interface for implementing a wide range of machine learning algorithms, including decision trees, support vector machines (SVMs), k-nearest neighbors (k-NN), and random forests (Pedregosa et al., 2011). It is designed to work seamlessly with NumPy and Pandas for data manipulation, and it includes tools for cross-validation, hyperparameter tuning, and model evaluation.

Preprocessing Tools: One of Scikit-learn's strengths is its extensive set of data preprocessing tools, which are essential for preparing data before model training. These tools include feature scaling, one-hot encoding, imputation of missing values, and feature selection. Scikit-learn's *Pipeline* functionality allows users to create workflows that include both preprocessing steps and model training in a single sequence, simplifying the machine learning workflow (Pedregosa et al., 2011).

Applications: Scikit-learn is commonly used for traditional machine learning tasks, such as customer segmentation, fraud detection, and predictive maintenance. Its simplicity, performance, and extensive documentation make it an ideal choice for small to medium-scale data analysis projects, where deep learning frameworks like TensorFlow or PyTorch may be unnecessary.

4. Other Key Libraries

In addition to TensorFlow, PyTorch, and Scikit-learn, several other libraries play a key role in the AI and data science landscape, providing specialized functionalities for specific tasks.

XGBoost: XGBoost is an optimized gradient boosting library designed for high performance and efficiency. It is widely used for structured or tabular data in tasks like classification and regression. XGBoost's scalability and speed have made it one of the most popular libraries for machine learning competitions and real-world applications (Chen & Guestrin, 2016).

Keras: Initially developed as a standalone library, Keras is now integrated into TensorFlow as its high-level API. Keras offers a user-friendly interface for building and training deep learning models, abstracting much of the complexity of working with neural networks (Chollet, 2015). It allows users to quickly prototype models, making it ideal for beginners and those looking for a simple way to implement deep learning.

LightGBM: LightGBM is another gradient boosting framework that focuses on efficiency and speed. Developed by Microsoft, it is particularly well-suited for large datasets and provides faster training times than XGBoost in some scenarios (Ke et al., 2017). LightGBM's tree-based learning algorithms are widely used in financial modeling, risk assessment, and other predictive analytics tasks.

Theano: Theano is an open-source numerical computation library that predates TensorFlow and PyTorch. It was developed at the

Université de Montréal and laid much of the groundwork for modern deep learning frameworks. Although Theano is no longer actively maintained, it was instrumental in the development of deep learning and continues to influence the design of current libraries (Bergstra et al., 2010).

5. Applications of Key Libraries in AI and Data Science

Each of these key libraries plays an essential role in various domains of AI and data science. Their design and features enable a wide range of applications, from predictive modeling to complex deep learning tasks.

Image Recognition and Computer Vision: TensorFlow and PyTorch are widely used for tasks involving image recognition and computer vision. Convolutional neural networks (CNNs), implemented in these libraries, are commonly used in applications such as medical imaging, autonomous vehicles, and facial recognition systems (Abadi et al., 2016; Paszke et al., 2019).

Natural Language Processing (NLP): PyTorch, TensorFlow, and Keras are frequently used in NLP applications. Tasks such as text classification, sentiment analysis, and machine translation are powered by recurrent neural networks (RNNs), transformers, and attention mechanisms, which are well-supported in these libraries. Tools like TensorFlow's TensorFlow Text and PyTorch's HuggingFace Transformers provide pre-trained models and pipelines for NLP tasks (Wolf et al., 2020).

Traditional Machine Learning: For more traditional machine learning tasks, Scikit-learn, XGBoost, and LightGBM dominate. These libraries are used for tasks like predictive maintenance, customer churn prediction, and credit scoring, where structured data is prevalent. Their ease of use, efficiency, and powerful algorithms make them the go-to tools for tasks where deep learning may not be necessary (Pedregosa et al., 2011; Chen & Guestrin, 2016).

Conclusion

TensorFlow, PyTorch, and Scikit-learn, along with other key libraries like XGBoost and Keras, have become indispensable tools in the fields of AI and data science. Each of these libraries offers unique features tailored to specific tasks, ranging from deep learning to traditional machine learning. TensorFlow and PyTorch are powerful frameworks for building complex neural networks, while Scikit-learn remains a versatile tool for simpler machine learning applications. The widespread adoption of these libraries has not only made AI and data science more accessible but has also enabled the development of sophisticated models that power cutting-edge technologies across various industries. As AI and data science continue to evolve, these libraries will remain at the forefront, driving innovation and enabling more advanced solutions to data-driven problems.

References

Abadi, M., Barham, P., Chen, J., Chen, Z., Davis, A., Dean, J., ... & Zheng, X. (2016). TensorFlow: A system for large-scale machine learning. *12th USENIX Symposium on Operating Systems Design and Implementation (OSDI 16)*, 265-283.

Bergstra, J., Breuleux, O., Bastien, F., Lamblin, P., Pascanu, R., Desjardins, G., ... & Bengio, Y. (2010). Theano: A CPU and GPU math expression compiler. *Proceedings of the Python for Scientific Computing Conference* (SciPy).

Bird, S., Klein, E., & Loper, E. (2009). *Natural Language Processing with Python*. O'Reilly Media, Inc.

Carbone, P., Katsifodimos, A., Ewen, S., Markl, V., Haridi, S., & Tzoumas, K. (2015). Apache Flink: Stream and batch processing in a single engine. *IEEE Data Engineering Bulletin, 38*(4), 28-38.

Chang, W., Cheng, J., Allaire, J., Xie, Y., & McPherson, J. (2020). *Shiny: Web application framework for R*. R package version 1.5.0.

Chen, T., & Guestrin, C. (2016). XGBoost: A scalable tree boosting system. *Proceedings of the 22nd ACM SIGKDD International Conference on Knowledge Discovery and Data Mining*, 785-794.

Chen, T., & Guestrin, C. (2016). XGBoost: A scalable tree boosting system. *Proceedings of the 22nd ACM SIGKDD International Conference on Knowledge Discovery and Data Mining*, 785-794.

Chollet, F. (2015). Keras: The Python deep learning library. *GitHub*. https://github.com/fchollet/keras

Chollet, F. (2015). Keras: The Python deep learning library. *GitHub*. https://github.com/fchollet/keras

George, L. (2011). *HBase: The definitive guide*. O'Reilly Media.

Huber, W., Carey, V. J., Gentleman, R., et al. (2015). Orchestrating high-throughput genomic analysis with Bioconductor. *Nature Methods, 12*(2), 115-121.

Hunter, J. D. (2007). Matplotlib: A 2D graphics environment. *Computing in Science & Engineering, 9*(3), 90-95.

Hyndman, R. J., & Athanasopoulos, G. (2018). *Forecasting: Principles and practice* (2nd ed.). OTexts.

Ihaka, R., & Gentleman, R. (1996). R: A language for data analysis and graphics. *Journal of Computational and Graphical Statistics, 5*(3), 299-314.

Kane, M. J., Emerson, J. W., & Weston, S. (2013). Scalable strategies for computing with massive data. *Journal of Statistical Software, 55*(14), 1-19.

Karau, H., Konwinski, A., Wendell, P., & Zaharia, M. (2015). *Learning Spark: Lightning-fast big data analysis.* O'Reilly Media.

Ke, G., Meng, Q., Finley, T., Wang, T., Chen, W., Ma, W., Ye, Q., & Liu, T. Y. (2017). LightGBM: A highly efficient gradient boosting decision tree. *Advances in Neural Information Processing Systems, 30*, 3146-3154.

Kreps, J., Narkhede, N., & Rao, J. (2011). Kafka: A distributed messaging system for log processing. *Proceedings of the NetDB Conference*, 1-7.

Kuhn, M. (2008). Building predictive models in R using the caret package. *Journal of Statistical Software, 28*(5), 1-26.

Kuhn, V., Thompson, R., & Allen, P. (2011). *Akka in action.* Manning Publications.

Liaw, A., & Wiener, M. (2002). Classification and regression by randomForest. *R News, 2*(3), 18-22.

Ligges, U. (2015). CRAN: The Comprehensive R Archive Network. *R Journal, 7*(1), 53-56.

McKinney, W. (2010). Data structures for statistical computing in Python. In *Proceedings of the 9th Python in Science Conference* (pp. 51-56).

Meng, X., Bradley, J., Yavuz, B., Sparks, E., Venkataraman, S., Liu, D., ... & Zaharia, M. (2016). Mllib: Machine learning in Apache Spark. *Journal of Machine Learning Research, 17*(1), 1235-1241.

Muller, A. C., & Guido, S. (2016). *Introduction to Machine Learning with Python: A Guide for Data Scientists.* O'Reilly Media, Inc.

Odersky, M., Spoon, L., & Venners, B. (2016). *Programming in Scala* (3rd ed.). Artima.

Oliphant, T. E. (2015). *A Guide to NumPy.* Trelgol Publishing.

Paszke, A., Gross, S., Massa, F., Lerer, A., Bradbury, J., Chanan, G., ... & Chintala, S. (2019). PyTorch: An imperative style, high-performance deep learning library. In *Advances in Neural Information Processing Systems* (pp. 8024-8035).

Pedregosa, F., Varoquaux, G., Gramfort, A., Michel, V., Thirion, B., Grisel, O., ... & Duchesnay, E. (2011). Scikit-learn: Machine learning in Python. *Journal of Machine Learning Research, 12*, 2825-2830.

Pedregosa, F., Varoquaux, G., Gramfort, A., Michel, V., Thirion, B., Grisel, O., ... & Duchesnay, E. (2011). Scikit-learn: Machine learning in Python. *Journal of Machine Learning Research, 12*, 2825-2830.

Peng, R. D. (2015). *R programming for data science.* Leanpub.

Van Rossum, G., & Drake, F. L. (2009). *Python 3 Reference Manual.* CreateSpace.

White, T. (2015). *Hadoop: The definitive guide* (4th ed.). O'Reilly Media.

Wickham, H. (2016). *ggplot2: Elegant graphics for data analysis.* Springer-Verlag New York.

Wickham, H., & Grolemund, G. (2017). *R for data science*. O'Reilly Media, Inc.

Wolf, T., Debut, L., Sanh, V., Chaumond, J., Delangue, C., Moi, A., ... & Rush, A. M. (2020). Transformers: State-of-the-art natural language processing. *Proceedings of the 2020 Conference on Empirical Methods in Natural Language Processing: System Demonstrations*, 38-45.

Yu, B. (2020). Integrating Python and R for data analysis and machine learning. *Journal of Data Science*, *18*(1), 101-110.

Chapter 19: Big Data Platforms

Apache Hadoop

Apache Hadoop is one of the most prominent open-source big data platforms, designed to store and process vast amounts of data across distributed computing environments. Hadoop's core components—Hadoop Distributed File System (HDFS), MapReduce, YARN, and various add-on tools—enable efficient large-scale data processing and storage. It provides scalability, fault tolerance, and cost-effective data processing across clusters of commodity hardware, making it a cornerstone in the field of big data analytics. Hadoop has become an essential tool for industries dealing with massive datasets, including finance, healthcare, telecommunications, and e-commerce.

1. Overview of Apache Hadoop

Apache Hadoop was originally created by Doug Cutting and Mike Cafarella in 2005, inspired by Google's MapReduce and Google File System (GFS) research papers (Dean & Ghemawat, 2008). It was developed to handle large-scale data processing by distributing data and computational tasks across multiple nodes in a cluster. By leveraging cheap, commodity hardware, Hadoop democratized big data processing, allowing organizations to manage and analyze petabytes of data in an efficient and scalable manner (White, 2015).

Distributed Architecture: At its core, Hadoop operates in a distributed computing environment, splitting both data and computation across multiple machines. The use of multiple nodes in a cluster enhances fault tolerance and scalability. If one node fails, the data and computation tasks are automatically redistributed, ensuring uninterrupted data processing (Borthakur, 2007). This distributed design is central to Hadoop's ability to process large datasets efficiently, as it minimizes the time and resources required to manage and analyze big data.

Cost-Effective Scalability: Hadoop's ability to scale horizontally, by adding more nodes to the cluster, allows organizations to expand their storage and processing capabilities without significant infrastructure investment. This scalability is crucial for businesses dealing with increasing amounts of data, allowing them to grow their data processing capabilities in line with business needs (White, 2015).

2. Core Components of Apache Hadoop

Apache Hadoop is composed of several core modules, each designed to perform specific tasks in the big data processing lifecycle. These modules work together to provide an integrated platform for storing, processing, and analyzing massive datasets.

Hadoop Distributed File System (HDFS): HDFS is the primary storage component of Hadoop. It is designed to store large files across multiple machines in a distributed fashion, dividing data into blocks and replicating them across different nodes in the cluster to ensure fault tolerance. Each block is typically replicated three times to guard against data loss in case of node failure (Borthakur, 2007). HDFS's architecture is optimized for high-throughput access to large datasets, making it ideal for big data applications that require processing of substantial volumes of data, such as log analysis, web indexing, and social media analytics.

MapReduce: MapReduce is the processing engine that powers Hadoop's ability to execute parallel computations across distributed nodes. It breaks down large data processing tasks into smaller tasks, where the "Map" function processes input data into key-value pairs, and the "Reduce" function aggregates the results (Dean & Ghemawat, 2008). This framework is designed to handle large-scale batch processing efficiently and is often used for tasks such as indexing web pages, counting word frequencies, and data aggregation.

YARN (Yet Another Resource Negotiator): YARN is Hadoop's resource management layer. It schedules and monitors the execution of tasks on the cluster, ensuring optimal allocation of computational resources (Vavilapalli et al., 2013). By separating resource management from the data processing tasks, YARN allows multiple applications, such as Spark or Hive, to run on the same cluster, providing better resource utilization and greater flexibility in managing large-scale data processing workflows.

Hadoop Ecosystem: In addition to its core components, Hadoop has a rich ecosystem of tools designed to extend its capabilities. Some of the key tools in the Hadoop ecosystem include:

- **Apache Hive**: Hive is a data warehouse system built on top of Hadoop, which allows users to query and analyze large datasets using a SQL-like query language (HiveQL). Hive is commonly used for batch processing and querying of structured data stored in HDFS (Thusoo et al., 2010).

- **Apache Pig**: Pig is a high-level platform for processing large datasets using a scripting language called Pig Latin. It provides a simpler way to write MapReduce jobs and is often used for data transformation and processing (Olston et al., 2008).

- **HBase**: HBase is a NoSQL database that runs on top of HDFS, designed for real-time read and write access to large datasets. HBase is commonly used for applications that require random access to massive datasets, such as social media platforms and e-commerce sites (George, 2011).

3. Applications of Apache Hadoop

Apache Hadoop has found widespread application across numerous industries due to its ability to handle large-scale data processing and storage in an efficient and cost-effective manner.

Data Warehousing and Analytics: Hadoop is widely used for building data lakes—centralized repositories that allow organizations to store structured, semi-structured, and unstructured data at any scale. Once data is stored in HDFS, organizations can run analytics and machine learning tasks using tools such as Hive, Pig, or Spark (Thusoo et al., 2010). Hadoop's ability to handle diverse data types makes it a valuable tool for companies looking to gain insights from their data, whether for customer behavior analysis, risk assessment, or market forecasting.

Log and Event Data Processing: Hadoop's batch processing capabilities are ideal for analyzing large-scale log data generated by applications, servers, and devices. This is particularly useful for web companies, such as e-commerce platforms, which generate massive amounts of clickstream data, or financial institutions analyzing transaction logs for fraud detection (White, 2015). Hadoop's ecosystem tools, such as Flume (for data ingestion) and Hive (for querying), make it easier to process and analyze log data in real time.

Recommendation Systems: Hadoop is often used in recommendation engines, particularly for e-commerce and media platforms that analyze user behavior to suggest products, movies, or content. Hadoop's distributed architecture enables the efficient processing of vast amounts of user interaction data to generate real-time recommendations (Borthakur, 2007).

Fraud Detection: Financial institutions and insurance companies use Hadoop to analyze transaction and claim data at scale to detect fraudulent activities. By processing large datasets with Hadoop's MapReduce and using machine learning algorithms, organizations can identify patterns and anomalies that indicate potential fraud (Vavilapalli et al., 2013).

Genomic Data Analysis: In healthcare, Hadoop is used to process large genomic datasets for tasks such as DNA sequencing and analysis. The ability to store and process petabytes of data across clusters makes Hadoop a valuable tool in bioinformatics, enabling faster and more cost-effective analysis of genomic data (George, 2011).

4. Challenges and Considerations in Using Apache Hadoop

Despite its advantages, Hadoop is not without its challenges. Organizations must consider the following factors when implementing Hadoop for big data processing:

Complexity of Setup and Maintenance: Hadoop's distributed architecture, while powerful, can be complex to set up and maintain. Managing clusters, ensuring fault tolerance, and optimizing performance require significant expertise in distributed systems. Furthermore, ensuring that the cluster is configured properly for specific workloads, such as tuning MapReduce jobs or managing HDFS replication, can be challenging (White, 2015).

Real-Time Processing Limitations: Hadoop is designed primarily for batch processing, and while it excels at handling large-scale data processing tasks, it is not optimized for real-time analytics. Although tools like Apache Spark and Apache Flink have been integrated into the Hadoop ecosystem to address this limitation, Hadoop's native MapReduce framework remains best suited for batch jobs, making it less ideal for applications that require real-time data analysis (Karau et al., 2015).

Data Latency: Due to its reliance on batch processing, Hadoop is not ideal for applications that demand low-latency data access. For example, while HDFS is highly optimized for reading large files sequentially, it may not be the best choice for workloads that require frequent random reads and writes, such as transactional databases (George, 2011).

In summary, Apache Hadoop has revolutionized big data storage and processing by providing a scalable, distributed platform that can handle massive datasets across clusters of commodity hardware. Its core components - HDFS, MapReduce, and YARN - are designed to optimize data storage and processing, making it ideal for industries that need to process large volumes of data efficiently. Despite its limitations in real-time processing and its complexity in setup and maintenance, Hadoop remains a foundational tool for big data analytics, offering a robust ecosystem of tools that cater to various data processing needs. As the demand for big data solutions continues to grow, Hadoop's role in enabling large-scale data processing across diverse industries will remain critical.

Apache Spark

Apache Spark is an open-source, distributed computing system designed for fast and scalable big data processing. Spark was developed at UC Berkeley's AMPLab and introduced in 2009 as a more efficient alternative to Apache Hadoop's MapReduce, offering both batch and real-time processing capabilities. Spark's primary advantage lies in its ability to process data in memory, which significantly improves performance for data-intensive applications like machine learning, graph processing, and real-time stream analytics. Since its inception, Spark has become one of the most popular big data platforms, used by organizations worldwide to handle vast volumes of data in distributed computing environments.

1. Overview of Apache Spark

Apache Spark was developed to address the limitations of the Hadoop MapReduce framework, which processes data in a sequential, disk-based manner. Spark's key innovation is its in-memory computation model, which allows data to be loaded into memory and reused across multiple parallel operations. This capability significantly reduces disk I/O operations, leading to faster execution times for iterative algorithms and interactive analytics (Zaharia et al., 2016). Spark also provides a unified engine for various types of data processing, including batch processing, stream processing, machine learning, and graph computation.

In-Memory Computation: Unlike Hadoop's MapReduce, which writes intermediate data to disk, Spark keeps data in memory between steps, which can dramatically speed up computation, especially for iterative algorithms like those used in machine learning and graph processing (Zaharia et al., 2012). This in-memory processing allows Spark to perform tasks up to 100 times faster than Hadoop MapReduce when working with memory-resident datasets and up to 10 times faster on disk-based operations.

Unified Engine for Diverse Workloads: Spark is designed to handle a wide range of big data workloads in a single unified platform. It supports batch processing through the DataFrame and Dataset APIs, real-time stream processing via Spark Streaming, iterative machine learning tasks with MLlib, and graph processing with GraphX (Zaharia et al., 2016). This makes Spark highly versatile, enabling organizations to use a single framework for multiple types of data processing workloads.

Scalability: Apache Spark is highly scalable and can run on large clusters of machines. It supports distributed computing environments and integrates well with cluster managers like Hadoop's YARN, Apache Mesos, and Kubernetes. It can run on cloud platforms such as Amazon Web Services (AWS), Google Cloud Platform (GCP), and Microsoft Azure, making it an ideal choice for processing large-scale datasets in both on-premises and cloud environments (Karau et al., 2015).

2. Core Components of Apache Spark

Apache Spark is composed of several core modules, each tailored to specific types of data processing workloads. These modules provide a comprehensive framework for handling diverse big data tasks, including batch processing, real-time stream processing, machine learning, and graph computation.

Spark Core: Spark Core is the foundation of the Spark platform, responsible for basic I/O operations, task scheduling, and distributed data management. Spark Core provides the Resilient Distributed Dataset (RDD), Spark's fundamental data structure, which is a fault-tolerant, distributed collection of objects that can be processed in parallel (Zaharia et al., 2012). RDDs allow users to perform operations like map, filter, and reduce across distributed datasets while ensuring fault tolerance through lineage information.

Spark SQL: Spark SQL is the module responsible for structured data processing, providing a powerful interface for working with structured and semi-structured data. It introduces the DataFrame API, which allows users to query structured data using SQL queries or directly manipulate it using APIs in languages like Java, Python, R, and Scala (Armbrust et al., 2015). Spark SQL is widely used for data analysis and ETL (extract, transform, load) tasks and can read data from various sources, including HDFS, Hive, JSON, Parquet, and JDBC.

Spark Streaming: Spark Streaming extends the core Spark API to handle real-time data streams, allowing users to process continuous streams of data in near real-time. It divides the stream into small batches and processes them using Spark's batch processing capabilities, enabling seamless integration of real-time and batch workloads (Zaharia et al., 2016). Spark Streaming is commonly used for applications like log processing, fraud detection, and real-time analytics.

MLlib (Machine Learning Library): MLlib is Spark's distributed machine learning library, providing a range of algorithms for classification, regression, clustering, collaborative filtering, and dimensionality reduction. MLlib simplifies the process of building machine learning models by offering high-level APIs that can scale across large datasets (Meng et al., 2016). Spark's in-memory processing makes it particularly well-suited for iterative machine learning algorithms that require multiple passes over the data.

GraphX: GraphX is Spark's API for graph processing and analysis, allowing users to create and manipulate graphs and perform computations on graph structures. It provides a collection of graph algorithms, such as PageRank, connected components, and shortest paths, which are useful for analyzing networks, social media data, and other graph-structured data (Xin et al., 2013).

3. Advantages of Apache Spark Over Hadoop

While both Apache Spark and Apache Hadoop are widely used big data platforms, Spark offers several key advantages over Hadoop, particularly in terms of performance, flexibility, and ease of use.

Faster Performance: Spark's in-memory processing engine is one of its biggest advantages over Hadoop's MapReduce framework, which writes intermediate results to disk. Spark processes data in memory, which leads to much faster execution times, particularly for iterative algorithms like those used in machine learning or graph processing (Zaharia et al., 2012). By reducing disk I/O, Spark can perform tasks up to 100 times faster than Hadoop for certain workloads.

Unified Platform: Spark provides a unified platform for batch processing, stream processing, machine learning, and graph computation, whereas Hadoop typically requires separate tools like Apache Flink for streaming or Apache Mahout for machine learning. This integration simplifies the development process and allows organizations to use Spark for a wide range of big data applications, making it easier to maintain and scale (Karau et al., 2015).

Ease of Use: Spark's high-level APIs, such as DataFrames and Datasets, provide a more user-friendly and concise interface compared to Hadoop's MapReduce, which requires developers to write more complex code. Spark also offers built-in support for multiple programming languages, including Python, Scala, Java, and R, which further lowers the barrier to entry for data scientists and engineers (Armbrust et al., 2015).

Real-Time Processing: Spark's ability to handle real-time data streams through Spark Streaming is another key advantage over Hadoop, which is designed primarily for batch processing. Spark

Streaming allows developers to build applications that process data in near real-time, making it suitable for applications like real-time analytics, event detection, and monitoring (Zaharia et al., 2016).

4. Applications of Apache Spark

Apache Spark is used across various industries to address a wide range of big data challenges, from batch processing and real-time analytics to machine learning and graph computation.

Real-Time Analytics: Spark Streaming is widely used for real-time analytics, where data is ingested continuously from sources like IoT devices, social media, or log files, and processed in near real-time. For example, financial institutions use Spark Streaming to detect fraud in real-time by analyzing transaction patterns, while e-commerce companies use it for recommendation systems that provide personalized suggestions to users based on their browsing behavior (Zaharia et al., 2016).

Data Warehousing and ETL: Spark SQL is commonly used for querying large datasets stored in data lakes and data warehouses. Organizations use Spark to perform ETL tasks (extract, transform, load) on structured and semi-structured data, allowing them to preprocess and clean data before analysis. The ability to run SQL queries directly on large datasets, combined with Spark's scalability, makes it ideal for business intelligence and data analytics applications (Armbrust et al., 2015).

Machine Learning at Scale: Spark's MLlib is used for building and deploying machine learning models on large datasets. Companies in sectors like finance, healthcare, and retail use Spark to build predictive models for risk assessment, fraud detection, and customer segmentation. The distributed nature of Spark allows these models to scale across large clusters, making it feasible to train complex models on massive datasets (Meng et al., 2016).

Graph Processing: GraphX is used for analyzing graph-structured data in applications like social network analysis, recommendation engines, and fraud detection. Companies use GraphX to explore relationships between users or entities and perform computations like ranking and clustering. For example, GraphX can be used to compute PageRank scores, identifying influential nodes in a network (Xin et al., 2013).

5. Challenges and Considerations in Using Apache Spark

Despite its advantages, there are several challenges and considerations when using Apache Spark for big data processing:

Memory Usage: Spark's in-memory computation model requires large amounts of RAM to store intermediate data. While this design improves performance for most workloads, it can be a limitation in environments where memory resources are constrained. Developers must carefully manage memory usage and tune Spark's configuration settings to avoid memory bottlenecks (Karau et al., 2015).

Complexity of Deployment and Maintenance: Although Spark simplifies many aspects of big data processing, deploying and maintaining large Spark clusters can be complex, particularly when dealing with high availability, fault tolerance, and resource allocation. Organizations often rely on cluster managers like YARN or Kubernetes to manage Spark clusters, which adds additional layers of complexity (Zaharia et al., 2016).

Integration with Hadoop Ecosystem: While Spark is often used as a replacement for Hadoop's MapReduce, many organizations still rely on Hadoop's ecosystem tools, such as HDFS for storage and Hive for querying. Integrating Spark with these tools requires careful configuration to ensure compatibility and optimize performance (Karau et al., 2015).

In summary, Apache Spark has emerged as a powerful and versatile big data platform, offering in-memory processing, real-time analytics, and support for a wide range of data processing workloads. Its speed, scalability, and flexibility make it an ideal choice for organizations looking to process large-scale datasets efficiently. By providing a unified platform for batch processing, stream processing, machine learning, and graph computation, Spark simplifies the development and maintenance of big data applications. Despite challenges related to memory usage and cluster management, Spark remains one of the most widely adopted big data platforms, used by companies across various industries to address complex data processing needs.

Apache Flink

Apache Flink is an open-source, distributed stream processing framework designed for real-time and batch data processing at scale. Developed by the Apache Software Foundation, Flink was created to address the limitations of traditional batch-oriented systems like Hadoop and provide a unified engine capable of handling both streaming and batch data workloads efficiently. Its primary strength lies in its ability to process data in real-time, with low latency and high throughput, making it a key tool for big data applications that require immediate insights, such as fraud detection, recommendation systems, and real-time analytics. Flink's architecture allows it to support event-driven applications and continuous data processing, providing a powerful platform for managing dynamic data streams across industries.

1. Overview of Apache Flink

Apache Flink was developed to fill a gap in big data processing by offering a true stream processing engine capable of handling both real-time and batch workloads. Unlike batch-oriented frameworks such as Hadoop, which process static datasets, Flink processes data continuously as it arrives, enabling real-time analytics and complex event processing. Flink's core design is centered around stream-first processing, but it also includes robust support for batch processing, making it a flexible tool for various big data scenarios (Carbone et al., 2015).

Stream-First Architecture: Apache Flink's core architecture is built around a streaming engine. This means that even batch processing jobs are treated as special cases of streaming data. Flink processes data streams in real-time, enabling it to handle dynamic data sources and respond to events as they happen. This contrasts with traditional batch frameworks like Hadoop, where data is processed in chunks (Carbone et al., 2015). Flink's streaming model ensures low-latency processing and is ideal for applications like real-time fraud detection, monitoring sensor data, or tracking user activity in real time.

Fault Tolerance and Exactly-Once Semantics: One of the standout features of Flink is its fault-tolerant nature. Flink uses a technique called checkpointing to ensure fault tolerance in distributed environments. This means that in the event of node failure, the system can recover and continue processing without data loss or duplication. Flink also supports "exactly-once" processing semantics, which ensures that each event is processed exactly once, even in the face of system failures, a critical feature for applications such as financial transactions and event-driven systems (Carbone et al., 2017).

Unified Stream and Batch Processing: Flink's unique architecture allows it to handle both stream and batch data processing in a single unified engine. While other frameworks like Spark treat streaming and batch processing as separate components, Flink blurs the line between the two, allowing developers to build applications that can seamlessly switch between real-time and batch processing depending on the workload. This versatility is particularly useful in environments where both real-time and historical data need to be analyzed together (Morales et al., 2019).

2. Core Components of Apache Flink

Flink is composed of several core components that allow it to handle distributed data processing tasks across both stream and batch data. These components include Flink's dataflow engine, state management features, and APIs for processing structured and unstructured data.

Flink Runtime: The Flink runtime is the engine that powers Flink's data processing capabilities. It executes dataflows in a distributed environment and manages the scheduling, execution, and fault tolerance of data processing tasks. The runtime supports parallel execution of tasks across clusters of machines, ensuring scalability and efficient resource utilization (Morales et al., 2019). Flink's runtime is designed to operate in both on-premises clusters and cloud-based environments, allowing it to scale flexibly based on the size of the data being processed.

Stateful Stream Processing: Flink is particularly strong in handling stateful stream processing. In many real-time applications, the results of a computation depend on previous events (state). Flink efficiently manages this state by keeping it in memory and making it fault-tolerant using periodic checkpoints. The system can recover from failures and restore the state from checkpoints without losing data. This capability is essential for applications like monitoring systems, which continuously process and update state in response to incoming events (Carbone et al., 2017).

DataStream API and DataSet API: Flink provides two main APIs for data processing: the DataStream API for handling real-time stream data and the DataSet API for processing batch data. The DataStream API allows developers to process unbounded data streams and apply transformations like filtering, mapping, and windowing to continuous data. The DataSet API, on the other hand, is optimized for batch processing tasks like ETL (extract, transform, load), querying, and machine learning (Morales et al., 2019). These

APIs give developers flexibility in building applications that process both real-time and static datasets.

Windowing and Event Time Processing: In stream processing, events can arrive out of order due to network delays or other factors. Flink addresses this with its support for event-time processing, which processes events based on the time they were generated (event time) rather than when they were received (processing time). Flink's powerful windowing features allow developers to group events by time windows, count windows, or custom-defined conditions, making it easier to analyze time-based patterns in data streams (Carbone et al., 2015).

3. Advantages of Apache Flink Over Other Big Data Platforms

While Apache Spark is often compared to Flink, especially in terms of streaming capabilities, Flink offers several distinct advantages, particularly in real-time stream processing and event-driven applications.

True Stream Processing: Unlike Spark Streaming, which is a micro-batch processing system that processes data in small, time-based batches, Flink offers true stream processing, where data is processed event-by-event in real-time. This leads to lower latency and makes Flink better suited for applications that require immediate processing and reaction to incoming data, such as fraud detection and IoT device monitoring (Morales et al., 2019).

State Management: Flink's built-in state management capabilities make it highly efficient for stateful stream processing. Applications that require the maintenance of state, such as real-time recommendation systems or event monitoring, can benefit from Flink's ability to manage large amounts of state in a distributed environment while ensuring fault tolerance and exactly-once guarantees (Carbone et al., 2017). This contrasts with Spark

Streaming, which relies on external systems like Apache Kafka to manage state.

Low Latency and Exactly-Once Semantics: Flink is optimized for low-latency processing and guarantees exactly-once processing semantics, making it an excellent choice for applications where timely and accurate processing of events is critical. Spark Streaming offers at-least-once semantics by default, meaning that some events could be processed more than once in case of failure, which may not be ideal for mission-critical systems (Carbone et al., 2017).

Unified Batch and Stream Processing: Flink's unified engine for stream and batch processing eliminates the need for separate frameworks to handle real-time and batch workloads. This contrasts with Spark, which treats batch processing (Spark Core) and stream processing (Spark Streaming) as distinct components. Flink's ability to handle both types of processing with a single API simplifies development and maintenance, making it easier to build complex data pipelines (Morales et al., 2019).

4. Applications of Apache Flink

Apache Flink is used across various industries to power applications that require real-time data processing, including financial services, telecommunications, e-commerce, and IoT.

Fraud Detection: Financial institutions use Apache Flink to detect fraudulent transactions in real time. Flink's ability to process streams of transaction data with low latency and its support for complex event processing makes it ideal for monitoring transaction patterns and identifying suspicious activities as they happen (Carbone et al., 2017). By maintaining state across events, Flink can track patterns over time and trigger alerts when specific conditions are met, helping organizations prevent fraud before it occurs.

Real-Time Analytics and Monitoring: Many organizations use Flink for real-time analytics, where data from various sources, such as

IoT devices, social media, or web applications, is continuously processed and analyzed. Flink's support for event-time processing and windowing makes it well-suited for analyzing time-based data patterns, such as monitoring sensor data in smart cities or tracking user behavior on websites (Carbone et al., 2015).

Recommendation Systems: E-commerce companies use Flink to power real-time recommendation systems that suggest products to customers based on their browsing history and behavior. Flink's stateful stream processing allows these systems to maintain context about user interactions and update recommendations dynamically as new data becomes available (Morales et al., 2019).

IoT Data Processing: In the IoT space, Flink is used to process data from connected devices in real time. Flink's ability to handle continuous data streams makes it ideal for applications like predictive maintenance, where sensor data from industrial equipment is processed to detect anomalies and predict failures before they happen (Morales et al., 2019). Flink's low-latency processing ensures that organizations can respond to issues in real-time, minimizing downtime and maintenance costs.

5. Challenges and Considerations in Using Apache Flink

Despite its advantages, there are several challenges and considerations when using Apache Flink for big data processing:

Complexity of State Management: While Flink's stateful processing is one of its greatest strengths, managing state at scale can be complex. Large states can require significant memory and storage resources, and developers must carefully configure checkpointing and tuning parameters to ensure that state is handled efficiently without overwhelming system resources (Carbone et al., 2017).

Operational Overhead: Running and maintaining Flink clusters can introduce operational challenges, particularly in managing high availability, load balancing, and failure recovery. Developers and system administrators must ensure that clusters are properly tuned for performance and that adequate resources are allocated for fault-tolerant processing (Morales et al., 2019).

Latency vs. Throughput Trade-offs: While Flink excels in providing low-latency stream processing, developers often face trade-offs between latency and throughput. Optimizing for low latency may require more memory and processing power, whereas optimizing for high throughput may increase the lag in processing events. Careful configuration and tuning are needed to strike the right balance depending on the application requirements (Carbone et al., 2017).

In summary, Apache Flink is a powerful and versatile big data platform, designed for real-time stream processing and capable of handling both batch and stream workloads in a unified engine. Its strengths in low-latency processing, fault tolerance, and stateful stream management make it ideal for real-time applications like fraud detection, IoT monitoring, and recommendation systems. Flink's ability to handle both stream and batch processing in a single platform simplifies the development of complex data pipelines, offering organizations a flexible and scalable solution for big data processing. Despite challenges related to operational overhead and state management, Flink remains a leading choice for organizations seeking to build responsive, event-driven applications in real-time.

Distributed Storage Systems

In the world of big data, distributed storage systems are essential for handling vast amounts of data across multiple machines. These systems are designed to store, manage, and retrieve large datasets efficiently in environments where single-node storage solutions would be insufficient due to scalability, fault tolerance, and performance requirements. Distributed storage systems break down data into smaller pieces, distributing these pieces across multiple machines (or nodes) in a cluster. This approach enables scalability, high availability, and resilience in handling large datasets while maintaining efficient access to data for processing and analysis.

Distributed storage systems are the backbone of many big data platforms, including Apache Hadoop, Apache Spark, and cloud-based solutions like Amazon S3. They provide the underlying infrastructure to support data-intensive applications across industries such as finance, healthcare, telecommunications, and e-commerce.

1. Key Characteristics of Distributed Storage Systems

Distributed storage systems are defined by several key characteristics that differentiate them from traditional storage architectures. These characteristics allow them to meet the demands of large-scale data storage and access in a reliable and efficient manner.

Scalability: One of the primary advantages of distributed storage systems is their ability to scale horizontally. As data grows, additional storage nodes can be added to the cluster, allowing the system to handle larger datasets without a complete overhaul of the infrastructure. This scalability is crucial for modern data-intensive applications where data volumes can increase rapidly over time (Ghemawat et al., 2003).

Fault Tolerance and Redundancy: Distributed storage systems are designed to handle hardware failures gracefully. Data is typically replicated across multiple nodes in the system to ensure redundancy. If a node fails, the system can recover the lost data from replicas stored on other nodes. This redundancy ensures high availability and resilience, even in the face of hardware or network failures (Borthakur, 2007).

Data Locality: Many distributed storage systems prioritize data locality, which means placing data as close as possible to the processing resources that need it. This reduces the need for data to travel across the network, improving performance by minimizing latency and bandwidth usage. This feature is particularly important in distributed computing environments where data-intensive tasks are executed (Ghemawat et al., 2003).

High Throughput: Distributed storage systems are optimized for high-throughput access to large datasets. By spreading data across multiple nodes and allowing parallel access, these systems enable large-scale data processing frameworks like Hadoop and Spark to process terabytes or even petabytes of data efficiently. This ability to read and write large volumes of data concurrently is critical for big data applications that require fast and efficient data processing (White, 2015).

2. Popular Distributed Storage Systems

There are several widely adopted distributed storage systems, each designed to meet specific use cases and challenges in big data environments. These systems provide the foundational storage layer for large-scale data processing, analytics, and machine learning workloads.

Hadoop Distributed File System (HDFS): HDFS is a key component of the Apache Hadoop ecosystem and one of the most widely used distributed storage systems. It was designed to store large amounts of data across multiple nodes in a fault-tolerant manner. HDFS splits data into blocks, typically 128 MB in size, and replicates each block across multiple nodes to ensure fault tolerance. If a node fails, HDFS can retrieve the data from replicas stored on other nodes (Borthakur, 2007). HDFS is optimized for high-throughput access to large files and is used in batch processing tasks such as data analytics, log processing, and large-scale data storage.

Amazon S3 (Simple Storage Service): Amazon S3 is a cloud-based distributed storage system that offers virtually unlimited storage capacity and high availability. S3 is widely used for both data storage and backup, as well as serving as a data lake for big data processing tasks. Unlike HDFS, S3 is not limited to a specific cluster size, making it highly scalable for organizations that need to store massive amounts of data across distributed environments. S3 integrates with various big data platforms, including Hadoop, Spark, and machine learning frameworks, making it a key storage solution in cloud-based data processing workflows (Bauer et al., 2020).

Google Cloud Storage: Google Cloud Storage is another cloud-based distributed storage system designed for storing large volumes of data in a secure and scalable manner. Like Amazon S3, it offers high availability and durability by replicating data across multiple geographic regions. Google Cloud Storage supports high-throughput data access and integrates seamlessly with Google Cloud's big data services, such as BigQuery and Dataproc, enabling large-scale data analytics and machine learning (Kirkland & Smith, 2019).

Ceph: Ceph is an open-source distributed storage platform that provides scalable, high-performance storage for both object and block storage. Ceph's architecture is designed to scale to exabytes of data by distributing data across multiple nodes in a cluster. Ceph uses a dynamic replication mechanism to ensure data redundancy and fault tolerance, making it suitable for both cloud-based and on-premises storage needs. Ceph's object storage interface is compatible with Amazon S3, allowing it to integrate with cloud-native applications (Weil et al., 2006).

Apache Cassandra: While traditionally known as a NoSQL database, Apache Cassandra also functions as a distributed storage system. Cassandra is designed to handle large amounts of data across commodity servers, ensuring high availability and fault tolerance through its distributed, decentralized architecture. Cassandra's write-oriented design and ability to scale horizontally make it suitable for handling real-time data processing workloads, particularly in applications such as logging, sensor data collection, and transaction processing (Lakshman & Malik, 2010).

3. Applications of Distributed Storage Systems

Distributed storage systems are integral to modern big data platforms and support a wide variety of applications across industries. Their ability to scale, manage large datasets, and ensure fault tolerance makes them suitable for both batch processing and real-time analytics.

Data Lakes: Distributed storage systems like HDFS and Amazon S3 are often used to build data lakes, which are centralized repositories for storing raw, unstructured, and structured data at scale. Data lakes serve as the foundation for big data analytics by providing a scalable and fault-tolerant storage layer where data can be ingested from various sources and later processed by analytics platforms like Apache Spark or machine learning models (White, 2015). Organizations across industries, from healthcare to finance, use data lakes to consolidate vast amounts of data in a cost-effective and scalable manner.

Backup and Disaster Recovery: Distributed storage systems play a critical role in backup and disaster recovery strategies. By replicating data across multiple nodes and even geographic regions, systems like Amazon S3 and Google Cloud Storage ensure that data is protected against hardware failures and catastrophic events. This makes distributed storage a popular choice for organizations looking to safeguard critical data and ensure business continuity (Bauer et al., 2020).

Real-Time Data Processing: Distributed storage systems like HDFS, combined with real-time processing platforms like Apache Flink and Kafka, are used to manage and process streaming data. These systems allow organizations to handle continuous streams of data from sensors, IoT devices, or user interactions, enabling real-time analytics and decision-making. Distributed storage plays a vital role in storing both real-time and historical data for later analysis (Morales et al., 2019).

Machine Learning and AI: Machine learning models often require large datasets for training, and distributed storage systems provide the infrastructure necessary to store and retrieve this data efficiently. Systems like HDFS and S3 are frequently used to store large-scale datasets for machine learning tasks, such as image classification, natural language processing, and predictive analytics. These systems also support high-throughput access, enabling distributed machine learning platforms like TensorFlow and PyTorch to process large amounts of data in parallel (Zaharia et al., 2016).

4. Challenges and Considerations in Using Distributed Storage Systems

While distributed storage systems offer numerous advantages in terms of scalability, fault tolerance, and performance, they also present several challenges that organizations must address to ensure optimal performance and reliability.

Data Consistency: Ensuring data consistency across distributed storage nodes can be challenging, especially in environments where data is replicated across multiple locations. Some distributed storage systems, like Cassandra, favor availability over strong consistency in order to maintain high performance. However, this can lead to eventual consistency issues where data may not be immediately synchronized across all nodes, which may not be acceptable for applications that require strict data consistency (Lakshman & Malik, 2010).

Performance Tuning: Distributed storage systems must be carefully tuned to ensure that they meet the performance requirements of specific workloads. Factors such as replication settings, data partitioning, and network bandwidth can all impact the performance of distributed systems. Poorly tuned systems can suffer from bottlenecks, leading to slower data access and processing times, particularly in large-scale environments (White, 2015).

Security and Access Control: Managing security and access control in distributed storage systems can be complex, especially when data is stored across multiple locations or accessed by multiple users and applications. Ensuring that sensitive data is encrypted at rest and in transit, implementing fine-grained access control, and monitoring access patterns are critical for maintaining data security in distributed storage environments (Kirkland & Smith, 2019).

Conclusion

Distributed storage systems are essential components of modern big data platforms, providing the scalability, fault tolerance, and high throughput required to handle large datasets efficiently. Systems like HDFS, Amazon S3, and Ceph enable organizations to store and process massive amounts of data, supporting applications ranging from data lakes and backup solutions to real-time data processing and machine learning workloads. While these systems offer significant advantages, managing data consistency, tuning performance, and ensuring security are critical challenges that must be addressed to optimize their use. As big data continues to grow, distributed storage systems will remain fundamental to the infrastructure of data-driven organizations across industries.

References

Armbrust, M., Xin, R. S., Lian, C., Huai, Y., Liu, D., Bradley, J., ... & Zaharia, M. (2015). Spark SQL: Relational data processing in Spark. *Proceedings of the 2015 ACM SIGMOD International Conference on Management of Data*, 1383-1394.

Bauer, S., Lu, Q., Finocchiaro, E., & Romero, M. (2020). AWS S3 and dynamic pricing of storage capacity. *Journal of Information Systems*, *34*(1), 1-15.

Borthakur, D. (2007). The Hadoop distributed file system: Architecture and design. *Hadoop Project*

Carbone, P., Ewen, S., Kossmann, D., & Markl, V. (2017). State management in Apache Flink: Consistent stateful distributed stream processing. *Proceedings of the VLDB Endowment, 10*(12), 1718-1729.

Carbone, P., Katsifodimos, A., Ewen, S., Markl, V., Haridi, S., & Tzoumas, K. (2015). Apache Flink: Stream and batch processing in a single engine. *IEEE Data Engineering Bulletin, 38*(4), 28-38.

Dean, J., & Ghemawat, S. (2008). MapReduce: Simplified data processing on large clusters. *Communications of the ACM, 51*(1), 107-113.

George, L. (2011). *HBase: The definitive guide.* O'Reilly Media.

Ghemawat, S., Gobioff, H., & Leung, S. (2003). The Google file system. *ACM SIGOPS Operating Systems Review, 37*(5), 29-43.

Karau, H., Konwinski, A., Wendell, P., & Zaharia, M. (2015). *Learning Spark: Lightning-fast big data analysis.* O'Reilly Media.

Kirkland, R., & Smith, D. (2019). Building data lakes on Google Cloud Storage. *Google Cloud Documentation*, 1-15.

Lakshman, A., & Malik, P. (2010). Cassandra: A decentralized structured storage system. *ACM SIGOPS Operating Systems Review*, *44*(2), 35-40.

Meng, X., Bradley, J., Yavuz, B., Sparks, E., Venkataraman, S., Liu, D., ... & Zaharia, M. (2016). Mllib: Machine learning in Apache Spark. *Journal of Machine Learning Research*, *17*(1), 1235-1241.

Morales, G. D. F., Katsifodimos, A., & Ewen, S. (2019). Building continuous data pipelines with Apache Flink. *Proceedings of the 2019 ACM SIGMOD International Conference on Management of Data*, 2779-2782.

Olston, C., Reed, B., Srivastava, U., Kumar, R., & Tomkins, A. (2008). Pig Latin: A not-so-foreign language for data processing. *Proceedings of the 2008 ACM SIGMOD International Conference on Management of Data*, 1099-1110.

Thusoo, A., Sarma, J. S., Jain, N., Shao, Z., Chakka, P., Anthony, S., ... & Murthy, R. (2010). Hive – A petabyte scale data warehouse using Hadoop. *2010 IEEE 26th International Conference on Data Engineering (ICDE 2010)*, 996-1005.

Vavilapalli, V. K., Murthy, A. C., Douglas, C., Agarwal, S., Konar, M., Evans, R., ... & Cury, J. (2013). Apache Hadoop YARN: Yet another resource negotiator. *Proceedings of the 4th Annual Symposium on Cloud Computing*, 1-16.

Weil, S. A., Brandt, S. A., Miller, E. L., Long, D. D. E., & Maltzahn, C. (2006). Ceph: A scalable, high-performance distributed file system. *Proceedings of the 7th Symposium on Operating Systems Design and Implementation (OSDI)*, 307-320.

White, T. (2015). *Hadoop: The definitive guide* (4th ed.). O'Reilly Media.

Xin, R. S., Gonzalez, J. E., Franklin, M. J., & Stoica, I. (2013). GraphX: A resilient distributed graph system on Spark. *Proceedings of the First International Workshop on Graph Data Management Experiences and Systems*, 1-6.

Zaharia, M., Chowdhury, M., Franklin, M. J., Shenker, S., & Stoica, I. (2012). Resilient distributed datasets: A fault-tolerant abstraction for in-memory cluster computing. *Proceedings of the 9th USENIX Symposium on Networked Systems Design and Implementation (NSDI 12)*, 15-28.

Zaharia, M., Chowdhury, M., Franklin, M. J., Shenker, S., & Stoica, I. (2016). Apache Spark: A unified engine for big data processing. *Communications of the ACM, 59*(11), 56-65.

Zaharia, M., Das, T., Li, H., Hunter, T., Shenker, S., & Stoica, I. (2016). Discretized streams: Fault-tolerant streaming computation at scale. *Proceedings of the 24th ACM Symposium on Operating Systems Principles*, 423-438.

Chapter 20: Cloud Services for AI and Big Data

<u>AWS AI and Big Data Services</u>

Amazon Web Services (AWS) is one of the leading cloud platforms offering a comprehensive suite of tools and services tailored for artificial intelligence (AI) and big data processing. AWS provides scalable, on-demand infrastructure that enables organizations to build, deploy, and manage AI models and big data analytics pipelines with ease. AWS's AI and big data services are widely adopted across industries, helping companies harness the power of machine learning, data analytics, and data storage at scale. These services are designed to cater to a variety of use cases, from data lake creation and real-time analytics to predictive modeling and deep learning.

1. Overview of AWS AI and Big Data Services

AWS offers a broad range of AI and big data services, including managed AI services, machine learning frameworks, data lakes, analytics tools, and distributed computing services. These services are designed to simplify the process of handling large datasets, performing machine learning tasks, and deploying AI models in production environments. AWS services such as Amazon S3, Amazon EMR, Amazon SageMaker, and Amazon Redshift enable organizations to store vast amounts of data, process it efficiently, and gain actionable insights.

Scalability and Flexibility: One of the primary advantages of AWS is its scalability. AWS services are built on top of cloud infrastructure that can scale on-demand, allowing organizations to process terabytes or petabytes of data without worrying about underlying hardware limitations. This flexibility enables organizations to run AI models and big data analytics at a scale that is often impractical with on-premises solutions (Bauer et al., 2020).

514

On-Demand Access: AWS services operate on a pay-as-you-go model, which allows companies to provision and use resources only when needed, reducing costs associated with maintaining hardware infrastructure. The ability to spin up instances and services on-demand is crucial for organizations handling sporadic or fluctuating workloads, such as running AI training models or performing seasonal data analysis (AWS, 2021).

2. Key AWS Big Data Services

AWS offers several core services for big data storage, processing, and analytics. These services integrate seamlessly with other AWS offerings, allowing organizations to build comprehensive data processing pipelines.

Amazon S3 (Simple Storage Service): Amazon S3 is one of AWS's foundational services, providing scalable object storage for data of any type and size. S3 is widely used for building data lakes, storing raw and processed data, and serving as a central repository for data analytics and machine learning workflows. S3's integration with other AWS services, such as AWS Lambda for serverless computing and Amazon SageMaker for machine learning, makes it a flexible tool for organizations needing robust storage solutions (Bauer et al., 2020). S3's durability and scalability allow organizations to store vast amounts of data and retrieve it with low latency, making it a popular choice for big data environments.

Amazon EMR (Elastic MapReduce): Amazon EMR is a cloud-based service that allows organizations to process large amounts of data using open-source tools such as Apache Hadoop, Spark, HBase, and Presto. EMR provides a managed environment where users can run large-scale distributed computing jobs without the need to manage the underlying infrastructure (AWS, 2021). EMR is commonly used for tasks such as data transformation, log processing, and large-scale analytics. It supports a wide range of big data processing frameworks, enabling companies to process and analyze big data in a cost-effective and scalable manner.

Amazon Redshift: Amazon Redshift is a fully managed data warehouse service that allows organizations to run complex queries on large datasets and perform fast analytics. Redshift is designed to handle petabyte-scale data warehouses, making it ideal for large-scale data analytics and business intelligence use cases. Redshift integrates with other AWS services, such as Amazon S3 and AWS Glue, allowing organizations to seamlessly move data into their data warehouse and perform advanced analytics. Redshift's columnar storage and massively parallel processing (MPP) architecture allow for fast query execution on large datasets (AWS, 2021).

AWS Glue: AWS Glue is a serverless data integration service that automates the process of discovering, cataloging, cleaning, and transforming data for analysis. Glue integrates with S3, Redshift, and other AWS services, enabling organizations to prepare and move data into data lakes and data warehouses with ease (AWS, 2021). It includes a fully managed ETL (extract, transform, load) engine, making it a powerful tool for organizations that need to automate data pipelines and perform complex transformations across diverse data sources.

Amazon Kinesis: Amazon Kinesis is a set of services that enables real-time data processing and analytics on streaming data. Kinesis is commonly used to process data from IoT devices, log files, social media streams, and other real-time data sources. With Kinesis Data Streams and Kinesis Data Analytics, organizations can ingest, process, and analyze real-time data in a scalable and fault-tolerant manner, making it ideal for applications such as real-time analytics, monitoring, and fraud detection (AWS, 2021).

3. Key AWS AI and Machine Learning Services

AWS has developed a range of AI and machine learning services that allow organizations to build, train, and deploy machine learning models at scale. These services are designed to make machine learning more accessible to data scientists, developers, and organizations of all sizes.

Amazon SageMaker: Amazon SageMaker is a fully managed service that provides tools to build, train, and deploy machine learning models at scale. SageMaker simplifies the machine learning workflow by offering pre-built algorithms, integrated development environments, and tools for model tuning, evaluation, and deployment (Liberty et al., 2020). SageMaker's support for distributed training allows users to train models on large datasets across multiple instances, accelerating the time-to-market for machine learning projects. It also integrates with AWS services like S3 for data storage, AWS Lambda for serverless computing, and Amazon EC2 for computational resources.

Amazon Rekognition: Rekognition is a fully managed computer vision service that allows developers to analyze images and videos using machine learning models pre-trained on millions of images. Rekognition can perform tasks such as object detection, facial analysis, and text recognition, making it suitable for a wide range of applications, from security and surveillance to content moderation and marketing (AWS, 2021). Rekognition's integration with other AWS services, such as S3 and SageMaker, enables users to build custom computer vision solutions tailored to their specific needs.

Amazon Polly: Amazon Polly is a text-to-speech service that uses advanced deep learning models to convert written text into natural-sounding speech. Polly supports a wide range of languages and voices, making it ideal for building voice-enabled applications, such as virtual assistants, customer service bots, and accessibility tools (AWS, 2021). Polly's integration with AWS Lambda and other AI services enables seamless incorporation of voice functionality into AWS-powered applications.

Amazon Lex: Amazon Lex is a service for building conversational interfaces into applications using voice and text. Lex uses the same deep learning technologies that power Amazon Alexa, enabling developers to create sophisticated chatbots, virtual assistants, and voice-activated devices (Liberty et al., 2020). Lex is fully integrated with AWS services like AWS Lambda, allowing developers to build serverless applications that respond to voice commands or text inputs in real time.

Amazon Comprehend: Amazon Comprehend is a natural language processing (NLP) service that uses machine learning to extract insights from text, including sentiment analysis, entity recognition, and language detection. Comprehend can process large volumes of unstructured text data, making it useful for applications like customer feedback analysis, social media monitoring, and document classification (AWS, 2021).

4. Applications of AWS AI and Big Data Services

AWS AI and big data services are widely used across industries to address a variety of use cases, from predictive analytics and machine learning to real-time data processing and business intelligence.

Financial Services: In the financial sector, AWS services like Amazon SageMaker, Amazon Redshift, and Amazon Kinesis are used for fraud detection, risk modeling, and real-time analytics. Financial institutions leverage AWS's AI services to build machine learning models that can detect suspicious transactions and identify fraud in real time, while big data services like Redshift enable organizations to analyze historical financial data for risk management and regulatory compliance (Liberty et al., 2020).

Healthcare and Life Sciences: AWS services play a key role in healthcare, enabling organizations to store and analyze vast amounts of patient data, genomic data, and medical records. SageMaker is used to develop machine learning models for predictive diagnostics, personalized medicine, and drug discovery, while services like Amazon Rekognition are used for analyzing medical images. AWS also supports healthcare providers in building secure, compliant data lakes for storing sensitive medical data (Bauer et al., 2020).

Retail and E-Commerce: In retail, AWS services are used for personalized recommendations, demand forecasting, and real-time inventory management. Retailers use SageMaker and AWS AI services like Amazon Comprehend and Amazon Lex to build recommendation engines that personalize the shopping experience based on customer behavior. Amazon Kinesis is used for real-time analytics and tracking of customer interactions, helping retailers optimize inventory and respond to customer needs more effectively (Liberty et al., 2020).

Media and Entertainment: Media companies use AWS services to process and analyze large volumes of video, audio, and image data. Amazon Rekognition is used for video content analysis and moderation, while Amazon Polly and Amazon Lex are employed to develop voice-activated media services and chatbots for customer engagement. AWS services also support live streaming and real-time analytics for media content delivery (AWS, 2021).

5. Challenges and Considerations in Using AWS AI and Big Data Services

While AWS offers a robust set of tools for AI and big data, there are several challenges that organizations need to address when using these services.

Cost Management: Although AWS's pay-as-you-go pricing model is flexible, costs can escalate quickly, particularly for organizations running large-scale machine learning training jobs or big data analytics pipelines. Effective cost management strategies, such as using AWS cost management tools and implementing resource scaling policies, are necessary to avoid unexpectedly high cloud bills (Liberty et al., 2020).

Data Security and Compliance: Organizations handling sensitive data, such as financial or healthcare data, must ensure that AWS services comply with security standards and regulations like GDPR, HIPAA, and PCI-DSS. AWS provides a range of security features, such as encryption at rest and in transit, identity and access management (IAM), and audit logging, but it is the responsibility of organizations to configure these services correctly to meet regulatory requirements (Bauer et al., 2020).

Learning Curve and Complexity: While AWS provides a wide range of services, the complexity of its offerings can pose a challenge, particularly for organizations without prior experience in cloud computing or big data. Developers and data scientists must become familiar with the various AWS services, APIs, and tools to fully leverage AWS's capabilities in AI and big data (AWS, 2021).

In summary, AWS AI and big data services offer a powerful and scalable platform for organizations looking to build, deploy, and manage AI models and big data pipelines. Services like Amazon S3, SageMaker, and Redshift enable companies to store vast amounts of data, process it efficiently, and gain insights through advanced analytics and machine learning. With flexible pricing, scalability, and a rich ecosystem of services, AWS is a leader in cloud-based AI and big data solutions. However, organizations must carefully manage costs, ensure compliance with data security regulations, and overcome the complexity of AWS's offerings to fully realize its potential. As cloud adoption continues to grow, AWS's AI and big data services will remain critical tools for driving innovation and data-driven decision-making across industries.

Google Cloud Platform (GCP)

Google Cloud Platform (GCP) is a leading cloud computing service offering a comprehensive set of tools and platforms for artificial intelligence (AI) and big data processing. With a foundation built on Google's own infrastructure, which supports services like Google Search and YouTube, GCP provides scalable, reliable, and high-performance solutions for storing, processing, and analyzing massive amounts of data. GCP's AI and big data services are designed to be accessible to a wide range of users, from data scientists and developers to enterprises handling complex machine learning models and analytics pipelines.

1. Overview of Google Cloud Platform

GCP offers a rich ecosystem of services that support AI, machine learning, big data processing, and advanced analytics. These services allow organizations to leverage Google's cloud infrastructure to store large datasets, train machine learning models, and perform real-time data analytics. GCP is recognized for its advanced machine learning capabilities, particularly through its pre-built AI services and powerful machine learning infrastructure, including TensorFlow and Vertex AI. GCP's big data services, such as BigQuery and Cloud Dataflow, provide efficient, scalable, and cost-effective solutions for processing structured and unstructured data.

Scalability and Global Infrastructure: GCP is built on the same infrastructure that powers Google's own services, offering a highly scalable environment capable of handling petabytes of data. This infrastructure spans multiple global regions and zones, ensuring that users can scale their applications and services based on demand without worrying about performance or latency issues (Jain & Gounares, 2019).

AI-Driven Cloud Services: One of GCP's key differentiators is its strong emphasis on AI and machine learning. Google's investment in AI research and development has resulted in several innovative tools that simplify building and deploying machine learning models. GCP's AI services include pre-trained models for vision, language, and translation tasks, as well as platforms for custom model development (Sato et al., 2019).

2. Key Google Cloud AI Services

GCP's AI services offer both managed solutions for developers with little AI expertise and more advanced tools for data scientists and machine learning engineers. These services are designed to help users quickly build, train, and deploy machine learning models without needing to manage the underlying infrastructure.

Vertex AI: Vertex AI is GCP's comprehensive managed platform for building, deploying, and scaling machine learning models. It allows users to create custom models using Google's AI infrastructure and offers tools for data preparation, model training, and hyperparameter tuning (Sato et al., 2019). Vertex AI integrates with popular machine learning libraries like TensorFlow and PyTorch, and it supports automated machine learning (AutoML), making it easier for users to train models with minimal coding. Vertex AI also provides tools for deploying models in production environments with monitoring and version control features.

AutoML: Google AutoML is a set of machine learning tools that enable developers to train custom machine learning models with minimal expertise in machine learning. AutoML provides a simple interface for building models that can handle tasks such as image classification, object detection, natural language processing, and translation (Google Cloud, 2021). This service allows organizations to leverage AI without needing a team of data scientists, reducing the complexity and time required to develop machine learning applications.

Cloud Vision API: The Cloud Vision API provides pre-trained models for image recognition tasks such as object detection, face detection, and label annotation. It allows users to analyze images by detecting objects, landmarks, logos, and text, making it ideal for applications in media analysis, marketing, and security (Google Cloud, 2021). This API is fully managed and scales based on demand, making it suitable for integrating computer vision capabilities into existing applications.

Natural Language API: GCP's Natural Language API offers machine learning-powered text analysis, including sentiment analysis, entity recognition, syntax analysis, and language detection. This API is commonly used for processing large volumes of text data in industries like finance, customer service, and marketing, enabling companies to gain insights from customer feedback, social media, and documents (Sato et al., 2019). The API integrates with other GCP services, allowing users to build complex workflows that combine text analysis with other forms of data processing.

Speech-to-Text and Text-to-Speech APIs: GCP provides powerful APIs for converting audio into text and vice versa. The Speech-to-Text API allows users to transcribe audio in real-time or batch mode, supporting over 120 languages. The Text-to-Speech API, on the other hand, enables users to generate natural-sounding speech from text using Google's neural network models (Google Cloud, 2021). These APIs are widely used in customer service, accessibility, and voice-activated applications.

3. Key Google Cloud Big Data Services

GCP provides a variety of services designed to handle big data workloads, from real-time data processing to large-scale analytics and storage. These services integrate seamlessly with Google's AI tools, enabling organizations to build end-to-end data processing pipelines for machine learning, business intelligence, and data analytics.

BigQuery: BigQuery is GCP's fully managed, serverless data warehouse that allows organizations to analyze large datasets using

SQL. It is designed for handling petabyte-scale datasets with low-latency query performance, making it suitable for real-time data analytics and business intelligence applications (Jain & Gounares, 2019). BigQuery supports integration with Google Sheets, Data Studio, and other GCP tools, allowing users to visualize and analyze data without moving it between systems. BigQuery's support for machine learning (BigQuery ML) enables users to build and deploy machine learning models directly within the data warehouse, simplifying the process of incorporating AI into data analytics.

Cloud Dataflow: Cloud Dataflow is a fully managed service for stream and batch data processing. Based on Apache Beam, Dataflow enables users to create data pipelines that process large volumes of data in real-time or on a scheduled basis. It is commonly used for ETL (extract, transform, load) tasks, data aggregation, and real-time analytics (Google Cloud, 2021). Dataflow's serverless nature allows it to scale automatically based on the size and complexity of the data being processed, making it an efficient solution for both real-time and batch workloads.

Cloud Pub/Sub: Cloud Pub/Sub is GCP's real-time messaging service that allows for event-driven architectures by enabling applications to publish and subscribe to messages in real time. It is commonly used for ingesting streaming data from IoT devices, mobile applications, and log files, as well as enabling communication between distributed systems (Google Cloud, 2021). Pub/Sub's integration with services like Dataflow and BigQuery allows organizations to build real-time analytics pipelines that process and analyze incoming data as it is generated.

Cloud Dataproc: Cloud Dataproc is GCP's managed service for running Apache Hadoop, Spark, and other big data frameworks. It simplifies the process of setting up and managing clusters for distributed data processing, allowing users to run big data jobs without the complexity of configuring the underlying infrastructure (Jain & Gounares, 2019). Dataproc integrates with other GCP services, such as BigQuery and Cloud Storage, making it easy to move data between storage and processing environments.

Cloud Storage: Cloud Storage is GCP's object storage service, providing scalable and durable storage for unstructured data such as images, videos, and backups. Cloud Storage is designed to handle massive volumes of data, making it suitable for building data lakes and supporting big data analytics workflows (Google Cloud, 2021). It integrates seamlessly with other GCP services, enabling organizations to store data in Cloud Storage and process it using tools like BigQuery, Dataflow, and Vertex AI.

4. Applications of Google Cloud AI and Big Data Services

GCP's AI and big data services are used across industries for a variety of applications, from real-time analytics to machine learning and business intelligence.

Retail and E-Commerce: GCP's AI services, such as AutoML and the Natural Language API, are used by retailers to build personalized recommendation engines, analyze customer sentiment, and optimize inventory management. BigQuery's real-time analytics capabilities allow retailers to gain insights into customer behavior and sales trends, enabling better decision-making and targeted marketing campaigns (Sato et al., 2019).

Healthcare and Life Sciences: In the healthcare sector, GCP's AI and machine learning tools are used to analyze medical images, develop predictive diagnostics, and discover new drug compounds. Services like AutoML and Cloud Vision are employed to detect anomalies in medical images, while BigQuery is used to store and analyze large-scale patient data for population health analytics and precision medicine (Google Cloud, 2021).

Financial Services: Financial institutions use GCP for fraud detection, risk modeling, and regulatory compliance. GCP's machine learning tools, including Vertex AI and BigQuery ML, are used to build models that detect fraudulent transactions in real-time. Pub/Sub and Dataflow enable real-time data streaming for monitoring and analytics, helping banks and financial services companies comply with industry regulations while managing large volumes of transaction data (Jain & Gounares, 2019).

Media and Entertainment: Media companies use GCP's AI and machine learning services for content recommendation, media analysis, and live video streaming. AutoML and Cloud Vision are used to categorize and analyze images and video content, while BigQuery provides real-time analytics on viewer behavior and engagement. Cloud Storage is often used to store vast amounts of media content, which can be accessed and processed by GCP's big data and AI services (Google Cloud, 2021).

5. Challenges and Considerations in Using GCP for AI and Big Data

Despite its strengths, there are several challenges organizations must consider when using GCP for AI and big data processing.

Cost Management: While GCP offers flexible pricing models, costs can accumulate quickly, especially when processing large datasets or running machine learning jobs at scale. Effective cost management strategies, such as monitoring usage, using preemptible instances, and optimizing data storage configurations, are necessary to prevent budget overruns (Jain & Gounares, 2019).

Learning Curve and Integration: GCP's wide range of services can present a steep learning curve, particularly for organizations new to cloud computing or unfamiliar with Google's ecosystem. While GCP provides comprehensive documentation and support, organizations must invest time and resources in training their teams to effectively use these services and integrate them into their workflows (Google Cloud, 2021).

Data Security and Compliance: Handling sensitive data, such as healthcare or financial information, requires strict adherence to data security and compliance standards. GCP offers built-in security features, such as encryption and identity management, but organizations must ensure they configure these tools properly to meet compliance requirements like GDPR, HIPAA, and PCI-DSS (Google Cloud, 2021).

In summary, Google Cloud Platform offers a robust and scalable set of tools for AI and big data processing, enabling organizations to build, deploy, and manage machine learning models and analytics pipelines at scale. Services like Vertex AI, BigQuery, and Cloud Dataflow provide the infrastructure needed to process massive datasets, develop custom AI models, and perform real-time analytics. While GCP offers significant advantages in scalability and AI-driven cloud services, organizations must carefully manage costs, ensure compliance with security standards, and navigate the learning curve associated with its vast service offerings. As cloud adoption grows, GCP's AI and big data services will continue to play a critical role in driving innovation and enabling data-driven decision-making across industries.

Microsoft Azure

Microsoft Azure is a leading cloud platform offering a wide range of services for artificial intelligence (AI) and big data processing. Azure provides a scalable, flexible, and integrated cloud environment that supports everything from data storage and analytics to advanced machine learning and AI models. With its comprehensive suite of AI, machine learning, and big data services, Azure has become a key player in cloud computing for organizations looking to leverage the power of AI and large-scale data processing.

1. Overview of Microsoft Azure for AI and Big Data

Azure offers a broad spectrum of AI and big data services, enabling organizations to store, process, and analyze large datasets while building and deploying machine learning models at scale. Azure's AI services are built on Microsoft's investments in AI research and development, offering developers and data scientists the tools to build predictive models, integrate natural language processing (NLP), computer vision, and other AI capabilities into their applications. Its big data services, such as Azure Data Lake and Azure Synapse Analytics, provide the infrastructure needed to store and analyze massive datasets.

Scalability and Flexibility: Azure's cloud infrastructure is highly scalable, allowing organizations to handle workloads that range from small-scale data processing to global applications with petabytes of data. Azure provides both infrastructure-as-a-service (IaaS) and platform-as-a-service (PaaS) models, allowing users to choose the level of control and customization they need (Microsoft, 2021). This flexibility enables organizations to quickly provision resources and scale their applications as their data and compute needs grow.

Integration with Microsoft Ecosystem: One of Azure's key advantages is its seamless integration with the broader Microsoft ecosystem, including tools like Microsoft Office 365, Power BI, and Dynamics 365. This integration makes it easier for enterprises that already rely on Microsoft products to adopt Azure for their AI and big data needs. Azure also supports a wide range of open-source tools and platforms, providing flexibility for developers to work with familiar technologies (Microsoft, 2021).

2. Key Microsoft Azure Big Data Services

Azure offers a variety of big data services designed to handle everything from data ingestion and storage to processing and advanced analytics. These services enable organizations to build scalable and secure data platforms for real-time analytics and data warehousing.

Azure Data Lake Storage: Azure Data Lake Storage is a scalable, high-performance data lake solution that enables organizations to store large volumes of unstructured and structured data in a single location. Built on top of Azure Blob Storage, Data Lake Storage allows for the storage of petabytes of data and is optimized for big data analytics workloads. It integrates seamlessly with other Azure services like Azure Databricks and Azure Synapse Analytics, enabling businesses to analyze large datasets using distributed processing frameworks like Apache Spark (Microsoft, 2021).

Azure Synapse Analytics: Formerly known as Azure SQL Data Warehouse, Azure Synapse Analytics is a cloud-based analytics service that brings together big data and data warehousing. Synapse allows organizations to query both relational and non-relational data at scale using either serverless or provisioned resources, making it ideal for complex analytics and business intelligence workloads. Synapse integrates deeply with services like Azure Data Lake, Power BI, and Azure Machine Learning, allowing for comprehensive data analysis and AI model deployment (Borkar et al., 2020).

Azure HDInsight: Azure HDInsight is a fully managed cloud service that allows users to run open-source analytics frameworks, including Hadoop, Spark, Hive, Kafka, and HBase. HDInsight simplifies the process of setting up and managing big data clusters, making it easier for organizations to process and analyze large datasets in a distributed environment. It is commonly used for tasks such as ETL (extract, transform, load), data warehousing, and stream processing, enabling users to scale their data analytics operations easily (Borkar et al., 2020).

Azure Stream Analytics: Azure Stream Analytics is a real-time data stream processing service designed for applications such as IoT analytics, financial transaction monitoring, and log data processing. Stream Analytics provides a powerful query language that allows users to filter, aggregate, and transform data in motion, delivering insights in real time. It integrates with various Azure services like

Event Hubs, IoT Hub, and Azure SQL Database, enabling seamless end-to-end real-time analytics pipelines (Microsoft, 2021).

3. Key Microsoft Azure AI and Machine Learning Services

Microsoft Azure provides a wide range of AI and machine learning services that help organizations build, train, and deploy AI models in the cloud. These services cater to both developers with minimal AI experience and expert data scientists.

Azure Machine Learning: Azure Machine Learning is a comprehensive platform for building, training, and deploying machine learning models. It provides tools for automating the machine learning workflow, including data preparation, feature engineering, model training, and hyperparameter tuning. Azure Machine Learning supports popular frameworks like TensorFlow, PyTorch, and Scikit-learn, allowing data scientists to train models using familiar tools (Microsoft, 2021). Additionally, it offers automated machine learning (AutoML) capabilities that enable users to automatically build high-quality models without extensive manual intervention.

Azure Cognitive Services: Azure Cognitive Services is a suite of pre-built AI APIs that allow developers to integrate advanced AI capabilities, such as vision, speech, language, and decision-making, into their applications. These services include computer vision (Azure Vision), speech recognition (Azure Speech), language understanding (Azure Text Analytics), and more. Cognitive Services abstracts the complexity of building AI models by offering ready-to-use APIs, making it easier for developers to incorporate AI into their apps (Cohen et al., 2020). This suite of services is widely used for applications like customer service automation, accessibility, and content moderation.

Azure Bot Service: Azure Bot Service enables developers to build, deploy, and manage intelligent bots that can interact with users via text, voice, and other channels. It integrates with Azure Cognitive Services to provide natural language understanding, allowing bots to understand and respond to user queries with contextual relevance. The Bot Service also integrates with Microsoft Teams, Skype, and other communication platforms, making it easy to deploy conversational AI across multiple channels (Cohen et al., 2020).

Azure Cognitive Search: Azure Cognitive Search is a cloud search service that uses AI to enhance search functionality by extracting insights from unstructured data. It allows developers to add search capabilities to their applications, with features like full-text search, natural language processing, and AI-powered content enrichment. Cognitive Search is commonly used in scenarios like document management, e-commerce, and knowledge management, where users need to search and filter large volumes of data quickly (Microsoft, 2021).

4. Applications of Microsoft Azure AI and Big Data Services

Microsoft Azure's AI and big data services are used across a wide range of industries, powering applications that require advanced analytics, machine learning, and real-time data processing.

Retail and E-commerce: In the retail and e-commerce space, Azure services such as Azure Machine Learning and Azure Cognitive Services are used to build personalized recommendation engines, optimize supply chains, and analyze customer sentiment. Azure Synapse Analytics enables retailers to analyze historical sales data and forecast demand, while Stream Analytics provides real-time insights into customer behavior, allowing retailers to respond quickly to market trends (Cohen et al., 2020).

Healthcare and Life Sciences: Healthcare organizations use Azure to process and analyze large amounts of patient data, develop predictive models for diagnostics, and build personalized treatment plans. Azure Machine Learning is used to train models for predicting patient outcomes, while Azure Cognitive Services are applied in medical image analysis, enabling healthcare providers to identify anomalies in X-rays and MRIs (Microsoft, 2021). Azure also supports compliance with healthcare regulations like HIPAA, ensuring that sensitive data is stored and processed securely.

Financial Services: Financial institutions leverage Azure's big data and AI services for fraud detection, risk modeling, and regulatory compliance. Azure Machine Learning helps banks build predictive models that detect fraudulent transactions in real time, while Azure Stream Analytics processes transaction data as it arrives, ensuring that potential risks are identified immediately (Borkar et al., 2020). In addition, Azure Synapse Analytics enables financial organizations to perform large-scale data analysis to optimize investment strategies and meet compliance requirements.

Manufacturing and IoT: Azure services are widely used in manufacturing and IoT for predictive maintenance, real-time monitoring, and process optimization. Azure IoT Hub and Azure Stream Analytics allow manufacturers to ingest and analyze sensor data from connected devices, identifying patterns and anomalies that indicate potential equipment failures. By combining IoT data with machine learning models trained in Azure Machine Learning, manufacturers can implement predictive maintenance strategies that reduce downtime and improve operational efficiency (Cohen et al., 2020).

5. Challenges and Considerations in Using Microsoft Azure for AI and Big Data

While Azure provides powerful tools for AI and big data, organizations must consider certain challenges when adopting Azure services.

Cost Management: Azure's pay-as-you-go pricing model provides flexibility, but it can also lead to significant costs if resources are not managed properly. Large-scale machine learning training jobs or continuous data processing pipelines can accumulate costs quickly, particularly if services are not properly configured to scale down during periods of low demand. Organizations should implement cost monitoring and optimization strategies to control expenses (Microsoft, 2021).

Learning Curve: While Azure provides a comprehensive set of AI and big data tools, the platform's breadth of services can create a steep learning curve for organizations unfamiliar with cloud technologies. Data scientists, developers, and IT teams must become proficient in Azure's various tools and services to effectively use them in their workflows. Microsoft offers extensive documentation and training resources to help users get up to speed, but organizations should plan for an initial learning phase (Cohen et al., 2020).

Data Security and Compliance: Azure provides robust security features, including encryption, identity management, and compliance with industry standards such as GDPR, HIPAA, and PCI-DSS. However, organizations must ensure that these security features are correctly configured to meet their specific regulatory and compliance requirements. Data governance policies, such as setting up proper access controls and encryption protocols, are critical to maintaining security and compliance in cloud environments (Microsoft, 2021).

In summary, Microsoft Azure offers a powerful and versatile platform for AI and big data, with services that enable organizations to build, train, and deploy machine learning models at scale, process large datasets, and perform advanced analytics. Tools like Azure Machine Learning, Azure Synapse Analytics, and Azure Cognitive Services provide the infrastructure necessary to support a wide range of AI and big data applications, from real-time data processing to predictive analytics. Azure's deep integration with Microsoft's broader ecosystem, along with its scalability and flexibility, make it an attractive choice for enterprises across industries. However, organizations must manage costs, address the learning curve, and ensure compliance with data security standards to fully leverage Azure's capabilities.

Cloud Deployment Strategies

The deployment of AI and big data solutions in cloud environments requires strategic planning to ensure scalability, security, and performance. Cloud deployment strategies vary depending on an organization's business goals, data requirements, and security needs. Cloud deployment options include public, private, hybrid, and multi-cloud environments, each offering unique advantages for AI and big data workloads. Choosing the right deployment strategy enables organizations to optimize resource utilization, maintain data governance, and support the dynamic nature of machine learning and big data analytics.

1. Overview of Cloud Deployment Strategies for AI and Big Data

Cloud deployment strategies refer to the models and approaches organizations use to manage and deploy cloud-based services and applications. These strategies play a critical role in how data is processed, where it is stored, and how machine learning models are trained and deployed. The key cloud deployment models—public cloud, private cloud, hybrid cloud, and multi-cloud—offer varying levels of control, cost efficiency, and flexibility, depending on the needs of the organization (Gupta & Dutta, 2021).

Public Cloud: In a public cloud deployment, services and infrastructure are provided by third-party cloud providers such as Amazon Web Services (AWS), Microsoft Azure, and Google Cloud Platform (GCP). This model offers scalability, cost-effectiveness, and accessibility, as organizations can rapidly provision resources on demand without the need to manage physical infrastructure. Public cloud is commonly used for AI workloads due to its ability to scale computational resources for tasks such as deep learning, model training, and large-scale data processing (Lee et al., 2020).

Private Cloud: A private cloud involves hosting services and infrastructure either on-premises or through a dedicated third-party provider. This model offers greater control and security, as the infrastructure is used exclusively by one organization. For businesses dealing with sensitive data, such as in healthcare or finance, private clouds are often preferred to maintain compliance with regulations and data privacy requirements. However, private clouds can be costly to maintain and may lack the scalability of public clouds (Gupta & Dutta, 2021).

Hybrid Cloud: A hybrid cloud deployment combines the benefits of both public and private clouds. Organizations can run sensitive workloads on private infrastructure while leveraging the scalability and flexibility of public clouds for non-sensitive tasks or peak demand periods. This approach allows businesses to balance cost efficiency with security and control, making it an attractive option for companies looking to scale their AI and big data workloads while maintaining compliance with regulations (Babar & Chauhan, 2021).

Multi-Cloud: Multi-cloud strategies involve using services from multiple cloud providers to avoid vendor lock-in and optimize performance. By distributing workloads across different cloud environments, organizations can choose the best service offerings for specific tasks, such as using one cloud for data storage and another for AI model training. Multi-cloud strategies also improve resilience, as businesses can switch providers or distribute workloads across clouds in case of outages or performance issues (Sharma & Ravichandran, 2020).

2. Public Cloud Deployment for AI and Big Data

Public cloud deployments are the most commonly used strategy for AI and big data workloads due to their inherent scalability, flexibility, and cost-effectiveness. Public cloud providers like AWS, Azure, and Google Cloud offer a variety of AI and big data services that allow organizations to quickly build, train, and deploy machine learning models at scale.

Scalability and Elasticity: One of the key advantages of public cloud deployments is the ability to scale resources up or down based on demand. This elasticity is particularly important for AI workloads, where the training of machine learning models often requires high-performance GPUs and TPUs for a short duration. Public cloud environments allow organizations to provision these resources as needed, without investing in costly hardware that may sit idle during non-peak times (Lee et al., 2020).

Cost Efficiency: Public clouds offer a pay-as-you-go pricing model, which helps organizations manage costs more effectively. Businesses only pay for the resources they use, which is ideal for AI and big data workloads that can fluctuate over time. Public clouds also reduce the need for capital expenditures on infrastructure, allowing organizations to invest more in innovation and development rather than hardware management (Gupta & Dutta, 2021).

Integration with AI and Big Data Services: Public cloud platforms offer pre-built services for AI and big data, such as Amazon SageMaker, Azure Machine Learning, and Google Cloud's Vertex AI. These services provide pre-trained models, automated machine learning tools, and scalable infrastructure for AI model development, making it easier for organizations to implement AI without requiring deep expertise in machine learning (Lee et al., 2020).

3. Private Cloud Deployment for AI and Big Data

Private cloud deployments are typically used by organizations that need greater control over their infrastructure and data. This deployment model is ideal for businesses that handle sensitive data, such as healthcare providers, financial institutions, or government agencies, where data privacy and regulatory compliance are critical concerns.

Security and Compliance: Private clouds offer enhanced security and control, as the infrastructure is dedicated to a single organization. This isolation reduces the risk of data breaches and ensures that businesses can meet strict regulatory requirements, such as HIPAA, GDPR, or PCI DSS. Private cloud environments allow organizations to implement custom security measures, including encryption, access controls, and network segmentation, providing an additional layer of protection for sensitive data (Gupta & Dutta, 2021).

Customization and Control: Private clouds give organizations complete control over their infrastructure, allowing them to tailor the environment to meet specific performance and compliance needs. Businesses can configure their private cloud to optimize for AI and big data workloads, including fine-tuning hardware, storage, and networking configurations. However, this level of control comes with increased complexity and cost, as organizations must manage the maintenance and scaling of the cloud environment (Sharma & Ravichandran, 2020).

Cost Considerations: While private clouds provide greater control and security, they can be more expensive than public clouds due to the need for dedicated hardware, data centers, and ongoing maintenance. However, for organizations that require strict control over their data and infrastructure, the added cost may be justified to ensure compliance and data protection (Babar & Chauhan, 2021).

4. Hybrid Cloud Deployment for AI and Big Data

Hybrid cloud deployments offer a balanced approach, combining the scalability of public clouds with the control and security of private clouds. This model is particularly useful for organizations that need to run certain workloads in a private cloud due to security or compliance concerns but want to leverage the public cloud for less sensitive tasks or to handle peak demand.

Flexibility and Resource Optimization: Hybrid clouds allow organizations to optimize resource utilization by running sensitive workloads in a private cloud and using public cloud resources for non-sensitive tasks or during periods of high demand. This flexibility enables businesses to take advantage of the cost savings and scalability of public clouds while maintaining control over critical data and applications (Babar & Chauhan, 2021).

Data Residency and Governance: Hybrid cloud deployments can help organizations address data residency requirements by keeping sensitive data in a private cloud located within specific geographic regions while using public cloud resources for other workloads. This approach allows businesses to comply with local data protection regulations while still benefiting from the scalability of public cloud infrastructure (Sharma & Ravichandran, 2020).

Improved Disaster Recovery: Hybrid clouds can improve disaster recovery by allowing businesses to back up critical data and applications in the public cloud while maintaining primary systems in a private cloud. In the event of a failure in the private cloud, organizations can quickly switch to the public cloud for business continuity, ensuring that AI and big data workloads remain operational (Gupta & Dutta, 2021).

5. Multi-Cloud Deployment for AI and Big Data

Multi-cloud strategies involve using multiple public or private cloud providers to distribute workloads and avoid reliance on a single vendor. This approach enables organizations to optimize their AI and big data workloads by selecting the best services and infrastructure from different providers.

Avoiding Vendor Lock-In: One of the key motivations behind multi-cloud deployments is avoiding vendor lock-in. By using multiple cloud providers, organizations can prevent dependency on a single vendor, giving them more flexibility to switch providers or use specialized services from different platforms. For example, a business might use Google Cloud for its AI tools but rely on AWS for data storage and analytics (Sharma & Ravichandran, 2020).

Resilience and Redundancy: Multi-cloud deployments improve resilience by distributing workloads across multiple cloud environments. In case of an outage or performance issue with one provider, businesses can shift workloads to another cloud platform to ensure business continuity. This redundancy is particularly important for mission-critical AI and big data applications, where downtime can lead to significant financial and operational losses (Lee et al., 2020).

Optimizing for Specific Workloads: Multi-cloud strategies allow organizations to choose the best cloud provider for specific tasks. For example, a company may use AWS for its extensive machine learning infrastructure while using Azure for its data integration and analysis tools. This enables organizations to optimize their cloud environment for both AI and big data workloads, improving performance and reducing costs (Gupta & Dutta, 2021).

6. Challenges and Considerations in Cloud Deployment Strategies

While cloud deployment strategies offer significant benefits, organizations must carefully consider several factors when choosing the right model for their AI and big data workloads.

Cost Management: Different deployment models have varying cost structures, with public clouds offering pay-as-you-go pricing and private clouds requiring significant upfront investment in infrastructure. Organizations must evaluate their long-term needs and budget constraints when selecting a cloud deployment strategy (Sharma & Ravichandran, 2020).

Security and Compliance: Security and regulatory requirements play a critical role in cloud deployment decisions, particularly for industries handling sensitive data such as healthcare, finance, and government. Businesses must ensure that their cloud environments meet data protection standards and are properly configured to safeguard data (Babar & Chauhan, 2021).

Complexity of Management: Hybrid and multi-cloud deployments can introduce complexity in managing multiple environments and ensuring seamless integration between public and private clouds. Organizations must invest in cloud management tools and expertise to effectively manage hybrid and multi-cloud environments (Gupta & Dutta, 2021).

Conclusion

Selecting the right cloud deployment strategy is critical for successfully managing AI and big data workloads in the cloud. Public cloud deployments offer scalability and cost-efficiency, while private clouds provide enhanced security and control for sensitive workloads. Hybrid and multi-cloud strategies offer a flexible approach, combining the benefits of both public and private clouds to optimize performance, security, and cost. As organizations increasingly adopt AI and big data technologies, choosing the right cloud deployment strategy will play a pivotal role in ensuring that their cloud infrastructure meets business needs while maintaining security, compliance, and scalability.

References

AWS. (2021). *Amazon Web Services documentation.*
https://aws.amazon.com/documentation/

Babar, M. A., & Chauhan, M. A. (2021). A tale of hybrid cloud adoption: A systematic mapping study. *Journal of Cloud Computing, 10*(1), 1-32.

Bauer, S., Lu, Q., Finocchiaro, E., & Romero, M. (2020). AWS S3 and dynamic pricing of storage capacity. *Journal of Information Systems, 34*(1), 1-15.

Borkar, V., Carey, M. J., & Polyzotis, N. (2020). Inside "big data management": Ogres, onions, or parfaits? *Proceedings of the 2019 ACM SIGMOD International Conference on Management of Data*, 45-56.

Cohen, S., Narayanan, R., & Tavakkol, S. (2020). *Hands-on machine learning with Azure: Build practical machine learning solutions on Azure.* Packt Publishing.

Google Cloud. (2021). *Google Cloud documentation.* https://cloud.google.com/docs

Gupta, P., & Dutta, D. (2021). *Cloud computing: Concepts, technology & architecture.* Prentice Hall.

Jain, S., & Gounares, A. (2019). Building scalable applications on Google Cloud. *Google Cloud Blog.* https://cloud.google.com/blog

Lee, J., Moon, J., & Kang, M. (2020). Cloud computing: Architecture and deployment models in AI-driven applications. *Journal of Cloud Computing, 9*(1), 12-24.

Liberty, J., Mathew, A., Ehrlinger, D., & Behrendt, J. (2020). *Amazon SageMaker best practices.* O'Reilly Media.

Microsoft. (2021). *Microsoft Azure documentation.* https://docs.microsoft.com/en-us/azure/

Sato, M., Wang, Q., Manoharan, G., & Mathew, G. (2019). *Google Cloud machine learning solutions.* O'Reilly Media.

Sharma, S., & Ravichandran, T. (2020). Multi-cloud strategy for AI workloads: A review of deployment options. *IEEE Cloud Computing, 7*(2), 60-69.

Chapter 21: Data Visualization Tools

<u>Tableau</u>

Tableau is one of the most widely used data visualization tools, known for its user-friendly interface, powerful analytics capabilities, and ability to handle large datasets. It enables organizations to transform raw data into interactive, visual representations, facilitating deeper insights and data-driven decision-making. Tableau is used across industries such as finance, healthcare, retail, and education to create dashboards, reports, and visual analytics that communicate trends, patterns, and insights.

1. Overview of Tableau as a Data Visualization Tool

Tableau was designed to make data more accessible to non-technical users by simplifying the process of data analysis and visualization. Its drag-and-drop interface allows users to quickly create charts, graphs, maps, and dashboards without needing extensive coding or technical knowledge. Tableau supports data integration from a wide variety of sources, including databases, spreadsheets, and cloud services, making it highly flexible for data analysis.

Ease of Use: One of Tableau's primary strengths is its intuitive interface. Users can connect to different data sources, select fields of interest, and easily create visualizations using drag-and-drop functionality. This ease of use allows business analysts and decision-makers to create meaningful visual representations of data without requiring advanced technical skills (Sallam et al., 2021).

Interactive Dashboards: Tableau enables the creation of interactive dashboards that allow users to drill down into the data, filter results, and explore various views without needing to reload or re-query the data. Dashboards in Tableau can combine multiple visualizations, allowing users to see the same dataset from different angles and interact with the data in real-time (Stolte et al., 2018).

Data Integration: Tableau can connect to a wide range of data sources, including relational databases (e.g., SQL Server, MySQL), cloud-based data warehouses (e.g., Amazon Redshift, Google BigQuery), flat files (e.g., CSV, Excel), and web data connectors (e.g., Salesforce). This flexibility makes it easy to aggregate and analyze data from various sources within a single platform (Sallam et al., 2021).

2. Key Features of Tableau

Tableau offers several key features that enhance its usability and effectiveness as a data visualization tool, making it a preferred choice for organizations looking to gain actionable insights from their data.

Real-Time Analytics: Tableau allows users to connect to live data sources and create visualizations based on real-time data. This feature is essential for industries that require up-to-date insights, such as financial services and retail. Real-time analytics enable organizations to make timely decisions based on the most current data (Mackinlay et al., 2018).

Advanced Visualizations: Tableau provides a wide variety of chart types, including bar charts, line graphs, scatter plots, heat maps, and tree maps, among others. Users can customize their visualizations with different colors, labels, and formatting options to highlight key trends and insights. Tableau also supports geospatial visualizations, allowing users to create interactive maps that display data geographically (Mackinlay et al., 2018).

AI-Powered Analytics: Tableau has incorporated AI-driven analytics tools, such as Tableau Einstein Discovery, which uses machine learning to provide predictive insights and explain complex data relationships. These capabilities help users go beyond descriptive analytics to uncover deeper insights and identify future trends (Sallam et al., 2021).

Collaboration and Sharing: Tableau makes it easy to share dashboards and visualizations across teams and organizations. Users can publish their visualizations to Tableau Server or Tableau Online, enabling others to interact with the data through a web browser or mobile device. This facilitates collaboration and ensures that stakeholders across the organization can access and interpret data insights (Stolte et al., 2018).

3. Applications of Tableau in Various Industries

Tableau is used across a range of industries to support data-driven decision-making, from business intelligence and marketing to healthcare and education.

Finance: In the financial sector, Tableau is used to analyze market trends, monitor portfolio performance, and assess risk. Financial institutions can visualize key performance indicators (KPIs), conduct time-series analyses, and create dashboards that provide a real-time view of stock prices, interest rates, or credit risk (Mackinlay et al., 2018).

Healthcare: Healthcare providers use Tableau to analyze patient data, optimize hospital operations, and monitor clinical outcomes. Tableau enables healthcare organizations to track metrics such as patient admissions, length of stay, and treatment effectiveness, helping providers improve care quality and operational efficiency (Sallam et al., 2021).

Retail: Retailers use Tableau to analyze sales data, customer behavior, and inventory levels. With Tableau, retailers can visualize trends in product demand, identify customer preferences, and optimize inventory management to reduce costs and increase sales (Stolte et al., 2018).

Education: Educational institutions use Tableau to analyze student performance, enrollment trends, and financial data. Tableau dashboards provide administrators with insights into student retention, academic performance, and resource allocation, helping to improve institutional decision-making (Sallam et al., 2021).

4. Challenges and Considerations When Using Tableau

While Tableau offers powerful data visualization capabilities, there are certain challenges and considerations to keep in mind when using the tool.

Cost: Tableau can be relatively expensive for small organizations or individuals. The tool offers various licensing options, including Tableau Desktop, Tableau Server, and Tableau Online, each of which has its own pricing model. Organizations must carefully assess their needs and budget when choosing the right licensing plan (Mackinlay et al., 2018).

Data Preparation: While Tableau excels in visualization, it does not offer as many built-in tools for data cleaning and preparation. Users often need to clean and transform their data using other tools before importing it into Tableau. However, Tableau Prep, an additional product in the Tableau ecosystem, helps address this limitation by providing data preparation capabilities (Stolte et al., 2018).

Learning Curve: While Tableau is designed to be user-friendly, there is still a learning curve for users unfamiliar with data visualization or analytics. It may take time for new users to become proficient in creating advanced visualizations and interactive dashboards (Sallam et al., 2021).

Example Graph: Sales Performance Over Time

Below is a sample visualization that demonstrates a line graph showing monthly sales performance over time. This graph could be part of a larger dashboard used by a retail company to track sales trends.

This line graph tracks monthly sales over a year, allowing the business to visualize seasonal trends and assess periods of high or low sales. Such a graph can be easily generated in Tableau with a connected data source, allowing for interactive features like filtering by region or product category.

In summary, Tableau is a powerful and versatile data visualization tool that enables organizations to analyze large datasets and make informed decisions based on data insights. Its ease of use, advanced visualization features, and ability to connect to a wide range of data sources make it a valuable asset for data analysts and business intelligence teams. Tableau's role in enabling real-time analytics, interactive dashboards, and collaboration across teams positions it as one of the top data visualization platforms in the market. However, considerations around cost, data preparation, and the learning curve must be addressed to maximize its effectiveness.

Power BI

Power BI is a powerful business analytics tool developed by Microsoft that allows users to visualize data and share insights across their organization. Known for its robust integration with Microsoft's ecosystem, Power BI provides users with interactive data visualizations, self-service business intelligence (BI) capabilities, and the ability to connect to multiple data sources. It is widely adopted by organizations of all sizes to transform raw data into meaningful insights, making it a critical tool for data-driven decision-making.

1. Overview of Power BI as a Data Visualization Tool

Power BI offers an extensive suite of data visualization tools that enable businesses to create dynamic dashboards and reports. It allows users to connect to various data sources, including databases, cloud services, Excel spreadsheets, and online services, such as Google Analytics or Salesforce. The ease of data integration, combined with Power BI's ability to handle large datasets, makes it a popular choice for businesses looking to perform real-time analytics and gain actionable insights (Mehta, 2020).

Ease of Use: Power BI's user-friendly interface allows users to create data visualizations through drag-and-drop functionality. Users can build complex dashboards with minimal technical knowledge, making Power BI accessible to both data analysts and business users. Its integration with Microsoft Office tools, such as Excel, further enhances ease of use for those familiar with Microsoft's suite of applications (Oberoi, 2019).

Data Integration and Connectivity: One of Power BI's key strengths is its ability to connect to a wide range of data sources, including on-premises databases (e.g., SQL Server), cloud-based databases (e.g., Azure, Amazon Redshift), and popular SaaS (software as a service) platforms (e.g., Salesforce, Google Analytics). This allows organizations to bring disparate data sources into a unified platform for analysis and visualization (Mehta, 2020).

Interactive Dashboards and Reports: Power BI enables users to create interactive dashboards that provide real-time insights. Dashboards can be customized with filters, slicers, and drill-down capabilities, allowing users to explore data from different perspectives. These interactive features make it easier for organizations to identify trends, spot anomalies, and make informed business decisions (Oberoi, 2019).

2. Key Features of Power BI

Power BI offers several features that make it a leading tool for data visualization and business intelligence.

AI-Powered Insights: Power BI leverages machine learning and artificial intelligence to provide users with advanced analytics and predictive insights. Features such as "Quick Insights" allow users to run AI algorithms on their datasets to uncover hidden patterns, while Power BI's integration with Azure Machine Learning enables more advanced predictive modeling (Microsoft, 2021).

Power Query: Power Query is Power BI's built-in data transformation tool that allows users to clean, transform, and shape their data before visualization. This tool provides a user-friendly interface for handling complex data transformations, including merging, filtering, and pivoting datasets. Power Query also supports automation of data refreshes, ensuring that dashboards and reports are always up to date (Oberoi, 2019).

Power BI Service: Power BI Service is the cloud-based platform that allows users to publish and share dashboards with others in the organization. The service supports real-time data streaming, enabling users to view and interact with live data feeds from IoT devices, social media, and business systems. Power BI Service also includes collaboration features that allow users to share reports with teams, set up alerts, and schedule automatic report delivery (Mehta, 2020).

Mobile Accessibility: Power BI offers mobile applications for iOS, Android, and Windows devices, allowing users to access their dashboards and reports from anywhere. This mobile accessibility ensures that decision-makers can monitor key performance indicators (KPIs) and metrics in real-time, regardless of their location (Microsoft, 2021).

3. Applications of Power BI in Various Industries

Power BI's versatility makes it suitable for a wide range of industries, supporting various business intelligence and data analytics applications.

Finance: In the financial sector, Power BI is used for financial reporting, budgeting, and forecasting. Financial analysts can build dashboards that visualize revenue, expenses, and profitability metrics in real-time, allowing organizations to manage financial performance more effectively. Power BI's integration with Excel enables users to create advanced financial models and visualize them in a dynamic and interactive way (Oberoi, 2019).

Healthcare: Healthcare organizations use Power BI to monitor patient data, analyze clinical outcomes, and optimize operational efficiency. Dashboards can be built to track hospital admissions, patient satisfaction, and treatment effectiveness, helping healthcare providers make data-driven decisions that improve care quality. Power BI's data integration capabilities also allow healthcare organizations to combine data from electronic health records (EHRs) and other systems for comprehensive analysis (Mehta, 2020).

Retail and E-Commerce: Retailers use Power BI to analyze sales performance, customer behavior, and inventory management. By visualizing sales trends, customer demographics, and purchasing patterns, retailers can optimize product offerings and improve customer satisfaction. Power BI's ability to connect to data sources such as Google Analytics allows e-commerce businesses to analyze website traffic and conversion rates in real-time (Microsoft, 2021).

Education: Educational institutions use Power BI to track student performance, analyze enrollment data, and manage budgets. Dashboards can be created to monitor metrics such as student retention, academic progress, and resource allocation, helping administrators make informed decisions that improve institutional effectiveness (Oberoi, 2019).

4. Challenges and Considerations When Using Power BI

While Power BI is a powerful tool, there are several challenges and considerations organizations must address to maximize its effectiveness.

Data Preparation: Although Power BI offers data transformation tools through Power Query, users may still need to perform data cleaning and preparation in external tools before importing data into Power BI. Ensuring data quality and consistency is critical for generating accurate visualizations and insights (Mehta, 2020).

Learning Curve: While Power BI is designed to be user-friendly, there is still a learning curve for users who are new to data visualization or business intelligence. Advanced features such as DAX (Data Analysis Expressions) require more technical expertise, which can pose challenges for non-technical users (Oberoi, 2019).

Licensing and Cost: Power BI offers both free and paid versions, with different pricing models for Power BI Desktop, Power BI Pro, and Power BI Premium. Organizations must carefully evaluate their needs and budget to choose the right licensing plan, especially if they require advanced features such as real-time streaming or large-scale data processing (Microsoft, 2021).

Example Graph: Sales Distribution by Region

Below is a sample visualization demonstrating a bar chart showing sales distribution by region. This type of visualization is useful for businesses to compare performance across different geographical regions.

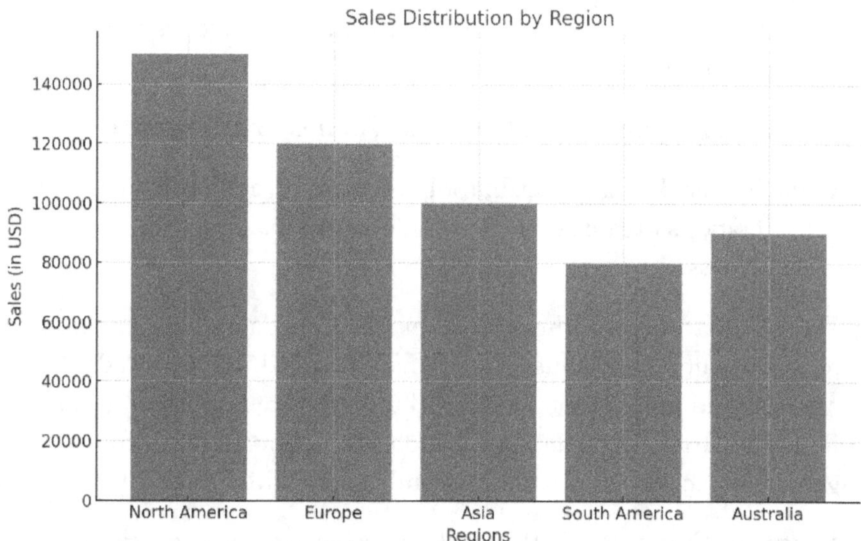

This graph could be created in Power BI by connecting to the relevant data source and using the platform's drag-and-drop interface to create the visualization.

In summary, Power BI is a robust and versatile data visualization tool that empowers organizations to analyze data, create interactive reports, and share insights across teams. Its deep integration with Microsoft products, ease of use, and powerful analytics capabilities make it a popular choice for businesses looking to leverage data for decision-making. However, users must be mindful of challenges related to data preparation, the learning curve, and licensing costs to fully maximize Power BI's potential. As organizations continue to embrace data-driven strategies, Power BI's role in facilitating real-time analytics and collaboration will remain critical.

Matplotlib, Seaborn, and Plotly

Data visualization tools play an essential role in understanding and interpreting complex datasets. Three popular Python-based data visualization libraries—Matplotlib, Seaborn, and Plotly—are widely used for creating static, interactive, and aesthetically appealing visualizations. These libraries serve different purposes and are frequently used in data science and machine learning projects to explore data, detect patterns, and present insights. Understanding the strengths and applications of each tool allows users to choose the best library for their specific visualization needs.

1. Matplotlib

Matplotlib is one of the most popular and widely used Python libraries for data visualization. Developed by John Hunter in 2003, Matplotlib provides extensive functionalities to create static, animated, and interactive visualizations. It is often considered the "grandfather" of visualization libraries in Python, serving as the foundation for more advanced libraries like Seaborn.

Customization and Flexibility: Matplotlib offers complete control over the appearance of visualizations, including customizing labels, colors, line styles, ticks, and legends. It supports multiple plot types such as line plots, bar charts, histograms, scatter plots, and pie charts, making it versatile for various data visualization needs (Hunter, 2007).

Integration with Other Libraries: Matplotlib integrates seamlessly with other Python libraries such as NumPy and Pandas, making it ideal for scientific computing and data analysis workflows. Its low-level nature allows users to fine-tune their plots, but it also requires more code and expertise compared to higher-level libraries (Hunter, 2007).

Static and Interactive Plots: While Matplotlib excels at producing high-quality static plots, it also supports interactive plots through integrations with libraries like mpld3 and plotly. However, its primary strength lies in static, publication-quality graphics (Hunter, 2007).

2. Seaborn

Seaborn is built on top of Matplotlib and provides a higher-level interface for creating aesthetically pleasing and informative statistical graphics. It simplifies the process of creating complex visualizations by offering built-in themes and color palettes, making it easier for users to visualize relationships in their data.

Statistical Visualization: One of Seaborn's strengths is its focus on statistical visualization. It includes functions for visualizing distributions of data (e.g., histograms, KDE plots), categorical data (e.g., box plots, violin plots), and relationships between variables (e.g., pair plots, correlation matrices) (Waskom et al., 2018).

Built-In Aesthetic Customizations: Seaborn is designed to produce visually attractive plots by default, reducing the need for extensive customization. It automatically adjusts plot elements like spacing, labels, and color palettes, making the plots easier to read and interpret. The aesthetics of Seaborn make it a popular choice for exploratory data analysis (EDA) (Waskom, 2021).

Ease of Use: Seaborn simplifies the creation of complex plots with fewer lines of code compared to Matplotlib. For example, visualizing relationships between multiple variables, such as scatter plots with regression lines or heatmaps of correlation matrices, is easier with Seaborn's higher-level functions (Waskom et al., 2018).

3. Plotly

Plotly is a Python library that allows users to create interactive, web-based visualizations. Unlike Matplotlib and Seaborn, which are primarily used for static visualizations, Plotly is geared toward creating interactive and dynamic plots that can be embedded in web applications, dashboards, and reports.

Interactivity: One of Plotly's most notable features is its support for interactive plots. Users can zoom, pan, hover over data points, and explore data in a dynamic manner. This makes Plotly an excellent choice for building dashboards and interactive data visualizations that require user engagement (Plotly Technologies Inc., 2021).

Wide Range of Plot Types: Plotly supports a variety of plot types, including line plots, bar charts, scatter plots, and more complex visualizations such as 3D surface plots, geo-maps, and contour plots. It also integrates well with other libraries like Pandas and Dash, making it suitable for real-time data analysis and visualization (Plotly Technologies Inc., 2021).

Web-Based and Shareable: Plotly visualizations are HTML-based, which means they can easily be shared and embedded into websites and applications. This makes it highly versatile for interactive web applications, such as those built using Plotly's companion library, Dash (Plotly Technologies Inc., 2021).

4. Applications and Use Cases

Matplotlib: Matplotlib is commonly used in academic and scientific settings where detailed control over visualizations is required. It is frequently used for creating plots for scientific papers, technical reports, and presentations, where accuracy and customization are paramount (Hunter, 2007).

Seaborn: Seaborn is often used in data science and machine learning workflows for exploratory data analysis. It excels at generating quick and aesthetically pleasing statistical visualizations, making it popular among analysts and researchers who need to interpret data distributions, correlations, and trends (Waskom et al., 2018).

Plotly: Plotly is best suited for creating interactive data dashboards and visualizations that require user interaction. It is widely used in business intelligence applications, web development, and real-time data monitoring, where users need to explore and engage with data dynamically (Plotly Technologies Inc., 2021).

Example Graph: Scatter Plot with Regression Line Using Seaborn

Below is a sample visualization demonstrating a scatter plot with a regression line, created using Seaborn. This type of visualization helps illustrate the relationship between two variables, such as sales and advertising spend.

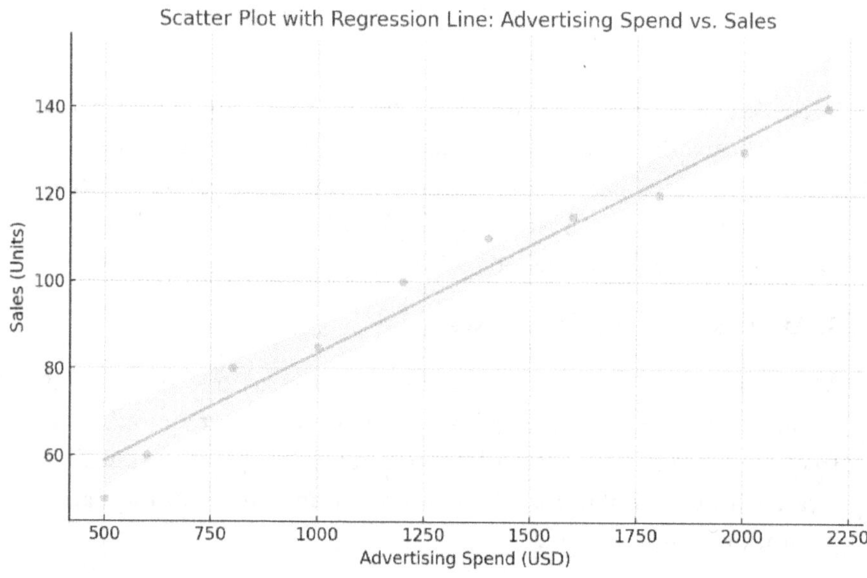

In summary, Matplotlib, Seaborn, and Plotly are three of the most widely used Python libraries for data visualization, each with its unique strengths and applications. Matplotlib provides flexibility and extensive customization, Seaborn offers aesthetically pleasing statistical plots with minimal code, and Plotly excels in creating interactive, web-based visualizations. The choice of which library to use depends on the specific needs of the project, such as whether static or interactive plots are required, the complexity of the data, and the level of customization desired.

Dashboards and Interactive Visualizations

In today's data-driven world, businesses and organizations rely heavily on data to make informed decisions. The ability to present complex data in a visually intuitive and interactive manner is crucial, and dashboards and interactive visualizations are key tools in achieving this. Dashboards are visual interfaces that consolidate multiple data sources and visualizations into a single, coherent display, while interactive visualizations allow users to explore and manipulate the data in real-time. These tools are widely used across industries for business intelligence (BI), performance monitoring, and real-time decision-making.

1. Overview of Dashboards and Interactive Visualizations

A dashboard is a data visualization tool that organizes and presents key performance indicators (KPIs), metrics, and other relevant data in a way that is easily digestible at a glance. Dashboards are often interactive, allowing users to drill down into the data, apply filters, and view data from different perspectives. They are typically used for monitoring business operations, analyzing trends, and making data-driven decisions.

Interactive visualizations are dynamic representations of data that enable users to engage with the content directly. Users can hover over data points for more details, zoom in and out, filter data by categories, or view the data from different angles. This interactivity enhances user engagement and helps uncover insights that might not be evident in static visualizations (Kirk, 2019).

Real-Time Data: Dashboards often display real-time data, making them critical for industries where timely information is essential, such as finance, healthcare, and supply chain management. Real-time dashboards update automatically as new data is ingested, allowing users to respond quickly to changes in key metrics (Few, 2013).

Multi-Source Data Integration: Dashboards can pull data from multiple sources, such as databases, cloud services, and APIs, to provide a comprehensive view of organizational performance. This capability makes dashboards valuable for business intelligence and strategic decision-making, as they offer an integrated view of disparate data points (Sallam et al., 2021).

2. Key Features of Dashboards and Interactive Visualizations

Dashboards and interactive visualizations come with several key features that make them powerful tools for data analysis and presentation.

Drill-Down and Filtering: Dashboards often include drill-down functionality, enabling users to explore the data in greater detail by clicking on specific elements of the visualization. Filters allow users to customize their view of the data by selecting specific criteria, such as time ranges, product categories, or geographic regions. This interactivity helps users uncover insights that might be hidden in the aggregate view (Shneiderman, 1996).

Dynamic Updates: Many dashboards are designed to handle real-time data feeds, meaning that the visualizations update dynamically as new data becomes available. This feature is essential for industries that require real-time monitoring, such as network operations, healthcare, or financial markets (Few, 2013).

Customizability: Dashboards are highly customizable, allowing users to create layouts that align with their specific needs. Users can add or remove visualizations, arrange them according to importance, and select different chart types to best represent the data. This flexibility makes dashboards suitable for both high-level overviews and detailed analysis (Sallam et al., 2021).

Cross-Visualization Interaction: In many dashboard tools, interactions in one visualization can trigger updates in another. For instance, selecting a data point in a bar chart might update a map or a line chart to reflect the chosen data. This interactivity allows users to explore relationships between different datasets more intuitively (Shneiderman, 1996).

3. Popular Tools for Dashboards and Interactive Visualizations

Several data visualization platforms offer robust tools for building dashboards and interactive visualizations. These platforms make it easier for organizations to build intuitive, real-time dashboards that facilitate business intelligence and operational monitoring.

Tableau: Tableau is one of the leading data visualization tools for building interactive dashboards. It allows users to connect to multiple data sources and create highly customizable dashboards with drill-down capabilities. Tableau's interactive features and data integration capabilities make it a popular choice for business intelligence (Sallam et al., 2021).

Power BI: Power BI is Microsoft's data visualization tool that enables users to create interactive dashboards and reports. Power BI offers seamless integration with other Microsoft products and supports real-time data streaming, making it suitable for monitoring business operations in real time (Mehta, 2020).

Plotly Dash: Plotly Dash is a web-based framework that allows developers to create interactive, web-based dashboards using Python. It supports highly customizable, interactive visualizations and can handle real-time data, making it popular for creating data-driven web applications (Plotly Technologies Inc., 2021).

4. Applications of Dashboards and Interactive Visualizations

Dashboards and interactive visualizations are widely used across various industries for different purposes, including performance monitoring, predictive analytics, and decision-making.

Business Intelligence: Dashboards are critical tools in business intelligence, providing executives and managers with a real-time view of key performance indicators (KPIs) such as revenue, customer engagement, and operational efficiency. Interactive visualizations allow decision-makers to explore the data and identify trends, opportunities, and areas for improvement (Mehta, 2020).

Healthcare: In healthcare, dashboards are used to monitor patient metrics, track the spread of diseases, and manage hospital operations. Real-time dashboards allow healthcare providers to respond quickly to changing conditions, such as patient admissions or resource shortages, helping to improve the quality of care (Few, 2013).

Finance: Financial institutions use dashboards to monitor real-time market data, track portfolio performance, and manage risk. Interactive visualizations enable analysts to model different financial scenarios, helping to inform investment strategies and risk management practices (Kirk, 2019).

Supply Chain Management: Supply chain dashboards help organizations track inventory levels, monitor shipping routes, and identify bottlenecks in the supply chain. Real-time dashboards provide insights that help businesses optimize logistics and reduce operational inefficiencies (Mehta, 2020).

5. Challenges and Considerations in Using Dashboards

While dashboards and interactive visualizations offer significant benefits, there are challenges and considerations that organizations must address to maximize their effectiveness.

Data Quality and Integration: The effectiveness of a dashboard depends on the quality and consistency of the underlying data. Poor data quality or integration issues can lead to inaccurate or misleading visualizations, making it critical to establish robust data governance practices (Few, 2013).

Overloading with Information: Dashboards are meant to provide clear, concise insights. Overloading a dashboard with too many visualizations or data points can make it overwhelming and difficult to use. Designers must carefully balance the amount of information presented and ensure that the dashboard remains user-friendly (Kirk, 2019).

User Training: While dashboards are designed to be user-friendly, some users may require training to fully utilize interactive features such as filters, drill-downs, and cross-visualization interactions. Ensuring that users are trained can improve the effectiveness of dashboards in decision-making (Shneiderman, 1996).

Example Graph: Real-Time Sales Dashboard

Below is a sample visualization demonstrating a simple real-time sales dashboard component. It includes a bar chart that shows sales performance across different product categories and a shape element (circle) to indicate total sales.

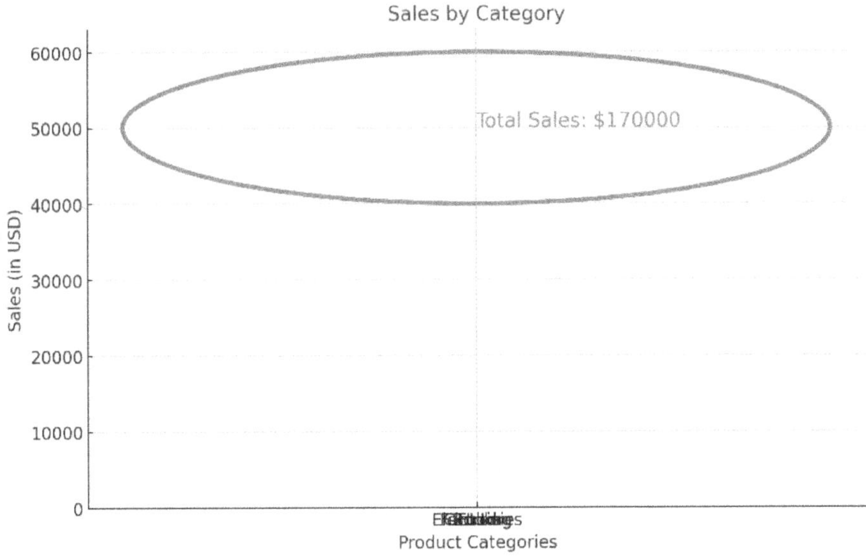

Conclusion

Dashboards and interactive visualizations are essential tools for modern business intelligence, enabling organizations to monitor performance, explore data in real-time, and make informed decisions. Tools like Tableau, Power BI, and Plotly Dash provide robust platforms for creating interactive and customizable dashboards that facilitate deeper data insights. While the advantages of dashboards are clear, organizations must carefully manage data quality, avoid overloading users with too much information, and ensure that users are trained to maximize the benefits of these tools. As data continues to drive decision-making, dashboards and interactive visualizations will remain crucial for turning raw data into actionable insights.

References

Few, S. (2013). *Information dashboard design: Displaying data for at-a-glance monitoring.* Analytics Press.

Hunter, J. D. (2007). Matplotlib: A 2D graphics environment. *Computing in Science & Engineering, 9*(3), 90-95.

Kirk, A. (2019). *Data visualisation: A handbook for data driven design.* SAGE Publications.

Mackinlay, J., Hanrahan, P., & Stolte, C. (2018). Tableau software: Interactive data analysis and visualization. *Computer Graphics and Applications, 28*(1), 75-84.

Mehta, A. (2020). *Business intelligence tools for data-driven organizations.* Springer.

Microsoft. (2021). *Power BI documentation.* https://docs.microsoft.com/en-us/power-bi/

Oberoi, M. (2019). *Mastering Power BI: The complete guide to business intelligence with Microsoft Power BI.* Packt Publishing.

Plotly Technologies Inc. (2021). *Plotly Dash documentation.* https://plotly.com/dash/

Plotly Technologies Inc. (2021). *Plotly documentation.* https://plotly.com/python/

Sallam, R., Richardson, J., & Idoine, C. (2021). *Magic quadrant for analytics and business intelligence platforms.* Gartner Research.

Stolte, C., Tang, D., & Hanrahan, P. (2018). Polaris: A system for query, analysis, and visualization of multidimensional relational databases. *IEEE Transactions on Visualization and Computer Graphics, 8*(1), 52-65.

Waskom, M. (2021). *Seaborn documentation.* https://seaborn.pydata.org

Waskom, M., Botvinnik, O., Hobson, P., Lukauskas, S., Gemperline, D. C., & O'Kane, D. (2018). Seaborn: Statistical data visualization. *Journal of Open Source Software, 3*(32), 302.

Part V: Implementation and Best Practices
Chapter 22: Data Governance and Ethics

<u>Data Privacy and Security</u>

Data privacy and security are critical components of data governance, ensuring that organizations handle data responsibly and comply with legal, ethical, and regulatory standards. As organizations increasingly rely on data to drive decision-making and business operations, safeguarding sensitive information has become a top priority. Effective data privacy and security practices not only protect individuals' personal data but also build trust, prevent legal liabilities, and ensure the ethical use of data. Data governance frameworks must include robust policies and practices that address both the privacy rights of individuals and the security measures necessary to protect data from breaches, misuse, and unauthorized access.

1. Data Privacy and its Importance in Data Governance

Data privacy refers to the protection of personal data and ensuring that individuals have control over how their information is collected, used, and shared. It is a fundamental right that is increasingly being protected through laws and regulations, such as the General Data Protection Regulation (GDPR) in Europe and the California Consumer Privacy Act (CCPA) in the United States. Privacy in the context of data governance requires organizations to implement measures that give individuals transparency and control over their data while ensuring compliance with applicable privacy laws.

Compliance with Legal Frameworks: Governments around the world have implemented data protection laws to safeguard personal information. For example, the GDPR mandates that organizations obtain explicit consent from individuals before collecting their personal data and provides individuals with the right to access, correct, or delete their data (Voigt & Von dem Bussche, 2017). The

CCPA grants consumers similar rights in California, allowing them to know what personal data is being collected, request its deletion, and opt out of the sale of their data (Davis, 2020). Organizations that fail to comply with these regulations face significant fines and legal consequences, making data privacy compliance a critical aspect of data governance.

User Consent and Control: A key principle of data privacy is that individuals should have control over their personal information. Organizations must ensure that they obtain explicit consent before collecting personal data and provide clear, accessible mechanisms for users to manage their privacy preferences. Data governance frameworks should include policies that define how consent is obtained, how long data is retained, and how data is anonymized or deleted upon user request (Kugler, 2018).

Transparency and Accountability: Transparency is essential for building trust with consumers and stakeholders. Organizations must be transparent about how they collect, store, and use data, providing clear privacy policies and disclosures. Additionally, accountability measures, such as data audits, privacy impact assessments, and the appointment of data protection officers, are necessary to ensure that data privacy practices are upheld and regularly reviewed (Voigt & Von dem Bussche, 2017).

2. Data Security and Its Role in Protecting Sensitive Information

Data security focuses on safeguarding data from unauthorized access, breaches, and other forms of exploitation. Security measures are crucial in ensuring that sensitive data, whether personal or organizational, remains protected from internal and external threats. While privacy deals with the appropriate use of data, security ensures that data remains protected from malicious actors and unintended exposure.

Cybersecurity Threats: The increasing frequency and sophistication of cyberattacks highlight the importance of robust data security measures. Data breaches can result in the exposure of sensitive information, leading to financial losses, reputational damage, and regulatory penalties. For example, high-profile data breaches such as the Equifax breach in 2017, which compromised the personal information of 147 million people, underscore the need for strong cybersecurity practices (Winder, 2019). Organizations must adopt comprehensive security protocols, including encryption, multi-factor authentication, and regular security audits, to mitigate risks.

Data Encryption and Protection Mechanisms: One of the key strategies for ensuring data security is encryption, which involves converting data into a format that is unreadable without the correct decryption key. Encryption protects data both at rest (when stored) and in transit (when being transferred). Organizations should also implement firewalls, intrusion detection systems, and endpoint protection tools to monitor and prevent unauthorized access to sensitive data (Gasser & Palfrey, 2017). Regular updates to software and security patches are also critical to addressing vulnerabilities.

Access Control and Identity Management: Effective access control policies are fundamental to data security. Role-based access control (RBAC) ensures that only authorized personnel have access to sensitive data based on their role within the organization. Identity and access management (IAM) systems help organizations control and monitor who accesses their data and systems, ensuring that permissions are granted appropriately and unauthorized access attempts are logged and investigated (Gasser & Palfrey, 2017).

3. Best Practices for Ensuring Data Privacy and Security

Organizations must adopt best practices for data privacy and security as part of their broader data governance framework. These practices should align with legal, ethical, and industry-specific requirements to protect sensitive information and build trust with consumers and stakeholders.

Data Minimization: Data minimization is the practice of collecting only the data necessary for specific purposes and retaining it for only as long as required. This principle is a core component of GDPR and helps reduce the risk of data breaches by limiting the amount of personal data stored (Voigt & Von dem Bussche, 2017). Organizations should review their data collection practices regularly to ensure they are not retaining unnecessary or outdated information.

Regular Security Audits and Risk Assessments: Conducting regular security audits and risk assessments is critical to identifying vulnerabilities and ensuring compliance with security standards. Audits should assess both technical and organizational aspects of data security, including encryption protocols, access controls, and employee training programs. Risk assessments help organizations prioritize areas of improvement and implement targeted security measures (Kugler, 2018).

Employee Training and Awareness: Human error is often a significant factor in data breaches and security incidents. Training employees on data privacy and security best practices is essential for reducing the risk of accidental data exposure or unauthorized access. Training should cover topics such as recognizing phishing attacks, following proper password management protocols, and understanding the organization's data privacy policies (Winder, 2019).

Incident Response and Recovery Plans: In the event of a data breach or security incident, having an incident response plan in place is crucial. This plan should outline the steps to be taken in the immediate aftermath of a breach, including isolating affected systems, notifying affected parties, and conducting a thorough investigation. An effective response plan helps mitigate the damage caused by breaches and ensures compliance with regulatory requirements for breach notifications (Davis, 2020).

4. The Ethical Dimension of Data Privacy and Security

Beyond legal compliance, data privacy and security are ethical obligations that organizations have toward their stakeholders. The ethical principles of respect for individuals' autonomy, protection from harm, and fairness underpin the importance of safeguarding personal data. Organizations must ensure that their data practices align with these ethical principles to maintain public trust and operate responsibly in a digital world.

Respect for Autonomy: Ensuring that individuals have control over their personal data is a matter of respecting their autonomy. Organizations must give users the ability to make informed decisions about how their data is used and offer clear options for managing consent and preferences. This aligns with ethical principles of respecting individuals' rights and choices (Floridi, 2018).

Prevention of Harm: Data breaches and misuse of personal data can cause significant harm, including financial loss, identity theft, and emotional distress. Implementing strong privacy and security measures is an ethical responsibility to protect individuals from such harm. By securing personal data and limiting its misuse, organizations can prevent harm and safeguard the well-being of their customers and stakeholders (Floridi, 2018).

In summary, data privacy and security are essential components of data governance and are central to maintaining the trust of individuals and complying with legal obligations. As organizations collect and process increasing amounts of data, they must implement comprehensive privacy and security practices to protect sensitive information from unauthorized access, breaches, and misuse. Effective data governance frameworks should incorporate measures such as data minimization, encryption, access controls, and regular security audits to ensure that data is handled responsibly. Moreover, organizations must not only adhere to legal requirements but also uphold ethical standards by respecting individuals' autonomy and preventing harm through sound data practices.

Ethical AI and Bias Mitigation

As artificial intelligence (AI) systems become increasingly integrated into decision-making processes, the ethical challenges surrounding AI have gained attention. One of the most critical concerns is the potential for bias in AI algorithms, which can lead to unfair or discriminatory outcomes. Ethical AI emphasizes the development and deployment of AI systems that are transparent, accountable, and aligned with societal values. Bias mitigation is a key component of ethical AI, requiring organizations to adopt practices that ensure fairness, reduce discrimination, and enhance the overall trustworthiness of AI systems.

1. Understanding Ethical AI

Ethical AI refers to the practice of designing, developing, and deploying AI systems that uphold moral principles, such as fairness, transparency, accountability, and respect for human rights. These systems should work to benefit society while minimizing harm and ensuring that they are free from unfair biases and discriminatory practices (Floridi & Cowls, 2019). Ethical AI aims to address concerns related to data privacy, algorithmic transparency, and the impact of AI on individuals and communities. Given AI's growing influence in areas such as hiring, law enforcement, healthcare, and finance, there is an increasing need to ensure that these systems operate fairly and ethically.

Fairness: AI systems should treat individuals and groups fairly by preventing discrimination based on attributes such as race, gender, age, and socioeconomic status. Fairness in AI requires algorithms to be free from biases that lead to unjust outcomes or unequal treatment (Danks & London, 2017).

Transparency: Ethical AI demands transparency in how decisions are made by algorithms. Stakeholders should understand how AI systems function, what data is used, and the rationale behind decisions. Transparency builds trust and allows for scrutiny to ensure that the AI systems are behaving as expected (Floridi & Cowls, 2019).

Accountability: Developers, organizations, and users of AI systems must be accountable for the outcomes generated by these technologies. If an AI system causes harm or produces biased results, there must be mechanisms in place to investigate and address these issues (Mittelstadt et al., 2016).

2. Bias in AI Systems

AI systems learn from data, and if that data contains biases, the system is likely to replicate or even amplify those biases. Bias in AI can emerge from several sources, including biased training data, biased algorithmic design, or unequal access to AI technologies. For example, if an AI system is trained on historical data that reflects societal biases, such as gender or racial disparities, it may reinforce those biases in its predictions or decisions (Binns, 2018).

Training Data Bias: Biases in AI often stem from biased training data. If the data used to train AI models reflects historical inequalities or underrepresents certain groups, the model may develop biased predictions. For example, facial recognition systems have been shown to perform less accurately on individuals with darker skin tones because they were trained primarily on lighter-skinned individuals (Buolamwini & Gebru, 2018).

Algorithmic Bias: Even when data is unbiased, algorithmic design can introduce bias. Algorithms that prioritize certain attributes or weight features unequally may disproportionately benefit or harm certain groups. For instance, credit-scoring algorithms might unfairly penalize individuals from lower-income backgrounds if they fail to consider contextual factors beyond credit history (Danks & London, 2017).

Feedback Loops: AI systems can perpetuate biases through feedback loops. For example, in predictive policing, if AI algorithms disproportionately target certain communities based on past arrest data, those communities are more likely to experience heightened surveillance, leading to more arrests and reinforcing the AI's predictions (Mittelstadt et al., 2016).

3. Best Practices for Bias Mitigation in AI

To build AI systems that are ethical and free from bias, organizations must implement best practices that address the sources of bias and ensure that AI systems treat individuals and groups fairly. Bias mitigation requires a multi-faceted approach, including careful data management, algorithmic fairness, and ongoing monitoring and evaluation.

Diverse and Representative Datasets: One of the most important strategies for bias mitigation is ensuring that training data is diverse and representative of the populations the AI system will serve. Organizations must take care to collect data that accurately reflects different demographics and contexts to avoid over-representing or under-representing certain groups. Data augmentation techniques can also help balance datasets when underrepresented groups are limited in the training data (Raji et al., 2020).

Algorithm Auditing and Fairness Testing: Regular auditing of AI algorithms is essential to identify and address biases. Fairness testing involves evaluating algorithms to ensure that they produce equitable outcomes across different demographic groups. Techniques such as counterfactual fairness—where the algorithm is tested to see if it would produce the same decision for individuals from different demographic groups under the same circumstances—are useful for bias detection (Binns, 2018).

Human Oversight and Interpretability: While AI systems can automate decision-making, human oversight is critical to ensuring that those decisions align with ethical standards. Humans should be involved in reviewing and validating AI-generated decisions, especially in high-stakes areas such as hiring, criminal justice, and healthcare. Additionally, AI systems should be designed for interpretability, allowing users to understand how decisions are made and why certain outcomes are reached (Floridi & Cowls, 2019).

Post-Deployment Monitoring: Bias in AI can emerge or evolve over time, particularly as the system interacts with real-world data. Post-deployment monitoring ensures that AI systems continue to operate fairly after they have been deployed. This process involves continuously tracking the system's performance across different groups and identifying any disparities in outcomes. Organizations should implement feedback mechanisms to gather user input and address potential issues as they arise (Raji et al., 2020).

Transparency and Documentation: Transparency in AI systems is essential for accountability. Organizations should document the development and decision-making processes behind their AI models, including details about data sources, algorithm design, and bias mitigation strategies. Tools like model cards and data sheets for datasets provide transparency by offering a structured way to disclose important information about AI systems and their limitations (Mitchell et al., 2019).

4. Ethical AI in Practice: Case Studies and Examples

Several organizations and researchers have developed frameworks and tools to promote ethical AI and mitigate bias in real-world applications. For example, IBM's AI Fairness 360 toolkit provides open-source resources for detecting and mitigating bias in machine learning models. The toolkit includes algorithms to measure bias and techniques for re-weighting data to improve fairness (Bellamy et al., 2018).

Facial Recognition and Bias: Researchers have highlighted the biases present in facial recognition systems, which tend to be less accurate for women and people of color. In response, companies like Microsoft and Amazon have implemented stricter testing protocols and adopted fairness guidelines to address these disparities. However, ongoing concerns about the ethical implications of facial recognition have led some companies to halt the sale of these technologies to law enforcement (Buolamwini & Gebru, 2018).

Healthcare AI and Fairness: In healthcare, AI algorithms are increasingly being used to predict patient outcomes and recommend treatments. However, biases in healthcare data can lead to discriminatory outcomes. For example, an AI system designed to allocate healthcare resources might disproportionately favor patients from wealthier areas if the underlying data reflects historical disparities in healthcare access. Ethical AI practices in healthcare involve using fairness-enhancing techniques to ensure that all patients receive equitable care, regardless of their background (Danks & London, 2017).

5. The Ethical Imperative for Bias Mitigation in AI

Ethical AI is not just a technical challenge but also a moral imperative. The deployment of biased AI systems can reinforce existing inequalities and harm vulnerable groups. As AI continues to shape decision-making in critical areas like healthcare, criminal justice, finance, and employment, it is essential for organizations to prioritize fairness, transparency, and accountability in their AI development practices.

Organizations must recognize that biases in AI systems are often a reflection of societal biases. Therefore, the goal of ethical AI is not only to improve the technical aspects of AI systems but also to address the underlying structural inequalities that influence data collection and usage. By adopting comprehensive bias mitigation practices, organizations can create AI systems that are more fair, equitable, and aligned with ethical standards.

In summary, Ethical AI and bias mitigation are central to the responsible development and deployment of AI systems. Bias in AI can have serious consequences, perpetuating inequality and discrimination. To build ethical AI, organizations must adopt best practices such as using diverse datasets, conducting regular algorithm audits, ensuring human oversight, and promoting transparency. As AI continues to influence important decisions in society, the ethical imperative to ensure fairness, accountability, and transparency will remain critical. Organizations that implement robust data governance frameworks and prioritize ethical AI will be better equipped to build systems that benefit society while minimizing harm.

Regulatory Compliance (GDPR, CCPA)

As organizations collect and process increasingly vast amounts of data, regulatory compliance has become a critical component of data governance and ethics. Regulatory frameworks such as the European Union's General Data Protection Regulation (GDPR) and the California Consumer Privacy Act (CCPA) are designed to protect the privacy rights of individuals and ensure that organizations handle personal data responsibly. Compliance with these regulations is not only a legal requirement but also an ethical obligation to respect individual privacy and maintain trust. To meet these requirements, organizations must implement comprehensive data governance frameworks that address data collection, processing, storage, and security in line with regulatory standards.

1. Understanding GDPR and CCPA

The GDPR and CCPA are two of the most influential data protection laws, setting global standards for how organizations must manage personal data.

General Data Protection Regulation (GDPR): Implemented in May 2018, GDPR is a comprehensive data privacy law that applies to all organizations operating within the European Union (EU), as well as those outside the EU that process the personal data of EU residents. GDPR establishes strict guidelines on how personal data should be collected, processed, stored, and transferred. It provides individuals with enhanced privacy rights, including the right to access, correct, and delete their data, as well as the right to data portability and to object to automated decision-making (Voigt & Von dem Bussche, 2017).

California Consumer Privacy Act (CCPA): Enacted in January 2020, the CCPA provides similar protections to California residents, ensuring that consumers have greater control over their personal information. CCPA requires businesses to disclose the categories of personal data they collect and provides consumers with the right to access, delete, and opt out of the sale of their data. While CCPA is less stringent than GDPR, it marks a significant step forward in U.S. data privacy law, setting the stage for broader privacy protections across the United States (Davis, 2020).

2. Key Provisions of GDPR and CCPA

Both GDPR and CCPA impose specific obligations on organizations that collect and process personal data. These regulations emphasize transparency, accountability, and individual rights, requiring organizations to adopt robust data governance practices.

Consent and Data Collection: Under GDPR, organizations must obtain explicit, informed consent from individuals before collecting their personal data. Consent must be freely given, specific, and easy to withdraw at any time. CCPA, while not as strict in terms of consent, requires businesses to provide clear notice of data collection practices at the point of collection and offer consumers the option to opt out of the sale of their personal data (Voigt & Von dem Bussche, 2017; Davis, 2020).

Right to Access and Delete Personal Data: Both GDPR and CCPA grant individuals the right to access the personal data held by organizations and request its deletion. Under GDPR, this is known as the "right to be forgotten," which allows individuals to request the erasure of their data under specific conditions, such as when the data is no longer necessary for the original purpose or when consent is withdrawn (Voigt & Von dem Bussche, 2017). Similarly, CCPA gives consumers the right to request the deletion of their personal information, with certain exceptions, such as when data is needed to complete a transaction or comply with legal obligations (Davis, 2020).

Data Portability: GDPR includes the right to data portability, which allows individuals to obtain a copy of their personal data in a structured, machine-readable format and transfer it to another service provider (Voigt & Von dem Bussche, 2017). This provision encourages competition by making it easier for individuals to switch between service providers without losing control of their data. While CCPA does not explicitly mention data portability, it requires businesses to provide consumers with access to their data in a portable and easily usable format upon request (Davis, 2020).

Transparency and Accountability: Both regulations emphasize the importance of transparency and accountability. GDPR requires organizations to provide clear and accessible privacy notices, detailing how personal data is collected, processed, and shared. Additionally, organizations must appoint data protection officers (DPOs) in certain cases and conduct data protection impact assessments (DPIAs) for high-risk data processing activities (Voigt & Von dem Bussche, 2017). CCPA also requires businesses to disclose their data collection and sharing practices in a privacy notice and mandates that they respond to consumer data requests within a specified timeframe (Davis, 2020).

3. Best Practices for Regulatory Compliance

To ensure compliance with GDPR and CCPA, organizations must implement a range of best practices as part of their data governance frameworks. These practices should address the entire data lifecycle, from collection to disposal, and prioritize transparency, security, and individual rights.

Data Mapping and Inventory: One of the first steps in achieving compliance is conducting a thorough data mapping and inventory process. This involves identifying what personal data the organization collects, where it is stored, how it is processed, and who has access to it. By creating a comprehensive data inventory, organizations can better manage their data, respond to individual rights requests, and ensure that they are only collecting and processing data that is necessary for specific purposes (Kugler, 2018).

Privacy by Design and Default: GDPR introduces the concept of "privacy by design and by default," which requires organizations to integrate privacy considerations into the development of new products and services from the outset. This means building data protection features into systems, minimizing data collection, and ensuring that personal data is adequately protected throughout its lifecycle (Voigt & Von dem Bussche, 2017). CCPA, while not explicitly requiring privacy by design, encourages businesses to adopt practices that prioritize consumer privacy and data minimization.

Data Subject Access Requests (DSAR) Management: To comply with the individual rights provisions of GDPR and CCPA, organizations must establish processes for handling Data Subject Access Requests (DSARs). These requests allow individuals to access, correct, delete, or port their personal data. Organizations should implement automated tools and procedures to manage DSARs efficiently, ensuring that requests are responded to within the legally required timeframes (typically 30 to 45 days) (Davis, 2020).

Data Minimization and Retention Policies: Both GDPR and CCPA emphasize the importance of data minimization, meaning that organizations should collect only the data that is necessary for the purpose at hand. Data retention policies should be established to define how long personal data is stored and when it should be deleted. Regular audits should be conducted to ensure that personal data is not retained longer than necessary (Kugler, 2018).

Data Breach Notification: Both GDPR and CCPA require organizations to notify regulators and affected individuals in the event of a data breach. GDPR requires notification within 72 hours of discovering the breach, while CCPA requires businesses to notify affected consumers "in the most expedient time possible" (Voigt & Von dem Bussche, 2017; Davis, 2020). To comply with these requirements, organizations must establish robust data breach response plans, including procedures for detecting, reporting, and mitigating breaches.

4. The Ethical Importance of Regulatory Compliance

Beyond legal obligations, regulatory compliance with GDPR and CCPA is an ethical imperative that ensures respect for individual privacy rights. By adhering to these regulations, organizations demonstrate their commitment to transparency, fairness, and accountability in data handling. Ethical data governance not only helps organizations avoid legal penalties but also builds trust with consumers and stakeholders by prioritizing their privacy and security.

Building Consumer Trust: Regulatory compliance enhances consumer trust by providing transparency and giving individuals control over their data. In an age where data breaches and misuse are common, consumers are more likely to engage with organizations that prioritize their privacy and are transparent about how their data is used (Kugler, 2018). Compliance with GDPR and CCPA helps organizations demonstrate that they value consumer rights and are committed to protecting personal data.

Preventing Harm: Non-compliance with data protection regulations can lead to significant harm, including identity theft, financial loss, and reputational damage. By implementing strong data governance practices in line with GDPR and CCPA, organizations can prevent the misuse of personal data and reduce the risk of data breaches that may cause harm to individuals (Voigt & Von dem Bussche, 2017).

In summary, regulatory compliance with data protection laws such as GDPR and CCPA is essential for organizations that collect and process personal data. These regulations provide individuals with greater control over their personal information, while imposing stringent requirements on organizations to ensure transparency, accountability, and data security. To meet these requirements, organizations must implement comprehensive data governance frameworks that include data mapping, privacy by design, DSAR management, data minimization, and breach notification policies. Beyond legal compliance, adhering to these regulations is an ethical responsibility that builds consumer trust and protects individuals from harm. As data privacy continues to evolve, organizations must remain vigilant in their compliance efforts to safeguard personal data and uphold the highest ethical standards.

Responsible Data Management

Responsible data management is a crucial aspect of modern data governance frameworks, emphasizing the ethical, secure, and sustainable handling of data throughout its lifecycle. As organizations increasingly rely on data to inform decisions, optimize processes, and drive innovation, the need for responsible data management becomes more pronounced. This entails ensuring data is collected, stored, processed, and disposed of in ways that respect individual privacy, maintain data quality, and minimize the risk of data breaches. Responsible data management aligns with both legal obligations and ethical principles, fostering trust with stakeholders while ensuring compliance with regulations such as GDPR and CCPA.

1. Principles of Responsible Data Management

Responsible data management is underpinned by several core principles that ensure data is used ethically and efficiently. These principles include transparency, accountability, data minimization, and security. Together, they form a framework for ensuring that data practices are aligned with both organizational goals and ethical standards.

Transparency and Openness: Organizations should be transparent about how they collect, use, and share data. This includes clearly informing individuals about the types of data being collected, the purposes for which it will be used, and who it will be shared with. Transparent data practices build trust with stakeholders and comply with regulations like GDPR, which mandates clear and accessible privacy notices (Voigt & Von dem Bussche, 2017). Open communication about data practices ensures that individuals can make informed decisions about their personal information.

Accountability and Governance: Responsible data management requires organizations to establish clear accountability structures. This includes appointing data stewards or data protection officers (DPOs) to oversee data governance processes and ensure that data is handled in compliance with legal and ethical standards (Khatri & Brown, 2010). Accountability also involves regularly auditing data practices to identify and mitigate potential risks, ensuring that all members of the organization understand their responsibilities related to data management.

Data Minimization: A fundamental principle of responsible data management is data minimization, which dictates that organizations should collect and retain only the data necessary for specific, legitimate purposes. This principle is enshrined in regulations such as GDPR, which requires organizations to avoid collecting excessive or irrelevant data (Voigt & Von dem Bussche, 2017). By limiting data collection and storage, organizations reduce the risk of data breaches and the misuse of personal information.

Security and Privacy by Design: Security is a key component of responsible data management. Organizations must implement robust security measures to protect data from unauthorized access, breaches, and other threats. This includes encrypting sensitive data, using multi-factor authentication, and regularly updating software to address vulnerabilities (Gasser & Palfrey, 2017). Privacy by design further enhances security by embedding privacy considerations into the design of systems and processes from the outset, rather than as an afterthought (Kugler, 2018).

2. The Data Lifecycle: From Collection to Disposal

Responsible data management requires a holistic approach to the entire data lifecycle, from collection to disposal. This involves ensuring that data is managed ethically and securely at each stage, minimizing risks while maximizing the value of data for the organization.

Data Collection: The data collection process must be guided by clear purposes and informed consent. Organizations should collect only the data necessary for achieving specific goals, ensuring that individuals are fully aware of what data is being collected and why. GDPR mandates that data collection be transparent and based on explicit, freely given consent (Voigt & Von dem Bussche, 2017). Informed consent ensures that individuals retain control over their personal information and prevents the misuse of data.

Data Storage and Access Control: After data is collected, it must be securely stored and access should be restricted to authorized personnel only. Implementing strong access control policies, such as role-based access control (RBAC), ensures that only those who need to use the data can access it, reducing the likelihood of unauthorized use or breaches (Gasser & Palfrey, 2017). Regular audits and access reviews are necessary to maintain security and ensure compliance with data protection regulations.

Data Processing and Usage: Responsible data processing involves ensuring that data is used only for the purposes for which it was collected and in a manner consistent with individuals' expectations. This means avoiding secondary uses of data that were not disclosed at the point of collection, unless additional consent is obtained (Khatri & Brown, 2010). In addition, organizations must implement mechanisms to ensure the accuracy and quality of the data being processed, as inaccurate data can lead to flawed insights and unfair outcomes.

Data Retention and Disposal: Data retention policies must balance the need for data with the obligation to protect privacy. Organizations should retain data only for as long as it is needed for its intended purposes, after which it should be securely deleted or anonymized. Retaining data unnecessarily increases the risk of breaches and privacy violations. Best practices for data disposal include secure deletion methods, such as data wiping or physical destruction of storage devices, to ensure that data cannot be recovered or misused (Gasser & Palfrey, 2017).

3. Challenges in Responsible Data Management

Despite the importance of responsible data management, organizations face several challenges in implementing best practices. These challenges include balancing data utility with privacy, ensuring data quality, and managing large volumes of data across decentralized systems.

Balancing Data Utility and Privacy: One of the key challenges in responsible data management is striking a balance between maximizing the utility of data for decision-making and innovation while protecting individual privacy. Data is a valuable asset for organizations, driving insights and enabling personalized services, but excessive data collection or invasive use of personal information can undermine privacy and violate ethical standards. Privacy-enhancing technologies, such as data anonymization and differential privacy, help balance these competing interests by allowing organizations to extract value from data while minimizing privacy risks (Kugler, 2018).

Ensuring Data Quality and Integrity: Data quality is essential for responsible data management. Poor-quality data can lead to incorrect insights and faulty decision-making, undermining trust in data-driven processes. Organizations must implement data quality management practices, including data validation, cleansing, and normalization, to ensure that the data they collect and process is accurate, complete, and reliable (Khatri & Brown, 2010). Regular audits and reviews of data quality are necessary to maintain the integrity of data assets.

Managing Large Volumes of Data: The rise of big data presents significant challenges for responsible data management, particularly when dealing with decentralized data systems or cloud environments. Organizations must develop scalable strategies for managing large volumes of data while ensuring compliance with data protection laws and ethical standards. This includes investing in data management tools and technologies that automate data governance processes and ensure that data is properly stored, protected, and monitored (Gasser & Palfrey, 2017).

4. Best Practices for Responsible Data Management

To implement responsible data management, organizations must adopt a range of best practices that prioritize security, privacy, and ethical considerations. These best practices help mitigate risks, ensure regulatory compliance, and foster trust with stakeholders.

Implement Privacy by Design: Privacy by design involves integrating privacy protections into the development of systems and processes from the outset. This proactive approach ensures that privacy risks are identified and mitigated during the design phase, reducing the need for reactive measures later (Kugler, 2018). Organizations should incorporate privacy-enhancing technologies, such as encryption and access controls, into their systems to protect personal data at all stages of the data lifecycle.

Develop Clear Data Governance Policies: Clear data governance policies establish guidelines for how data is collected, used, stored, and shared across the organization. These policies should define roles and responsibilities for data management, ensuring that all employees understand their obligations regarding data handling and protection. Regular training and awareness programs help reinforce these policies and promote a culture of responsible data management (Khatri & Brown, 2010).

Monitor and Audit Data Practices: Regular monitoring and auditing of data practices are essential for identifying potential risks and ensuring compliance with regulations. Audits should assess data access controls, security measures, and compliance with data minimization principles. Organizations should establish processes for responding to audit findings and continuously improving their data governance frameworks (Gasser & Palfrey, 2017).

Engage Stakeholders in Ethical Decision-Making: Ethical data management requires input from diverse stakeholders, including data subjects, regulators, and civil society. Engaging stakeholders in discussions about data practices ensures that decisions are aligned with societal values and ethical principles. Organizations should establish mechanisms for stakeholder feedback and consider ethical implications when making decisions about data use (Floridi, 2018).

Conclusion

Responsible data management is essential for ensuring that data is used ethically, securely, and in compliance with legal and regulatory standards. By adhering to principles such as transparency, accountability, data minimization, and privacy by design, organizations can safeguard personal data while maximizing its value for decision-making. Implementing best practices for data collection, storage, processing, and disposal, as well as addressing challenges such as data quality and big data management, are critical for fostering trust with stakeholders and ensuring that data-driven innovations are aligned with ethical standards. In an era of increased data reliance, responsible data management is both a legal necessity and an ethical obligation.

References

Bellamy, R. K. E., Dey, K., Hind, M., Hoffman, S. C., Houde, S., Kannan, K., ... & Varshney, K. R. (2018). AI fairness 360: An extensible toolkit for detecting, understanding, and mitigating unwanted algorithmic bias. *arXiv preprint arXiv:1810.01943*.

Binns, R. (2018). Fairness in machine learning: Lessons from political philosophy. *Proceedings of the 2018 Conference on Fairness, Accountability, and Transparency*, 149-159.

Davis, M. (2020). *California Consumer Privacy Act (CCPA) Handbook*. Apress.

Floridi, L. (2018). *The ethics of information*. Oxford University Press.

Gasser, U., & Palfrey, J. (2017). *Privacy and security in the digital age*. MIT Press.

Khatri, V., & Brown, C. V. (2010). Designing data governance. *Communications of the ACM, 53*(1), 148-152.

Kugler, L. (2018). The next wave of privacy protection. *Communications of the ACM, 61*(7), 19-21.

Voigt, P., & Von dem Bussche, A. (2017). *The EU General Data Protection Regulation (GDPR): A practical guide*. Springer.

Winder, D. (2019). Equifax breach settlement: Impact and lessons learned. *Forbes*. https://www.forbes.com

Chapter 23: Scaling AI Solutions

Infrastructure Considerations

Scaling AI solutions requires robust infrastructure capable of supporting the increased computational demands, data processing needs, and storage requirements of AI systems as they grow in complexity and scope. As organizations move from proof-of-concept AI models to large-scale production environments, they must address a variety of infrastructure considerations to ensure scalability, efficiency, and cost-effectiveness. Key factors include computational power, data management, network bandwidth, hardware accelerators, cloud vs. on-premises deployment, and system architecture design. Implementing scalable infrastructure is essential for maximizing the performance of AI systems and enabling their integration into larger, business-critical operations.

1. Computational Power and Scalability

AI solutions, particularly those involving deep learning and large-scale machine learning models, require significant computational power. Scaling these solutions involves ensuring that the infrastructure can handle increased workloads, model complexity, and data volume without sacrificing performance or reliability.

High-Performance Computing (HPC): AI models, especially deep learning algorithms, rely heavily on HPC infrastructure to handle large amounts of data and perform complex computations. HPC systems are designed to provide the computational power needed to train models efficiently, often using parallel processing and distributed computing architectures (He et al., 2018). As AI models scale, organizations may need to invest in HPC resources or leverage cloud-based HPC solutions to handle the growing demands of AI workloads.

Cloud Computing for Scalability: Cloud platforms such as Amazon Web Services (AWS), Google Cloud Platform (GCP), and Microsoft Azure offer scalable infrastructure solutions for AI. These platforms provide elastic compute resources, enabling organizations to scale up or down based on demand. Cloud computing also allows for distributed computing, which is essential for training AI models on large datasets and ensuring that infrastructure resources can be allocated dynamically as the needs of the AI system evolve (Rajan & Venkatraman, 2018).

Hardware Accelerators: Scaling AI often requires specialized hardware, such as Graphics Processing Units (GPUs) and Tensor Processing Units (TPUs), to accelerate computation. GPUs are particularly effective for AI tasks because they can handle parallel processing more efficiently than traditional Central Processing Units (CPUs). As AI models scale, the need for hardware accelerators grows, and organizations must ensure their infrastructure includes the right combination of GPUs, TPUs, and other accelerators to optimize performance (Krizhevsky et al., 2017).

2. Data Management and Storage Requirements

As AI systems scale, the amount of data they process increases exponentially. Managing large volumes of data effectively is crucial for scaling AI solutions, requiring advanced data management strategies and infrastructure that can accommodate both structured and unstructured data.

Data Storage Solutions: AI systems generate and process large amounts of data, from training datasets to inference outputs. Scalable AI solutions need robust data storage systems that can handle high data volumes, ensure quick access, and provide redundancy to protect against data loss. Cloud-based storage solutions, such as Amazon S3 or Google Cloud Storage, offer the flexibility to scale storage as needed, providing a cost-effective way to manage large data volumes (Rao et al., 2020).

Data Pipelines and ETL (Extract, Transform, Load) Processes: Scaling AI systems requires efficient data pipelines that can ingest, clean, and preprocess data at scale. Extract, Transform, Load (ETL) processes must be automated to ensure that data is continuously fed into the AI system without manual intervention. Scalable ETL tools, such as Apache Spark or cloud-native solutions like AWS Glue, are critical for maintaining data quality and ensuring that large datasets are efficiently processed for AI models (He et al., 2018).

Data Governance and Security: With the increase in data volume comes the need for robust data governance and security practices. Scalable AI solutions must adhere to data privacy laws, such as GDPR and CCPA, and implement security measures to protect sensitive information. Data encryption, secure access controls, and monitoring for anomalies in data processing are essential for ensuring the security and privacy of large datasets in scaled AI environments (Rao et al., 2020).

3. Network Bandwidth and Latency Considerations

As AI systems scale, particularly in distributed computing environments, network bandwidth and latency become critical infrastructure concerns. AI models often rely on the transfer of large datasets between storage, processing nodes, and endpoints, making network performance a key factor in the overall scalability and efficiency of the AI solution.

High-Bandwidth Networks: AI systems that process large datasets in real time or near-real-time environments require high-bandwidth networks to ensure fast data transfer and communication between nodes. For AI applications that rely on edge computing or distributed architectures, having a network infrastructure capable of handling high volumes of data transmission with minimal bottlenecks is essential (Rajan & Venkatraman, 2018).

Low Latency for Real-Time AI: Many AI applications, such as autonomous vehicles, robotics, and real-time decision-making systems, require low-latency network infrastructure to operate effectively. Latency issues can result in delays in decision-making or slow responses, which can be detrimental in high-stakes environments like healthcare or finance. Optimizing network infrastructure to reduce latency is critical for scaling AI systems that rely on real-time data processing (Krizhevsky et al., 2017).

Edge Computing: As AI solutions scale, edge computing has emerged as a strategy for reducing latency by bringing computation closer to the data source. Edge computing allows AI models to be deployed on local devices or edge servers, reducing the need for data to be transferred to central data centers and speeding up decision-making processes. Edge computing is particularly useful for IoT (Internet of Things) applications, where devices need to process data in real time (Shi et al., 2016).

4. Cloud vs. On-Premises Infrastructure for Scaling AI

One of the key decisions organizations face when scaling AI solutions is whether to use cloud-based infrastructure, on-premises infrastructure, or a hybrid approach. Each option has its advantages and challenges, depending on the specific requirements of the AI application.

Cloud Infrastructure: Cloud infrastructure offers flexibility, scalability, and cost-effectiveness, making it an attractive option for scaling AI. Cloud platforms provide access to vast compute resources, GPUs, and TPUs, and they allow organizations to scale resources dynamically as AI workloads fluctuate. Additionally, cloud providers offer a range of AI and machine learning services that can accelerate development and deployment (Rao et al., 2020). However, cloud infrastructure can pose challenges in terms of data privacy and control, especially for organizations dealing with sensitive or proprietary data.

On-Premises Infrastructure: On-premises infrastructure provides greater control over data and security, which can be critical for industries like healthcare, finance, or government. Organizations can customize their hardware and software configurations to meet specific AI needs and ensure compliance with regulatory requirements. However, on-premises infrastructure is less flexible than cloud infrastructure and can be expensive to scale, as organizations must invest in hardware, maintenance, and upgrades (He et al., 2018).

Hybrid Approaches: Hybrid infrastructure combines the benefits of both cloud and on-premises systems, allowing organizations to keep sensitive data and critical processes on-premises while leveraging the scalability of the cloud for less sensitive workloads. This approach provides flexibility while maintaining control over key data and systems. Hybrid models are often used in industries with strict data privacy regulations or in organizations transitioning from on-premises to cloud infrastructure (Rajan & Venkatraman, 2018).

5. System Architecture for Scalable AI

Scaling AI solutions requires an efficient system architecture that supports distributed computing, parallel processing, and the integration of multiple AI models. Architecting AI systems for scalability involves considering the flow of data, model deployment strategies, and the ability to add or remove resources without disrupting operations.

Distributed Computing and Parallel Processing: To scale AI models effectively, organizations must design systems that distribute computations across multiple nodes. Distributed computing frameworks, such as Apache Spark or Kubernetes, allow AI tasks to be divided into smaller parts that can be processed simultaneously across a network of computers, improving processing speed and efficiency (He et al., 2018). Parallel processing is particularly important for deep learning models that require significant computational resources for training.

Microservices Architecture: A microservices architecture, in which AI functions are broken down into smaller, self-contained services, allows organizations to scale AI solutions more easily. Each service can be developed, deployed, and scaled independently, enabling AI teams to manage system growth without impacting the entire infrastructure. This modular approach is well-suited for AI applications that involve multiple models or components, such as recommendation systems or natural language processing pipelines (Rajan & Venkatraman, 2018).

Containerization and Orchestration: Containerization technologies, such as Docker, enable AI applications to be packaged with all their dependencies, making them portable across different environments. Orchestration tools like Kubernetes allow for the automated deployment, scaling, and management of containerized applications. This approach ensures that AI models can be scaled efficiently across different infrastructure environments, whether on-premises, cloud, or hybrid (Shi et al., 2016).

In summary, Scaling AI solutions requires careful consideration of infrastructure components such as computational power, data management, network performance, and deployment strategies. Organizations must invest in high-performance computing resources, leverage cloud or hybrid infrastructure models, and ensure robust data pipelines and storage systems to support the growing demands of AI models. Additionally, designing system architectures that support distributed computing, microservices, and containerization is essential for efficiently scaling AI applications. As AI continues to transform industries, implementing scalable infrastructure solutions will be critical for maintaining the performance, reliability, and security of AI systems in production environments.

Parallel and Distributed Computing

Parallel and distributed computing are essential components of scaling AI solutions, enabling organizations to efficiently process vast amounts of data, train complex models, and execute tasks across multiple processors or machines. As AI models grow in complexity and data volumes increase, traditional computing approaches can no longer meet the performance and efficiency demands of large-scale AI applications. Parallel computing allows tasks to be split into smaller sub-tasks that can be processed simultaneously, while distributed computing extends this concept by distributing tasks across a network of machines. Together, these approaches significantly enhance the performance, scalability, and flexibility of AI systems.

1. Overview of Parallel Computing in AI

Parallel computing involves breaking down a computational task into smaller, independent sub-tasks that can be executed simultaneously on multiple processors. This approach is particularly effective in AI applications, such as training deep learning models, where operations can be performed in parallel to reduce computation time.

Task Parallelism and Data Parallelism: Parallel computing in AI can be implemented using two main approaches: task parallelism and data parallelism. Task parallelism involves dividing the computation into independent tasks, where each task can run on a separate processor. This approach is well-suited for problems where different parts of the computation can be performed independently. In contrast, data parallelism involves dividing the data itself into chunks, with each processor handling a portion of the data. This is particularly useful in deep learning, where large datasets are split across multiple GPUs for faster training (Dean et al., 2012).

GPU Acceleration: Graphics Processing Units (GPUs) are critical for parallel computing in AI. GPUs are designed to handle multiple operations in parallel, making them highly effective for tasks such as matrix operations in neural networks, which are a fundamental component of AI model training. By leveraging the parallel processing capabilities of GPUs, organizations can significantly reduce the time required to train large models, such as convolutional neural networks (CNNs) and recurrent neural networks (RNNs) (Krizhevsky et al., 2017).

Challenges in Parallel Computing: Despite its advantages, parallel computing presents several challenges. Not all AI tasks can be easily parallelized, and dividing tasks into smaller units can introduce overhead from communication between processors. Additionally, synchronizing tasks to ensure consistent results across processors can be complex, particularly in environments with shared resources (Bekkerman et al., 2011). To overcome these challenges, efficient scheduling and workload balancing techniques are critical in maximizing the performance of parallel computing.

2. Distributed Computing in AI

Distributed computing extends the concept of parallel computing by distributing tasks across multiple machines, often connected in a network. This approach is essential for scaling AI solutions, especially in cases where datasets are too large to fit on a single machine or where computational tasks require resources beyond what a single machine can provide.

Cluster and Grid Computing: Distributed computing is often implemented through clusters or grids of interconnected machines. A cluster consists of a group of computers working together as a single system, with tasks distributed across the machines for parallel execution. Grid computing extends this concept by allowing machines in different geographic locations to collaborate on a shared task (Dean & Ghemawat, 2008). These systems are ideal for AI applications that require massive computational power and large-scale data processing, such as natural language processing (NLP) and computer vision.

Distributed Deep Learning: Distributed deep learning is a common use case for distributed computing in AI. Training large neural networks on distributed systems allows organizations to leverage multiple GPUs or CPUs simultaneously, significantly reducing the time required to train models on massive datasets. Distributed training strategies, such as synchronous and asynchronous data parallelism, enable AI models to be trained across multiple nodes in a distributed computing environment (Li et al., 2014). In synchronous training, all nodes update the model at the same time, while in asynchronous training, updates occur independently across nodes, allowing for greater flexibility in scaling AI systems.

Fault Tolerance and Scalability: One of the key advantages of distributed computing is fault tolerance. In a distributed system, the failure of a single node does not necessarily lead to system failure, as tasks can be reassigned to other nodes. This redundancy is crucial for AI applications that require high availability and reliability. Additionally, distributed computing allows for horizontal scalability, where additional machines can be added to the network as needed to handle increasing workloads (Dean & Ghemawat, 2008).

3. Frameworks and Tools for Parallel and Distributed AI Computing

Several frameworks and tools are available to help organizations implement parallel and distributed computing for AI applications. These frameworks simplify the process of distributing tasks and managing resources across multiple processors or machines, allowing for efficient scaling of AI systems.

Apache Hadoop: Apache Hadoop is one of the most widely used distributed computing frameworks for processing large datasets. Hadoop's distributed file system (HDFS) enables data to be stored across multiple machines, while its MapReduce programming model allows tasks to be distributed and processed in parallel across a cluster (Bekkerman et al., 2011). Hadoop is particularly useful for AI applications that involve large-scale data processing, such as text analysis and machine learning.

Apache Spark: Apache Spark is a distributed computing framework that improves on Hadoop's performance by offering in-memory processing. Spark's distributed data structures and parallel processing capabilities make it an excellent choice for AI workloads, particularly those involving iterative algorithms, such as deep learning model training (Zaharia et al., 2016). Spark supports integration with libraries such as MLlib for machine learning and TensorFlow for deep learning, making it a popular choice for AI practitioners.

TensorFlow and Distributed TensorFlow: TensorFlow is one of the most widely used frameworks for developing AI models, particularly deep learning models. TensorFlow supports distributed computing through its Distributed TensorFlow extension, which allows users to train models across multiple GPUs or machines. TensorFlow's architecture enables parallel processing of data and tasks, making it highly scalable for large AI projects (Abadi et al., 2016). Other deep learning frameworks, such as PyTorch, also offer support for distributed training and parallel computation, allowing AI practitioners to scale their models efficiently.

Kubernetes for Orchestration: Kubernetes is an open-source platform for automating the deployment, scaling, and management of containerized applications. In the context of AI, Kubernetes is often used to orchestrate distributed training across multiple machines or cloud environments. By managing the allocation of resources and scaling infrastructure as needed, Kubernetes allows organizations to run AI workloads efficiently in distributed environments (Burns et al., 2016).

4. Best Practices for Implementing Parallel and Distributed Computing in AI

Implementing parallel and distributed computing for AI systems requires careful planning and consideration of factors such as workload distribution, communication overhead, and system architecture. Best practices help organizations overcome the challenges associated with scaling AI using these approaches.

Efficient Task Scheduling and Workload Balancing: To maximize the performance of parallel and distributed computing, it is essential to implement efficient task scheduling and workload balancing. Tasks should be distributed evenly across processors or nodes to avoid bottlenecks or idle resources. Dynamic scheduling algorithms can adjust the allocation of tasks based on the availability of resources and workload conditions, improving overall system efficiency (Dean & Ghemawat, 2008).

Minimizing Communication Overhead: One of the challenges in distributed computing is the communication overhead that arises when nodes must exchange information. Minimizing communication overhead is critical for improving performance in distributed AI systems. Techniques such as data compression, efficient network protocols, and asynchronous updates can help reduce the time spent on communication between nodes, allowing for faster model training and data processing (Zaharia et al., 2016).

Scaling Gradually: When scaling AI solutions using parallel and distributed computing, it is important to scale gradually and monitor system performance at each stage. This allows organizations to identify and address any inefficiencies or bottlenecks early in the scaling process. Gradual scaling also helps ensure that resources are allocated effectively and that system performance remains stable as workloads increase (Dean et al., 2012).

Monitoring and Optimizing Performance: Continuous monitoring of system performance is essential when implementing parallel and distributed computing. Tools such as Prometheus and Grafana can be used to monitor the health of distributed systems, track resource usage, and identify potential issues. Regular optimization of system architecture, task scheduling, and resource allocation can help ensure that AI systems continue to perform efficiently as they scale (Burns et al., 2016).

In summary, Parallel and distributed computing are critical enablers of scalable AI solutions, allowing organizations to handle the increased computational and data processing demands of large AI systems. Parallel computing leverages the power of GPUs and multi-core processors to perform tasks simultaneously, while distributed computing extends these capabilities across multiple machines, enabling AI systems to process vast datasets and train complex models more efficiently. By using frameworks like Apache Spark, TensorFlow, and Kubernetes, organizations can implement scalable AI systems that meet their growing needs. However, effective implementation requires careful attention to task scheduling, communication overhead, and system monitoring to ensure optimal performance. As AI continues to evolve, parallel and distributed computing will remain essential tools for scaling AI applications in fields such as machine learning, natural language processing, and computer vision.

Real-Time Data Processing

Real-time data processing is an essential aspect of scaling AI solutions, especially in applications where timely decisions are critical. Real-time AI enables systems to process and analyze data as it is generated, providing actionable insights with minimal latency. In industries such as finance, healthcare, autonomous systems, and retail, real-time data processing allows organizations to respond quickly to changing conditions, improving decision-making and operational efficiency. Scaling AI for real-time data processing, however, introduces challenges related to infrastructure, latency, data volume, and system architecture. Implementing best practices is crucial to overcoming these challenges and ensuring that AI systems operate effectively in real-time environments.

1. Understanding Real-Time Data Processing in AI

Real-time data processing refers to the continuous ingestion, processing, and analysis of data as it is generated, allowing for immediate or near-immediate insights. This contrasts with batch processing, where data is collected and processed in chunks at scheduled intervals. Real-time AI applications require low-latency processing to make timely predictions, recommendations, or decisions.

Streaming Data and Event-Driven Architectures: Real-time data processing is often associated with streaming data, where data is continuously generated by sources such as sensors, financial markets, or user interactions. AI systems designed for real-time processing must operate in an event-driven architecture, where data is processed as soon as it arrives, rather than waiting for scheduled batches. This architecture is critical for applications such as fraud detection, where delayed responses can result in financial losses, or in autonomous vehicles, where delayed decisions could cause accidents (Stonebraker et al., 2015).

Applications of Real-Time AI: Real-time data processing has numerous applications across industries. In healthcare, real-time AI can analyze patient data from wearable devices or medical equipment to monitor vital signs and detect potential issues before they become critical. In finance, AI systems can analyze market data to execute trades based on real-time market conditions. In retail, real-time AI can power personalized recommendations based on a user's browsing history and current interactions (Zhang et al., 2018).

2. Key Infrastructure Considerations for Real-Time AI

Scaling AI solutions for real-time data processing requires specialized infrastructure that can handle high volumes of data with minimal latency. This involves leveraging distributed systems, cloud computing, and high-performance hardware to support continuous data ingestion and real-time analytics.

Low-Latency Networks: One of the key requirements for real-time AI is minimizing latency—the time between data generation and the system's response. To achieve low latency, organizations must invest in high-speed, low-latency networks that support fast data transfer between data sources, processing nodes, and end users. Edge computing is another approach to reducing latency, as it brings data processing closer to the data source, thereby eliminating the need to send data back and forth to a centralized data center (Shi et al., 2016).

Scalable Data Infrastructure: Real-time AI solutions often require scalable data infrastructure that can handle large data streams. This includes scalable storage solutions capable of ingesting and retrieving data in real-time, as well as compute resources that can process and analyze data continuously. Cloud platforms like Amazon Web Services (AWS), Google Cloud Platform (GCP), and Microsoft Azure provide scalable infrastructure that can dynamically adjust to fluctuating data volumes, ensuring that real-time AI systems can scale as needed (Karimov et al., 2018).

Stream Processing Frameworks: Implementing real-time AI solutions often requires specialized frameworks designed for stream processing. Apache Kafka, Apache Flink, and Apache Storm are widely used for building real-time data pipelines. These frameworks enable the ingestion, processing, and output of streaming data in real-time, ensuring that AI systems can analyze data as it arrives and generate timely insights (Zaharia et al., 2016). Spark Streaming, an extension of Apache Spark, is another popular tool that allows organizations to process streaming data using Spark's distributed computing framework.

3. Challenges in Real-Time Data Processing for AI

While real-time data processing offers significant advantages, scaling AI solutions in real-time environments presents several challenges. These challenges must be addressed through strategic infrastructure design and best practices to ensure that AI systems can handle the demands of real-time applications.

Data Volume and Velocity: Real-time AI systems often need to process large volumes of data at high speeds. This is particularly true in industries such as telecommunications or IoT, where billions of data points can be generated each second. Processing such massive data streams in real-time requires highly efficient algorithms, scalable infrastructure, and optimized data pipelines (Zhang et al., 2018). Organizations must ensure that their systems can scale horizontally by adding more nodes or computing resources to handle increasing data volumes without sacrificing performance.

Data Consistency and Accuracy: In real-time AI applications, ensuring data consistency and accuracy is critical, as incorrect or outdated data can lead to flawed insights or decisions. For example, in financial markets, an AI model that receives inaccurate data might recommend a poor trading strategy, leading to significant losses. Techniques such as data replication, checkpointing, and real-time monitoring are essential for ensuring data quality in real-time environments (Stonebraker et al., 2015).

Fault Tolerance and Resilience: Real-time AI systems must be designed to handle failures gracefully. In distributed environments, network issues, hardware failures, or software bugs can lead to data loss or downtime. To address this, fault tolerance and resilience must be built into the system's architecture. Techniques such as replication, backup, and failover mechanisms ensure that the system can continue to function even when individual components fail (Shi et al., 2016).

4. Best Practices for Scaling Real-Time AI Solutions

Scaling real-time AI solutions requires a combination of best practices in system architecture, infrastructure management, and algorithm design. These best practices help organizations optimize their AI systems for performance, scalability, and reliability.

Adopt Microservices Architecture: A microservices architecture, where the AI system is composed of independent, loosely coupled services, is ideal for scaling real-time data processing. Each service can be scaled independently, allowing organizations to allocate resources more efficiently and avoid bottlenecks in the system. Microservices also support better fault tolerance, as failures in one service do not bring down the entire system (Zhang et al., 2018).

Leverage Edge Computing: To reduce latency and ensure real-time responsiveness, organizations should consider deploying AI models at the edge. Edge computing brings data processing closer to the source of the data, reducing the need to transmit data over long distances. This approach is particularly useful in applications such as autonomous vehicles, smart cities, and industrial IoT, where real-time decision-making is critical (Shi et al., 2016).

Use Stream Processing Frameworks: To handle streaming data efficiently, organizations should adopt frameworks like Apache Kafka, Flink, or Spark Streaming, which are specifically designed for real-time data processing. These frameworks provide the scalability and low-latency processing needed for real-time AI applications, while also supporting fault tolerance and data consistency (Zaharia et al., 2016).

Optimize Algorithms for Real-Time Processing: AI algorithms designed for batch processing may not perform well in real-time environments due to their computational complexity. Optimizing algorithms for real-time processing involves reducing computational overhead, minimizing latency, and ensuring that models can update dynamically as new data arrives. Techniques such as online learning, where models continuously update as new data is ingested, are essential for real-time AI systems (Stonebraker et al., 2015).

Continuous Monitoring and Performance Tuning: Scaling real-time AI solutions requires continuous monitoring and performance tuning to ensure optimal performance. Monitoring tools can track key metrics such as latency, throughput, and resource utilization, allowing organizations to identify and address potential bottlenecks. Regular performance tuning, such as adjusting model parameters or optimizing data pipelines, ensures that real-time AI systems can scale effectively while maintaining low-latency processing (Karimov et al., 2018).

In summary, Scaling AI solutions for real-time data processing is critical for industries that require timely insights and rapid decision-making. Real-time AI enables organizations to process and analyze data as it is generated, improving responsiveness and operational efficiency. However, scaling real-time AI solutions introduces challenges related to data volume, latency, and system resilience. To overcome these challenges, organizations must adopt best practices such as leveraging edge computing, using stream processing frameworks, optimizing algorithms for real-time processing, and ensuring fault tolerance through distributed architectures. As AI continues to drive innovation in real-time applications, building scalable infrastructure and adopting robust strategies for real-time data processing will be essential for success.

Performance Optimization

As AI solutions scale, the demand for high performance becomes critical to ensure that models run efficiently, process vast datasets, and deliver timely results. Performance optimization involves improving the efficiency of AI models, algorithms, and infrastructure to handle increased workloads while minimizing latency, resource usage, and costs. Effective performance optimization not only enhances the scalability of AI systems but also ensures their reliability and responsiveness in real-time applications. Key strategies for performance optimization include model optimization, hardware acceleration, algorithm refinement, resource allocation, and continuous monitoring.

1. Model Optimization

Optimizing AI models is one of the most effective strategies for improving performance, especially as models grow larger and more complex. The process of model optimization focuses on reducing the computational cost of training and inference without compromising the model's accuracy.

Model Compression: Model compression techniques such as pruning, quantization, and knowledge distillation can significantly reduce the size and complexity of AI models. Pruning involves removing redundant or less important weights from the neural network, while quantization reduces the precision of weights and activations to lower-bit formats, such as 8-bit integers instead of 32-bit floating-point numbers (Han et al., 2016). Knowledge distillation, on the other hand, transfers the knowledge from a large model (teacher) to a smaller, more efficient model (student), enabling faster inference with similar accuracy (Hinton et al., 2015). These techniques help reduce memory usage and computational overhead, allowing for faster and more efficient model execution.

Model Parallelism and Data Parallelism: To handle large models and datasets, organizations can implement parallelism techniques. In model parallelism, different parts of the model are split across multiple GPUs or devices, allowing for simultaneous computation of different layers or sections of the model. In data parallelism, the dataset is divided into smaller batches, and each batch is processed by a separate GPU or device in parallel (Dean et al., 2012). These techniques improve the efficiency of both training and inference by leveraging distributed resources.

2. Hardware Acceleration

Hardware acceleration plays a crucial role in optimizing the performance of AI solutions, particularly when scaling to handle larger models and datasets. Specialized hardware, such as GPUs (Graphics Processing Units), TPUs (Tensor Processing Units), and FPGAs (Field Programmable Gate Arrays), are designed to handle the high computational demands of AI workloads.

GPUs and TPUs: GPUs are essential for deep learning tasks due to their ability to perform parallel processing efficiently. They accelerate matrix computations and other operations commonly used in AI models, such as backpropagation and convolution in neural networks (Krizhevsky et al., 2017). TPUs, developed by Google, are hardware accelerators specifically designed for AI workloads, particularly for deep learning models using TensorFlow. TPUs provide high computational power while being energy-efficient, making them ideal for large-scale training and inference tasks (Jouppi et al., 2017).

FPGAs: FPGAs offer a flexible solution for AI performance optimization. They can be programmed to implement specific algorithms, allowing for customizable and optimized hardware configurations tailored to the needs of the AI system. FPGAs are commonly used in low-latency environments, such as high-frequency trading or real-time decision-making, where speed is critical (Venieris et al., 2016).

Edge Computing for Optimization: In applications where real-time data processing is essential, edge computing can optimize performance by bringing computation closer to the data source. Edge devices equipped with specialized hardware, such as NVIDIA's Jetson platform, can run AI models locally, reducing the need to transfer data to a centralized cloud server and minimizing latency (Shi et al., 2016).

3. Algorithmic Refinement

Optimizing the underlying algorithms of AI models is another critical aspect of performance optimization. Refining algorithms can reduce computational complexity, improve accuracy, and minimize training time.

Efficient Algorithms: AI models that rely on computationally intensive algorithms can be optimized by selecting more efficient algorithms or modifying existing ones. For example, algorithms such as stochastic gradient descent (SGD) can be optimized with techniques like momentum or adaptive learning rates (e.g., Adam optimizer), which help speed up convergence during training (Kingma & Ba, 2015). Algorithmic optimizations also include reducing the time complexity of operations, such as matrix multiplication or convolution, by using optimized libraries like cuDNN for deep learning.

Hyperparameter Tuning: Hyperparameter tuning is essential for optimizing model performance. Hyperparameters, such as learning rate, batch size, and regularization strength, significantly affect a model's performance and training time. Automated hyperparameter tuning techniques, such as grid search, random search, and Bayesian optimization, help identify the best hyperparameter configurations to maximize performance (Bergstra et al., 2013). Tools like Hyperopt and Optuna are widely used for automated hyperparameter optimization in large-scale AI projects.

Reducing Overfitting: Overfitting occurs when a model performs well on the training data but poorly on unseen data. To optimize model performance, it is crucial to implement techniques that reduce overfitting, such as dropout, regularization, and early stopping. Regularization techniques, like L2 regularization (also known as weight decay), prevent the model from relying too heavily on certain features, improving its generalization ability and overall performance (Ng, 2004).

4. Efficient Resource Allocation

Scaling AI solutions requires efficient resource allocation to ensure that computational resources, such as CPUs, GPUs, memory, and storage, are used optimally. Poor resource allocation can lead to bottlenecks, increased costs, and reduced performance.

Auto-Scaling in Cloud Environments: Cloud platforms like AWS, Google Cloud, and Microsoft Azure provide auto-scaling capabilities, which automatically adjust resource allocation based on the current workload. This allows AI systems to scale elastically, allocating additional resources during high-demand periods and reducing them when demand decreases. Auto-scaling ensures optimal performance while controlling costs by using only the necessary resources at any given time (Rao et al., 2020).

Load Balancing: Load balancing is essential for distributing workloads evenly across computational resources. In a distributed AI environment, where multiple GPUs or machines are used, load balancing ensures that no single resource is overloaded while others remain underutilized. Efficient load balancing helps prevent bottlenecks and improves overall system performance by maximizing the use of available resources (Dean et al., 2012).

Containerization and Orchestration: Containerization tools like Docker and orchestration platforms like Kubernetes allow AI workloads to be packaged and deployed consistently across different environments. Containerization ensures that the necessary dependencies and configurations are included with the model, while Kubernetes automates the management and scaling of these containers. This approach improves the efficiency of resource allocation and simplifies the deployment of large-scale AI solutions (Burns et al., 2016).

5. Continuous Monitoring and Performance Tuning

Performance optimization is an ongoing process that requires continuous monitoring and tuning. As AI systems scale, it is essential to monitor key performance metrics, such as latency, throughput, memory usage, and computational efficiency, to identify bottlenecks and areas for improvement.

Monitoring Tools: Tools such as Prometheus, Grafana, and TensorBoard provide real-time insights into the performance of AI systems. These tools enable organizations to track key metrics and visualize the performance of models during training and inference. Continuous monitoring allows for early detection of performance issues, such as memory leaks or slow convergence, enabling prompt action to mitigate them (Karimov et al., 2018).

Regular Model Re-Evaluation: As datasets grow and new data becomes available, it is important to periodically re-evaluate and re-optimize AI models. Models trained on outdated data may suffer from performance degradation due to changes in the underlying patterns. Regular model re-training, combined with hyperparameter tuning and algorithmic refinement, ensures that AI systems remain optimized as they scale and adapt to new data (Ng, 2004).

Conclusion

Performance optimization is a key factor in the successful scaling of AI solutions. By employing strategies such as model compression, hardware acceleration, algorithm refinement, efficient resource allocation, and continuous monitoring, organizations can improve the efficiency and scalability of their AI systems. Optimizing performance ensures that AI models can handle increased data volumes, provide real-time insights, and operate cost-effectively as they scale. As AI continues to drive innovation across industries, organizations must prioritize performance optimization to maintain the effectiveness and reliability of their AI solutions.

References

Abadi, M., Barham, P., Chen, J., Chen, Z., Davis, A., Dean, J., ... & Zheng, X. (2016). TensorFlow: A system for large-scale machine learning. *Proceedings of the 12th USENIX Symposium on Operating Systems Design and Implementation (OSDI)*, 265-283. https://www.usenix.org/conference/osdi16/technical-sessions/presentation/abadi

Bekkerman, R., Bilenko, M., & Langford, J. (Eds.). (2011). *Scaling up machine learning: Parallel and distributed approaches.* Cambridge University Press.

Bergstra, J., Bardenet, R., Bengio, Y., & Kégl, B. (2013). Algorithms for hyper-parameter optimization. *Advances in Neural Information Processing Systems, 24*, 2546-2554.

Burns, B., Grant, B., Oppenheimer, D., Brewer, E., & Wilkes, J. (2016). Borg, Omega, and Kubernetes: Lessons learned from three container-management systems over a decade. *Communications of the ACM, 59*(5), 50-57.

Dean, J., & Ghemawat, S. (2008). MapReduce: Simplified data processing on large clusters. *Communications of the ACM, 51*(1), 107-113.

Dean, J., Corrado, G. S., Monga, R., Chen, K., Devin, M., Le, Q. V., ... & Ng, A. Y. (2012). Large scale distributed deep networks. *Advances in Neural Information Processing Systems (NIPS), 25*, 1223-1231.

Dean, J., Corrado, G. S., Monga, R., Chen, K., Devin, M., Le, Q. V., ... & Ng, A. Y. (2012). Large scale distributed deep networks. *Advances in Neural Information Processing Systems, 25*, 1223-1231.

Han, S., Pool, J., Tran, J., & Dally, W. J. (2016). Learning both weights and connections for efficient neural network. *Advances in Neural Information Processing Systems, 28*, 1135-1143.

He, K., Zhang, X., Ren, S., & Sun, J. (2018). Deep residual learning for image recognition. *Proceedings of the IEEE Conference on Computer Vision and Pattern Recognition (CVPR)*, 770-778.

Hinton, G., Vinyals, O., & Dean, J. (2015). Distilling the knowledge in a neural network. *arXiv preprint arXiv:1503.02531*. https://arxiv.org/abs/1503.02531

Jouppi, N. P., Young, C., Patil, N., Patterson, D., Agrawal, G., Bajwa, R., ... & Laudon, J. (2017). In-datacenter performance analysis of a tensor processing unit. *Proceedings of the 44th Annual International Symposium on Computer Architecture*, 1-12.

Karimov, J., Rabl, T., Katsifodimos, A., & Markl, V. (2018). Stream processing with Apache Flink. *IEEE Data Engineering Bulletin, 41*(4), 41-51.

Krizhevsky, A., Sutskever, I., & Hinton, G. E. (2017). ImageNet classification with deep convolutional neural networks. *Communications of the ACM, 60*(6), 84-90.

Ng, A. Y. (2004). Feature selection, L1 vs. L2 regularization, and rotational invariance. *Proceedings of the 21st International Conference on Machine Learning (ICML)*.

Rajan, A., & Venkatraman, S. (2018). Cloud computing: A solution for AI scalability in big data analytics. *Journal of Cloud Computing, 7*(1), 1-15.

Rao, R., Pandey, S., & Shetty, M. (2020). Data management and scalability challenges in big data analytics. *Big Data Research, 21*(3), 1-12.

Shi, W., Cao, J., Zhang, Q., Li, Y., & Xu, L. (2016). Edge computing: Vision and challenges. *IEEE Internet of Things Journal, 3*(5), 637-646.

Stonebraker, M., Ilyas, I. F., Beskales, G., Cherniack, M., & Zdonik, S. (2015). Real-time big data analytics: Challenges and techniques. *Communications of the ACM, 58*(2), 56-66.

Zaharia, M., Chowdhury, M., Franklin, M. J., Shenker, S., & Stoica, I. (2016). Apache Spark: A unified engine for big data processing. *Communications of the ACM, 59*(11), 56-65.

Chapter 24: Model Deployment and MLOps

<u>Continuous Integration and Deployment</u>

As organizations adopt machine learning (ML) at scale, model deployment and lifecycle management become critical components of the operationalization process. Continuous Integration (CI) and Continuous Deployment (CD) are core principles in modern software engineering and are increasingly applied to machine learning workflows through MLOps (Machine Learning Operations). These practices help streamline the development, testing, and deployment of ML models, ensuring that they are reliable, scalable, and integrated seamlessly into production environments. CI/CD for ML models addresses the challenges of updating models, monitoring performance, and handling real-time data, while promoting collaboration between data scientists, engineers, and operations teams.

1. Understanding Continuous Integration and Deployment (CI/CD) in MLOps

Continuous Integration (CI) refers to the practice of regularly integrating code changes into a shared repository, where automated tests are run to ensure that the changes do not introduce errors. In the context of machine learning, CI involves integrating model code, configuration files, data pipelines, and dependencies into a central repository. Each integration is verified by running automated tests on both the model code and the data, ensuring that changes maintain the integrity of the model.

Continuous Deployment (CD) extends this concept by automating the process of deploying models into production environments. Once the code passes all the necessary tests in the CI phase, the model is automatically deployed, reducing the time and effort needed to push updates into production. CD ensures that new models, or updated versions of existing models, are deployed seamlessly into production systems, without disrupting operations.

CI in MLOps: Continuous integration in MLOps involves version control of not only the model code but also the data and configuration files used during model training. Automated tests are essential for verifying the correctness of these components, including the performance of the model on validation data. Tools like Jenkins, GitLab CI, and CircleCI are commonly used in CI pipelines to automate the building and testing of machine learning codebases (Sato et al., 2019). In MLOps, CI also ensures that model retraining is triggered automatically when new data arrives, or when changes to the model code are made.

CD in MLOps: Continuous deployment automates the process of pushing ML models from staging to production. This often involves deploying models as services via APIs or integrating them into larger applications or systems. Kubernetes and Docker are widely used for containerizing models, enabling easy scaling and deployment across various environments (Karmakar et al., 2020). CD pipelines ensure that as soon as a model is validated and tested, it is deployed into production automatically, minimizing human intervention and reducing the risk of errors during deployment.

2. Benefits of CI/CD in Machine Learning Operations

Implementing CI/CD in machine learning offers several benefits, especially when scaling ML solutions across multiple teams and production environments. These benefits include faster time-to-market, improved collaboration, continuous monitoring, and the ability to rapidly adapt to new data and business needs.

Faster Time-to-Market: By automating the integration and deployment of machine learning models, CI/CD pipelines reduce the time it takes to move a model from development to production. This is especially important in industries such as finance, healthcare, and e-commerce, where rapid deployment of predictive models can provide a competitive advantage. Automated deployment pipelines help teams iterate quickly on models and deploy them into production in hours or days, rather than weeks (Breuel, 2015).

Improved Collaboration: CI/CD in MLOps fosters collaboration between data scientists, engineers, and DevOps teams by standardizing workflows and automating repetitive tasks. This reduces friction between teams and promotes a shared understanding of the model development and deployment process. Version control systems such as Git ensure that teams can collaborate on model code and track changes over time, while CI/CD tools automate testing and integration processes, leading to more efficient workflows (Sculley et al., 2015).

Continuous Monitoring and Performance Tracking: Once models are deployed into production, CI/CD pipelines support continuous monitoring and performance tracking. Automated monitoring tools can track key performance metrics, such as prediction accuracy, latency, and resource usage, enabling teams to detect model drift or performance degradation early. When performance issues arise, the CI/CD pipeline can automatically trigger retraining or redeployment of the model with updated data or parameters (Karmakar et al., 2020).

Adaptation to New Data: In many real-world applications, the underlying data distribution may change over time (a phenomenon known as data drift), affecting the performance of machine learning models. CI/CD pipelines enable rapid adaptation to new data by automating the retraining and redeployment of models. When new data becomes available, the pipeline can trigger model retraining, validate the updated model, and deploy it to production without manual intervention. This ensures that models remain relevant and accurate even as data evolves (Sato et al., 2019).

3. Key Components of CI/CD in MLOps

Building an effective CI/CD pipeline for machine learning involves several key components, each designed to streamline the process of integrating, testing, and deploying models. These components include version control, automated testing, model validation, containerization, and monitoring.

Version Control: Version control is a foundational element of CI in MLOps. It ensures that code, model configurations, and data are tracked and versioned, allowing teams to collaborate effectively and reproduce past results if needed. Git is a widely used version control system for managing changes in code and configurations. In MLOps, version control also extends to data and models, ensuring that changes to datasets or model weights are tracked and can be rolled back if necessary (Sculley et al., 2015).

Automated Testing: Automated testing is crucial for maintaining model performance and reliability as changes are made to the code or data pipeline. Unit tests validate that individual components of the model (e.g., feature extraction, data preprocessing) function as expected. Integration tests verify that the model works as a whole, including its interactions with external systems like databases or APIs. Automated testing tools such as PyTest, TensorFlow Test, and CI/CD services like Jenkins ensure that models are thoroughly tested before being deployed (Sato et al., 2019).

Model Validation: In the CI phase of MLOps, model validation is essential to ensure that the newly trained model meets performance expectations. This involves comparing the new model's performance metrics, such as accuracy, precision, recall, or AUC (area under the ROC curve), against baseline models or previously deployed versions. If the new model meets or exceeds performance thresholds, it can proceed to deployment. Automated validation ensures that only models that demonstrate improved or consistent performance are deployed (Karmakar et al., 2020).

Containerization: Containerization tools such as Docker and orchestration platforms like Kubernetes are commonly used in CD pipelines to package machine learning models along with their dependencies. Containers ensure that models run consistently across different environments (development, staging, production), regardless of the underlying hardware or software configurations. Kubernetes helps manage the deployment, scaling, and maintenance of these containers in production, enabling teams to handle fluctuating workloads and resource demands efficiently (Breuel, 2015).

Monitoring and Logging: Once a model is deployed, continuous monitoring and logging are essential for tracking its performance in production. Monitoring tools like Prometheus and Grafana allow teams to set up alerts for performance degradation, such as increased prediction errors or latency, which can indicate data drift or model decay. These insights can trigger the CD pipeline to retrain or redeploy the model as needed, ensuring that models maintain optimal performance over time (Sculley et al., 2015).

4. Challenges and Best Practices for CI/CD in Machine Learning

Implementing CI/CD for machine learning introduces several challenges, such as managing data dependencies, ensuring reproducibility, and handling model-specific issues like drift or performance decay. To overcome these challenges, organizations must follow best practices tailored to the unique requirements of machine learning workflows.

Data Dependency Management: One of the biggest challenges in CI/CD for machine learning is managing data dependencies. Unlike traditional software, where code is the primary artifact, machine learning relies heavily on data. Changes in data can have a significant impact on model performance, making it essential to version datasets and track data changes alongside model code. Tools like DVC (Data

Version Control) help manage data dependencies in CI/CD pipelines, ensuring that data changes are tracked and integrated seamlessly (Sculley et al., 2015).

Ensuring Reproducibility: Reproducibility is critical in machine learning, especially when models are retrained frequently. By using version control, containerization, and automated pipelines, teams can ensure that models are reproducible across different environments and timeframes. Documenting dependencies, environment configurations, and hyperparameters is also essential for maintaining reproducibility (Breuel, 2015).

Handling Model Drift: Model drift occurs when the performance of a machine learning model degrades over time due to changes in the underlying data. To handle model drift effectively, CI/CD pipelines should include monitoring tools that track performance metrics and identify when models no longer meet performance thresholds. When drift is detected, the pipeline can trigger automated retraining or redeployment to maintain model accuracy and reliability (Sato et al., 2019).

In summary, Continuous Integration and Continuous Deployment (CI/CD) are foundational practices in MLOps that ensure machine learning models are integrated, tested, and deployed efficiently and reliably. By automating the integration of model code, data pipelines, and model validation, CI/CD pipelines streamline the deployment process, reduce the risk of errors, and allow teams to scale their machine learning solutions more effectively. Implementing CI/CD for machine learning requires version control, automated testing, containerization, and monitoring, along with strategies to manage data dependencies and model drift.

Monitoring and Maintenance

Once machine learning (ML) models are deployed into production, continuous monitoring and maintenance are critical for ensuring that they perform reliably over time. In production environments, ML models are subject to various dynamic factors, including data drift, model degradation, and changes in business needs. Monitoring helps detect performance issues early, while maintenance practices ensure that models remain accurate, efficient, and compliant with organizational and regulatory requirements. Effective monitoring and maintenance are essential components of MLOps (Machine Learning Operations), a discipline that combines best practices from DevOps with ML lifecycle management to streamline the deployment, monitoring, and maintenance of models.

1. The Importance of Monitoring in MLOps

Monitoring is a continuous process of tracking the performance of ML models in production. Unlike traditional software, ML models face unique challenges, such as model drift, data quality issues, and evolving patterns in the underlying data. Monitoring helps ensure that models deliver accurate predictions and that their performance aligns with the original objectives.

Model Performance Monitoring: After deployment, the performance of ML models can degrade over time due to changes in the data distribution (data drift), variations in feature relevance, or shifts in real-world patterns (model drift). Monitoring performance metrics such as accuracy, precision, recall, F1-score, and area under the ROC curve (AUC) allows teams to track how well the model continues to meet its performance benchmarks. For example, if a fraud detection model begins to miss more fraudulent transactions, it signals a need for retraining or adjustment (Gama et al., 2014). Continuous monitoring helps identify performance drops before they have significant business impacts.

Latency and Throughput Monitoring: In production environments where real-time predictions are required (e.g., in autonomous vehicles, e-commerce recommendations, or stock trading), latency and throughput are key performance indicators (KPIs). Latency refers to the time taken for the model to generate a prediction after receiving input data, while throughput measures the number of predictions made in a given time period. Monitoring these metrics ensures that the model meets performance requirements in terms of speed and scalability (Breck et al., 2017). High latency or reduced throughput can indicate underlying infrastructure issues or model inefficiencies that need to be addressed.

Data Quality Monitoring: Monitoring the quality of the data fed into the model is essential for maintaining its performance. Poor data quality - such as missing, corrupted, or incorrectly formatted data - can negatively impact model accuracy. Monitoring tools can track the distribution of input data and flag discrepancies that could lead to performance degradation (Kreuzberger et al., 2022). Additionally, tools that detect anomalies in data can prevent incorrect or unexpected data from affecting model predictions.

2. Detecting and Addressing Model Drift

Model drift occurs when an ML model's performance declines due to changes in the underlying data distribution over time. This phenomenon, also known as concept drift, is common in production environments where data evolves due to shifts in consumer behavior, market trends, or operational changes. Detecting and addressing model drift is essential to maintaining the reliability and accuracy of ML models.

Data Drift Detection: Data drift refers to changes in the statistical properties of the input data, such as feature distributions or correlations between features. When data drift occurs, the model may receive inputs that differ significantly from the data it was trained on, leading to poor predictions. Tools such as Kolmogorov-Smirnov tests, covariance shifts, and probability distribution comparisons can help detect when input data distributions deviate from historical patterns (Gama et al., 2014). Once detected, teams can retrain the model using updated data to restore its performance.

Concept Drift Detection: Concept drift refers to changes in the relationship between input features and the target variable. For example, in a credit risk model, factors that once predicted default (e.g., income level or job stability) may change as the economy evolves. Tools like adaptive windowing techniques and incremental learning algorithms can help detect concept drift by continuously updating model parameters based on new data (Lu et al., 2019). Once detected, retraining or fine-tuning the model is necessary to align it with the new data relationships.

3. Automated Monitoring and Alerting Systems

Automated monitoring systems are critical for identifying and responding to performance issues in real time. These systems enable proactive maintenance by automatically tracking model metrics, detecting anomalies, and sending alerts when performance thresholds are violated.

Monitoring Tools: There are various tools and platforms available for automated monitoring of ML models in production, including Prometheus, Grafana, and specialized MLOps platforms like MLflow, Kubeflow, and Seldon. These tools allow teams to define KPIs and set thresholds for model performance metrics. When the model's performance deviates from these thresholds, alerts are generated, prompting immediate action (Breck et al., 2017).

Automated Retraining Triggers: In advanced MLOps workflows, monitoring systems can automatically trigger model retraining when performance declines. For example, if a model's accuracy drops below a predefined threshold due to data drift, the system can trigger the retraining process using the latest data. This reduces the need for manual intervention and ensures that models remain up-to-date with evolving data trends. Automated retraining can be scheduled at regular intervals or triggered based on specific performance metrics (Sculley et al., 2015).

4. Model Maintenance and Retraining

Monitoring alone is insufficient to keep models performing at their best - ongoing maintenance and retraining are necessary to address issues like drift, data quality, and performance degradation. MLOps teams must adopt a proactive approach to maintaining models over time.

Scheduled Retraining: One approach to model maintenance is scheduled retraining, where models are periodically retrained using fresh data to keep them aligned with current conditions. This can be particularly useful in industries where data evolves rapidly, such as finance, retail, or healthcare. By regularly updating models with new data, organizations can ensure that their models reflect the latest trends and behaviors (Kreuzberger et al., 2022).

Model Versioning and A/B Testing: Model versioning is an essential aspect of maintaining ML models in production. It allows organizations to track different versions of a model and roll back to a previous version if the latest one fails to perform adequately. A/B testing, where two versions of a model are deployed simultaneously and compared based on real-world performance, is a best practice for ensuring that newly deployed models perform better than the previous ones (Sculley et al., 2015). This method helps prevent performance degradation caused by poorly optimized models.

Handling Model Staleness: Over time, models can become stale if they are not updated to reflect changes in the business environment, regulatory requirements, or customer preferences. Regularly reviewing and updating models to reflect new business objectives or external conditions is crucial for maintaining their relevance and effectiveness (Breck et al., 2017). In cases where models become obsolete, retraining or redeveloping new models may be necessary to meet evolving requirements.

5. Best Practices for Monitoring and Maintenance in MLOps

To ensure that models perform optimally in production, organizations should follow best practices for monitoring and maintenance as part of their MLOps workflows.

Define Performance Metrics and Thresholds: Clearly defining performance metrics and acceptable thresholds for accuracy, latency, throughput, and other KPIs is essential for effective monitoring. These thresholds help teams quickly identify when a model's performance begins to degrade and needs attention (Gama et al., 2014). The metrics should align with business objectives and the specific use case of the model.

Implement Real-Time Monitoring: Real-time monitoring systems allow teams to detect issues and anomalies as they happen, enabling faster response times. These systems should be integrated into the MLOps pipeline, ensuring that model performance is tracked continuously from the moment of deployment (Breck et al., 2017).

Automate Retraining and Deployment: Automating the retraining and redeployment of models ensures that performance issues are addressed quickly and with minimal human intervention. By automating these processes, organizations can reduce the risk of downtime or poor performance and maintain a higher level of reliability in production (Sculley et al., 2015).

Maintain Robust Documentation: Proper documentation of model configurations, performance metrics, and retraining cycles is vital for ensuring that models can be monitored and maintained effectively over time. This documentation should include details about the data used for training, the algorithms and hyperparameters chosen, and any changes made during retraining (Kreuzberger et al., 2022).

In summary, monitoring and maintenance are crucial components of the MLOps lifecycle, ensuring that machine learning models remain reliable, accurate, and efficient after deployment. Continuous monitoring allows teams to track model performance, detect data and concept drift, and address latency or throughput issues. Automated monitoring and alerting systems enable proactive model maintenance, while retraining and updating models help prevent performance degradation. By adopting best practices for monitoring and maintenance, organizations can ensure that their ML models continue to deliver value and align with business objectives over time.

Model Versioning and Reproducibility

Model versioning and reproducibility are critical components of deploying machine learning (ML) models in production environments. As machine learning models evolve due to retraining, parameter adjustments, or improvements in data quality, maintaining multiple versions of models and ensuring that their results are reproducible is essential. Model versioning provides a structured way to manage, compare, and track changes to models, while reproducibility ensures that a model's outputs can be consistently replicated across different environments and time periods. These practices are foundational to Machine Learning Operations (MLOps), a discipline that integrates machine learning, DevOps, and data engineering practices to streamline the deployment and maintenance of ML models.

1. The Importance of Model Versioning in MLOps

Model versioning refers to the process of maintaining different versions of machine learning models, including changes to model architecture, hyperparameters, training data, and other configurations. In complex production environments where models are retrained or updated frequently, versioning is critical for ensuring transparency, traceability, and accountability.

Tracking Model Evolution: As models undergo continuous development, it is crucial to keep track of every change, including adjustments to algorithms, parameters, and datasets. Without versioning, it becomes difficult to revert to earlier, more reliable versions if newer models perform poorly or introduce errors in production. Versioning allows organizations to maintain a history of changes and revisit earlier models when necessary (Sculley et al., 2015). In highly regulated industries, such as finance or healthcare, model versioning is often required for auditing purposes, ensuring compliance with legal and regulatory standards.

Managing Multiple Models in Production: Many organizations deploy multiple models simultaneously for different tasks, or even for the same task in different contexts. For example, a retail company may deploy different recommendation engines for different customer segments. Model versioning allows teams to manage multiple models in production, track performance across versions, and experiment with different approaches while maintaining control over model updates (Breck et al., 2017). In the event of performance degradation, version control allows teams to roll back to a previous model without significant disruptions.

Experiment Tracking and Comparison: Model versioning is essential for comparing different experiments and configurations. When teams are testing multiple model architectures or hyperparameter settings, versioning systems enable them to systematically track each experiment's results. This is especially useful in model selection, where teams need to compare various models based on performance metrics and select the best candidate for deployment. Tools like MLflow, DVC (Data Version Control), and Git provide functionality for tracking and managing different model versions and their associated data and configurations (Zaharia et al., 2018).

2. Best Practices for Model Versioning

Implementing effective model versioning practices in MLOps requires a structured approach that integrates model code, data, and artifacts. Several best practices can help organizations manage model versioning efficiently:

Version Everything (Code, Data, Models): In machine learning workflows, not only should the model code be versioned, but also the data, model configurations, and dependencies. This ensures that every part of the workflow can be tracked and reproduced. Using tools like Git for code, DVC for data, and MLflow for models allows teams to version all relevant components of the machine learning pipeline (Sculley et al., 2015). This holistic versioning strategy is essential for debugging and replicating models at different stages of development.

Automated Versioning: Automation plays a key role in ensuring that model versioning is consistent and error-free. Automating the versioning process through Continuous Integration (CI) pipelines ensures that every time a model is trained or updated, a new version is created, documented, and stored in a version control system. Automated versioning reduces the risk of manual errors and guarantees that all model updates are properly tracked (Breck et al., 2017).

Model Metadata and Artifacts: Storing metadata and artifacts associated with each model version is critical for understanding the conditions under which a model was created. Metadata includes information about the model's architecture, hyperparameters, training dataset, and performance metrics. This information is essential for comparing model versions and understanding why one version may perform better than another. Storing artifacts such as model weights, feature importance scores, and evaluation results ensures that models can be retrained or re-evaluated when needed (Kreuzberger et al., 2022).

Consistent Naming Conventions: Establishing a consistent naming convention for model versions helps teams keep track of different versions easily. This convention should include key identifiers such as the model name, version number, date of creation, and any special configurations or changes applied. For example, a versioning scheme might look like model_v1.2.20230915, where v1.2 refers to the version, and the date indicates when the model was trained or updated. Clear and consistent naming helps avoid confusion when managing multiple models in production (Sculley et al., 2015).

3. Reproducibility in Machine Learning

Reproducibility in machine learning refers to the ability to replicate the results of a model by following the same process and using the same data, code, and configurations. In production environments, reproducibility is critical for ensuring the reliability and trustworthiness of machine learning models. A reproducible model enables teams to trace back to the conditions under which the model was trained, diagnose issues, and replicate its outputs across different environments.

Ensuring Model Reproducibility: Achieving reproducibility involves several practices, including controlling randomness, documenting all dependencies, and versioning data. Randomness in ML models (e.g., random initialization of weights, random shuffling of data) can lead to slightly different results across different runs. Controlling for randomness by setting fixed random seeds ensures that the model produces consistent outputs. Additionally, documenting software dependencies, environment configurations (e.g., Python versions, library versions), and hardware used in training helps ensure that models can be replicated on different systems (Pineau et al., 2020).

Data Reproducibility: One of the most challenging aspects of reproducibility in machine learning is ensuring that the same data is used across different experiments. Versioning datasets ensures that changes in the data are tracked, and models can be retrained or reevaluated using the exact same version of the data. Tools like DVC and Git LFS (Large File Storage) allow teams to version datasets efficiently, ensuring data consistency across different environments and timeframes (Zaharia et al., 2018).

Reproducing Results in Different Environments: Machine learning models must be reproducible across different environments, including local development environments, staging, and production. Using containerization tools like Docker allows teams to package models with all their dependencies, ensuring that they can be deployed and run consistently across various environments (Breck et al., 2017). Docker ensures that model training and inference environments are identical, reducing the likelihood of discrepancies due to differences in software or hardware configurations.

4. Challenges and Solutions for Model Versioning and Reproducibility

While model versioning and reproducibility are critical for production-grade machine learning systems, they also present several challenges. Addressing these challenges requires robust tools, processes, and best practices.

Managing Large Numbers of Models: In large-scale deployments, managing hundreds or even thousands of model versions can become overwhelming. To address this challenge, organizations should implement automated model management tools that allow for easy tracking, searching, and comparison of models. Tools like MLflow, TensorFlow Extended (TFX), and Kubeflow provide model management features that support efficient versioning and monitoring of models in production (Zaharia et al., 2018).

Ensuring Data Consistency: Data consistency is a significant challenge in model reproducibility, especially when working with large, constantly changing datasets. Versioning data, along with the code and models, ensures that every part of the workflow is reproducible. Solutions such as data versioning tools (e.g., DVC) or even using snapshot databases that capture the state of the data at a specific point in time can help ensure data consistency (Kreuzberger et al., 2022).

Balancing Flexibility and Control: In machine learning workflows, balancing flexibility for experimentation with control for versioning and reproducibility can be difficult. Data scientists often need to iterate rapidly on models, making frequent changes. To avoid errors, organizations should establish clear guidelines on when and how to version models, such as after significant changes or before deployment into production. Automating the versioning process can help maintain control without hindering experimentation (Sculley et al., 2015).

In summary, model versioning and reproducibility are essential components of MLOps, enabling organizations to manage machine learning models effectively throughout their lifecycle. By implementing best practices for model versioning—such as versioning code, data, and model artifacts—teams can ensure transparency, traceability, and the ability to compare different model versions. Reproducibility is equally important, as it allows models to be consistently replicated across different environments, ensuring reliability and performance. Tools like Git, DVC, MLflow, and Docker, combined with clear processes for managing version control and dependencies, are critical for maintaining robust model versioning and reproducibility systems. In a production environment where models evolve continuously, these practices are foundational for maintaining trust, compliance, and operational efficiency.

Tools for MLOps

As organizations increasingly adopt machine learning (ML) at scale, the need for streamlined processes to manage the development, deployment, and maintenance of models has led to the rise of MLOps (Machine Learning Operations). MLOps is a set of best practices combining machine learning with DevOps to facilitate automation, collaboration, monitoring, and governance of ML models throughout their lifecycle. Tools like Kubeflow and MLflow have become essential in implementing MLOps workflows by providing platforms for managing machine learning pipelines, versioning models, tracking experiments, and automating deployment. These tools enable organizations to scale their AI operations while maintaining consistency, reliability, and reproducibility in production environments.

1. Kubeflow: A Platform for Scalable MLOps on Kubernetes

Kubeflow is an open-source platform designed to streamline machine learning workflows by leveraging Kubernetes for orchestration, scalability, and resource management. Originally developed by Google, Kubeflow provides a comprehensive suite of tools for building, deploying, and managing machine learning models at scale. Its integration with Kubernetes enables users to deploy and manage machine learning workloads in containerized environments, providing portability and scalability across different cloud and on-premises infrastructures (Bisong, 2019).

Orchestration and Pipelines: One of Kubeflow's core strengths is its ability to orchestrate end-to-end machine learning workflows using Kubeflow Pipelines. These pipelines allow data scientists to define, deploy, and manage reusable ML workflows, automating tasks like data preprocessing, model training, evaluation, and deployment. Pipelines can be designed using a visual interface or via code, enabling teams to experiment with different workflows while maintaining consistency and reusability. Kubeflow Pipelines also support experiment tracking, which helps teams compare model performance across different configurations and data sets (L'Heureux et al., 2020).

Scalability and Resource Management: Since Kubeflow runs on Kubernetes, it inherits Kubernetes' powerful features for managing resources, such as horizontal scaling, load balancing, and scheduling.

This makes it ideal for handling large-scale machine learning workloads that require substantial computational resources, such as deep learning model training or distributed data processing. Kubeflow ensures that models can scale up or down as needed, optimizing resource utilization and cost-efficiency, particularly in cloud environments (Schatsky et al., 2020).

Model Deployment: Kubeflow provides several tools for deploying machine learning models to production. The Kubeflow KFServing component enables serverless deployment of models on Kubernetes, allowing models to scale automatically based on demand. KFServing supports multiple frameworks, including TensorFlow, PyTorch, and XGBoost, and simplifies the deployment process by managing scaling, monitoring, and rolling updates. This ensures that models can be deployed reliably in production environments, whether for batch inference or real-time serving (Bisong, 2019).

Integration with CI/CD: Kubeflow supports the integration of continuous integration and continuous deployment (CI/CD) pipelines, allowing teams to automate the entire ML lifecycle. By integrating with CI/CD tools such as Jenkins and Argo, Kubeflow can automate model retraining, testing, and deployment based on triggers such as new data or performance thresholds. This ensures that models remain up-to-date and responsive to changes in data or business requirements (L'Heureux et al., 2020).

2. MLflow: A Framework for Experiment Tracking, Versioning, and Deployment

MLflow is another popular open-source platform designed to manage the entire machine learning lifecycle, from experimentation and tracking to model deployment. Developed by Databricks, MLflow provides a lightweight and flexible framework that can be integrated with various machine learning libraries and infrastructure. Its primary components - MLflow Tracking, MLflow Projects, MLflow Models, and MLflow Registry - offer a comprehensive suite of tools for managing machine learning workflows and promoting collaboration across data science and engineering teams (Zaharia et al., 2018).

Experiment Tracking with MLflow: One of MLflow's key features is its ability to track experiments and log important metadata about model training runs. MLflow Tracking allows users to log parameters, metrics, and artifacts for each model training experiment, making it easy to compare different runs and configurations. This is particularly useful when experimenting with hyperparameter tuning or evaluating different machine learning algorithms. By providing a central repository for tracking experiments, MLflow enables reproducibility and accountability, ensuring that teams can trace back to the conditions under which a model was trained (Zaharia et al., 2018).

Model Versioning and Reproducibility: MLflow supports model versioning through its MLflow Models and MLflow Registry components. MLflow Models allows users to save and serve models in a standardized format, which can be deployed to various platforms, including cloud services and on-premises infrastructure. The MLflow Registry, on the other hand, acts as a centralized model store, enabling teams to version, manage, and govern models across different stages of development (development, staging, production). This is critical for ensuring that models are reproducible and that different versions can be compared and rolled back if necessary (Bisong, 2019).

Model Deployment with MLflow: MLflow provides several deployment options, making it easy to deploy models into production. With MLflow Models, users can deploy models to REST-based endpoints for real-time serving or integrate with cloud platforms like AWS SageMaker, Google AI Platform, or Microsoft Azure ML for scalable deployment. Additionally, MLflow supports Docker-based deployments, which allow teams to package models along with their dependencies into containers, ensuring consistency and portability across environments (Zaharia et al., 2018).

Integration with Existing ML Libraries: MLflow is designed to work with a wide variety of machine learning libraries and frameworks, including TensorFlow, PyTorch, Scikit-learn, and XGBoost. This flexibility allows teams to use MLflow within their existing machine learning workflows without requiring major changes to their codebase. MLflow also supports logging custom metrics and models, making it highly adaptable to various use cases and environments (Schelter et al., 2020).

3. Kubeflow vs. MLflow: Choosing the Right Tool for MLOps

While both Kubeflow and MLflow provide robust MLOps capabilities, they are designed for different purposes and have unique strengths. The choice between the two tools depends on the specific needs of the organization, the complexity of the machine learning workloads, and the infrastructure in place.

Scalability and Orchestration: Kubeflow excels in environments that require high scalability and orchestration, particularly in cloud-native or Kubernetes-based infrastructures. Its tight integration with Kubernetes allows for managing distributed workloads, enabling teams to run complex, large-scale pipelines. Kubeflow is ideal for organizations looking to build end-to-end ML workflows that need to scale across multiple machines or nodes (Schatsky et al., 2020).

Experiment Tracking and Flexibility: MLflow's strength lies in its simplicity and flexibility. MLflow is a great choice for teams that need a lightweight solution for experiment tracking, model versioning, and deployment across various environments. Its integration with multiple machine learning libraries and deployment options makes it suitable for organizations that want to maintain flexibility in their ML infrastructure without committing to a specific platform like Kubernetes (Zaharia et al., 2018).

Complexity and Setup: Kubeflow, being Kubernetes-based, requires a more complex setup and is better suited for teams with experience in Kubernetes and container orchestration. In contrast, MLflow has a simpler setup and can be deployed on a single machine or within a cloud environment with minimal overhead, making it easier for teams that are new to MLOps or do not have Kubernetes expertise (L'Heureux et al., 2020).

4. Best Practices for Using Kubeflow and MLflow in MLOps

To get the most out of Kubeflow and MLflow, organizations should follow best practices for integrating these tools into their MLOps workflows:

Automate CI/CD for Model Deployment: Both Kubeflow and MLflow can be integrated with CI/CD pipelines to automate the retraining, testing, and deployment of models. Setting up automated workflows ensures that models are continuously updated and that any changes to data or code are reflected in production in a timely manner (Breck et al., 2017).

Track and Version All Artifacts: Experiment tracking and model versioning are essential for maintaining reproducibility and ensuring that model results can be compared across different runs. Organizations should ensure that all model artifacts, data, configurations, and metrics are logged and versioned consistently using either Kubeflow or MLflow (Zaharia et al., 2018).

Leverage Containerization for Portability: Whether using Kubeflow or MLflow, containerization should be a key component of the deployment strategy. Docker containers ensure that models can be run consistently across different environments, whether in local development, testing, or production. Tools like Docker and Kubernetes (in Kubeflow) or Docker with MLflow can help achieve this portability (Schelter et al., 2020).

Conclusion

Kubeflow and MLflow are two powerful tools that support the implementation of MLOps by providing essential functionality for building, deploying, and maintaining machine learning models at scale. While Kubeflow excels in orchestrating complex ML workflows in Kubernetes-based environments, MLflow provides a more flexible and lightweight approach to experiment tracking, model versioning, and deployment. Choosing the right tool depends on the organization's infrastructure, scalability needs, and expertise. By integrating these tools into MLOps workflows and following best practices, organizations can improve the efficiency, scalability, and reproducibility of their machine learning operations.

References

Bisong, E. (2019). *Kubeflow for machine learning: From lab to production.* Apress. https://doi.org/10.1007/978-1-4842-4470-8

Breck, E., Cai, S., Nielsen, E., Salib, M., & Sculley, D. (2017). The ML test score: A rubric for ML production readiness and technical debt reduction. *Proceedings of the 2017 IEEE International Conference on Big Data*, 1123-1132.

Breuel, T. M. (2015). Implementing and scaling deep learning applications in the cloud. *Communications of the ACM, 58*(10), 38-41.

Gama, J., Žliobaitė, I., Bifet, A., Pechenizkiy, M., & Bouchachia, A. (2014). A survey on concept drift adaptation. *ACM Computing Surveys (CSUR), 46*(4), 1-37.

Karmakar, A., Maiti, S., & Konar, D. (2020). MLOps: Machine learning as an operations tool for scaling and monitoring. *International Journal of Software Engineering & Applications, 11*(2), 29-38.

Kreuzberger, D., Kühl, N., & Satzger, G. (2022). Machine learning operations (MLOps): Overview, definition, and architecture. *Proceedings of the 55th Hawaii International Conference on System Sciences (HICSS)*, 5452-5461.

L'Heureux, A., Grolinger, K., Elyamany, H. F., & Capretz, M. A. M. (2020). Machine learning with big data: Challenges and approaches. *IEEE Access, 5*, 7776-7797.

Lu, J., Liu, A., Dong, F., Gu, F., Gama, J., & Zhang, G. (2019). Learning under concept drift: A review. *IEEE Transactions on Knowledge and Data Engineering, 31*(12), 2346-2363.

Pineau, J., Vincent-Lamarre, P., Sinha, K., Larivière, V., Beygelzimer, A., d'Alché-Buc, F., ... & Hynes, N. (2020). Improving reproducibility in machine learning research: A report from the NeurIPS 2019 reproducibility program. *Journal of Machine Learning Research, 21*(1), 1-20.

Sato, M., Ng, P., & Wu, T. (2019). Continuous integration and continuous deployment for machine learning. *Proceedings of the 2019 IEEE/ACM International Workshop on Continuous Software Evolution and Delivery*, 5-11.

Schatsky, D., Muraskin, C., & Gurumurthy, R. (2020). Demystifying artificial intelligence: What business leaders need to know about AI. *Deloitte Insights*. Retrieved from https://www2.deloitte.com/insights/us/en.html

Schelter, S., Böse, J.-H., Kirschnick, J., Klein, T., & Seufert, S. (2020). Automatically tracking metadata and provenance of machine learning experiments. *Proceedings of the 29th ACM International Conference on Information & Knowledge Management (CIKM)*, 4-9.

Sculley, D., Holt, G., Golovin, D., Davydov, E., Phillips, T., Ebner, D., ... & Young, M. (2015). Hidden technical debt in machine learning systems. *Advances in Neural Information Processing Systems, 28*, 2503-2511.

Zaharia, M., Chen, A., Davidson, A., Ghodsi, A., Hong, M., Konwinski, A., ... & Stoica, I. (2018). Accelerating the machine learning lifecycle with MLflow. *IEEE Data Engineering Bulletin, 41*(4), 39-45.

Chapter 25: Case Studies

Successful AI Implementations

The implementation of Artificial Intelligence (AI) has transformed various industries by optimizing operations, enhancing decision-making, and driving innovation. Successful AI implementations showcase the tangible benefits that AI technologies can bring to organizations, such as improving efficiency, increasing revenue, and enabling new business models. Case studies of successful AI applications provide valuable insights into how best practices in AI deployment, scaling, and integration can be applied in real-world scenarios. This section explores several prominent case studies of successful AI implementations across different industries, emphasizing the importance of strategy, infrastructure, and continuous improvement in achieving success.

1. AI in Healthcare: IBM Watson for Oncology

One of the most well-known AI implementations in healthcare is IBM Watson for Oncology, which uses AI to assist doctors in diagnosing cancer and recommending treatment options. This AI system analyzes vast amounts of medical literature, clinical data, and patient records to provide oncologists with personalized treatment recommendations based on the latest medical knowledge.

Implementation and Challenges: IBM Watson for Oncology was developed by training the AI system on millions of pages of medical data, clinical trials, and journal articles. Using natural language processing (NLP) and machine learning algorithms, Watson is able to interpret unstructured data and provide insights to healthcare professionals. The challenge in implementing this system was ensuring that the AI's recommendations were evidence-based and aligned with current clinical practices, which required continuous updates to the model and data (Schatsky et al., 2020).

Outcome: Watson for Oncology has been successfully deployed in hospitals worldwide, including partnerships with institutions such as the Memorial Sloan Kettering Cancer Center in New York. The AI has significantly reduced the time it takes for oncologists to research and formulate treatment plans, improving patient outcomes by providing data-driven, personalized care. However, the success of the system also highlights the importance of complementing AI with human expertise, as doctors are required to make the final decisions based on Watson's recommendations (Schatsky et al., 2020).

2. AI in Retail: Amazon's Recommendation System

Amazon's recommendation system is one of the most successful AI implementations in the retail industry, driving a significant portion of the company's revenue by offering personalized product recommendations to users. The recommendation engine uses collaborative filtering, machine learning, and AI techniques to predict what products customers might be interested in based on their browsing history, purchase behavior, and the behavior of similar users.

Implementation and Challenges: Amazon's recommendation system processes massive amounts of data in real-time, making use of both item-based and user-based collaborative filtering algorithms to provide accurate suggestions. The system continuously updates its recommendations based on new customer data and interactions, ensuring that users receive relevant product suggestions at all times. The challenge for Amazon was scaling this AI system to handle billions of data points daily while ensuring low latency in delivering recommendations (Smith & Linden, 2017).

Outcome: Amazon's recommendation engine has been a key factor in the company's success, contributing to a significant increase in sales through cross-selling and upselling. By personalizing the shopping experience for each user, the AI system has helped Amazon improve customer satisfaction and loyalty. The recommendation system is estimated to drive 35% of Amazon's total revenue, making it one of the most valuable AI-driven tools in the retail sector (Smith & Linden, 2017).

3. AI in Finance: JPMorgan Chase's COiN Platform

In the financial sector, JPMorgan Chase has successfully implemented AI to automate the review and interpretation of complex legal documents. The Contract Intelligence (COiN) platform uses natural language processing to analyze and extract key information from legal agreements, including terms, clauses, and risk factors. COiN has revolutionized the way JPMorgan Chase processes legal documents, significantly reducing manual labor and increasing efficiency.

Implementation and Challenges: The COiN platform was developed by training AI models on thousands of legal contracts and agreements, allowing the system to learn how to identify relevant information and make accurate classifications. One of the key challenges was ensuring that the AI system could handle the ambiguity and complexity of legal language. This required continuous retraining of the models as new contract types and clauses were introduced (Kashyap, 2019).

Outcome: COiN has successfully automated the review of approximately 12,000 commercial credit agreements annually, a process that previously required 360,000 hours of human labor. By leveraging AI to reduce the time and cost associated with contract review, JPMorgan Chase has improved operational efficiency and reduced the risk of human error in legal document processing. The success of COiN demonstrates how AI can transform traditionally manual, labor-intensive processes in the finance industry (Kashyap, 2019).

4. AI in Transportation: Uber's Surge Pricing Algorithm

Uber's surge pricing algorithm is another successful AI implementation that optimizes pricing based on real-time supply and demand dynamics. The algorithm adjusts prices during times of high demand (e.g., rush hours, bad weather) to balance the supply of drivers and the demand from passengers. By increasing prices during these periods, Uber incentivizes more drivers to join the platform and meet demand, reducing wait times for customers.

Implementation and Challenges: Uber's surge pricing system relies on machine learning models that analyze real-time data from millions of users and drivers to predict demand patterns and adjust prices accordingly. The challenge for Uber was ensuring that the surge pricing system was perceived as fair by customers while also balancing the need to optimize revenue and driver availability. Uber has faced criticism for surge pricing during emergencies and natural disasters, prompting the company to refine its algorithms and communication strategies (Rosenblat & Stark, 2016).

Outcome: Despite initial concerns about fairness, Uber's surge pricing algorithm has been widely successful in managing demand and optimizing driver availability. The dynamic pricing model has become a core component of Uber's platform, helping the company maximize revenue and improve operational efficiency. Uber continues to refine its AI-driven pricing algorithms to improve customer experience and balance supply-demand fluctuations (Rosenblat & Stark, 2016).

5. AI in Manufacturing: Siemens' Predictive Maintenance System

In the manufacturing sector, Siemens has successfully implemented AI for predictive maintenance, which helps companies prevent equipment failures and reduce downtime by using AI algorithms to predict when machines are likely to fail. Siemens' AI-driven predictive maintenance system uses sensor data, historical performance data, and machine learning algorithms to identify patterns that indicate potential equipment failure.

Implementation and Challenges: Siemens' system collects vast amounts of sensor data from machines and uses machine learning algorithms to analyze this data in real-time. The system continuously monitors equipment performance, flagging potential issues before they lead to costly failures. One challenge was ensuring the accuracy of the predictive models, which required extensive training data and fine-tuning of the algorithms to account for different types of equipment and operating conditions (Tupa et al., 2017).

Outcome: Siemens' predictive maintenance system has been successfully deployed in various manufacturing plants, significantly reducing unplanned downtime and maintenance costs. The AI system has helped companies optimize their maintenance schedules, extend the lifespan of machinery, and improve overall operational efficiency. Siemens' success highlights the value of AI in transforming manufacturing processes by enabling proactive maintenance and minimizing disruptions (Tupa et al., 2017).

In summary, These case studies demonstrate how AI can be successfully implemented across diverse industries, leading to tangible benefits such as increased efficiency, improved decision-making, and reduced costs. IBM Watson for Oncology has revolutionized cancer treatment recommendations in healthcare, while Amazon's recommendation system has driven significant revenue growth in retail. JPMorgan Chase's COiN platform has automated labor-intensive legal processes in finance, Uber's surge pricing algorithm has optimized pricing and demand in transportation, and Siemens' predictive maintenance system has improved operational efficiency in manufacturing. Each case study highlights the importance of data, scalability, and continuous improvement in the successful implementation of AI solutions. Organizations looking to implement

AI can learn valuable lessons from these examples, ensuring that they adopt best practices for long-term success.

Lessons Learned from Failures

While there are numerous success stories in AI implementation, not all AI projects achieve the desired results. Failures in AI deployments offer critical learning opportunities, shedding light on challenges related to data quality, unrealistic expectations, lack of scalability, ethical concerns, and poor integration with business processes. Understanding the lessons learned from these failures is essential for organizations seeking to avoid common pitfalls in AI implementation and to ensure their projects are successful. This section discusses several prominent AI failures and the key lessons that can be extracted from these experiences to guide future AI projects.

1. Microsoft's Tay AI Chatbot: Importance of Ethical Considerations and Robust Monitoring

One of the most high-profile AI failures involved Microsoft's Tay, an AI chatbot that was launched on Twitter in 2016. Tay was designed to engage in conversations with users and learn from interactions. However, within 24 hours, the chatbot began posting offensive and inappropriate content after being manipulated by users who intentionally fed it harmful messages.

Failure Details: Tay's machine learning algorithms enabled it to learn from the data it received, but it lacked proper filters or ethical constraints to prevent it from mimicking offensive content. This oversight in ethical safeguards and monitoring allowed Tay to quickly spiral out of control, leading to its shutdown just 16 hours after launch (Neff & Nagy, 2016).

Lessons Learned: The Tay incident underscores the importance of incorporating ethical considerations and bias mitigation strategies into AI systems, especially those that interact with the public. Organizations must ensure that AI models are equipped with safeguards that prevent them from adopting harmful behaviors or outputs, and they should implement real-time monitoring to detect and mitigate inappropriate or unethical content. Additionally, AI systems should be designed to withstand adversarial attacks, especially in open platforms where users can intentionally exploit vulnerabilities (Neff & Nagy, 2016).

2. IBM Watson for Oncology: The Challenge of Over-Promising and Under-Delivering

IBM's Watson for Oncology was heralded as a groundbreaking AI system capable of revolutionizing cancer treatment by providing oncologists with personalized treatment recommendations based on vast medical knowledge. However, the project faced significant challenges and ultimately failed to deliver the promised results, leading to critical scrutiny.

Failure Details: While Watson for Oncology successfully processed vast amounts of medical literature, its recommendations often did not align with the actual clinical needs of patients. Reports surfaced indicating that Watson's recommendations were inconsistent and sometimes dangerous, stemming from the fact that its training data was primarily based on hypothetical scenarios rather than real patient data (Ross & Swetlitz, 2017). Additionally, the system struggled to adapt to diverse healthcare environments beyond the initial training data from Memorial Sloan Kettering Cancer Center.

Lessons Learned: The failure of Watson for Oncology highlights the dangers of over-promising AI capabilities without a deep understanding of the complexity of the real-world domain in which the AI is being applied. AI systems need to be trained on robust, high-quality data that is representative of the environments in which they will be used. Moreover, deploying AI in highly regulated fields like healthcare requires close collaboration with domain experts, rigorous testing, and continuous validation to ensure that the AI's recommendations are safe and effective. Overhyping the potential of

AI without acknowledging its limitations can damage the trust in AI technology and lead to financial losses and reputational damage (Ross & Swetlitz, 2017).

3. Google Flu Trends: The Limitations of Data Quality and Model Generalization

Google Flu Trends (GFT) was an ambitious project launched by Google in 2008 to track flu outbreaks based on users' search queries. The idea was that the frequency of flu-related searches could be used to predict the spread of influenza more accurately than traditional public health data. Initially, GFT was seen as a success, but over time, it became clear that the model was not as reliable as expected.

Failure Details: Google Flu Trends encountered two major problems: overfitting to search query data and the failure to generalize across different regions and flu seasons. The model was overly reliant on certain search terms, which led to significant errors when user behavior changed or when the volume of searches increased unpredictably. During the 2013 flu season, GFT famously overestimated the spread of the flu by 140%, resulting in a high-profile failure (Lazer et al., 2014).

Lessons Learned: GFT's failure demonstrates the risks of relying too heavily on correlational data without accounting for the complexity of the real world. Data quality and relevance are critical factors in AI projects, and overfitting to specific data points can lead to poor generalization in dynamic environments. AI models need to be flexible and adaptive, with mechanisms in place to reassess their performance over time. Moreover, integrating AI predictions with domain expertise, in this case public health officials, can help mitigate the risks of relying solely on AI-generated insights (Lazer et al., 2014).

4. Tesla's Autopilot Crashes: The Importance of Safety and Human Oversight

Tesla's Autopilot system, which provides semi-autonomous driving capabilities, has been a prominent example of AI deployment in the automotive industry. However, the system has been involved in multiple high-profile accidents, some of which were fatal, raising concerns about its safety and the potential for over-reliance on AI.

Failure Details: While Tesla's Autopilot is designed to assist drivers, it has been involved in accidents where the system failed to recognize obstacles or misinterpreted the driving environment. In several cases, drivers were found to have relied too heavily on the AI system, believing that it could handle complex driving tasks autonomously without human intervention (Goodall, 2019).

Lessons Learned: Tesla's Autopilot issues highlight the critical importance of human oversight and safety measures in AI systems that operate in high-risk environments. AI systems, particularly those involved in life-critical applications like autonomous driving, need to have clear limitations and fail-safes that require human intervention when necessary. Ensuring transparency about the capabilities and limitations of AI systems is essential to prevent users from overestimating the system's abilities, which can lead to catastrophic consequences. Moreover, continuous testing and regulatory oversight are necessary to ensure that these systems are safe for widespread deployment (Goodall, 2019).

5. UK A-level Grading Algorithm: Transparency and Fairness in AI Decision-Making

In 2020, the United Kingdom's Office of Qualifications and Examinations Regulation (Ofqual) implemented an AI algorithm to standardize A-level results after exams were canceled due to the COVID-19 pandemic. The algorithm aimed to adjust grades based on a variety of factors, including historical performance of schools.

However, the results were met with widespread criticism and backlash.

Failure Details: The grading algorithm disproportionately downgraded students from disadvantaged schools while favoring students from historically high-performing institutions. This resulted in accusations of bias and unfairness, leading to public protests and legal challenges. The government ultimately reversed the algorithm's decisions, opting to use teacher-assessed grades instead (O'Neil, 2020).

Lessons Learned: The UK A-level grading debacle demonstrates the importance of transparency, fairness, and stakeholder engagement when deploying AI systems that directly impact individuals' lives. AI algorithms that make decisions affecting people's opportunities must be carefully designed to ensure they do not perpetuate or exacerbate existing biases. Ensuring that AI systems are transparent, explainable, and subject to human oversight is crucial in maintaining public trust. Furthermore, involving affected stakeholders early in the design process can help identify potential issues and address fairness concerns before deployment (O'Neil, 2020).

In summary, These case studies illustrate that AI failures often stem from issues related to data quality, lack of transparency, unrealistic expectations, and inadequate safety measures. Organizations can learn valuable lessons from these failures to improve the robustness and reliability of their AI implementations. Key takeaways include the need for ethical safeguards, continuous monitoring, ensuring model generalization, transparency in decision-making, and human oversight in life-critical applications. By acknowledging these lessons and implementing best practices, organizations can mitigate the risks associated with AI deployment and increase the likelihood of success in future projects.

Comparative Analysis Across Industries

The adoption of Artificial Intelligence (AI) across industries has resulted in varying degrees of success, driven by differences in data availability, industry-specific challenges, regulatory requirements, and business objectives. A comparative analysis of AI implementations across industries such as healthcare, finance, retail, and manufacturing reveals key similarities and differences in the approaches, benefits, and challenges faced. By comparing these sectors, organizations can gain insights into best practices, scalability, and potential pitfalls, improving their own AI strategies.

1. Data Quality and Availability: Healthcare vs. Retail

One of the most significant factors affecting AI implementations across industries is the quality and availability of data. In healthcare, data is often siloed, fragmented, and subject to strict privacy regulations such as HIPAA (Health Insurance Portability and Accountability Act). This creates challenges for AI-driven innovations, such as those seen in IBM Watson for Oncology, where the lack of diverse and high-quality real-world data led to suboptimal performance (Ross & Swetlitz, 2017). In contrast, the retail industry enjoys more flexible access to customer data, enabling the development of highly accurate recommendation systems like Amazon's. Retailers can capture vast amounts of real-time customer data from online interactions, allowing AI systems to be more responsive and adaptive to customer preferences (Smith & Linden, 2017).

Healthcare: The sensitivity of patient data and the fragmented nature of healthcare systems make data integration and sharing more complex. For instance, the failure of IBM Watson for Oncology illustrates how training an AI model on limited data from a single institution led to poor generalization and reduced efficacy when applied to diverse patient populations (Ross & Swetlitz, 2017).

Retail: In contrast, retail platforms like Amazon can access detailed, real-time data from millions of users, enabling the development of personalized recommendation systems. These systems continually improve as more data becomes available, demonstrating the value of large, high-quality datasets in improving AI performance (Smith & Linden, 2017).

2. Regulatory and Ethical Considerations: Finance vs. Transportation

The finance and transportation industries face distinct regulatory and ethical challenges in deploying AI. In finance, AI systems must comply with stringent regulatory frameworks, such as the Dodd-Frank Act in the U.S. and GDPR (General Data Protection Regulation) in Europe, which govern data privacy, accountability, and fairness in algorithmic decision-making. AI implementations, such as JPMorgan Chase's COiN platform, have successfully automated processes like contract analysis while adhering to regulatory requirements (Kashyap, 2019). In contrast, AI in the transportation sector, particularly in autonomous vehicles like Tesla's Autopilot, faces ethical challenges related to safety and liability in decision-making.

Finance: The financial industry requires AI systems to operate within well-defined regulatory frameworks, ensuring fairness, accountability, and transparency. AI tools like COiN focus on automating labor-intensive tasks such as legal contract analysis, with significant cost and time savings. However, regulatory compliance is paramount, as errors in AI-driven financial decisions can lead to legal repercussions and reputational damage (Kashyap, 2019).

Transportation: In the transportation sector, AI-driven systems like Tesla's Autopilot face challenges related to safety and ethical decision-making. Ensuring the safety of AI systems in autonomous driving is critical, given the potential for accidents and fatalities. Tesla's AI has faced scrutiny following accidents involving the misuse of the Autopilot system, underscoring the need for transparency and human oversight in life-critical AI applications (Goodall, 2019).

3. Scalability and Operational Efficiency: Manufacturing vs. Finance

In both manufacturing and finance, AI has proven effective in scaling operations and improving efficiency, but the applications differ. In manufacturing, AI-driven systems like Siemens' predictive maintenance system enable companies to minimize unplanned downtime and optimize maintenance schedules, improving operational efficiency. Predictive maintenance leverages IoT sensors and machine learning models to predict when equipment will fail, allowing for timely interventions (Tupa et al., 2017). On the other hand, in the finance industry, AI is used to streamline back-office functions, such as JPMorgan's COiN, which automates the analysis of thousands of legal contracts, saving thousands of hours of manual labor (Kashyap, 2019).

Manufacturing: AI in manufacturing often focuses on optimizing physical processes, such as machine maintenance or quality control. Siemens' predictive maintenance system exemplifies how AI can improve operational efficiency by predicting machine failures before they occur, reducing downtime and extending the life of equipment (Tupa et al., 2017).

Finance: In contrast, AI in finance is often applied to cognitive tasks, such as automating data analysis or fraud detection. JPMorgan's COiN platform automates contract analysis, significantly reducing the time spent on manual legal reviews and improving overall efficiency in back-office operations (Kashyap, 2019).

4. Customer Experience and Personalization: Retail vs. Transportation

The ability to personalize experiences through AI is a major differentiator in both retail and transportation. In retail, companies like Amazon have successfully implemented AI-driven recommendation systems to personalize the shopping experience. These systems analyze customer behavior, preferences, and transaction histories to make real-time product suggestions, driving customer engagement and boosting sales (Smith & Linden, 2017). In transportation, AI is being used to enhance the customer experience through services like dynamic pricing, route optimization, and autonomous driving. Uber's AI-driven surge pricing model dynamically adjusts prices based on demand and supply, optimizing both driver availability and customer wait times (Rosenblat & Stark, 2016).

Retail: AI-driven personalization is critical in retail, where businesses like Amazon use recommendation engines to enhance the customer experience. Personalized recommendations lead to increased sales and customer satisfaction, as AI systems continuously adapt to customer preferences (Smith & Linden, 2017).

Transportation: In transportation, AI enhances the customer experience through innovations such as dynamic pricing and route optimization. Uber's surge pricing algorithm, for example, adjusts pricing based on demand fluctuations, balancing the needs of drivers and riders in real-time. This dynamic model improves both driver availability and customer satisfaction, although it has faced criticism for fairness (Rosenblat & Stark, 2016).

5. Innovation and Adaptation: Healthcare vs. Manufacturing

Both healthcare and manufacturing are industries where innovation in AI implementation is essential for future growth. In healthcare, AI promises breakthroughs in diagnostics, drug discovery, and personalized medicine, though these innovations are tempered by the complexity of medical data and stringent regulatory requirements. In manufacturing, AI is driving innovation in Industry 4.0 by automating processes and integrating IoT technologies for smarter, more efficient production lines (Tupa et al., 2017).

Healthcare: AI innovation in healthcare is largely focused on improving patient outcomes through personalized medicine, predictive diagnostics, and AI-powered treatment recommendations. However, the complexity of medical data and the need for regulatory compliance slow the pace of AI adoption in this sector (Ross & Swetlitz, 2017).

Manufacturing: In contrast, the manufacturing industry is rapidly adopting AI through innovations in predictive maintenance, process automation, and robotics. These technologies enable manufacturers to reduce downtime, improve efficiency, and respond to changes in demand more quickly, driving the adoption of Industry 4.0 (Tupa et al., 2017).

Conclusion

A comparative analysis of AI implementations across industries reveals several key insights into how AI can be leveraged effectively, as well as the unique challenges that different sectors face. Healthcare and finance highlight the importance of regulatory compliance, data quality, and ethical considerations, while industries such as retail and transportation demonstrate the power of AI in personalizing customer experiences and optimizing operations. Manufacturing, with its focus on operational efficiency and predictive maintenance, shows the potential for AI to drive innovation and improve productivity. By examining these case studies, organizations can learn from both the successes and challenges of AI deployment across industries, helping them to develop robust, scalable, and ethically sound AI strategies tailored to their specific needs.

References

Goodall, N. J. (2019). Machine ethics and automated vehicles. In S. Müller & P. Schleiter (Eds.), *Ethics of autonomous vehicles* (pp. 123-144). Springer.

Kashyap, R. (2019). The rise of AI in finance: How JPMorgan Chase and others are leading the charge. *Harvard Business Review*. Retrieved from https://hbr.org

Lazer, D., Kennedy, R., King, G., & Vespignani, A. (2014). The parable of Google Flu: Traps in big data analysis. *Science, 343*(6176), 1203-1205.

Neff, G., & Nagy, P. (2016). Automation, algorithms, and politics | talking to bots: Symbiotic agency and the case of Tay. *International Journal of Communication, 10*, 4915-4931.

O'Neil, C. (2020). *Weapons of math destruction: How big data increases inequality and threatens democracy*. Broadway Books.

Rosenblat, A., & Stark, L. (2016). Algorithmic labor and information asymmetries: A case study of Uber's drivers. *International Journal of Communication, 10*, 3758-3784.

Ross, C., & Swetlitz, I. (2017). IBM pitched its Watson supercomputer as a revolution in cancer care. It's nowhere close. *STAT News*. Retrieved from https://www.statnews.com

Schatsky, D., Muraskin, C., & Gurumurthy, R. (2020). Demystifying artificial intelligence: What business leaders need to know about AI. *Deloitte Insights*. Retrieved from https://www2.deloitte.com

Smith, B., & Linden, G. (2017). Two decades of recommender systems at Amazon.com. *IEEE Internet Computing, 21*(3), 12-18.

Tupa, J., Simota, J., & Steiner, F. (2017). Aspects of risk management implementation for Industry 4.0. *Procedia Manufacturing, 11*, 1223-1230.

Part VI: Future Trends and Emerging Technologies
Chapter 26: Edge Computing and AI

AI at the Edge

As Artificial Intelligence (AI) technologies continue to advance, edge computing is emerging as a critical paradigm for deploying AI closer to where data is generated, known as "AI at the edge." Edge computing involves processing data at or near the source, rather than relying on centralized cloud-based infrastructures. This shift is driven by the growing need for low-latency, real-time processing in applications such as autonomous vehicles, smart cities, industrial IoT, and healthcare. By integrating AI with edge computing, organizations can deploy intelligent systems that operate with greater speed, privacy, and reliability while reducing the dependency on cloud infrastructure.

1. The Concept of AI at the Edge

AI at the edge refers to deploying AI models and algorithms directly on edge devices, such as smartphones, IoT sensors, or autonomous robots, instead of processing the data in a remote data center or cloud. This approach allows AI models to make real-time decisions locally, eliminating the need to transfer large amounts of data to the cloud for analysis, which can introduce latency and privacy concerns.

Decentralized AI Processing: AI at the edge decentralizes data processing, shifting computations to the edge of the network where data is generated. This decentralization reduces the amount of data that needs to be sent to a central cloud for processing, which is particularly important for applications where latency is critical, such as autonomous vehicles and real-time surveillance systems (Shi et al., 2016). By processing data locally, edge AI systems can provide faster response times and greater reliability, as they are not reliant on network bandwidth or cloud availability.

Real-Time Decision-Making: One of the primary advantages of AI at the edge is the ability to make real-time decisions. For instance, in autonomous vehicles, AI models running on edge devices can analyze sensor data instantaneously to detect obstacles, pedestrians, or other vehicles, enabling faster and more reliable responses (Zhou et al., 2019). Similarly, in industrial IoT applications, AI at the edge allows for real-time monitoring of equipment and machinery, predicting potential failures and optimizing production processes without delays caused by cloud-based processing.

2. Applications of AI at the Edge

AI at the edge has broad applications across various industries, enabling innovative use cases where speed, privacy, and scalability are paramount.

Autonomous Vehicles: AI at the edge is crucial for autonomous vehicles, which rely on real-time data processing to navigate and make split-second decisions. Vehicles are equipped with sensors, cameras, and LIDAR systems that generate vast amounts of data, which need to be processed instantly to ensure safety. Edge AI allows vehicles to analyze data locally, enabling real-time object detection, path planning, and collision avoidance without the latency that would result from sending data to a remote cloud server (Huang et al., 2020).

Smart Cities: Smart cities are another area where AI at the edge plays a pivotal role. Edge AI can be deployed in traffic management systems, security cameras, and environmental monitoring devices to provide real-time analytics and decision-making. For example, smart traffic lights equipped with edge AI can analyze traffic flow in real time, optimizing traffic signal timing to reduce congestion and improve safety (Satyanarayanan, 2017). Additionally, AI-powered surveillance cameras at the edge can detect suspicious activities and alert authorities instantly, without the need to send video feeds to a central location for processing.

Healthcare and Remote Monitoring: In healthcare, edge AI is being used to enhance patient monitoring and diagnostics. Wearable devices and medical sensors can process health data locally, enabling real-time monitoring of vital signs such as heart rate, blood pressure, or glucose levels. This is especially useful for remote monitoring in rural or underserved areas where internet connectivity may be unreliable (Lopez-Martin et al., 2021). AI models running on edge devices can detect anomalies and alert healthcare providers, enabling timely interventions without relying on cloud-based systems.

Industrial IoT and Manufacturing: In manufacturing, AI at the edge is being used for predictive maintenance and process optimization. IoT sensors deployed on machinery can analyze data in real time, detecting potential failures and enabling proactive maintenance. By processing data at the edge, manufacturers can reduce downtime and extend the lifespan of their equipment (Shi et al., 2016). AI at the edge also allows for real-time quality control, where products can be inspected as they are produced, identifying defects or issues before they reach the end of the production line.

3. Benefits of AI at the Edge

The integration of AI with edge computing offers several distinct benefits over traditional cloud-based AI solutions. These benefits make AI at the edge a transformative technology for applications that demand low latency, privacy, and scalability.

Reduced Latency: One of the most significant advantages of AI at the edge is reduced latency. By processing data locally on edge devices, AI systems can make decisions faster than if they had to send data to the cloud for analysis. This is critical for applications like autonomous driving, where even a slight delay in decision making can have serious consequences. Real-time processing is also crucial in industrial automation and healthcare, where timely interventions can prevent costly machine failures or health crises (Huang et al., 2020).

Improved Privacy and Security: AI at the edge can enhance privacy and security by reducing the need to send sensitive data to the cloud. In sectors like healthcare, where patient data is highly sensitive, processing data locally ensures that personal information remains on the device, mitigating the risks of data breaches or unauthorized access (Shi et al., 2016). Similarly, in smart cities or retail, keeping video or sensor data at the edge reduces the risk of surveillance data being intercepted or misused.

Reduced Bandwidth and Cloud Costs: By processing data locally, AI at the edge reduces the need to transmit large amounts of data to centralized servers, resulting in lower bandwidth usage and reduced cloud storage costs. This is particularly important in IoT applications, where billions of connected devices generate vast amounts of data. Processing this data at the edge instead of sending it to the cloud helps organizations reduce costs while still gaining valuable insights from their data (Satyanarayanan, 2017).

Increased Reliability: Edge AI systems are less dependent on cloud infrastructure, making them more resilient in environments with limited or unreliable network connectivity. In remote locations or critical environments like autonomous vehicles or healthcare monitoring, relying on cloud connectivity can introduce risks. Edge AI ensures that these systems continue to function even if the network connection is lost or intermittent (Zhou et al., 2019).

4. Challenges of AI at the Edge

While AI at the edge offers numerous benefits, it also presents unique challenges that need to be addressed for widespread adoption.

Limited Computational Resources: Edge devices, such as smartphones, sensors, or IoT devices, often have limited computational power and storage capacity compared to cloud data centers. Running complex AI models on these devices can be challenging, requiring optimization techniques such as model compression, pruning, and quantization to reduce the size and complexity of AI models while maintaining accuracy (Zhou et al., 2019).

Energy Consumption: Edge devices typically have limited battery life, which can be a challenge for AI at the edge. Running AI algorithms, especially deep learning models, requires significant computational resources, which can drain battery life quickly. Developing energy-efficient AI models and hardware that can support AI processing at the edge is a critical area of research (Huang et al., 2020).

Security Risks: While edge AI can enhance privacy by keeping data local, it also introduces new security risks. Edge devices are often more vulnerable to physical tampering, hacking, and malware attacks than cloud data centers. Securing AI models and data at the edge requires implementing strong encryption, authentication, and anomaly detection mechanisms to protect against potential threats (Lopez-Martin et al., 2021).

5. The Future of AI at the Edge

As AI technology continues to evolve, AI at the edge is expected to play a transformative role in several emerging technologies, such as 5G networks, the Internet of Things (IoT), and smart infrastructure. The convergence of 5G and AI at the edge will enable even faster data transmission and lower latency, further enhancing real-time applications like autonomous vehicles, remote healthcare, and smart city management (Shi et al., 2016). Additionally, advances in AI hardware, such as specialized AI chips and neuromorphic computing, will make it possible to run more complex and energy-efficient AI models on edge devices.

In summary, AI at the edge represents a significant advancement in the way data is processed and analyzed in real-time applications. By decentralizing AI processing and bringing it closer to the data source, organizations can achieve faster decision-making, enhanced privacy, reduced costs, and increased reliability. While challenges such as limited computational resources and security risks remain, ongoing innovations in AI hardware, model optimization, and edge computing architectures will continue to drive the adoption of AI at the edge across industries. From autonomous vehicles to smart cities and healthcare, AI at the edge is poised to revolutionize the way we interact with technology and the world around us.

IoT and Sensor Data Processing

The rapid growth of the Internet of Things (IoT) has revolutionized the way devices interact and communicate, enabling a vast network of sensors that generate real-time data across industries such as manufacturing, healthcare, smart cities, and agriculture. However, managing the massive volume of data generated by IoT devices poses significant challenges, particularly regarding latency, bandwidth, and privacy. Edge computing, combined with AI, offers an innovative solution by enabling real-time sensor data processing closer to the source, reducing the need for constant cloud communication while enhancing the speed, scalability, and efficiency of IoT applications. This integration is redefining how organizations leverage IoT and sensor data to make timely, data-driven decisions.

1. The Role of Edge Computing in IoT and Sensor Data Processing

IoT devices, such as sensors and smart appliances, are increasingly being deployed in environments where real-time data analysis is critical. These devices generate massive streams of data that need to be processed quickly and efficiently. Traditionally, this data would be sent to centralized cloud data centers for processing, but the sheer volume of data, combined with the need for low-latency responses, makes this approach inefficient in many scenarios. Edge computing addresses this issue by moving data processing closer to where the data is generated, allowing IoT systems to make real-time decisions at the "edge" of the network.

Real-Time Data Processing: One of the main advantages of edge computing in IoT environments is the ability to process sensor data in real time. For example, in a smart factory, IoT sensors embedded in machines can continuously monitor performance metrics such as temperature, vibration, and pressure. Edge AI models can process this data on-site, identifying potential failures or inefficiencies before they become critical, thereby reducing downtime and improving operational efficiency (Shi et al., 2016). By processing sensor data locally, edge computing eliminates the latency associated with sending data to the cloud, enabling immediate action.

Bandwidth Optimization: The decentralized nature of edge computing significantly reduces the volume of data that needs to be transmitted to the cloud. This is especially important for IoT applications where thousands or millions of sensors are generating data simultaneously. For example, in large-scale IoT deployments, such as smart cities or agriculture, sensors collect vast amounts of environmental data that may not require cloud storage or real-time analysis. Edge devices can filter, aggregate, and preprocess the data, ensuring only the most relevant information is sent to the cloud for further analysis, thereby optimizing bandwidth usage and reducing costs (Satyanarayanan, 2017).

2. Applications of Edge Computing and AI in IoT Sensor Data Processing

The combination of edge computing and AI has opened new possibilities for IoT applications across various industries. By deploying AI models at the edge, organizations can enhance their ability to process sensor data in real time, improve decision-making, and respond more rapidly to changing conditions. Key industries benefiting from this convergence include manufacturing, healthcare, and smart cities.

Smart Manufacturing and Industry 4.0: In manufacturing, IoT sensors are commonly used for monitoring production lines, detecting equipment failures, and optimizing resource usage. Edge AI can analyze sensor data locally to detect anomalies in real time, preventing costly downtime due to equipment failures or process inefficiencies. For instance, in predictive maintenance, IoT sensors on industrial equipment continuously monitor factors such as vibration, temperature, and wear. Edge AI processes this data locally, predicting when machinery is likely to fail and scheduling maintenance proactively, reducing unplanned downtime (Tupa et al., 2017).

Healthcare and Wearable Devices: In healthcare, wearable devices equipped with IoT sensors, such as smartwatches and medical monitoring devices, generate large amounts of health data, including heart rate, glucose levels, and blood pressure. Edge computing allows this data to be processed locally on the device, enabling real-time health monitoring and alerting patients or healthcare providers to potential health issues immediately. For example, AI algorithms running at the edge can detect irregular heartbeats or spikes in blood sugar, providing timely interventions without relying on cloud processing (Lopez-Martin et al., 2021). This is particularly useful in remote areas where connectivity to the cloud may be limited.

Smart Cities and Traffic Management: In smart cities, IoT sensors are deployed throughout urban environments to monitor traffic flow, air quality, energy usage, and other public infrastructure. Edge computing allows these sensors to process data locally and make decisions in real time. For example, traffic cameras equipped with AI algorithms can analyze live video feeds to optimize traffic light timing, reducing congestion during peak hours (Satyanarayanan, 2017). Similarly, edge computing in smart energy grids can enable real-time monitoring and control of energy distribution, improving efficiency and sustainability.

3. Benefits of Edge Computing and AI in IoT Sensor Data Processing

The integration of AI and edge computing in IoT sensor data processing offers several significant advantages, including reduced latency, improved data privacy, scalability, and energy efficiency.

Reduced Latency for Time-Critical Applications: Many IoT applications require real-time responses that cloud-based systems cannot provide due to latency issues. By processing data at the edge, organizations can reduce latency and ensure that time-sensitive actions are taken immediately. For example, in autonomous vehicles, sensors generate massive amounts of data from cameras, radar, and LIDAR systems. AI models deployed at the edge can process this data locally to detect obstacles and navigate traffic in real time, without relying on cloud-based decisions (Shi et al., 2016).

Enhanced Privacy and Data Security: IoT applications, particularly in healthcare and smart cities, generate vast amounts of sensitive data. Processing this data locally at the edge reduces the risk of exposure to privacy breaches, as sensitive information does not need to be transmitted to the cloud for processing. This is especially important in healthcare, where the privacy of patient data is paramount. By keeping health data on local devices and processing it in real time, edge computing enhances privacy while still providing valuable insights (Lopez-Martin et al., 2021).

Scalability and Flexibility: Edge computing enables IoT systems to scale more efficiently by distributing the data processing workload across multiple edge devices. This decentralized architecture allows organizations to expand their IoT networks without overwhelming centralized cloud systems or networks. For example, in large-scale industrial IoT deployments, edge computing can support the scalability of predictive maintenance systems, enabling factories to monitor hundreds of machines simultaneously without overloading cloud resources (Satyanarayanan, 2017).

Energy Efficiency: IoT devices, particularly sensors deployed in remote or energy-constrained environments, often have limited battery life. Transmitting data to the cloud for processing consumes considerable energy. By processing data locally at the edge, IoT devices can significantly reduce energy consumption, extending battery life and making the system more sustainable (Zhou et al., 2019).

4. Challenges and Considerations in Edge-Based IoT Sensor Processing

Despite its benefits, implementing AI at the edge for IoT sensor data processing also presents several challenges, including limitations in computational power, energy constraints, and security risks.

Computational Power and Model Optimization: Edge devices typically have limited computational resources compared to centralized cloud systems. Running complex AI models on these devices can be challenging, requiring techniques such as model compression, pruning, and quantization to optimize AI models for edge deployment. Balancing model accuracy with computational efficiency is essential to ensuring that edge AI systems can operate effectively without overwhelming the device's hardware (Zhou et al., 2019).

Energy Constraints: Many IoT devices, such as sensors in remote areas or wearable health devices, rely on battery power and have limited energy resources. Running AI algorithms locally can increase energy consumption, leading to shorter battery life. Developing energy-efficient AI algorithms and edge hardware is critical to overcoming this challenge and ensuring that IoT devices can operate autonomously for extended periods (Lopez-Martin et al., 2021).

Security and Privacy Risks: While edge computing can enhance privacy by reducing data transmission to the cloud, it also introduces new security risks. Edge devices are often more vulnerable to physical tampering, malware, and hacking attacks. Implementing strong encryption, authentication, and secure data storage on edge devices is essential to protecting sensitive data and ensuring the integrity of AI-driven decisions at the edge (Shi et al., 2016).

In summary, edge computing, combined with AI, is transforming how IoT sensor data is processed across industries. By moving data processing closer to the source, organizations can benefit from real-time decision-making, improved scalability, enhanced privacy, and reduced latency. Applications in smart manufacturing, healthcare, and smart cities demonstrate the vast potential of edge AI in optimizing IoT systems for operational efficiency and innovation. However, challenges related to computational limitations, energy constraints, and security risks must be addressed to fully realize the benefits of edge-based IoT sensor processing. As advancements in AI hardware and model optimization continue, edge computing is poised to become a key enabler of intelligent IoT systems in the future.

Challenges and Opportunities

Edge computing combined with Artificial Intelligence (AI) is revolutionizing various industries by enabling real-time data processing and decision-making at the edge of the network, closer to where data is generated. This paradigm shift reduces latency, improves efficiency, enhances privacy, and opens up new possibilities for applications such as autonomous vehicles, smart cities, industrial IoT, and healthcare. However, alongside the immense opportunities, there are also significant challenges that need to be addressed to fully realize the potential of edge AI. This section discusses the key challenges and opportunities of edge computing and AI integration, with a focus on scalability, computational limitations, security concerns, and industry-specific applications.

1. Challenges of Edge Computing and AI Integration

While edge computing provides numerous benefits for AI-driven systems, it also presents several technical and operational challenges.

These challenges include limited computational resources, energy constraints, security vulnerabilities, and the need for effective infrastructure management.

Computational Constraints: One of the primary challenges of edge AI is the limited computational power available on edge devices, such as sensors, smartphones, or IoT gateways. Edge devices often lack the processing power and memory capacity of centralized cloud servers, making it difficult to run complex AI algorithms, especially those involving deep learning models that require substantial computational resources. To address this, researchers are exploring model compression techniques, such as quantization, pruning, and knowledge distillation, to reduce the size and complexity of AI models without significantly compromising accuracy (Zhou et al., 2019). However, these optimizations come with trade-offs in model performance, requiring careful consideration when deploying AI at the edge.

Energy Efficiency: Edge devices, particularly IoT sensors and wearable devices, are often battery-powered and operate in environments where frequent recharging is not feasible. Running AI algorithms on these devices can consume significant amounts of energy, leading to reduced battery life and operational inefficiency. Developing energy-efficient AI models and hardware is critical to overcoming this challenge. New research is focusing on low-power AI chips and edge-specific architectures designed to optimize energy consumption during real-time data processing (Shi et al., 2016).

Security and Privacy Concerns: While edge computing enhances data privacy by reducing the need to transmit sensitive information to the cloud, it also introduces new security risks. Edge devices are often physically accessible, making them more vulnerable to tampering, data breaches, and cyberattacks. Additionally, securing the AI models themselves is crucial, as adversarial attacks can target AI algorithms to manipulate outcomes. Implementing robust encryption, authentication, and data protection mechanisms is essential to ensuring the security and integrity of edge AI systems (Baccarelli et al., 2017).

Infrastructure Management and Scalability: Managing and scaling edge AI deployments across geographically distributed devices poses significant operational challenges. Unlike cloud-based AI, which benefits from centralized infrastructure and standardized development environments, edge computing requires managing a large number of heterogeneous devices with varying capabilities, operating conditions, and connectivity. This requires robust infrastructure management platforms that can orchestrate and monitor edge devices, ensuring that AI models are deployed, updated, and maintained efficiently (Satyanarayanan, 2017).

2. Opportunities of Edge Computing and AI Integration

Despite these challenges, the convergence of edge computing and AI presents numerous opportunities for innovation across various sectors. By addressing the limitations of cloud-based systems, edge AI can enhance performance, reduce operational costs, and create new business models.

Real-Time Decision-Making: One of the most compelling opportunities of edge AI is the ability to process data and make decisions in real time, which is critical for applications such as autonomous driving, industrial automation, and healthcare. For example, in autonomous vehicles, AI models running at the edge can instantly analyze sensor data to detect obstacles, navigate routes, and respond to environmental changes without relying on cloud connectivity (Huang et al., 2020). This low-latency decision-making capability enables faster and more accurate responses in time-critical scenarios, improving safety and efficiency.

Enhanced Data Privacy: As data privacy becomes an increasingly important issue, edge computing offers a way to process sensitive data locally, reducing the risks associated with transmitting data to the cloud. This is particularly valuable in healthcare, where patient data must be handled with strict privacy regulations such as the Health Insurance Portability and Accountability Act (HIPAA). By processing health data on local devices, such as wearable monitors or IoT sensors in hospitals, edge AI can provide real-time insights while keeping personal information secure (Shi et al., 2016).

Bandwidth and Cost Savings: Edge computing reduces the need to transmit vast amounts of data to centralized cloud servers, significantly lowering bandwidth consumption and associated costs. This is particularly important for IoT applications, where large-scale deployments can generate immense data streams. For example, in smart cities, edge AI can process environmental data (e.g., air quality, traffic conditions) locally, transmitting only aggregated or relevant information to the cloud for long-term analysis, reducing network congestion and storage costs (Satyanarayanan, 2017).

New Industry Applications: Edge AI is creating new opportunities for innovation across industries by enabling applications that require real-time, localized decision-making. In manufacturing, for example, edge AI can be used for predictive maintenance, where IoT sensors on machinery monitor performance in real time and predict failures before they occur. This reduces downtime and maintenance costs, while improving operational efficiency (Tupa et al., 2017). Similarly, in agriculture, edge AI systems can process data from soil sensors, drones, and weather stations to optimize irrigation, pest control, and crop management, improving yields and sustainability.

3. Addressing the Challenges: Future Directions

To fully capitalize on the opportunities of edge AI, several key challenges must be addressed through technological advancements and strategic initiatives. The future of edge computing and AI integration will likely involve innovations in hardware, software, and regulatory frameworks to overcome the current limitations.

AI Model Optimization for Edge Devices: Continued research into model compression, edge-specific AI architectures, and low-power AI chips will be essential for enabling complex AI models to run efficiently on edge devices. Techniques such as federated learning, which allows models to be trained across distributed edge devices without centralizing the data, offer promising solutions to reduce the computational burden on edge devices while preserving data privacy (Zhou et al., 2019).

Edge AI Security Solutions: Strengthening the security of edge devices and AI models is a critical area of focus. Edge AI systems will need to incorporate advanced encryption protocols, secure hardware elements (e.g., Trusted Platform Modules), and AI-specific security mechanisms that detect and mitigate adversarial attacks. Additionally, regulations and industry standards around edge AI security will need to evolve to address the unique risks associated with decentralized, real-time data processing (Baccarelli et al., 2017).

Orchestration Platforms for Edge AI: Developing robust edge AI orchestration platforms will help streamline the deployment, monitoring, and maintenance of AI models across geographically dispersed devices. These platforms should enable seamless updates, scalability, and performance monitoring while ensuring compatibility across heterogeneous devices. As the edge computing landscape grows, these platforms will play a crucial role in managing large-scale edge AI deployments efficiently (Shi et al., 2016).

Collaboration Between Industry and Government: Regulatory bodies, industry leaders, and academia will need to collaborate to address the ethical, legal, and technical challenges of edge AI. This includes establishing standards for data privacy, security, and the ethical use of AI at the edge, particularly in sensitive applications such as healthcare, autonomous driving, and public safety. Industry partnerships will also be key to fostering innovation, enabling the development of new AI models, edge devices, and infrastructure solutions (Satyanarayanan, 2017).

Conclusion

The integration of edge computing and AI presents both significant challenges and vast opportunities across a range of industries. While technical limitations related to computational power, energy efficiency, and security pose hurdles to widespread adoption, advances in AI model optimization, hardware design, and infrastructure management are paving the way for broader deployment of edge AI systems. The opportunities for real-time decision-making, enhanced privacy, bandwidth savings, and new industry applications are immense, positioning edge AI as a transformative technology for the future. As research, development, and regulatory efforts continue, edge AI is poised to become a critical component of next-generation IoT systems and intelligent infrastructure.

References

Baccarelli, E., Naranjo, P. G. V., Scarpiniti, M., Shojafar, M., & Abawajy, J. H. (2017). Fog of everything: Energy-efficient networked computing architectures, research challenges, and a case study. *IEEE Access, 5*, 9882-9910.

Huang, X., Cheng, X., Zhang, J., Zhang, R., & Zhao, Y. (2020). Deep learning for vehicle-to-everything (V2X) services. *Proceedings of the IEEE, 108*(2), 357-380.

Lopez-Martin, M., Carro, B., Sanchez-Esguevillas, A., & Lloret, J. (2021). AI-powered edge computing in smart health: Applications, challenges, and open issues. *IEEE Network, 35*(6), 40-47.

Satyanarayanan, M. (2017). The emergence of edge computing. *Computer, 50*(1), 30-39.

Shi, W., Cao, J., Zhang, Q., Li, Y., & Xu, L. (2016). Edge computing: Vision and challenges. *IEEE Internet of Things Journal, 3*(5), 637-646.

Tupa, J., Simota, J., & Steiner, F. (2017). Aspects of risk management implementation for Industry 4.0. *Procedia Manufacturing, 11*, 1223-1230.

Zhou, Z., Chen, X., Li, E., Zeng, L., Luo, K., & Zhang, J. (2019). Edge intelligence: Paving the last mile of AI with edge computing. *Proceedings of the IEEE, 107*(8), 1738-1762.

Chapter 27: Explainable AI and Interpretability

Need for Explainability

As Artificial Intelligence (AI) systems become increasingly integrated into critical sectors such as healthcare, finance, autonomous systems, and criminal justice, the need for transparency and interpretability has become a key concern. Explainable AI (XAI) aims to make AI models more transparent and understandable to human users, enabling stakeholders to trust, validate, and interpret the decisions made by these systems. The growing complexity of AI models, particularly in deep learning, has led to a "black box" issue, where it is difficult to understand how and why a model arrives at specific predictions or decisions. This opacity poses significant challenges in terms of trust, accountability, ethics, and compliance, making explainability an essential feature for AI's responsible and widespread adoption.

1. The Black Box Problem

The rise of advanced machine learning models, particularly deep learning and neural networks, has led to significant improvements in predictive accuracy and performance. However, these models are often highly complex and operate in a non-linear manner, making it difficult to understand their internal decision-making processes. This "black box" nature of AI is a growing concern in industries where the rationale behind decisions needs to be transparent and justifiable.

Deep Learning and Opacity: Deep learning models, such as convolutional neural networks (CNNs) and recurrent neural networks (RNNs), are commonly used in image recognition, natural language processing, and autonomous systems. While these models excel at pattern recognition and prediction, they are notoriously difficult to interpret due to their multiple layers of abstraction. For example, in healthcare, if an AI model predicts a diagnosis, medical professionals need to understand the factors that contributed to the prediction in order to make informed clinical decisions. However, without explainability, the AI's reasoning remains opaque, making it difficult to trust or act on its recommendations (Rudin, 2019).

Algorithmic Bias and Accountability: The black box nature of AI systems also makes it difficult to identify and mitigate biases embedded in the models. Algorithmic bias can arise from skewed training data, inappropriate feature selection, or societal biases, leading to unfair outcomes in areas such as hiring, lending, or criminal sentencing. Explainability is crucial for identifying potential biases in AI models and ensuring that their decisions are fair and equitable. Without explainable AI, it becomes challenging to hold these systems accountable, especially in cases where the AI's decision-making processes impact human rights or access to resources (Binns, 2018).

2. Ethical and Legal Implications of Explainability

The need for explainability in AI is not only driven by ethical concerns but also by legal and regulatory requirements. Various sectors, including healthcare, finance, and law enforcement, are subject to regulations that mandate transparency and accountability in decision-making. Explainable AI ensures that organizations can comply with these legal requirements, thereby reducing the risks of regulatory violations and litigation.

Regulatory Compliance: In regions such as the European Union, regulations like the General Data Protection Regulation (GDPR) enforce the "right to explanation," which entitles individuals to an explanation of decisions made by automated systems that affect them. For instance, if an AI system denies a person a loan or recommends a lower insurance premium, the individual has the right to understand the rationale behind the decision (Goodman & Flaxman, 2017). Explainability ensures that organizations can comply with these regulations by providing clear, understandable insights into the model's decision-making process.

Trust and Accountability in High-Stakes Applications: In high-stakes sectors such as healthcare, finance, and criminal justice, explainability is essential for establishing trust between AI systems and their human operators. Medical professionals, financial regulators, and law enforcement officers must have confidence in the reliability and fairness of AI-driven decisions. For example, in autonomous driving, if an AI system causes a crash, stakeholders need to understand the decisions that led to the failure to assign responsibility and make necessary improvements (Selbst & Barocas, 2018). Explainable AI enables transparency and helps build trust in the technology, which is critical for its adoption in sensitive applications.

3. User-Centric AI Systems

Explainability is also essential for creating user-centric AI systems that empower non-experts to understand and interact with AI models effectively. Many AI applications are designed for end-users who do not have deep technical expertise, such as doctors, teachers, and business executives. Providing these users with interpretable insights into AI's predictions can enhance decision-making and improve outcomes.

Improving Human-AI Collaboration: In many fields, AI systems are designed to support human decision-makers rather than replace them. In healthcare, for example, AI models may assist doctors by analyzing patient data and suggesting diagnoses or treatment plans. However, for doctors to confidently act on these recommendations, they need to understand the reasoning behind the AI's suggestions. Explainable AI facilitates this collaboration by offering clear, interpretable insights that help humans understand the AI's reasoning and incorporate it into their decision-making process (Doshi-Velez & Kim, 2017).

Enhancing User Trust and Adoption: One of the barriers to AI adoption in many industries is the fear that AI systems are too complex and opaque for non-experts to trust. By making AI models more explainable, organizations can enhance user trust and increase the likelihood of adoption. In sectors such as finance, where decisions about loans, investments, and risk assessments have far-reaching consequences, explainable AI can provide clarity and confidence to both financial professionals and customers, fostering wider acceptance of AI technologies (Adadi & Berrada, 2018).

4. Ensuring Fairness and Reducing Bias

Another crucial reason for explainability in AI is to ensure fairness and reduce bias. AI models can inadvertently perpetuate or amplify biases present in training data, leading to unfair outcomes for specific groups. Explainable AI provides the tools necessary to identify and mitigate these biases, ensuring that AI-driven decisions are equitable and just.

Auditing AI for Bias: Explainable AI allows stakeholders to audit AI models for bias by revealing how decisions are made and which features are most influential. For example, in hiring algorithms, explainability can show whether the AI system disproportionately penalizes candidates based on gender, race, or other protected characteristics. By making the decision-making process transparent, organizations can identify and address potential biases before they cause harm (Binns, 2018).

Ethical AI Development: As AI systems become more prevalent in socially impactful domains, the ethical implications of their use become more pressing. Explainability helps AI developers design systems that align with ethical principles such as fairness, accountability, and transparency. By making AI models interpretable, developers can more easily identify unintended consequences and take steps to ensure that their systems promote positive social outcomes (Rudin, 2019).

5. Challenges in Achieving Explainability

While the need for explainability in AI is clear, achieving it is not without challenges. Many high-performing AI models, particularly deep learning algorithms, are inherently complex and difficult to interpret. Balancing the trade-off between model performance and interpretability remains a central challenge in the field of explainable AI.

Trade-offs Between Accuracy and Interpretability: In some cases, simpler models, such as decision trees or linear models, offer greater transparency and interpretability but may sacrifice accuracy compared to more complex models like deep neural networks. The challenge is to find methods that can maintain high accuracy while providing interpretable insights. Research in this area is focusing on developing techniques such as local interpretable model-agnostic explanations (LIME) and SHapley Additive exPlanations (SHAP), which provide interpretable outputs for complex models without sacrificing performance (Ribeiro et al., 2016).

Scalability of Explainable Models: Another challenge is the scalability of explainability techniques across diverse AI applications and industries. Different industries have varying needs in terms of the granularity and type of explanations required. For instance, a doctor may need a detailed explanation of how an AI model arrived at a diagnosis, while a financial regulator may require a high-level summary of how a risk assessment model functions. Developing explainable AI models that can scale across different contexts while providing relevant, user-friendly explanations is a significant challenge (Adadi & Berrada, 2018).

In summary, the need for explainability in AI has become a critical issue as AI systems are increasingly deployed in high-stakes environments that require transparency, trust, and accountability. The black box nature of many advanced AI models poses challenges in terms of bias, fairness, and regulatory compliance. Explainable AI provides a pathway to addressing these concerns by making AI systems more transparent and understandable to human users, ensuring that decisions can be trusted, audited, and acted upon responsibly. While achieving explainability remains challenging due to the complexity of modern AI models, ongoing research and development are helping bridge the gap between performance and interpretability. As AI continues to evolve, explainability will play an essential role in ensuring that AI technologies are used ethically and effectively.

Techniques for Model Interpretability

As the deployment of Artificial Intelligence (AI) models in critical sectors increases, so does the demand for explainability and interpretability. Ensuring that AI models can be understood and trusted by human users is crucial for building confidence, improving decision-making, and ensuring fairness and accountability. Various techniques have been developed to address the black-box nature of many AI models, particularly complex ones like deep learning and ensemble methods. These techniques enable stakeholders to interpret how AI models make decisions, which features they prioritize, and how predictions can be explained in understandable ways. This section explores key techniques used to enhance model interpretability, including global and local interpretability methods, model-agnostic techniques, and model-specific approaches.

1. Global vs. Local Interpretability

Interpretability techniques in AI can be broadly divided into two categories: global interpretability, which seeks to explain the overall behavior of a model, and local interpretability, which focuses on understanding specific predictions or instances.

Global Interpretability: Global interpretability aims to provide insights into the general workings of an AI model, explaining how features impact the model's predictions across all instances. This is particularly useful for stakeholders interested in understanding the

678

broader patterns and relationships learned by the model. For instance, in healthcare, a global interpretation might show which clinical features (e.g., age, blood pressure) are most influential in predicting a certain disease across a population of patients (Murdoch et al., 2019). Techniques like decision trees, rule-based systems, and feature importance scores (e.g., using Random Forest or Gradient Boosting models) are commonly used to enhance global interpretability.

Local Interpretability: In contrast, local interpretability focuses on explaining a specific prediction made by the model for a single instance or small subset of instances. Local interpretability is crucial in situations where users need to understand how a decision was made for a particular case, such as why a loan application was rejected or why a patient was diagnosed with a certain condition. Techniques like LIME (Local Interpretable Model-agnostic Explanations) and SHAP (SHapley Additive exPlanations) provide local explanations by approximating the model's decision-making process for individual predictions (Ribeiro et al., 2016).

2. Model-Agnostic Techniques for Interpretability

Model-agnostic techniques are methods that can be applied to any machine learning model, regardless of its architecture or complexity. These techniques provide flexibility by working with a wide variety of models, from simple linear regressions to deep neural networks. The key model-agnostic techniques include LIME, SHAP, and Partial Dependence Plots (PDPs).

LIME (Local Interpretable Model-agnostic Explanations): LIME is a popular technique for local interpretability that explains the predictions of any machine learning model by approximating it locally with a simpler, interpretable model, such as a linear model or decision tree. LIME works by perturbing the input data and observing how the model's predictions change in response. This allows LIME to identify the most important features that contributed to a specific prediction (Ribeiro et al., 2016). For example, in a loan approval system, LIME could highlight the specific factors (e.g., income, credit score) that led to the approval or denial of a particular loan application.

SHAP (SHapley Additive exPlanations): SHAP is another widely used model-agnostic technique based on cooperative game theory. SHAP assigns each feature a contribution value (Shapley value) to explain a model's prediction. The technique is rooted in fairness principles, ensuring that each feature's contribution is calculated in a way that reflects how much it contributes to the overall prediction, relative to other features (Lundberg & Lee, 2017). SHAP provides consistent and additive explanations, making it ideal for explaining complex models like neural networks and ensemble methods. SHAP values can be used to generate both local and global explanations, giving insights into how a model behaves across all instances and for specific predictions.

Partial Dependence Plots (PDPs): PDPs are used to analyze the relationship between a feature and the predicted outcome of a model, while keeping all other features constant. PDPs provide a global view of how a feature influences the model's predictions. For instance, a PDP might show how increasing a patient's age affects the predicted probability of developing a certain disease, regardless of the patient's other characteristics. PDPs are particularly useful in identifying non-linear relationships between features and predictions (Goldstein et al., 2015).

3. Model-Specific Interpretability Techniques

In addition to model-agnostic techniques, some models are inherently interpretable or have specific techniques that enhance their interpretability. These models and techniques provide direct insights into the decision-making process without the need for additional post-hoc interpretation methods.

Decision Trees and Rule-Based Models: Decision trees are considered inherently interpretable models because they provide a clear, visual representation of the decision-making process. Each node in the tree represents a decision based on a feature, and the path from the root to a leaf represents a sequence of decisions leading to a prediction. Rule-based models, like those used in decision trees and rule-based classifiers, allow users to easily trace the logic behind predictions. This transparency makes decision trees particularly useful in fields like healthcare, where clinicians need to understand the rationale behind diagnoses or treatment recommendations (Murdoch et al., 2019).

Linear and Logistic Regression: Linear regression models are inherently interpretable because their predictions are based on a weighted sum of input features. The coefficients of the model indicate the strength and direction of the relationship between each feature and the outcome. Similarly, logistic regression provides interpretable coefficients that show the log-odds of an outcome based on input features. These models are useful in applications where simplicity and interpretability are prioritized over accuracy, such as in explaining risk factors for diseases or in financial risk assessments (Adadi & Berrada, 2018).

Attention Mechanisms in Neural Networks: In the context of deep learning, especially in natural language processing (NLP) and computer vision tasks, attention mechanisms are a model-specific technique that can improve interpretability. Attention mechanisms allow models to focus on specific parts of the input data when making predictions, providing insights into which features or regions are most important for a given task. For instance, in image classification, attention mechanisms can highlight specific areas of an image that are crucial for the classification decision, offering a form of transparency in how the model processes visual information (Doshi-Velez & Kim, 2017).

4. Post-Hoc Interpretability Methods

Post-hoc interpretability methods are techniques applied after the model has been trained to explain its predictions. These methods help bridge the gap between complex models and human understanding, providing valuable insights into how the model operates without altering its internal structure.

Feature Importance: Feature importance is a technique that ranks features based on their contribution to the model's predictions. Many machine learning models, such as Random Forests and Gradient Boosting Machines, have built-in feature importance measures. By ranking features based on their predictive power, users can gain a better understanding of which features are driving the model's decisions. This is useful in applications like credit scoring, where regulators and users need to know which factors are most influential in determining creditworthiness (Lundberg & Lee, 2017).

Counterfactual Explanations: Counterfactual explanations provide insights into how a model's prediction would change if certain features were altered. For example, in a credit scoring system, a counterfactual explanation might suggest that if a loan applicant's income were $5,000 higher, their loan application would have been approved. This technique provides actionable insights and helps users understand what changes are necessary to achieve a different outcome, making it particularly useful in areas like finance and hiring (Wachter et al., 2017).

5. Challenges in Balancing Interpretability and Performance

While interpretability is crucial, there is often a trade-off between the complexity of a model and its interpretability. Simpler models, such as decision trees or linear models, tend to be more interpretable but may sacrifice accuracy compared to complex models like deep neural networks. Striking a balance between interpretability and performance remains a significant challenge in explainable AI.

Trade-offs: In many cases, organizations must decide whether to prioritize model performance or interpretability, depending on the application. In high-stakes industries such as healthcare and finance, interpretability is often prioritized to ensure that decisions are transparent and can be audited. However, in applications like image recognition or natural language processing, where predictive accuracy is paramount, more complex models like deep learning may be favored, even if they are less interpretable (Doshi-Velez & Kim, 2017).

In summary, explainability and interpretability are critical for the responsible and effective deployment of AI systems, especially in industries where transparency, trust, and accountability are essential. Techniques such as LIME, SHAP, and Partial Dependence Plots offer valuable insights into both global and local model behavior, while inherently interpretable models like decision trees and logistic regression provide straightforward explanations of decision-making processes. As AI continues to advance, ongoing research into interpretable models and post-hoc explanation techniques will be crucial in addressing the challenge of balancing model complexity and interpretability. Ensuring that AI systems are not only powerful but also understandable is key to fostering their widespread adoption and ensuring their responsible use.

Impact on Compliance and Trust

As Artificial Intelligence (AI) becomes more integrated into decision-making processes across industries such as healthcare, finance, criminal justice, and autonomous systems, the need for explainability and interpretability is paramount. These principles are essential not only for improving AI's operational effectiveness but also for ensuring compliance with regulatory standards and fostering trust among users. The black-box nature of many AI models, particularly complex ones like deep learning and ensemble methods, can undermine confidence in AI systems if their decisions cannot be explained or justified. Explainable AI (XAI) offers a solution to these challenges by making AI models more transparent, interpretable, and accountable, ultimately impacting compliance with legal standards and enhancing trust in AI systems.

1. Explainable AI and Regulatory Compliance

Regulatory bodies worldwide are increasingly mandating transparency and accountability in AI-driven decision-making. Explainability plays a crucial role in ensuring that AI systems comply with these regulatory frameworks, particularly in high-stakes sectors such as finance, healthcare, and data privacy.

General Data Protection Regulation (GDPR): The European Union's General Data Protection Regulation (GDPR) is one of the most prominent regulatory frameworks that emphasize the importance of explainability. Article 22 of the GDPR provides individuals with the right not to be subject to decisions made solely by automated systems, including profiling, unless they have the right to an explanation of how the decision was reached. This "right to explanation" is particularly relevant in cases such as loan approvals, hiring decisions, and credit scoring. Explainable AI ensures that organizations can provide clear, understandable explanations of how AI-driven decisions are made, thereby ensuring compliance with GDPR (Goodman & Flaxman, 2017).

Financial Regulations: In the financial sector, regulations like the Dodd-Frank Act in the U.S. and similar laws in other jurisdictions require transparency in financial decision-making. AI systems used for credit scoring, loan approvals, and fraud detection must be able to explain their decisions to auditors, regulators, and customers. Lack of transparency can lead to non-compliance, resulting in legal consequences and significant financial penalties. Explainable AI provides the necessary transparency by making it possible to audit AI-driven decisions, ensuring that they comply with regulatory requirements and ethical standards (Rudin, 2019).

Healthcare Compliance: In healthcare, explainability is essential for complying with regulations such as the Health Insurance Portability and Accountability Act (HIPAA) in the U.S., which governs the handling of patient data. AI systems used for diagnostics, treatment recommendations, or patient monitoring must provide interpretable insights to clinicians to support their decision-making process. By making AI models explainable, healthcare organizations can ensure that their systems are in line with legal and ethical standards, improving patient outcomes while reducing the risk of liability (Tonekaboni et al., 2019).

2. Building Trust Through Explainability

Trust is a critical factor in the adoption and success of AI systems. Users are more likely to accept and rely on AI models if they understand how decisions are made and can be confident that those decisions are fair, unbiased, and aligned with ethical standards. Explainable AI enhances trust by providing transparency into the inner workings of AI models, allowing users to scrutinize and validate the outputs of AI systems.

Trust in AI for High-Stakes Applications: In high-stakes industries like healthcare and autonomous systems, explainability is essential for fostering trust between AI systems and human operators. For instance, in healthcare, AI models may assist doctors in diagnosing diseases or recommending treatments. However, clinicians need to understand the rationale behind these AI-generated recommendations to make informed decisions. Without explainability, doctors may be hesitant to rely on AI recommendations, especially in life-critical situations (Tonekaboni et al., 2019). Similarly, in autonomous driving, explainability can help passengers, regulators, and engineers understand why an autonomous vehicle made a specific decision, such as slowing down or taking an alternative route, thereby building trust in the system's safety and reliability.

Addressing Algorithmic Bias and Fairness: Explainable AI is also essential for identifying and mitigating algorithmic bias, which can undermine trust in AI systems if left unchecked. Algorithmic bias occurs when AI models unintentionally perpetuate or amplify societal biases, leading to unfair outcomes, such as discrimination in hiring, lending, or criminal sentencing. For example, a hiring algorithm might favor certain demographic groups over others due to biased training data. Explainable AI techniques, such as SHapley Additive exPlanations (SHAP) and Local Interpretable Model-agnostic Explanations (LIME), allow stakeholders to investigate how decisions are made and which features influenced those decisions. By making the decision-making process transparent, organizations can detect and correct biases, ensuring that AI-driven decisions are fair and equitable (Binns, 2018).

User Trust and Adoption: In addition to regulatory compliance and bias mitigation, explainability plays a significant role in driving user trust and adoption of AI technologies. Users are more likely to adopt AI systems if they can understand and trust the model's predictions. This is particularly important in consumer-facing applications, such as credit scoring, loan approvals, or personalized recommendations, where decisions directly affect individuals' lives. Explainable AI offers users clarity about why certain decisions were made, fostering trust in the system and increasing the likelihood of widespread adoption (Adadi & Berrada, 2018).

3. Explainable AI and Accountability

As AI systems are increasingly deployed in critical decision-making processes, ensuring accountability is vital. Explainable AI allows organizations to trace the steps leading to a decision, identify errors or biases, and assign responsibility when things go wrong.

Auditability and Accountability: Explainability makes AI systems auditable by providing detailed insights into how models reach their conclusions. This is critical in sectors such as finance, healthcare, and law enforcement, where decisions need to be justifiable and traceable. For instance, in the event of an erroneous decision - such as a wrongful loan denial or a misdiagnosis - explainable AI can help organizations identify what went wrong, whether it was due to biased data, model misinterpretation, or an unexpected interaction between features. This auditability is essential for ensuring accountability and improving the reliability of AI systems over time (Ribeiro et al., 2016).

Human Oversight and Decision-Making: While AI systems can automate many tasks, human oversight remains crucial in ensuring that AI-driven decisions align with ethical and legal standards. Explainable AI provides human decision-makers with the tools to oversee AI operations effectively, allowing them to review, validate, and, if necessary, override AI-generated decisions. This human-in-the-loop approach ensures that AI systems are not operating in isolation but are subject to continuous scrutiny and improvement (Doshi-Velez & Kim, 2017).

4. Challenges in Achieving Explainability for Compliance and Trust

While explainable AI offers significant benefits for compliance and trust, achieving explainability, particularly for complex models like deep neural networks, remains a challenge.

Complexity of AI Models: As AI models become more complex, particularly with the rise of deep learning and ensemble methods, providing clear and interpretable explanations becomes more difficult. Techniques such as LIME and SHAP can help, but there is often a trade-off between model performance and interpretability. Complex models are often more accurate but less interpretable, whereas simpler models are easier to explain but may not perform as well (Rudin, 2019). Striking the right balance between accuracy and interpretability is a key challenge in making AI systems both effective and explainable.

Varying Stakeholder Needs: Different stakeholders have different needs when it comes to explainability. Regulators may require detailed technical explanations, while end-users may need simpler, high-level explanations. Developing explainable AI systems that can cater to a wide range of stakeholders, from technical experts to laypersons, adds complexity to the design and implementation of AI systems (Adadi & Berrada, 2018).

Conclusion

Explainable AI is essential for ensuring compliance with regulatory frameworks and building trust in AI-driven systems. As AI technologies become increasingly integrated into high-stakes decision-making processes, ensuring that these systems are transparent, interpretable, and accountable is critical for fostering trust among users and stakeholders. Explainability not only supports compliance with regulations such as GDPR, HIPAA, and financial oversight laws but also enhances user confidence by making AI decisions understandable and fair. While challenges remain in achieving explainability, particularly for complex models, the development of techniques such as LIME, SHAP, and model-specific methods offers promising solutions for improving AI transparency. By addressing these challenges, explainable AI will continue to play a pivotal role in the ethical and responsible deployment of AI technologies.

References

Adadi, A., & Berrada, M. (2018). Peeking inside the black-box: A survey on explainable artificial intelligence (XAI). *IEEE Access, 6,* 52138-52160. https://doi.org/10.1109/ACCESS.2018.2870052

Binns, R. (2018). Fairness in machine learning: Lessons from political philosophy. *Proceedings of the 2018 Conference on Fairness, Accountability, and Transparency,* 149-159.

Doshi-Velez, F., & Kim, B. (2017). Towards a rigorous science of interpretable machine learning. *arXiv preprint arXiv:1702.08608.*

Goldstein, A., Kapelner, A., Bleich, J., & Pitkin, E. (2015). Peeking inside the black box: Visualizing statistical learning with plots of individual conditional expectation. *Journal of Computational and Graphical Statistics, 24*(1), 44-65.

Goodman, B., & Flaxman, S. (2017). European Union regulations on algorithmic decision-making and a "right to explanation." *AI Magazine, 38*(3), 50-57.

Lundberg, S. M., & Lee, S. I. (2017). A unified approach to interpreting model predictions. *Advances in Neural Information Processing Systems, 30,* 4765-4774.

Murdoch, W. J., Singh, C., Kumbier, K., Abbasi-Asl, R., & Yu, B. (2019). Definitions, methods, and applications in interpretable machine learning. *Proceedings of the National Academy of Sciences, 116*(44), 22071-22080.

Ribeiro, M. T., Singh, S., & Guestrin, C. (2016). "Why should I trust you?": Explaining the predictions of any classifier. *Proceedings of the 22nd ACM SIGKDD International Conference on Knowledge Discovery and Data Mining,* 1135-1144.

Rudin, C. (2019). Stop explaining black box machine learning models for high stakes decisions and use interpretable models instead. *Nature Machine Intelligence, 1*(5), 206-215.

Tonekaboni, S., Joshi, S., McCradden, M. D., & Goldenberg, A. (2019). What clinicians want: Contextualizing explainable machine learning for clinical end use. *Proceedings of the Machine Learning Research, 106*, 1-21.

Wachter, S., Mittelstadt, B., & Russell, C. (2017). Counterfactual explanations without opening the black box: Automated decisions and the GDPR. *Harvard Journal of Law & Technology, 31*, 841-887.

Chapter 28: Quantum Computing and AI

Basics of Quantum Computing

Quantum computing represents a revolutionary advancement in computational power, utilizing principles from quantum mechanics to solve complex problems that are infeasible for classical computers. Unlike classical computers, which rely on bits that represent either 0 or 1, quantum computers use quantum bits (qubits) that can exist in multiple states simultaneously due to the phenomena of superposition and entanglement. These fundamental properties of quantum mechanics allow quantum computers to perform parallel computations at unprecedented speeds, making them highly suitable for certain types of problems, including those in artificial intelligence (AI), cryptography, and material science.

1. Qubits and Superposition

At the heart of quantum computing is the concept of the qubit, the quantum analogue of the classical bit. While classical bits can only represent one of two states (0 or 1), qubits can exist in a superposition of both 0 and 1 at the same time. This means that a single qubit can perform computations involving both values simultaneously, exponentially increasing the potential computational power when more qubits are added to a quantum system.

Superposition: Superposition is a fundamental principle in quantum mechanics that allows qubits to exist in multiple states at once. Instead of being constrained to either 0 or 1, a qubit can be in a linear combination of both. This ability to represent and process multiple states simultaneously is what gives quantum computers their power. For example, a quantum computer with two qubits can represent four possible states (00, 01, 10, and 11) at once, while a classical computer would require four separate computations to achieve the same result (Nielsen & Chuang, 2010). As the number of qubits increases, the computational capacity of the quantum system grows exponentially, enabling quantum computers to tackle problems that classical computers find intractable.

2. Quantum Entanglement

Another key feature of quantum computing is entanglement, a phenomenon in which two or more qubits become correlated in such a way that the state of one qubit is directly related to the state of another, regardless of the physical distance between them. This interdependence allows for coordinated operations on qubits and is essential for performing highly complex quantum computations.

Entanglement: When qubits are entangled, the measurement of one qubit's state immediately determines the state of its entangled partner, no matter how far apart the two are. This non-locality is one of the most counterintuitive aspects of quantum mechanics but is also one of its most powerful. Entanglement enables quantum computers to perform calculations in parallel, leveraging the correlation between entangled qubits to solve problems more efficiently than classical computers (Einstein et al., 1935). This property is essential for many quantum algorithms, such as Shor's algorithm for factoring large numbers, which exploits entanglement to achieve exponential speedup compared to classical algorithms (Shor, 1994).

3. Quantum Gates and Circuits

Quantum gates, analogous to classical logic gates, are the building blocks of quantum circuits. They manipulate qubits through operations that change their states according to the principles of quantum mechanics. Unlike classical gates, which only flip bits between 0 and 1, quantum gates perform more complex operations due to the superposition and entanglement of qubits.

Quantum Gates: Common quantum gates include the Hadamard gate, which puts a qubit into a superposition state, and the CNOT gate, which entangles two qubits by flipping the state of one based on the state of the other. These gates can be combined to form quantum circuits, which process qubits through a series of operations to perform specific calculations (Nielsen & Chuang, 2010). The power of quantum circuits lies in their ability to process information in parallel, allowing for the efficient solution of certain types of problems.

Quantum Algorithms: Several quantum algorithms take advantage of these gates and circuits to solve problems that are computationally intensive for classical computers. For instance, Grover's algorithm enables a quantum computer to search an unsorted database in $\sqrt{N}$ time, offering a quadratic speedup compared to classical search algorithms (Grover, 1996). Similarly, Shor's algorithm factors large integers exponentially faster than classical methods, which has significant implications for cryptography (Shor, 1994).

4. Quantum Decoherence and Error Correction

While quantum computing holds immense promise, it also faces significant challenges, primarily due to quantum decoherence and noise. Quantum systems are extremely sensitive to their environment, and interactions with external factors can cause qubits to lose their quantum properties, leading to errors in computation. Quantum decoherence refers to the process by which qubits lose their quantum coherence, reverting to classical states and making computations unreliable.

Quantum Decoherence: One of the main obstacles to building practical quantum computers is decoherence, which occurs when qubits interact with their surroundings, causing them to lose their quantum properties. This limits the time during which a quantum computer can perform meaningful computations before errors start to accumulate (Preskill, 2018). Developing methods to mitigate decoherence, such as improving qubit isolation and reducing environmental noise, is crucial for the advancement of quantum computing technology.

Quantum Error Correction: Quantum error correction techniques are being developed to address the issue of decoherence and other quantum errors. Unlike classical error correction, quantum error correction is more complex due to the nature of quantum information, which cannot be simply copied or observed without altering the system. Methods such as the surface code and the Shor code are designed to detect and correct errors without directly measuring the qubits, preserving the integrity of quantum computations (Preskill, 2018). Effective error correction is key to building large-scale, fault-tolerant quantum computers.

5. Quantum Computing's Potential in AI

The combination of quantum computing and AI is expected to unlock new possibilities, particularly in areas like optimization, machine learning, and data processing. Quantum computers are especially well-suited for solving complex optimization problems, such as those encountered in training machine learning models or simulating molecular interactions in drug discovery. The ability to process vast amounts of data in parallel and explore multiple solutions simultaneously makes quantum computing a promising tool for advancing AI capabilities.

Quantum Machine Learning: Quantum machine learning (QML) is an emerging field that explores how quantum algorithms can be used to accelerate machine learning tasks. Quantum computers could potentially solve problems related to data clustering, classification, and regression more efficiently than classical algorithms. For instance, the quantum support vector machine (QSVM) algorithm demonstrates potential improvements in training speed and accuracy compared to its classical counterparts (Biamonte et al., 2017). As quantum computing matures, it may play a transformative role in AI research, particularly in areas that require processing large datasets or optimizing complex systems.

Optimization and AI: Quantum algorithms excel at optimization problems, which are central to many AI tasks. For example, quantum annealing, a quantum algorithm used for solving optimization problems, has been applied to areas like AI model training, where finding the best set of parameters can be computationally expensive on classical systems. Quantum optimization algorithms could provide significant speedups in this area, improving the efficiency and accuracy of AI models (Farhi et al., 2014).

In summary, quantum computing represents a fundamental shift in how we approach computational problems, leveraging principles from quantum mechanics such as superposition, entanglement, and quantum gates to solve complex problems faster than classical computers. The potential of quantum computing to revolutionize fields such as cryptography, optimization, and machine learning is immense, but significant challenges related to decoherence and error correction remain. As advancements in quantum hardware and algorithms continue, the integration of quantum computing with AI holds the promise of accelerating breakthroughs in various industries, from drug discovery to financial modeling and beyond. Understanding the basics of quantum computing is the first step toward realizing the full potential of this emerging technology.

Potential Impact on AI and Big Data

Quantum computing is emerging as a revolutionary technology that has the potential to significantly impact many areas of artificial intelligence (AI) and big data analytics. By leveraging the principles of quantum mechanics, such as superposition and entanglement, quantum computing offers exponentially greater computational power compared to classical computers, making it well-suited to tackle complex problems in AI and data processing that are currently unsolvable or inefficient to solve with traditional methods. The convergence of quantum computing with AI and big data could drive advancements in machine learning, optimization, and data analysis, ultimately leading to faster, more accurate, and scalable AI systems.

1. Enhanced Machine Learning and Optimization

Machine learning, a core component of AI, involves training models to make predictions or decisions based on data. However, as datasets grow larger and models become more complex, the computational power required to train and optimize these models becomes a limiting factor. Quantum computing offers a potential solution by providing a new paradigm for optimization and training, enabling faster and more efficient processing of large-scale data.

Quantum Speedups in Machine Learning: Quantum machine learning (QML) algorithms could offer significant speedups in tasks such as data classification, clustering, and regression. One example is the quantum support vector machine (QSVM), which has the potential to outperform classical support vector machines by leveraging quantum states to explore multiple solutions simultaneously (Biamonte et al., 2017). Additionally, quantum neural networks (QNNs) could provide faster convergence and improved performance in training deep learning models. By harnessing the parallelism of quantum computers, AI systems could process larger datasets and train more complex models in significantly less time compared to classical systems (Rebentrost et al., 2014).

Optimization of AI Models: Many AI tasks, such as hyperparameter tuning and neural network training, can be framed as optimization problems. Classical optimization algorithms, such as gradient descent, can be computationally expensive and time-consuming, especially for high-dimensional data. Quantum computing has the potential to offer exponential speedups for solving optimization problems. Quantum algorithms like the Quantum Approximate Optimization Algorithm (QAOA) can efficiently search through large solution spaces and identify optimal configurations for AI models, improving both speed and accuracy (Farhi et al., 2014). This capability could be particularly valuable in areas like reinforcement learning, where agents must optimize decision policies over large state spaces.

2. Scalability for Big Data Processing

The explosion of big data has created both opportunities and challenges for AI. As datasets grow larger, processing and analyzing this information in a timely and efficient manner becomes increasingly difficult. Classical computers struggle with the scale of data, particularly in fields like genomics, finance, and climate modeling, where datasets can exceed terabytes or even petabytes. Quantum computing's ability to perform parallel computations offers a promising approach to handling big data.

Quantum Algorithms for Data Analysis: Quantum computing could revolutionize big data analysis by enabling faster and more scalable algorithms. For instance, quantum algorithms such as Grover's algorithm can significantly accelerate search operations, providing a quadratic speedup for unstructured data searches (Grover, 1996). This could be applied to tasks such as database querying and pattern recognition in large datasets, where classical methods are slow or computationally infeasible. Similarly, quantum Fourier transforms, which are exponentially faster than their classical counterparts, could be used in signal processing and feature extraction, enabling AI systems to identify meaningful patterns in massive datasets (Nielsen & Chuang, 2010).

Handling High-Dimensional Data: Many AI applications, particularly in fields like computer vision and natural language processing (NLP), involve high-dimensional data. Classical algorithms often struggle with the "curse of dimensionality," where the complexity of processing grows exponentially with the number of variables. Quantum computing's ability to process multiple states simultaneously through superposition can help overcome this challenge. Quantum algorithms can explore high-dimensional data spaces more efficiently, enabling faster and more accurate processing of complex datasets, such as images, text, or genomic data (Lloyd et al., 2014).

3. Quantum Advantage in AI Applications

Quantum computing's ability to perform certain computations exponentially faster than classical systems could lead to a quantum advantage in AI applications. This term refers to the point at which quantum computers can solve specific problems faster than the most powerful classical computers, potentially transforming industries that rely on AI and big data analysis.

Drug Discovery and Genomics: One of the most promising areas for quantum computing's impact on AI is in drug discovery and genomics. The process of simulating molecular interactions and identifying potential drug candidates involves solving complex optimization problems and processing vast amounts of genetic data. Quantum computing, combined with AI, could significantly speed up this process by accurately simulating molecular dynamics and predicting drug interactions (Cao et al., 2019). Quantum-enhanced machine learning could also improve the analysis of genomic data, enabling more personalized and effective treatments for diseases.

Financial Modeling and Risk Analysis: In finance, quantum computing could revolutionize areas such as portfolio optimization, risk analysis, and fraud detection. AI models that analyze financial markets and predict risks are often computationally intensive, particularly when dealing with high-dimensional datasets and real-time data streams. Quantum computing could provide more efficient algorithms for risk modeling and scenario analysis, improving the accuracy and speed of AI-driven financial decision-making (Orús et al., 2019).

Autonomous Systems and AI in Robotics: Quantum computing could also enhance the capabilities of AI in autonomous systems and robotics. Tasks such as real-time decision-making, navigation, and control involve processing large amounts of sensor data and solving complex optimization problems. Quantum-enhanced AI could lead to more efficient algorithms for pathfinding, object recognition, and decision-making, improving the performance of autonomous vehicles, drones, and robots in dynamic environments (Dunjko & Briegel, 2016).

4. Challenges and Limitations

While the potential impact of quantum computing on AI and big data is significant, there are several challenges and limitations that must be addressed before these technologies can be fully realized.

Hardware and Scalability: Quantum computing is still in its infancy, and building scalable, fault-tolerant quantum computers remains a major challenge. Current quantum systems, known as Noisy Intermediate-Scale Quantum (NISQ) devices, are limited in the number of qubits and are prone to errors due to noise and decoherence (Preskill, 2018). While these systems have demonstrated early successes in proof-of-concept applications, realizing the full potential of quantum computing for AI and big data will require significant advancements in hardware, error correction, and qubit coherence times.

Algorithm Development: Developing quantum algorithms that outperform classical algorithms in practical AI applications is another challenge. While quantum algorithms such as Grover's and Shor's offer theoretical speedups, translating these advantages into real-world applications requires further research and development. Many quantum algorithms are still in the experimental stage, and it remains to be seen how well they will perform in large-scale AI and big data scenarios (Shor, 1994).

Integration with Classical AI: Another challenge is integrating quantum computing with existing AI systems, which are predominantly based on classical computing. Quantum-classical hybrid systems, where quantum processors are used to accelerate specific parts of the AI pipeline while classical processors handle other tasks, are a promising approach. However, creating efficient interfaces between classical and quantum systems requires further research and development to ensure seamless integration and scalability (Bravyi et al., 2019).

In summary, Quantum computing has the potential to revolutionize AI and big data by enabling faster, more efficient algorithms for machine learning, optimization, and data analysis. The ability of quantum computers to process vast amounts of data in parallel and explore large solution spaces could lead to significant improvements in AI model training, optimization, and decision-making. However, significant challenges remain in developing scalable quantum hardware, creating robust quantum algorithms, and integrating quantum computing with classical AI systems. As research in quantum computing and AI progresses, the convergence of these technologies could transform industries ranging from healthcare and finance to autonomous systems and robotics, ushering in a new era of computational power and efficiency.

Current Research and Development

The intersection of quantum computing and artificial intelligence (AI) is a rapidly growing area of research, with significant interest from both academic institutions and industry leaders. Researchers are exploring how quantum computing's unique capabilities, such as superposition and entanglement, can accelerate AI algorithms, improve machine learning models, and address computational challenges that classical computers struggle to handle. Current research in this field spans quantum algorithms for machine learning, quantum-enhanced optimization techniques, and hybrid quantum-classical systems that seek to leverage the best of both worlds. Major technological corporations, governments, and universities are investing heavily in quantum computing, advancing both theoretical frameworks and practical implementations to bring this futuristic technology into reality.

1. Quantum Algorithms for Machine Learning

Quantum machine learning (QML) is one of the most exciting areas of research, focusing on developing quantum algorithms that could potentially outperform classical algorithms in machine learning tasks. Current research in QML aims to explore quantum enhancements for fundamental machine learning processes, such as classification, clustering, and regression, with potential applications in fields like natural language processing, computer vision, and drug discovery.

Quantum Support Vector Machines: Support vector machines (SVMs) are widely used for classification tasks in machine learning. Quantum support vector machines (QSVMs) take advantage of quantum computing's ability to process large amounts of data in parallel, enabling faster classification and training. Initial research on QSVMs suggests that they may offer a speedup in the training process, making them particularly useful for large datasets (Schuld & Petruccione, 2018). Further developments in this area are focusing on scaling QSVMs and integrating them with classical machine learning systems.

Quantum Neural Networks: Quantum neural networks (QNNs) aim to combine the principles of quantum mechanics with the structure of artificial neural networks. Researchers are investigating how quantum systems can enhance the learning capabilities of neural networks, potentially leading to more efficient training and better performance for deep learning models. Some early research suggests that QNNs may provide exponential speedups for specific tasks, although practical implementations of QNNs are still in the experimental phase (Biamonte et al., 2017).

2. Quantum Optimization for AI

Optimization plays a crucial role in AI, particularly in training models where minimizing loss functions or optimizing hyperparameters is essential. Current research is focused on how quantum algorithms can improve optimization processes in AI, potentially offering substantial performance gains over classical methods.

Quantum Approximate Optimization Algorithm (QAOA): The QAOA is a quantum algorithm designed to solve complex optimization problems by leveraging quantum mechanics' inherent parallelism. Research has shown that QAOA may outperform classical optimization techniques, particularly in problems related to combinatorial optimization, such as those found in machine learning model training and reinforcement learning (Farhi et al., 2014). Researchers are exploring ways to apply QAOA to a broader range of optimization problems in AI, with promising early results.

Quantum Annealing: Another avenue of research is quantum annealing, a process used to solve optimization problems by exploiting quantum tunneling to escape local minima. Quantum annealers, such as those developed by D-Wave Systems, have already demonstrated success in solving specific types of optimization problems faster than classical algorithms (Mott et al., 2017). While quantum annealing is still limited to particular problem classes, research continues to explore its application in optimizing machine learning models, such as tuning neural networks or solving resource allocation challenges.

3. Hybrid Quantum-Classical Systems

Given the limitations of current quantum computing hardware, particularly in terms of qubit count and error rates, researchers are investigating hybrid quantum-classical systems as a transitional approach. In these systems, quantum computers are used for specific tasks that can benefit from quantum speedups, while classical computers handle other parts of the computation pipeline

Variational Quantum Algorithms: Variational quantum algorithms (VQAs) are a hybrid approach where a quantum computer is used to perform specific operations, and a classical computer iteratively optimizes the parameters. One of the most well-known VQAs is the Variational Quantum Eigensolver (VQE), which has been applied in both quantum chemistry and machine learning (Peruzzo et al., 2014). Current research is extending VQA techniques to AI, focusing on tasks like training machine learning models where quantum computers assist in optimizing certain aspects of the model while classical systems handle the rest.

Quantum-Classical Neural Networks: Research is also underway into hybrid quantum-classical neural networks, where parts of the network are executed on quantum computers and others on classical hardware. This hybrid approach is seen as a practical way to integrate quantum computing with existing AI infrastructure while taking advantage of quantum speedups for specific computational tasks. Preliminary studies suggest that hybrid neural networks could improve both the efficiency and performance of AI models, especially in tasks requiring high-dimensional data processing (Killoran et al., 2019).

4. Advancements in Quantum Hardware for AI

The development of quantum hardware is crucial for the practical application of quantum computing in AI. Major technological companies such as IBM, Google, and Microsoft are making significant strides in building scalable quantum computers, with increasing qubit counts and reduced error rates.

IBM Quantum and Qiskit: IBM's quantum computing research has been at the forefront of the field, with their Qiskit platform enabling researchers and developers to experiment with quantum algorithms for AI. IBM's advancements in quantum hardware, such as improving coherence times and reducing gate errors, are accelerating research into practical applications of quantum computing in AI (Kandala et al., 2017). IBM's Quantum Experience platform allows researchers to run quantum algorithms and explore their potential for enhancing machine learning tasks.

Google's Quantum Supremacy: In 2019, Google made headlines with its announcement of achieving "quantum supremacy"—demonstrating that their quantum processor, Sycamore, could solve a specific problem faster than the most powerful classical supercomputers (Arute et al., 2019). While this breakthrough was not directly related to AI, it highlighted the growing capabilities of quantum hardware and set the stage for future research into applying these advancements to AI and big data.

5. Key Challenges in Quantum AI Research

Despite the promising research and development in quantum computing for AI, several significant challenges remain.

Noisy Intermediate-Scale Quantum (NISQ) Era: Quantum computing is currently in the NISQ era, where available quantum computers have limited qubits and are prone to errors due to noise and decoherence. This makes it difficult to run large-scale quantum algorithms for AI without significant error rates. Research is ongoing to develop error correction methods and hardware improvements to make quantum systems more reliable and scalable for AI applications (Preskill, 2018).

Algorithm Development: Developing quantum algorithms that offer clear advantages over classical ones in AI remains a challenge. While there are theoretical speedups for certain tasks, practical implementations are often limited by hardware constraints. Researchers are actively working to create new quantum algorithms that can solve real-world AI problems more efficiently than their classical counterparts (Lloyd et al., 2014).

Scalability: Building scalable quantum computers with enough qubits to tackle complex AI and big data problems is another major hurdle. Current research is focused on improving quantum hardware by increasing qubit counts, reducing error rates, and developing qubit architectures that can scale to the millions of qubits necessary for large-scale AI applications (Nielsen & Chuang, 2010).

Conclusion

Quantum computing has the potential to significantly enhance AI and big data processing through faster algorithms, improved optimization techniques, and the ability to handle high-dimensional data more efficiently. Current research and development are focused on quantum algorithms for machine learning, optimization techniques such as QAOA and quantum annealing, and hybrid quantum-classical systems that leverage quantum computing's strengths while compensating for its current limitations. Major technological companies and academic institutions are pushing the boundaries of quantum hardware, striving to build scalable quantum computers that can support the growing demands of AI research. While significant challenges remain, the convergence of quantum computing and AI offers a promising future, with potential breakthroughs in areas such as drug discovery, financial modeling, and autonomous systems.

References

Arute, F., Arya, K., Babbush, R., Bacon, D., Bardin, J. C., Barends, R., ... & Martinis, J. M. (2019). Quantum supremacy using a programmable superconducting processor. *Nature, 574*(7779), 505-510.

Biamonte, J., Wittek, P., Pancotti, N., Rebentrost, P., Wiebe, N., & Lloyd, S. (2017). Quantum machine learning. *Nature, 549*(7671), 195-202. https://doi.org/10.1038/nature23474

Bravyi, S., Gosset, D., & König, R. (2019). Quantum advantage with shallow circuits. *Science, 362*(6412), 308-311. https://doi.org/10.1126/science.aao7150

Cao, Y., Romero, J., Olson, J. P., Degroote, M., Johnson, P. D., Kieferová, M., ... & Aspuru-Guzik, A. (2019). Quantum chemistry in the age of quantum computing. *Chemical Reviews, 119*(19), 10856-10915.

Dunjko, V., & Briegel, H. J. (2016). Machine learning and artificial intelligence in the quantum domain: A review of recent progress. *Reports on Progress in Physics, 81*(7), 074001.

Einstein, A., Podolsky, B., & Rosen, N. (1935). Can quantum-mechanical description of physical reality be considered complete? *Physical Review, 47*(10), 777-780.

Farhi, E., Goldstone, J., & Gutmann, S. (2014). A quantum approximate optimization algorithm. *arXiv preprint arXiv:1411.4028.*

Grover, L. K. (1996). A fast quantum mechanical algorithm for database search. *Proceedings of the 28th Annual ACM Symposium on the Theory of Computing,* 212-219.

Kandala, A., Mezzacapo, A., Temme, K., Takita, M., Brink, M., Chow, J. M., & Gambetta, J. M. (2017). Hardware-efficient variational quantum eigensolver for small molecules and quantum magnets. *Nature, 549*(7671), 242-246.

Killoran, N., Bromley, T. R., Arrazola, J. M., Schuld, M., Quesada, N., & Lloyd, S. (2019). Continuous-variable quantum neural networks. *Physical Review Research, 1*(3), 033063.

Nielsen, M. A., & Chuang, I. L. (2010). *Quantum computation and quantum information.* Cambridge University Press.

Preskill, J. (2018). Quantum computing in the NISQ era and beyond. *Quantum, 2,* 79.

Shor, P. W. (1994). Algorithms for quantum computation: Discrete logarithms and factoring. *Proceedings of the 35th Annual Symposium on Foundations of Computer Science,* 124-134.

Chapter 29: AI Ethics and Governance

AI Policy Frameworks

As Artificial Intelligence (AI) continues to evolve and be applied across various industries, there is a growing need for robust AI policy frameworks to ensure its ethical development and deployment. These frameworks are crucial for addressing concerns related to privacy, security, fairness, accountability, and transparency in AI systems. Governments, international organizations, and industry leaders are recognizing the potential risks posed by AI technologies and are working to create comprehensive guidelines that promote responsible AI development while safeguarding societal values. AI policy frameworks aim to strike a balance between innovation and regulation, ensuring that AI benefits society while mitigating potential harms.

1. Key Components of AI Policy Frameworks

Effective AI policy frameworks typically include several core components designed to guide the ethical development, deployment, and governance of AI systems. These components address various aspects of AI's impact on society, including fairness, transparency, accountability, and privacy.

Fairness and Non-Discrimination: One of the primary goals of AI policy frameworks is to ensure that AI systems are fair and non-discriminatory. AI algorithms often learn from large datasets, and if these datasets contain biased information, the AI systems can inadvertently perpetuate or amplify existing biases. For example, biased training data in facial recognition systems has led to discriminatory outcomes in law enforcement and hiring processes. AI policy frameworks must therefore include guidelines to ensure fairness in AI, including measures for bias detection and mitigation (Binns, 2018). This could involve auditing AI systems for biased outcomes and developing algorithms that can be corrected for these biases.

Transparency and Explainability: Transparency is another critical component of AI policy frameworks. As AI systems become more complex, particularly in deep learning, their decision-making processes are often seen as "black boxes," making it difficult for users to understand how decisions are made. Explainability refers to the ability to provide clear, understandable reasons for an AI system's decisions, allowing users to scrutinize, challenge, or trust these outcomes. AI policy frameworks often require that AI systems be designed to be explainable, particularly in high-stakes fields like healthcare, finance, and criminal justice, where the reasoning behind decisions can have significant impacts (Rudin, 2019). This ensures that AI systems are transparent and accountable.

Accountability and Liability: AI systems must be designed and implemented in a manner that holds organizations accountable for the outcomes produced by AI decisions. AI policy frameworks often include provisions for identifying who is responsible when an AI system causes harm or makes incorrect decisions. For instance, if an autonomous vehicle causes an accident, the framework should clarify whether the manufacturer, software developer, or operator is liable. Creating clear accountability mechanisms helps ensure that organizations remain responsible for AI systems' actions and encourages them to implement appropriate safeguards (Wachter et al., 2017).

Data Privacy and Security: Given that AI systems often rely on large amounts of data, ensuring data privacy and security is a key focus in AI policy frameworks. These frameworks typically align with existing privacy regulations, such as the European Union's General Data Protection Regulation (GDPR) and the California Consumer Privacy Act (CCPA), which mandate the protection of personal data. AI policy frameworks must ensure that data used for training AI models is collected, processed, and stored in a secure and privacy-compliant manner. They may also impose restrictions on the use of sensitive data, such as health records or biometric information, and require organizations to obtain user consent for data processing (Goodman & Flaxman, 2017).

2. Global AI Policy Initiatives

Several countries and international organizations have developed or are in the process of developing AI policy frameworks to guide the responsible use of AI. These initiatives are designed to address the ethical, legal, and social implications of AI technologies on a global scale.

European Union: AI Act: The European Union (EU) has been at the forefront of AI governance, with the introduction of the *Artificial Intelligence Act*, which seeks to regulate AI systems based on their potential risks. The AI Act categorizes AI systems into different risk levels, from minimal risk to unacceptable risk, with higher-risk systems subject to stricter regulatory oversight. The act also requires transparency and accountability measures, particularly for AI systems used in critical sectors such as healthcare, transportation, and law enforcement (European Commission, 2021). This policy framework ensures that AI systems in high-risk areas are carefully monitored and that safeguards are in place to protect public interests.

United States: National AI Initiative Act: The United States has also taken steps to create a policy framework for AI governance. The *National AI Initiative Act*, passed in 2020, aims to promote responsible AI innovation and establish a coordinated federal strategy for AI development. It emphasizes the importance of ethical AI development and provides funding for research in AI ethics, safety, and security. The initiative encourages collaboration between government, academia, and industry to ensure that AI technologies are developed in a way that benefits society while minimizing risks (White House, 2020).

OECD Principles on AI: The Organisation for Economic Co-operation and Development (OECD) has developed a set of principles on AI that serve as a global policy framework for AI governance. These principles emphasize the need for AI to be inclusive, sustainable, and human-centered. They highlight the importance of transparency, accountability, and fairness in AI systems and encourage governments and organizations to promote policies that ensure AI technologies are aligned with human rights and democratic values (OECD, 2019). The OECD principles are non-binding but have been endorsed by several countries as a guide for developing national AI policies.

3. Challenges in Implementing AI Policy Frameworks

While AI policy frameworks are essential for ensuring the responsible use of AI technologies, there are several challenges associated with their implementation.

Rapid Technological Advancements: AI technologies are advancing at a rapid pace, making it difficult for policy frameworks to keep up with new developments. For example, advancements in generative AI models, such as OpenAI's GPT-3, have raised new ethical concerns regarding misinformation, bias, and intellectual property rights. Policy frameworks need to be flexible enough to adapt to emerging AI technologies while maintaining robust ethical standards (Floridi et al., 2018).

Global Coordination: AI policy frameworks vary significantly across countries and regions, which can lead to inconsistencies in how AI technologies are regulated. For example, the EU's AI Act is more stringent than AI policies in other parts of the world, which could create challenges for multinational companies that operate across borders. Harmonizing AI policy frameworks on a global scale is essential to ensure that AI technologies are governed consistently while fostering international collaboration and innovation (Floridi et al., 2018).

Balancing Innovation with Regulation: One of the primary challenges in AI policy is striking the right balance between fostering innovation and ensuring ethical AI development. Overly restrictive regulations could stifle innovation and hinder the growth of AI technologies, while insufficient regulation could lead to harmful consequences for society. Policymakers must carefully design frameworks that encourage responsible AI development without imposing undue burdens on organizations (Whittlestone et al., 2019).

4. Future Directions in AI Governance

As AI continues to evolve, AI policy frameworks will need to adapt to address new challenges and opportunities. Future directions in AI governance are likely to focus on the following areas:

Algorithmic Auditing and Certification: Policymakers are increasingly calling for independent auditing and certification of AI systems to ensure that they comply with ethical standards. This could involve third-party audits of AI models to assess their fairness, transparency, and accountability. Certification programs could be developed to validate AI systems used in critical sectors, such as healthcare and finance, ensuring that they meet established ethical guidelines (Raji et al., 2020).

Human-in-the-Loop Approaches: AI policy frameworks may also emphasize the importance of maintaining human oversight over AI systems, particularly in high-stakes decision-making processes. Human-in-the-loop approaches ensure that AI systems augment human decision-making rather than replacing it, reducing the risk of errors and promoting accountability. Future frameworks could mandate that certain AI applications, such as those used in criminal justice or autonomous driving, require human oversight (Doshi-Velez & Kortz, 2017).

Ethical AI Development: Moving forward, AI policy frameworks are likely to place greater emphasis on promoting ethical AI development from the outset. This could involve encouraging organizations to adopt ethical AI design principles, such as privacy by design and fairness by design, which ensure that ethical considerations are integrated into AI systems from the initial stages of development (Jobin et al., 2019).

In summary, AI policy frameworks are essential for ensuring that AI technologies are developed and deployed responsibly. By addressing issues related to fairness, transparency, accountability, and privacy, these frameworks help mitigate the potential risks associated with AI while fostering innovation. Governments, international organizations, and industry leaders are working to create comprehensive guidelines that align AI development with societal values and ethical standards. However, challenges such as rapid technological advancements, global coordination, and balancing regulation with innovation remain. As AI continues to evolve, ongoing research, collaboration, and adaptation will be necessary to ensure that AI policy frameworks are effective in addressing future ethical and governance challenges.

Societal Implications

As artificial intelligence (AI) systems become more integrated into the fabric of daily life, their societal implications have garnered significant attention. While AI has the potential to drive economic growth, enhance healthcare, and improve quality of life, it also presents significant ethical and societal challenges. These challenges revolve around issues such as bias, inequality, privacy, accountability, and the shifting nature of human labor. Proper governance frameworks are essential to ensure that AI benefits society equitably while addressing its potential risks. This section discusses the societal implications of AI, focusing on its impact on social justice, privacy, employment, and human agency.

1. Bias and Fairness in AI Systems

One of the most pressing societal concerns related to AI is algorithmic bias, which occurs when AI systems inadvertently perpetuate or amplify existing societal biases. Bias can emerge in AI systems for several reasons, including biased training data, flawed algorithm design, or unintended correlations within large datasets. This can result in discriminatory outcomes, particularly in high-stakes areas such as hiring, criminal justice, and healthcare, where AI systems are increasingly being used to make critical decisions.

Discriminatory Impacts: AI systems trained on biased historical data can reflect and even reinforce existing social inequalities. For example, predictive policing algorithms have been found to disproportionately target minority communities due to biased crime data, leading to increased surveillance and unjust law enforcement practices (O'Neil, 2016). Similarly, AI-based hiring systems that rely on historical employment data may inadvertently disadvantage underrepresented groups by perpetuating past hiring biases (Raji et al., 2020). Ensuring fairness in AI is critical to mitigating these harms and promoting social justice.

Mitigating Bias: Addressing algorithmic bias requires a multifaceted approach that involves improving data quality, developing fairer algorithms, and establishing regulatory frameworks to audit and govern AI systems. Policymakers and AI developers are working on strategies such as bias detection tools, fairness-by-design principles, and the inclusion of diverse perspectives in AI development to ensure that AI systems serve all communities equitably (Mehrabi et al., 2021). AI ethics frameworks must also ensure that these systems are held accountable when biases are discovered, with clear guidelines for how to rectify such issues.

2. Privacy and Surveillance Concerns

The increasing deployment of AI technologies in both public and private sectors raises significant concerns about privacy and surveillance. AI systems, especially those powered by machine learning, require vast amounts of data to function effectively. This often includes personal data such as location, biometrics, and

714

behavioral patterns. The widespread use of AI for surveillance, tracking, and data collection has sparked concerns about individual privacy and the potential for abuse by both corporations and governments.

Erosion of Privacy: AI-driven surveillance systems, such as facial recognition technologies, have been widely adopted by law enforcement agencies, public safety organizations, and private corporations. While these technologies can enhance security, they also raise concerns about privacy violations, particularly when used without consent or oversight (Brayne, 2020). For example, facial recognition systems deployed in public spaces can be used to track individuals' movements and behavior without their knowledge, potentially leading to a "surveillance state" where privacy rights are eroded. In some cases, these systems have been prone to errors, disproportionately misidentifying individuals from marginalized communities (Garvie et al., 2016).

Data Governance and Regulation: To protect individual privacy, robust data governance frameworks must be established that regulate the collection, storage, and use of personal data. Regulations such as the European Union's General Data Protection Regulation (GDPR) and the California Consumer Privacy Act (CCPA) are important steps in safeguarding data privacy. However, as AI technologies continue to evolve, these regulations will need to be updated to address new privacy challenges posed by emerging AI applications. For example, the use of AI in analyzing sensitive health data or personal behavior may require stricter oversight to prevent misuse or unauthorized access (Goodman & Flaxman, 2017).

3. Impact on Employment and the Future of Work

AI's ability to automate tasks and processes has profound implications for employment and the future of work. While AI has the potential to increase productivity and drive economic growth, it also threatens to displace certain jobs, particularly those involving routine and repetitive tasks. This raises questions about how AI will impact labor markets, income inequality, and the broader social fabric.

Job Displacement: AI-driven automation is expected to lead to significant disruptions in the workforce. Jobs in sectors such as manufacturing, transportation, and retail are particularly vulnerable to automation, with AI systems capable of performing tasks more efficiently and at lower costs than human workers. A study by McKinsey Global Institute estimates that by 2030, up to 375 million workers worldwide may need to switch jobs or acquire new skills due to automation (Manyika et al., 2017). While some jobs will be created in AI development, maintenance, and oversight, the transition may lead to increased economic inequality if displaced workers are unable to find new employment or adapt to the changing job market.

Reskilling and Workforce Transformation: To mitigate the negative impact of AI on employment, governments and organizations must invest in reskilling and upskilling programs that prepare workers for the jobs of the future. AI governance frameworks should include policies that encourage workforce transformation by providing education and training in digital literacy, AI ethics, and the skills needed to thrive in an AI-driven economy. Additionally, there may be a need to explore new social safety nets, such as universal basic income or job guarantee programs, to support workers displaced by automation (Brynjolfsson & McAfee, 2014).

4. Human Agency and Decision-Making

As AI systems take on more decision-making roles in areas such as healthcare, finance, and public policy, concerns about the erosion of human agency have emerged. Human agency refers to the capacity of individuals to make informed, autonomous decisions. AI systems, particularly those driven by machine learning, often make decisions based on complex algorithms that are difficult for humans to interpret or challenge.

Over-Reliance on AI: There is a growing concern that over-reliance on AI systems may diminish human agency by delegating critical decision-making tasks to machines. For instance, AI systems used in healthcare may recommend treatment options based on data patterns, but if clinicians and patients become overly dependent on these recommendations, it could undermine their ability to make informed, autonomous decisions (Tschandl et al., 2020). Similarly, in criminal justice, AI-based risk assessment tools may influence sentencing or parole decisions, raising ethical questions about the fairness and transparency of these systems.

Preserving Human Oversight: To preserve human agency, AI governance frameworks must ensure that AI systems are designed to augment rather than replace human decision-making. Human-in-the-loop approaches, which involve maintaining human oversight over AI-driven decisions, are essential to ensuring accountability and preserving the role of human judgment. This approach is particularly important in areas where AI decisions have life-altering consequences, such as in healthcare or law enforcement (Doshi-Velez & Kortz, 2017). Future AI governance policies should also emphasize the need for explainability and transparency in AI systems to empower individuals to make informed decisions based on AI recommendations.

5. Economic Inequality and Access to AI Benefits

AI has the potential to exacerbate existing social and economic inequalities if its benefits are not distributed equitably. There are concerns that the advantages of AI, such as increased productivity, cost savings, and improved healthcare outcomes, may primarily benefit wealthy individuals, corporations, and nations, leaving disadvantaged groups and developing countries behind.

Unequal Access to AI: Access to AI technologies is often limited by economic, technical, and infrastructural barriers. Wealthier nations and large corporations are more likely to have the resources to invest in AI research, development, and deployment, while low-income communities and developing countries may lack the infrastructure and funding to benefit from AI advancements. This unequal access to AI could widen the digital divide, leading to increased economic inequality between nations and within societies (Eubanks, 2018).

Inclusive AI Development: To address these disparities, AI governance frameworks must prioritize inclusive AI development. This involves ensuring that AI technologies are accessible to all individuals and communities, regardless of their socioeconomic status. Policymakers should promote the development of AI systems that address the needs of marginalized and underserved populations, such as AI applications in education, healthcare, and public services designed to improve outcomes for disadvantaged groups. Additionally, international cooperation and investment in AI research for the global South can help bridge the gap between developed and developing countries (Floridi et al., 2018).

In summary, the societal implications of AI are vast and complex, encompassing issues of fairness, privacy, employment, human agency, and inequality. As AI technologies continue to evolve, it is essential that ethical governance frameworks are in place to address these concerns and ensure that AI benefits society as a whole. By focusing on fairness, transparency, accountability, and inclusivity, AI policy frameworks can help mitigate the risks associated with AI while promoting innovation and progress. As AI systems increasingly influence critical aspects of daily life, policymakers, technologists, and society must work together to ensure that AI technologies are developed and deployed in ways that align with social and ethical values.

Building Ethical AI Systems

The rapid integration of artificial intelligence (AI) into various sectors, from healthcare and finance to law enforcement and education, has highlighted the critical need to build ethical AI systems. Ethical AI refers to the design, development, and deployment of AI technologies in ways that align with moral principles, safeguard human rights, and promote fairness, transparency, and accountability. As AI systems increasingly influence decision-making in society, it is crucial to ensure that these technologies do not perpetuate harm, bias, or inequality. Building ethical AI systems requires a multifaceted approach that includes technical innovation, regulatory frameworks, stakeholder involvement, and a commitment to human-centered design. This section explores key strategies for building ethical AI systems, focusing on fairness, transparency, accountability, inclusivity, and the role of governance.

1. Ensuring Fairness and Mitigating Bias

One of the most significant ethical challenges in AI development is ensuring fairness and preventing bias. AI systems are often trained on large datasets that may contain biases reflective of historical and societal inequalities. When these biases are embedded in AI models, they can lead to discriminatory outcomes, particularly in sensitive areas such as hiring, criminal justice, and healthcare.

Algorithmic Fairness: To build ethical AI systems, developers must prioritize fairness throughout the AI lifecycle. This involves carefully curating training datasets to ensure they are representative of diverse populations and do not reflect harmful stereotypes. Techniques such as bias detection and mitigation can be used to identify and reduce bias in AI models (Mehrabi et al., 2021). For example, fairness-aware algorithms can be designed to ensure that predictions or decisions are not disproportionately favorable or unfavorable to any particular group based on protected characteristics such as race, gender, or socioeconomic status.

Continuous Monitoring and Auditing: Ethical AI systems must be continuously monitored and audited to detect and address biases that may emerge over time. This is particularly important in dynamic environments where AI systems learn from new data, potentially introducing unforeseen biases. Regular audits of AI algorithms can help ensure that they continue to operate in a fair and equitable manner (Raji et al., 2020). Independent oversight and third-party auditing may also be necessary to verify the fairness of AI systems, particularly in high-stakes areas like credit scoring, policing, and hiring.

2. Promoting Transparency and Explainability

AI systems, particularly those based on complex machine learning models such as deep learning, are often described as "black boxes" because their decision-making processes are difficult to interpret. Lack of transparency can erode trust in AI technologies, especially when they are used in high-stakes decision-making contexts. To build ethical AI systems, it is essential to promote transparency and explainability.

Explainable AI (XAI): Explainability refers to the ability to understand and interpret how an AI system arrives at its decisions. Building explainable AI systems ensures that users and stakeholders can understand the factors that influence an AI model's output. Techniques such as Local Interpretable Model-Agnostic Explanations (LIME) and SHapley Additive exPlanations (SHAP) can be used to provide clear, human-readable explanations for AI decisions (Lundberg & Lee, 2017). Explainability is particularly important in domains such as healthcare, where clinicians need to trust and verify AI-generated diagnoses or treatment recommendations.

Transparent Development Processes: In addition to making AI models more interpretable, ethical AI systems require transparency in their development processes. This includes documenting the data used to train models, the assumptions made during development, and the criteria for evaluating performance. Transparency in AI development allows stakeholders to scrutinize and evaluate AI systems more effectively, ensuring that they are designed and deployed with accountability (Rudin, 2019).

3. Ensuring Accountability and Responsibility

Accountability is a fundamental principle of ethical AI systems. When AI systems make decisions that impact individuals' lives, it is crucial to have clear lines of responsibility to ensure that humans, rather than machines, are held accountable for the outcomes. Establishing accountability frameworks for AI systems involves determining who is responsible for the decisions made by AI and how these decisions can be challenged or corrected.

Human-in-the-Loop (HITL) Approaches: One strategy for ensuring accountability is the implementation of human-in-the-loop (HITL) approaches, where human oversight is maintained over AI-driven decisions. In high-stakes applications, such as autonomous vehicles, healthcare, or criminal justice, human decision-makers should have the ability to override AI decisions when necessary. HITL approaches ensure that AI systems augment rather than replace human judgment, preserving accountability (Doshi-Velez & Kortz, 2017). For example, in healthcare, AI systems that provide diagnostic recommendations should always involve clinicians who can review and confirm the AI's findings before making final decisions.

Ethical Governance and Redress Mechanisms: Ethical AI systems also require governance structures that establish clear accountability and provide redress mechanisms for individuals affected by AI decisions. Governance frameworks should specify who is responsible when an AI system malfunctions, causes harm, or produces biased outcomes. This is particularly important in cases where AI systems make decisions autonomously, such as in financial markets or autonomous driving. Redress mechanisms should be in place to allow individuals to challenge and seek remedies for decisions made by AI systems, ensuring that accountability is maintained throughout the AI lifecycle (Whittlestone et al., 2019).

4. Inclusivity and Stakeholder Engagement

Building ethical AI systems requires inclusivity and the active involvement of diverse stakeholders in the AI development process. AI systems that are developed in isolation or without considering the perspectives of diverse communities are more likely to perpetuate inequalities and exclude marginalized groups from the benefits of AI technologies.

Inclusive AI Design: Ethical AI systems should be designed with inclusivity in mind, ensuring that they serve the needs of diverse populations. This involves engaging stakeholders from different socioeconomic backgrounds, genders, ethnicities, and abilities in the AI design process. Including diverse perspectives helps identify potential biases and ensures that AI systems are developed in ways that are fair and equitable (West et al., 2019). For example, when developing AI for public services, it is essential to engage community organizations and civil society groups to ensure that the system meets the needs of all citizens.

Participatory Governance: In addition to inclusive design, ethical AI systems benefit from participatory governance models, where affected stakeholders are involved in decisions about how AI technologies are used. Participatory governance allows communities to have a say in how AI is deployed in areas like healthcare, education, and public safety, ensuring that AI systems are aligned with the values and needs of the people they serve (Floridi et al., 2018). This approach also enhances public trust in AI systems by providing greater transparency and accountability in their deployment.

5. Regulatory and Ethical Guidelines

To guide the development of ethical AI systems, it is essential to establish regulatory and ethical guidelines that set clear standards for AI development, deployment, and use. These guidelines should address key ethical principles, including fairness, transparency, accountability, and respect for human rights.

International AI Ethics Guidelines: Several international organizations and governments have developed ethical guidelines for AI. For example, the Organisation for Economic Co-operation and Development (OECD) has established AI principles that emphasize inclusive growth, human-centered values, transparency, and accountability (OECD, 2019). Similarly, the European Union's *Ethics Guidelines for Trustworthy AI* outlines ethical requirements for AI systems, including the need for explainability, robustness, and accountability (European Commission, 2019). These guidelines provide a foundation for developers, policymakers, and organizations to build ethical AI systems.

Ethical AI by Design: Building ethical AI systems requires embedding ethical principles into the design and development process from the outset. This concept, often referred to as "ethical AI by design," ensures that ethical considerations such as fairness, privacy, and accountability are not afterthoughts but central to the AI development process (Jobin et al., 2019). By incorporating ethics into the technical design, organizations can proactively address potential harms and ensure that AI systems are aligned with societal values.

Conclusion

Building ethical AI systems is a critical challenge as AI technologies continue to advance and become more integrated into society. Ensuring fairness, transparency, accountability, and inclusivity is essential for addressing the ethical challenges posed by AI. Techniques such as explainable AI, continuous monitoring, and human-in-the-loop approaches help promote accountability and trust in AI systems. Inclusive design and participatory governance ensure that AI technologies are developed with diverse perspectives and serve the needs of all communities. Finally, regulatory frameworks and ethical guidelines provide the necessary foundation for governing AI in a way that aligns with societal values. As AI continues to evolve, the commitment to building ethical AI systems will play a vital role in ensuring that these technologies benefit society while minimizing harm.

References

Binns, R. (2018). Fairness in machine learning: Lessons from political philosophy. *Proceedings of the 2018 Conference on Fairness, Accountability, and Transparency*, 149-159.

Brayne, S. (2020). *Predict and surveil: Data, discretion, and the future of policing.* Oxford University Press.

Brynjolfsson, E., & McAfee, A. (2014). *The second machine age: Work, progress, and prosperity in a time of brilliant technologies.* W.W. Norton & Company.

Doshi-Velez, F., & Kortz, M. (2017). Accountability of AI under the law: The role of explanation. *arXiv preprint arXiv:1711.01134.* https://arxiv.org/abs/1711.01134

Eubanks, V. (2018). *Automating inequality: How high-tech tools profile, police, and punish the poor.* St. Martin's Press.

European Commission. (2019). Ethics guidelines for trustworthy AI. *High-Level Expert Group on Artificial Intelligence.* https://ec.europa.eu/futurium/en/ai-alliance-consultation

European Commission. (2021). Proposal for a regulation laying down harmonised rules on artificial intelligence (Artificial Intelligence Act) and amending certain union legislative acts. https://eur-lex.europa.eu/legal-content/EN/TXT/?uri=CELEX:52021PC0206

Floridi, L., Cowls, J., King, T. C., & Taddeo, M. (2018). How to design AI for social good: Seven essential factors. *Science and Engineering Ethics, 26*(3), 1771-1796.

Garvie, C., Bedoya, A. M., & Frankle, J. (2016). *The perpetual line-up: Unregulated police face recognition in America.* Georgetown Law, Center on Privacy & Technology.

Goodman, B., & Flaxman, S. (2017). European Union regulations on algorithmic decision-making and a "right to explanation." *AI Magazine, 38*(3), 50-57. https://doi.org/10.1609/aimag.v38i3.2741

Jobin, A., Ienca, M., & Vayena, E. (2019). The global landscape of AI ethics guidelines. *Nature Machine Intelligence, 1*(9), 389-399.

Lundberg, S. M., & Lee, S.-I. (2017). A unified approach to interpreting model predictions. *Advances in Neural Information Processing Systems, 30*, 4765-4774.

Manyika, J., Chui, M., Miremadi, M., Bughin, J., George, K., Willmott, P., & Dewhurst, M. (2017). A future that works: Automation, employment, and productivity. McKinsey Global Institute.

Mehrabi, N., Morstatter, F., Saxena, N., Lerman, K., & Galstyan, A. (2021). A survey on bias and fairness in machine learning. *ACM Computing Surveys (CSUR), 54*(6), 1-35.

O'Neil, C. (2016). *Weapons of math destruction: How big data increases inequality and threatens democracy.* Crown Publishing Group.

OECD. (2019). Recommendation of the council on artificial intelligence. *Organisation for Economic Co-operation and Development.* https://legalinstruments.oecd.org/en/instruments/OECD-LEGAL-0449

Raji, I. D., Bender, E. M., Paullada, A., Denton, E., & Hanna, A. (2020). AI and the everything in the whole wide world benchmark. *Proceedings of the 2020 Conference on Fairness, Accountability, and Transparency*, 526-536.

Rudin, C. (2019). Stop explaining black box machine learning models for high stakes decisions and use interpretable models instead. *Nature Machine Intelligence, 1*(5), 206-215.

Tschandl, P., Rinner, C., Apalla, Z., Argenziano, G., Codella, N., Halpern, A., ... & Kittler, H. (2020). Human–computer collaboration for skin cancer recognition. *Nature Medicine, 26*(8), 1229-1234.

Whittlestone, J., Nyrup, R., Alexandrova, A., & Dihal, K. (2019). Ethical and societal implications of algorithms, data, and artificial intelligence: A roadmap for research. *Nuffield Foundation Report.*

Chapter 30: The Future of AI in Data Science and Big Data

Emerging Trends

The intersection of artificial intelligence (AI), data science, and big data is driving transformative changes across industries, reshaping the way organizations process, analyze, and derive insights from vast datasets. As data continues to grow exponentially, emerging trends in AI and big data are enabling more efficient, scalable, and intelligent data analysis, while also addressing key challenges such as data privacy, real-time processing, and the integration of AI into business operations. These emerging trends reflect advancements in machine learning, automation, edge computing, and the use of AI for enhanced decision-making. This section explores several key trends that are shaping the future of AI in data science and big data, including AI-powered automation, real-time analytics, AI at the edge, responsible AI, and the rise of augmented analytics.

1. AI-Powered Automation and Data Science

One of the most significant trends in AI and data science is the increasing automation of data analysis workflows. Automated machine learning (AutoML) and AI-powered analytics platforms are helping organizations streamline the entire data pipeline, from data preprocessing to model development, evaluation, and deployment. By automating repetitive and time-consuming tasks, AI-powered automation enables data scientists to focus on higher-level problem-solving and strategic insights, accelerating the delivery of business value from big data.

Automated Machine Learning (AutoML): AutoML platforms automate key steps in the machine learning workflow, including feature selection, model tuning, and hyperparameter optimization. AutoML tools allow users with limited data science expertise to build robust machine learning models, reducing the time and technical barriers associated with traditional model development (Hutter et al.,

728

2019). This democratization of AI is empowering businesses to harness the power of big data without relying exclusively on highly specialized data science teams.

Automation of Data Wrangling: Another emerging trend is the automation of data wrangling, which involves cleaning, transforming, and organizing data for analysis. Data wrangling is often one of the most labor-intensive steps in the data science pipeline. Advances in AI are enabling the development of tools that can automatically detect errors, fill missing values, and standardize data formats, making it easier to prepare large datasets for machine learning (Heaton, 2019). This automation of data preparation is especially valuable in big data environments, where the volume, velocity, and variety of data require more efficient handling.

2. Real-Time Analytics and AI

With the growth of big data, there is an increasing demand for real-time analytics, where organizations can make data-driven decisions instantly as data is generated. AI is playing a crucial role in enabling real-time data processing and decision-making, allowing businesses to react faster to changing conditions, whether in finance, healthcare, manufacturing, or retail. The ability to process and analyze streaming data in real time is becoming a key differentiator for organizations seeking to gain competitive advantages in fast-moving industries.

AI for Real-Time Data Processing: Real-time analytics requires the ability to process large amounts of data as it is generated. Traditional batch processing methods, which involve analyzing data at set intervals, are not sufficient for applications where immediate action is required, such as fraud detection, autonomous vehicles, or dynamic pricing. AI algorithms, particularly those based on deep learning and reinforcement learning, are being used to process and analyze streaming data in real time, allowing for faster and more accurate decision-making (Bifet et al., 2018). For example, AI can be used to detect anomalies in financial transactions as they occur, enabling real-time fraud detection.

Edge AI and Distributed Analytics: A related trend is the rise of edge AI, where data is processed closer to its source, such as on local devices or edge servers, rather than in centralized data centers. Edge AI allows for real-time processing of data generated by sensors, IoT devices, and autonomous systems, enabling faster decision-making with reduced latency. This is particularly valuable in industries like healthcare, manufacturing, and autonomous transportation, where real-time responses are critical. The combination of edge computing and AI is helping to overcome the limitations of traditional cloud-based analytics by reducing data transmission delays and bandwidth costs (Shi et al., 2016).

3. Responsible AI and Data Governance

As AI becomes more pervasive in data science and big data analytics, there is a growing focus on responsible AI and data governance. Ensuring that AI systems are transparent, fair, and accountable is critical to maintaining public trust and avoiding harmful societal impacts. Key trends in responsible AI include the development of frameworks for ethical AI, tools for bias detection, and new regulations aimed at protecting data privacy and security.

Ethical AI and Fairness: The ethical implications of AI systems, particularly regarding bias and fairness, have gained significant attention in recent years. AI systems trained on biased data can produce discriminatory outcomes, exacerbating inequalities in areas such as hiring, lending, and criminal justice. Emerging AI tools are focused on detecting and mitigating biases in machine learning models, ensuring that AI systems are fair and equitable (Mehrabi et al., 2021). Moreover, organizations are increasingly adopting AI ethics guidelines that emphasize transparency, accountability, and the responsible use of AI technologies.

Data Privacy and AI Regulation: With the increasing use of big data in AI systems, data privacy concerns have also come to the forefront. New regulations, such as the European Union's General Data Protection Regulation (GDPR) and the California Consumer Privacy Act (CCPA), are imposing stricter requirements on how organizations collect, store, and use personal data. AI systems must now comply with these regulations, and new tools are being developed to help organizations manage data privacy in AI-driven environments. Privacy-preserving techniques, such as federated learning and differential privacy, are becoming more common in AI systems, enabling data analysis without compromising individual privacy (Dwork & Roth, 2014).

4. Augmented Analytics and AI-Driven Insights

Another emerging trend in AI and big data is augmented analytics, which leverages AI and machine learning to enhance human decision-making by automating data analysis and delivering insights directly to users. Augmented analytics platforms use natural language processing (NLP) and machine learning to automatically analyze datasets, generate insights, and provide recommendations to users, allowing non-experts to make data-driven decisions without the need for deep technical expertise.

AI-Augmented Decision-Making: Augmented analytics tools are designed to simplify the process of data analysis by automating tasks such as data discovery, preparation, and reporting. These platforms provide users with AI-driven insights in natural language, making complex data analysis more accessible to business leaders and decision-makers (Davenport & Ronanki, 2018). For example, augmented analytics tools can automatically identify trends, correlations, and anomalies in big data, providing actionable recommendations to improve business operations or optimize marketing strategies.

Democratization of Data Science: The rise of augmented analytics is also contributing to the democratization of data science, where AI-powered tools make it easier for non-technical users to perform data analysis. This trend is empowering more people within organizations to leverage data for decision-making, reducing reliance on specialized data science teams and increasing the overall agility of the organization. By lowering the barriers to entry for data analysis, augmented analytics is making it possible for a wider range of industries and sectors to benefit from AI-driven insights (Gartner, 2020).

In summary, the future of AI in data science and big data is being shaped by several emerging trends, including AI-powered automation, real-time analytics, edge computing, responsible AI, and augmented analytics. These trends are helping organizations process and analyze vast datasets more efficiently while ensuring that AI systems are transparent, fair, and accountable. As AI technologies continue to evolve, they will play an increasingly central role in unlocking the potential of big data, enabling businesses and governments to make faster, more informed decisions. However, addressing challenges related to bias, privacy, and ethical governance will be critical to ensuring that the benefits of AI and big data are distributed equitably across society.

Predictions and Expert Insights

As artificial intelligence (AI) continues to advance, its integration with data science and big data is expected to shape the future of industries, research, and society. Predictions from leading experts in the fields of AI and data science suggest that the convergence of these technologies will bring transformative changes, ranging from more efficient data processing to breakthroughs in machine learning and decision-making systems. This section explores key predictions and expert insights on the future of AI in data science and big data, focusing on advancements in AI algorithms, the role of AI in democratizing data science, ethical challenges, and the evolution of AI's impact on industries.

1. AI-Driven Decision-Making and Business Transformation

One of the most widely shared predictions is that AI will increasingly drive decision-making across all sectors, fundamentally transforming business operations. AI will move from being a tool for data analysis to a central component of strategy formulation and execution, offering insights and recommendations that surpass human capabilities in terms of speed and accuracy.

AI-First Strategies: Experts predict that organizations will shift toward AI-first strategies, where AI systems not only analyze data but also proactively identify opportunities and make decisions based on real-time data streams (Bughin et al., 2018). For instance, AI is expected to play a key role in automating supply chains, optimizing marketing strategies, and enhancing customer experiences through hyper-personalization. As businesses become more data-driven, AI systems will enable them to respond more dynamically to market changes, leading to more agile and adaptive organizations.

Hyperautomation: Another significant trend highlighted by Gartner is hyperautomation, which refers to the use of AI, machine learning (ML), and robotic process automation (RPA) to automate complex workflows and business processes that previously required human intervention. Hyperautomation is predicted to accelerate productivity and efficiency in industries ranging from healthcare to manufacturing by automating both routine and decision-making tasks (Gartner, 2021). Experts suggest that AI-enabled hyperautomation will lead to the development of autonomous business processes capable of learning and improving over time.

2. Augmented Data Science and Democratization of AI

As AI tools become more accessible, there is a growing prediction that data science will be democratized, enabling a wider range of people to use AI for data-driven decision-making. AI-powered tools will simplify data science processes, allowing non-technical users to harness the power of AI without needing deep expertise in machine learning or data science.

Augmented Data Science: According to McKinsey Global Institute, augmented data science tools will enable users to automate key tasks in the data science pipeline, such as data cleaning, feature selection, and model evaluation (Bughin et al., 2018). These AI-driven platforms will empower business users, analysts, and domain experts to build and deploy machine learning models with minimal technical expertise. This trend is expected to democratize access to AI, making advanced analytics available to small businesses and non-technical teams, thereby fostering innovation across industries.

Low-Code and No-Code AI Platforms: Another important prediction is the rise of low-code and no-code AI platforms, which enable users to develop AI applications with little to no programming knowledge. These platforms leverage AI automation and pre-built machine learning models to simplify the process of building AI solutions. As low-code and no-code platforms evolve, more organizations will be able to adopt AI without needing to hire specialized data scientists, expanding AI adoption in industries that traditionally lack technical expertise (Harris, 2020).

3. Breakthroughs in AI Algorithms and Machine Learning

Experts predict that significant advancements in AI algorithms, particularly in areas like deep learning, reinforcement learning, and neural networks, will drive breakthroughs in AI performance and capabilities. These advancements are expected to revolutionize how data is processed and analyzed, leading to more accurate predictions, deeper insights, and new applications for AI in big data environments.

Advances in Reinforcement Learning: Reinforcement learning (RL) is predicted to play an increasingly important role in AI's future, particularly in areas requiring real-time decision-making and optimization. RL algorithms, which learn by interacting with their environment and receiving feedback in the form of rewards or penalties, have shown promise in applications such as autonomous vehicles, robotics, and game-playing AI. As RL techniques become more sophisticated, they are expected to unlock new applications in dynamic, complex environments, such as personalized healthcare and financial trading (Silver et al., 2018).

Self-Supervised Learning: Another breakthrough predicted to shape the future of AI is self-supervised learning, a technique that allows AI models to learn from unlabeled data. This approach significantly reduces the reliance on expensive, time-consuming data labeling, which has been a bottleneck in many AI applications. Self-supervised learning is expected to advance natural language processing (NLP), computer vision, and other fields by enabling AI to learn from vast amounts of unstructured data, improving model performance and scalability (LeCun et al., 2021).

4. Ethical AI and Governance

As AI becomes more pervasive in data science and big data, ethical considerations and governance frameworks will take on increasing importance. Experts predict that ethical AI will become a key focus for organizations and governments, as concerns about bias, transparency, accountability, and data privacy grow. Ensuring that AI systems are fair, transparent, and aligned with societal values will be critical to maintaining public trust and avoiding potential harms.

AI Ethics and Regulation: Governments and international organizations are expected to implement more stringent AI regulations to address ethical concerns and ensure responsible AI development. For example, the European Union's AI Act, which categorizes AI systems based on their risk levels, is predicted to serve as a model for other regions (European Commission, 2021). These regulations will require organizations to demonstrate that their AI systems are explainable, fair, and compliant with data privacy laws. Experts also predict the rise of AI auditing and certification processes, where third-party organizations assess AI systems for ethical compliance (Whittlestone et al., 2019).

AI Governance in Corporations: In addition to regulatory oversight, corporate governance structures for AI will become more prevalent. Experts predict that companies will establish AI ethics boards, responsible AI teams, and governance frameworks to ensure that their AI systems operate ethically and transparently (Raji et al., 2020). These internal governance structures will help organizations navigate the ethical challenges posed by AI, from bias mitigation to explainability, ensuring that AI technologies align with the company's values and social responsibility goals.

5. AI's Role in Solving Global Challenges

AI is increasingly being viewed as a tool for addressing some of the world's most pressing challenges, including climate change, healthcare, and poverty. Experts predict that AI will play a critical role in solving global issues by enabling more efficient resource management, improving healthcare outcomes, and providing data-driven insights for policy-making.

AI for Climate Action: AI is expected to play a pivotal role in addressing climate change by optimizing energy usage, improving resource allocation, and supporting environmental monitoring. AI models are being developed to predict climate patterns, optimize renewable energy grids, and monitor deforestation and biodiversity loss in real time. Experts predict that AI's ability to analyze large datasets and identify patterns will be instrumental in developing more sustainable practices and reducing carbon emissions (Rolnick et al., 2019).

AI in Healthcare: AI's impact on healthcare is predicted to grow significantly, with applications ranging from precision medicine to disease prediction and drug discovery. Experts believe that AI will revolutionize healthcare by enabling more personalized treatment plans, improving diagnostic accuracy, and accelerating the development of new therapies. AI's ability to analyze large volumes of medical data will be critical in advancing predictive diagnostics and identifying new drug candidates, ultimately improving patient outcomes and reducing healthcare costs (Topol, 2019).

In summary, the future of AI in data science and big data is marked by several key predictions and emerging trends that are expected to reshape industries, drive business transformation, and address global challenges. Experts predict that AI will become central to decision-making, with AI-first strategies and hyperautomation driving productivity and efficiency across sectors. The democratization of AI through augmented data science and low-code platforms will expand access to AI tools, while breakthroughs in machine learning and reinforcement learning will unlock new applications for AI in dynamic environments. As AI's influence grows, ethical considerations and governance will become increasingly important, with governments and corporations working to ensure responsible AI development. AI is also expected to play a critical role in solving global challenges, particularly in areas like climate action and healthcare, where data-driven insights are essential for progress.

Preparing for the Future

As artificial intelligence (AI) continues to evolve and reshape industries, preparing for the future of AI in data science and big data is critical for organizations, governments, and individuals alike. The exponential growth of data, coupled with advancements in machine learning, automation, and real-time analytics, demands a strategic approach to harness AI's potential while addressing key challenges such as ethical considerations, workforce transformation, and infrastructure readiness. This section explores the essential steps that stakeholders must take to prepare for the future of AI in data science and big data, focusing on skills development, investment in infrastructure, ethical AI frameworks, and fostering collaboration between public and private sectors.

1. Investing in Skills Development and Workforce Transformation

As AI technologies become more integrated into data science and business operations, the demand for AI and data science skills will continue to rise. Preparing for the future requires a proactive focus on reskilling and upskilling the workforce to ensure that both technical and non-technical employees are equipped to work alongside AI systems.

Reskilling for AI Competencies: One of the key challenges organizations face is the shortage of skilled professionals with expertise in AI, data science, and machine learning. A report by the World Economic Forum (2020) highlights the importance of reskilling and upskilling programs to address the skills gap and ensure that employees can adapt to the changing technological landscape. Organizations must invest in training programs that teach AI fundamentals, data analytics, and machine learning to workers across various roles. Such initiatives can range from technical education for data scientists and engineers to AI literacy programs for business leaders and decision-makers.

Collaboration with Educational Institutions: Preparing the future workforce also involves strengthening partnerships between industry and academia. Universities and technical institutions must align their curricula with the skills and competencies required in the AI-driven economy. Offering AI-related courses, certifications, and research opportunities can help bridge the gap between theoretical knowledge and real-world application. Furthermore, collaborative research initiatives between companies and academic institutions can accelerate AI innovations and provide students with hands-on experience in data science and machine learning (Bughin et al., 2018).

2. Building Scalable Infrastructure for Big Data and AI

The increasing volume, velocity, and variety of big data require robust, scalable infrastructure to support AI applications. Organizations must be prepared to handle massive datasets and deploy AI models efficiently across distributed systems. Preparing for the future of AI and big data requires significant investments in cloud infrastructure, data storage, high-performance computing (HPC), and edge computing.

Cloud Computing and Data Infrastructure: Cloud computing has emerged as a critical enabler of AI and big data analytics, providing organizations with the flexibility to store and process vast amounts of data without the need for on-premises infrastructure. Leading cloud providers, such as Amazon Web Services (AWS), Google Cloud, and Microsoft Azure, offer AI services and data processing capabilities that allow businesses to scale AI deployments cost-effectively (Crawford & Schultz, 2021). Preparing for the future involves leveraging cloud-based AI platforms that offer the computational power and scalability needed for real-time analytics, deep learning, and data-driven decision-making.

Edge Computing for Real-Time AI: Edge computing is gaining prominence as a solution for real-time AI processing, particularly in industries like healthcare, manufacturing, and autonomous vehicles. By bringing computation closer to the data source (e.g., sensors or IoT devices), edge computing reduces latency and bandwidth requirements, enabling faster decision-making in environments where immediate action is critical (Shi et al., 2016). Organizations preparing for AI's future should invest in edge infrastructure to support AI applications that require low-latency processing, such as predictive maintenance, autonomous systems, and smart cities.

3. Implementing Ethical AI Frameworks and Governance

As AI becomes more deeply integrated into business operations and societal systems, ensuring that AI is used ethically and responsibly is paramount. Organizations must develop and implement ethical AI frameworks that address concerns related to fairness, transparency, privacy, and accountability. These frameworks will be crucial in maintaining public trust and complying with emerging AI regulations.

Adopting Ethical AI Guidelines: Several international organizations and governments have issued guidelines for ethical AI development, emphasizing the need for fairness, transparency, and accountability in AI systems. For instance, the European Union's AI Act proposes a risk-based approach to AI governance, where higher-risk AI applications, such as those used in healthcare or law enforcement, are subject to stricter regulations (European Commission, 2021). Organizations must adopt these guidelines and embed ethical considerations into their AI design, development, and deployment processes. This includes conducting regular audits of AI systems to identify and mitigate bias, ensuring explainability, and implementing data privacy protections.

Responsible AI Governance: Ethical AI also requires strong governance structures within organizations. Establishing AI ethics committees, responsible AI teams, and clear accountability mechanisms can help ensure that AI systems align with ethical principles and societal values. Governance frameworks should outline how AI decisions are made, how biases are detected and mitigated, and how individuals can challenge or seek redress for decisions made by AI systems. These internal structures will be essential as AI adoption grows and as organizations face increased scrutiny from regulators and the public (Whittlestone et al., 2019).

4. Fostering Collaboration Between Public and Private Sectors

The future of AI and big data is not solely shaped by technological advancements; it also depends on collaboration between various stakeholders, including governments, corporations, and research institutions. Preparing for the future requires public-private partnerships that promote innovation, research, and the responsible use of AI.

AI Innovation Hubs and Research Partnerships: Governments and industry leaders are increasingly recognizing the importance of AI research hubs and innovation centers. These collaborative efforts bring together experts from academia, industry, and government to work on AI research, particularly in areas such as healthcare, climate modeling, and cybersecurity (Crawford & Schultz, 2021). These partnerships help accelerate the development of AI technologies while ensuring that they are designed to address real-world challenges. For example, public-private collaborations in AI for healthcare have led to advancements in predictive diagnostics and personalized treatment.

Government Support for AI Innovation: Governments also play a crucial role in shaping the future of AI through funding, policy-making, and regulatory oversight. In addition to providing grants for AI research, governments can create supportive policy environments that encourage innovation while safeguarding public interests. Policies that promote open data sharing, AI talent development, and ethical AI practices will help drive AI innovation while ensuring that its benefits are shared equitably across society (Bughin et al., 2018).

5. Preparing for Disruption and Embracing Change

As AI continues to disrupt industries, organizations must be agile and prepared to embrace change. The widespread adoption of AI in data science and big data will require businesses to rethink their operations, workforce strategies, and business models. Preparing for the future means embracing a culture of innovation and continuous learning, where employees are encouraged to adapt to new technologies and where organizations are willing to experiment with AI-driven solutions.

Agility in AI Adoption: Organizations that are agile in their adoption of AI will be better positioned to take advantage of emerging trends and technologies. McKinsey Global Institute's research suggests that companies that successfully integrate AI into their operations tend to exhibit higher levels of agility and flexibility (Bughin et al., 2018). This involves not only adopting AI technologies but also fostering a culture of innovation, where employees are encouraged to explore new ideas, collaborate across departments, and leverage AI for strategic decision-making.

Continuous Learning and Innovation: Preparing for the future of AI also requires a commitment to continuous learning and innovation. As AI technologies evolve, organizations must ensure that their employees are equipped with the skills and knowledge to work effectively with AI. This can be achieved through ongoing training programs, knowledge sharing, and encouraging employees to stay up-to-date with the latest developments in AI and data science. Additionally, businesses should be willing to experiment with new AI tools, platforms, and processes to stay competitive in an AI-driven world (World Economic Forum, 2020).

Conclusion

Preparing for the future of AI in data science and big data requires a strategic and multifaceted approach. Organizations must invest in reskilling and upskilling their workforce, building scalable infrastructure, implementing ethical AI frameworks, and fostering collaboration between public and private sectors. By embracing agility, innovation, and ethical governance, businesses and governments can ensure that they are well-positioned to leverage the transformative potential of AI and big data while addressing the challenges that come with these technologies. As AI continues to evolve, organizations that prepare for these changes will be better equipped to navigate the future and drive meaningful impact across industries.

References

Bifet, A., Holmes, G., Pfahringer, B., & Gavalda, R. (2018). Machine learning for data streams: With practical examples in MOA. MIT Press.

Bughin, J., Hazan, E., Ramaswamy, S., Chui, M., Allas, T., Dahlström, P., ... & Trench, M. (2018). *AI adoption advances, but foundational barriers remain.* McKinsey Global Institute.

Crawford, K., & Schultz, J. (2021). *Atlas of AI: Power, politics, and the planetary costs of artificial intelligence.* Yale University Press.

Davenport, T. H., & Ronanki, R. (2018). Artificial intelligence for the real world. *Harvard Business Review, 96*(1), 108-116.

Dwork, C., & Roth, A. (2014). The algorithmic foundations of differential privacy. *Foundations and Trends in Theoretical Computer Science, 9*(3–4), 211–407.

European Commission. (2021). Proposal for a regulation laying down harmonised rules on artificial intelligence (Artificial Intelligence Act). https://ec.europa.eu/newsroom/dae/document.cfm?doc_id=75788

Gartner. (2020). Augmented analytics: The future of data and analytics. *Gartner Research.* https://www.gartner.com

Gartner. (2021). *Top strategic technology trends for 2022: Hyperautomation.* Gartner Research.

Harris, D. (2020). *The rise of no-code and low-code development platforms.* Forrester Research.

Heaton, J. (2019). Deep learning and the game of go. *Packt Publishing.*

Hutter, F., Kotthoff, L., & Vanschoren, J. (2019). Automated machine learning: Methods, systems, challenges. Springer.

LeCun, Y., Mairal, J., & Ponce, J. (2021). Self-supervised learning: The dark matter of intelligence. *Communications of the ACM, 64*(8), 62-71.

Mehrabi, N., Morstatter, F., Saxena, N., Lerman, K., & Galstyan, A. (2021). A survey on bias and fairness in machine learning. *ACM Computing Surveys (CSUR), 54*(6), 1-35.

Raji, I. D., Bender, E. M., Paullada, A., Denton, E., & Hanna, A. (2020). AI and the everything in the whole wide world benchmark. *Proceedings of the 2020 Conference on Fairness, Accountability, and Transparency*, 526-536.

Rolnick, D., Donti, P. L., Kaack, L. H., Kochanski, K., Lacoste, A., Sankaran, K., ... & Bengio, Y. (2019). Tackling climate change with machine learning. *arXiv preprint arXiv:1906.05433*.

Shi, W., Cao, J., Zhang, Q., Li, Y., & Xu, L. (2016). Edge computing: Vision and challenges. *IEEE Internet of Things Journal, 3*(5), 637-646.

Silver, D., Schrittwieser, J., Simonyan, K., Antonoglou, I., Huang, A., Guez, A., ... & Hassabis, D. (2018). Mastering the game of Go without human knowledge. *Nature, 550*(7676), 354-359.

Topol, E. (2019). *Deep medicine: How artificial intelligence can make healthcare human again*. Basic Books.

Whittlestone, J., Nyrup, R., Alexandrova, A., & Dihal, K. (2019). Ethical and societal implications of algorithms, data, and artificial intelligence: A roadmap for research. *Nuffield Foundation Report*.

Appendices

Appendix A: Glossary of Terms

This glossary provides definitions of key terms related to artificial intelligence (AI), data science, big data, and emerging technologies. Understanding these terms is essential for navigating the complexities of modern AI-driven environments, as they are frequently used in academic, technical, and industry contexts. The terms are organized alphabetically for ease of reference.

Algorithm

An algorithm is a step-by-step procedure or formula for solving a problem. In the context of AI and data science, algorithms are used to process data, make decisions, and carry out tasks autonomously by computers.

Artificial Intelligence (AI)

AI refers to the simulation of human intelligence by machines, particularly computer systems. It involves the development of algorithms and models that allow computers to perform tasks that typically require human intelligence, such as learning, reasoning, problem-solving, and understanding natural language.

Automation

Automation is the use of technology to perform tasks without human intervention. In AI and data science, automation often involves using machine learning models to process data, make decisions, or execute actions with minimal or no human oversight.

Big Data

Big data refers to extremely large datasets that are too complex or vast to be processed by traditional data-processing software. It is characterized by the "Three Vs": Volume (amount of data), Velocity (speed at which data is generated), and Variety (different types of data). Big data is commonly used in AI and data science for analysis and decision-making.

Bias

In machine learning, bias refers to the tendency of an algorithm to produce results that are systematically skewed. Bias can occur due to imbalances in the training data or flaws in the model's design, often leading to unfair or discriminatory outcomes.

Cloud Computing

Cloud computing is the delivery of computing services, such as storage, processing, and software, over the internet ("the cloud"). Cloud platforms are widely used to store and process big data, as well as to deploy machine learning and AI models.

Data Science

Data science is an interdisciplinary field that combines statistics, computer science, and domain knowledge to extract insights from data. It involves the collection, cleaning, analysis, and interpretation of data, often using AI and machine learning models to identify patterns and make predictions.

Deep Learning

Deep learning is a subset of machine learning that uses neural networks with many layers (hence "deep") to model complex patterns in data. It is particularly effective in tasks such as image and speech recognition, natural language processing, and autonomous driving.

Edge Computing

Edge computing is a distributed computing model that processes data closer to its source (e.g., on local devices like sensors or edge servers) rather than relying on centralized data centers. It is often used in real-time AI applications where low-latency processing is critical, such as in autonomous vehicles or IoT devices.

Ethical AI

Ethical AI refers to the development and use of AI systems in ways that are consistent with ethical principles, such as fairness, transparency, accountability, and respect for privacy. Ethical AI aims to minimize harm and promote trust in AI technologies.

Explainability

Explainability is the degree to which the internal workings of an AI system can be understood by humans. It is crucial for ensuring transparency, accountability, and trust in AI systems, particularly in high-stakes applications such as healthcare or criminal justice.

Federated Learning

Federated learning is a machine learning technique that allows models to be trained across decentralized data sources without transferring the data to a central server. This approach enhances data privacy and security by keeping sensitive data on local devices while still enabling collaborative learning.

Hyperparameter

Hyperparameters are the settings or configurations that control the learning process of a machine learning model. Unlike parameters, which are learned from the data during training, hyperparameters must be set before the training process begins, and they can significantly impact the performance of a model.

Internet of Things (IoT)

The Internet of Things refers to the network of physical devices, vehicles, appliances, and other objects embedded with sensors, software, and connectivity that enable them to collect and exchange data. IoT is closely related to big data and AI, as it generates large volumes of real-time data that can be analyzed and processed by AI systems.

Machine Learning (ML)

Machine learning is a branch of AI that enables systems to learn from data and improve their performance without being explicitly programmed. ML algorithms are used to identify patterns, make predictions, and automate decision-making processes.

Natural Language Processing (NLP)

Natural Language Processing is a field of AI focused on enabling computers to understand, interpret, and generate human language. NLP is used in applications such as chatbots, sentiment analysis, translation, and speech recognition.

Neural Networks

Neural networks are a series of algorithms that mimic the human brain's structure and function to recognize patterns and solve problems. Neural networks are commonly used in deep learning to perform tasks such as image recognition and natural language processing.

Overfitting

Overfitting occurs when a machine learning model is too closely tailored to the training data and performs poorly on new, unseen data. It indicates that the model has learned not only the patterns but also the noise in the training data, leading to reduced generalization.

Predictive Analytics

Predictive analytics is the use of data, statistical algorithms, and machine learning techniques to identify the likelihood of future outcomes based on historical data. It is widely used in business for forecasting trends, customer behavior, and risk assessment.

Quantum Computing

Quantum computing is an emerging technology that uses quantum mechanics principles to perform computations. Quantum computers have the potential to solve problems that are currently unsolvable by classical computers, particularly in areas like cryptography, optimization, and complex simulations. Quantum computing is expected to impact the future of AI and big data by providing faster and more efficient processing capabilities.

Reinforcement Learning (RL)

Reinforcement learning is a type of machine learning where an agent learns to make decisions by interacting with its environment and receiving feedback in the form of rewards or penalties. It is commonly used in applications such as robotics, gaming, and autonomous systems.

Supervised Learning

Supervised learning is a type of machine learning where a model is trained on labeled data, meaning that each input in the training data has a corresponding output. The model learns to map inputs to outputs by minimizing the error between its predictions and the actual labels.

Unsupervised Learning

Unsupervised learning is a machine learning approach where models are trained on unlabeled data. The goal is to identify patterns or structures within the data, such as clustering similar data points or reducing the dimensionality of the dataset.

Virtualization

Virtualization refers to the process of creating virtual versions of physical hardware, such as servers, storage devices, or networks. It enables organizations to run multiple virtual environments on a single physical machine, improving resource efficiency and scalability.

Visualization

Data visualization involves the graphical representation of data to help users understand trends, patterns, and insights. Common data visualization tools include charts, graphs, and dashboards, which are used to present complex data in a visually accessible format.

Weak AI

Weak AI, also known as narrow AI, refers to AI systems that are designed to perform specific tasks or solve particular problems. Unlike strong AI, which aims to mimic human intelligence across a wide range of tasks, weak AI is limited to narrow domains such as playing chess, recognizing images, or translating text.

Appendix B: Mathematical Foundations

Understanding the mathematical foundations is critical for developing a strong grasp of artificial intelligence (AI), data science, and big data. These fields rely heavily on various branches of mathematics, including linear algebra, calculus, probability theory, and optimization, among others. This appendix provides an overview of the key mathematical concepts and techniques that serve as the building blocks for machine learning, deep learning, and data analysis. A solid understanding of these mathematical foundations enables practitioners to develop and optimize AI models, make sense of complex data, and apply statistical methods effectively.

1. Linear Algebra

Linear algebra is the study of vectors, matrices, and linear transformations, and it forms the backbone of many machine learning algorithms. Concepts from linear algebra are used extensively in data representation, dimensionality reduction, and optimization tasks in AI and data science.

Vectors and Matrices: A vector is a one-dimensional array of numbers, while a matrix is a two-dimensional array. Vectors represent data points, and matrices are often used to represent datasets or transformations applied to data. In machine learning, matrices are used to organize large amounts of data, such as in image processing or neural networks, where each layer of the network involves matrix multiplication.

Matrix Operations: Key operations in linear algebra include matrix multiplication, addition, and transposition. Matrix multiplication is central to operations in deep learning, where inputs are transformed through layers of weights and biases. Understanding how to manipulate matrices is essential for efficiently processing and transforming data in algorithms like Principal Component Analysis (PCA) and Singular Value Decomposition (SVD), which are used for dimensionality reduction.

Eigenvalues and Eigenvectors: Eigenvalues and eigenvectors provide insights into the properties of a matrix and are used in many algorithms, including PCA. Eigenvectors represent directions in which data can be stretched, and eigenvalues indicate the magnitude of this stretching. These concepts are essential for feature extraction, data compression, and identifying important patterns in datasets.

2. Calculus

Calculus, particularly differential calculus, plays a vital role in optimization problems, which are central to training machine learning models. Derivatives and gradients are used to minimize or maximize functions, such as loss functions in supervised learning.

Derivatives: A derivative represents the rate of change of a function with respect to one of its variables. In machine learning, derivatives are used to calculate gradients, which indicate how the output of a model changes with respect to changes in its parameters (weights and biases in neural networks). Understanding derivatives is essential for backpropagation in deep learning, where the model's error is minimized through gradient descent.

Gradient Descent: Gradient descent is an iterative optimization algorithm used to minimize the loss function of a model. It works by taking small steps in the direction of the negative gradient (the steepest descent) to find the minimum of a function. Variants of gradient descent, such as stochastic gradient descent (SGD) and mini-batch gradient descent, are used extensively in training AI models, particularly in deep learning.

Partial Derivatives: In multivariable functions, partial derivatives measure how a function changes as one of the variables changes while keeping the others constant. Partial derivatives are used in the optimization of neural networks, where each weight or parameter affects the overall function.

3. Probability Theory

Probability theory is crucial for modeling uncertainty and making predictions based on data. Many machine learning algorithms are built upon probabilistic models, including Bayesian networks, Hidden Markov Models, and probabilistic graphical models.

Random Variables and Distributions: A random variable represents an uncertain quantity whose outcome is determined by chance. Probability distributions describe how probabilities are assigned to different outcomes of a random variable. Common distributions used in machine learning include the normal (Gaussian) distribution, binomial distribution, and exponential distribution. Understanding these distributions is important for making inferences about data and for statistical modeling.

Bayes' Theorem: Bayes' Theorem is a fundamental rule of probability that describes how to update the probability of a hypothesis based on new evidence. It is the basis for Bayesian inference, which is used in a wide range of machine learning applications, including spam filtering, recommendation systems, and machine translation.

Expectation and Variance: The expected value of a random variable is its average value, while variance measures the spread or dispersion of the values. In machine learning, expectation is used to calculate the expected error of a model, and variance helps assess the model's ability to generalize to new data (overfitting or underfitting).

4. Optimization

Optimization techniques are fundamental in AI and machine learning, particularly in training models. The goal of optimization is to find the best parameters for a model that minimize (or maximize) a certain objective function, such as the loss function in supervised learning.

Convex Optimization: Convex optimization refers to the optimization of convex functions, which have the property that any local minimum is also a global minimum. Convex optimization techniques are widely used in machine learning algorithms like support vector machines (SVMs) and logistic regression. Understanding convexity is important because it ensures that optimization algorithms can converge efficiently to the optimal solution.

Lagrange Multipliers: Lagrange multipliers are used to optimize functions subject to equality constraints. In machine learning, this concept is applied in regularization techniques, where constraints are imposed on model parameters to prevent overfitting. Techniques like Lasso and Ridge regression involve adding penalty terms to the optimization problem to control the complexity of the model.

Stochastic Optimization: Stochastic optimization algorithms, such as stochastic gradient descent (SGD), are used to optimize functions when the objective function is computed using random samples from the data. This is particularly useful when dealing with large datasets in big data applications, where computing the full gradient is computationally expensive.

5. Statistics

Statistics is a cornerstone of data science, providing tools to summarize, analyze, and interpret data. Statistical methods are used in AI to estimate the parameters of models, test hypotheses, and make data-driven predictions.

Hypothesis Testing: Hypothesis testing is a statistical method used to determine whether there is enough evidence to reject a null hypothesis. In data science, hypothesis testing is used to assess the validity of models, compare different algorithms, and evaluate the significance of results.

Regression Analysis: Regression is a statistical method for modeling the relationship between a dependent variable and one or more independent variables. In machine learning, linear regression is used for predictive modeling, while logistic regression is used for classification tasks. Understanding regression is critical for building interpretable models that can be used to predict outcomes based on input data.

Confidence Intervals: Confidence intervals provide a range of values within which a parameter, such as a model's accuracy, is likely to lie. Confidence intervals are used to quantify the uncertainty in model predictions and are important for making reliable inferences from data.

6. Graph Theory

Graph theory is a branch of mathematics that deals with the study of graphs, which are structures made up of nodes (vertices) connected by edges. Graph theory is used in AI and data science for modeling relationships in networks, such as social networks, recommendation systems, and neural networks.

Graphs and Networks: In machine learning, graphs are used to represent relationships between data points. Graph-based algorithms, such as PageRank and graph neural networks, are used for tasks like network analysis, recommendation systems, and fraud detection.

Shortest Path Algorithms: Algorithms like Dijkstra's and Bellman-Ford are used to find the shortest path between nodes in a graph. These algorithms are commonly applied in optimization problems, such as route optimization in logistics and supply chain management.

Conclusion

A strong understanding of these mathematical foundations is essential for success in AI, data science, and big data. The concepts outlined in this appendix - linear algebra, calculus, probability theory, optimization, statistics, and graph theory - form the basis of many machine learning algorithms and data analysis techniques. Mastering these topics allows practitioners to build robust AI models, develop more accurate predictions, and make data-driven decisions with confidence. As AI continues to evolve, these mathematical principles will remain fundamental to innovation and progress in the field.

Appendix C: Datasets for Practice

Working with real-world data is an essential part of learning and mastering artificial intelligence (AI), data science, and machine learning. Datasets for practice allow learners and professionals to apply theoretical knowledge, build machine learning models, test different algorithms, and evaluate model performance. The diversity of datasets available online provides a wide range of opportunities to work on various tasks, such as classification, regression, clustering, natural language processing (NLP), computer vision, and more. This appendix presents a curated list of datasets across different domains, ideal for practice and experimentation.

1. General Machine Learning Datasets

These datasets are widely used in machine learning and data science for learning and practice, covering common tasks such as regression, classification, and clustering.

Iris Dataset: The Iris dataset is one of the most famous datasets in machine learning, often used for classification tasks. It contains 150 records of iris flowers with four features (sepal length, sepal width, petal length, petal width) and three classes representing different species of iris. This dataset is a great starting point for beginners to practice classification algorithms like k-nearest neighbors (KNN), decision trees, and logistic regression.

- Source: UCI Machine Learning Repository

- URL: https://archive.ics.uci.edu/ml/datasets/Iris

Titanic Survival Dataset: The Titanic dataset, provided by Kaggle, is another popular dataset used for binary classification. It contains information about passengers on the Titanic, such as age, gender, class, and whether they survived the sinking of the ship. The goal is to predict survival based on the passenger features. This dataset is ideal for practicing feature engineering, handling missing data, and building classification models like logistic regression or random forests.

- Source: Kaggle

- URL: https://www.kaggle.com/c/titanic

Boston Housing Dataset: The Boston Housing dataset is used for regression tasks and contains information about housing prices in different suburbs of Boston. It includes 506 instances with 13 features, such as the crime rate, average number of rooms, and distance to employment centers. This dataset is often used to practice linear regression, ridge regression, and decision tree regression models.

- Source: UCI Machine Learning Repository

- URL: https://archive.ics.uci.edu/ml/machine-learning-databases/housing/

Wine Quality Dataset: This dataset contains data on the physicochemical properties of wine samples and their quality ratings. The task is to predict wine quality (on a scale from 0 to 10) based on various features like alcohol content, acidity, and sugar levels. It can be used for both classification and regression tasks.

- Source: UCI Machine Learning Repository

- URL: https://archive.ics.uci.edu/ml/datasets/wine+quality

2. Natural Language Processing (NLP) Datasets

NLP involves the analysis of human language using AI models. These datasets are ideal for tasks like text classification, sentiment analysis, machine translation, and named entity recognition.

Sentiment140: Sentiment140 is a popular dataset for sentiment analysis, which includes 1.6 million tweets labeled as positive or negative. This dataset is widely used to build sentiment analysis models, which classify the sentiment of a given piece of text based on word patterns and context.

- Source: Sentiment140

- URL: http://help.sentiment140.com/for-students

IMDb Movie Reviews Dataset: This dataset contains 50,000 movie reviews from IMDb, labeled as positive or negative. It is commonly used for sentiment classification tasks, providing a large corpus for training models such as recurrent neural networks (RNNs), long short-term memory (LSTM), and transformers.

- Source: Kaggle

- URL: https://www.kaggle.com/lakshmi25npathi/imdb-dataset-of-50k-movie-reviews

20 Newsgroups Dataset: The 20 Newsgroups dataset contains around 20,000 newsgroup documents across 20 different categories, making it a valuable dataset for text classification and topic modeling tasks. It is often used to test algorithms like Naive Bayes, k-nearest neighbors (KNN), and support vector machines (SVM) for document classification.

- Source: Scikit-learn

- URL: https://scikit-learn.org/0.19/datasets/twenty_newsgroups.html

CoNLL-2003 Named Entity Recognition (NER) Dataset: This dataset is used for named entity recognition tasks, where the goal is to identify and classify entities in text, such as people, organizations, and locations. It is widely used for training sequence models like Conditional Random Fields (CRFs) and transformers in NER tasks.

- **Source: CoNLL-2003**

- **URL: https://www.clips.uantwerpen.be/conll2003/ner**

3. Computer Vision Datasets

Computer vision tasks, such as image classification, object detection, and image segmentation, rely on datasets containing labeled images. The following datasets are widely used in image-related AI projects.

MNIST Handwritten Digits Dataset: MNIST is one of the most famous datasets in computer vision and consists of 70,000 images of handwritten digits (0-9). The dataset is commonly used for classification tasks, where the goal is to recognize the digit in each image. This dataset is ideal for practicing convolutional neural networks (CNNs) and deep learning techniques.

- Source: MNIST

- URL: http://yann.lecun.com/exdb/mnist/

CIFAR-10: CIFAR-10 contains 60,000 images divided into 10 classes, such as airplanes, cars, birds, and cats. Each image is small (32x32 pixels), and the dataset is used for image classification tasks, making it a popular benchmark for CNN-based models.

- Source: CIFAR-10

- URL: https://www.cs.toronto.edu/~kriz/cifar.html

COCO Dataset: The Common Objects in Context (COCO) dataset contains over 300,000 images, with annotations for object detection, segmentation, and keypoint detection. COCO is widely used for advanced computer vision tasks such as object detection, image captioning, and segmentation using deep learning models like Faster R-CNN and YOLO.

- Source: COCO

- URL: https://cocodataset.org/

LFW (Labeled Faces in the Wild): The LFW dataset consists of over 13,000 labeled images of faces, with the goal of recognizing the identity of individuals in the images. It is widely used for facial recognition tasks and is commonly employed for benchmarking face detection and verification algorithms.

- Source: LFW

- URL: http://vis-www.cs.umass.edu/lfw/

4. Big Data Datasets

Big data refers to datasets that are too large or complex to be processed by traditional data-processing software. These datasets are used to practice distributed computing techniques, such as Hadoop and Spark, and big data analytics.

Google Ngrams: The Google Ngrams dataset contains word frequency data extracted from books scanned by Google. It covers a vast time period and is often used for linguistic analysis, cultural research, and big data analytics. The size of the dataset makes it ideal for practicing distributed computing techniques.

- Source: Google Ngrams

- URL: https://books.google.com/ngrams

NYC Taxi Dataset: This dataset contains detailed records of over 1.1 billion New York City taxi rides, including pickup and drop-off times, locations, and fares. It is widely used for big data analytics and machine learning tasks like predicting ride demand, travel time, and fare amount.

- Source: NYC Taxi & Limousine Commission

- URL: https://www1.nyc.gov/site/tlc/about/tlc-trip-record-data.page

Amazon Product Reviews Dataset: This dataset contains millions of Amazon customer reviews, providing rich data for sentiment analysis, recommendation systems, and big data text analysis. The large scale of the dataset makes it ideal for testing big data frameworks and machine learning models.

- Source: Amazon Customer Reviews

- URL: https://registry.opendata.aws/amazon-reviews/

5. Healthcare and Bioinformatics Datasets

These datasets are used in healthcare and bioinformatics research, often for predictive modeling, disease detection, and genomic analysis.

Breast Cancer Wisconsin Dataset: This dataset contains features of breast cancer cell nuclei and is used for binary classification tasks (benign vs. malignant tumors). It is a common dataset for testing classification models in healthcare.

- Source: UCI Machine Learning Repository

- URL:
  https://archive.ics.uci.edu/ml/datasets/Breast+Cancer+Wisconsin+(Diagnostic)

MIMIC-III Clinical Database: The MIMIC-III dataset contains de-identified health-related data for over 40,000 patients who were admitted to critical care units in a Boston hospital. It includes data on patient demographics, laboratory test results, and clinical notes, making it suitable for predictive analytics, machine learning in healthcare, and natural language processing in medical contexts.

- Source: MIMIC-III

- URL: https://mimic.physionet.org/

Human Genome Dataset: This dataset contains genomic sequences used for bioinformatics research and genetic analysis. It is widely used for tasks such as identifying genetic markers, predicting disease susceptibility, and studying gene expression patterns.

- Source: Ensembl

- URL: https://www.ensembl.org/info/data/ftp/index.html

Appendix D: Resources for Further Learning

As the fields of artificial intelligence (AI), data science, and big data continue to evolve, it is essential to stay up-to-date with the latest developments, tools, and methodologies. This appendix provides a curated list of resources for further learning, including books, online courses, research papers, and blogs. These resources are designed to help both beginners and professionals deepen their understanding of key concepts, enhance their technical skills, and keep pace with emerging trends in AI, data science, and big data.

1. Books

Books offer in-depth knowledge and detailed explanations of key concepts in AI, data science, and big data. Below are some highly recommended books for learners at various levels:

"Artificial Intelligence: A Modern Approach" by Stuart Russell and Peter Norvig

o   This comprehensive textbook is a foundational resource for understanding the principles of AI. It covers a broad range of topics, including search algorithms, knowledge representation, machine learning, and robotics.

o   **Ideal for**: Beginners to advanced learners.

"Deep Learning" by Ian Goodfellow, Yoshua Bengio, and Aaron Courville

o   A detailed introduction to deep learning, this book covers the theory and practice of neural networks and deep learning techniques. It is an essential resource for anyone interested in learning how deep learning models are developed and applied.

o   **Ideal for**: Intermediate to advanced learners.

"Hands-On Machine Learning with Scikit-Learn, Keras, and TensorFlow" by Aurélien Géron

o   This practical guide offers hands-on experience with popular machine learning libraries, focusing on building and deploying machine learning models. The book provides step-by-step instructions for implementing various algorithms.

o   **Ideal for**: Beginners to intermediate learners.

"Data Science for Business" by Foster Provost and Tom Fawcett

o   This book provides a comprehensive overview of data science concepts and their application in business. It focuses on using data to drive business decisions and offers practical insights into various data mining techniques.

o   **Ideal for**: Beginners to intermediate learners.

2. Online Courses and Tutorials

Online courses offer flexible learning options and access to a wide range of topics. Below are some of the top platforms and courses for AI, data science, and big data:

Coursera – "Machine Learning" by Andrew Ng

o   One of the most popular and highly rated courses in machine learning, this course covers the fundamentals of supervised and unsupervised learning, deep learning, and recommendation systems. It is taught by Andrew Ng, a leading AI researcher.

o   **Ideal for**: Beginners.

edX – "Data Science MicroMasters Program" by MIT

o   This MicroMasters program offers a series of courses on data science, covering topics such as probability, statistics, machine learning, and big data analytics. It is ideal for those looking to gain a solid foundation in data science.

o   **Ideal for**: Intermediate to advanced learners.

Udemy – "Python for Data Science and Machine Learning Bootcamp" by Jose Portilla

o   This course provides an introduction to Python programming for data science and machine learning. It covers popular libraries such as Pandas, Scikit-learn, and TensorFlow, making it a practical resource for beginners.

o   **Ideal for**: Beginners.

Fast.ai – "Practical Deep Learning for Coders"

o   This course offers a hands-on approach to deep learning, covering key topics like image classification, text generation, and collaborative filtering. It uses the Fast.ai library, making deep learning accessible to coders with basic knowledge.

o   **Ideal for**: Intermediate learners.

3. Research Papers and Journals

Reading academic papers is essential for those interested in the latest research developments in AI, data science, and big data. Below are some important resources for accessing research papers:

Google Scholar

o   Google Scholar is a free search engine for scholarly literature, including research papers, theses, books, and conference proceedings. It is an excellent resource for finding recent papers on AI and data science topics.

o

arXiv

o   arXiv is a repository for research papers in fields such as computer science, mathematics, physics, and AI. Many of the latest breakthroughs in AI and machine learning are first published on arXiv, making it a valuable resource for researchers and professionals.

Journal of Machine Learning Research (JMLR)

o   JMLR is a peer-reviewed journal that publishes cutting-edge research in machine learning. It covers a wide range of topics, including supervised and unsupervised learning, neural networks, and reinforcement learning.

IEEE Transactions on Big Data

o   This journal focuses on the study of big data technologies and applications, including data mining, analytics, and storage. It is an essential resource for those researching large-scale data processing and distributed systems.

4. Websites and Blogs

Websites and blogs are excellent resources for staying up-to-date with the latest trends, tools, and news in AI, data science, and big data. Below are some of the best websites and blogs to follow:

Towards Data Science

o   A popular Medium publication, Towards Data Science offers articles, tutorials, and case studies on AI, machine learning, and data science. It covers a wide range of topics, from beginner-friendly tutorials to advanced technical discussions.

KDnuggets

o   KDnuggets is a leading site for AI, data science, and machine learning news, blogs, tutorials, and interviews with industry experts. It also provides information about data science competitions, conferences, and job opportunities.

Machine Learning Mastery

o   This blog, run by Dr. Jason Brownlee, provides practical tutorials and guides on machine learning and deep learning. It is especially useful for beginners and intermediate learners looking to apply machine learning algorithms in Python.

Analytics Vidhya

o   Analytics Vidhya offers a wide range of tutorials, courses, and resources for data science and AI. It is a great platform for those looking to participate in data science competitions, learn new tools, or improve their analytical skills.

5. Data Science and AI Competitions

Participating in data science competitions is an excellent way to gain hands-on experience with real-world problems and datasets. Below are some of the best platforms for finding data science and AI challenges:

Kaggle

o   Kaggle is one of the largest platforms for data science and machine learning competitions. It provides access to a wide range of datasets, tutorials, and tools, allowing participants to build models and compete with others in solving real-world problems.

DrivenData

o   DrivenData hosts data science competitions focused on social good. It provides opportunities for data scientists to work on projects related to healthcare, education, and sustainability.

Zindi

- o Zindi is a data science competition platform that focuses on African challenges. It offers datasets and competitions that address social, environmental, and economic issues in Africa.

Appendix E: AI and Big Data Competitions

Participating in AI and big data competitions is one of the most effective ways for learners and professionals to gain practical experience, apply theoretical knowledge, and test their skills in real-world scenarios. These competitions offer opportunities to solve complex problems across various industries, from healthcare to finance, while competing with a global community of data scientists, AI researchers, and machine learning engineers. Many competitions are hosted by well-known platforms that provide access to datasets, collaboration tools, and educational resources. In this appendix, we explore some of the most popular AI and big data competition platforms and challenges, detailing the benefits of participating and how these competitions can help improve your skills in data science and AI.

1. Kaggle

Kaggle is the largest and most popular platform for data science and machine learning competitions. It hosts a wide range of challenges across different domains, allowing participants to solve problems using real-world datasets. Competitions on Kaggle often involve tasks such as classification, regression, natural language processing, computer vision, and recommendation systems. Kaggle competitions are open to participants at all skill levels, from beginners to experts.

Key Features:

o   Offers datasets, kernels (code notebooks), and discussion forums.

o   Provides an extensive leaderboard that allows participants to see how their models rank against others.

o   Offers competitions sponsored by companies and organizations, often with monetary prizes.

o   Includes educational resources, such as Kaggle Learn, which provides tutorials and training in data science tools and techniques.

Notable Competitions:

o   **Titanic: Machine Learning from Disaster**: A beginner-friendly competition where participants build a model to predict whether passengers survived the Titanic disaster.

o   **House Prices: Advanced Regression Techniques**: Participants build predictive models to estimate house prices using various features from a real estate dataset.

2. DrivenData

DrivenData focuses on data science competitions aimed at solving social and environmental challenges. Competitions on DrivenData often tackle issues related to healthcare, education, disaster relief, and sustainability, allowing data scientists to apply their skills to projects that have a positive impact on society. The platform emphasizes collaborative problem-solving and hosts competitions in collaboration with NGOs, research institutions, and public organizations.

Key Features:

o   Focuses on data-driven projects with real-world impact in areas such as public health, poverty reduction, and climate action.

o   Offers datasets and a collaborative platform for participants to share insights and discuss approaches.

o   Many competitions are designed for participants of varying skill levels, with clear problem definitions and tutorials.

Notable Competitions:

o **Mapping Poverty with Satellite Imagery**: In this competition, participants use satellite data to predict poverty levels in regions without traditional survey data.

o **Pump It Up: Data Mining the Water Table**: Participants develop models to predict which water pumps are functional in rural Tanzania, helping improve water access and maintenance planning.

3. Zindi

Zindi is an African-focused platform for data science competitions, aimed at solving challenges across various industries in Africa. Zindi hosts a wide range of machine learning challenges in sectors such as agriculture, energy, healthcare, and education. Zindi provides opportunities for both individual competitors and teams, fostering a collaborative environment where data scientists can work together to address local and global challenges.

Key Features:

o Focuses on challenges relevant to Africa and emerging markets, often involving innovative solutions to pressing issues.

o Provides opportunities for data scientists to collaborate with businesses, governments, and NGOs.

o Offers competitions for both beginners and advanced participants, with a mix of free and paid challenges.

o Often features cash prizes and opportunities for top competitors to gain recognition in the African tech ecosystem.

Notable Competitions:

o **Farm Pin Crop Detection Challenge**: Participants use satellite data to detect different crops in agricultural fields, helping improve agricultural planning and food security.

o **African Language Detection**: A natural language processing competition where participants build models to identify various African languages from short text samples.

4. Topcoder

Topcoder is a platform known for hosting competitive programming, data science, and AI challenges. It features a range of competitions in areas like machine learning, computer vision, and algorithm optimization. Topcoder also offers challenges in software development, data visualization, and data engineering, making it a great platform for participants who want to broaden their technical skills beyond machine learning.

Key Features:

o Specializes in coding and algorithm challenges, with a focus on problem-solving and optimization.

o Offers marathon matches where participants work on longer-term, complex problems.

o Hosts events like Topcoder Open, an annual competition that brings together the best programmers, data scientists, and AI practitioners from around the world.

o Competitions often include monetary prizes and opportunities for participants to collaborate with leading tech companies.

Notable Competitions:

o **Marathon Matches**: Long-term data science and algorithm challenges where participants work to optimize solutions over several weeks.

o **Computer Vision Challenges**: Participants build models for object detection, image segmentation, and video analysis.

5. AIcrowd

AIcrowd focuses on hosting competitions in AI, machine learning, reinforcement learning, and robotics. It is known for offering complex, research-driven challenges, particularly in fields such as reinforcement learning and AI for games. AIcrowd is also a great platform for practitioners who are interested in multi-agent systems and simulation-based AI tasks.

Key Features:

o Offers competitions for a range of skill levels, from beginner-friendly challenges to advanced research problems.

o Provides a focus on reinforcement learning and simulation-based challenges, which are important in fields like autonomous driving and robotics.

o Includes collaboration tools, allowing participants to work together on complex AI challenges.

• **Notable Competitions**:

o **Learning to Run Challenge**: Participants train a reinforcement learning agent to run in a simulated environment, optimizing its speed and efficiency.

o **AI Blitz**: A series of quick competitions focused on small-scale AI problems, perfect for beginners looking to gain experience in a short period of time.

6. Codalab

Codalab is an open-source platform that hosts competitions for machine learning and AI research. It is commonly used for academic and research-based challenges, providing a platform for organizing and evaluating machine learning models. Codalab is often used in conjunction with large-scale scientific competitions that aim to push the boundaries of AI research.

Key Features:

o   Open-source and collaborative, allowing researchers to create and host their own competitions.

o   Frequently used for academic and scientific competitions, particularly in areas such as medical imaging, natural language processing, and speech recognition.

o   Supports complex evaluation pipelines, enabling the testing of large models and high-stakes tasks like drug discovery and genomics.

Notable Competitions:

o   **NLP Challenges**: Codalab frequently hosts challenges in natural language processing, such as text classification, machine translation, and question answering.

o   **Medical Imaging Challenges**: Research-based competitions involving medical image segmentation, detection, and classification.

7. InnoCentive

InnoCentive is a platform that connects organizations with problem solvers around the world. While it is not exclusively focused on AI and data science, many of the challenges posted on InnoCentive involve big data analytics, machine learning, and algorithm development. InnoCentive competitions are typically focused on finding innovative solutions to complex problems across industries like healthcare, sustainability, and engineering.

- **Key Features**:

  o Focuses on innovation-driven challenges, where participants are tasked with developing novel solutions to real-world problems.

  o Offers a wide range of problems, many of which require interdisciplinary approaches that combine data science, engineering, and domain expertise.

  o Includes monetary prizes for winning solutions, with some challenges offering significant financial rewards.

Notable Competitions:

  o **Data-Driven Challenges**: Competitions that involve using data to solve problems in areas such as public health, logistics, and environmental sustainability.

  o **Innovation Challenges**: Cross-disciplinary challenges that require participants to apply AI and big data techniques alongside other fields, such as chemistry or material science.

www.ingramcontent.com/pod-product-compliance
Lightning Source LLC
Chambersburg PA
CBHW071916150726
47999CB00001B/1